Lecture Notes in C

Edited by G. Goos, J. Har

Springer
Berlin
Heidelberg
New York
Hong Kong
London
Milan
Paris
Tokyo

Catuscia Palamidessi (Ed.)

Logic Programming

19th International Conference, ICLP 2003
Mumbai, India, December 9-13, 2003
Proceedings

Springer

Series Editors

Gerhard Goos, Karlsruhe University, Germany
Juris Hartmanis, Cornell University, NY, USA
Jan van Leeuwen, Utrecht University, The Netherlands

Volume Editor

Catuscia Palamidessi
INRIA-Futurs and LIX
École Polytechnique
Rue de Saclay
91128 Palaiseau Cedex
France
E-mail:catuscia@lix.polytechnique.fr

Cataloging-in-Publication Data applied for

A catalog record for this book is available from the Library of Congress.

Bibliographic information published by Die Deutsche Bibliothek
Die Deutsche Bibliothek lists this publication in the Deutsche Nationalbibliografie;
detailed bibliographic data is available in the Internet at <http://dnb.ddb.de>.

CR Subject Classification (1998): D.1.6, I.2.3, D.3, F.3, F.4

ISSN 0302-9743
ISBN 3-540-20642-6 Springer-Verlag Berlin Heidelberg New York

Springer-Verlag is a part of Springer Science+Business Media

springeronline.com

© Springer-Verlag Berlin Heidelberg 2003
Printed in Germany

Typesetting: Camera-ready by author, data conversion by PTP-Berlin, Protago-TeX-Production GmbH
Printed on acid-free paper   SPIN: 10973417   06/3142   5 4 3 2 1 0

Preface

This volume contains the proceedings of the 19th International Conference on Logic Programming, ICLP 2003, which was held at the Tata Institute of Fundamental Research in Mumbai, India, during 9–13 December, 2003. ICLP 2003 was colocated with the 8th Asian Computing Science Conference, ASIAN 2003, and was followed by the 23rd Conference on Foundations of Software Technology and Theoretical Computer Science, FSTTCS 2003. The latter event was hosted by the Indian Institute of Technology in Mumbai.

In addition, there were five satellite workshops associated with ICLP 2003:

- PPSWR 2003, Principles and Practice of Semantic Web Reasoning, 8th Dec. 2003, organized by François Bry, Nicola Henze, and Jan Maluszynski.
- COLOPS 2003, COnstraint & LOgic Programming in Security, 8th Dec. 2003, organized by Martin Leucker, Justin Pearson, Fred Spiessens, and Frank D. Valencia.
- WLPE 2003, Workshop on Logic Programming Environments, organized by Alexander Serebrenik and Fred Mesnard.
- CICLOPS 2003, Implementation of Constraint and LOgic Programming Systems, 14th Dec. 2003, organized by Michel Ferreira and Ricardo Lopes.
- SVV 2003, Software Verification and Validation, 14th Dec. 2003, organized by Sandro Etalle, Supratik Mukhopadhyay, and Abhik Roychoudhury.

Starting with the first conference held in Marseilles in 1982, ICLP has been the premier international conference for presenting research into logic programming. ICLP 2003 received 81 submissions, from which the Program Committee selected 23 papers for presentation and inclusion in the proceedings. In addition, these proceedings contain the abstracts of 18 selected posters. For the first time, these posters have been organized into a series of short presentations complementing the usual display session at the conference. Credit is due to Poster Chair M.R.K. Krishna Rao for the extreme care with which he managed all matters related to the posters, including their selection, the editing of the abstracts for the proceedings, and the organization of the poster session itself.

Finally, the proceedings contain the contributions of the invited speakers and invited tutorial speakers. We were privileged to have Greg Morriset as keynote speaker, in common with ASIAN 2003. The other invited talks were given by Rolf Backofen, Maurizio Gabbrielli, Olivier Ridoux, and William Winsborough. The tutorial speakers were Paola Bruscoli, François Fages, Kung-Kiu Lau, and Frank S. Valencia.

In addition, the conference program contained some special sessions: a Programming Contest, organized by Bart Demoen; an open session on the next LP language, organized by Bart Demoen and Peter Stuckey; and a Teaching Panel, organized by Mireille Ducassé.

The Association of Logic Programming sponsored some awards assigned to the authors of the best works accepted at ICLP 2003 in the categories of student papers and application papers.

- The best student paper awards were received by:
    - Frank D. Valencia, for the paper *Timed Concurrent Constraint Programming: Decidability Results and Their Application to LTL*, and
    - Brigitte Pientka, for the paper *Higher-Order Substitution Tree Indexing*.
- The best application paper award was received by: Frej Drejhammar, Christian Schulte, Per Brand, and Seif Haridi for the paper *Flow Java: Declarative Concurrency for Java*.

On behalf of the Program Committee I would like to thank the authors of the submitted papers and the external referees, whose timely and expert reviews were indispensable in the evaluation of the submissions. Many thanks also to the Conference Chair, R.K. Shyamasundar, to the Poster Chair, and to the Publicity Chair, Jan-Georg Smaus, for the extraordinary work they did. Furthermore we want to express our appreciation to the invited speakers and to the invited tutorial speakers, whose excellent talks contributed greatly to the success of the conference. Special thanks go to the workshops organizers, to the Workshop Chairs, N. Raja and Vitor Santos Costa, and to the organizers of the special sessions. The Poster Chair, M.R.K. Krishna Rao, gratefully acknowledges the excellent support provided by the King Fahd University of Petroleum and Minerals in his activities related to ICLP 2003. Finally, we would like to thank Richard van de Stadt for his conference management software, Cyber-Chair, which was extremely useful for dealing with the electronic submissions and with the selection process.

September 2003   Catuscia Palamidessi

Organization

ICLP 2003 was organized by the Tata Institute of Fundamental Research (TIFR) in Mumbai (India).

Organizing Committee

Conference Chair	R.K. Shyamasundar (TIFR, India)
Program Chair	Catuscia Palamidessi (INRIA-Futurs and LIX, France)
Poster Chair	M.R.K. Krishna Rao (King Fahd Univ. of Petroleum and Minerals, Saudi Arabia)
Publicity Chair	Jan-Georg Smaus (Universität Freiburg, Germany)
Workshop Chairs	N. Raja (TIFR, India)
	Vitor Santos Costa (Fed. Univ. Rio de Janeiro, Brazil)
Programming Contest	Bart Demoen (Catholic University of Leuven, Belgium)
Teaching Panel Chair	Mireille Ducassé (IRISA/INSA, France)

Program Committee

Bart Demoen (Catholic University of Leuven, Belgium)
Agostino Dovier (University of Udine, Italy)
Mireille Ducassé (IRISA/INSA, France)
Sandro Etalle (University of Twente, and CWI, The Netherlands)
Moreno Falaschi (University of Udine, Italy)
Maria García de la Banda (Monash University, Australia)
Andy King (University of Kent, UK)
Kung-Kiu Lau (University of Manchester, UK)
Catuscia Palamidessi (INRIA-Futurs and LIX, France)
Enrico Pontelli (New Mexico State University, USA)
German Puebla (Technical University of Madrid, Spain)
Mario Rodriguez Artalejo (Universidad Complutense de Madrid, Spain)
Francesca Rossi (University of Padova, Italy)
Dietmar Seipel (University of Würzburg, Germany)
R.K. Shyamasundar (TIFR, India)
Zoltan Somogyi (University of Melbourne, Australia)
Hudson Turner (University of Minnesota, Duluth, USA)
Kazunori Ueda (Waseda University, Japan)
David Scott Warren (University of Stony Brook, and XSB, Inc., USA)

External Referees

M. Balduccini
D. Ballis
R. Becket
S. Boyd
D. Cabeza
D. Calvanese
D. Cantone
S. Cao Tran
M. Carlsson
M. Carro
J. Chong
M. Comini
J. Correas
P. Cox
A. Dal Palù
M. Denecker
L. Di Gaspero
A. Formisano
M. Gabbrielli
J. Gallagher
R. Gennari
U. Geske
P.-Y. Glorennec
M. Hanus
B. Heumesser
P. Hill
M. Hopfner
M.T. Hortalá González
J. Howe
J.J. Ruz-Ortiz
N. Kato

L. Llana-Díaz
P. López-García
N. Leone
M. Leuschel
J. Lipton
M. Liu
M. Marchiori
K. Marriott
N. Martí-Oliet
N. Mazur
B. Meyer
D. Miller
A. Montanari
S. Muñoz
G. Nadathur
E. Omodeo
M. Ornaghi
J. Pan
N. Pelov
S. Perri
C. Piazza
E. Pimentel-Sánchez
I. Pivkina
A. Policriti
M. Proietti
E. Quintarelli
F. Ranzato
O. Ridoux
G. Rossi
M. Rueher
S. Ruggieri

F. Sáenz-Pérez
F. Sadri
K. Sagonas
C. Sakama
V. Santos Costa
M.L. Sapino
K. Satoh
A. Schaerf
T. Schrijvers
A. Serebrenik
K. Shen
E. Shibayama
I. Shioya
A. Simon
J.-G. Smaus
F. Spoto
U. Straccia
P. Stuckey
V.S. Subrahmanian
K. Taguchi
P. Tarau
P. Torroni
B. Van Nuffelen
W. Vanhoof
S. Verbaeten
A. Villanueva
J. Wielemaker
C. Witteveen
C.G. Zarba
Y. Zhang

Sponsoring Institutions

ICLP 2003 was sponsored by the Association of Logic Programming.

Table of Contents

Invited Talks

Invited Tutorials

Regular Papers

Posters

Achieving Type Safety for Low-Level Code

Greg Morrisett

Cornell University, Ithaca NY 14853, USA

Abstract. Type-safe, high-level languages such as Java ensure that a wide class of failures, including buffer overruns and format string attacks, simply cannot happen. Unfortunately, our computing infrastructure is built with type-unsafe low-level languages such as C, and it is economically impossible to throw away our existing operating systems, databases, routers, etc. and re-code them all in Java.

Fortunately, a number of recent advances in static analysis, language design, compilation, and run-time systems have given us a set of tools for achieving type safety for legacy C code. In this talk, I will survey some of the progress that has been made in the last few years, and focus on the issues that remain if we are to achieve type safety, and more generally, security for our computing infrastructure.

1 Overview

In November of 1988, Robert Morris, Jr. released a worm into the Internet. One of the ways the worm propagated was by overflowing an input buffer for the gets routine of the finger daemon. The worm also took advantage of a flaw in the configuration of the sendmail program, where remote debugging was enabled by default, as well as a password cracking program. Based on infection rates at MIT, some have concluded that roughly 10% of the supposedly 60,000 machines connected to the Internet were infected by the worm over a period of a few days. During those few days, heroic engineers disassembled the worm, figured out what it was doing, and took steps to block its propagation by pushing out changes to various sites [1].

Not much has changed in 15 years, except that there are many more hosts on the Internet, we are more dependent on these hosts, and the worms are a lot faster. For instance, in January 2003, someone released the so-called "Sapphire" worm (also known as the SQL-Slammer worm) which took advantage of a buffer overrun in Microsoft's SQL servers. This worm doubled in size every 8.5 seconds and managed to traverse and infect about 90% of the 100,000 susceptible hosts on the Internet in about 10 minutes [2]. There simply wasn't time to determine what the worm was doing, construct a patch, and get the patch in place before the whole Internet had been hit. In fact, a patch to prevent the flaw Sapphire took advantage of had been out for a number of months, but many users had failed to apply the patch, perhaps in fear that the cure was worse than the poison, or perhaps out of simple laziness.

C. Palamidessi (Ed.): ICLP 2003, LNCS 2916, pp. 1–2, 2003.

In the case of the Blaster worm, released in August of 2003 and which took advantage of a buffer overrun in Windows 2000 and XP, a counter-worm was released in a vain attempt to patch machines. Unfortunately, it managed to clog networks in the same way that Blaster did. At Cornell University, about 1,000 out of a roughly 30,000 Windows machines were infected by Blaster and even though the infection rate was so low, we estimate that it has cost about $133,000 in IT time so far to contain and deal with the damage. Other universities have reported as much as $800,000 in IT costs [3].

Security and reliability are hard issues. Misconfiguration, social issues, and many other problems will not be solved by technology alone. But surely after 15 years, we should be able to prevent buffer overruns and other "simple" errors in a proactive fashion before we ship code. In this talk, I will survey some of the approaches that people have used or are proposing for addressing buffer overruns and related problems in legacy C and C++ code.

References

1. Spafford, E. The Internet Worm Program: An Analysis. Purdue Technical Report CSD-TR-823, 1988.
2. Moore, D., Paxson, V., Savage, S., Shannon, C., Staniford, S., Weaver, N. The Spread of the Sapphire/Slammer Worm.
   http://www.cs.berkeley.edu/ nweaver/sapphire/.
3. http://whodunit.uchicago.edu/misc/infection-costs.html.

Logic Information Systems for Logic Programmers

Olivier Ridoux

IRISA/IFSIC, Campus de Beaulieu, 35042 RENNES cedex, FRANCE,
ridoux@irisa.fr

Abstract. Logic Information Systems (LIS) use logic in a uniform way to describe their contents, to query it, to navigate through it, to analyze it, and to update it. They can be given an abstract specification that does not depend on the choice of a particular logic, and concrete instances can be obtained by instantiating this specification with a particular logic. In fact, a logic plays in a LIS the role of a schema in data-bases. We present the principles of LIS, and a system-level implementation. We compare with the use of logic in Logic Programming, in particular through the notions of intention and extension.

1 Introduction

The goal of this invited article is to present the notion of Logic Information System (LIS), that we have developed in the past four years, to a Logic Programming (LP) audience. At a very general level, LP and LIS attack their respective problems in the same way: using logic. This is not a very distinctive property, and does not help much in introducing LIS to Logic Programmers. We believe that the interplay of the logical notions of *intention* and of *extension* gives a better approach.

Logic, more precisely set-theory, put to the front the notions of intention (also called comprehension) and extension. Roughly speaking, an intention expresses a property, and an extension is a set of items that have a property in common.

Logic-based computing systems are often "intention engines". They are filled in with an intention, and they compute the corresponding extension. Intentions considered in these systems are finite, though extensions may not be finite, or at least may be very large. Moreover, intentions are thought of as expressive and structured, though extensions are flat and unstructured.

Logic programming engines (e.g., a PROLOG interpreter) take intentions that are Horn programs (including a query), and they return answers (often called computed answers) that are sets of substitutions. The substitutions represent items such that the query holds for the program; i.e., computed answers represent the extension of the queries. Similarly, deductive data-base engines take intentions that are DATALOG programs, and they return extensions that are sets of answers.

This applies to all sorts of computing systems, including non-logical ones. In fact, going from intentions to extensions is simply the logical version of going

C. Palamidessi (Ed.): ICLP 2003, LNCS 2916, pp. 3–19, 2003.

from the implicit to the explicit. These computations go the easy way: down-stream. To go up-stream from the explicit to the implicit is often much more difficult. However, the ability to go up-stream is also crucial.

Consider for instance the debugging of logic programs. A programmer composes an intention, a program and query, and feeds it to a PROLOG interpreter. He checks the computed extension, the answers, and finds out that it contains wrong answers, or that intended answers are missing. To isolate the fault in the program given the incorrect computed extension and the intended extension is to go up-stream; this is the goal of Declarative Debugging. Similarly, to infer a general rule from examples is to go up-stream; this is the goal of Automated Learning and Inductive Logic Programming.

The debugging example is interesting because it shows a situation where there are not only pairs of intentions and extensions. There are *intended intentions, expressed intentions, intended extensions*, and *computed extensions*. The programmer has a goal, his intended intention. He expresses an intention, which may not be equivalent to the intended intention (*errare humanum est*). The computer yields a computed extension, which may not match the intended extension. If the programmer observes the discrepancy, he will strive to find out a better expression of his intended intention.

All this applies crucially to Information Retrieval. A user has an information goal. He expresses it as a query to, say, a data-base, or to the Web. The goal and the query may not match; this is just because the goal is expressed as thoughts, and the query is expressed in SQL or as a set of keywords. The computer yields an answer that the user checks against the intended extension. In case of discrepancy, the user will try another (hopefully better) query. The process repeats itself until the user is happy with the answer. Each iteration entails a step up-stream from an intended extension to an expressed intention. Data-bases and Web browsers provide no help for going up-stream.

Navigation systems, such as Hierarchical File Systems, go half-way from an intention to an extension. For instance, with UNIX file systems the answer to ls *path* is not the set of all files that can be reached from *path* (which is in fact the answer to ls -R *path*). The answer to ls *path* is the set of all files that are exactly at address *path*, plus directory names that can be concatenated to *path* in order to refine the query. So, in his process to formally express his intended intention, the user has less needs to go up-stream. Such systems answer intentional queries in the language of intentions. The user starts with a vague expressed intention, and the system answers it with hints to make the expressed intention more precise. This sounds good, but navigation in hierarchical file systems has drawbacks anyway. Since information is organized as a tree, there is a unique path to every information element. The goal of navigation is to find this unique path. This is often difficult because the hierarchy may have been designed by somebody else, or even by the user himself with another purpose in mind. Worse, the hierarchical organization may be used to store a data that is not hierarchical in itself. In fact, with Hierarchical File Systems, the difference between the physical model, the disk, and the logical model, the tree, is tiny.

With a hierarchical file system, the intentional part of navigation answers is not really computed; it has been statically decided by the user who created the hierarchy of directories. This is the result of a manual classification that can be outdated or even bogus. It would be better if the system really computed the extension, and then computed the possible refinements to the expressed intention in order to help the user expressing his intended intention. Again, this requires the ability to go up-stream from extensions to intentions.

In fact, a theory of coherent pairs of intention and extension exists; it is called *Formal Concept Analysis* (FCA [14]). In this theory, going up-stream is no longer a problem because intentions and extensions are at the same level.

The objective of this research was not to play with intentions and extensions. The initial objective was to design a storage and retrieval model that could offer the progressive search process of navigation, without the rigidity of static navigation links, and that could combine it with the use of rich descriptions. So doing, collections of objects could be classified according to the needs of different users with possibly conflicting purposes.

LIS are a combination of three ingredients:

1. logic, as in LP or Deductive Data-Bases, is used to offer a flexible and expressive language for intentions, and a rich theory of extensions,
2. navigation, as in Hierarchical File Systems, is used to provide a process of refining expressed intentions,
3. FCA is used to maintain symmetric relations between intentions and extensions.

As a result, LIS offer means for a progressive expression of ones intended intention, without the rigidity of a static organization; and it offers means to describe and locate information elements logically, without compromising the possibility to go up-stream. LIS also offers a logic-based variant of data-mining operations like the search for association rules, and the measurement of their confidence and support.

After a first intuition of LIS given in Section 2, we present a logic-based variant of FCA in Section 3, and the definition of LIS in Section 4, with a rapid survey of their capabilities. Then, we describe a file system implementation in Section 5, with a few experimental results. We present a few points of the relation between LP and LIS in Section 6, and we conclude in Section 7.

2   The Intuition of Logic Information Systems

We expose informally the intuition of LIS before giving formal definitions in next sections. A complete account of LIS can be found in [13,7].

The content of a LIS is a collection of *objects*; e.g., files, recipes in a cook-book, entries in a data-bases. Every object has attached to it a *description*, which is a closed logical formula (see Definition 3). A LIS may be queried and updated. In this article, we will focus on querying.

There are a few requirements on what kind of logic a description should belong to (see Definition 1), but in this section we will only postulate that the logic has an *entailment relation* and a *conjunction*, written $\sqsubseteq$ and $\sqcap$. Queries are also logical formulas, so that the entailment relation serves to retrieve objects. Note that the logic may have an infinite language. Propositional logic is a possible choice for a logic, but we also have experienced (combinations of) other logics like types, intervals, sets, and strings.

The extension of a query is the set of all objects in a LIS whose description entails the query, but this is not the actual answer to the query. The actual answer to a query is a collection of logical formulas that can be $\sqcap$'ed with the query to refine it, plus files whose description match the query. The files are called the *local files*. To match the query is not exactly to be equivalent to it, but it comes close (see Definition 15). The logical formulas are called *navigation links*; they must be so that the union of their extensions is the extension of the query, minus the local files, otherwise files could be inaccessible to navigation (see Definition 14). In short, local files are *there*, and navigation links point to somewhere *farther*.

The purpose of this scheme is that the user will recognize that some navigation links match his intended intention, whereas others do not. He will then form new more precise queries $\sqcap$'ing his former expressed query and the selected navigation links. The process goes on until the intended query is formed.

The process may even start with zero initial knowledge from the user. He sends query *true*, and the system answers with navigation links. By simply cutting and pasting links, the user may form increasingly complex queries without even knowing the language of the descriptions. All what is required from the user is that he can read the descriptions.

The description of objects is made of the conjunction of two parts: an *intrinsic* part and an *extrinsic* part. The intrinsic part is a function of the content of each object. The extrinsic part is arbitrary. When an object is added to a LIS, its intrinsic description is computed automatically, but its extrinsic part is left to the user. This may be a tedious task, especially if extrinsic description are rich. An induction process has been defined for deriving most of the extrinsic part from the intrinsic one [12].

All these operations require to be able to manage logical entailment, intention, and extension in a coherent framework. This is what Logic Concept Analysis offers.

3 Logic Concept Analysis

The basis of Formal Concept Analysis is a *formal context* that associates attributes to objects. FCA has received attention for its application in many domains such as in software engineering [25,21,18]. The interest of FCA as a navigation tool in general has also been recognized [16,21,26]. However, we feel it is not flexible enough as far as the language of attributes is concerned. In this section, we present an extension to FCA that allows for a richer attribute language.

See [9] for a complete account of this extension. We first define what we call a *logic* in this article.

Definition 1 (logic) *A logic is a 6-tuple* $(\mathcal{L}, \sqsubseteq, \sqcap, \sqcup, \top, \bot)$, *where*

- $\mathcal{L}$ *is the language of formulas,*
- $\sqsubseteq$ *is the* entailment *relation (pre-order over* $\mathcal{L}$*); we will write* $\sqsubset$ *when it is strict,*
- $\sqcap$ *and* $\sqcup$ *are respectively* conjunction *and* disjunction *(binary operations),*
- $\top$ *and* $\bot$ *are respectively* tautology *and* contradiction *(constant formulas).*

Such a logic must form a lattice [4], whose order is derived in the usual way from the pre-order $\sqsubseteq$*, and such that* $\sqcap$ *and* $\sqcup$ *are respectively the* infimum *(greatest lower bound) and the* supremum *(least upper bound), and* $\top$ *and* $\bot$ *are respectively the* top *and the* bottom*.*

That the entailment relation induces a lattice forbids non-monotonous logics. This is the only formal restriction on the logic. There is also a practical restriction; the logic must be decidable, and even tractable. The entailment relation also induces an equivalence relation, which we will write $\equiv$.

Example 2 (Propositional logic) *An example of logic that can be used in* LCA *is propositional logic. On the syntactic side, the set of propositions* $\mathcal{P}$ *contains atomic propositions (taken in a set* $\mathcal{A}$*), formulas 0 and 1, and is closed under binary connectives* $\land$ *and* $\lor$*, and unary connective* $\neg$*. We say that a proposition p entails q if* $\neg p \lor q$ *is a valid proposition (* $p \vDash q$*). Then,* $(\mathcal{P}, \vDash, \land, \lor, 1, 0)$ *satisfies Definition 1, because it is the well-known boolean algebra.*

This example shows that though the interface of the logic is limited to the tuple $(\mathcal{L}, \sqsubseteq, \sqcap, \sqcup, \top, \bot)$*, an actual logic may have more connectives:* $\neg$ *in this example.*

In our experiments, the logic is always a variant of $\mathcal{P}$ where formulas of domain-specific logics play the role of propositional variables; e.g., logics on intervals, string containment, sets. For instance, $] - \infty, 1999] \lor [2001, \infty[$ can be used to express a year that is not 2000.

We now define the main notions and results of LCA: *context* and *concept lattice*. A *context* plays the role of tables in a database, as it gathers the knowledge one has about objects of interest (e.g., files, BibTeX references, recipes).

Definition 3 (context) *A context is a triple* $K = (\mathcal{O}, \mathcal{L}, d)$ *where:*

- $\mathcal{O}$ *is a finite set of objects; most theoretical results still hold when* $\mathcal{O}$ *is infinite, but we believe the notion is easier to grasp when* $\mathcal{O}$ *is finite*
- $\mathcal{L}$ *is a logic (as in Definition 1); it may have an infinite language, and infinitely many non-equivalent formulas,*
- *d is a mapping from* $\mathcal{O}$ *to* $\mathcal{L}$ *that describes each object by a formula.*

Then, we define two mappings between extensions ($2^{\mathcal{O}}$) and intentions ($\mathcal{L}$) in a context K, that we prove to be a Galois connection [4]. A first mapping τ connects each formula f to its *instances*, i.e., objects whose description entails f; $\tau(f)$ is the *extension* of f. A second mapping σ connects each set of objects $O \subseteq \mathcal{O}$ to the most precise formula entailed by all descriptions of objects in O; $\sigma(O)$ is the *intention* of O.

Definition 4 (mappings τ and σ) *Let* $K = (\mathcal{O}, \mathcal{L}, d)$ *be a context,* $O \subseteq \mathcal{O}$, *and* $f \in \mathcal{L}$,

- $\sigma : 2^{\mathcal{O}} \to \mathcal{L}$, $\sigma(O) := \bigsqcup_{o \in O} d(o)$
- $\tau : \mathcal{L} \to 2^{\mathcal{O}}$, $\tau(f) := \{o \in \mathcal{O} \mid d(o) \sqsubseteq f\}$

Lemma 5 (Galois connection) *Let* $K = (\mathcal{O}, \mathcal{L}, d)$ *be a context,* (σ, τ) *is a* Galois connection *because* $\forall O \subseteq \mathcal{O}, f \in \mathcal{L} : \sigma(O) \sqsubseteq f \iff O \subseteq \tau(f)$.

Example 6 ($Triv$) *An example context will illustrate the rest of our development on* LCA. *The logic used in this context is propositional logic* $\mathcal{P}$ *(see Example 2) with a set of atomic propositions* $\mathcal{A} = \{a, b, c\}$. *We define context* K_{Triv} *by* $(\mathcal{O}_{Triv}, \mathcal{P}, d_{Triv})$, *where* $\mathcal{O}_{Triv} = \{x, y, z\}$, *and where* $d_{Triv} = \{x \mapsto a, y \mapsto b, z \mapsto c \wedge (a \vee b)\}$.

A LIS instance is essentially a context equipped with navigation and management tools.

A *formal concept*, central notion of LCA, is a pair of a set of objects and of a formula, which is stable for the Galois connection (σ, τ).

Definition 7 (formal concept) *In a context* $K = (\mathcal{O}, \mathcal{L}, d)$, *a formal concept (concept for short) is a pair* $c = (O, f)$ *where* $O \subseteq \mathcal{O}$, *and* $f \in \mathcal{L}$, *such that* $\sigma(O) \equiv f$ *and* $\tau(f) = O$.

The set of objects O *is the concept* extension *(written* $ext(c)$*), whereas formula* f *is its* intention *(written* $int(c)$*).*

Not every set of objects is a concept extension. Symmetrically, not every formula is a concept intention. If one is restricted to only consider concept intentions/extensions, to go up-stream from an extension to an intention is done by applying function σ. If a set is not a concept extension, then it can be normalized to the closest larger concept extension by applying function $\tau \circ \sigma$. This function is idempotent.

We write $=^c$ for concept equality. The set of all concepts that can be built in a context K is denoted by $\mathcal{C}_K$, and is partially ordered by $\leq^c$ defined below. The fundamental theorem of LCA is that $\langle \mathcal{C}_K; \leq^c \rangle$ forms a complete *lattice*. Completeness comes for free when $\mathcal{O}$ is finite, but the result holds as well when $\mathcal{O}$ is not finite.

Definition 8 (partial order $\leq^c$) *Let c_1 and c_2 be in $\mathcal{C}_K$,*
$$c_1 \leq^c c_2 \iff ext(c_1) \subseteq ext(c_2) \text{ (could be defined equivalently by } int(c_1) \sqsubseteq int(c_2)).$$

Theorem 9 (concept lattice) *Let K be a context. The partially ordered set $\langle \mathcal{C}_K; \leq^c \rangle$ is a finite lattice, whose supremum and infimum are as follows for every set of indexes J:*

- $\bigvee^c_{j \in J}(O_j, f_j) =^c (\tau(\sigma(\bigcup_{j \in J} O_j)), \sqcup_{j \in J} f_j)$
- $\bigwedge^c_{j \in J}(O_j, f_j) =^c (\bigcap_{j \in J} O_j, \sigma(\tau(\sqcap_{j \in J} f_j)))$

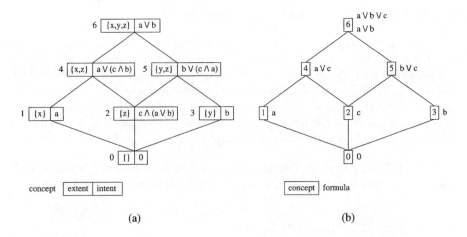

(a)   (b)

Fig. 1. The concept lattice of context K_{Triv} (a) and a possible labeling (b).

Example 10 *(Triv) Figure 1.(a) represents the Hasse diagram of the concept lattice of context K_{Triv} (see Example 6). Concepts are represented by a box containing their extension on the left, and their intention on the right. The higher concepts are placed in the diagram the greater they are for partial order $\leq^c$. Note that the concept lattice is not isomorphic to the power-set lattice of objects $\langle 2^O; \subseteq \rangle$; there are less concepts than parts of a set. For instance, set $\{x, y\}$ is not the extension of any concept, because $\tau(\sigma(\{x, y\})) = \tau(a \vee b) = \{x, y, z\}$.*

To make the concept lattice more readable, it is possible to label it with formulas and objects. Mapping μ labels with a formula f the concept whose extension is the extension of f. Mapping γ labels with an object o the concept whose intention is the intention of $\{o\}$, i.e., its description.

Definition 11 (labeling) *Let $K = (\mathcal{O}, \mathcal{L}, d)$ be a context, $o \in \mathcal{O}$, and $f \in \mathcal{L}$,*

- $\mu : \mathcal{L} \to \mathcal{C}_K$, $\mu(f) = \langle \tau(f); \sigma(\tau(f)) \rangle$
- $\gamma : \mathcal{O} \to \mathcal{C}_K$, $\gamma(o) = \langle \tau(d(o)); d(o) \rangle$.

The interesting thing with this labeling is that it enables to retrieve all data of the context: an object o satisfies ($\sqsubseteq$) a formula f in some context K if and only if the concept labeled with o is below ($\leq^c$) the concept labeled with f in the concept lattice of K.

Lemma 12 (labeling) *Under the conditions of Definition 11,*
$$d(o) \sqsubseteq f \iff \gamma(o) \leq^c \mu(f) \ .$$

So, the information in the concept lattice is equivalent to the information in the context. It is only a matter of presentation: rather extensional for the context, and more intentional for the concept lattice.

Example 13 *(Triv) Figure 1.(b) represents the same concept lattice as Figure 1.(a) (see also Example 10), but its concepts are decorated with labeling μ instead of with the extensions and intentions. Formulas of the form $\bigvee A$ where $A \subseteq \mathcal{A}$ ($\bigvee \emptyset \equiv 0$) are placed on the right of the concept that they label. For instance, concept 1 is labeled by formula a (i.e., $\mu(a) =^c 1$). We have only printed labels of the form $\bigvee A$, but it is only to have a finite number of labels that are not all in the formal context.*

In the following sections, formal contexts will be used to formalize the content of an information system, and the concept lattice will be used to organize objects.

4   Logical Information Systems

The contents of a LIS instance is a context (see Definition 3). The choice of a particular logic is left to the user, or to an administrator. The average user or administrator cannot invent arbitrary logics, and their theorem provers. So, we defined the notion of *logic functor* for building logics and their theorem provers by composing functors [10].

Once objects have been logically described and recorded in a logical context $K = (\mathcal{O}, \mathcal{L}, d)$, one wants to retrieve them. One way to do this is *navigating* in the context. The aim of navigation is to guide the user from a *current place* to a *target place*, which contains the object(s) of interest.

In a hierarchical file system, a "place" is a directory. In our case, a "place" is a formal concept (see Definition 7). In large contexts, concepts cannot be referred to by enunciating either their extension or their intention, because both are generally too large. However, formulas of the logic $\mathcal{L}$ refer concisely to concepts *via* the labeling map μ (see Definition 11).

First of all, going from place to place implies to remember the current place, which corresponds to the working directory. In a LIS, we introduce the *working query, wq*, and the *working concept, wc* $:= \mu(wq)$; we say that *wq* refers to *wc*. This working query is taken into account in the interpretation of most LIS commands, and it is initialized to the formula ⊤, which refers to the concept whose extension is the set of all objects.

Changing place uses a query formula q saying in which place to go, and it changes the working query accordingly. We call l_{wq} (i.e., *elaboration* w.r.t. *wq*) the mapping that associates to the query q a new working query w.r.t. the current working query *wq*. The query q can be seen as a *link* between the current and the new working query. Usually, navigating is used to refine the working concept, i.e., to select a subset of its extension. In this case, the mapping l_{wq} is defined by $l_{wq}(q) := wq \sqcap q$, which is equivalently characterized by

$$\mu(l_{wq}(q)) =^c wc \wedge^c \mu(q) \quad \text{and} \quad \tau(l_{wq}(q)) = \tau(wq) \cap \tau(q).$$

Note again the duality between the intentional vision, on the left, and the extensional one, on the right.

It is useful to allow for other interpretations of the query argument. For instance, we can allow for the distinction between *relative* and *absolute* queries, similarly to relative and absolute paths in file systems. The previous definition of the mapping l_{wq} concerns relative queries, but can be extended to handle absolute queries by $l_{wq}(/q) := q$, where '/' denotes the absolute interpretation of queries. This allows to forget the working query. We can also imagine less usual interpretations of queries like $l_{wq}(|q) := wq \sqcup q$.

The main navigation operation is to guide the user toward his goal. More precisely, it suggests queries that refine the working query. We call these queries *navigation links*. They are formulas of $\mathcal{L}$. A set of navigation links should be finite, of course (whereas $\mathcal{L}$ is usually infinite), even small if possible, and complete for navigation (i.e., each object of the context must be accessible by navigating from ⊤).

The following notion of *link* corresponds to the case where the elaboration mapping satisfies $l_{wq}(q) = wq \sqcap q$. To avoid to go in a concept whose extension is empty (a dead-end), we must impose the following condition on a link x: $\tau(wq \sqcap x) \neq \emptyset$. Furthermore, to avoid to go in a concept whose extension is equal to the extension of *wq* (a false start), we must impose this other condition: $\tau(wq \sqcap x) \neq \tau(wq)$. Note that $\tau(wq \sqcap x) \neq \tau(wq) \implies wq \sqcap x \sqsubset wq$, but not the reverse. Imagine, for instance, a context where every object has description $a \sqcap b$; then $\tau(a \sqcap b) = \tau(a)$. These conditions state that the extension of the new working query must be strictly between the empty set and the extension of the current working query.

Note that $\mathcal{L}$ is a too wide search space (it is often infinite) for links. In fact, links can be searched in the descriptions of the current context without loss of completeness. Furthermore, we retain only greatest links (in the entailment order) as they correspond to smallest navigation steps. Following this principle, every conjunctive formula $x \sqcap y$ can be excluded from the search space for links, because it is redundant with x and y. Thus, a way to build the set of possible links is to split object descriptions on outermost conjunctions (i.e., $a \wedge b$ is split into a and b, whereas $(c \wedge d) \vee e$ cannot be split this way).

Definition 14 (Navigation links) *Let $K = (\mathcal{O}, \mathcal{L}, d)$ be a context. The set of* navigation links *for every working query $wq \in \mathcal{L}$ is defined by*
$$Links(wq) := Max_{\sqsubseteq}\{x \in Descriptions(K) \mid \emptyset \neq \tau(wq \sqcap x) \neq \tau(wq)\}.$$
where $Descriptions(K)$ is the set of all formulas and sub-formulas used in context K.

As navigation aims at finding objects, it must not only suggest links to other places, but also present the objects belonging to the current place, called the *objects of wq* or the *local objects*. We define a local object as an object that is in the current place, but in no place reachable through a link.

Definition 15 (local object) *Let $K = (\mathcal{O}, \mathcal{L}, d)$ be a context. The set of* local objects *is defined for every working query $wq \in \mathcal{L}$ by*
$$Files(wq) := \tau(wq) \setminus \bigcup_{x \in Links(wq)} \tau(x).$$
Alternatively, $Files(wq) := \{o \mid \gamma(o) = wq\}$, the set of all objects that label wq.

A user can reach every intended singleton intention only by following links given by the system.

Theorem 16 (navigation completeness) *Let $K = (\mathcal{O}, \mathcal{L}, d)$ be a context. For every working query $wq \in \mathcal{L}$, the following holds*
$$\forall o \in \tau(wq) \exists q \in Links(wq) : \tau(d(o)) \subseteq \tau(wq \wedge q).$$

In the case where all objects have different descriptions, there is never more than one local object. This must be contrasted to *Web* querying where the number of objects returned in response to a query is generally large. This is because with navigation, non-local objects are hidden behind the intentional properties that enable to distinguish these objects. It is the end-user who selects an intentional property to reveal its content.

This definition of links forms a framework in which operations of data-analysis or data-mining can also be expressed [11]. Using this framework, purely symbolic navigation as well as statistical exploration can be integrated smoothly as variants of the same generic operation.

5   A File System Implementation of a Logic Information System

A first prototype of a LIS has been implemented in λPROLOG [22,2] as a generic system in which a theorem-prover and a syntax analyzer can be plugged-in for every logic used in descriptions. Contrary to other tools based on CA, it does not create the concept lattice. It only manages a Hasse diagram of the formulas used so far. The Hasse diagram serves as a *logical cache* to prevent calling every-time a theorem prover for checking $f \models g$.

In experiments with BibTeX contexts, where all BibTeX fields [19] are represented and there are several thousand bibliographical references, the Hasse diagram has an average of 15 nodes per object, 3 arcs per node, and a height of about 5. This experiment and others support the idea that the number f of features (roughly speaking, sub-formulas) per object is nearly constant for a given application; e.g., f is about 60 in BibTeX contexts. This has a positive implication on the complexity of LIS operations, because under this hypothesis their time complexity is either constant, or linear with the number of objects.

This prototype was promising but still had performance limitations. It was not easily connected to applications that actually produce data, it had no provision for protection of data, and it could hardly operate on context of more than a few thousand objects. So, we designed a file system that offers the operations of a LIS at the operating system level [8,23]. In doing so, applications that actually produce data simply create files, protection of data is an extrapolation of usual file system protections, and performances could be improved.

In modern operating systems, a file system is a set of methods for managing files and directories. For instance, with LINUX a Virtual File System (VFS) acts as an interface whose every method is virtual; an actual file system (e.g., EXT2 or /PROC) is simply an implementation of these virtual methods (file system operations `lookup`, `readdir`, `create`, `rename`, ...). However, this interface reveals technical details that are not interesting in this article (see [23] for these details). To avoid this, we will describe the LIS file system (LISFS) at the shell level, and give only a few hints on the actual file systems operations.

The shell commands are those of the UNIX shell, reinterpreted in the LIS framework. Main changes are the replacement of *paths* by formulas of $\mathcal{L}$ referring to concepts via mapping μ, and the use of concept ordering. For the rest, commands have essentially the same effects. The correspondence between a UNIX file system and LISFS is as follows:

$$\begin{array}{rcl}
\text{UNIX shell} & \longrightarrow & \text{UNIX shell} \\
& & \text{The shell is left unchanged.} \\
\text{file} & \longrightarrow & \text{file} \\
& & \text{Files also.} \\
\text{path} & \longrightarrow & \text{logical formula} \in \mathcal{L} \\
\text{absolute name of a file} & \longrightarrow & \text{object description} = d(\text{file}) \in \mathcal{L} \\
\text{directory} & \longrightarrow & \text{formula/concept} \\
\text{root} & \longrightarrow & \text{formula } \top / \text{concept } \mu(\top) \\
\text{working directory} & \longrightarrow & \text{working query/concept}
\end{array}$$

We now describe LISFS operations in terms of shell commands (commands `pwd`, `cd`, `ls`, `touch`, `mkdir`, `mv`) and a few file systems operations.

– *path formula* (or *path*) — every object has a *path formula* that fully identifies the object, including access rights and system properties like date of last modification. $\top$ is the path to the *root directory*. A path is *relative* to a formula f if it must be $\sqcap$'ed with f to fully identify an object. It is *absolute* otherwise.

- *directory* — A directory is a formal concept. To belong to a directory (i.e., to inhabit a directory) is governed by functions *Files* and *Links* (see Definitions 7, 14, and 15).
- *inode* — every file and directory has an internal name called its *inode number*. We write $\mathtt{inode}(p)$ the internal name of an object whose path is p.
- lookup — given the internal name i of a directory, and a string s, $\mathtt{lookup}(i, s)$ checks that an object with relative path s exists in the directory, and returns its internal name.
- create — given the internal name i of a directory, and a string s, $\mathtt{create}(i, s)$ checks that no object with relative path s exists in the directory, and creates one.
- readdir — given the internal name i of a directory, $\mathtt{readdir}(i)$ lists the names (internal name and relative path) of every inhabitant of the directory.
- rename — given the internal names i and j of two directories, and two strings s and t, $\mathtt{rename}(i, s, j, t)$ checks that an object with relative path s exists in directory i, and moves it to directory j at relative path t.
- pwd — the shell manages a variable called PWD that contains the path to its current working directory. Command pwd returns the content of PWD.
- cd *path* — changes PWD to PWD⊓*path*. Usually the shell asks the file system whether *path* is a valid argument using $\mathtt{lookup}(\mathtt{inode}(\mathtt{PWD}), path)$ which checks that *path* is a known navigation link of PWD, and returns the file system internal name of PWD⊓*path*, i.e., $\mathtt{inode}(\mathtt{PWD}⊓path)$. These ⊓'s are written '/' when PWD is printed.
- ls *path* — returns the local files and the navigation links to more precise queries, $Files(\mathtt{PWD}⊓path) \bigcup Links(\mathtt{PWD}⊓path)$. The corresponding file system operation is $\mathtt{readdir}(\mathtt{inode}(\mathtt{PWD}⊓path))$.
- ls -R *path* — returns the extension of the query, $\tau(\mathtt{PWD}⊓path)$ (see Definition 4). This is the extension of concept $\mu(\mathtt{PWD}⊓path)$. With hierarchical file systems, option -R is interpreted by the shell that performs a recursive traversal of a tree; there is no corresponding dedicated file system operation. With LISFS, the option is better interpreted by the file system who knows about formal concepts.
- touch *path/file* — adds an object $file : d(file) = \mathtt{PWD}⊓path$ to the context. The corresponding file system operation is $\mathtt{create}(\mathtt{inode}(\mathtt{PWD}⊓path), file)$. Command touch is only one of the many ways of creating a file at the shell level; they all boil down to file system operation create. Note that if *file* already exists in PWD⊓*path*, touch will change its last modification time to the current time.

  A file is always created empty, then filled in, then possibly updated using file system operation release. Every time a file is updated, a routine called a *transducer* is called to compute the new intrinsic description of the updated file. (The inference of an extrinsic description is not implemented yet in LISFS.) So, a file may "move" as a consequence of an update.
- mkdir *name* — adds an axiom $name \models \mathtt{PWD}$ to the logic of the file system. This yields the possibility to include taxonomies and ontologies in LISFS.

- mv p_1/f_1 p_2/f_2 — renames local file f_1 of PWD$\sqcap p_1$ into f_2, and moves it to PWD$\sqcap p_2$. The corresponding file system operation is rename(inode(PWD$\sqcap p_1$),f_1,inode(PWD$\sqcap p_2$),f_2). Command mv also uses file system operation lookup to make sure that f_1 is a local file of PWD$\sqcap p_1$, and also to check that an f_2 does not already exist with the new description, PWD$\sqcap p_2$.
- *other commands* — like rm, are defined in the same style.

The neat effect of LISFS is that directories are virtual. They are not represented on disk, but they result from a computation. For instance, doing cd /bin under LISFS places a user in a virtual directory where local files are files of UNIX directory /bin, and links are usr/, local/, X11R4/, prolog/, etc. In a further development of LISFS we have proposed that files also are virtual [24]. Navigation goes inside files and select views that the user sees as regular files. The user can update the views, and the effect is retro-propagated to the master file. For instance, one can navigate inside a BibTeX file, or enter in all definitions of Section 2 of a LaTeX file, update them, and save the modification to the LaTeX file. One can enter in, say, a PROLOG file, and form a view on all clauses that call a given predicate.

6   Discussion for Logic Programmers

Beyond the trivial affinity of two approaches that solve their own problems using logic, we believe that there are deeper common interests between LIS and LP.

First, organizing software objects (e.g., classes and packages) is a classical application of FCA. We have pursued this track with LIS using richer descriptions than simply attributes. For instance, we have used a logic of type entailment based on Di Cosmo's works on type isomorphism [5] to describe Java methods and retrieve them by their types. Then, cd in:Button/out:int could be used to search for a method that takes at least a Button as a parameter, and returns an int. The answer will not be a list of all methods that satisfy the query, but relevant links to them. This can be combined with other kinds of description, e.g., protection modifiers and keywords from the comments, to navigate in large Java packages. This could be transposed to PROLOG packages using types (when available), modes, and abstract properties, and all kinds of descriptions that can be extracted from PROLOG programs.

Second, logic programming can be used in LISFS to form rich queries, especially queries with existential variables. In doing so, objects are described by formulas of a decidable and tractable logic (i.e., not PROLOG), but queries are programmed in PROLOG. For instance, imagine a context of geometric shapes; quadrilaterals have two valued attributes length and width. One needs an existential variable to express square quadrilaterals, cd length:X/width:X. We could have added this feature to the interpretation of *paths*, but we believe it is more expedient to simply allow PROLOG queries in paths, as in cd prolog:"length(X),width(X)".

Third, concept lattices could form a nice computation domain to an LCA-based logic programming language. In this case, unification amounts to apply operator ⊓ and check that the result is not ⊥. This is similar in effects with the LOGIN attempt to combine inheritance and unification [1]. The main difference is that with LOGIN the domain lattice was expressed directly by its Hasse diagram, though with CA the domain lattice is expressed by a formal context. In other words, LOGIN concepts where expressed by their names (e.g., *queen*, *witch* and *wicked queen* in the LOGIN literature), though CA concepts are computed. For this reason, we believe that CA concepts are easier to manage.

Fourth is an issue that takes a very large place in LP, non-monotony. It conciliates the need for negation with an easy and efficient execution scheme, negation-as-failure (NAF). NAF is related to the Closed-World Assumption (CWA). In LIS, we also found the needs for a form of CWA, but we could not abandon monotony. On the one hand, the needs for CWA comes from users. E.g., when a user describes a bibliography entry as `author is "Smith"` he really expects that this implies ¬ `author is "Jones"`, though this is not logically true. On the other hand, the LCA theory collapses if the logic is not monotonous. So, we adapted a modal logic initially proposed by Levesque under the name "All I know" [20]. This logic gives a monotonous rendering of CWA. The trick is to use a modality to reflect the fact that a given formula expresses all the truth, or only the known part of it. We developed a modality that applies to formulas of an almost arbitrary logic, and is easy to implement [6]. We believe that the "All I know" modality can also be applied to LP.

7   Conclusion

7.1   Summary of LIS

We have presented the specifications of a Logical Information System based on (Logical) Concept Analysis. It is generic w.r.t. a logic for describing objects. In this framework, navigation/querying and creation/updating can be seamlessly integrated.

As opposed to previous attempts of using CA for organizing data, we do not propose to navigate directly in the concept lattice. Instead, we use concept ordering to compute navigation links that can be used to come closer to some place of interest. The definition of links can be generalized to encompass data-mining notions like necessary and sufficient conditions, and association rules.

The advantage of LIS is a great flexibility which comes from two factors:

1. the integration of operations that were exclusive in most systems,
2. the use of logic with CA,

We have experimented it in various contexts: e.g., cook-books, bibliographical repository, software repository (search by keywords, types, etc.), music repository (search by style, author, etc.), and simply a note-pad. Various logics were used in these contexts: atoms, intervals, strings, propositional logic, type entailment, taxonomies (e.g., for ingredients). In all cases, a LIS goes beyond any a priori structure and permits many kinds of views on the same information. For instance, in the case of a cook-book, if every recipe is described by its ingredients, its process, the required kitchen utensils, its dietetic value, its place in a meal, and more cultural information, then a cook, a dietitian, and a gourmet can have very different views on the same data, and acquire new information by data-mining and learning, simply by using a few LIS shell commands. Similarly, if software components have intrinsic descriptions like their types and languages, the modules they use, parts of specification, and requirements, and extrinsic descriptions like their testing status, and who is using them, then several software engineering operations like developing and testing, versioning and configuring, and maintenance and evolution can be done using the same repository under different views, and also going smoothly from one view to another.

LIS operations can be implemented by a file system, which we call LISFS. It offers the LIS semantics under the usual file system interface.

7.2   Related Works

There have been several other proposal of navigation/querying based on CA. In [21], Lindig designed a concept-based component retrieval based on sets of *significant keywords* which are equivalent to links for the logic of attributes underlying FCA. In [16], Godin *et al.* propose a direct navigation in the lattice of concepts, which is in fact very similar to Lindig's approach except that only greatest significant keywords, according to context ordering, are displayed to the user. They have also notions common to LIS such as working query, direct query specification, and history of selected queries.

However, the main difference with all of these approaches is that we use an (almost) arbitrary logic to express properties. This enables us to have automatic entailment relations (e.g., (author is "Wille, Ganter") ⊑ (author contains "Wille")). Another difference is that LIS handle in a uniform way, based on CA, navigation and querying as above, but also, updating, data-mining, learning, etc.

On the file system side, many works on file organization have been made to permit more flexible organizations than hierarchies. SFS [15], HAC [17], or NEBULA [3], mix querying and navigation in a file system. For instance, SFS has transducers that extract automatically properties from file contents, such as the names of the functions in a C file. This makes it easy to search for a file using a query such as cd function:foo. However, these systems do not propose a progressive navigation among the query results. In short, they behave like *Google* vs. *Yahoo!*. The contribution of LISFS is to combine querying and navigation in a fully logic framework.

7.3   On-Going Work

The *World Wide Web* can also be explored using our techniques if one considers answers to Web-queries as a formal context into which to navigate. More ambitious is to think of a Web-based LIS. In this case, the main issues will be distribution of data and computation on a large scale.

In all this article, descriptions are essentially unary predicates. However, several applications require to express relations between objects, i.e., n-ary predicates. For instance, a LIS for a software environment should permit to express such relations as `calls` f or `is connected to` x, where f and x are objects. These relations form concrete links between objects, which we plan to consider for navigation in a future work. The main difficulty is to manage the concrete links in a way that remains compatible with the other navigation links. This will also permit to represent topological informations, e.g., `West of` x or `10 miles from` y, that are used in Geographical Information Systems.

Acknowledgments. The results presented here owe much to two PhD students: Sébastien Ferré and Yoann Padioleau. Sébastien Ferré contributed in the theoretical model of LIS, and many more good things that are not presented here. Yoann Padioleau managed to make a round peg enter a square hole by designing a system level LIS that is compatible with existing system interfaces.

References

1. H. Aït-Kaci and R. Nasr. Login: A logic programming language with built-in inheritance. *J. Logic Programming*, 3:187–215, 1986.
2. C. Belleannée, P. Brisset, and O. Ridoux. A pragmatic reconstruction of λProlog. *The Journal of Logic Programming*, 41:67–102, 1999.
3. C.M. Bowman, C. Dharap, M. Baruah, B. Camargo, and S. Potti. A File System for Information Management. In *ISMM Int. Conf. Intelligent Information Management Systems*, 1994.
4. B. A. Davey and H. A. Priestley. *Introduction to Lattices and Order*. Cambridge University Press, 1990.
5. R. Di Cosmo. Deciding type isomorphisms in a type assignment framework. *J. Functional Programming*, 3(3):485–525, 1993.
6. S. Ferré. Complete and incomplete knowledge in logical information systems. In S. Benferhat and P. Besnard, editors, *Symbolic and Quantitative Approaches to Reasoning with Uncertainty*, LNCS 2143, pages 782–791. Springer, 2001.
7. S. Ferré. *Systèmes d'information logiques : un paradigme logico-contex tuel pour interroger, naviguer et apprendre*. PhD thesis, Université de Rennes 1, 2003.
8. S. Ferré and O. Ridoux. A file system based on concept analysis. In Y. Sagiv, editor, *Int. Conf. Rules and Objects in Databases*, LNCS 1861, pages 1033–1047. Springer, 2000.
9. S. Ferré and O. Ridoux. A logical generalization of formal concept analysis. In *Int. Conf. Conceptual Structures*, LNCS 1867, pages 371–384, 2000.
10. S. Ferré and O. Ridoux. A framework for developing embeddable customized logics. In *LOPSTR*, LNCS 2372, pages 191–215. Springer, 2001.
11. S. Ferré and O. Ridoux. Searching for objects and properties with logical concept analysis. In *Int. Conf. Conceptual Structures*, LNCS 2120. Springer, 2001.
12. S. Ferré and O. Ridoux. The use of associative concepts in the incremental building of a logical context. In U. Priss, D. Corbett, and G. Angelova, editors, *Int. Conf. Conceptual Structures*, LNCS 2393, pages 299–313. Springer, 2002.

13. S. Ferré and O. Ridoux. Introduction to logic information systems. *Elsevier J. Information Processing & Management,* In Press (available at http://www.sciencedirect.com/science).
14. B. Ganter and R. Wille. *Formal Concept Analysis — Mathematical Foundations.* Springer, 1999.
15. D.K. Gifford, P. Jouvelot, M.A. Sheldon, and J.W. O'Toole Jr. Semantic file systems. In *13th ACM Symp. on Operating Systems Principles,* pages 16–25. ACM SIGOPS, 1991.
16. R. Godin, R. Missaoui, and A. April. Experimental comparison of navigation in a Galois lattice with conventional information retrieval methods. *International Journal of Man-Machine Studies,* 38(5):747–767, 1993.
17. B. Gopal and U. Manber. Integrating content-based access mechanisms with hierarchical file systems. In *3rd ACM Symp. Operating Systems Design and Implementation,* pages 265–278, 1999.
18. M. Krone and G. Snelting. On the inference of configuration structures from source code. In *Int. Conf. Software Engineering,* pages 49–58. IEEE Computer Society Press, May 1994.
19. L. Lamport. *LaTeX — A Document Preparation System.* Addison-Wesley, 1994. 2nd edition.
20. H. Levesque. All I know: a study in autoepistemic logic. *Artificial Intelligence,* 42(2), March 1990.
21. C. Lindig. Concept-based component retrieval. In *IJCAI95 Workshop on Formal Approaches to the Reuse of Plans, Proofs, and Programs,* 1995.
22. D. A. Miller and G. Nadathur. Higher-order logic programming. In E. Shapiro, editor, *In Third Int. Conf. Logic Programming,* LNCS, pages 448–462, London, 1986. Springer-Verlag.
23. Y. Padioleau and O. Ridoux. A logic file system. In *Usenix Annual Technical Conference,* 2003.
24. Y. Padioleau and O. Ridoux. The parts-of-file file system. Rapport de recherche 4783, INRIA, 2003.
25. G. Snelting. Concept analysis — A new framework for program understanding. *ACM SIGPLAN Notices,* 33(7):1–10, July 1998.
26. F. Vogt and R. Wille. TOSCANA — a graphical tool for analyzing and exploring data. In *Symposium on Graph Drawing,* LNCS 894, pages 226–233, 1994.

A Logic Programming View of Authorization in Distributed Systems

William H. Winsborough

Center for Secure Information Systems, George Mason University wwinsborough@acm.edu

Abstract. An approach to authorization that is based on attributes of the resource requester provides flexibility and scalability that is essential in the context of large distributed systems. Logic programming provides an elegant, expressive, and well-understood framework in which to work with attribute-based authorization policy. We summarize one specific attribute-based authorization framework built on logic programming: RT, a family of Role-based Trust-management languages. RT's logic programming foundation has facilitated the conception and specification of several extensions that greatly enhance its expressivity with respect to important security concepts such as parameterized roles, thresholds, and separation of duties. After examining language design issues, we consider the problem of assessing authorization policies with respect to vulnerability of resource owners to a variety of security risks due to delegations to other principals, risks such as undesired authorizations and unavailability of critical resources. We summarize analysis techniques for assessing such vulnerabilities.

1 Introduction

The problem of authorization is that of determining whether a given subject (typically a user or a software agent) is permitted to access a given resource. Thus there are the questions of how authorization policy is expressed and evaluated. Traditionally, authorization has been based on the identity of the principal requesting access to a resource, although abstractions such as groups and roles [29] have long been recognized as helping to organize the problem by providing layers of abstraction. Still, as many researchers have noted, the problem remains unmanagably cumbersome in highly distributed contexts, where the security domains of the resource and the requester are often not the same. Moreover, it is increasingly typical that distributed systems span multiple organizations, or include individuals acting in their private capacity, *e.g.*, on the Web. The basic problem is one of scale. When the pool of potential requesters is sufficiently large, it is impractical for a resource provider to administer an access control system that requires it to maintain records for every member of the pool.

An alternative is to grant resources based on attributes of the requester that may be more relevant or more universally recognized than one's identity—attributes such as roles within one's home organization, project assignments, degrees held, credit status, nationality, or date of birth. We call this approach attribute-based access control (ABAC). ABAC avoids the need for permissions to be assigned to individual requesters before the request is made. Instead, when a stranger requests access, the ABAC-enabled resource provider can make an authorization decision about an unfamiliar requester (*i.e.*, a

C. Palamidessi (Ed.): ICLP 2003, LNCS 2916, pp. 20–46, 2003.

stranger) based on properties that are familiar, and perhaps more relevant to the decision than the requester's identity.

True scalability is obtained only when authority to define attributes is decentralized. By delegating authority appropriately to representatives of other organizations, policy authors in the multi-centric context can avoid the need to replicate effort, *e.g.*, for background checks and maintenance of personnel data, such as current project assignments or other roles. In decentralized, open systems, there may be no possibility of replicating all the relevant information about would-be resource requesters. For example, obtaining current registration data concerning all university students in the world would be out of the question for, say, a small Internet subscription service that wishes to offer discount student subscription rates.

Attribute credentials provide a means for distributing verifiable attributes to resource providers. Credentials can be obtained as needed, and need not be obtained directly from their issuers to ensure authenticity (*i.e.*, the statement contained in the credentials was made by the issuer) and integrity (*i.e.*, the credential content has not been modified). For instance, the resource requester may supply the necessary credentials to authorize his request.

Principals are entities such as users and software agents that can issue credentials and request resources. A principal is typically represented as a public key; the corresponding private key is known only to that principal, enabling it to sign arbitrary data yeilding a signature that is unforgable and verifiable. A principal demonstrates its intentions by signing various content. For instance, by signing a resource request (together with some additional content included to prevent replay attacks), a principal can demonstrate that it is really him that is making the request. By signing a credential the principal demonstrates it is making a claim about attributes.

A central issue in ABAC policy design is managing decisions about whose assessment of someone's attributes should be trusted. For instance, a principal that is a trustworthy authority on whether someone is a student may not also be a reliable authority on whether someone is a loan officer.

In [3], Blaze, Feigenbaum, and Lacy coined the term "trust management" (TM) to group together some principles dealing with decentralized authorization. In TM systems, principals have ultimate authority over policy statements they issue. However, decentralization is achieved by allowing principals to delegate some of this authority to others. Such delegations determine whether statements of others are significant for determining if a requester is authorized. Early TM languages (notably KeyNote [2] and the original SPKI) emphasized delegation of permissions to access specific resources. Permissions are a restricted form of attribute. Some later trust management systems, such as RT [21, 23], explicitly support ABAC in general, and others, such as SPKI/SDSI 2.0 [7,8], can be used as ABAC systems. In these languages, attributes are established by policy statements about the attributes of principals. Credentials are simply policy statements that have been signed by their issuers. Other policy statements, such as those issued and used locally, need not be signed, for instance, if they will be stored in trusted local storage.

Li et al. [21] designed the RT family of policy languages, which combines the strengths of role-based access control (RBAC) [29] and trust-management systems. RT can be viewed as an extension of a subset of SPKI/SDSI, whose semantics was originally given in terms of reductions or rewrite rules. Later, a set-theoretic semantics was sketched [7] and then formalized [23,19]. The semantics of RT is given by translating policies into datalog programs a restricted form of logic programming. These two later approaches–sets and logic programming–each in turn yield increasing degrees of flexibility. The translation to datalog also shows that the semantics is algorithmically tractable. It is more extensible than a rewriting approach, which allows RT to use conjunction "for free" and to support key security concepts, such as parameterized roles and separation of duty. Furthermore, it enables constraints to be added, as discussed in [18].

While the use of delegation greatly enhances flexibility and scalability, it may also reduce the control that a principal has over the resources it owns. Since delegation gives a certain degree of control to a principal that may be only partially trusted, a natural security concern is whether an individual or organization nevertheless has some guarantees about who can access its resources. Thus, after introducing RT and discussing its relationship to SDSI, we go on to discuss a family of recently developed security analysis techniques [22] that provide the user with an alternative view of policy that can provide such guarantees. If we think of the set of all policy statements of all principals as the state of a TM system, then an individual or organization always has control over some part of the state, but not necessarily all parts. With these limitations in mind, Li et al. [22] developed an analysis of several security properties of policies written in RT, such as safety (access restrictions), availability (access guarantees), and mutual exclusion among roles. We review here algorithms that efficiently decide these properties in several cases. These algorithms are formulated by translating RT policies in the efficiently decidable cases to datalog programs, yielding what can be viewed as a non-standard semantics for those policies. Here we see an additional advantage of taking a logic programming view: the close similarity between the standard and non-standard semantics facilitates their comparison. Finally, we also discuss the complexity classes of certain cases that cannot be decided efficiently.

In Section 2, we present the simplest member of the RT family of ABAC policy languages, giving the syntax and semantics, discussing support for attribute vocabularies, and illustrating the language's features. In Section 3, we discuss some of the language features provided by richer members of the family, including parameterized roles, and support for thresholds and separation of duties. In Section 4, we discuss related trust management systems. In Section 5, we introduce security analysis. In Section 6, we present techniques for answering simple forms of security analysis queries. In Section 7, we show how to answer complex queries for simplified languages and summarize results concerning the computational complexity of answering complex queries richer languages. Section 8 concludes.

2 RT: An ABAC Language

The introduction of abstractions such as groups and roles has long been recognized as essential to increasing the scalability of authorization management. Attributes serve a similar function. A distinguishing feature of ABAC is its emphasis on management of authority to define these abstractions. We argue that an ABAC system should be able to express the following:

1. Decentralized attributes: a principal states that another principal has a certain attribute.
2. Delegation of attribute authority: a principal delegates the authority over an attribute to another principal, *i.e.*, the principal trusts another principal's judgement on the attribute.
3. Inference of attributes: a principal states that one or more attributes can be used to make inferences about another attribute.
4. Attribute parameters. It is often useful to have attributes carry parameter values, such as age and credit limit. It is also useful to infer additional attributes based on these parameters and to delegate attribute authority to a certain principal only for certain specific parameter values, *e.g.*, only when spending level is below a certain limit.
5. Attribute-based delegation of attribute authority: a key to ABAC's scalability is the ability to delegate to strangers whose trustworthiness is determined based on their own certified attributes. For example, a principal may delegate authority on identifying students to principals that are certified universities, and delegate the authority on identifying universities to an accrediting board. By doing so, one avoids having to know all the universities to be able to recognize their students.

The RT framework [21], a family of Role-based Trust-management languages for distributed authorization policies, was the proposal of Li et al. for meeting the desiderata of ABAC systems listed above. RT combines the strengths of role-based access control (RBAC) [29] and trust-management (TM) systems. From RBAC, RT barrows the notion of roles. A *role* in RT defines a set of principals who are members of this role. This notion of roles also captures the notions of groups in many systems. A role can be viewed as an attribute: a principal is a member of a role if and only if it has the attribute identified by the role. In some contexts in the current discussion, we find it natural to talk about a principal having or satisfying an attribute, and in others it is more convenient to use set terminology to talk about role membership.

Membership in a role also entails certain permissions, which in RT are simply modeled as additional roles whose membership decides access to associated resources. Thus, a role can be viewed as the set of permissions it entails. Like RBAC, some members of the RT family provide constructs for sessions and selective role activations (see [21] for discussion of the latter). The thing that is lacking from RBAC is the ability to scale further to coalition contexts and open systems, in which authority is respectively multi-centric or decentralized.

From TM, RT barrows concepts for organizing delegation of authority that can be used to support scalability in decentralized and multi-centric systems. These include the principle of managing distributed authority through the use of credentials, as well as some clear notation denoting relationships between those authorities.

The simplest member of the RT family is RT_0 [23], which satisfies all but one of the desiderata listed above: it does not have attribute parameters. We present RT_0 in this section. In Section 3, we discuss some of the extensions by which other RT family members are constructed.

2.1 RT_0 Syntax

The RT_0 syntax we use in this paper is an abstract syntax designed for understanding the framework. The representation used in practice [20] can take various forms, *e.g.*, XML. We present a simpler, but equivalent variant of the version of RT_0 presented in [23]. The basic constructs of RT_0 include *principals* and *role names*. In this paper, we use A, B, D, X, Y, and Z, sometimes with subscripts, as well as longer names starting with capital letters, to denote principals. A role name is a word over some given standard alphabet. We use r, and u, sometimes with subscripts, as well as longer names starting with lowercase letters, to denote role names. A *role* takes the form of a principal followed by a role name, separated by a dot, *e.g.*, $A.r$ and $X.u$. A *role* defines a set of principals that are members of this role. Each principal A has the authority to define who are the members of each role of the form $A.r$. Thus, A has control over role definition in a namespace of roles of the form $A.r$ for arbitrary r. An access control permission is represented as a role as well; for example, that B is a member of the role of $A.r$ may represent that B has the permission to do action r on the object A.

There are four types of policy statements in RT_0, each corresponding to a different way of defining role membership:

-   *Simple Member*: $A.r \longleftarrow D$
    This statement means that A defines D to be a member of A's r role. We read "$\longleftarrow$" as includes.
-   *Simple Inclusion*: $A.r \longleftarrow B.r_1$
    This statement means that A defines its r role to include (all members of) B's r_1 role. This represents a delegation from A to B, since B may affect who is a member of the role $A.r$ by issuing statements. In other words, A defines the role $B.r_1$ to be more powerful than $A.r$, in the sense that a member of $B.r_1$ is automatically a member of $A.r$ and thus can do anything that the role $A.r$ is authorized to do.
-   *Linking Inclusion*: $A.r \longleftarrow A.r_1.r_2$
    We call $A.r_1.r_2$ a *linked role*. This statement means that A defines $A.r$ to include $A_1.r_2$ for every A_1 that is a member of $A.r_1$. This represents a delegation from A to all the members of the role $A.r_1$, *i.e.*, attribute-based delegation.
-   *Intersection Inclusion*: $A.r \longleftarrow B_1.r_1 \cap B_2.r_2$
    We call $B_1.r_1 \cap B_2.r_2$ an *intersection*. This statement means that A defines $A.r$ to include every principal who is a member of both $B_1.r_1$ and $B_2.r_2$. This represents partial delegations from A to B_1 and to B_2.

A *role expression* is a principal, a role, a linked role, or an intersection. We say that each policy statement *defines* the role $A.r$. Given a set $\mathcal{P}$ of policy statements, we define the following: $\mathsf{Principals}(\mathcal{P})$ is the set of principals in $\mathcal{P}$, $\mathsf{Names}(\mathcal{P})$ is the set of role names in $\mathcal{P}$, and $\mathsf{Roles}(\mathcal{P}) = \{\mathsf{A.r} \mid \mathsf{A} \in \mathsf{Principals}(\mathcal{P}), \mathsf{r} \in \mathsf{Names}(\mathcal{P})\}$.

2.2   Semantics of RT_0

In the original presentation of RT_0 [23], Li et al. presented a set-based semantics, as well as a graph-theoretic semantics. Li and Mitchell showed the logic programming semantics given below to be equivalent to the set theoretic semantics [19]. The logic programming semantics of a set $\mathcal{P}$ of policy statements is given by translating each policy statement into a datalog clause. (Datalog is a restricted form of logic programming (LP) with variables, predicates, and constants, but without function symbols of higher arity.) We call the resulting program the *semantic program* of $\mathcal{P}$. As discussed in the introduction, using the LP-based approach yields many benefits. Perhaps the most pronounced is that it generalizes easily to the case in which role names contain parameters, as we shall see in Section 3. It also is very convenient for working with non-standard semantics, as we do below when we take up policy analysis in Section 5.

Definition 1 (Semantic Program). Given a set $\mathcal{P}$ of policy statements, the *semantic program*, $SP(\mathcal{P})$, of $\mathcal{P}$, has one ternary predicate m. Intuitively, $m(A, r, D)$ represents that D is a member of the role $A.r$. As a convenience below when we discuss extensions to RT_0, we use macro $isMember(D, A.r)$ to represent $m(A, r, D)$. $SP(\mathcal{P})$ is constructed as follows. (Symbols that start with "?" represent logical variables.)

For each $A.r \longleftarrow D$ in $\mathcal{P}$, add
$$isMember(D, A.r) \tag{m1}$$
For each $A.r \longleftarrow B.r_1$ in $\mathcal{P}$, add
$$isMember(?z, A.r) :- isMember(?z, B.r_1) \tag{m2}$$
For each $A.r \longleftarrow A.r_1.r_2$ in $\mathcal{P}$, add
$$isMember(?z, A.r) :- isMember(?y, A.r_1), isMember(?z, ?y.r_2) \tag{m3}$$
For each $A.r \longleftarrow B_1.r_1 \cap B_2.r_2$ in $\mathcal{P}$, add
$$isMember(?z, A.r) :- isMember(?z, B_1.r_1), isMember(?z, B_2.r_2) \tag{m4}$$

A datalog program is a set of datalog clauses. Given a datalog program, $\mathcal{DP}$, its semantics can be defined through several equivalent approaches. The model-theoretic approach views $\mathcal{DP}$ as a set of first-order sentences and uses the minimal Herbrand model as the semantics. We write $SP(\mathcal{P}) \models isMember(Z, X.u)$ when $isMember(Z, X.u)$ is in the minimal Herbrand model of $SP(\mathcal{P})$.

2.3   An Example of Attribute-Based Delegation

In this section we give a small example that illustrates the power of attribute-based delegation to leverage judgements of third-parties that may not be identified by name, but by some other attribute.

Example 1. EPub is an electronic publisher that wishes to offer discount subscription rates to university students. To accept a student ID from a university, EPub needs to indicate which principals are universities. Enumerating these in the policy is impractical and would require EPub to assess the legitimacy of universities. For both these reasons, EPub is motivated to delegate authority to identify legitimate universities to an accrediting board for universities (ABU). Thus, authority to identify students is delegated to universities based not on their identities, but on the attribute of being accredited.

> EPub.studentDiscount $\longleftarrow$ EPub.university.student
> EPub.university $\longleftarrow$ ABU.accredited
> ABU.accredited $\longleftarrow$ StateU
> StateU.student $\longleftarrow$ Alice   ∎

There has to be agreement on the meaning and name of the student attribute for this to work. In Section 2.4, we discuss a mechanism that disambiguates whether such agreement exists. In general, such agreement can be established in practice only incrementally, as the need for agreement is shown and interested parties settle on a standard that is acceptable to many of them.

2.4   Globally Unique Role Names

We now discuss the issue of establishing agreement on the intended meaning of role names. Attaining agreement on terminology often facilitates collaboration. Of course, agreement is not always attainable because of differences in nuance between conceptual referents, and even when there is conceptual uniformity, different communities may have historical attachments to their customary usage. At minimum, what a participant requires is the ability to use terms from the vocabulary of other communities and collaborators unambiguously.

In ABAC, it is essential to be able to refer unambiguously to roles whose membership is defined by other individuals or organizations, such as coalition partners. The need to support this is illustrated by the following statement barrowed from Example 1:

$$\text{EPub.studentDiscount} \longleftarrow \text{EPub.university.student}$$

If some universities use student to mean currently enrolled students, but others include alumni, EPub does not obtain the desired result from its policy (which is, presumably, to grant discounts to students currently enrolled). This is clearly unacceptable.

RT addresses this problem through a scheme inspired by XML namespaces [5], *viz.*, *application domain specification documents (ADSDs)*. Each ADSD defines a vocabulary, which is a suite of related data types (which are used in role parameters in RT_1), role identifiers (role ids for short) with the name and the data type of each of its parameters, *etc.* An ADSD may also declare other common characteristics of role ids, such as storage type information, as studied in [23]. An ADSD generally should give natural-language explanations of these role ids, including the conditions under which policy statements defining them should be issued. Credentials contain a preamble in which vocabulary identifiers are defined to refer to a particular ADSD, *e.g.*, by giving its URI. Each use of a role id inside the credential then incorporates such a vocabulary identifier as a prefix. Thus, a relatively short role id specifies a globally unique role id. An ADSD can refer to other ADSDs and use data types defined in it, using the mechanism just described. A concrete RT system is defined by multiple ADSDs. ADSDs allow multiple individuals and organizations to use the same role name in the roles they define, as well as to refer unambiguously to roles defined by one another, without requiring universal acceptance. They also allow for incremental adoption and evolution of role vocabularies.

2.5   An Example Using Credentials Representing Rules

Notice that simple-member statements translate to atomic clauses (facts), while the various inclusion statements translate to rules. In RT, any of these forms of statement can be signed to form a credential. Several prior languages [4,25,30] only allowed credentials

Table 1. A set of policy statements illustrating the utility of having credentials encode implications

BankWon.deferGSL ⟵ BankWon.university.fulltimeStudent
BankWon.university ⟵ ABU.accredited
ABU.accredited ⟵ StateU
StateU.fulltimeStudent ⟵ Registrar.fulltimeLoad
StateU.fulltimeStudent ⟵ Registrar.parttimeLoad ∩ StateU.phdCandidate
StateU.phdCandidate ⟵ StateU.gradOfficer.phdCandidate
Registrar.parttimeLoad ⟵ Bob
StateU.gradOfficer ⟵ Carol
Carol.phdCandidate ⟵ Bob

to carry data about a single, specified principal, like RT's simple-member statements. The logic programming-based languages of this kind [4,30] do allow policies to be expressed such as the one defined by EPub in Example 1. However, the role student must be defined directly by credentials issued to each student by each university.

By contrast, RT's inclusion statements provide rules for inferring attributes of arbitrary principals based on other attributes that may be defined by others. This expressive power to delegate authority to others is a significant advantage when it comes to writing policies that scale. It enables policy writers to invoke policies written by others who may have greater expertise, particularly with respect to how foreign organizations are structured, what kinds of credentials they issue, and who within them issues those credentials. The following example is intended to illustrate this point.

Example 2. A bank wants to know whether a principal is a full-time student, to determine whether the principal is eligible to defer repayment on a guaranteed student loan (GSL). (The US government insures banks against default of GSLs and requires participating banks to allow full-time students to defer repayments.) Table 1 shows a set of policy statements that might be written by various participants in this scenario. Other universties, not illustrated here, may define fulltimeStudent using different rules and delegating authority differently to internal university bodies. (Nevertheless, the overall effect of their definitions are assumed to be consistent with the description of the role name in the associated ADSD.) StateU allows fulltimeStudents to register for a light course load once they are formally accepted as Ph.D. candidates. Thus, Bob is authorized to defer his GSL.   ∎

Note that the bank does not need to understand the way authority is delegated by the university to graduate officers and the registrar.

3   Extensions to RT_0

The logic programming basis for defining the semantics of RT facilitates several extension that provide useful expressive power. These include adding attribute (role) parameters and roles containing as members sets of principals whose concurrence is required for an authorization. The latter are called *manifold roles* [21]. In this section we outline the addition of attribute parameters to RT_0, which yields RT_1. We then discuss another member of the family, RT^T, which introduces role-product operators and manifold roles, allowing us to express some policies that cannot be expressed in other systems at all, and some that cannot be expressed in such succinct and intuitive a way. Role product operators can be added to either RT_0 or RT_1, obtaining as a result languages called RT_0^T and RT_1^T, respectively.

There are additional RT family members that we will not discuss here. One allows sets of objects to be defined and used in constraints on variables that range over resources. A second captures the notion of delegation of role activations. This would be used, for instance, to tranfer some of one's access rights to a server so that it could access backend a database on one's behalf. For details of these two RT extension, the reader is referred to [21].

3.1 RT_1: Adding Role Parameters

Parameters are added to roles in a rather straightforward manner. Role names now have the form $R = r(h_1, \ldots, h_k)$ in which r is required to be a role identifier and for each i in $1..n$, h_i is a data term having the type of the ith parameter of r. Parameter types of role identifiers are declared in ADSDs. A data term is either a constant, a variable, or the keyword this. The latter is permitted only in linking inclusions, $A.R \longleftarrow A.R_1.R_2$, where it can appear only in R_1. When a variable occurs as a parameter to a role name, it is implicitly assigned to have the type of that parameter. In any RT system, a statement that is not well-formed is ignored. An RT_1 statement is *well-formed* if all named variables are well-typed and safe. A named variable is *well-typed* if it has the same type across all occurances in one statement. Two types are the same if they have the same name. A variable in a statement is *safe* if it appears in the body. This safety requirement ensures that RT_1 statements can be translated into safe datalog rules, which helps to guarantee tractability of RT_1.

Example 3. A company Alpha allows the manager of an employee to evaluate an employee by issuing the following statement, which cannot be expressed in RT_0:

Alpha.evaluatorOf(?Y) $\longleftarrow$ Alpha.managerOf(?Y)

In the semantics for RT_1, several versions of the predicate m are created, each with different arity; to represent membership in a given role, one additional parameter is needed by m for each of the role's parameters. The macro $isMember(D, A.r(h_1, \ldots, h_k))$ now stands for $m(A, r, h_1, \ldots, h_k, D)$. In translation rule (m3), occurances this are replaced by the variable $?z$. Constraints are also added to clauses defined by (m1) through (m4). These come from constraints on variables and are discussed in [21]. Li and Mitchell [18] have shown that parameters can range over simple constraint domains, such as numeric ranges and trees. This requires extending the translation target to datalog with constraints, which is shown to be efficient.

Example 4. As part of its annual review process, Alpha gives a pay raise to an employee if someone authorized to evaluate the employee says that his performance was good.

Alpha.payRaise $\longleftarrow$ Alpha.evaluatorOf(this).goodPerformance

Proposition 1 ([21]). *Given a set $\mathcal{P}$ of RT_1 statements, assuming that each statement in $\mathcal{P}$ has at most v variables and that each role name has at most p arguments, then the atomic implications of $\mathcal{P}$ can be computed in time $O(MN^{v+2})$, where $N = \max(N_0, pN_0)$, N_0 is the number of statements in $\mathcal{P}$, and M is the size of $\mathcal{P}$.*

3.2 RT^T: Supporting Threshold and Separation-of-Duty Policies

Threshold structures, which require agreement among k out of a list of principals, are common in trust-management systems. Some systems, such as Delegation Logic [17], also have the more expressive dynamic threshold structures, which are satisfied by the agreement of k out of a set of principals that satisfy a specified condition.

A related yet distinct policy concept is separation of duty (SoD) [6,31]. This security principle requires that two or more different people be responsible for the completion of a sensitive task, such as ordering and paying for a purchase. SoD can be used to discourage fraud by requiring collusion among principals to commit fraud. In RBAC, SoD is often achieved by using constraints such as mutual exclusion among roles [29, 31] and requiring cooperation of mutually exclusive roles to complete sensitive tasks. Because no principal is allowed to simultaneously occupy two mutually exclusive roles, sensitive tasks can be completed only by cooperation of principals.

Though the problems are related, the threshold structures of existing TM systems cannot generally be used to express SoD policies. Threshold structures can require agreement only of two different principals drawn from a single set, while SoD policies typically are concerned with agreement among members of two different sets. For similar reasons, mutually exclusive roles cannot be used to achieve thresholds either.

In a distributed environment, it is often very difficult to ensure one has complete information in the form of every policy statement that may be relevant to an authorization decision. Thus, trust management systems are generally monotonic, in the sense that the more statements there are, the more role memberships and authorizations there are. Constraints such as mutual exclusion of roles are nonmonotonic in nature: a principal cannot be a member of one role if it is a member of another role. To enforce such constraints, complete information about role memberships is needed. Since we allow only monotonic constructs in RT, we cannot use such constraints. Instead, we use what we call *manifold roles* to achieve thresholds and separation of duty. Similar to a role, which defines a set of principals, a manifold role defines a set of principal collections, each of which is a set of principals whose cooperation satisfies the manifold role. Manifold roles are defined by role expressions constructed using either of the two *role-product operators*: $\odot$ and $\otimes$.

The role expression

$$\overbrace{A.R \otimes A.R \otimes \cdots \otimes A.R}^{k}$$

represents the dynamic threshold structure that requires k (different) principals out of members of $A.R$. The role expression "$A.R_1 \otimes A.R_2$" represents the set of principal collections each of which has two different principals, one from $A.R_1$ and the other from $A.R_2$. This can be used to force cooperation to complete a sensitive task (the goal of SoD) without forcing roles to be mutually disjoint. This could permit important flexibility, particularly in small organizations where individuals may need to fulfill several roles. Such flexibility motivates mutual exclusion in role activations (also known as dynamic separation of duty) [31]. Also, because the constructs are monotonic, they allow SoD to be supported in a de-centralized framework, where role membership information may be partial or incomplete.

The operator $\odot$ can be used to implement policies such as the following: An action is allowed if it gets approval from two roles. This approval might come from one principal who is a member of both roles, or it might come from two different principals who are each members of one role.

Example 5. The graduate school says that a student has passed his doctoral defense if the sudent's advisor and two other members of the student's doctoral committee approves the student's dissertation:

gradscl.docComMajority$(?s)\longleftarrow$
    gradscl.Advisor$(?s) \otimes$ gradscl.CommMbr$(?s) \otimes$ gradscl.CommMbr$(?s)$.
gradscl.passedDocDefense$\longleftarrow$
    gradscl.docComMajority(this).approveDisseration.

Again, the value of a manifold role is a set of principal collections. A *principal collection* is either a principal, which can be viewed as a singleton set, or a set of two or more principals. This allows us to view a single-element role as a special-case manifold role whose value is a set of singletons. In this section, we extend the notion of *roles* to include both manifold roles and single-element roles, and (allowing for role parameters) we continue to use R to denote role name of this generalized notion of roles. RT^T introduces two new types of statements:

–   *Type-5:* $A.R \longleftarrow B_1.R_1 \odot \cdots \odot B_k.R_k$
    In which R and the R_i's are (single-element or manifold) role names. This statement means:

    $members(A.R) \supseteq members(B_1.R_1 \odot \cdots \odot B_k.R_k) = \{s_1 \cup \cdots \cup s_k \mid s_i \in members(B_i.R_i)$ for $1 \le i \le k\}$.

    Here, when s_i is an individual principal, say, D, it is implicitly converted to the singleton $\{D\}$.
–   *Type-6:* $A.R \longleftarrow B_1.R_1 \otimes \cdots \otimes B_k.R_k$
    This statement means:

    $members(A.R) \supseteq members(B_1.R_1 \otimes \cdots \otimes B_k.R_k) = \{s_1 \cup \cdots \cup s_k \mid (s_i \in members(B_i.R_i)$ & $s_i \cap s_j = \emptyset)$ for $1 \le i \ne j \le k\}$

Example 6. A says that a principal has attribute R if one member of $A.R_1$ and two different members of $A.R_2$ all say so. This can be represented using the following statements:

    $A.R_3 \longleftarrow A.R_2 \otimes A.R_2, \quad A.R_4 \longleftarrow A.R_1 \odot A.R_3, \quad A.R \longleftarrow A.R_4.R.$

Suppose that in addition one has the following statements:

    $A.R_1 \longleftarrow B, \quad A.R_1 \longleftarrow E,$
    $A.R_2 \longleftarrow B, \quad A.R_2 \longleftarrow C, \quad A.R_2 \longleftarrow D.$

Then one can conclude the following:

$members(A.R_1) \supseteq \{B, E\}$,
$members(A.R_2) \supseteq \{B, C, D\}$,
$members(A.R_3) \supseteq \{\{B, C\}, \{B, D\}, \{C, D\}\}$,
$members(A.R_4) \supseteq \{\{B, C\}, \{B, D\}, \{B, C, D\}$,
$\qquad\qquad\qquad \{B, C, E\}, \{B, D, E\}, \{C, D, E\}\}$.

Now suppose one further has the following statements:

$B.R \longleftarrow B, \quad B.R \longleftarrow C$,
$C.R \longleftarrow C, \quad C.R \longleftarrow D, \quad C.R \longleftarrow E$,
$D.R \longleftarrow D, \quad D.R \longleftarrow E$,
$E.R \longleftarrow E$.

Then one can conclude that $members(A.R) \supseteq \{C, E\}$, but one cannot conclude $members(A.R) \supseteq \{B\}$ or $members(A.R) \supseteq \{D\}$.

In RT^T, type 1 through 4 statements are also generalized in that a manifold role name can appear where a role name is allowed, except when as a constraint to a variable.

Each role identifier has a *size*. The size of a manifold role id should be specified when the role id is declared in an ADSD. A single-element role id always has size one. A role name $r(t_1, \ldots, t_h)$ has the same size as r, and we have $size(A.R) = size(R)$. The size of a role limits the maximum size of each principal set in the role's value. For example, if $size(A.R) = 2$, then $members(A.R)$ can never contain $\{B_1, B_2, B_3\}$.

For an RT^T role-definition statement to be well-formed, it has to satisfy the additional requirement that the size of its head is always greater than or equal to the size of its body. And the size of its body is defined as follows:

$$
\begin{cases}
size(D) = 1 \\
size(A.R_1.R_2) = size(R_2) \\
size(B_1.R_1 \cap \cdots \cap B_k.R_k) = \max_{i=1..k} size(R_i) \\
size(B_1.R_1 \odot \cdots \odot B_k.R_k) = \sum_{i=1..k} size(R_i) \\
size(B_1.R_1 \otimes \cdots \otimes B_k.R_k) = \sum_{i=1..k} size(R_i)
\end{cases}
$$

3.3   Translating RT^T into Horn Clauses

We extend the predicate *isMember* in the output language to allow the first argument to be a principal collection, and to allow the second argument to be a manifold role as well as a single-element role. Let t be the maximum size of all manifold roles in the system, we also introduce $2(t-1)$ new predicates set_k and $niset_k$ for $k = 2..t$. Each set_k takes $k+1$ principal collections as arguments, and $set_k(s, s_1, \ldots, s_k)$ is true if and only if $s = s_1 \cup \cdots \cup s_k$; where when s_i is a principal, it is treated as a single-element set. Each $niset_k$ is similar to set_k, except that $niset_k(s, s_1, \ldots, s_k)$ is true if and only if $s = s_1 \cup \cdots \cup s_k$ and for any $1 \le i \ne j \le k$, $s_i \cap s_j = \emptyset$.

The translation for type 1, 2, and 4 statements is the same as that in Section 2.2. The other three types are translated as follows:

- For each $A.R \longleftarrow A.R_1.R_2$ in $\mathcal{P}$,
  when $size(R_1) = 1$, add

$$isMember(?z, A.R) \longleftarrow isMember(?x, A.R_1), isMember(?z, ?x.R_2).$$

when $size(R_1) = k > 1$, add

$$isMember(?z, A.R) \longleftarrow$$
$$isMember(?x, A.R_1),$$
$$isMember(?z, ?x_1.R_2), \cdots, isMember(?z, ?x_k.R_2),$$
$$set_k(?x, ?x_1, \ldots, ?x_k).$$

- For each $A.R \longleftarrow B_1.R_1 \odot \cdots \odot B_k.R_k$ in $\mathcal{P}$, add

$$isMember(?z, A.R) \longleftarrow$$
$$isMember(?z_1, B_1.R_1), \cdots, isMember(?z_k, B_k.R_k),$$
$$set_k(?z, ?z_1, \ldots, ?z_k).$$

- For each $A.R \longleftarrow B_1.R_1 \otimes \cdots \otimes B_k.R_k$ in $\mathcal{P}$, add

$$isMember(?z, A.R) \longleftarrow$$
$$isMember(?z_1, B_1.R_1), \cdots, isMember(?z_k, B_k.R_k),$$
$$niset_k(?z, ?z_1, \ldots, ?z_k).$$

It is easy to see that this translation is an extension to that in section 2.2. When a statement contains no manifold roles, the resulting rule is the same.

Proposition 2 ([21]). *Given a set $\mathcal{P}$ of RT^T statements, let t be the maximal size of all roles in $\mathcal{P}$. The atomic implications of $\mathcal{P}$ can be computed in time $O(MN^{v+2t})$.*

4   SPKI/SDSI and Other Work Related to RT

Using KeyNote, SPKI 1.0[1], or X.509 attribute certificates [9], one cannot express inference of attributes or attribute-based delegation. SDSI 1.0 or even SPKI/SDSI 2.0 do not support attribute parameters. Neither TPL [12] nor the language of Bonatti and Samarati [4] supports delegation of authority over arbitrary attributes. Although one can use Delegation Logic (DL) [15,16] to express all of the above, it is not very convenient. Through a basic attribute credential, a designated issuer should be able to express the judgement that a subject has a certain attribute. A basic certificate in DL has only an issuer and a statement. Although one can encode the subject and attribute together in a statement, DL lacks the explicit subject abstraction, which we desire for the following reasons. The explicit abstraction allows clear, concise representation of attribute-based delegation, *e.g.*, in the form of linked local names in SDSI. The subject abstraction also enables distributed storage and discovery of credentials, as shown in [23]. It also enables us to view attributes similarly to roles in role-based access control (RBAC) [29], and to use concepts similar to role activations to enable principals to make selective use of those roles. Another TM system SD3 [13] can be viewed as Delegation Logic without delegation constructs; it does not have the subject abstraction either.

---

[1] We use SPKI 1.0 to denote the part of SPKI/SDSI 2.0 [7,8] originally from SPKI, *i.e.*, 5-tuples, and SDSI 1.0 to denote the part of SDSI originally from SDSI, *i.e.*, name certificates (or 4-tuples as called in [8]).

5   Security Analysis

In this section, we consider the *security analysis* problem, which asks what accesses may be allowed or prevented by prospective changes in the state of a TM system. A few definitions are useful for stating the security analysis problem more precisely. In general, a TM language has a syntax for specifying *policy statements* and *queries*, together with an entailment relation $\vdash$. We call a set $\mathcal{P}$ of policy statements a *state* of a TM system. Given a state $\mathcal{P}$ and a query $\mathcal{Q}$, the relation $\mathcal{P} \vdash \mathcal{Q}$ means that $\mathcal{Q}$ is true in $\mathcal{P}$. When $\mathcal{Q}$ arises from an access request, $\mathcal{P} \vdash \mathcal{Q}$ means that access $\mathcal{Q}$ is allowed in $\mathcal{P}$; a proof demonstrating $\mathcal{P} \vdash \mathcal{Q}$ is then called a *proof-of-compliance*.

Recognizing that a principal or an organization of cooperating principals may control only a part of the global state, we assume there is a *restriction rule*, $\mathcal{R}$, that defines how states may be changed. For example, the principal in question may consider the part of the state controlled by fully trusted principals to be fixed, while considering that other principals may remove some policy statements and/or add new ones. We define one step of change as adding or removing one policy statement. Given a state $\mathcal{P}$ and a restriction rule $\mathcal{R}$, we write $\mathcal{P} \mapsto_{\mathcal{R}} \mathcal{P}'$ if the change from $\mathcal{P}$ to $\mathcal{P}'$ is allowed by $\mathcal{R}$, and $\mathcal{P} \overset{*}{\mapsto}_{\mathcal{R}} \mathcal{P}'$ if a sequence of zero or more allowed changes leads from $\mathcal{P}$ to $\mathcal{P}'$. If $\mathcal{P} \overset{*}{\mapsto}_{\mathcal{R}} \mathcal{P}'$, we say that $\mathcal{P}'$ is $\mathcal{R}$-*reachable* from P, or simply $\mathcal{P}'$ is *reachable*, when $\mathcal{P}$ and $\mathcal{R}$ are clear from context.

Definition 2. Let $\mathcal{P}$ be a state, $\mathcal{R}$ a restriction rule, and $\mathcal{Q}$ a query. *Existential security analysis* takes the form: Does there exist $\mathcal{P}'$ such that $\mathcal{P} \overset{*}{\mapsto}_{\mathcal{R}} \mathcal{P}'$ and $\mathcal{P}' \vdash \mathcal{Q}$? When the answer is affirmative, we say $\mathcal{Q}$ is *possible* given $\mathcal{P}$ and $\mathcal{R}$. *Universal security analysis* takes the form: For every $\mathcal{P}'$ such that $\mathcal{P} \overset{*}{\mapsto}_{\mathcal{R}} \mathcal{P}'$, does $\mathcal{P}' \vdash \mathcal{Q}$? If so, we say $\mathcal{Q}$ is *necessary* given $\mathcal{P}$ and $\mathcal{R}$.

Here are some motivating examples of security analysis problems.

Simple Safety (Existential). Does there exist a reachable state in which a specific (presumably untrusted) principal has access to a given resource?

Simple Availability (Universal). In every reachable state, does a specific (presumably trusted) principal have access to a given resource?

Bounded Safety (Universal). In every reachable state, is the set of all principals that have access to a given resource bounded by a given set of principals?

Liveness (Existential). Does there exist a reachable state in which no principal has access to a given resource?

Mutual Exclusion (Universal). In every reachable state, are two given properties (resources) mutually exclusive, *i.e.*, no principal has both properties (access to both resources) at the same time?

Containment (Universal). In every reachable state, does every principal that has one property (*e.g.*, has access to a resource) also have another property (*e.g.*, being an employee)? Containment can express safety or availability (*e.g.*, by interchanging the two example properties in the previous sentence).

Simple safety analysis was first formalized by Harrison et al. [11] in the context of the well-known access matrix model [14,10]. Simple safety analysis was referred to as *safety analysis* since other analysis problems were not considered. The model in [11] is commonly known as the HRU model. In the general HRU model, *safety analysis* is undecidable [11]. A number of protection models were developed to address this. Lipton and Snyder introduced the take-grant model [24], in which simple safety can be decided in linear time. Sandhu introduced the Schematic Protection Model [27], and the Typed Access Matrix model [28]. In these previous works, only simple safety analysis are considered; the other kinds of analysis listed above were not. Since some of the analysis problems are about properties other than safety (e.g., availability), we use the term *security analysis* rather than safety analysis.

The first investigation of security analysis for TM systems was presented by Li et al. [22]. We summarize their model, some of the main results, and discuss usage scenarios. The policy languages considered in those results are RT_0 and three of its sub-languages: BRT (for Basic RT) has only simple member and simple inclusion statements, LRT (for Linking RT) adds to BRT linking inclusion statements, and NRT (for iNtersection RT) adds to BRT intersection inclusion statements.

5.1 Summary of Security Analysis Results

All the security analysis problems listed above are considered in [22]. The TM language we are studying, RT supports delegation and is more expressive than the access matrix model in certain ways. Moreover, the kinds of analysis problems we are considering are more general than those discussed in the access matrix context. Nevertheless, somewhat surprisingly, they are decidable for RT_0. Simple safety, simple availability, bounded safety, liveness, and mutual exclusion analysis for RT_0 (and hence for the three sub-languages of RT_0) can all be answered in time polynomial in the size of $\mathcal{P}$. These analysis problems are answered by evaluating queries against logic programs derived from $\mathcal{P}$ and $\mathcal{R}$.

Containment analysis is the most interesting case, both in terms of usefulness and in terms of technical challenge. The computational complexity of containment analysis depends on the language features. In BRT, the most basic language, containment analysis is in **P**. Containment analysis becomes more complex when additional policy language features are used. Containment analysis is **coNP**-complete for NRT, **coNP**-hard for LRT, and in **coNEXP** for RT_0. To derive these complexity results, we found that techniques and results from logic programming, formal languages, and automata theory are useful. For BRT, we use logic programs derived from $\mathcal{P}$ and $\mathcal{R}$ to do containment analysis. These logic programs use negation-as-failure in a stratified manner [1]. For NRT, containment analysis is essentially equivalent to determining validity of propositional logic formulas. The LRT language is expressively equivalent to SDSI (Simple Distributed Security Infrastructure) [7,26]. We show that containment analysis for LRT can be used to determine validity of propositional logic formulas. For the case of RT_0, we show that if a containment does not hold, then there must exist a counter example state (*i.e.*, a reachable state in which the containment does not hold) of size at most exponential in the size of the input.

5.2   Restriction Rules on State Changes

Before discussing how we model restrictions on changes in policy state, we consider one motivating scenario. Additional discussion of ways that security analysis can be used in practical situations appears in Section 5.5. Suppose that the users within an organization control certain principals, and that these principals delegate partial control to principals outside the organization. In this situation, roles defined by principals within the organization can be viewed as unchanging, since the analysis will be repeated before any future candidate change is made to those roles. Roles defined by principals outside the organization, however, may change in arbitrary ways, since they are beyond the organization's control. By using security analysis, the organization can ensure that delegations to principals outside the organization do not violate desired security properties, which are specified by a collection of security analysis problem instances and the correct answers to them.

To model control over roles, we use restriction rules of the form $\mathcal{R} = (\mathcal{G}_{\mathcal{R}}, \mathcal{S}_{\mathcal{R}})$, which consist of a pair of finite sets of roles. (In the rest of the paper we drop the subscripts from $\mathcal{G}$ and $\mathcal{S}$, as $\mathcal{R}$ is clear from context.)

- Roles in $\mathcal{G}$ are called *growth-restricted* (or *g-restricted*); no policy statements defining these roles can be added. Roles not in $\mathcal{G}$ are called *growth-unrestricted* (or *g-unrestricted*).
- Roles in $\mathcal{S}$ are called *shrink-restricted* (or *s-restricted*); policy statements defining these roles cannot be removed. Roles not in $\mathcal{S}$ are called *shrink-unrestricted* (or *s-unrestricted*).

One example of $\mathcal{R}$ is $(\emptyset, \emptyset)$, under which every role is g/s-unrestricted, *i.e.*, both g-unrestricted and s-unrestricted. Another example is $\mathcal{R} = (\emptyset, \mathrm{Roles}(\mathcal{P}))$, *i.e.*, every role may grow without restriction, and no statement defining roles in $\mathrm{Roles}(\mathcal{P})$ can be removed. This models the case of having incomplete knowledge of a fixed policy state. A third example, corresponding to the scenario discussed above, is $\mathcal{R} = (\mathcal{G}, \mathcal{S})$, where $\mathcal{G} = \mathcal{S} = \{X.u \mid X \in \{X_1, \dots, X_k\}, u \in \mathrm{Names}(\mathcal{P})\}$, *i.e.*, $X_1, \dots, X_k$ are trusted (controlled); therefore, every role $X.u$ such that $X \in \{X_1, \dots, X_k\}$ is restricted, all other roles are unrestricted. If a principal X does not appear in $\mathcal{R}$, then for every role name r, by definition $X.r$ is *g/s-unrestricted*. This models the fact that the roles of unknown principals may be defined arbitrarily.

We allow some roles controlled by one principal to be g-restricted while other roles controlled by the same principal may be g-unrestricted. This provides more flexibility than simply identifying principals as trusted and untrusted, and permits one in practice to perform security analysis only when changing certain roles. Similarly, we allow a role to be both g-restricted and s-unrestricted, which has the effect of making a safety check necessary when modifying the definition of the role only if adding a new statement.

The above kinds of restrictions are *static* in the sense that whether or not a state-change step is allowed by $\mathcal{R}$ does not depend on the current state. A dynamic restriction could, for instance, have $B.r_2$ be g-restricted if B is a member of $A.r_1$, which depends on the current state. Security analysis with dynamic restrictions is potentially interesting future work.

5.3   Queries

We consider the following three forms of query $\mathcal{Q}$:

–   *Membership*: $members(A.r) \sqsupseteq \{D_1, \ldots, D_n\}$
    Intuitively, this means that all the principals $D_1, \ldots, D_n$ are members of $A.r$. Formally, $\mathcal{P} \vdash members(A.r) \sqsupseteq \{D_1, \ldots, D_n\}$ if and only if $\{Z \mid SP(\mathcal{P}) \models m(A, r, Z)\} \supseteq \{D_1, \ldots, D_n\}$.
–   *Boundedness*: $\{D_1, \ldots, D_n\} \sqsupseteq members(A.r)$
    Intuitively, this means that the member set of $A.r$ is bounded by the given set of principals. Formally, $\mathcal{P} \vdash members(A.r) \sqsupseteq \{D_1, \ldots, D_n\}$ if and only if $\{D_1, \ldots, D_n\} \supseteq \{Z \mid SP(\mathcal{P}) \models m(A, r, Z)\}$.
–   *Inclusion*: $members(X.u) \sqsupseteq members(A.r)$
    Intuitively, this means that all the members of $A.r$ are also members of $X.u$. Formally, $\mathcal{P} \vdash members(X.u) \sqsupseteq members(A.r)$ if and only if $\{Z \mid SP(\mathcal{P}) \models m(X, u, Z)\} \supseteq \{Z \mid SP(\mathcal{P}) \models m(A, r, Z)\}$.

A membership query $members(A.r) \sqsupseteq \{D_1, \ldots, D_n\}$ can be translated to an inclusion query $members(A.r) \sqsupseteq B.u$, in which $B.u$ is a new role, by adding $B.u \longleftarrow D_1, \ldots, B.u \longleftarrow D_n$ to $\mathcal{P}$ and making $B.u$ g/s-restricted. Similarly, boundedness queries can be translated to inclusion queries as well. We include membership and bounded queries because they can be answered more efficiently.

Each form of query can be generalized to involve compound role expressions that use linking and intersection; these generalized queries can be answered by adding some new roles and statements to the policy, and posing a query of one of the restricted forms above. For instance, $\{\} \sqsupseteq members(A.r \cap A_1.r_1.r_2)$ can be answered by adding $B.u_1 \longleftarrow A.r \cap B.u_2, B.u_2 \longleftarrow B.u_3.r_2$, and $B.u_3 \longleftarrow A_1.r_1$ to $\mathcal{P}$, in which $B.u_1, B.u_2$, and $B.u_3$ are new g/s-restricted roles, and by posing the query $\{\} \sqsupseteq members(B.u_1)$.

Simple safety analysis and simple availability analysis use special cases of membership queries; they have the form $members(A.r) \sqsupseteq \{D\}$. Simple safety analysis is existential, and simple availability analysis is universal. Bounded safety analysis and mutual exclusion analysis use universal boundedness queries. (For instance, universally quantifying the example query in the previous paragraph yields a mutual exclusion analysis.) Liveness analysis uses existential boundedness queries. Containment analysis use universally quantified inclusion queries.

The three forms of queries can be varied to consider cardinality of roles rather than exact memberships. A cardinality variant of membership queries has the form "$|members(A.r)| \geq n$", which means that the number of principals who are members of $A.r$ is no less than n. A cardinality variant of boundedness queries has the form "$n \geq |members(A.r)|$". Cardinality variant of membership and boundedness queries can be answered similarly to the base queries. We do not consider a cardinality variant of inclusion queries in this paper.

5.4   An Example

Example 7. The system administrator of a company, SA, controls access to some resource, which we abstractly denote by SA.access. The company policy is that managers always have access to the resource, managers can delegate the access to other principals, but only to employees of the company. HR is trusted for defining employees and managers. The state $\mathcal{P}$ consists of the following statements:

SA.access $\longleftarrow$ SA.manager

SA.access $\longleftarrow$ SA.delegatedAccess $\cap$ HR.employee

SA.manager $\longleftarrow$ HR.manager

SA.delegatedAccess $\longleftarrow$ SA.manager.access

HR.employee $\longleftarrow$ HR.manager   HR.employee $\longleftarrow$ HR.programmer

HR.manager $\longleftarrow$ Alice

HR.programmer $\longleftarrow$ Bob   HR.programmer $\longleftarrow$ Carl

Alice.access $\longleftarrow$ Bob

Given the state $\mathcal{P}$ above, Alice and Bob have access, Carl does not. One possible restriction rule has $\mathcal{G}$ = { SA.access, SA.manager, SA.delegatedAccess, HR.employee } and $\mathcal{S}$ = { SA.access, SA.manager, SA.delegatedAccess, HR.employee, HR.manager }. We now list some example analysis problem instances, together with the answers:

Simple safety analysis: Is "SA.access $\sqsupseteq$ {Eve}" possible?   (Yes.)

Simple availability analysis: Is "SA.access $\sqsupseteq$ {Alice}" necessary?   (Yes.)

Bounded safety analysis: Is "{Alice, Bob} $\sqsupseteq$ SA.access" necessary? (No.)

Containment analysis: Is "HR.employee $\sqsupseteq$ SA.access" necessary? (Yes.)

Intuitively, these answers may be considered bad, good, bad, and good, respectively. ∎

5.5   Usage of Security Analysis

Security analysis provides a means to ensure that safety and availability requirements are met and will continue to be met after policy changes are made by autonomous authorities. Security analysis is also useful when the global state of a TM system is fixed, but only partially known. For instance, previously unknown statements may be presented along with new access requests. In this case, although the global state does not change, one's view of that state is changing. Thus, there are many reasons why an individual or organization using a TM system may be unable to determine a fixed state of that system. Whatever the reason, security analysis techniques can be used to ensure that basic requirements such as safety, availability, and mutual exclusion are not violated by prospective changes one is considering making, before putting those changes into effect. Let us make this more concrete.

A security analysis problem instance is given by a state $\mathcal{P}$, a query $\mathcal{Q}$, a quantifier for the query (universal or existential), and a restriction rule $\mathcal{R}$. Basic security requirements can be formalized as instances of security analysis, together with answers that are acceptable for secure operation. For instance, one safety requirement might be formalized as asking whether anyone outside the organization can access a particular confidential resource, in which case the acceptable answer would be "no." Once a policy state has been established that leads the analysis to produce no unacceptable answers, if prospective changes to g/s-restricted roles result in any unacceptable answers, the changes are considered to be in violation of the corresponding requirement, and should not be applied.

By definition of the analysis, changes to g/s-unrestricted roles cannot cause unacceptable answers when starting from a policy state that gives none.

One possible usage scenario for this approach is as follows. An organization's System Security Officer (SSO) writes a restriction rule restricting change of some of the roles that are under the control of principals in the organization, as well as a set of analysis-instance/acceptable-answer pairs. The SSO then uses these pairs and obtains the assistance of principals within the organization to bring the current policy into compliance. This is done by changing the policy as needed to make the analysis yield acceptable answers for all the analysis instances. If this cannot be done, the requirements are inconsistent or outside the organization's control, and must be revised. Once the policy has been brought into compliance, principals that control restricted roles are trusted to ensure that subsequent changes to such roles do not lead to unacceptable answers. By restricting only roles controlled within the organization, the SSO may be able to rely on software enforcement and other means to ensure that this trust is justified.

In the above usage, the SSO determines an analysis configuration consisting of a set of analysis-instance/acceptable-answer pairs and a restriction rule. In general, many such configurations can be used, each specified by a different interested party having a different set of principals it is willing to trust to run the analysis and to enforce the analysis-instance/acceptable-answer pairs, and hence having a different restriction rule.

It is significant to note that the usage pattern we are suggesting enables the enforcement of requirements that cannot be enforced by constructs in RT_0, or most other trust management languages. This is because those languages are monotonic in the sense that policies with more statements derive more role membership facts. By contrast, many of the requirements expressible using analysis-instance/acceptable-answer pairs are non-monotonic, in the sense that adding statements to a policy that satisfies such a requirement can yield a policy that does not. Thus, there is no way to enforce such a requirement within the language itself. This is illustrated by the example of mutual exclusion of two roles. Monotonicity makes it impossible to express within RT_0 that a principal cannot be added to both roles. However, this is easily prevented through the usage pattern described above.

6   Answering Form-1 and Form-2 Queries

RT_0 and its sub-languages are all monotonic in the sense that more statements will derive more role memberships (*i.e.*, logical atoms of the form $m(A, r, D)$). This follows from the fact that the semantic program is a positive logic program. Form-1 queries are monotonic; given a form-1 query Q, if $\mathcal{P} \vdash Q$, then for every $\mathcal{P}'$ such that $\mathcal{P} \subseteq \mathcal{P}'$, $\mathcal{P}' \vdash Q$. Form-2 queries are anti-monotonic; given a form-2 query Q, if $\mathcal{P} \vdash Q$, then for every $\mathcal{P}' \subseteq \mathcal{P}$, $\mathcal{P}' \vdash Q$.

Intuitively, universal form-1 (simple availability) queries and existential form-2 queries can be answered by considering the lower bound of role memberships. A role's lower bound is the set of principals that are members of the role in every reachable state. Because $\mathcal{R}$ is static, there exists a minimal state that is reachable from $\mathcal{P}$ and $\mathcal{R}$, which is obtained from $\mathcal{P}$ by removing all statements defining s-unrestricted roles. We denote this state by $\mathcal{P}|_{\mathcal{R}}$. Clearly, $\mathcal{P}|_{\mathcal{R}}$ is reachable; furthermore, $\mathcal{P}|_{\mathcal{R}} \subseteq \mathcal{P}'$ for every reachable

$\mathcal{P}'$. Since RT_0 is monotonic, one can compute the lower bound by computing the role memberships in $\mathcal{P}|_{\mathcal{R}}$.

Similarly, existential form-1 (simple safety) queries and universal form-2 (bounded safety) queries can be answered by computing an "upper bound" of role memberships. The upper bound of a role is the set of principals that could become a member of the role in some reachable state. Intuitively, such bounds can be computed by considering a "maximal reachable state". However, such a "state" is not well-defined since it would contain an infinite set of policy statements, and we only allow a state to contain a finite set of policy statements. We will show that one can simulate the "maximal reachable state" by a finite state and derive correct answers.

6.1   The Lower Bound

Definition 3 (The Lower Bound Program). Given $\mathcal{P}$ and $\mathcal{R}$, the *lower bound program* for them, $LB(\mathcal{P}, \mathcal{R})$, is constructed as follows:

> For each $A.r \longleftarrow D$ in $\mathcal{P}|_{\mathcal{R}}$, add
> $$lb(A, r, D) \tag{b1}$$
> For each $A.r \longleftarrow B.r_1$ in $\mathcal{P}|_{\mathcal{R}}$, add
> $$lb(A, r, ?Z) :- lb(B, r_1, ?Z) \tag{b2}$$
> For each $A.r \longleftarrow A.r_1.r_2$ in $\mathcal{P}|_{\mathcal{R}}$, add
> $$lb(A, r, ?Z) :- lb(A, r_1, ?Y), \ lb(?Y, r_2, ?Z) \tag{b3}$$
> For each $A.r \longleftarrow B_1.r_1 \cap B_2.r_2$ in $\mathcal{P}|_{\mathcal{R}}$, add
> $$lb(A, r, ?Z) :- lb(B_1, r_1, ?Z), \ lb(B_2, r_2, ?Z) \tag{b4}$$

The worst-case complexity of evaluating the lower bound program is $O(|\mathcal{P}|^3)$.

Observe that the above lower bound program is essentially the same as the semantic program for the minimal state $\mathcal{P}|_{\mathcal{R}}$. They differ in that anywhere $LB(\mathcal{P}, \mathcal{R})$ uses the predicate lb, $SP(\mathcal{P}|_{\mathcal{R}})$ uses the predicate m. Therefore, we have the following fact.

Proposition 3. $LB(\mathcal{P}, \mathcal{R}) \models lb(A, r, D)$ *if and only if* $SP(\mathcal{P}|_{\mathcal{R}}) \models m(A, r, D)$.

Proposition 4. $LB(\mathcal{P}, \mathcal{R}) \models lb(A, r, D)$ *if and only if for every* $\mathcal{P}'$ *such that* $\mathcal{P} \overset{*}{\mapsto}_{\mathcal{R}} \mathcal{P}'$, $SP(\mathcal{P}') \models m(A, r, D)$.

See [22] for the proof of this and other results stated below. Proposition 4 means that the lower bound program can be used to answer universal form-1 queries and existential form-2 queries. We have not found an intuitive security meaning of existential form-2 queries, but include answering method for them here for completeness.

Corollary 1. *Given* $\mathcal{P}$ *and* $\mathcal{R}$, *a form-1 query* members$(A.r) \sqsupseteq \{D_1, \ldots, D_n\}$ *is necessary if and only if* $LB(\mathcal{P}, \mathcal{R}) \models lb(A, r, D_i)$ *for every* i, $1 \leq i \leq n$.

Corollary 2. *Given* $\mathcal{P}$ *and* $\mathcal{R}$, *a form-2 query* $\{D_1, \ldots, D_n\} \sqsupseteq$ members$(A.r)$ *is possible if and only if* $\{D_1, \ldots, D_n\} \supseteq \{Z \mid LB(\mathcal{P}, \mathcal{R}) \models lb(A, r, Z)\}$.

Consider Example 7. The simple availability query "is SA.access $\sqsupseteq$ {Alice} necessary" is true when SA.access, SA.manager, and HR.manager are s-restricted, since then the statements "SA.access $\longleftarrow$ SA.manager", "SA.manager $\longleftarrow$ HR.manager", and "HR.manager $\longleftarrow$ Alice" exist in the minimal state. On the other hand, it is not necessary that Bob has access, even when SA.delegatedAccess, HR.employee, and HR.programmer are also s-restricted, since Alice could remove her statement "Alice.access $\longleftarrow$ Bob".

6.2 The Upper Bound

To compute the upper bound of roles, we introduce the following notion: A role is *g-unbounded* if for every principal Z, there exists a reachable $\mathcal{P}'$ such that $SP(\mathcal{P}') \models m(A, r, Z)$. In other words, $A.r$ could have every principal as its member. A g-unrestricted role is clearly g-unbounded. A g-restricted role may also be g-unbounded, as it may be defined to include a g-unbounded role.

The following fact about g-unbounded roles says that one only needs to consider one principal that does not occur in $\mathcal{P}$ (instead of every principal) to determine whether a role is g-unbounded.

Proposition 5. *Given $\mathcal{P}$, $\mathcal{R}$, a role $A.r$, and a principal E that does not occur in $\mathcal{P}$, $A.r$ is g-unbounded if and only if there exists a reachable state $\mathcal{P}'$ such that $SP(\mathcal{P}') \models m(A, r, E)$.*

We now show how to compute the upper bound, which simulates an infinite state.

Definition 4 (The Upper Bound Program). Given $\mathcal{P}$, $\mathcal{R} = (\mathcal{G}, \mathcal{S})$, their upper bound program, $UB(\mathcal{P}, \mathcal{R})$, is constructed as follows. ($\top$ is a special principal symbol not occurring in $\mathcal{P}$, $\mathcal{R}$, or any query $\mathcal{Q}$.)

$$\text{Add}$$
$$ub(\top, ?r, ?Z) \qquad\qquad (u)$$
$$\text{For each } A.r \in \text{Roles}(\mathcal{P}) - \mathcal{G}, \text{ add}$$
$$ub(A, r, ?Z) \qquad\qquad (u0)$$
$$\text{For each } A.r \longleftarrow D \text{ in } \mathcal{P}, \text{ add}$$
$$ub(A, r, D) \qquad\qquad (u1)$$
$$\text{For each } A.r \longleftarrow B.r_1 \text{ in } \mathcal{P}, \text{ add}$$
$$ub(A, r, ?Z) :- ub(B, r_1, ?Z) \qquad\qquad (u2)$$
$$\text{For each } A.r \longleftarrow A.r_1.r_2 \text{ in } \mathcal{P}, \text{ add}$$
$$ub(A, r, ?Z) :- ub(A, r_1, ?Y), ub(?Y, r_2, ?Z) \qquad\qquad (u3)$$
$$\text{For each } A.r \longleftarrow B_1.r_1 \cap B_2.r_2 \text{ in } \mathcal{P}, \text{ add}$$
$$ub(A, r, ?Z) :- ub(B_1, r_1, ?Z), ub(B_2, r_2, ?Z) \qquad\qquad (u4)$$

The computational complexity for evaluating $UB(\mathcal{P}, \mathcal{R})$ is $O(|\mathcal{P}|^3)$. Note that Roles$(\mathcal{P})$ has $O(|\mathcal{P}|^2)$ elements, since there are $O(|\mathcal{P}|)$ principals and $O(|\mathcal{P}|)$ role names in $\mathcal{P}$. Therefore, there are $O(N^2)$ instance rules of $(u0)$; however, each such rule has only one variable.

Proposition 6. *Given any* $\mathcal{P}$, $\mathcal{R} = (\mathcal{G}, \mathcal{S})$, $A.r \in$ Roles$(\mathcal{P})$, *and* $Z \in$ Principals$(\mathcal{P}) \cup$ $\{\top\}$, $UB(\mathcal{P}, \mathcal{R}) \models ub(A, r, Z)$ *if and only if there exists* $\mathcal{P}'$ *such that* $\mathcal{P} \overset{*}{\mapsto}_{\mathcal{R}} \mathcal{P}'$ *and* $SP(\mathcal{P}') \models m(A, r, Z)$.

From Fact 5 and Proposition 6, we have the following.

Corollary 3. *A role* $A.r$ *is g-unbounded if and only if* $UB(\mathcal{P}, \mathcal{R}) \models ub(A, r, \top)$.

Corollary 4. *Given* $\mathcal{P}$ *and* $\mathcal{R} = (\mathcal{G}, \mathcal{S})$, *a form-1 query* $members(A.r) \sqsupseteq$ $\{D_1, \ldots, D_n\}$ *is possible if and only if one of the following three conditions hold: (1)* $A.r \notin \mathcal{G}$, *(2)* $UB(\mathcal{P}, \mathcal{R}) \models ub(A, r, \top)$, *or (3)* $UB(\mathcal{P}, \mathcal{R}) \models ub(A, r, D_i)$ *for every* $i, 1 \le i \le n$.

Corollary 5. *Given* $\mathcal{P}$ *and* $\mathcal{R} = (\mathcal{G}, \mathcal{S})$, *a form-2 query* $\{D_1, \ldots, D_n\} \sqsupseteq$ $members(A.r)$ *is necessary if and only if* $A.r \in \mathcal{G}$ *and* $\{D_1, \ldots, D_n\} \supseteq$ $\{Z | UB(\mathcal{P}, \mathcal{R}) \models ub(A, r, Z)\}$.

Consider Example 7 again and observe that the policy is not safe according to either the simple safety query or the bounded safety query. One reason is that the role HR.manager is g-unrestricted, meaning that new managers may be added. Another reason is that the role HR.programmer is g-unrestricted; therefore, new programmers may be added and access may be delegated to them. However, if the company knows that Eve is an enemy, then the company probably will not hire Eve as a manager or a programmer.

In fact, simple safety is quite unnatural: to use it effectively, one has to be able to identify the principals that should never have access, the number of such principals could be arbitrary large. Bounded safety is also unnatural, one does not know, for example, who in the future the company will hire as a manager. A more natural policy is to ensure that, for example, only employees of the company are allowed to access the resource. This can be done by using form-3 queries.

7 Answering Universal Form-3 Queries

Form-3 queries (*i.e.*, role inclusion queries) are neither monotonic nor anti-monotonic. Given a form-3 query $members(X.u) \sqsupseteq members(Z.w)$ and three states $\mathcal{P}' \subseteq \mathcal{P} \subseteq \mathcal{P}''$, it is possible that $\mathcal{P} \vdash Q$, but both $\mathcal{P}' \nvdash Q$ and $\mathcal{P}'' \nvdash Q$. As a result, the approach taken with form-1 and form-2 queries is not applicable here. We cannot simply look at a specific minimal (or maximal) state and answer the query.

In this paper, we restrict our attention to universal role inclusion queries. We have not found meaningful readings of existential role inclusion queries in terms of security properties. We say that a role $X.u$ *contains* another role $A.r$ if $members(X.u) \sqsupseteq$ $members(A.r)$ is necessary, *i.e.*, $X.u$ includes $A.r$ in every reachable state. And we call the problem of answering containment queries *containment analysis*.

The case that one of $X.u$ and $A.r$ is not in Roles$(\mathcal{P})$ is uninteresting. If $A.r \notin$ Roles$(\mathcal{P})$, then $X.u$ contains $A.r$ if and only if $A.r$ is g-restricted. If $A.r \in$ Roles$(\mathcal{P})$ and $X.u \notin$ Roles$(\mathcal{P})$, then $X.u$ contains $A.r$ if and only if $A.r$ has an upper bound that is empty. In the rest of this section, we only consider the case that both $X.u$ and $A.r$ are in Roles($\mathcal{P}$).

Intuitively, there are two cases in which a role $X.u$ contains a role $A.r$. The first case is that this containment is *forced* by the statements that are in $\mathcal{P}$. For example, if a statement $X.u \longleftarrow A.r$ exists and cannot be removed, then $X.u$ contains $A.r$. A containment may be forced by a chain of credentials. Forced containment can be computed similarly to role memberships.

In the second case, containment is caused by the nonexistence of statements in $\mathcal{P}$. In the extreme case, if $A.r$ has no definition and is g-restricted, then $A.r$ is contained in every role, since the member set of $A.r$ is empty in every reachable state. To compute this kind of containment, observe that a g-restricted role $A.r$ is contained in another role $X.u$ if every definition of $A.r$ is contained in $X.u$. If $A.r$ has no definition at all, then it is contained in every role. However, a straightforward translation of this into a positive logic program does not work. Consider the following example: $\mathcal{P} = \{A.r \longleftarrow B.r_1,\ A.r \longleftarrow D,\ B.r_1 \longleftarrow A.r,\ X.u \longleftarrow D\}$ and $\mathcal{R}$ is such that $\mathcal{G} = \{A.r, B.r_1\}$ and $\mathcal{S} = \{A.r, B.r_1, X.u\}$. In any $\mathcal{P}'$ that is $\mathcal{R}$-reachable from $\mathcal{P}$, the member sets of $A.r$ and $B.r_1$ are always $\{D\}$, and so both roles are contained by $X.u$. A straightforward positive logic program cannot derive this, since $X.u$ contains $A.r$ only if it contains $B.r_1$ and vice versa. As a result, neither containment relationship will be in the minimal model. To deal with this problem, we take the approach to prove non-containment using the minimal model of a logic program, and derive containment using negation-as-failure. Intuitively, $X.u$ contains $A.r$ unless we can find a witness principal E that is a member of $A.r$ in some state but not a member of $X.u$ in the same state.

Intuitively, containment queries that have the character of availability should be proven by forced containment. That a manager always has access to a resource should be due to a credential chain forcing this. In Example 7, SA.access contains HR.manager as long as SA.access and SA.manager are s-restricted. On the other hand, policy statements are unlikely to force everyone who has access to a resource to be an employee; the orientation of the forced containment does not naturally correspond to this practical dependency. In Example 7, HR.employee contains SA.access as long as SA.access and SA.manager are g-restricted and HR.employee is s-restricted. This is because, as long as no new rule defining SA.access or SA.mamnager is added, any member of SA.access is either a member of HR.manager or a member of HR.employee; if furthermore, the statement "HR.employee $\longleftarrow$ HR.manager" cannot be removed, then HR.employee contains SA.access.

7.1 Answering Containment Queries in BRT

Recall that the language BRT has only type-1 and type-2 statements.

Definition 5. (The Role Containment Program for BRT) Given a BRT state $\mathcal{P}$ and $\mathcal{R}$, the role containment program, $BCP(\mathcal{P}, \mathcal{R})$, includes the lower bound program $LB(\mathcal{P}, \mathcal{R})$ in Definition 3. In addition, it defines two predicates: $fc/4$ and $nc/4$. An atom $fc(X, u, Z, w)$ means that $X.u$ is forced to contain $Z.w$. An atom $nc(X, u, Z, w)$ means that $X.u$ does not contain $Z.w$. The program $BCP(\mathcal{P}, \mathcal{R})$ is derived from $LB(\mathcal{P}, \mathcal{R})$ as follows.

Add

$$fc(?X, ?u, ?X, ?u) \qquad\qquad (c)$$

For each $A.r \longleftarrow B.r_1$ in $\mathcal{P}|_{\mathcal{R}}$, add

$$fc(A, r, ?Z, ?w) :- fc(B, r_1, ?Z, ?w) \qquad\qquad (c2)$$

For each $A.r \in \text{Roles}(\mathcal{P}) - \mathcal{G}$, add

$$nc(?X, ?u, A, r) :- \sim fc(?X, ?u, A, r) \qquad\qquad (n0)$$

For each $A.r \in \mathcal{G}$, do the following:

For each $A.r \longleftarrow D$ in $\mathcal{P}$, add

$$nc(?X, ?u, A, r) :- \sim fc(?X, ?u, A, r), \sim lb(?X, ?u, D) \quad (n1)$$

For each $A.r \longleftarrow B.r_1$ in $\mathcal{P}$, add

$$nc(?X, ?u, A, r) :- \sim fc(?X, ?u, A, r), nc(?X, ?u, B, r_1) \ (n2)$$

Rules (c) and $(c2)$ are straightforward. The intuition behind $(n0)$ is that for $X.u$ to contain a g-unrestricted role $A.r$, $X.u$ has to be forced to contain $A.r$, since arbitrary new members may be added to $A.r$. The intuition behind $(n1)$ is that, since $A.r$ contains D, if $X.u$'s lower bound does not contain D, and $X.u$ is not forced to contain $A.r$, then $X.u$ does not contain $A.r$. The "$\sim fc$" part is needed, since it may be the case that $A.r \longleftarrow D$ can be removed and $X.u \longleftarrow A.r$ exists and cannot be removed, in which case D may not be in $X.u$'s lower bound. Rule $(n2)$ means that $X.u$ does not contain $A.r$ if it does not contain $B.r_1$ and is not forced to contain $A.r$.

The datalog program $BCP(\mathcal{P}, \mathcal{R})$ uses negation-as-failure in a stratified manner. Most commonly accepted semantics for logic programming with negation-as-failure agree on stratified programs. The semantics of $BCP(\mathcal{P}, \mathcal{R})$ can be computed in poliynomial time.

The following lemma says that the fc predicate in BCP is always sound for role containment, and it is complete when the second role is g-unrestricted.

Lemma 1. *Given a BRT state $\mathcal{P}$, $\mathcal{R}$, two roles $X.u$ and $A.r$, if $BCP(\mathcal{P}, \mathcal{R}) \models fc(X, u, A, r)$, then $X.u$ contains $A.r$. If $X.u$ contains $A.r$ and $A.r$ is g-unrestricted, then $BCP(\mathcal{P}, \mathcal{R}) \models fc(X, u, A, r)$.*

The following proposition says that role containment in BRT can be answered by using the program $BCP(\mathcal{P}, \mathcal{R})$.

Proposition 7. *Given a BRT state $\mathcal{P}$, $\mathcal{R}$, and two roles $X.u$ and $A.r$ in $\text{Roles}(\mathcal{P})$, $BCP(\mathcal{P}, \mathcal{R}) \models nc(X, u, A, r)$ if and only if $X.u$ does not contain $A.r$.*

7.2   Complexity Results for Containment Analysis in NRT, LRT, and RT_0

NRT adds to BRT type-4 statements. Intersections in type-4 statements have the effect of conjunction. A role can be defined by multiple statements, which have the effect of disjunction. As a result, NRT can simulate formulas in propositional logic, and answering containment queries subsumes determining validity of propositional formulas, which is coNP-complete.

Theorem 1. *Containment analysis in NRT is coNP-complete.*

The coNP-hard part is by reducing the monotone 3SAT problem, which is NP-complete, to the complement of containment analysis in NRT.

LRT adds to BRT type-3 statements. Linked roles in type-3 statements add the ability to simulate logical conjunction. Recall that the semantic rule for type-3 statements, $(m3)$, has a conjunction in the body, similar to that for type-4 statements, $(m4)$.

Theorem 2. *Containment analysis in LRT is coNP-hard.*

We now give an upper bound on the computational complexity of containment analysis in RT_0. This shows that containment analysis in RT_0 (and thus the sub-language LRT) is decidable.

Theorem 3. *Containment analysis in RT_0 is in coNEXP.*

8   Conclusions and Future Work

We have discussed an attribute-based authorization system, RT, that is built on logic programming and that derives clarity and extensibility from that foundation. We have also discussed security analyses for policies written in RT that use their own logic programming foundation to great advantage. By using policy analysis techniques to understand the potential for security violations, exposure due to delegation of authority can be managed. Because containment analysis is **coNP**-hard for RT_0, no efficient analysis technique that is sound will also be complete. A sound, but incomplete tool would admit the possibility of false positives in checking for violations of security requirements. Additional research is needed to develop efficient heuristic analysis techniques that make the number and importance of such false positives acceptable. A larger, equally important area for future work will be automated assistance with bringing policies into compliance with security requirements. This could amount to simply pointing out why the requirement is currently violated, or, ideally, suggesting changes to the policy that would achieve or restore compliance.

References

1. Krzysztof R. Apt, Howard A. Blair, and Adrian Walker. Towards a theory of declarative knowledge. In J. Minker, editor, *Foundations of Deductive Databases and Logic Programming*, pages 89–148. Morgan Kaufmann, Los Altos, CA, 1988.
2. Matt Blaze, Joan Feigenbaum, John Ioannidis, and Angelos D. Keromytis. The KeyNote trust-management system, version 2. IETF RFC 2704, September 1999.
3. Matt Blaze, Joan Feigenbaum, and Jack Lacy. Decentralized trust management. In *Proceedings of the 1996 IEEE Symposium on Security and Privacy*, pages 164–173. IEEE Computer Society Press, May 1996.
4. Piero Bonatti and Pierangela Samarati. A uniform framework for regulating service access and information release on the web. *Journal of Computer Security*, 10(3):241–274, 2002. Extended abstract appeared in *Proceedings of the 7th ACM Conference on Computer and Communications Security*, November 2000.

5. Tim Bray, Dave Hollander, and Andrew Layman. Namespaces in XML. W3C Recommendation, January 1999.
6. David D. Clark and David R. Wilson. A comparision of commercial and military computer security policies. In *Proceedings of the 1987 IEEE Symposium on Security and Privacy*, pages 184–194. IEEE Computer Society Press, May 1987.
7. Dwaine Clarke, Jean-Emile Elien, Carl Ellison, Matt Fredette, Alexander Morcos, and Ronald L. Rivest. Certificate chain discovery in SPKI/SDSI. *Journal of Computer Security*, 9(4):285–322, 2001.
8. Carl Ellison, Bill Frantz, Butler Lampson, Ron Rivest, Brian Thomas, and Tatu Ylonen. SPKI certificate theory. IETF RFC 2693, September 1999.
9. Stephen Farrell and Russell Housley. An Internet attribute certificate profile for authorization, 2001.
10. G. Scott Graham and Peter J. Denning. Protection – principles and practice. In *Proceedings of the AFIPS Spring Joint Computer Conference*, volume 40, pages 417–429. AFIPS Press, May 16–18 1972.
11. Michael A. Harrison, Walter L. Ruzzo, and Jeffrey D. Ullman. Protection in operating systems. *Communications of the ACM*, 19(8):461–471, August 1976.
12. Amir Herzberg, Yosi Mass, Joris Mihaeli, Dalit Naor, and Yiftach Ravid. Access control meets public key infrastructure, or: Assigning roles to strangers. In *Proceedings of the 2000 IEEE Symposium on Security and Privacy*, pages 2–14. IEEE Computer Society Press, May 2000.
13. Trevor Jim. SD3: A trust management system with certified evaluation. In *Proceedings of the 2001 IEEE Symposium on Security and Privacy*, pages 106–115. IEEE Computer Society Press, May 2001.
14. Butler W. Lampson. Protection. In *Proceedings of the 5th Princeton Conference on Information Sciences and Systems*, 1971. Reprinted in ACM Operating Systems Review, 8(1):18–24, Jan 1974.
15. Ninghui Li. *Delegation Logic: A Logic-based Approach to Distributed Authorization*. PhD thesis, New York University, September 2000.
16. Ninghui Li, Benjamin N. Grosof, and Joan Feigenbaum. A practically implementable and tractable Delegation Logic. In *Proceedings of the 2000 IEEE Symposium on Security and Privacy*, pages 27–42. IEEE Computer Society Press, May 2000.
17. Ninghui Li, Benjamin N. Grosof, and Joan Feigenbaum. Delegation Logic: A logic-based approach to distributed authorization. *ACM Transaction on Information and System Security (TISSEC)*, 6(1):128–171, February 2003.
18. Ninghui Li and John C. Mitchell. Datalog with constraints: A foundation for trust management languages. In *Proceedings of the Fifth International Symposium on Practical Aspects of Declarative Languages (PADL 2003)*, pages 58–73. Springer, January 2003.
19. Ninghui Li and John C. Mitchell. Understanding spki/sdsi using first-order logic. In *Proceedings of the 16th IEEE Computer Security Foundations Workshop*, pages 89–103. IEEE Computer Society Press, June 2003.
20. Ninghui Li, John C. Mitchell, Yu Qiu, William H. Winsborough, Kent E. Seamons, Michael Halcrow, and Jared Jacobson. RTML: A Role-based Trust-management Markup Language, August 2002. Unpublished manuscript. Available at
http://crypto.stanford.edu/~ninghui/papers/rtml.pdf.
21. Ninghui Li, John C. Mitchell, and William H. Winsborough. Design of a role-based trust management framework. In *Proceedings of the 2002 IEEE Symposium on Security and Privacy*, pages 114–130. IEEE Computer Society Press, May 2002.
22. Ninghui Li, William H. Winsborough, and John C. Mitchell. Beyond proof-of-compliance: Safety and availability analysis in trust management. In *Proceedings of IEEE Symposium on Security and Privacy*, pages 123–139. IEEE Computer Society Press, May 2003.

23. Ninghui Li, William H. Winsborough, and John C. Mitchell. Distributed credential chain discovery in trust management. *Journal of Computer Security*, 11(1):35–86, February 2003. Extended abstract appeared in *Proceedings of the Eighth ACM Conference on Computer and Communications Security*, November 2001.

24. Richard J. Lipton and Lawrence Snyder. A linear time algorithm for deciding subject security. *Journal of ACM*, 24(3):455–464, 1977.

25. ITU-T Rec. X.509 (revised). *The Directory - Authentication Framework*. International Telecommunication Union, 1993.

26. Ronald L. Rivest and Bulter Lampson. SDSI — a simple distributed security infrastructure, October 1996. Available at http://theory.lcs.mit.edu/~rivest/sdsi11.html.

27. Ravi S. Sandhu. The Schematic Protection Model: Its definition and analysis for acyclic attenuating systems. *Journal of ACM*, 35(2):404–432, 1988.

28. Ravi S. Sandhu. The typed access matrix model. In *Proceedings of the 1992 IEEE Symposium on Security and Privacy*, pages 122–136. IEEE Computer Society Press, May 1992.

29. Ravi S. Sandhu, Edward J. Coyne, Hal L. Feinstein, and Charles E. Youman. Role-based access control models. *IEEE Computer*, 29(2):38–47, February 1996.

30. Kent E. Seamons, William H. Winsborough, and Marianne Winslet. Internet credential acceptance policies. In *Proceedings of the 2nd International Workshop on on Logic Programming Tools for Internet Applications*, July 1997. http://clip.dia.fi.upm.es/lpnet/proceedings97/proceedings.html.

31. Tichard T. Simon and Mary Ellen Zurko. Separation of duty in role-based environments. In *Proceedings of The 10th Computer Security Foundations Workshop*, pages 183–194. IEEE Computer Society Press, June 1997.

Compositional Verification of Infinite State Systems

Giorgio Delzanno[1], Maurizio Gabbrielli[2], and Maria Chiara Meo[3]

[1] Università di Genova
DISI
Via Dodecanneso 35, 16146 Genova, Italy
delzanno@disi.unige.it
[2] Università di Bologna
Dipartimento di Scienze dell'Informazione
Mura A. Zamboni 7, 40127 Bologna, Italy
gabbri@cs.unibo.it
[3] Università di Chieti
Dipartimento di Scienze
Viale Pindaro 42, 65127 Pescara, Italy
cmeo@unich.it

Abstract. The verification of infinite state systems is one of the most challenging areas in the field of computer aided verification. In fact these systems arise naturally in many application fields, ranging from communication protocols to multi-threaded programs and time-dependent systems, and are quite difficult to analyze and to reason about.

The main approaches developed so far consist in the extension to the infinite case of techniques already developed for finite state systems, notably model checking suitably integrated with abstractions which allow to finitely represent infinite sets of states. Constraints have also been quite useful in representing and manipulating infinite sets of states, both directly and indirectly.

Particularly relevant in this context is the issue of compositionality: In fact, a compositional methodology could allow to reduce the complexity of the verification procedure by splitting a big system into smaller pieces. Moreover, when considering systems such as those arising in distributed and mobile computing, compositional verification is imperative in some cases, as the environment in which software agents operate cannot be fixed in advance.

In this talk we will first illustrate some techniques based on constraints and multi set rewriting (MSR) for the automatic verification of systems and protocols parametric in several directions. Then we will discuss some ongoing research aiming at developing a compositional model for reasoning on MSR specifications.

References

1. F.S. de Boer, M. Gabbrielli, and M. C. Meo. A Temporal Logic for reasoning about Timed Concurrent Constraint Programs. In Proc *8th International Symposium on Temporal Representation and Reasoning (TIME 2001)*. IEEE Press, 2001.
2. F. S. de Boer, M. Gabbrielli, and M. C. Meo. A Denotational Semantics for a Timed Linda Language. In *Proc. PPDP*. ACM Press, 2001.

C. Palamidessi (Ed.): ICLP 2003, LNCS 2916, pp. 47–48, 2003.
© Springer-Verlag Berlin Heidelberg 2003

3. G. Delzanno. An Assertional Language for Systems Parametric in Several Dimensions. VEPAS'01, *ENTCS* volume 50, issue 4, 2001.
4. G. Delzanno and A. Podelski. Model checking in CLP. In *Proc. TACAS'99, LNCS* 1579, pp. 223–239, 1999.
5. L. Fribourg. Constraint Logic Programming Applied to Model Checking. In *Proc. LOPSTR'99, LNCS* 1817, pp. 30–41, 1999.

A Constraint-Based Approach to Structure Prediction for Simplified Protein Models That Outperforms Other Existing Methods

Rolf Backofen and Sebastian Will

Friedrich-Schiller-Universitaet Jena
Institute of Computer Science, Chair for Bioinformatics
Ernst-Abbe-Platz 1-4, D-07743 Jena, Germany,
backofen@inf.uni-jena.de

Abstract Lattice protein models are used for hierarchical approaches to protein structure prediction, as well as for investigating general principles of protein folding. So far, one has the problem that either the lattice does not model real protein conformations with good quality, or there is no efficient method known for finding native conformations.

We present a constraint-based method that largely improves this situation. It outperforms all existing approaches in lattice protein folding on the type of model we have chosen (namely the HP-model by Lau and Dill[34], which models the important aspect of hydrophobicity). It is the only exact method that has been applied to two different lattices. Furthermore, it is the only exact method for the face-centered cubic lattice. This lattice is important since it has been shown [38] that the FCC lattice can model real protein conformations with coordinate root mean square deviation below 2 Å.

Our method uses a constraint-based approach. It works by first calculating maximally compact sets of points (hydrophobic cores), and then threading the given HP-sequence to the hydrophobic cores such that the core is occupied by H-monomers.

1 Introduction

1.1 Proteins

Proteins are sequences composed of an alphabet of 20 amino acids. An amino acid is a chemical group of the form where R is a chemical group (called *chain residue*) specifying the type of the amino-acid. The central carbon atom is the *α-carbon* (short Cα), the left NH_2 groups is the *amino group*, and the left COOH the *carboxy group*. There are 20 different chain residues, which have different chemical properties. Residues can be hydrophobic or hydrophilic, small or large, charged or uncharged.

Two amino acids can be connected via a *peptide bond*, where the carboxy group of the first amino acid reacts with the amino group of the second. The result is a group of the form

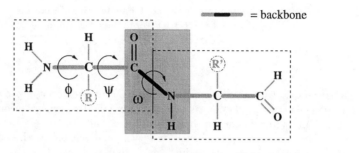

(1)

Using the peptide bond, long sequences of amino acids (i.e., proteins) can be generated.

The peptide bond itself (indicated with a grey rectangle in (1)) is usually planar, which means that there is no free rotation around this bond.[1] There is more flexibility for rotation around the N-Cα-bond (called the φ-angle), and around the Cα–C bond (called the ψ-angle). But even there, the allowed values of combinations of φ and ψ angles are restricted to small regions in natural proteins (which are displayed on so-called Ramachandran plots).

Using this freedom of rotation, the protein can *fold* into a specific three-dimensional structure (also called *conformation*). For natural proteins, the final structure that is achieved is uniquely determined by the sequence of amino acids. For this reason, one speaks of the *native structure* of a given amino acid sequence. The native structure itself uniquely determines the function of the protein.

1.2 Simplified Models of Proteins

The protein structure prediction is one of the most important unsolved problems of computational biology. It can be specified as follows: Given a protein by its sequence of amino acids, what is its native structure? NP-completeness of the problem has been proven for many different models (including lattice and off-lattice models) [17,21]. These results strongly suggest that the protein folding problem is NP-hard in general. Therefore, it is unlikely that a general, efficient algorithm for solving this problem can be given. Actually, the situation

---

[1] There are two conformations for the peptide bond, namely *trans* (corresponding to a rotation angle of 180°), and *cis* (corresponding to a rotation angle of 0°). The *cis* conformation is rare and occurs usually in combination with a specific amino acid, namely Proline.

is even worse, since the general principles why natural proteins fold into a native structure are unknown. This is cumbersome since rational design is commonly viewed to be of paramount importance e.g. for drug design, where one faces the difficulty to design proteins that have a unique and stable native structure.

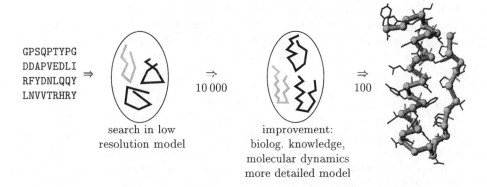

GPSQPTYPG
DDAPVEDLI ⇒
RFYDNLQQY
LNVVTRHRY

⇒
10 000

⇒
100

search in low
resolution model

improvement:
biolog. knowledge,
molecular dynamics
more detailed model

Fig. 1. Hierarchical Approach to Protein Structure Prediction

To tackle structure prediction and related problems simplified models have been introduced. These simplified models have been successfully used by several groups in the international contest on automated structure prediction (see the meeting review of CASP3 [33]). They are used in hierarchical approaches for protein folding [46] as follows (see also Figure 1). Given a protein sequence, then one first enumerates all low (or minimal) energy conformations in a simplified model. In the simplified model, only some aspects of the protein structure are modeled (for which reason they are also called low-resolution or coarse-grained protein models). Then, the say 10 000 best structures are taken and fine-tuned using other methods. These methods usually incorporate biological knowledge and simulation of protein folding on full atomic detail (i.e. molecular dynamics simulation).

The most important class of simplified models are the so-called lattice models. The simplifications commonly used in this class of models are: 1) monomers (or residues) are represented using a unified size 2) bond length is unified 3) the positions of the monomers are restricted to lattice positions and 4) a simplified energy function. Apart from their use in structure prediction, they have became a major tool for investigating general properties of protein folding. They constitute a genotype (protein sequence) versus phenotype (protein conformation) mapping that can be dealt using computational methods. Thus, they can be used to investigate evolutionary processes. An example is [18], where so-called neutral networks have been investigated. The edges of the network are pairs of sequences which differ only in one positions, but have the same minimal energy conformation. Thus, a neutral network represents all protein sequences encoding the same protein conformation. The question is whether one can switch between two different neutral networks using only a small number of amino-acid substitutions. If this is the case, then this suggest a way evolution could have produced the diversity of protein conformations found in nature.

In the literature, many different lattice models, (i.e., lattices and energy functions) have been used (see related work). Of course, the question arises which lattice and energy functions has to be preferred. There are two (somewhat conflicting) aspects that have to be evaluated when choosing a model: 1) the accuracy of the lattice in approximating real protein conformations, and the ability of the energy function to discriminate native from non-native conformations, and 2) the availability and quality of search algorithm for finding minimal (or low) energy conformations.

While the first aspect is well-investigated in the literature (e.g., [38,23]), the second aspect is underrepresented. By and large, there are mainly two different heuristic search approaches used in the literature: 1) Ad hoc restriction of the search space to compact or quasi-compact conformations. A good example is [43], where the search space is restricted to conformations forming an $n \times n \times n$-cube. The main drawback here is that the restriction to compact conformation is not biologically motivated for a complete amino acid sequence (as done in these approaches), but only for the hydrophobic amino acids. In consequence, the restriction either has to be relaxed and then leads to an inefficient algorithm, or is chosen to strong and thus may exclude minimal conformations. 2.) Stochastic sampling like Monte Carlo methods with simulated annealing, genetic algorithms etc. Here, the degree of optimality for the best conformations and the quality of the sampling cannot be determined by state of the art methods.[2]

In this work, we introduce a constraint-based approach that completely outperforms existing approaches in lattice protein folding (on the type of model we have chosen). It outperforms them even in several ways, namely flexibility, completeness and efficiency.

1.3   Contribution of the Paper: A Constraint-Based Approach

We have considered the HP-model, which is an important representative of lattice models. It has been introduced by Lau and Dill in [34]. In this model, the 20 letter alphabet of amino acids is reduced to a two letter alphabet, namely H and P. H represents *hydrophobic* amino acids, whereas P represent *polar* or hydrophilic amino acids. The energy function for the HP-model is given by the matrix as shown in Figure 2(a). It simply states that the energy contribution of a contact between two monomers is -1 if both are H-monomers, and 0 otherwise. Two monomers form a *contact* in some specific conformation if they are not connected via a bond, and the euclidian distance of the positions is 1. A conformation with *minimal energy* (also called *optimal conformation*) is just a conformation with the maximal number of contacts between H-monomers. Just recently, the

---

[2] Despite there are mathematical treatments of Monte Carlo methods with simulated annealing, the partition function of the ensemble (which is needed for a precise statement) is in general unknown.

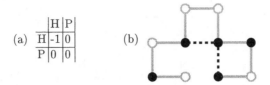

(a)

	H	P
H	-1	0
P	0	0

(b)

Fig. 2. Energy matrix and sample conformation for the HP-model

structure prediction problem has been shown to be NP-complete even for the HP-model [17,21].

A sample conformation for the sequence PHPHPPHHPH in the two-dimensional lattice with energy -2 is shown in Figure 2(b). The white beads represent P, the black ones H monomers. The two contacts are indicated via dashed lines.

Concerning flexibility, our method is the only one that works for two different but important lattices. These are the cubic lattice and the face-centered-cubic lattice (FCC). The cubic lattice is important for comparability to other existing approaches since it is the lattice which is explored most. However, the ability of this lattice to approximate real protein conformations is poor. For example, [4] pointed out especially the parity problem in the cubic lattice. This drawback of the cubic lattice is that every two monomers with chain positions of the same parity cannot form a contact.

The FCC on the other hand is important since it can model real protein conformations with good quality (see [38], where it was shown that FCC can model protein conformations with coordinate root mean square deviation below 2 Å). Recently, [15,16] have shown that neighborship of amino acids in proteins closely resembles a distorted FCC-lattice, and that the FCC is best suited for modeling proteins. This is an immediate effect of hydrophobic packing. Just recently, it was shown that the FCC is the lattice allowing the densest packing of identical spheres, approximately 400 years after the original conjecture by Kepler [40,20] (see Figure 3 for a description of the FCC lattice).

Concerning completeness, we have applied the method to existing structures and found additional optimal conformations not found by other existing approaches. Only for the HP-model on the cubic lattice, there is one other method that can provably find and enumerate optimal conformations [49]. In the HP-model, a sequence usually does not have a unique minimal energy conformation. Instead, there are many minimal energy conformation, and [49] have given a lower bound for the number of such conformations for specific sequences. We have applied our approach to this problem and strongly improved this lower bound.

Concerning efficiency, we have successfully applied our algorithm to sequences up to length 200 in the face-centered cubic lattice (FCC). For these sequences, we can provably find a minimal energy conformation. For the FCC, so far there existed only heuristic algorithms (for an example of a genetic algorithm for arbitrary Bravais lattices see [14]). Usually, these algorithms are applied to sequence of say length at most 80 (where they usually find only a low but *not* minimal energy conformation). Since the search space for conformations in the cubic lat-

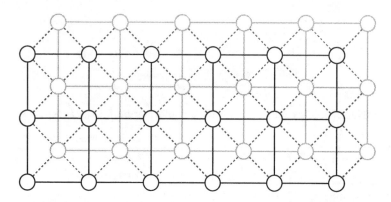

Fig. 3. Two layers of the face-centered-cubic lattice (FCC). It can be seen as two layers of the cubic lattice, which are arranged in such a way that every position of the second layer has contacts to 4 positions in the previous layer and vice versa (shown as dashed lines). Hence, every position has 12 neighbors in the FCC.

tice grows with approximately 4.5^n (where n is the length of the sequence), this implies that our method handles a search space that at least by the factor 4.5^{120} higher than the search space handled by other methods for the face-centered cubic lattice.[3]

1.4   Related Work

A discussion of lattice proteins can be found in [23]. There is a bunch of groups working with lattice proteins. Examples of how lattice proteins can be used for predicting the native structure or for investigating principles of protein folding are [44,1,25,42,31,28,2,37]. Most of them use heuristic methods, ranging from Monte-Carlo simulated annealing (e.g. [35,25]) to genetic algorithms (e.g. [42]), purely heuristic methods like hydrophobic zipper [24] and the chain growth algorithm [19], as well as complete enumeration (often restricted to subset of all conformations, e.g. [43,46]).

First steps have been made to improve the situation on the algorithmic part. The first improvement was the introduction of an exact algorithm for find minimal energy conformations in the cubic HP-Model [49]. The algorithm is called CHCC for "Constraint Hydrophobic Core Construction) (albeit it doesn't use constraint-based methods). This approach works only for the cubic lattice, but not for the FCC-lattice which is much better suited for modeling real protein conformations. The second improvement is the appearance of a bunch of approximation algorithms [30,3] for different lattice models. Also they are a very

---

[3] The number 4.5^n has been estimated for cubic lattice [36]; for the FCC, we do not know of any good estimation of the number of conformations. But one knows that it must be higher than the number of conformations in the cubic lattice.

important first step in the right direction, their approximation ratio is still not good enough to be used in practice.

Another interesting approach is to combine secondary structure predictions with lattice models. The secondary structure consists of local structure motifs like α-helices and β-sheets. One searches for conformations in the lattice model with low energy having the predicted secondary structure elements. Here, major improvements have been achieved using again a constraint-based approach and the FCC lattice [26].

2   Overview over the Algorithm

2.1   Formal Model

The original HP-model is defined for the cubic lattice. But it is easy to use the HP-energy function for other lattices. In [4], this has been done for the face-centered cubic lattice (FCC). For this reason, we have applied our approach to the HP-model in both the cubic and face-centered cubic lattice. For simplicity, we introduce the formal model for the cubic lattice only. The description for the face-centered-cubic is analogous if one applies the appropriate transformation (for details see [7]). A sequence is an element in $\{H, P\}^*$. With s_i we denote the ith element of a sequence s. We say that a monomer with number i in s is even (resp. odd) if i is even (resp. odd). A conformation c of a sequence s is a function

$$c : [1..|s|] \rightarrow \mathbb{Z}^d$$

(where $d = 2$ or $d = 3$ depending on whether we consider a 2-dimensional or a 3-dimensional lattice) such that

1. $\forall 1 \leq i < |s| : ||c(i) - c(i+1)|| = 1$ (where $|| \cdot ||$ is the euclidian norm on $\mathbb{Z}^d$)
2. and $\forall i \neq j : c(i) \neq c(j)$.

The first condition is imposed by the lattice constraint and implies that the distance vector between two successive elements must be a unit-vector (or a negative unit-vector) in every admissible conformation. The second condition is the constraint that the conformation must be self-avoiding.

Given a conformation c of a sequence s, the number of contacts $\text{Contact}_s(c)$ in c is defined as the number of pairs (i, j) with $i + 1 < j$ such that

$$s_i = H \wedge s_j = H \wedge ||c(i) - c(j)|| = 1$$

(in other words, the number of pairs of H-monomers that have distance 1 in the conformation c, but are not successive in the sequence s). The energy of c is just $-\text{Contact}_s(c)$. With e_x, e_y and e_z we denote the unit vectors $(1, 0, 0)$, $(0, 1, 0)$ or $(0, 0, 1)$, respectively. We say that two points $p, p' \in \mathbb{Z}^3$ are *neighbors* if $||p - p'|| = 1$. This is equivalent to the proposition that $p = p' \pm e$ with $e \in \{e_x, e_y, e_z\}$.

This can now be directly encoded as a constraint problem. Our constraint problem consists of finite domain variables. We use also Boolean constraint and reified constraints. With *reified constraints* we mean a constraint $\mathbf{x} =: (\phi)$, where ϕ is a finite domain constraint. $\mathbf{x}$ is a Boolean variable which is 1 if and only if ϕ holds. Technically, this can be achieved via setting x to 1 if the constraint store entails ϕ, and to 0 if the constraint store disentails ϕ. A constraint store *entails* a constraint ϕ if every valuation that makes the constraint store valid also makes ϕ valid. We use also entailment constraints of the form $\phi \to \psi$, which are interpreted as follows. If a constraint store entails ϕ, then ψ is added to the constraint store. We have implemented the problem using the language Oz [41], which supports finite domain variables, Boolean constraints, reified constraints, entailment constraints and a programmable search module.

Now we can encode the space of all possible conformations for a given sequence as a constraint problem as follows. We introduce for every monomer i new variables X_i, Y_i and Z_i, which denote the x-, y-, and z-coordinate of $c(i)$. Since we are using a cubic lattice, we know that these coordinates are all integers. But we can even restrict the possible values of these variables to the finite domain $[1..2n]$.[4] This is expressed by introducing the constraints

$$X_i \in [1..(2 \cdot \text{length}(s)] \wedge Y_i \in [1..(2 \cdot \text{length}(s)] \wedge Z_i \in [1..(2 \cdot \text{length}(s)]$$

for every $1 \leq i \leq n$. The self-avoidingness is just $(X_i, Y_i, Z_i) \neq (X_j, Y_j, Z_j)$ for $i \neq j$.[5]

For expressing that the distance between two successive monomers is 1, we introduce for every monomer i with $1 \leq i < \text{length}(s)$ three variables Xdiff_i, Ydiff_i and Zdiff_i. The value range of these variables is $[0..1]$. Then we can express the unit-vector distance constraint by

$$\text{Xdiff}_i =: |X_i - X_{i+1}| \qquad \text{Zdiff}_i =: |Z_i - Z_{i+1}|$$
$$\text{Ydiff}_i =: |Y_i - Y_{i+1}| \qquad 1 =: \text{Xdiff}_i + \text{Ydiff}_i + \text{Zdiff}_i.$$

The constraints described above span the space of all possible conformations. I.e., every valuation of X_i, Y_i, Z_i satisfying the constraints introduced above is an *admissible* conformation for the sequence s, i.e. a self-avoiding walk of s. Given partial information about X_i, Y_i, Z_i (expressed by additional constraints as introduced by the search algorithm), we call a conformation c *compatible* with these constraints on X_i, Y_i, Z_i if c is admissible and c satisfies the additional constraints.

The most simplest way to search for conformations with maximal number of contacts would be to add constraints for counting the number of contacts. Then one can directly enumerate the variables X_i, Y_i and Z_i. For HP-type models, we have to count contacts which are always generated between two neighboring H-monomers. For this purpose, one introduces a variable $\text{Contact}_{i,j}$ that is 1

---

[4] We even could have used $[1..n]$. But the domain $[1..2n]$ is more flexible since we can assign an arbitrary monomer the vector (n, n, n), and still have the possibility to represent all possible conformations.

[5] This cannot be directly encoded in Oz [41], but we reduce these constraints to difference constraints on integers.

if i and j have a contact in every conformation which is compatible with the valuations of X_i, Y_i, Z_i, and 0 otherwise. Then

$$\texttt{Xdiff}_{i,j} = |X_i - X_j| \qquad \texttt{Zdiff}_{i,j} = |Z_i - Z_j|$$
$$\texttt{Ydiff}_{i,j} = |Y_i - Y_j| \qquad \texttt{Contact}_{i,j} \in \{0,1\}$$
$$(\texttt{Contact}_{i,j} = 1) \leftrightarrow (\texttt{Xdiff}_i + \texttt{Ydiff}_i + \texttt{Zdiff}_i = 1) \tag{2}$$

where $\texttt{Xdiff}_{i,j}, \texttt{Xdiff}_{i,j}$ and $\texttt{Zdiff}_{i,j}$ are new variables. The variable $\texttt{HHContacts}$ counts the number of contacts between H-monomers, and is defined by

$$\texttt{HHContacts} = \sum_{\substack{i+1<j \wedge \\ s(i)=H \wedge s(j)=H}} \texttt{Contact}_{i,j}. \tag{3}$$

Now we could start to apply constraint-based enumeration on X_i, Y_i, Z_i searching for a conformation with maximal number of contacts.

The main problem using this approach alone is that it is very difficult to define good bounds and to find a search heuristic for enumerating low-energy conformation first. Nevertheless, this formulation is in part required for lattice models with an extended alphabet like the HPNX-model [13], which models also electrostatic contacts in addition to hydrophobicity.

To overcome this problem, one has to find a way to restrict the set of all conformations in a pre-processing step to a subset of conformations that contains provably all minimal energy conformations. For this purpose, we apply a technique that has been used first by the CHCC algorithm [48]. There, one calculates first the so-called hydrophobic cores, which are the positions occupied by H-monomers. Formally, a *hydrophobic core* $\mathcal{C}$ is just a set of positions. The number of contacts in a hydrophobic core $\mathcal{C}$ is defined by

$$\texttt{Contact}(\mathcal{C}) = \frac{1}{2}|\{(\boldsymbol{p}, \boldsymbol{p}') \mid \boldsymbol{p}, \boldsymbol{p} \in \mathcal{C} \wedge \boldsymbol{p} \text{ and } \boldsymbol{p} \text{ are neighbors}\}|$$

Of course, one has to consider all possible hydrophobic cores with a sufficient number of contacts (where generating the cores is a problem by its own). Luckily, the number of cores that have to be visited is usually feasible and can be precalculated, especially if symmetric solutions are discarded. In [9,12], we have introduced the first general method for breaking symmetries in constraint-based search, which has now become sort of a standard method.

For each core, one has then to find a conformation of the sequence considered that has exactly the corresponding core. This process is called to *thread* the sequence onto the core. We have found good constraint formulations to solve the threading problem (which will be described in section 5). Of course, if we start with a core that is maximally compact (i.e., has the maximal number of contacts between the positions occupied by H-monomers), then it is clear that a conformation generated by threading the sequence onto this core must be a minimal energy conformation. If one starts with all maximally compact cores,

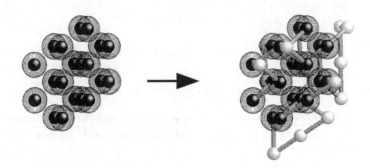

Fig. 4. The threading step for the HP-sequence 'HHPPPPHHHHPHHHPHHHP-PHHPHHPPPHHHPH'. The sequence contains 20 H-monomers. To the left a maximally compact hydrophobic core for 20 H-monomers is shown. The core is simply a set of 20 positions occupied by H-monomers. To the right, a conformation for this sequence having the select core is shown. H-monomers are indicated as black beads, and P-monomers as white beads.

and continue with the next best cores, then it is clear that we provably find the minimal energy conformations this way.

The remaining problem is to generate the hydrophobic cores. Without any additional efforts, we would have a huge search space again, since nothing is know about the shape of the hydrophobic core. Hence, one has to find again some restriction on the search space that allows us to calculate bounds and to apply constraint-bases optimization (i.e., branch-and-bound together with constraint propagation). The first idea for restricting the hydrophobic core is to define the surrounding cuboid that contains the hydrophobic core. If one has a very tight cuboid, then it is clear that the hydrophobic core in this cuboid must be very compact (at least in the cubic lattice, in the FCC it is more complicated).

Albeit this helps for the compact conformations, this approach is not fine-grained enough for the FCC as well as for sub-optimal hydrophobic cores in the cubic lattice. We introduce therefore a more precise boundary for the hydrophobic core, which is generated by splitting the lattice into layers. A layer is just a plane orthogonal to the x-dimension. For each layer, we define the *frame* to be the minimal rectangle around all positions of the core in this layer. The corresponding *frame sequence* consists of the height and width of each frame in each layer, together with the number of H-monomers in this layer (see Figure 5). Please note that the exact position of the frames is **not** part of the frame sequence. The sequence of number $n_1 \ldots n_l$ will be called *number sequence* in the following.

For finding all hydrophobic cores, one enumerates all frame sequences with the property that $\sum_i n_i$ is the number of H-monomers in the HP-sequence s. In addition, we have to enumerate in principle all possible ways of combining the frames for every frame sequence. Of course, we apply a branch-and-bound

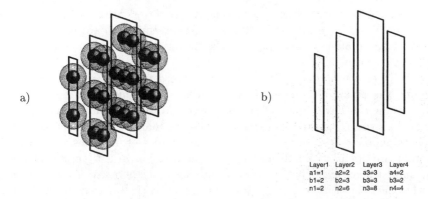

Layer1	Layer2	Layer3	Layer4
a1=1	a2=2	a3=3	a4=2
b1=2	b2=3	b3=3	b3=2
n1=2	n2=6	n3=8	n4=4

Fig. 5. Hydrophobic cores and frame sequences. a) a hydrophobic core with frames. b) the corresponding frame sequence. a_i is the width and b_i is the height of the frame in the i-th layer. And n_i is the number of H-monomers in this layer.

approach to discard combinations which do not yield a sufficient number of contacts. These bound are of course lattice specific and will be described in the next section. In the following section, we will describe the construction of the hydrophobic cores, followed by the description of the threading method.

3   The Lattice-Specific Part: Upper Bound for Frame Sequences

We will now consider the problem of enumerating the frame sequence using branch-and-bound, starting with the cubic lattice. We need some definitions first. In Figure 6a), a the hydrophobic core for the cubic lattice is shown together with the two layers. All contacts between positions in the same layer are called *layer*

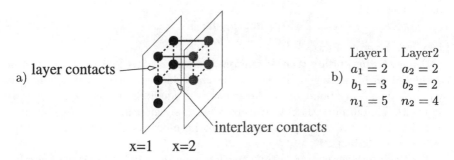

Layer1	Layer2
$a_1 = 2$	$a_2 = 2$
$b_1 = 3$	$b_2 = 2$
$n_1 = 5$	$n_2 = 4$

Fig. 6. a) Layer and Interlayer Contacts   b) Corresponding Frame Sequence

contacts. All contacts between positions in successive layers are called *interlayer contacts.* To give an upper bound for a specific frame sequence, one give separate bounds for the number of layer *and* interlayer contacts for hydrophobic cores have this frame sequence.

For the layer contacts, consider a frame of size $a \times b$ with n H-monomers. For finding the maximal number of layer contacts that any hydrophobic core with this frame can have, Yue and Dill [48] observed that it is much simpler to calculate the surface instead of the number of layer contacts. The *layer surface* of an hydrophobic core C in layer $x = k$ is the number of positions p in layer $x = k$ that are not in C, but neighbors of some position $p' \in C$ (p is called a *surface point*). Since every position in the core has 4 neighbors, which are filled by another member of the core or by a surface point, it is clear that surface and contacts are related via the equation

$$4n = 2\text{Contact} + 2a + 2b.$$

Hence, minimizing the surface maximizes the number of contacts.

Now whenever we have a layer where a surface point is buried between two position from the core, this core cannot be maximal. We can achieve a more compact one by resorting the core positions in this layer in a way that the gap generated by this surface point is closed (recall that a hydrophobic core is just a set of positions, with no other conditions imposed on them). Under the condition of a maximal compact layer core, this implies that every horizontal and vertical line that goes through the core in some layer must generate 2 surface points. Hence, a frame of size $a \times b$ must generate at least $2a + 2b$ surface points. Furthermore, one can conclude that an optimal frame for n points must minimize $a + b$, which is the case for a nearly quadratic frame. I.e., the best possible adaption of a quadratic frame with $a = \lceil \sqrt{n} \rceil$ and $b = \lceil \frac{n}{a} \rceil$ will have minimal surface, which used as a bound when enumerating number sequences.

Concerning the interlayer contacts for the cubic lattice, the situation is simple. Given two successive layers $x = k$ and $x = k + 1$, then every position in layer $x = k$ has exactly one neighbor position in $x = k + 1$ and vice versa. Hence, there can be at most n_k interlayer contacts between $x = k$ and $x = k + 1$ if $n_k \leq n_{k+1}$. Otherwise, if $n_k \geq n_{k+1}$, then there can be at most n_{k+1} interlayer contacts. Thus, for two successive layers with n_k and n_{k+1} core positions, there are at most

$$\min(n_i, n_{i+1})$$

many interlayer contacts.

Using an appropriate transformation, the face-centered-cubic lattice can be considered as consisting of layers of the cubic lattice, which are arranged in way such that every point in one layer has four neighbors in the next layer (see Figure 3). This implies that we can use the same definitions of layer sequences as well as layer and interlayer contacts. Furthermore, we have the same bound for the layer contacts.

For the interlayer contacts, the situation is more complicated since every position in one layer can have up to 4 neighbors in the next layer. This problem

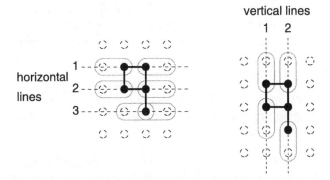

Fig. 7. Horizontal and Vertical Surface. Every horizontal and vertical line through the hydrophobic core produces 2 surface points (if no surface point is buried in the core). The grey ovals include a surface point and the corresponding position of the core.

was only recently solved in [7,11]. In order to calculate the number of interlayer contacts, we have to consider in principle every possible form of the hydrophobic core in the first layer. Then, for each such form, we have to calculate how many points there are in the following layer with $1, 2, 3$ and 4 possible contacts. Formally, we define a position p in layer $x = k + 1$ to be an *i-point for the core C_k in layer x_k* (with $i = 1, 2, 3$ or 4) if p has i neighbors in $x = k$ that are contained in C_k (see Figure 8).

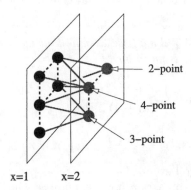

Fig. 8. Definition of *i*-points

Of course, we don't want to enumerate all possible forms for the hydrophobic core in order to calculate a bound on the number of interlayer contacts (recall that this is intended as a first step *before* enumerating the hydrophobic cores).

But we can show that it is possible to calculate a bound on the number of i-points in layer $x = k + 1$ without knowing the *exact* form of the hydrophobic core in layer $x = k$. Instead, it is sufficient to know just the frame in layer $x = k$, which is exactly what is needed when enumerating frame sequences. This bound is given in the next theorem.

Theorem 1 ([7]). *Let $x = k$ be a layer containing n_k points in a frame with height a_k and width b_k. Furthermore, let ℓ be the number of 3-points in layer $x = k$. Then*

number 3-points $= \ell$ $\qquad\qquad$ number 1-points $= \ell + 4$.
number 4-points $= n_k + 1 - a_k - b_k$ $\quad$ number 2-points $= 2a_k + 2b_k - 2\ell - 4$

It would go beyond the scope of this paper to explain this equations in detail, and the reader is referred to [7] for details. Using the above theorem, it is clear for a fixed number ℓ of 3-points, the placement of n_{k+1} in the next layer that maximizes the number of interlayer contacts is as follows. First, one fills as many 4-points as possible, then, with the remaining points, one fills the 3-points and so on. Note that this placement might *not* be optimal for the layer contacts in layer $x = k + 1$, which isn't necessary since we are calculating an upper bound. The remaining question which number of 3-points to choose. Consider the effects of going from ℓ 3-points to $(\ell + 1)$ 3-points. By the theorem, this gives us one point 3-point and one 1-point more, but we loose two 2-points. If we have enough elements in layer $x = k$ to fill even all 2-points in the case of ℓ 3-points, then we do not loose anything by going to $(\ell + 1)$ 3-points. If not, then it is better to have more 3-points. Hence, by the optimal placement strategy described above, this implies that it is best to have as much 3-points as possible. This number is also determined by the frame in $x = k$ and given in the next theorem.

Theorem 2 ([7]). *Let $x = k$ be a layer containing n_k points in a frame with height a_k and width b_k. W.l.o.g., we assume that $a_k \le b_k$. Then the maximum number of 3-points $\ell_{\max}$ is given by*

$$\ell_{\max} = \begin{cases} 4e + r & \text{if } 4e + r < 2(a_k - 1) \\ 2(a_k - 1) & \text{else.} \end{cases}$$

where $e = \max\{s \in \mathbb{N} \mid a_k b_k - 4\frac{s(s+1)}{2} \ge n_k\}$, and $r = \lfloor \frac{a_k b_k - 4\frac{e(e+1)}{2} - n}{e+1} \rfloor$.

Again, the details go beyond the scope of this paper. But there is a more or less simple geometric explanation for this number which is as follows. 3-points are generated at outer diagonals of the hydrophobic core in layer $x = k$. The lengths of the diagonals depends on their distances from the corner of the frame. This is the same as the number of diagonal lines at this corner that are *not* occupied by core elements. Then e is the maximal number of diagonals that can be left unoccupied in all corners of the frame (when distributing the unoccupied diagonals equally on all corners). $r \le 3$ is the number of times that we can add one additional unoccupied diagonal. To give an example, consider the core for

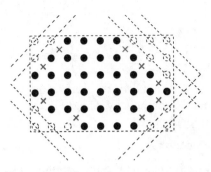

Fig. 9. Diagonals and 3-points. The figure shows one specific layer of an hydrophobic core (indicated by black beads) together with it frames. × indicate 3-points in the *next* layer. One can see that in each corner, the number of 3-points is exactly the number of diagonals in that corner that do not contain a core position.

one layer in Figure 9 with $n = 38$, $a = 6$ and $b = 9$. Then e is 2. That means, in each corner we can have at least 2 diagonal lines that are not occupied by core positions. r is 1, which means that in one corner, we can add a third unoccupied diagonal.

Thus, we can calculate boundaries for every number sequences (by assuming the optimal frames for layer and interlayer contacts independently) and for frame sequences. Furthermore, we can calculate (using a dynamic programming approach, for details see [10]) optimal or near optimal frame sequences.

4   Constructing the Hydrophobic Cores

Once we have a frame sequence a_k, b_k, n_k for $k = 1 \ldots m$, one has to enumerate the possible hydrophobic cores for this frame sequence. The first step is to fix the frame positions in each layer. That is, we have finite domain variables sy_k and sy_k for the lower left corner of the frame in layer $x = k$. We can choose $sy_1 = sz_1 = 0$ for the first frame. For the remaining frames, we have to enumerate in principle all possible starting positions. But again, we can use bounds to discard combination of values for sy_k, sz_k that may not result in a maximal compact hydrophobic core.

An example of such a bound is the following. A combination is unfavorable if a frame does not completely overlap with the previous frame. Then only the part of the two frames that do overlap can generate interlayer contacts. Hence, we can use the bounds on the interlayer contacts described in the last section to calculate the number of interlayer contacts for the overlapping sub-frames.

Once we have fixed the frames (via determining their lower left corners), we start be enumerating the positions that are actually contained in the core. This can be done by inserting for every position a Boolean variable c_p for every position p that is in one of the fixed frames. Then

$$c_p = 1 \quad \text{iff} \quad p \text{ is in the core.}$$

Clearly, we have

$$\left(\sum_{p \text{ is in Layer } x = k} c_p \right) = n_k.$$

Since a frame is usually tightly filled, this constraint provides good propagation. Finally, we have to encode contacts by using a Boolean variable $\texttt{Contact}_{p,p'}$ for each pair of neighbors p, p'. Then

$$\texttt{Contact}_{p,p'} = 1 \Leftrightarrow (c_p = 1 \wedge c_{p'} = 1).$$

Counting $\texttt{Contact}_{p,p'}$ will gives us the total number of contacts for the core.

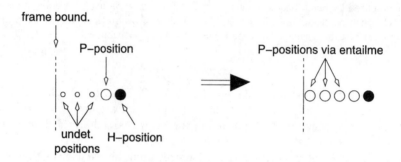

Fig. 10. Example of the caveat-freeness constraint

We can improve propagation by the following consideration. Usually, hydrophobic cores do not have too many caveats. A *caveat* is a P-monomer which is part of the hydrophobic core and thus buried by H-monomers. This usually produces a non-optimal core, but must be considered in the case that the optimal cores do not correspond to a valid sequence conformation. If a frame does not contain any caveat, then we know that for any line through the frame, the H-monomers must be consecutive on this line. Now suppose we have two positions p and p' in the same frame with the property that p is the left neighbor of p', $c_p = 0$ (P-position) and $c_{p'} = 1$ (H-position). Then all positions to the left of p on the line through p, p' must be P-positions as well (see Figure 10). For a given pair of left neighbors $p = (k, s, t)$ and $p' = (k, s+1, t)$, this can be simply expressed by the following entailment constraint:

$$c_p = 0 \wedge c_{p'} = 1 \implies \bigwedge_{\substack{p'' = (k, s, t) \\ \text{in frame} \\ \text{with } r < s}} c_{p''} = 0$$

Of course, we have to introduce such a constraint for every pair of left, right or vertical neighbors. For more details, the reader is referred to [5] and [45]. If caveats are allowed, then one can enumerate them explicitly and add the constraint for the remaining positions.

5   Threading the Sequence to a Hydrophobic Core

The final problem is the threading of the sequence to the hydrophobic core. Once we have fixed the core, it is clear that the set of positions that can be occupied by the monomers is finite. H-monomers must take positions *inside* the hydrophobic core, and P-monomers positions *outside* the hydrophobic core. To model this mapping, we introduce variables $x_1 \ldots x_n$ for a sequence s of length n that have positions as values. This can be achieved by assigning a unique number to each position. If the i-th mom omer is an H-mom omer (i.e. $s_i = H$), then x_i can of course have only II-positions as a values, and analogously for P-monomers.

Now we have to encode the properties of conformations, which are self-avoiding walks. The self-avoidingness is nothing else than an **alldifferent** constraint on $x_1 \ldots x_n$. The walk property implies that successive monomers must occupy neighboring positions. This this nothing else then a path on a graph E, which contains as nodes all positions, and an edge for two different nodes if they are neighboring positions. Thus, we have to require in addition that $x_1 \ldots x_n$ form a path in this graph E. For this purpose, we introduce the constraint $\mathrm{Path}(x_1, \ldots, x_n)$. The question is now how to guarantee hyper-arc consistency for this constraint. By a general result of Freuder [27], arc consistency amounts to global consistency in a tree-structured network of binary constraints. The next lemma is an instance of this result.

Lemma 1. *Let $x_1, \ldots, x_n$ be variables. $\mathrm{Path}(x_1, \ldots, x_n)$ is hyper-arc consistent, iff for $1 \leq i \leq n-1$ all constraints $\mathrm{Path}(x_i, x_{i+1})$ are arc consistent.*

Due to this lemma, the hyper-arc consistency of the n-ary path constraint is reduced to the arc consistency of the set of all 2-ary path constraints $\mathrm{Path}(x_i, x_{i+1})$.

The main problem is that we will not have enough propagation if self-avoiding walks are model using the two separate and unconnected constrains $\mathrm{AllDiff}(x_1, \ldots, x_n)$ and $\mathrm{Path}(x_1, \ldots, x_n)$. To improve this we have to consider the combined constraint

$$\mathrm{SAPath}(x_1, \ldots, x_n) = \mathrm{AllDiff}(x_1, \ldots, x_n) \wedge \mathrm{Path}(x_1, \ldots, x_n).$$

Unfortunately, we are not aware of any efficient arc consistency algorithm for this combined constraint in the literature. Furthermore, it is unlikely that there exists one. It is well known that many problems involving self-avoiding walks (we use the term path here), especially counting of such walks, are intrinsically hard and there are no efficient algorithms to solve them [36].

For this reason, we have considered in [10] a relaxation of this constraint that provides better propagation but is still tractable. We have searched for a class of walks that are between arbitrary walks and self-avoiding walks. Self-avoiding means that we have the AllDiff() constraint for every variable in the walk. But what happens if we enforce this only for a subset of variables? To this end, we introduced the concept of k-avoiding walks, which are walks that are self-avoiding for every subwalk of length k (but not necessarily for the complete walk). Figure 11 shows a walk that is 4-avoiding, but neither 5-avoiding nor self-avoiding.

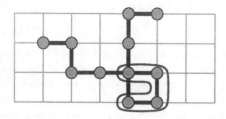

Fig. 11. A walk that is not self-avoiding but 4-avoiding. Encircled is a subwalk of length 4. Every subwalk of length 4 is self-avoiding.

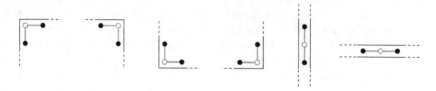

Fig. 12. All possible conformations for an HPH subsequence. The black lines indicate the minimal frame boundaries, showing that the P must be within the frame enclosing the two surrounding H-monomers.

The combination of cpaths[k]($x_1, \ldots, x_n$) (which expresses k-avoidingness) and AllDiff($x_1, \ldots, x_n$) provides much better propagation than the combination of Path($x_1, \ldots, x_n$) and AllDiff($x_1, \ldots, x_n$), which can be seen in the following example. The cubic lattice has the property that if we consider a HPH subsequence, then the middle P monomer must be contained in the frame that contains also the surrounding H-monomers (see Figure 12). The reason is that the only way we could have the P outside is to go back and forth, which is not allowed by the self-avoidingness condition. This property is detect via propagation of the 3-avoidingness constraint, but not using separate propagation on the constraints AllDiff($x_1, \ldots, x_n$) and Path($x_1, \ldots, x_n$).

6   Results

We have successfully applied the approach to sequences up to length 200. The hydrophobic cores are pre-calculated. Thus, when folding an HP-sequence, only the work for the threading step has to be done. Runtimes for this steps are given in Figure 13. The approach can be tested on our WWW-page

http://www.bio.inf.uni-jena.de/Software/Prediction/prediction.cgi

In Figure 14, a comparison with other approaches is given. Usually, no search times are given. For that reason, we have listed the maximal sequence length

Sequence	length	runtime
PPPHPHHPHHPPPHPHPPPPHPHHPPHPHHHHHHPPHHPPHHHHHHPPHPP HHPPHPHPHHHHHPHHPHHHPPPHHHPHHPPHPHPPHPPPHPPHPPHPPH HHPHPHHPPPHPHPHPHHPPHHPPPPHHHHHHPPPHHPPPPPPHHPPHPH HHPHPHHPPPPHPHPHPHHPPHPPPHHHHHHHPPPHHPPPPHPHPPHPPH	200	6.1 s
HPHHPHHPPPPPHPHPHPHHPPPPHHHHHHHPPHPHHPPHHHHHPHPPPP HHPPHHHPHHHHHHPPHHPHHPPHPHPPPPHHPHPHPHHHHHPPPPPHHHPP PPHHPPPPPHPHPPHPHPHHHHHHHHPHPPPPHPHHHHHHPHHHHHPHHP HHHPHPHHPPPPPHPHPHPHHPHPPPPHPPPPPHPPHPHHHHHPHHPPPHPPH	200	52.6 s
HPHHHPHHPHPHPPPHHHHHPHPHPHHHHPPPHHPPPPPHHPPPPHPHH HPPPHPPPHPHPHPPPHHPHPPPPHHHHPHPHPHPPPPHHPPPPHPHPPPP HPPHHHPHHHPHPHPPHHHPPPPPHHHHPHHPHPPPHHHHPPPHPHPPP HPHPPPPPHPHPHHHHHHHHHPHPHHHHHHHHHHPHHHPPPHPPPHPPPHHHPHH	200	17.6 s

Fig. 13. Example runtimes for the threading of 3 random sequences of length 200 onto a hydrophobic core of size 100 (on a Pentium IV 2.4Ghz).

handled in the references. Beside the HP model on the two-dimensional square, 3-dimensional cubic and 3-dimensional FCC lattice, we have in addition the so-called "Hetero" models. These models consider more types of interactions (not only hydrophobic/hydrophobic interactions like in the HP-model). In [39,43], the interactions where even generated by a random model resulting in one specific type of interaction for *every* pair of amino acids. This kind of models are used to make prediction about general properties of the protein folding problem.

Authors	Model	Dim.	maxlen	Algorithm	Comment
Structure Prediction Algorithms					
Shakhnovich et al. [39] Sali et al. [43]	cubic Hetero (max. compact)	3	27	compl. enum	fixed shape
Dinner et al. [25]	cubic Hetero (max. compact)	3	125	compl. enum	fixed shape
Yue&Dill [48]	cubic HP	3	36	branch-and-bound	optimality proven
Yue&Dill [49]	cubic HP	3	88	branch-and-bound	optimality proven
Xia et al. [46]	tetrahedral Hetero	3	?	enumeration	restricted shape
Kaya&Chan [32]	cubic Hetero	3	55	monte carlo	
Cui et al. [22]	square HP	2	18	compl. enum	
Approximation Algorithms					
Hart&Istrail [30]	cubic HP	3	—	approximation	$\frac{3}{8}$ of optimum
Hart&Istrail [29]	FCC-HP side chain	3	—	approximation	86% of optimum
Agarwala et al. [3]	FCC-HP	3	—	approximation	$\frac{3}{5}$ of optimum

Fig. 14. Results for difference lattice models by other groups.

Another distinction that has to be made when considering the sequence lengths in Figure 14 is the type of the algorithm, which is specified in the last two columns. We have all kinds of approaches including complete enumerations. The enumeration approaches either can be applied only to small sequence lengths (≤ 18), or to models, where the search space has been restricted artificially. An example here is the approach by [39,43], where only maximally compact conformations have been considered. I.e., only conformations on a $3 \times 3 \times 3$ cube have been considered, which drastically reduces the search space. This implies, that they consider only sequences of length 27, which equals the number of positions in a $3 \times 3 \times 3$ cube. For this model, one has to enumerate only all 103 346 maximally compact conformations [39]. In a later work, this was extended to $5 \times 5 \times 5$ cube having 125 positions [25].

Finally, we compare our work with the CHCC-algorithm [48,49], which is the only other approach that can find provably optimal conformations in the cubic lattice. The HP-model is not designed to generate one *single* minimal energy conformation. Instead, there are a lot of minimal energy conformations, suggesting possible topologies for a protein. The number of this minimal energy conformations for a specific sequences s is called the *degeneracy* of s. In [47], Yue et al. have given a lower bound on the degeneracy of some sequences. We have largely improved these bounds (see Figure 15).

Sequence	degeneracy found by	
	CHCC [47]	our approach
HPHHPPHHHHPHHHPPHHPPHPHHHHPHPHHPPHHPPPHPPPPPPPPHH	1500×10^3	$10,677,113$
HHHHPHHPHHHHHPPHHPPHHPPHPPPPPPPHPPHPPPPPHPHHPPHHHHPH	14×10^3	$28,180$
PHPHHPHHHHHHPPHPHPHPHHHPHPHPPPHPPPHHPPHHPPHHPHPHPPHP	5×10^3	$5,090$
PHHPPPPPPHHPPPHHHHPHPPHPHHPHPPHPPHHPPHHHHHHHHPPHH	188×10^3	$580,751$

Fig. 15. Comparison of lower bounds on the degeneracy.

References

1. V. I. Abkevich, A. M. Gutin, and E. I. Shakhnovich. Impact of local and non-local interactions on thermodynamics and kinetics of protein folding. *Journal of Molecular Biology*, 252:460–471, 1995.

2. V.I. Abkevich, A.M. Gutin, and E.I. Shakhnovich. Computer simulations of prebiotic evolution. In Russ B. Altman, A. Keith Dunker, Lawrence Hunter, and Teri E. Klein, editors, *PSB'97*, pages 27–38, 1997.

3. R. Agarwala, S. Batzoglou, V. Dancik, S. E. Decatur, S. Hannenhalli, M. Farach, S. Muthukrishnan, and S. Skiena. Local rules for protein folding on a triangular lattice and generalized hydrophobicity in the hp model. *Journal of Computational Biology*, 4(3):275–96, 1997.

4. Richa Agarwala, Serafim Batzoglou, Vlado Dancik, Scott E. Decatur, Martin Farach, Sridhar Hannenhalli, S. Muthukrishnan, and Steven Skiena. Local rules for protein folding on a triangular lattice and generalized hydrophobicity in the HP-model. *Journal of Computational Biology*, 4(2):275–296, 1997.

5. Rolf Backofen. Using constraint programming for lattice protein folding. In Russ B. Altman, A. Keith Dunker, Lawrence Hunter, and Teri E. Klein, editors, *Pacific Symposium on Biocomputing (PSB'98)*, volume 3, pages 387–398, 1998.

6. Rolf Backofen. *Optimization Techniques for the Protein Structure Prediction Problem*. Habilitationsschrift, University of Munich, 1999.

7. Rolf Backofen. An upper bound for number of contacts in the HP-model on the face-centered-cubic lattice (FCC). In Raffaele Giancarlo and David Sankoff, editors, *Proc. of the 11th Annual Symposium on Combinatorial Pattern Matching (CPM2000)*, volume 1848 of *Lecture Notes in Computer Science*, pages 277–292, Berlin, 2000. Springer–Verlag.

8. Rolf Backofen. The protein structure prediction problem: A constraint optimisation approach using a new lower bound. *Constraints*, 6:223–255, 2001.

9. Rolf Backofen and Sebastian Will. Excluding symmetries in constraint-based search. In Joxan Jaffar, editor, *Proceedings of 5ᵗʰ International Conference on Principle and Practice of Constraint Programming (CP'99)*, volume 1713 of *Lecture Notes in Computer Science*, pages 73–87, Berlin, 1999. Springer–Verlag.

10. Rolf Backofen and Sebastian Will. Fast, constraint-based threading of HP-sequences to hydrophobic cores. In *Proceedings of 7ᵗʰ International Conference on Principle and Practice of Constraint Programming (CP'2001)*, volume 2239 of *Lecture Notes in Computer Science*, Berlin, 2001. Springer–Verlag.

11. Rolf Backofen and Sebastian Will. Optimally compact finite sphere packings — hydrophobic cores in the FCC. In *Proc. of the 12th Annual Symposium on Combinatorial Pattern Matching (CPM2001)*, volume 2089 of *Lecture Notes in Computer Science*, Berlin, 2001. Springer–Verlag.

12. Rolf Backofen and Sebastian Will. Excluding symmetries in constraint-based search. *Constraints*, 7(3):333–349, 2002.

13. Rolf Backofen, Sebastian Will, and Erich Bornberg-Bauer. Application of constraint programming techniques for structure prediction of lattice proteins with extended alphabets. *J. Bioinformatics*, 15(3):234–242, 1999.

14. Rolf Backofen, Sebastian Will, and Peter Clote. Algorithmic approach to quantifying the hydrophobic force contribution in protein folding. In Russ B. Altman, A. Keith Dunker, Lawrence Hunter, and Teri E. Klein, editors, *Pacific Symposium on Biocomputing (PSB 2000)*, volume 5, pages 92–103, 2000.

15. Zerrin Bagci, Robert L. Jernigan, and Ivet Bahar. Residue coordination in proteins conforms to the closest packing of spheres. *Polymer*, 43:451–459, 2002.

16. Zerrin Bagci, Robert L. Jernigan, and Ivet Bahar. Residue packing in proteins: Uniform distribution on a coarse-grained scale. *J Chem Phys*, 116:2269–2276, 2002.

17. B. Berger and T. Leighton. Protein folding in the hydrophobic-hydrophilic (HP) modell is NP-complete. In *Proc. of the RECOMB'98*, pages 30–39, 1998.

18. E Bornberg-Bauer and HS Chan. Modeling evolutionary landscapes: mutational stability, topology, and superfunnels in sequence space. *Proc Natl Acad Sci U S A*, 96(19):10689–94, 1999.

19. Erich Bornberg-Bauer. Chain growth algorithms for HP-type lattice proteins. In *Proc. of the 1ˢᵗ Annual International Conference on Computational Molecular Biology (RECOMB)*, pages 47 – 55. ACM Press, 1997.

20. Barry Cipra. Packing challenge mastered at last. *Science*, 281:1267, 1998.

21. P. Crescenzi, D. Goldman, C. Papadimitriou, A. Piccolboni, and M. Yannakakis. On the complexity of protein folding. In *Proc. of STOC*, 1998. To appear. Short version in *Proc. of RECOMB'98*, pages 61–62.

22. Yan Cui, Wing Hung Wong, Erich Bornberg-Bauer, and Hue Sun Chan. Recombinatoric exploration of novel folded structures: a heteropolymer-based model of protein evolutionary landscapes. *Proc. Natl. Acad. Sci. USA*, 99(2):809–14, 2002.

23. K.A. Dill, S. Bromberg, K. Yue, K.M. Fiebig, D.P. Yee, P.D. Thomas, and H.S. Chan. Principles of protein folding – a perspective of simple exact models. *Protein Science*, 4:561–602, 1995.

24. Ken A. Dill, Klaus M. Fiebig, and Hue Sun Chan. Cooperativity in protein-folding kinetics. *Proc. Natl. Acad. Sci. USA*, 90:1942 – 1946, 1993.

25. A. R. Dinner, A Sali, and M Karplus. The folding mechanism of larger model proteins: role of native structure. *Proc. Natl. Acad. Sci. USA*, 93(16):8356–61, 1996.

26. A. Dovier, M. Burato, and F. Fogolari. Using secondary structure information for protein folding in clp(fd). In *Proc. of Workshop on Functional and Constraint Logic Programming*, volume ENTCS vol. 76, 2002.

27. Eugene C. Freuder. A sufficient condition for backtrack-free search. *Journal of the ACM*, 29:24–32, 1982.

28. S. Govindarajan and R. A. Goldstein. The foldability landscape of model proteins. *Biopolymers*, 42(4):427–438, 1997.

29. W. E. Hart and S. Istrail. Lattice and off-lattice side chain models of protein folding: linear time structure prediction better than 86 *Journal of Computational Biology*, 4(3):241–59, 1997.

30. W. E. Hart and S. C. Istrail. Fast protein folding in the hydrophobic-hydrophilic model within three-eighths of optimal. *Journal of Computational Biology*, 3(1):53–96, 1996.

31. David A. Hinds and Michael Levitt. From structure to sequence and back again. *Journal of Molecular Biology*, 258:201–209, 1996.

32. H. Kaya and H. S. Chan. Energetic components of cooperative protein folding. *Physical Review Letters*, 85(22):4823–6, 2000.

33. Patrice Koehl and Michael Levitt. A brighter future for protein structure prediction. *Nature Structural Biology*, 6:108–111, 1999.

34. Kit Fun Lau and Ken A. Dill. A lattice statistical mechanics model of the conformational and sequence spaces of proteins. *Macromolecules*, 22:3986 – 3997, 1989.

35. D. MacDonald, S. Joseph, D. L. Hunter, L. L. Moseley, N. Jan, and A. J. Guttmann. Self-avoiding walks on the simple cubic lattice. *J. Phys. A: Math. Gen.*, 33:5973–5983, 2000.

36. N. Madras and G. Slade. *The Self-Avoiding Walk*. Birkhäuser, Boston, 1993. 425 pages.

37. Angel R. Ortiz, Andrzej Kolinski, and Jeffrey Skolnick. Combined multiple sequence reduced protein model approach to predict the tertiary structure of small proteins. In Russ B. Altman, A. Keith Dunker, Lawrence Hunter, and Teri E. Klein, editors, *PSB'98*, volume 3, pages 375–386, 1998.

38. Britt H. Park and Michael Levitt. The complexity and accuracy of discrete state models of protein structure. *Journal of Molecular Biology*, 249:493–507, 1995.

39. E. I. Shakhnovich and A. M. Gutin. Enumeration of all compact conformations of copolymers with random sequence of links. *Journal Chemical Physics*, 8:5967–5971, 1990.

40. Neil J. A. Sloane. Kepler's conjecture confirmed. *Nature*, 395(6701):435–6, 1998.

41. Gert Smolka. The Oz programming model. In Jan van Leeuwen, editor, *Computer Science Today*, Lecture Notes in Computer Science, vol. 1000, pages 324–343. Springer-Verlag, Berlin, 1995.

42. Ron Unger and John Moult. Local interactions dominate folding in a simple protein model. *Journal of Molecular Biology*, 259:988–994, 1996.

43. A. Šali, E. Shakhnovich, and M. Karplus. Kinetics of protein folding. *Journal of Molecular Biology*, 235:1614–1636, 1994.

44. A. Šali, E. Shakhnovich, and M. Karplus. Kinetics of protein folding. *Journal of Molecular Biology*, 235:1614–1636, 1994.
45. Sebastian Will. Constraint-based hydrophobic core construction for protein structure prediction in the face-centered-cubic lattice. In Russ B. Altman, A. Keith Dunker, Lawrence Hunter, and Teri E. Klein, editors, *Proceedings of the Pacific Symposium on Biocomputing 2002 (PSB 2002)*, Singapore, 2002. World Scientific Publishing Co. Pte. Ltd.
46. Yu Xia, Enoch S. Huang, Michael Levitt, and Ram Samudrala. Ab initio construction of protein tertiary structures using a hierarchical approach. *Journal of Molecular Biology*, 300:171 – 185, 2000.
47. K. Yue, K. M. Fiebig, P. D. Thomas, H. S. Chan, E. I. Sha khnovich, and K. A. Dill. A test of lattice protein folding algorithms. *Proc. Natl. Acad. Sci. USA*, 92(1):325–9, 1995.
48. Kaizhi Yue and Ken A. Dill. Sequence-structure relationships in proteins and copolymers. *Physical Review E*, 48(3):2267–2278, September 1993.
49. Kaizhi Yue and Ken A. Dill. Forces of tertiary structural organization in globular proteins. *Proc. Natl. Acad. Sci. USA*, 92:146 – 150, 1995.

Concurrency, Time, and Constraints

Frank D. Valencia*

Dept. of Information Technology, Uppsala University
Box 337 SE-751 05 Uppsala, Sweden
frankv@it.uu.se   Fax: +46 18 511 925

Abstract. *Concurrent constraint programming* (ccp) is a model of concurrency for systems in which agents (also called processes) interact with one another by telling and asking information in a shared medium. *Timed* (or *temporal*) ccp extends ccp by allowing agents to be constrained by time requirements. The novelty of timed ccp is that it combines in one framework an *operational and algebraic* view based upon process calculi with a *declarative* view based upon temporal logic. This allows the model to benefit from two well-established theories used in the study of concurrency.

This essay offers an overview of timed ccp covering its basic background and central developments. The essay also includes an introduction to a temporal ccp formalism called the ntcc calculus.

1   Introduction

Concurrency theory has made progress by extending well-established models of computation to capture new and wider phenomena. These extensions should not come as a surprise since the field is indeed large and subject to the advents of new technology. One particular phenomenon, for which extensions of the very first theories of concurrency were needed, is the notion of *time*.

Time is not only a fundamental concept in concurrency but also in science at large. Just like modal extensions of logic for temporal progression study time in logic reasoning, mature models of concurrency were extended to study time in concurrent activity. For instance, neither Milner's CCS [23], Hoare's CSP [18], nor Petri Nets [31], in their original form, were concerned with temporal behavior but they all have been extended to incorporate an explicit notion of time. Namely, Timed CCS [52], Timed CSP [34], and Timed Petri Nets [53].

The notion of *constraint* is certainly not rare in concurrency. After all, concurrency is about the interaction of agents and such an interaction often involves constraints of some sort (e.g., synchronization constraints, access-control, actions that must eventually happen, actions that cannot happen, etc).

Saraswat's *concurrent constraint programming* (ccp) [44] is a well-established formalism for concurrency based upon the shared-variables communication model where interaction arises via constraint-imposition over shared-variables. In ccp, agents can interact by *adding* (or *telling*) partial information in a medium, a so-called *store*. Partial

---

* This work was supported by the **PROFUNDIS** Project.

information is represented by *constraints* (i.e., first-order formulae such as $x > 42$) on the shared variables of the system. The other way in which agents can interact is by *asking* partial information to the store. This provides the synchronization mechanism of the model; asking agents are suspended until there is enough information in the store to answer their query.

As other models of concurrency, ccp has been extended to capture aspects such as mobility [8,36,12], stochastic behavior [13], and most prominently time [39,5,41,14]. *Timed* ccp extends ccp by allowing agents to be constrained by time requirements.

A distinctive feature of timed ccp is that it combines in one framework an *operational and algebraic* view based upon process calculi with a *declarative* view based upon temporal logic. So, processes can be treated as computing agents, algebraic terms and temporal formulae. At this point it is convenient to quote Robin Milner:

> *I make no claim that everything can be done by algebra ... It is perhaps equally true that not everything can be done by logic; thus one of the outstanding challenges in concurrency is to find the right marriage between logic and behavioral approaches*
> — Robin Milner, [23]

In fact, the combination in one framework of the alternative views of processes mentioned above allows timed ccp to benefit from the large body of techniques of well established theories used in the study of concurrency and, in particular, *timed systems*.

Furthermore, timed ccp allows processes to be (1) expressed using a vocabulary and concepts appropriate to the *specific domain* (of some application under consideration), and (2) read and understood as temporal logic *specifications*. This feature is suitable for timed systems as they often involve *specific domains* (e.g., controllers, databases, reservation systems) and have time-constraints *specifying* their behavior (e.g., the lights must be switched on within the next three seconds). Indeed, several timed extensions of ccp have been developed in order to provide settings for the modeling, programming and specification of timed systems [39,42,5,14].

This paper offers an overview of timed ccp with its basic background and various approaches explored by researchers in this field. Furthermore, it offers an introduction to a timed ccp process calculus called ntcc. The paper is organized as follows. In Section 2 we discuss briefly those issues from models of concurrency, in particular process calculi, relevant to temporal ccp. In Sections 3 and 4 we give an overview of ccp and timed ccp. Section 5 is devoted to address, in the context of timed ccp and by using ntcc, those issues previously discussed in Section 2. Finally in Section 6 we discuss central developments in timed ccp.

2   Background: Models of Concurrency

Concurrency is concerned with the fundamental aspects of systems consisting of multiple computing agents, usually called *processes*, that interact among each other. This covers a vast variety of systems, so-called *concurrent systems*, which nowadays most people can easily relate to due to technological advances such as the Internet, programmable robotic devices and mobile computing . For instance, *timed* systems, in which agents are constrained by temporal requirements. Some example of timed systems are: Browser applications which are constrained by timer-based exit conditions (i.e., *time-outs*) for the case in which a sever cannot be contacted; E-mailer applications can be required to check for messages every k time units. Also, robots can be programmed with time-outs (e.g., to wait for some signal) and with timed instructions (e.g., to go forward for 42 time-units).

Because of the practical relevance, complexity and ubiquity of concurrent systems, it is crucial to be able to describe, analyze and, in general, reason about concurrent behavior. This reasoning must be precise and reliable. Consequently, it ought to be founded upon mathematical principles in the same way as the reasoning about the behavior of sequential programs is founded upon logic, domain theory and other mathematical disciplines.

Nevertheless, giving mathematical foundations to concurrent computation has become a serious challenge for computer science. Traditional mathematical models of (sequential) computation based on functions from inputs to outputs no longer apply. The crux is that concurrent computation, e.g., in a reactive system, is seldom expected to terminate, it involves constant interaction with the environment, and it is *nondeterministic* owing to unpredictable interactions among agents.

Models of Concurrency: Process Calculi. Computer science has therefore taken up the task of developing *models*, conceptually different from those of sequential computation, for the precise understanding of the behavior of concurrent systems. Such models, as other scientific models of reality, are expected to comply with the following criteria: They must be *simple* (i.e., based upon few basic principles), *expressive* (i.e., capable of capturing interesting real-world situations), *formal* (i.e., founded upon mathematical principles), and they must provide *techniques* to allow reasoning about their particular focus.

Process calculi are one of the most common frameworks for modeling concurrent activity. These calculi treat processes much like the λ-calculus treats computable functions. They provide a language in which the structure of *terms* represents the structure of processes together with an *operational semantics* to represent computational steps. For example, the term $P \parallel Q$, which is built from P and Q with the *constructor* $\parallel$, represents the process that results from the parallel execution of those represented by P and Q. An operational semantics may dictate that if P can evolve into P' in a computational step P' then $P \parallel Q$ can also evolve into $P' \parallel Q$ in a computational step.

An appealing feature of process calculi is their *algebraic* treatment of processes. The constructors are viewed as the *operators* of an algebraic theory whose equations and inequalities among terms relate process behavior. For instance, the construct $\parallel$ can be viewed as a commutative operator, hence the equation $P \parallel Q \equiv Q \parallel P$ states that the behavior of the two parallel compositions are the same. Because of this algebraic emphasis, these calculi are often referred to as *process algebras*.

There are many different process calculi in the literature mainly agreeing in their emphasis upon algebra. The main representatives are CCS [23], CSP [18], and the process algebra ACP [2]. The distinctions among these calculi arise from issues such as the process constructions considered (i.e., the language of processes), the methods used for giving meaning to process terms (i.e. the semantics), and the methods to reason about process behavior (e.g., process equivalences or process logics).

Semantics. The methods by which process terms are endowed with meaning may involve at least three approaches: *operational, denotational* and *algebraic* semantics. The *operational method* was pioneered by Plotkin [32]. An operational semantics interprets a given process term by using transitions (labeled or not) specifying its computational steps. A labeled transition $P \xrightarrow{a} Q$ specifies that P performs a and then behaves as Q. The *denotational method* was pioneered by Strachey and provided with a mathematical foundation by Scott. A denotational semantics interprets processes by using a function $[\![\cdot]\!]$ which maps them into a more abstract mathematical object (typically, a structured set or a category). The map $[\![\cdot]\!]$ is *compositional* in that the meaning of processes is determined from the meaning of its sub-processes. The *algebraic method* has been advocated by Bergstra and Klop [2]. An algebraic semantics attempts to give meaning by stating a set of laws (or axioms) equating process terms. The processes and their operations are then interpreted as structures that obey these laws.

Behavioral Analysis. Much work in the theory of process calculi, and concurrency in general, involves the analysis of process equivalences. Let us say that our equivalence under consideration is denoted by $\sim$. Two typical questions that arise are: (1) Is the equivalence decidable ? (2) Is the equivalence a congruence ? The first question refers to the issue as to whether there can be an algorithm that fully determines (or decides) for every P and Q if $P \sim Q$ or $P \nsim Q$. Since most process calculi can model Turing machines most natural equivalences are therefore undecidable. So, the interesting question is rather for what subclasses of processes is the equivalence decidable. The second question refers to the issue as to whether the fact that P and Q are equivalent implies that they are still equivalent in any process context. A process context C can be viewed as a term with a hole $[\cdot]$ such that placing a process in the hole yields a process term. Hence, the equivalence is a congruence if $P \sim Q$ implies $C[P] \sim C[Q]$ for every process context C. The congruence issue is fundamental for algebraic as well as practical reasons; one may not be content with having $P \sim Q$ equivalent but $R \parallel P \nsim R \parallel Q$ (here the context is $C = R \parallel [\cdot]$).

Specification and Logic. One often is interested in verifying whether a given process satisfies a specification; the so-called *verification problem*. But process terms themselves specify behavior, so they can also be used to express specifications. Then this verification problem can be reduced to establishing whether the process and the specification process are related under some behavioral equivalence (or pre-order). Another way of expressing process specifications, however, is by using temporal logics. These logics were introduced into computer science by Pnueli [33] and thereafter proven to be a good basis for specification as well as for (automatic and machine-assisted) reasoning about concurrent systems. Temporal logics can be classified into linear and branching time logics. In the *linear* case at each moment there is only one possible future whilst in the *branching* case at may split into alternative futures.

3   Concurrent Constraint Programming

In his seminal PhD thesis [38], Saraswat proposed concurrent constraint programming as a model of concurrency based on the shared-variables communication model and a few primitive ideas taking root in logic. As informally described in this section, the ccp model elegantly combines logic concepts and concurrency mechanisms.

Concurrent constraint programming traces its origins back to Montanari's pioneering work [26] leading to constraint programming and Shapiro's concurrent logic programming [45]. The ccp model has received a significant theoretical and implementational attention: Saraswat, Rinard and Panangaden [44] as well as De Boer, Di Pierro and Palamidessi [6] gave fixed-point denotational semantics to ccp whilst Montanari and Rossi [35] gave it a (true-concurrent) Petri-Net semantics; De Boer, Gabrielli et al [7] developed an inference system for proving properties of ccp processes; Smolka's Oz [47] as well as Haridi and Janson's AKL [17] programming languages are built upon ccp ideas.

Description of the model. A fundamental issue of the ccp model is the *specification of concurrent systems* in terms of constraints. A constraint is a first-order formula representing *partial information* about the shared variables of the system. For example, the constraint $x + y > 42$ specifies possible values for x and y (those satisfying the inequation). The ccp model is parameterized in a *constraint system* which specifies the constraints of relevance for the kind of system under consideration and an *entailment relation* $\models$ between constraints (e.g, $x + y > 42 \models x + y > 0$).

During computation, the state of the system is specified by an entity called the *store* where items of information about the variables of the system reside. The store is represented as a constraint and thus it may provide only partial information about the variables. This differs fundamentally from the traditional view of a store based on the Von Neumann memory model, in which each variable is assigned a uniquely determined value (e.g., $x = 42$ and $y = 7$) rather than a set of possible values.

Some readers may feel uneasy as the notion of store in ccp suggests a model of concurrency with central memory. This is, however, an abstraction that simplifies the presentation of the model. The store can be distributed in several sites according to the agents that share the same variables (see [38] for further discussions about this matter). Conceptually, the store in ccp is the *medium* through which agents interact with each other.

The ccp processes can update the state of the system only by *adding* (or *telling*) information to the store. This is represented as the (logical) conjunction of the constraint being added and the store representing the previous state. Hence, the update is not about changing the values of the variables but rather about ruling out some of the previously possible values. In other words, the store is *monotonically refined.*

Furthermore, processes can synchronize by *asking* information to the store. Asking is blocked until there is enough information in the store to *entail* (i.e., answer positively) their query. The ask operation is seen as determining whether the constraint representing the store entails the query.

A ccp computation terminates whenever it reaches a point, called *resting* or *quiescent* point, in which no more new information is added to the store. The final store, also called *quiescent store* (i.e,. the store at the quiescent point), is the output of the computation.

Example 1. To make the description of the ccp model clearer, consider the simple ccp scenario illustrated in Figure 1. We have four agents (or processes) wishing to interact through an initially empty medium. Let us name them, starting from the upper rightmost agent in a clockwise fashion, A_1, A_2, A_3 and A_4, respectively. Suppose that they are scheduled for execution in the same order they were named.

This way A_1 moves first and tells the others through the medium that the temperature value is greater than 42 degrees but without specifying the exact value. In other words A_1 gives the others partial information about the temperature. This causes the addition of the item "temperature>42" to the previously empty store.

Now A_2 asks whether the temperature is exactly 50 degrees, and if so it wishes to execute a process P. From the current information in the store, however, it cannot be determined what the exact value of the temperature is. The agent A_2 is then blocked and so is the agent A_3 since from the store it cannot be determined either whether the temperature is between 0 and 100 degrees.

The turn is for A_4 which tells that the temperature is less than 70 degrees. The store becomes "temperature $> 42 \wedge$ temperature < 70". Now A_3 can execute Q as its query is entailed by the information in the store . The other ask agent A_2 is doomed to be blocked forever unless Q adds enough information to the store to entail its query.   □

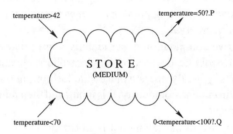

Fig. 1. A simple ccp scenario

The CCP Process Language. In the spirit of process calculi, the language of processes in the ccp model is given with a reduced number of primitive operators or combinators. Rather than giving the actual syntax of the language, we content ourselves with describing the basic intuition that each construct embodies. So, in ccp we have:

- *The tell action*, for expressing tell operations. E.g., agent A_1 above.
- *The ask action (or prefix action)*, for expressing an ask operation that prefixes another process; its continuation. E.g., the agent A_2 above.
- *Parallel composition*, which combines processes concurrently. E.g., the scenario in Figure 1 can be specified as the parallel composition of A_1, A_2, A_3 and A_4.
- *Hiding* (or *locality*), for expressing local variables that delimit the interface through which a process can interact with others.
- *Summation*, which expresses a disjunctive combination of agents to allow alternate courses of action.
- *Recursion*, for defining infinite behavior.

It is worth pointing out that without summation, the ccp model is deterministic in the sense that the quiescent or final store is always the same, independently from the execution order (scheduling) of the parallel components [44].

4   Timed Concurrent Constraint Programming

The first timed ccp model was introduced by Saraswat et al [39] as an extension of ccp aimed at programming and modeling timed, reactive systems. This model, which has attracted growing attention during the last five years or so, elegantly combines ccp with ideas from the paradigms of Synchronous Languages [3,15].

As any other model of computation, the tcc model makes an ontological commitment about computation. It emphasizes the view of reactive computation as proceeding *deterministically* in discrete time units (or time *intervals*). More precisely, time is conceptually divided into discrete intervals. In each time interval, a deterministic ccp process receives a stimulus (i.e. a constraint) from the environment, it executes with this stimulus as the *initial store*, and when it reaches its resting point, it responds to the environment with the *final store*. Also, the resting point determines a residual process, which is then executed in the next time interval.

This view of reactive computation is particularly appropriate for programming reactive systems such as robotic devices, micro-controllers, databases and reservation systems. These systems typically operate in a cyclic fashion; in each cycle they receive and input from the environment, compute on this input, and then return the corresponding output to the environment.

The fundamental move in the tcc model is to extend the standard ccp with *delay* and *time-out* operations. These operations are fundamental for programming reactive systems. The delay operation forces the execution of a process to be postponed to the next time interval. The time-out (or weak *pre-emption*) operation waits during the current time interval for a given piece of information to be present and if it is not, triggers a process in the *next time interval*.

Pre-emption and multi-form time. In spite of its simplicity, the tcc extension to ccp is far-reaching. Many interesting temporal constructs can be expressed, in particular:

- **do** P **watching** c. This interrupt process executes P continuously until the item of information (e.g, a signal) c is present (i.e., entailed by the information in the store); when c is present P is *killed* from the next time unit onwards. This corresponds to the familiar `kill` command in Unix or clicking on the stop bottom of your favorite web browser.
- $\mathbf{S}_c \mathbf{A}_d(P)$. This pre-emption process executes P continuously until c is present; when c is present P is *suspended* from the next time unit onwards. The process P is *reactivated* when d is present. This corresponds to the familiar (`ctrl -Z`, `fg`) mechanism in Unix.
- **time** P **on** c. This denotes a process whose *notion of time* is the occurrence of the item of information c. That is, P evolves only in those time intervals where c holds.

In general, tcc allows processes to be "clocked" by other processes. This provides meaningful pre-emption constructs and the ability of defining *multiple forms of time* instead of only having a unique global clock.

4.1 More Timed CCP Models

The ntcc calculus is generalization of the tcc model originated in [28] by Palamidessi, Nielsen and the present author. The calculus is built upon few basic ideas but it captures several aspects of timed systems. As tcc, ntcc can model unit delays, time-outs, pre emption and synchrony. Additionally, it can model *unbounded but finite delays, bounded eventuality, asynchrony* and *nondeterminism*. The applicability of the calculus has been illustrated with several examples of discrete-time systems involving , mutable data structures, robotic devices, multi-agent systems and music applications [37].

Another interesting extension of tcc, which does not consider nondeterminism or unbounded finite-delay, has been proposed in [42]. This extension adds strong pre-emption: the time-out operations can trigger activity in the current time interval. In contrast, ntcc can only express weak pre-emption. Other extensions of tcc have been proposed in [14]. In [14] processes can evolve continuously as well as discretely. None of these extensions consider nondeterminism or unbounded finite-delay.

The tccp framework, introduced in [5] by Gabrielli et al, is a fundamental representative model of (nondeterministic) timed ccp. The authors in [5] also advocate the need of nondeterminism in the context of timed ccp. In fact, they use tccp to model interesting applications involving nondeterministic timed systems (see [5]). The major difference between tccp and ntcc is that the former extends the original ccp while the latter extends the tcc model (so, except for allowing nondeterminism, it makes the same commitments about computation). In tccp the information about the store is carried through the time units, thus the semantic setting is completely different. The notion of time is also different; in tccp each time unit is identified with the time needed to ask and tell information to the store. As for the constructs, unlike ntcc, tccp provides for arbitrary recursion and does not have an operator for specifying unbounded but finite delays.

As briefly described in this section, there are several models of timed ccp, and it would be hard to introduce all of them in detail. I shall introduce in detail the generalization of Saraswat's tcc, the ntcc calculus, and then indicate as related work the developments in other models which appear to me to be central.

5 The ntcc Process Calculus

This section gives an introduction to the ntcc model. We shall give evidence of the compliance of ntcc with the criteria for models of concurrency previously mentioned (i.e., it is simple, expressive, formal and it provides reasoning techniques). First, we shall see that it captures fundamental aspects of concurrency (i.e., discrete-time reactive computations, nondeterminism, synchrony and asynchrony) whilst keeping a pleasant degree of *simplicity*. Second, the expressiveness of ntcc will be illustrated by modeling robotic devices. Furthermore, we shall see that ntcc is founded upon *formal* theories such as process calculi and first-order logic. Finally, we shall present some of the techniques that ntcc provides to reason about concurrent activity. Namely,

1. Several *equivalences*, characterized operationally, to compare the behavior of processes much like the behavioral equivalences for existing process calculi (e.g., bisimilarity and trace-equivalence).
2. A *denotational semantics* which interprets a given process as the set of sequences of actions it can potentially exhibit while interacting with arbitrary environments.
3. A *process logic* with an associated *inference system* than can be used much like the Hoare's program logic for sequential computation. The logic can be used to express required timed behaviors of processes, i.e., *temporal specifications*. The inference system can be used to prove that a process fulfills the specification.

We shall begin with an informal description of the process calculus with examples. These examples are also meant to give a flavor of the range of application of timed ccp.

5.1 Intuitive Description of Constraint Systems

In this section we introduce the basic ideas underlying the ntcc calculus in an informal way. We shall begin by introducing the notion of a constraint system, which is central to concurrent constraint programming. We then describe the basic process constructs by means of examples. Finally, we shall describe some convenient derived constructs.

The ntcc processes are parametric in a *constraint system*. A constraint system provides a *signature* from which syntactically denotable objects called *constraints* can be constructed and an *entailment relation* $\models$ specifying inter-dependencies between these constraints.

A constraint represents a piece of information (or *partial information*) upon which processes may act. For instance, processes modeling temperature controllers may have to deal with partial information such as $42 < \mathtt{tsensor} < 100$ expressing that the sensor registers an unknown (or not precisely determined) temperature value between 42 and 100. The inter-dependency $c \models d$ expresses that the information specified by d follows from that by c, e.g., $(42 < \mathtt{tsensor} < 100) \models (0 < \mathtt{tsensor} < 120)$.

We can set up the notion of constraint system by using first-order logic. Let us suppose that Σ is a signature (i.e., a set of constants, functions and predicate symbols) and that Δ is a consistent first-order theory over Σ (i.e., a set of sentences over Σ having at least one model). Constraints can be thought of as first-order formulae over Σ. We can then decree that $c \models d$ if the implication $c \Rightarrow d$ is valid in Δ. This gives us a simple and general formalization of the notion of constraint system as a pair (Σ, Δ).

In the examples below we shall assume that, in the underlying constraint system, Σ is the set $\{=, <, 0, 1 \dots\}$ and Δ is the set of sentences over Σ valid on the natural numbers.

Intuitive Description of Processes

We now proceed to describe with examples the basic ideas underlying the behavior of ntcc processes. For this purpose we shall model simple behavior of controllers such as Programmable Logic Controllers (PLC's) and RCX bricks.

PLC's are often used in timed systems of industrial applications [9], whilst RCX bricks are mainly used to construct autonomous robotic devices [20]. These controllers have external input and output ports. One can attach, for example, sensors of light, touch or temperature to the input ports, and motors, lights or alarms to the output ports. Typically PLC's and RCX bricks operate in a cyclic fashion. Each cycle consist of receiving an input from the environment, computing on this input, and returning the corresponding output to the environment.

Our processes will operate similarly. Time is conceptually divided into *discrete intervals (or time units)*. In a particular time interval, a process P_i receives a *stimulus* c_i from the environment (see Equation 1 below). The stimulus is some piece of information, i.e., a constraint. The process P_i executes with this stimulus as the initial store, and when it reaches its resting point (i.e., a point in which no further computation is possible), it *responds* to the environment with a resulting store d_i. Also the resting point determines a residual process P_{i+1}, which is then executed in the next time interval.

The following sequence illustrates the stimulus-response interactions between an environment that inputs $c_1, c_2, \ldots$ and a process that outputs $d_1, d_2, \ldots$ on such inputs as described above.

$$P_1 \xRightarrow{(c_1,d_1)} P_2 \xRightarrow{(c_2,d_2)} \ldots P_i \xRightarrow{(c_i,d_i)} P_{i+1} \xRightarrow{(c_{i+1},d_{i+1})} \ldots \qquad (1)$$

Communication: Telling and Asking Information. The ntcc processes communicate with each other by posting and reading partial information about the variables of system they model. The basic actions for communication provide the *telling* and *asking* of information. A tell action adds a piece of information to the common store. An ask action queries the store to decide whether a given piece of information is present in it. The store as a constraint itself. In this way addition of information corresponds to logic conjunction and determining presence of information corresponds to logic implication.

The tell and ask processes have respectively the form

$$\textbf{tell}(c) \text{ and } \textbf{when } c \textbf{ do } P. \qquad (2)$$

The only action of a tell process $\textbf{tell}(c)$ is to add, within a time unit, c to the current store d. The store then becomes $d \wedge c$. The addition of c is carried out even if the store becomes inconsistent, i.e., $(d \wedge c) = \texttt{false}$, in which case we can think of such an addition as generating a *failure*.

Example 2. Suppose that $d = (\texttt{motor}_1\_\texttt{speed} > \texttt{motor}_2\_\texttt{speed})$. Intuitively, d tells us that the speed of motor one is greater than that of motor two. It does not tell us what the specific speed values are. The execution in store d of process

$$\textbf{tell}(\texttt{motor}_2\_\texttt{speed} > 10)$$

causes the store to become $(\texttt{motor}_1\_\texttt{speed} > \texttt{motor}_2\_\texttt{speed} > 10)$ in the current time interval, thus increasing the information we know about the system – we now know that both speed values are greater than 10.

Notice that in the underlying constraint system $d \models \texttt{motor}_1\_\texttt{speed} > 0$, therefore the process

$$\textbf{tell}(\texttt{motor}_1\_\texttt{speed} = 0)$$

in store d causes a failure. $\square$

The process **when** c **do** P performs the action of asking c. If during the current time interval c can eventually be inferred from the store d (i.e., $d \models c$) then P is executed within the same time interval. Otherwise, **when** c **do** P is precluded from execution in any future time interval (i.e., it becomes constantly inactive).

Example 3. Suppose that $d = (\texttt{motor}_1\texttt{\_speed} > \texttt{motor}_2\texttt{\_speed})$ is the store. The process

$$P = \textbf{when } \texttt{motor}_1\texttt{\_speed} > 0 \textbf{ do } Q$$

will execute Q in the current time interval since $d \models \texttt{motor}_1\texttt{\_speed} > 0$, by contrast the process

$$P' = \textbf{when } \texttt{motor}_1\texttt{\_speed} > 10 \textbf{ do } Q$$

will not execute Q unless more information is added to the store, during the current time interval, to entail $\texttt{motor}_1\texttt{\_speed} > 10$.

The intuition is that any process in $d = (\texttt{motor}_1\texttt{\_speed} > \texttt{motor}_2\texttt{\_speed})$ can execute a given action if and only if it can do so whenever $\texttt{motor}_1\texttt{\_speed}$ and $\texttt{motor}_2\texttt{\_speed}$ are set to arbitrary values satisfying d. So, P above executes Q if $\texttt{motor}_1\texttt{\_speed}$ and $\texttt{motor}_2\texttt{\_speed}$ take on any value satisfying d. □

The above example illustrates the partial information allows us to model the actions that a system can perform, regardless of the alternative values a variable may assume, as long they comply with the constraint representing the store.

Nondeterminism. As argued above, partial information allows us to model behavior for alternative values that variables may take on. In concurrent systems it is often convenient to model behavior for *alternative courses* of action, i.e., nondeterministic behavior.

We generalize the processes of the form **when** c **do** P described above to guarded-choice summation processes of the form

$$\sum_{i \in I} \textbf{when } c_i \textbf{ do } P_i \tag{3}$$

where I is a finite set of indices. The expression $\sum_{i \in I} \textbf{when } c_i \textbf{ do } P_i$ represents a process that, in the current time interval, *must nondeterministically* choose a process P_j ($j \in I$) whose corresponding constraint c_j is entailed by the store. The chosen alternative, if any, precludes the others. If no choice is possible during the current time unit, all the alternatives are precluded from execution.

In the following example we shall use "+" for binary summations.

Example 4. Often RCX programs operate in a set of simple stimulus-response rules of the form **IF** E **THEN** C. The expression E is a condition typically depending on the sensor variables, and C is a command, typically an assignment. In [11] these programs respond to the environment by choosing a rule whose condition is met and executing its command.

If we wish to abstract from the particular implementation of the mechanism that chooses the rule, we can model the execution of these programs by using the summation process. For example, the program operating in the set

$$\left\{ \begin{array}{l} (\textbf{IF } \text{sensor}_1 > 0 \ \ \textbf{THEN } \text{motor}_1\_\text{speed} := 2), \\ (\textbf{IF } \text{sensor}_2 > 99 \ \textbf{THEN } \text{motor}_1\_\text{speed} := 0) \end{array} \right\}$$

corresponds to the summation process

$$P = \begin{array}{l} \textbf{when } \text{sensor}_1 > 0 \ \ \textbf{do tell}(\text{motor}_1\_\text{speed} = 2) \\ + \\ \textbf{when } \text{sensor}_2 > 99 \ \textbf{do tell}(\text{motor}_1\_\text{speed} = 0). \end{array}$$

In the store $d = (\text{sensor}_1 > 10)$, the process P causes the store to become $d \wedge (\text{motor}_1\_\text{speed} = 2)$ since $\textbf{tell}(\text{motor}_1\_\text{speed} = 2)$ is chosen for execution and the other alternative is precluded. In the store $\textbf{true}$, P cannot add any information. In the store $e = (\text{sensor}_1 = 10 \wedge \text{sensor}_2 = 100)$, P causes the store to become either $e \wedge (\text{motor}_1\_\text{speed} = 2)$ or $e \wedge (\text{motor}_1\_\text{speed} = 0)$. □

Parallel Composition. We need a construct to represent processes acting *concurrently*. Given P and Q we denote their parallel composition by the process

$$P \parallel Q \tag{4}$$

In one time unit (or interval) processes P and Q operate concurrently, "communicating" via the common store by telling and asking information.

Example 5. Let P be defined as in Example 4 and

$$Q = \begin{array}{l} \textbf{when } \text{motor}_1\_\text{speed} = 0 \ \textbf{do tell}(\text{motor}_2\_\text{speed} = 0) \\ + \\ \textbf{when } \text{motor}_2\_\text{speed} = 0 \ \textbf{do tell}(\text{motor}_1\_\text{speed} = 0). \end{array}$$

Intuitively Q turns off one motor if the other is detected to be off. The parallel composition $P \parallel Q$ in the store $d = (\text{sensor}_2 > 100)$ will, in one time unit, cause the store to become $d \wedge (\text{motor}_1\_\text{speed} = \text{motor}_2\_\text{speed} = 0)$. □

Local Behavior. Most process calculi have a construct to restrict the interface through which processes can interact with each other, thus providing for the modeling of *local (or hidden)* behavior. We introduce processes of the form

$$(\textbf{local } x)\, P \tag{5}$$

The process $(\textbf{local } x)\, P$ declares a variable x, private to P. This process behaves like P, except that all the information about x produced by P is hidden from external processes and the information about x produced by other external processes is hidden from P.

Example 6. In modeling RCX or PLC's one uses "global" variables to represent ports (e.g., sensor and motors). One often, however, uses variables which do not represent ports, and thus we may find it convenient to declare such variables as local (or private).

Suppose that R is a given process modeling some controller task. Furthermore, suppose that R uses a variable z, which is set at random, with some unknown distribution, to a value $v \in \{0, 1\}$. Let us define the process

$$P = (\sum_{v \in \{0,1\}} \textbf{when true do tell}(z = v)) \parallel R$$

to represent the behavior of R under z's random assignment.

We may want to declare z in P to be local since it does not represent an input or output port. Moreover, notice that if we need to run two copies of P, i.e., process $P \parallel P$, a failure may arise as each copy can assign a different value to z. Therefore, the behavior of R under the random assignment to z can be best represented as $P' = (\textbf{local } z) P$. In fact, if we run two copies of P', no failure can arise from the random assignment to the z's as they are private to each P'.   □

The processes hitherto described generate activity within the current time interval only. We now turn to constructs that can generate activity in future time intervals.

Unit Delays and Time-Outs. As in the Synchronous Languages [3] we have constructs whose actions can delay the execution of processes. These constructs are needed to model time dependency between actions, e.g., actions depending on the absence or presence of preceding actions. Time dependency is an important aspect in the modeling of timed systems.

The unit-delay operators have the form

$$\textbf{next } P \quad \text{and} \quad \textbf{unless } c \textbf{ next } P \tag{6}$$

The process **next** P represents the activation of P in the next time interval. The process **unless** c **next** P is similar, but P will be activated only if c cannot be inferred from the resulting (or final) store d in the current time interval, i.e., $d \not\models c$. The "unless" processes add time-outs to the calculus, i.e., they wait during the current time interval for a piece of information c to be present and if it is not, they trigger activity in the next time interval.

Notice that **unless** c **next** P is not equivalent to **when** $\neg c$ **do next** P since $d \not\models c$ does not necessarily imply $d \models \neg c$. Notice that $Q = \textbf{unless false next } P$ is not the same as $R = \textbf{next } P$ since unlike Q, even if the store contains false, R will still activate P in the next time interval (and the store in the next time interval may not contain false).

Example 7. Let us consider the following process:

$$P = \textbf{when false do next tell}(\text{motor}_1\_\text{speed} = \text{motor}_2\_\text{speed} = 0).$$

P turns the motors off by decreeing that $\text{motor}_1\_\text{speed} = \text{motor}_2\_\text{speed} = 0$ in the next time interval if a failure takes place in the current time interval. Similarly, the process

$$\textbf{unless false next } (\textbf{tell}(\text{motor}_1\_\text{speed} > 0) \parallel \textbf{tell}(\text{motor}_2\_\text{speed} > 0))$$

makes the motors move at some speed in the next time unit, unless a failure takes place in the current time interval.   □

Asynchrony. We now introduce a construct that, unlike the previous ones, can describe arbitrary (finite) delays. The importance of this construct is that it allows us to model asynchronous behavior across the time intervals.

We use the operator "$\star$" which corresponds to the unbounded but finite delay operator for synchronous CCS [24]. The process

$$\star P \tag{7}$$

represents an arbitrary long but finite delay for the activation of P. Thus, $\star$ **tell**(c) can be viewed as a message c that is eventually delivered but there is no upper bound on the delivery time.

Example 8. Let $S = \star$ **tell**(malfunction($motor_1\_status$)). The process S can be used to specify that $motor_1$, at some unpredictable point in time, is doomed to malfunction   □

Infinite Behavior. Finally, we need a construct to define infinite behavior. We shall use the operator "!" as a delayed version of the replication operator for the π−calculus [25]. Given a process P, the process

$$! P \tag{8}$$

represents $P \parallel (\textbf{next } P) \parallel (\textbf{next next } P) \parallel \cdots \parallel ! P$, i.e., unboundedly many copies of P, but one at a time. The process $! P$ executes P in one time unit and persists in the next time unit.

Example 9. The process R below repeatedly checks the state of $motor_1$. If a malfunction is reported, R tells that $motor_1$ must be turned off.

$$R = ! \textbf{ when } \text{malfunction}(motor_1\_status) \textbf{ do tell}(motor_1\_speed = 0)$$

Thus, $R \parallel S$ with $S = \star$ **tell**(malfunction($motor_1\_status$)) (Example 8) eventually tells that $motor_1$ is turned off.   □

Some Derived Forms

We have informally introduced the basic process constructs of ntcc and illustrated how they can be used to model or specify system behavior. In this section we shall illustrate how they can be used to obtain some convenient derived constructs.

In the following we shall omit "**when true do**" if no confusion arises. The "blind-choice" process $\sum_{i \in I} \textbf{when true do } P_i$, for example, can be written as $\sum_{i \in I} P_i$. We shall use $\prod_{i \in I} P_i$, where I is finite, to denote the parallel composition of all the P_i's. We use $\textbf{next}^n(P)$ as an abbreviation for $\textbf{next}(\textbf{next}(\ldots(\textbf{next } P)\ldots))$, where **next** is repeated n times.

Inactivity. The process doing nothing whatsoever, **skip** can be defined as an abbreviation of the empty summation $\sum_{i \in \emptyset} P_i$. This process corresponds to the inactive processes **0** of CCS and $STOP$ of CSP. We should expect the behavior of $P \parallel$ **skip** to be the same as that of P under any reasonable notion of behavioral equivalence.

Abortion. Another useful construct is the process **abort** which is somehow to the opposite extreme of **skip**. Whilst having **skip** in a system causes no change whatsoever, having **abort** can make the whole system fail. Hence **abort** corresponds to the $CHAOS$ operator in CSP. In Section 5.1 we mentioned that a tell process causes a failure, at the current time interval, if it leaves the store inconsistent. Therefore, we can define **abort** as ! **tell**(**false**), i.e., the process that once activated causes a constant failure. Therefore, any reasonable notion of behavioral equivalence should not distinguish between $P \parallel$ **abort** and **abort**.

Asynchronous Parallel Composition. Notice that in $P \parallel Q$ both P and Q are forced to move in the current time unit, thus our parallel composition can be regarded as being a synchronous operator. There are situations where an asynchronous version of "$\parallel$" is desirable. For example, modeling the interaction of several controllers operating concurrently where some of them could be faster or slower than the others at responding to their environment.

By using the star operator we can define a *(fair) asynchronous* parallel composition $P \mid Q$ as

$$(P \parallel \star Q) + (\star P \parallel Q)$$

A move of $P \mid Q$ is either one of P or one of Q (or both). Moreover, both P and Q are eventually executed (i.e. a fair execution of $P \mid Q$). This process corresponds to the asynchronous parallel operator described in [24].

We should expect operator "$\mid$" to enjoy properties of parallel composition. Namely, we should expect $P \mid Q$ to be the same as $Q \mid P$ and $P \mid (Q \mid R)$ to be the same as $(P \mid Q) \mid R$. Unlike in $P \parallel$ **skip**, however, in $P \mid$ **skip** the execution of P may be arbitrary postponed, therefore we may want to distinguish between $P \mid$ **skip** and P. Similarly, unlike in $P \parallel$ **abort**, in $P \mid$ **abort** the execution of **abort** may be arbitrarily postponed. In a timed setting we may want to distinguish between a process that aborts right now and one that may do so sometime later after having done some work.

Bounded Eventuality and Invariance. We may want to specify that a certain behavior is exhibited within a certain number of time units, i.e., *bounded eventuality*, or during a certain number of time units, i.e., *bounded invariance*. An example of bounded eventuality is "the light must be switched off within the next ten time units" and an example of bounded invariance is "the motor should not be turned on during the next sixty time units".

The kind of behavior described above can be specified by using the bounded versions of ! P and $\star P$, which can be derived using summation and parallel composition in the obvious way. We define !$_I P$ and $\star_I P$, where I is a closed interval of the natural numbers, as an abbreviation for

$$\prod_{i \in I} \textbf{next}^i P \quad \text{and} \quad \sum_{i \in I} \textbf{next}^i P$$

respectively. Intuitively, $\star_{[m,n]} P$ means that P is eventually active between the next m and $m + n$ time units, while $!_{[m,n]} P$ means that P is always active between the next m and $m + n$ time units.

Nondeterministic Time-Outs. The ntcc calculus generalizes processes of the form **when** c **do** P by allowing nondeterministic choice over them. It would therefore be natural to do the same with processes of the form **unless** c **next** P. In other words, one may want to have a *nondeterministic time-out operator*

$$\sum_{i \in I} \textbf{unless } c_i \textbf{ next } P_i$$

which chooses one P_i such that c_i cannot be eventually inferred from the store within the current time unit (if no choice is possible then the summation is precluded from future execution). Notice that this is not the same as having a blind-choice summation of the **unless** c_i **next** P_i operators. It is not difficult to see, however, that the behavior of such a nondeterministic time-out operator can be described by the ntcc process:.

$$(\textbf{local } I') \, (\prod_{i \in I} (\textbf{unless } c_i \textbf{ next tell}(i \in I')) \parallel \textbf{next} \sum_{i \in I} \textbf{when } i \in I' \textbf{ do } P_i)$$

where $i \in I'$ holds iff i is in the set I'.

5.2   The Operational Semantics of ntcc

In the previous section we gave an intuitive description of ntcc . In this section we shall make precise such a description. We shall begin by defining the notion of constraint system and the formal syntax of ntcc . We shall then give meaning to the ntcc processes by means of an operational semantics. The semantics, which resembles the reduction semantics of the π-calculus [25], provides *internal* and *external* transitions describing process evolutions. The internal transitions describe evolutions within a time unit and thus they are regarded as being unobservable. In contrast, the external transitions are regarded as being observable as they describe evolution across the time units.

Constraint Systems. For our purposes it will suffice to consider the notion of constraint system based on first-order logic, as was done in [46].

Definition 1 (Constraint System). *A constraint system (cs) is a pair* (Σ, Δ) *where* Σ *is a signature of function and predicate symbols, and* Δ *is a decidable theory over* Σ *(i.e., a decidable set of sentences over* Σ *with a least one model).*

Given a constraint system (Σ, Δ), let $(\Sigma, \mathcal{V}, \mathcal{S})$ be its underlying first-order language, where $\mathcal{V}$ is a countable set of variables $x, y, \ldots$, and $\mathcal{S}$ is the set of logic symbols $\neg, \wedge, \vee, \Rightarrow, \exists, \forall, \texttt{true}$ and $\texttt{false}$. *Constraints* $c, d, \ldots$ are formulae over this first-order language. We say that c *entails* d in Δ, written $c \models d$, iff $c \Rightarrow d$ is true in all models of Δ. The relation $\models$, which is decidable by the definition of Δ, induces an equivalence $\approx$ given by $c \approx d$ iff $c \models d$ and $d \models c$. Henceforth, $\mathcal{C}$ denotes *the set of constraints under consideration* modulo $\approx$ in the underlying cs. Thus, we simply write $c = d$ iff $c \approx d$.

Definition (Processes, *Proc*). *Processes P, Q, ... ∈ Proc are built from constraints c ∈ C and variables x ∈ V in the underlying constraint system by:*

$$P, Q, \ldots ::= \textbf{tell}(c) \mid \sum_{i \in I} \textbf{when } c_i \textbf{ do } P_i \mid P \parallel Q \mid (\textbf{local } x)\, P$$
$$\mid \quad \textbf{next } P \mid \textbf{unless } c \textbf{ next } P \quad \mid \star P \quad \mid \, !\, P$$

Intuitively, $\textbf{tell}(c)$ adds an item of information c to the store in the current time interval. The *guarded-choice summation* $\sum_{i \in I} \textbf{when } c_i \textbf{ do } P_i$, where I is a finite set of indexes, chooses in the current time interval one of the P_i's whose c_i is entailed by the store. If no choice is possible, the summation is precluded from execution. We write $\textbf{when } c_{i_1} \textbf{ do } P_{i_1} + \ldots + \textbf{when } c_{i_n} \textbf{ do } P_{i_n}$ if $I = \{i_1, \ldots, i_n\}$. We omit the "$\sum_{i \in I}$" if $|I| = 1$ and use $\textbf{skip}$ for $\sum_{i \in \emptyset} P_i$.

The process $P \parallel Q$ represents the *parallel execution* of P and Q. In one time unit P and Q operate concurrently, communicating through the store.

The process $(\textbf{local } x)\, P$ behaves like P, except that all the information about x produced by P can only be seen by P and the information about x produced by other processes cannot be seen by P. In other words $(\textbf{local } x)\, P$ declares an x *local* to P, and thus we say that it *binds* x in P. The *bound variables* $bv(Q)$ (*free variables* $fv(Q)$) are those with a bound (a not bound) occurrence in Q.

The *unit-delay* process $\textbf{next } P$ executes P in the next time interval. The *time-out* $\textbf{unless } c \textbf{ next } P$ is also a unit-delay, but P will be executed only if c cannot eventually be entailed by the store during the current time interval. Note that $\textbf{next } P$ is not the same as $\textbf{unless false next } P$ since an inconsistent store entails $\textbf{false}$. We use $\textbf{next}^n P$ for $\textbf{next}(\textbf{next}(\ldots(\textbf{next } P)\ldots))$, where $\textbf{next}$ is repeated n times.

The operator "$\star$" represents an *arbitrary (or unknown) but finite delay* (as "ϵ" in SCCS [24]) and allows asynchronous behavior across the time intervals. Intuitively, $\star P$ means $P + \textbf{next } P + \textbf{next}^2 P + \ldots$, i.e., an unbounded finite delay of P.

The *replication* operator "!" is a delayed version of that of the π-calculus [25]: $!\, P$ means $P \parallel \textbf{next } P \parallel \textbf{next}^2 P \parallel \ldots \parallel !\, P$, i.e., unboundedly many copies of P but one at a time.

A Transition Semantics

The structural operational semantics (SOS) of ntcc considers *transitions* between process-store *configurations* of the form $\langle P, c \rangle$ with stores represented as constraints and processes quotiented by $\equiv$ below. Intuitively $\equiv$ describes irrelevant syntactic aspects of processes.

Definition 2 (Structural Congruence). *Let $\equiv$ be the smallest congruence satisfying: (1) $P \parallel \textbf{skip} \equiv P$, (2) $P \parallel Q \equiv Q \parallel P$, and (3) $P \parallel (Q \parallel R) \equiv (P \parallel Q) \parallel R$. Extend $\equiv$ to configurations by decreeing that $\langle P, c \rangle \equiv \langle Q, c \rangle$ iff $P \equiv Q$.*

Following standard lines, we extend the syntax with a construct $\textbf{local } (x, d) \textbf{ in } P$, to represent the evolution of a process of the form $\textbf{local } x \textbf{ in } Q$, where d is the local information (or store) produced during this evolution. Initially d is "empty", so we regard $\textbf{local } x \textbf{ in } P$ as $\textbf{local } (x, \textbf{true}) \textbf{ in } P$.

The transitions of the SOS are given by the relations $\longrightarrow$ and $\Longrightarrow$ defined in Table 1. The *internal* transition $\langle P, d \rangle \longrightarrow \langle P', d' \rangle$ should be read as "P with store d reduces, in one internal step, to P' with store d' ". The *observable transition* $P \xrightarrow{(c,d)} R$ should be read as "P on input c, reduces in one *time unit* to R and outputs d". The observable transitions are obtained from terminating sequences of internal transitions.

Table 1. Rules for internal reduction $\longrightarrow$ (upper part) and observable reduction $\Longrightarrow$ (lower part). $\gamma \nrightarrow$ in OBS holds iff for no γ', $\gamma \longrightarrow \gamma'$. $\equiv$ and F are given in Definitions 2 and 3.

$$\text{TELL} \ \frac{}{\langle \mathbf{tell}(c), d \rangle \ \longrightarrow \ \langle \mathbf{skip}, d \wedge c \rangle} \qquad \text{SUM} \ \frac{d \models c_j \ j \in I}{\langle \sum_{i \in I} \mathbf{when} \ c_i \ \mathbf{do} \ P_i, d \rangle \ \longrightarrow \ \langle P_j, d \rangle}$$

$$\text{PAR} \ \frac{\langle P, c \rangle \longrightarrow \langle P', d \rangle}{\langle P \parallel Q, c \rangle \ \longrightarrow \ \langle P' \parallel Q, d \rangle} \qquad \text{LOC} \ \frac{\langle P, c \wedge \exists_x d \rangle \ \longrightarrow \ \langle P', c' \rangle}{\langle (\mathbf{local} \ x, c) \ P, d \rangle \ \longrightarrow \ \langle (\mathbf{local} \ x, c') \ P', d \wedge \exists_x c' \rangle}$$

$$\text{UNL} \ \frac{}{\langle \mathbf{unless} \ c \ \mathbf{next} \ P, d \rangle \ \longrightarrow \ \langle \mathbf{skip}, d \rangle} \ \text{if} \ d \models c$$

$$\text{REP} \ \frac{}{\langle \, ! \, P, d \rangle \ \longrightarrow \ \langle P \parallel \mathbf{next} \, ! \, P, d \rangle} \qquad \text{STAR} \ \frac{}{\langle \star \, P, d \rangle \ \longrightarrow \ \langle \mathbf{next}^n P, d \rangle} \ \text{if} \ n \geq 0$$

$$\text{STR} \ \frac{\gamma_1 \longrightarrow \gamma_2}{\gamma_1' \longrightarrow \gamma_2'} \ \text{if} \ \gamma_1 \equiv \gamma_1' \ \text{and} \ \gamma_2 \equiv \gamma_2'$$

$$\text{OBS} \ \frac{\langle P, c \rangle \longrightarrow^* \langle Q, d \rangle \nrightarrow}{P \xrightarrow{(c,d)} R} \ \text{if} \ R \equiv F(Q)$$

We shall only describe some of the rules of in Table 1 due to space restrictions (see [28] for further details). As clarified below, the seemingly missing cases for "next" and "unless" processes are given by OBS. The rule STAR specifies an arbitrary delay of P. REP says that $!P$ creates a copy of P and then persists in the next time unit. We shall dwell a little upon the description of Rule LOC as it may seem somewhat complex. Let us consider the process

$$Q = (\mathbf{local} \, x, c) \, P$$

in Rule LOC. The global store is d and the local store is c. We distinguish between the *external* (corresponding to Q) and the *internal* point of view (corresponding to P). From the internal point of view, the information about x, possibly appearing in the "global" store d, cannot be observed. Thus, before reducing P we should first hide the information about x that Q may have in d. We can do this by existentially quantifying x in d. Similarly, from the external point of view, the observable information about x that the reduction of internal agent P may produce (i.e., c') cannot be observed. Thus we hide it by existentially quantifying x in c' before adding it to the global store corresponding to the evolution of Q. Additionally, we should make c' the new private store of the evolution of the internal process for its future reductions.

Rule OBS says that an observable transition from P labeled with (c, d) is obtained from a terminating sequence of internal transitions from $\langle P, c \rangle$ to a $\langle Q, d \rangle$. The process R to be executed in the next time interval is equivalent to $F(Q)$ (the "future" of Q). $F(Q)$ is obtained by removing from Q summations that did not trigger activity and any local information which has been stored in Q, and by "unfolding" the sub-terms within "next" and "unless" expressions.

Definition 3 (Future Function). *Let* $F : Proc \rightharpoonup Proc$ *be defined by*

$$F(Q) = \begin{cases} \textbf{skip} & \text{if } Q = \sum_{i \in I} \textbf{when } c_i \textbf{ do } Q_i \\ F(Q_1) \parallel F(Q_2) & \text{if } Q = Q_1 \parallel Q_2 \\ (\textbf{local } x)\, F(R) & \text{if } Q = (\textbf{local } x, c)\, R \\ R & \text{if } Q = \textbf{next } R \text{ or } Q = \textbf{unless } c \textbf{ next } R \end{cases}$$

Remark 1. F need no to be total since whenever we need to apply F to a Q (OBS in Table 1), every tell(c), **abort**, $\star\, R$ *and* ! R *in Q will occur within a "next" or "unless" expression.*

5.3 Observable Behavior

In this section we recall some notions introduced in [29] of what an observer can see from a process behavior . We shall refer to such notions as *process observations*. We assume that what happens within a time unit cannot be directly observed, and thus we abstract from internal transitions. The ntcc calculus makes it easy to focus on the observation of input-output events in which a given process engages and the order in which they occur.

Notation 1 *Throughout this paper C^ω denotes the set of infinite (or ω) sequences of constraints in the underlying set of constraints C. We use $\alpha, \alpha', \ldots$ to range over C^ω.*

Let $\alpha = c_1.c_2.\ldots$ and $\alpha' = c_1'.c_2'.\ldots$. Suppose that P exhibits the following infinite sequence of observable transitions (or *run*): $P = P_1 \xrightarrow{(c_1, c_1')} P_2 \xrightarrow{(c_2, c_2')} \ldots$. Given this run of P, we shall use the notation $P \xrightarrow{(\alpha, \alpha')}{}_\omega$.

IO and Output Behavior. Observe the above run of P. At the time unit i, the environment *inputs* c_i to P_i which then responds with an output c_i'. As observers, we can see that on α, P responds with α'. We refer to the set of all (α, α') such that $P \xrightarrow{(\alpha, \alpha')}{}_\omega$ as the *input-output (io) behavior* of P. Alternatively, if $\alpha = \mathtt{true}^\omega$, we interpret the run as an interaction among the parallel components in P *without the influence of any (external) environment*; as observers what we see is that P produces α on its own. We refer to the set of all α' such that $P \xrightarrow{(\mathtt{true}^\omega, \alpha')}{}_\omega$ as the *output* behavior of P.

Quiescent Sequences and SP. Another observation we can make of a process is its quiescent input sequences. These are sequences on input of which P can run without adding any information; we observe whether $\alpha = \alpha'$ whenever $P \xrightarrow{(\alpha, \alpha')}{}_\omega$.

In [28] it is shown that the set of quiescent sequences of a given P can be alternatively characterized as *the set of infinite sequences that P can possibly output under arbitrary environments*; the strongest postcondition (sp) of P.

The following definition states the various notions of observable behavior mentioned above.

Definition 4 (Observable Behavior). *The behavioral observations that can be made of a process are:*

1. *The* input-output (or stimulus-response) behavior *of P, written, $io(P)$, defined as*

$$io(P) = \{(\alpha, \alpha') \mid P \xrightarrow{(\alpha,\alpha')} {}^{\omega}\}.$$

2. *The* (default) output behavior *of P, written $o(P)$, defined as*

$$o(P) = \{\alpha' \mid P \xrightarrow{(\text{true}^{\omega}, \alpha')} {}^{\omega}\}.$$

3. *The* strongest postcondition *behavior of P, written $sp(P)$, defined as*

$$sp(P) = \{\alpha \mid P \xrightarrow{(\alpha',\alpha)} {}^{\omega} \text{ for some } \alpha'\}.$$

The following are the obvious equivalences and congruences induced by our behavioral observations. (Recall the notion of congruence given in Section 2.)

Definition 5 (Behavioral Equivalences). *Let $l \in \{io, o, sp\}$. Define $P \sim_l Q$ iff $l(P) = l(Q)$. Furthermore, let $\approx_l$ the congruence induced by $\sim_l$, i.e., $P \approx_l Q$ iff $C[P] \sim_l C[Q]$ for every process context C.*

We shall refer to equivalences defined above as observational equivalences as they identify processes whose internal behavior may differ widely (e.g. in the number of internal actions). Such an abstraction from internal behavior is essential in the theory of several process calculi; most notably in weak bisimilarity for CCS [23].

Example 10. Let a, b, c, d and e be mutually exclusive constraints. Consider the processes P and Q below:

$$\underbrace{\textbf{when } a \textbf{ do next } \begin{array}{l} \textbf{when } b \textbf{ do next tell}(d) \\ + \\ \textbf{when } c \textbf{ do next tell}(e) \end{array}}_{P}, \quad \underbrace{\begin{array}{l} \textbf{when } a \textbf{ do next when } b \textbf{ do next tell}(d) \\ + \\ \textbf{when } a \textbf{ do next when } c \textbf{ do next tell}(e) \end{array}}_{Q}$$

The reader may care to verify that $P \sim_o Q$ since $o(P) = o(Q) = \{\text{true}^{\omega}\}$. However, $P \not\sim_{io} Q$ nor $P \not\sim_{sp} Q$ since if $\alpha = a.c.\,\text{true}^{\omega}$ then $(\alpha, \alpha) \in io(Q)$ and $\alpha \in sp(Q)$ but $(\alpha, \alpha) \notin io(P)$ and $\alpha \notin sp(P)$. □

Congruence and Decidability Issues. Several typical questions about these equivalence may then arise. For example, one may wonder which of them coincides with their corresponding induced congruences and whether there are interesting relationships between them.

In [28] it is proven that none of the equivalences is a congruence. However, $\sim_{sp}$ is a congruence in a restricted sense; Namely, if we confine our attention to the so-called *locally-independent* fragment of the calculus. This fragment only forbids non-unary summations (and "unless" processes) whose guards depend on local variables.

Definition 6 (Locally-Independent Processes). P *is* locally-independent *iff for every* **unless** c **next** Q *and* $\sum_{i \in I}$ **when** c_i **do** Q_i *($|I| \geq 2$) in P, neither c nor the c_i's contain variables in* $bv(P)$ *(i.e., the bound variables of P).*

The locally-independent fragment is indeed very expressive. Every summation process whose guards are either all equivalent or mutually exclusive can be encoded in this fragment [50]. Moreover, the applicability of this fragment is witnessed by the fact all the ntcc application the author is aware of [28,29,50] can be model as locally-independent processes. Also, the (parameterless-recursion) tcc model can be expressed in this fragment as, from the expressiveness point of view, the local operator is redundant in tcc with parameterless-recursion [27]. Furthermore, the fragment allows us to express infinite-state processes [51](i.e., processes that can evolve into infinitely many other processes). Hence, it is rather surprising that $\sim_{sp}$ is decidable for the local-independent fragment as recently proved in [51].

As for the input-output and output equivalences, in [50] it is shown how to characterize their induced congruence in a satisfactory way. Namely, $P \approx_o Q$ iff $U(P,Q)[P] \sim_o U(P,Q)[Q]$ where $U(P,Q)$ is a context which, given P and Q, can be effectively constructed. Also [50] shows that although $\sim_{io}$ is stronger than $\sim_o$, their induced congruences match. Perhaps the most significant theoretical value of these two results is its computational consequence:Both input-output and output congruence are decidable if output equivalence is decidable.

In fact, output equivalence is decidable for processes with a restricted form of nondeterminism [29]. Namely, $\star$-free processes in which local operators do not exhibit nondeterminism. This also represent a significant fragment of the calculus including all the application examples in [28,29,50] and the parameterless-recursion fragment of the tcc model. It then follows, from the previously mentioned results, that $\approx_{io}$ and $\approx_o$ are also decidable if we restrict our attention to these restricted nondeterministic processes.

5.4 Denotational Semantics

In the previous section we introduced the notion of strongest-postcondition of ntcc processes in operational terms. Let us now show the abstract denotational model of this notion first presented in [30]. Such a model is of great help when arguing about the strongest-postcondition of ntcc processes.

The denotational semantics is defined as a function $[\![\cdot]\!]$ which associates to each process a set of infinite constraint sequences, namely $[\![\cdot]\!] : Proc \to \mathcal{P}(\mathcal{C}^\omega)$. The definition of this function is given in Table 2. Intuitively, $[\![P]\!]$ is meant to capture the set of all sequences P can possibly output. For instance, the sequences that $\mathbf{tell}(c)$ can output are those whose first element is stronger than c (see DTELL, Table 2). Process **next** P has not influence in the first element of a sequence, thus $d.\alpha$ can be output by it iff α is can be output by P (see DNEXT, Table 2). A sequence can be output by $!\,P$ iff every suffix of it can be output by P (see DREP, Table 2). The other cases can be explained analogously.

From [7], however, we know that there cannot be a $f : Proc \to \mathcal{P}(\mathcal{C}^\omega)$, compositionally defined, such that $f(P) = sp(P)$ for all P. Nevertheless, as stated in the theorem below, Palamidessi et al [30] showed that that sp denotational semantics matches its

Table 2. Denotational semantics of ntcc. Symbols α and α' range over the set of infinite sequences of constraints $\mathcal{C}^\omega$; β ranges over the set of finite sequences of constraints $\mathcal{C}^*$. Notation $\exists_x \alpha$ denotes the sequence resulting by applying $\exists_x$ to each constraint in α.

DTELL:	$[\![\mathbf{tell}(c)]\!] = \{d.\alpha \mid d \models c\}$
DSUM:	$[\![\sum_{i \in I} \mathbf{when}\ c_i\ \mathbf{do}\ P_i]\!] = \bigcup_{i \in I} \{d.\alpha \mid d \models c_i \text{ and } d.\alpha \in [\![P_i]\!]\} \cup \bigcap_{i \in I} \{d.\alpha \mid d \not\models c_i\}$
DPAR:	$[\![P \parallel Q]\!] = [\![P]\!] \cap [\![Q]\!]$
DLOC:	$[\![(\mathbf{local}\ x)\ P]\!] = \{\alpha \mid \text{there exists } \alpha' \in [\![P]\!] \text{ s.t. } \exists_x \alpha' = \exists_x \alpha\}$
DNEXT:	$[\![\mathbf{next}\ P]\!] = \{d.\alpha \mid \alpha \in [\![P]\!]\}$
DUNL:	$[\![\mathbf{unless}\ c\ \mathbf{next}\ P]\!] = \{d.\alpha \mid d \models c\} \cup \{d.\alpha \mid d \not\models c \text{ and } \alpha \in [\![P]\!]\}$
DREP:	$[\![!\ P]\!] = \{\alpha \mid \text{for all } \beta, \alpha' \text{ s.t. } \alpha = \beta.\alpha', \text{ we have } \alpha' \in [\![P]\!]\}$
DSTAR:	$[\![\star\ P]\!] = \{\beta.\alpha \mid \alpha \in [\![P]\!]\}$

operational counter-part for the local independent-fragment, which as argued before is very expressive.

Theorem 1 (Full Abstraction). *For every* ntcc *process P, $sp(P) \subseteq [\![P]\!]$ and if P is locally-independent then $[\![P]\!] \subseteq sp(P)$.*

The full-abstraction result has an important theoretical value; i.e., for a significant fragment of the calculus we can abstract away from operational details by working with $[\![P]\!]$ rather than $sp(P)$. In fact, the congruence result for $\sim_{sp}$ mentioned in the previous section is a corollary of the above theorem.

5.5   LTL Specification and Verification

Processes in ntcc can be used to specify properties of timed systems, e.g., that an action must happen within some finite but not fixed amount of time. It is often convenient, however, to express specifications in another formalism, in particular a logical one. In this section we present the ntcc logic first introduced in [30]. We start by defining a linear-time temporal logic (LTL) to expresses temporal properties over infinite sequences of constraints. We then define what it means for a process to satisfy a specification given as a formula in this logic. We shall then say that P satisfies a specification F iff every infinite sequence P can possibly output (on inputs from arbitrary environments) satisfies F, i.e., iff the strongest-postcondition of P implies F. Finally, we present an inference system aimed at proving whether a process fulfills a given specification.

A Temporal Logic. The ntcc LTL expresses properties over sequences of constraints and we shall refer to it as **CLTL**. We begin by giving the syntax of LTL formulae and then interpret them with the **CLTL** semantics.

Definition 7 (LTL Syntax). *The formulae* $F, G, \ldots \in \mathcal{F}$ *are built from constraints* $c \in \mathcal{C}$ *and variables* $x \in \mathcal{V}$ *in the underlying constraint system by:*

$$F, G, \ldots := c \mid \texttt{true} \mid \texttt{false} \mid F \overset{.}{\wedge} G \mid F \overset{.}{\vee} G \mid \overset{.}{\neg} F \mid \overset{.}{\exists}_x F \mid \bigcirc F \mid \Box F \mid \Diamond F$$

The constraint c (i.e., a first-order formula in the cs) represents a *state formula*. The dotted symbols represent the usual (temporal) boolean and existential operators. As clarified later, the dotted notation is needed as in **CLTL** these operators do not always coincide with those in the cs. The symbols $\bigcirc$, $\Box$, and $\Diamond$ denote the LTL modalities *next*, *always* and *eventually*. We use $F \Rightarrow G$ for $\overset{.}{\neg} F \overset{.}{\vee} G$. Below we give the formulae a **CLTL** semantics. First, we need some notation and the notion of x-*variant*. Intuitively, d is an x-variant of c iff they are the same except for the information about x.

Notation 2 *Given a sequence* $\alpha = c_1.c_2.\ldots$, *we use* $\exists_x \alpha$ *to denote the sequence* $\exists_x c_1 \exists_x c_2 \ldots$. *We shall use* $\alpha(i)$ *to denote the i-th element of* α.

Definition 8 (x-variant). *A constraint d is an x-variant of c iff* $\exists_x c = \exists_x d$. *Similarly* α' *is an x-variant of α iff* $\exists_x \alpha = \exists_x \alpha'$.

Definition 9 (CLTL Semantics). *We say that the infinite sequence α satisfies (or that it is a model of) F in* **CLTL**, *written* $\alpha \models_{\mathrm{CLTL}} F$, *iff* $\langle \alpha, 1 \rangle \models_{\mathrm{CLTL}} F$, *where:*

$\langle \alpha, i \rangle \models_{\mathrm{CLTL}} \texttt{true}$		$\langle \alpha, i \rangle \not\models_{\mathrm{CLTL}} \texttt{false}$
$\langle \alpha, i \rangle \models_{\mathrm{CLTL}} c$	*iff*	$\alpha(i) \models c$
$\langle \alpha, i \rangle \models_{\mathrm{CLTL}} \overset{.}{\neg} F$	*iff*	$\langle \alpha, i \rangle \not\models_{\mathrm{CLTL}} F$
$\langle \alpha, i \rangle \models_{\mathrm{CLTL}} F \overset{.}{\wedge} G$	*iff*	$\langle \alpha, i \rangle \models_{\mathrm{CLTL}} F$ *and* $\langle \alpha, i \rangle \models_{\mathrm{CLTL}} G$
$\langle \alpha, i \rangle \models_{\mathrm{CLTL}} F \overset{.}{\vee} G$	*iff*	$\langle \alpha, i \rangle \models_{\mathrm{CLTL}} F$ *or* $\langle \alpha, i \rangle \models_{\mathrm{CLTL}} G$
$\langle \alpha, i \rangle \models_{\mathrm{CLTL}} \bigcirc F$	*iff*	$\langle \alpha, i+1 \rangle \models_{\mathrm{CLTL}} F$
$\langle \alpha, i \rangle \models_{\mathrm{CLTL}} \Box F$	*iff*	*for all $j \geq i$* $\langle \alpha, j \rangle \models_{\mathrm{CLTL}} F$
$\langle \alpha, i \rangle \models_{\mathrm{CLTL}} \Diamond F$	*iff*	*there is a $j \geq i$ such that* $\langle \alpha, j \rangle \models_{\mathrm{CLTL}} F$
$\langle \alpha, i \rangle \models_{\mathrm{CLTL}} \overset{.}{\exists}_x F$	*iff*	*there is an x-variant α' of α such that* $\langle \alpha', i \rangle \models_{\mathrm{CLTL}} F$.

Define $\llbracket F \rrbracket = \{\alpha \mid \alpha \models_{\mathrm{CLTL}} F\}$. *$F$ is* **CLTL** *valid iff* $\llbracket F \rrbracket = \mathcal{C}^\omega$, *and* **CLTL** *satisfiable iff* $\llbracket F \rrbracket \neq \emptyset$.

Let us discuss a little about the difference between the boolean operators in the constraint system and the temporal ones to justify our dotted notation. A state formula c is satisfied only by those $e.\alpha'$ such that $e \models c$. So, the state formula $\texttt{false}$ has at least one sequence that satisfies it; e.g. $\texttt{false}^\omega$. On the contrary the temporal formula $\texttt{false}$ has no models whatsoever. Similarly, $c \overset{.}{\vee} d$ is satisfied by those $e.\alpha'$ such that either $e \models c$ or $e \models d$ holds. Thus, in general $\llbracket c \overset{.}{\vee} d \rrbracket \neq \llbracket c \vee d \rrbracket$. The same holds true for $\neg c$ and $\overset{.}{\neg} c$.

Example 11. Let $e = c \vee d$ with $c = (x = 42)$ and $d = (x \neq 42)$. One can verify that $\mathcal{C}^\omega = \llbracket c \vee d \rrbracket \ni e^\omega \notin \llbracket c \overset{.}{\vee} d \rrbracket$ and also that $\llbracket \neg c \rrbracket \ni \texttt{false}^\omega \notin \llbracket \overset{.}{\neg} c \rrbracket$. □

From the above example, one may be tempted to think of **CLTL** as being intuitionistic. Notice, however, that statements like $\overset{.}{\neg} F \overset{.}{\vee} F$ and $\overset{.}{\neg} \overset{.}{\neg} F \Rightarrow F$ are **CLTL** valid.

Table 3. A proof system for linear-temporal properties of ntcc processes

LTELL: $\mathbf{tell}(c) \vdash c$	LPAR: $\dfrac{P \vdash F \qquad Q \vdash G}{P \parallel Q \vdash F \wedge G}$
LSUM: $\dfrac{\forall i \in I \;\; P_i \vdash F_i}{\sum_{i \in I} \mathbf{when}\ c_i\ \mathbf{do}\ P_i \;\vdash\; \bigvee_{i \in I}(c_i \wedge F_i)\,\dot{\vee}\,\bigwedge_{i \in I} \neg c_i}$	LLOC: $\dfrac{P \vdash F}{(\mathbf{local}\ x)\,P \;\vdash\; \dot{\exists}_x F}$
LNEXT: $\dfrac{P \vdash F}{\mathbf{next}\ P \vdash \bigcirc F}$	LUNL: $\dfrac{P \vdash F}{\mathbf{unless}\ c\ \mathbf{next}\ P \;\vdash\; c\,\dot{\vee}\,\bigcirc F}$
LREP: $\dfrac{P \vdash F}{!P \vdash \Box F}$	LSTAR: $\dfrac{P \vdash F}{\star P \vdash \Diamond F}$

$$\text{LCONS: } \dfrac{P \vdash F}{P \vdash G} \quad \text{if } F \Rightarrow G$$

Process Verification. Intuitively, $P \models_{\mathrm{CLTL}} F$ iff every sequence that P can possibly output, on inputs from arbitrary environments, satisfies F. In other words if every sequence in the strongest-postcondition of P is a model of A..

Definition 10 (Verification). *P satisfies F, written $P \models_{\mathrm{CLTL}} F$, iff $sp(P) \subseteq \llbracket F \rrbracket$.*

So, for instance, $\star\,\mathbf{tell}(c) \models_{\mathrm{CLTL}} \Diamond c$ as in every sequence output by $\star\,\mathbf{tell}(c)$ there must be an e entailing c. Also $P = \mathbf{tell}(c) + \mathbf{tell}(d) \models_{\mathrm{CLTL}} c \vee d$ and $P \models_{\mathrm{CLTL}} c\,\dot{\vee}\,d$ as every e output by P entails either c or d. Notice, however, that $Q = \mathbf{tell}(c \vee d) \models_{\mathrm{CLTL}} c \vee d$ but $Q \not\models_{\mathrm{CLTL}} (c\,\dot{\vee}\,d)$ in general, since Q can output an e which certainly entails $c \vee d$ and still entails neither c nor d - take e, c and d as in Example 11. Therefore, $c\,\dot{\vee}\,d$ distinguishes P from Q. The reader may now see why we wish to distinguish $c\,\dot{\vee}\,d$ from $c \vee d$.

Proof System for Verification. In order to reason about statements of the form $P \models_{\mathrm{CLTL}} F$, [30] proposes a *proof (or inference) system* for assertions of the form $P \vdash F$. Intuitively, we want $P \vdash F$ to be the "counterpart" of $P \models F$ in the inference system, namely $P \vdash F$ should approximate $P \models_{\mathrm{CLTL}} F$ as closely as possible (ideally, they should be equivalent). The system is presented in Table 3.

Definition 11 ($P \vdash F$). *We say that $P \vdash F$ iff the assertion $P \vdash F$ has a proof in the system in Table 3.*

Inference Rules. Let us now describe some of the inference rules of the proof system. The inference rule for the tell operator is given by

$$\text{LTELL: } \mathbf{tell}(c) \vdash c$$

Rule LTELL gives a proof saying that every output of $\mathbf{tell}(c)$ on inputs of arbitrary environments should definitely satisfy the atomic proposition c, i.e., $\mathbf{tell}(c) \models_{\mathrm{CLTL}} c$.

Consider now the rule for the choice operator:

$$\text{LSUM:} \quad \frac{\forall i \in I \quad P_i \vdash F_i}{\displaystyle\sum_{i \in I} \textbf{when } c_i \textbf{ do } P_i \vdash \bigvee_{i \in I}(c_i \wedge F_i) \dot{\vee} \bigwedge_{i \in I} \dot{\neg} c_i}$$

Rule LSUM can be explained as follows. Suppose that for $P = \sum_{i \in I} \textbf{when } c_i \textbf{ do } P_i$ we are given a proof that each P_i satisfies F_i. Then we certainly have a proof saying that every output of P on arbitrary inputs should satisfy either: (a) some of the guards c_i and their corresponding F_i (i.e., $\bigvee_{i \in I}(c_i \wedge F_i)$), or (b) none of the guards (i.e., $\bigwedge_{i \in I} \dot{\neg} c_i$).

The inference rule for parallel composition is defined as

$$\text{LPAR:} \quad \frac{P \vdash F \quad Q \vdash G}{P \parallel Q \vdash F \dot{\wedge} G}$$

The soundness of this rule can be justified as follows. Assume that each output of P, under the influence of arbitrary environments, satisfies F. Assume the same about Q and G. In $P \parallel Q$, the process Q can be thought as one of those arbitrary environment under which P satisfies F. Then $P \parallel Q$ must satisfy F. Similarly, P can be one of those arbitrary environment under which Q satisfies G. Hence, $P \parallel Q$ must satisfy G as well. We therefore have grounds to conclude that $P \parallel Q$ satisfies $F \wedge G$.

The inference rule for the local operator is

$$\text{LLOC:} \quad \frac{P \vdash F}{(\textbf{local } x)\, P \vdash \dot{\exists}_x F}$$

The intuition is that since the outputs of $(\textbf{local } x)\, P$ are outputs of P with x hidden then if P satisfies F, $(\textbf{local } x)\, P$ should satisfy F with x hidden, i.e., $\dot{\exists}_x F$.

The following are the inference rules for the temporal ntcc constructs:

$$\text{LNEXT:} \quad \frac{P \vdash F}{\textbf{next } P \vdash \circ F} \qquad \text{LUNL:} \quad \frac{P \vdash F}{\textbf{unless } c \textbf{ next } P \vdash c \dot{\vee} \circ F}$$

$$\text{LREP:} \quad \frac{P \vdash F}{!P \vdash \Box F} \qquad \text{LSTAR:} \quad \frac{P \vdash F}{\star P \vdash \Diamond F}$$

Assume that P satisfies F. Rule LNEXT says that if P is executed next, then in the next time unit it will also satisfy F. Hence, $\textbf{next } P$ satisfies $\circ F$. Rule LUNL is similar, except that P can also be precluded from execution if some environment provides c. Thus $\textbf{unless } c \textbf{ next } P$ satisfies either c or $\circ F$. Rule LREP says that if P is executed in each time interval, then F is always satisfied by P. Therefore, $!P$ satisfies $\Box F$. Rule LSTAR says that if P is executed in some time interval, then in that time interval P satisfies F. Therefore, $\star P$ satisfies $\Diamond F$.

Finally, we have a rule that allows reasoning about temporal formulae to be incorporated in proofs about processes satisfying specifications:

$$\text{LCONS:} \quad \frac{P \vdash F}{P \vdash G} \quad \text{if } F \Rightarrow G$$

Rule LCONS simply says that if P satisfies a specification F then it also satisfies any weaker specification G.

Notice that the inference rules reveal a pleasant correspondence between ntcc operators and the logic operators. For example, parallel composition and locality corresponds to conjunction and existential quantification. The choice operator corresponds to some special kind of conjunction. The next, replication and star operators correspond to the next, always, and eventuality temporal operator.

The Proof System at Work. Let us now give a simple example illustrating a proof in inference system.

Example 12. Recall Example 9. We have a process R which was repeatedly checking the state of $motor_1$. If a malfunction is reported, R would tell that $motor_1$ must be turned off. We also have a process S stating that motor $motor_1$ is doomed to malfunction. Let $R = !$ **when** c **do** $tell(e)$ and $S = \star tell(c)$ with the constraints $c = \texttt{malfunction}(motor_1\_\texttt{status})$ and $e = (motor_1\_\texttt{speed} = 0)$. We want to provide a proof of the assertion: $R \parallel S \vdash \Diamond e$. Intuitively, this means that the parallel execution of R and S satisfies the specification stating that $motor_1$ is eventually turned off. The following is a derivation of the above assertion.

$$
\cfrac{
  \cfrac{
    \cfrac{
      \cfrac{\textbf{when } c \textbf{ do tell}(e) \vdash (c \wedge e) \,\dot{\vee}\, \dot{\neg} c}{\textbf{when } c \textbf{ do tell}(e) \vdash c \Rightarrow e} \text{ LCONS}
    }{R \vdash \Box\,(c \Rightarrow e)} \text{ LREP}
    \qquad
    \cfrac{
      \cfrac{tell(c) \vdash c}{S \vdash \Diamond c} \text{ LSTAR}
    }{} \text{ LTELL}
  }{R \parallel S \vdash \Box\,(c \Rightarrow e) \wedge \Diamond c} \text{ LPAR}
}{R \parallel S \vdash \Diamond e} \text{ LCONS}
$$

(LSUM)

More complex examples of the use of the proof system for proving the satisfaction of processes specification can be found in [28]—in particular for proving properties of mutable data structures.   □

Let us now state how close the relation $\vdash$ to the verification relation $\models_{\text{CLTL}}$.

Theorem 2 (Relative Completeness). *Suppose that P is a locally-independent process. Then $P \vdash F$ iff $P \models_{\text{CLTL}} F$.*

The reason why the above result is called "relative completeness" is because we need to determine the validity of the temporal implication in the rule LCONS. This means that our proof system is complete, if we are equipped with an oracle that is guaranteed to provide a proof or a confirmation of each valid temporal implication. Because of the validity issues above mentioned, one may wonder about decidability of the validity problem for our temporal logic. We look at these issues next.

Decidability Results. In [51] it is shown that the verification problem (i.e., given P and F whether $P \models_{\text{CLTL}} F$) is decidable for the locally independent fragment and negation-free **CLTL** formulae. A noteworthy aspect of this result is that, as mentioned before, the ntcc fragment above admits infinite-state processes. Another interesting aspect is that **CLTL** is first-order. Most first-order LTL's in computer science are not recursively axiomatizable let alone decidable [1].

Furthermore, [51] proves the decidability of the validity problem for implication of negation-free **CLTL** formulae. This is done by appealing to the close connection between ntcc processes and LTL formulae to reduce the validity of implication to the verification problem. More precisely, it is shown that given two negation-free formulae F and G one can construct a process P_F such that $sp(P_F) = \llbracket F \rrbracket$ and then it follows that $P_F \models_{\text{CLTL}} G$ iff $F \Rightarrow G$. As a corollary of this result, we obtain the decidability of *satisfiability* for the negation-free first-order fragment of **CLTL** —recall G is satisfiable iff $G \Rightarrow$ false is not valid.

A theoretical application of the theory of ntcc is presented in [51] by stating a new positive decidability result for a first-order fragment of Pnueli's first-order **LTL** [21]. The result is obtained from a reduction to **CLTL** satisfiability and thus it also contributes to the understanding of the relationship between (timed) ccp and (temporal) classic logic.

6   Concluding Remarks and Related Work

There are several developments of timed ccp and, due to space restriction, it would be difficult to do justice to them all. I shall indicate a few which appear to me to be central.

Related Work.   Saraswat el al were the first proposing a denotational semantics and proof system for timed ccp in the context of tcc [39]. The denotational semantics is fully abstract and it was later generalized by Palemidessi et al for the ntcc case. The proof system of [39] is based on an intuitionistic logic enriched with a next operator—the logic for the ntcc case is classic. The system is complete for hiding-free and finite processes.

Gabrielli et al also provided a fully-abstract denotational semantics [5] and proof system [4] for the tccp model (see Section 4). The underlying second-order linear temporal logic in [4] can be used for describing input-output behavior. In contrast, the ntcc logic can only be used for the strongest-postcondition, but also it is semantically simpler and defined as the standard first-order linear-temporal logic of [21].

The decidability results for the ntcc equivalences here presented are based on reductions from ntcc processes into finite-state automata [29,27,51]. The work in [42] also shows how to compile tcc into finite-state machines. Rather than a direct way of verifying process equivalences, such machines provide an execution model of tcc.

Nielsen et al [27] compared, relatively to the notion of input-output behavior, the expressive power of various tcc variants differing in their way of expressing infinite behavior. It is shown that: (1) recursive procedures with parameters can be encoded into parameterless recursive procedures with dynamic scoping, and vice-versa. (2) replication can be encoded into parameterless recursive procedures with static scoping, and vice-versa. (3) the languages from (1) are strictly more expressive than the languages from (2). Furthermore, it is shown that behavioral equivalence is undecidable for the languages from (1), but decidable for the languages from (2). The undecidability result holds even if the process variables take values from a fixed finite domain.

Also Tini [48] explores the expressiveness of tcc languages, but focusing on the capability of tcc to encode synchronous languages. In particular, Tini shows that Argos [22] and a version of Lustre restricted to finite domains [16] can be encoded in tcc.

In the context of tcc, Tini [49] introduced a notion of bisimilarity, an elemental process equivalence in concurrency, with a complete and elegant axiomatization for the hiding-free fragment of tcc. The notion of bisimilarity has also been introduced for `ntcc` by the present author in his PhD thesis [50].

On the practical side, Saraswat el al introduced Timed Gentzen [40], a particular tcc-based programming language for reactive-systems implemented in PROLOG. More recently, Saraswat el al released jcc [43], an integration of timed (default) ccp into the popular JAVA programming language. Rueda et al [37] demonstrated that essential ideas of computer generated music composition can be elegantly represented in `ntcc`. Hurtado and Muñoz [19] in joint work with Fernández and Quintero [10] gave a design and efficient implementation of an `ntcc`-based reactive programming language for LEGO RCX robots [20]—the robotic devices chosen in Section 5.1 as motivating examples.

Future Work. Timed ccp is still under development and certainly much remain to be explored. I shall indicate briefly a few research directions that I believe are necessary for the development of timed ccp as a well-established model of concurrency. Future research in timed ccp should address those issues that are central to other matured models of concurrency. In particular, the development of solid theories and tools for behavioral equivalences, which at present time is still very immature. For instance, currently there are neither axiomatizations nor automatic tools for reasoning about process equivalences. Furthermore, the decision algorithms for the verification problem, are very costly as the initial interest in them was purely theoretical. For practical purposes, it is then fundamental to conduct studies on the design and implementation of efficient algorithms for this problem.

Acknowledgments. I am grateful to the people with whom I have worked on temporal ccp with great pleasure: Mogens Nielsen, Catuscia Palamidesi, and Camilo Rueda.

References

1. M. Abadi. The power of temporal proofs. *Theoretical Computer Science*, 65:35–84, 1989.
2. J.A. Bergstra and J.W. Klop. Algebra of communicating processes with abstraction. *Theoretical Computer Science*, 37(1):77–121, 1985.
3. G. Berry and G. Gonthier. The ESTEREL synchronous programming language: design, semantics, implementation. *Science of Computer Programming*, 19(2):87–152, 1992.
4. F. de Boer, M. Gabbrielli, and M. Chiara. A temporal logic for reasoning about timed concurrent constraint programs. In *TIME 01*. IEEE Press, 2001.
5. F. de Boer, M. Gabbrielli, and M. C. Meo. A timed concurrent constraint language. *Information and Computation*, 161:45–83, 2000.
6. F. de Boer, A. Di Pierro, and C. Palamidessi. Nondeterminism and infinite computations in constraint programming. *Theoretical Computer Science*, 151(1):37–78, 1995.
7. F. S. de Boer, M. Gabbrielli, E. Marchiori, and C. Palamidessi. Proving concurrent constraint programs correct. *ACM Transactions on Programming Languages and Systems*, 19(5), 1997.
8. J.F. Diaz, C. Rueda, and F. Valencia. A calculus for concurrent processes with constraints. *CLEI Electronic Journal*, 1(2), 1998.
9. H. Dierks. A process algebra for real-time programs. In *FASE*, volume 1783 of *LNCS*, pages 66–81. Springer Verlag, 2000.
10. D. Fernádez and L. Quintero. *VIN: An ntcc visual language for LEGO Robots*. BSc Thesis, Universidad Javeriana-Cali, Colombia, 2003. http://www.brics.dk/~fvalenci/ntcc-tools.

11. J. Fredslund. The assumption architecture. Progress Report, Department of Computer Science, University of Aarhus, 1999.
12. D. Gilbert and C. Palamidessi. Concurrent constraint programming with process mobility. In *Proc. of the CL 2000*, LNAI, pages 463–477. Springer-Verlag, 2000.
13. V. Gupta, R. Jagadeesan, and P. Panangaden. Stochastic processes as concurrent constraint programs. In *Symposium on Principles of Programming Languages*, pages 189–202, 1999.
14. V. Gupta, R. Jagadeesan, and V. A. Saraswat. Computing with continuous change. *Science of Computer Programming*, 30(1–2):3–49, 1998.
15. N. Halbwachs. Synchronous programming of systems. *LNCS*, 1427:1–16, 1998.
16. N. Halbwachs, P. Caspi, P. Raymond, and D. Pilaud. The synchronous data-flow programming language LUSTRE. *Proc. of the IEEE*, 79(9):1305–1320, 1991.
17. S. Haridi and S. Janson. Kernel andorra prolog and its computational model. In *Proc. of the International Conference on Logic Programming*, pages 301–309. MIT Press, 1990.
18. C. A. R. Hoare. *Communications Sequential Processes*. Prentice-Hall, Englewood Cliffs (NJ), USA, 1985.
19. R. Hurtado and M. Muñoz. *LMAN: An ntcc Abstract Machine for LEGO Robots*. BSc Thesis, Universidad Javeriana-Cali, Colombia, 2003. http://www.brics.dk/~fvalenci/ntcc-tools.
20. H. H. Lund and L. Pagliarini. Robot soccer with LEGO mindstorms. *LNCS*, 1604:141–151, 1999.
21. Z. Manna and A. Pnueli. *The Temporal Logic of Reactive and Concurrent Systems, Specification*. Springer, 1991.
22. F. Maraninchi. Operational and compositional semantics of synchronous automaton compositions. In *CONCUR '92*, volume 630 of *LNCS*, pages 550–564. Springer-Verlag, 1992.
23. R. Milner. *Communication and Concurrency*. International Series in Computer Science. Prentice Hall, 1989. SU Fisher Research 511/24.
24. R. Milner. A finite delay operator in synchronous ccs. Technical Report CSR-116-82, University of Edinburgh, 1992.
25. R. Milner. *Communicating and Mobile Systems: the π-calculus*. Cambridge University Press, 1999.
26. U. Montanari. Networks of constraints: Fundamental properties and applications to picture processing. *Information Science*, 7, 1974.
27. M. Nielsen, C. Palamidessi, and F. Valencia. On the expressive power of concurrent constraint programming languages. In *Proc. of PPDP'02*, pages 156–167. ACM Press, 2002.
28. M. Nielsen, C. Palamidessi, and F. Valencia. Temporal concurrent constraint programming: Denotation, logic and applications. *Nordic Journal of Computing*, 9(2):145–188, 2002.
29. M. Nielsen and F. Valencia. *Temporal Concurrent Constraint Programming: Applications and Behavior*, chapter 4, pages 298–324. Springer-Verlag, LNCS 2300, 2002.
30. C. Palamidessi and F. Valencia. A temporal concurrent constraint programming calculus. In *Proc. of CP'01*. Springer-Verlag, LNCS 2239, 2001.
31. C.A. Petri. Fundamentals of a theory of asynchronous information flow. In *Proc. IFIP Congress '62*, 1962.
32. G. Plotkin. A structural approach to operational semantics. Technical Report FN-19, DAIMI, University of Aarhus, 1981.
33. A. Pnueli. The temporal logic of programs. In *Proc. of FOCS-77*, pages 46–57. IEEE, IEEE Computer Society Press, 1977.
34. G.M. Reed and A.W. Roscoe. A timed model for communication sequential processes. *Theoretical Computer Science*, 8:249–261, 1988.
35. F. Rossi and U. Montanari. Concurrent semantics for concurrent constraint programming. In *Constraint Programming: Proc. 1993 NATO ASI*, pages 181–220, 1994.
36. J.H. Réty. Distributed concurrent constraint programming. *Fundamenta Informaticae*, 34(3), 1998.

37. C. Rueda and F. Valencia. Proving musical properties using a temporal concurrent constraint calculus. In *Proc. of the 28th International Computer Music Conference (ICMC2002)*, 2002.
38. V. Saraswat. *Concurrent Constraint Programming*. The MIT Press, Cambridge, MA, 1993.
39. V. Saraswat, R. Jagadeesan, and V. Gupta. Foundations of timed concurrent constraint programming. In *Proc. of LICS'94*, pages 71–80, 1994.
40. V. Saraswat, R. Jagadeesan, and V. Gupta. Programming in timed concurrent constraint languages. In *Constraint Programming*, NATO Advanced Science Institute Series, pages 361–410. Springer-Verlag, 1994.
41. V. Saraswat, R. Jagadeesan, and V. Gupta. Default timed concurrent constraint programming. In *Proc. of POPL'95*, pages 272–285, 1995.
42. V. Saraswat, R. Jagadeesan, and V. Gupta. Timed default concurrent constraint programming. *Journal of Symbolic Computation*, 22(5–6):475–520, 1996.
43. V. Saraswat, R. Jagadeesan, and V. Gupta. jcc: Integrating timed default concurrent constraint programming into java. http://www.cse.psu.edu/~saraswat/jcc.html, 2003.
44. V. Saraswat, M. Rinard, and P. Panangaden. The semantic foundations of concurrent constraint programming. In *POPL '91*, pages 333–352, 1991.
45. E. Shapiro. The Family of Concurrent Logic Programming Languages. *Computing Surveys*, 21(3):413–510, 1990.
46. G. Smolka. A Foundation for Concurrent Constraint Programming. In *Constraints in Computational Logics*, volume 845 of *LNCS*, 1994. Invited Talk.
47. G. Smolka. The Oz programming model. In Jan van Leeuwen, editor, *Computer Science Today*, volume 1000 of *LNCS*, pages 324–343. Springer-Verlag, 1995.
48. S. Tini. On the expressiveness of timed concurrent constraint programming. *Electronics Notes in Theoretical Computer Science*, 1999.
49. S. Tini. An axiomatic semantics for the synchronous language gentzen. In *FOSSACS'01*, volume 2030 of *LNCS*. Springer-Verlag, 2001.
50. F. Valencia. *Temporal Concurrent Constraint Programming*. PhD thesis, BRICS, University of Aarhus, 2003.
51. F. Valencia. Timed concurrent constraint programming: Decidability results and their application to LTL. In *Proc. of ICLP'03*. Springer-Verlag, LNCS, 2003.
52. W. Yi. *A Calculus for Real Time Systems*. PhD thesis, Chalmers Institute of Technology, Sweden, 1991.
53. W. M. Zuberek. Timed petri nets and preliminary performance evaluation. In *Proc. of the 7th Annual Symposium on Computer Architecture*, pages 88–96. ACM and IEEE, 1980.

Symbolic Model-Checking for Biochemical Systems

François Fages

Projet Contraintes, INRIA-Rocquencourt,
BP105, 78153 Le Chesnay Cedex, France,
Francois.Fages@inria.fr

In recent years, molecular biology has engaged in a large-scale effort to elucidate high-level cellular processes in terms of their biochemical basis at the molecular level. The mass production of post genomic data, such as ARN expression, protein production and protein-protein interaction, raises the need of a strong parallel effort on the formal representation of biological *processes*.

Several formalisms have been proposed for the modeling of metabolic pathways, cellular signaling pathways, or gene regulatory networks, ranging from boolean networks, rewriting logics, Petri nets, process calculi to systems of ordinary differential equations, hybrid automata or hybrid concurrent constraint languages.

In this tutorial, we will present some recent work done with our colleagues of the ARC CPBIO on the modeling of biomolecular processes and the use of automated reasoning tools for analyzing their properties. More specifically, we will examine

1. the modeling of biochemical networks with concurrent transition systems,
2. the use of the temporal logics CTL as a query language for such models,
3. the use of symbolic and constraint-based model-checkers for automatically evaluating CTL queries.

This approach will be illustrated with a boolean model of the mammalian cell cycle control involving several hundreds of proteins and interaction rules, and with quantitative models using constraint-based model checking.

We will conclude on some challenges raised by this programme to the logic programming community.

C. Palamidessi (Ed.): ICLP 2003, LNCS 2916, p. 102, 2003.
© Springer-Verlag Berlin Heidelberg 2003

Component-Based Software Development and Logic Programming

Kung-Kiu Lau

Department of Computer Science, University of Manchester
Manchester M13 9PL, United Kingdom
kung-kiu@cs.man.ac.uk

Abstract. Component-based Software Development (CBD) represents
a paradigm shift in software development. In the tutorial I will explain
what CBD is about, briefly survey current component technology, and
posit that Logic Programming can play a role in next-generation CBD.
In this abstract, I give an overview of the material that I plan to cover
in the tutorial.

1 Introduction

Software Engineering is entering a new era: the *component* era. Building on
the concepts of Object-Oriented Software Construction (e.g. [18]), Component-
based Software Development (CBD) aims to move Software Engineering into an
'industrial age', whereby software can be assembled from components, in the
manner that hardware systems are constructed from kits of parts nowadays.

Thus CBD represents a paradigm shift in software development: from building monolithic, single-platform, purpose-built-from-scratch systems to constructing assemblies of ready-made components that are platform-independent and
supplied by third-parties.

2 What Are Software Components?

The first thing to say is that there is as yet no universally accepted standard
definition of what a component is. Equally, there is no standard terminology for
CBD at present.

Nevertheless, the idea of using components to build software systems is as old
as Software Engineering itself. Indeed it is the motivation behind any program
units that purport to enable programmers to structure and to reuse their code.
These range from sub-routines, modules, packages, etc., that have been familiar
for a long time, to commercial off-the-shelf software, or COTS (e.g. [28]), and
web services, that are relatively recent. It may be too simplistic to describe
such components as just 'reusable blocks of software', but this does capture the
essence of what a component is.

Despite the lack of a standard definition and terminology, there is consensus
that to qualify as a software component, a piece of software should have the
following characteristics:

C. Palamidessi (Ed.): ICLP 2003, LNCS 2916, pp. 103–108, 2003.
© Springer-Verlag Berlin Heidelberg 2003

Encapsulation. The inner workings of a software component must be hidden from the outside world that it exists in.

Use of an Interface. A software component must present and make use of a useful *interface* which the outside world can interpret so that other components know what services it gives or *exports*.

The interface should also specify what the component needs to *import* in order to carry out its operations.

The interface must conform to the accepted standard used in the world which the component works in. Such a standard is sometimes called a *component model*. It specifies, among other things, how component interfaces are constructed, as well as the *middleware* that allows components to interact with one another via their interfaces.

Reusability. A software component must be *reusable* so that it can be used in multiple application contexts.

This enables developers to reduce the effort in developing new applications.

Replaceability. A software component must be able to *replace*, or be replaced by, other existing components.

The new component must at least be able to provide the same services as the old component so that components relying on the services of the old component will still work.

It must also have an interface that other components can still recognise and utilise.

Inter-operability. The services of a software component must be accessible on any platform.

Therefore software components must adhere to standards for component interfaces and middleware services.

A widely accepted definition of a software component is the following, due to Szyperski [26]:

"A software component is a unit of composition with contractually specified interfaces and explicit context dependencies only.
A software component can be deployed independently and is subject to composition by third parties."

This definition requires additionally that interfaces be specified contractually, i.e. with obligations and rights for both the component and its clients, and *context dependencies*, which define how and where the component can be deployed, be specified explicitly. Furthermore, components can be produced, acquired and deployed independently, and Szyperski argues that this in turn requires a component to be in binary form.

Heineman and Councill [10] define a component as:

"A software element that conforms to a component model and can be independently deployed and composed without modification according to a composition standard."

This definition is thus predicated on the existence of a component model.

3   Current Component Technology

A component model is a specification. For implementation, it has to be realised by a technology that provides the 'wiring' standard, or plumbing, for integrating software components according to the standards defined by the component model. In other words, a component technology provides the middleware that allows components to interact with one another (in accordance with the component model).

Implementing middleware requires enormous resources, and not surprisingly is the preserve of large industrial enterprises. Currently, there are 3 main industrial component models (and technologies):

- CORBA (Common Object Request Broker Architecture) [20,7]
  This is a standard defined by OMG (www.omg.org), the Object Management Group.
- COM (Component Object Model) [6,2]
  This is the standard marketed by Microsoft (www.microsoft.com).
- EJB (Enterprise JavaBeans) [25,9]
  This is marketed by Sun (www.sun.com).

All these are essentially wiring standards for integrating objects, in the sense of Object-Oriented Programming, distributed over networks, and therefore collectively constitute a distributed object technology. This technology is based on the *remote procedure call* (RPC) and *remote method invocation* (RMI) mechanisms. As a consequence, although the component models differ in various aspects, they can all access objects (and services) remotely and across platforms.

The details of these component models are extremely complicated. In the tutorial I will attempt to explain the basic underlying ideas and principles, and to outline the key characteristics, of each approach.

Naturally these component models are constantly evolving, CORBA is developing into the CORBA Component Model (CCM) [1], also called CORBA 3, and COM has metamorphosed into .NET [19,22].

4   Component-Based Software Development

For software development, the so-called Unified Methodology is the industry standard. It combines the Unified Software Development Process [11] with the Unified Modeling Language (UML) [23,27] which is used for specifying and designing software systems. UML also has its roots in Object-Oriented Software Construction, with objects as units of design and reuse.

Whether the Unified Methodology, in particular UML, can be used successfully for CBD remains to be seen. The notion of a component in the original UML was only an artefact at implementation time rather than design time, so strictly speaking it was not part of UML at all.

To introduce components into UML, i.e. to introduce them at design time, Cheesman and Daniels [4] define a component as a UML stereotype which consists of a class with an interface. However, it is not clear how this stereotype can be used to define components other than single classes, e.g. Catalysis frameworks [8] which are groups of interacting objects. The problem is that the Object Constraint Language (OCL) [29], part of UML, cannot deal with components that are not single objects, since it defines object constraints in the context of a single class.

However, here things are in flux, with a major upgrade of UML to UML 2.0 in the pipeline, and the introduction of OMG Model Driven Architecture (MDA) [21], which definitely aims to compose components. So we should 'watch this space'.

5   Is There a Role for Logic Programming?

Given that Logic Programming (LP) has never really made an impact on Software Engineering (SE), it would seem odd to posit that LP has a role to play in CBD [13,16], but that is precisely what I would like to do.

Firstly, as we said in [17], we believe LP's role in SE is to co-exist with the predominant imperative, in particular the OO, paradigm. Moreover, we believe LP's role in this co-existence is to address the critical kernel of a software system, for which there is no doubt that LP would be superior, for the reason that LP can deliver software correctness.

It is generally accepted that the critical kernel of a software system usually consists of some 20% of the code (see Figure 1), and it is this code that needs

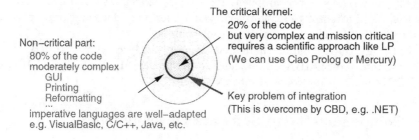

Fig. 1. The integration barrier between LP and predominant paradigms in SE.

a scientific approach such as LP affords. However, even if LP was used for the critical code, the problem of integrating (critical) LP code with (non-critical) code in the predominant (imperative) languages would at best be difficult. For example, we could use a foreign function interface, usually in C, but this is often difficult. Thus, as also shown in Figure 1, there is an integration barrier between LP and the predominant paradigm in SE. This barrier would have to be overcome even if we were to use LP just for the critical kernel.

We contend that CBD provides just the right impetus for removing this integration barrier. Since the the ultimate goal of CBD is third-party assembly of independently produced software components, which must be possible on any platform, it means that the components must be platform- and paradigm-independent. As a consequence, CBD offers a *level playing field* to all paradigms. Current approaches to industrial SE cannot address all the needs of CBD [3], so the playing field is level and LP is not at any disadvantage.

By definition, component technology supports the level playing field, and we believe that a feasible practicable approach is to interface a suitable LP language, such as Ciao Prolog [5] and Mercury [24], to a current component technology. For example, we think that .NET, Microsoft's new component platform, could give LP the necessary component technology (see Figure 1). As any language on a .NET platform can seamlessly interoperate with any other language on .NET (at least at a very low level), we have, for the first time, the possibility to build the critical components using the LP paradigm, while the non-critical, more mundane, components are still OOP-based.

In particular, we believe the declarative nature of LP, and Computational Logic in general, can play a crucial role in addressing key pre-requisites for CBD to succeed, such as component certification, predictable assembly [15], a priori reasoning [12], trusted components [14], etc.

References

1. BEA Systems *et al.* CORBA Components. Technical Report orbos/99-02-05, Object Management Group, 1999.
2. D. Box. *Essential COM*. Addison Wesley, 1998.
3. A.W. Brown and K.C. Wallnau. The current state of CBSE. *IEEE Software*, Sept/Oct 1998:37–46, 1998.
4. J. Cheesman and J. Daniels. *UML Components: A Simple Process for Specifying Component-based Software*. Addison-Wesley, 2001.
5. The Ciao Prolog Development System.
   http://clip.dia.fi.upm.es/Software/Ciao/.
6. COM web page. http://www.microsoft.com/com/.
7. CORBA FAQ web page. http://www.omg.org/gettingstarted/corbafaq.htm.
8. D.F. D'Souza and A.C. Wills. *Objects, Components, and Frameworks with UML: The Catalysis Approach*. Addison-Wesley, 1999.
9. EJB web page. http://java.sun.com/products/ejb/.
10. G.T. Heineman and W.T. Councill, editors. *Component-Based Software Engineering: Putting the Pieces Together*. Addison-Wesley, 2001.
11. I. Jacobson, G. Booch, and J. Rumbaugh. *The Unified Software Development Process*. Addison-Wesley, 1999.
12. K.-K. Lau. A priori reasoning for component-based software development. In M. Carro, C. Vaucheret, and K.-K. Lau, editors, *Proc. 1st CoLogNET Workshop on Component-based Software Development and Implementation Technology for Computational Logic Systems*, pages 5–19. Technical Report CLIP4/02.0, School of Computer Science, Technical University of Madrid, 2002.

13. K.-K. Lau. The role of logic programming in next-generation component-based software development. In G. Gupta and I.V. Ramakrishnan, editors, *Proc. Workshop on Logic Programming and Software Enginering, London, UK, July 2000.*
14. K.-K. Lau. Some ingredients of trusted components. In *Proc. Workshop on Trusted Components*, pages 1–5. January 2003, Prato, Italy.
15. K.-K. Lau. Component certification and system prediction: Is there a role for formality? In I. Crnkovic, H. Schmidt, J. Stafford, and K. Wallnau, editors, *Proc. 4th ICSE Workshop on Component-based Software Engineering*, pages 80–83. IEEE Computer Society Press, 2001.
16. K.-K. Lau and M. Ornaghi. Logic for component-based software development. In A. Kakas and F. Sadri, editors, *Computational Logic: Logic Programming and Beyond*, LNAI 2407, pages 347–373. Springer-Verlag, 2002.
17. K.-K. Lau and M. Vanden Bossche. Logic programming for software engineering: A second chance. In P.J. Stuckey, editor, *Proc. 18th Int. Conf. on Logic Programming*, LNCS 2401, pages 437–451. Springer-Verlag, 2002.
18. B. Meyer. *Object-oriented Software Construction*. Prentice-Hall, second edition, 1997.
19. Microsoft .NET web page. http://www.microsoft.com/net/.
20. Object Management Group. The Common Object Request Broker: Architecture and specification Revision 2.2, February 1998.
21. OMG Model Driven Architecture. http://www.omg.org/mda/.
22. D.S. Platt. *Introducing Microsoft .NET*. Microsoft Press, 3rd edition, 2003.
23. J. Rumbaugh, I. Jacobson, and G. Booch. *The Unified Modeling Language Reference Manual*. Addison-Wesley, 1999.
24. Z. Somogyi, F. Henderson, and T. Conway. Mercury – an efficient, purely declarative logic programming language. In *Proc. Australian Computer Science Comference*, pages 499–512, 1995.
25. Sun Microsystems. Enterprise JavaBeans Specification. Version 2.0, 2001.
26. C. Szyperski, D. Gruntz, and S. Murer. *Component Software: Beyond Object-Oriented Programming*. Addison-Wesley, second edition, 2002.
27. Introduction to OMG UML. http://www.omg.org/gettingstarted/what_is_uml.htm.
28. K. Wallnau, S. Hissam, and R. Seacord. *Building Systems from Commercial Components*. Addison-Wesley, 2001.
29. J. Warmer and A. Kleppe. *The Object Constraint Language*. Addison-Wesley, 1999.

A Tutorial on Proof Theoretic Foundations of Logic Programming

Paola Bruscoli and Alessio Guglielmi

Technische Universität Dresden
Hans-Grundig-Str. 25 - 01062 Dresden - German
{Paola.Bruscoli,Alessio.Guglielmi}@Inf.TU-Dresden.DE

Abstract. Abstract logic programming is about designing logic programming languages via the proof theoretic notion of uniform provability. It allows the design of purely logical, very expressive logic programming languages, endowed with a rich meta theory. This tutorial intends to expose the main ideas of this discipline in the most direct and simple way.

1 Introduction

Logic programming is traditionally introduced as an application of the resolution method. A limitation of this perspective is the difficulty of extending the pure language of Horn clauses to more expressive languages, without sacrificing logical purity.

After the work on abstract logic programming of Miller, Nadathur and other researchers (see especially [7,8,6]), we know that this limitation can largely be overcome by looking at logic programming from a proof theoretic perspective, through the idea of *uniform provability*. This way, one can make the declarative and operational meaning of logic programs coincide for large fragments of very expressive logics, like several flavours of higher order logics and linear logics. For these logics, proof theory provides a theoretical support, which is 'declarative' even in absence of a convenient semantics, like in the case of linear logic.

The essential tool is Gentzen's sequent calculus [2,1], for which one always requires the cut elimination property. Deductive systems can be defined in absence of their semantics, but they automatically possess the properties usually requested by computer scientists: a rigorous definition independent of specific implementations and a rich metatheory allowing formal manipulation. An important advantage of defining logic programming languages in the sequent calculus is the universality of this proof theoretic formalism. This allows for a much easier designing and comparing different languages than the corresponding situation in which a common formalism is not adopted.

Moreover, given the modularity properties induced by cut elimination and its consequences, it is conceivable to design tools for logic programming languages in a modular fashion, which is an obvious advantage. For example, a compiler can be produced by starting from some core sublanguage and proceeding by successive additions corresponding to modularly enlarging the core language. A

C. Palamidessi (Ed.): ICLP 2003, LNCS 2916, pp. 109–127, 2003.

first large scale language designed according to this principle is λ-Prolog [3], in intuitionistic higher order logic, and several others are available, especially in logics derived from linear logic (see [4] for a survey).

The purpose of this tutorial is to give a concise, direct and simple introduction to logic programming via uniform provability. This is a two phase operation: firstly, the sequent calculus of classical logic is introduced, then uniform provability and the related concept of *abstract logic programming*. The idea is that anybody familiar with classical logic in its basic, common exposition, and who also knows Prolog, should be able to find enough information for understanding how Prolog could be designed, and extended, using this proof theoretic methodology. The reader who is already acquainted with sequent calculus can skip the first section.

2   The Sequent Calculus

We deal here with the sequent calculus of first order classical logic; a good reference is [1]. This is enough to establish all the main ideas of abstract logic programming. For the higher order case, a great source of trouble is dealing with unification, but this issue does not directly affect the notion of uniform provability. The paper [8] studies the sequent calculus of the higher order logic at the basis of λ-Prolog.

2.1   Classical Logic

A sequent is an expression of the form $\Gamma \vdash \Delta$, where Γ and Δ are multisets of formulae. We can think of Γ and Δ as, respectively, a conjunction and a disjunction of formulae. The symbol $\vdash$ is called 'entailment' and corresponds to logical implication. Therefore 'Γ entails Δ' means that from all formulae in Γ some of the formulae in Δ follow.

A rule is a relation among sequents $S_1, \ldots, S_n$ and S

$$\rho \, \frac{S_1 \ \ldots \ S_n}{S},$$

where ρ is the name of the rule, $S_1, \ldots, S_n$ are its premises and S is its conclusion. If $n = 0$ the rule has no premises and we call it an axiom.

A system in the sequent calculus is a finite set of rules, that we can partition as follows: the axiom, the set of left rules and the set of right rules. Rules come in pairs for every logical connective, giving meaning to it depending on whether the connective appears at the left or at the right of the entailment symbol. Some more rules, called 'structural', model basic algebraic properties of sequents, like idempotency; they also belong to the sets of left and right rules. A further rule, called cut, may be present as well.

A derivation for a formula is obtained by successively applying instances of the given rules; if all branches of the derivation tree reach axioms then the derivation is a proof. We take a bottom-up perspective, i.e., we think of proofs as built from the bottom sequent up.

<table>
<tr><td colspan="2" align="center">Axiom</td><td colspan="2" align="center">Cut</td></tr>
</table>

$$A \vdash A$$

$$\text{cut} \; \frac{\Gamma \vdash \Delta, A \quad A, \Lambda \vdash \Theta}{\Gamma, \Lambda \vdash \Delta, \Theta}$$

Left Rules   Right Rules

$$c_L \; \frac{A, A, \Gamma \vdash \Delta}{A, \Gamma \vdash \Delta} \qquad\qquad c_R \; \frac{\Gamma \vdash \Delta, A, A}{\Gamma \vdash \Delta, A}$$

$$w_l \; \frac{\Gamma \vdash \Delta}{A, \Gamma \vdash \Delta} \qquad\qquad w_R \; \frac{\Gamma \vdash \Delta}{\Gamma \vdash \Delta, A}$$

$$\supset_L \; \frac{\Gamma \vdash \Delta, A \quad B, \Gamma \vdash \Delta}{A \supset B, \Gamma \vdash \Delta} \qquad\qquad \supset_R \; \frac{A, \Gamma \vdash \Delta, B}{\Gamma \vdash \Delta, A \supset B}$$

$$\wedge_{LL} \; \frac{A, \Gamma \vdash \Delta}{A \wedge B, \Gamma \vdash \Delta} \qquad \wedge_{LR} \; \frac{B, \Gamma \vdash \Delta}{A \wedge B, \Gamma \vdash \Delta} \qquad \wedge_R \; \frac{\Gamma \vdash \Delta, A \quad \Gamma \vdash \Delta, B}{\Gamma \vdash \Delta, A \wedge B}$$

$$\vee_L \; \frac{A, \Gamma \vdash \Delta \quad B, \Gamma \vdash \Delta}{A \vee B, \Gamma \vdash \Delta} \qquad \vee_{RL} \; \frac{\Gamma \vdash \Delta, A}{\Gamma \vdash \Delta, A \vee B} \qquad \vee_{RR} \; \frac{\Gamma \vdash \Delta, B}{\Gamma \vdash \Delta, A \vee B}$$

$$\neg_L \; \frac{\Gamma \vdash \Delta, A}{\neg A, \Gamma \vdash \Delta} \qquad\qquad \neg_R \; \frac{A, \Gamma \vdash \Delta}{\Gamma \vdash \Delta, \neg A}$$

$$\forall_L \; \frac{A[x/t], \Gamma \vdash \Delta}{\forall x. A, \Gamma \vdash \Delta} \qquad\qquad \forall_R \; \frac{\Gamma \vdash \Delta, A}{\Gamma \vdash \Delta, \forall x. A}$$

$$\exists_L \; \frac{A, \Gamma \vdash \Delta}{\exists x. A, \Gamma \vdash \Delta} \qquad\qquad \exists_R \; \frac{\Gamma \vdash \Delta, A[x/t]}{\Gamma \vdash \Delta, \exists x. A}$$

where in $\forall_R$ and $\exists_L$ the variable x is not free in the conclusion

Fig. 1. First Order Classical Sequent Calculus with Multiplicative Cut LK

We focus on classical logic, assuming that the reader is acquainted with some basic notions related to substitutions, instantiations and the like. We introduce a system for first-order classical logic, called LK, which is a slight modification of the system bearing the same name proposed by Gentzen in 1934. By means of examples we will see how the proof construction process works in the system and we will shortly discuss cut elimination.

From now on we consider the language of classical logic built over $\supset$, $\wedge$, $\vee$, $\neg$, $\forall$, $\exists$, and we denote formulae by A, B, ... , and atoms by a, b, ... , and by $p(x)$, $q(y)$. The system LK of *first order classical sequent calculus with multiplicative cut* is defined in fig. 1. The rules c_L and c_R are called *left* and *right contraction*; w_L and w_R are called *left* and *right weakening*; the other rules, except for —cut—, get the name from the connective they work on.

Regarding the use of the rules $\forall_R$ and $\exists_L$, one should remember that bound variables can always be renamed, i.e., one can consider, say, $\forall x.p(x)$ the same as $\forall y.p(y)$.

The first example shows the behaviour of several rules, in particular it shows how several structural rules operate. To see $\mathsf{c_L}$ in action, please wait until the next section.

Example 2.1. In LK, the tautologies $A \vee \neg A$ and $\forall x.(q(y) \supset p(x)) \supset (q(y) \supset \forall x.p(x))$ have these proofs:

$$
\cfrac{\cfrac{\cfrac{\cfrac{A \vdash A}{\vdash A, \neg A}\ {\scriptstyle \neg_R}}{\vdash A, A \vee \neg A}\ {\scriptstyle \vee_{RR}}}{\vdash A \vee \neg A, A \vee \neg A}\ {\scriptstyle \vee_{RL}}}{\vdash A \vee \neg A}\ {\scriptstyle \mathsf{c_R}}
$$

and

$$
\cfrac{\cfrac{\cfrac{\cfrac{\cfrac{\cfrac{q(y) \vdash q(y)}{q(y) \vdash q(y), p(x)}\ {\scriptstyle \mathsf{w_R}} \quad \cfrac{p(x) \vdash p(x)}{p(x), q(y) \vdash p(x)}\ {\scriptstyle \mathsf{w_L}}}{q(y) \supset p(x), q(y) \vdash p(x)}\ {\scriptstyle \supset_L}}{\forall x.(q(y) \supset p(x)), q(y) \vdash p(x)}\ {\scriptstyle \forall_L}}{\forall x.(q(y) \supset p(x)), q(y) \vdash \forall x.p(x)}\ {\scriptstyle \forall_R}}{\forall x.(q(y) \supset p(x)) \vdash q(y) \supset \forall x.p(x)}\ {\scriptstyle \supset_R}}{\vdash \forall x.(q(y) \supset p(x)) \supset (q(y) \supset \forall x.p(x))}\ {\scriptstyle \supset_R} \quad .
$$

The second tautology proven above is an instance of one of Hilbert axiom schemes: $\forall x.(A \supset B) \supset (A \supset \forall x.B)$, where x is not free in A.

In the next example, please pay special attention to the role played by the provisos of the $\forall_R$ and $\exists_L$ rules. In case more than one quantifier rule is applicable during the proof search, try first to apply a rule which has a proviso, while building a proof bottom-up, i.e., starting from its bottom sequent.

Example 2.2. We prove in LK that $(\forall x.p(x) \supset q(y)) \equiv \exists x.(p(x) \supset q(y))$. We need to prove both implications:

$$
\cfrac{\cfrac{\cfrac{\cfrac{\cfrac{\cfrac{p(x) \vdash p(x)}{p(x) \vdash p(x), q(y)}\ {\scriptstyle \mathsf{w_R}}}{\vdash p(x), p(x) \supset q(y)}\ {\scriptstyle \supset_R}}{\vdash p(x), \exists x.(p(x) \supset q(y))}\ {\scriptstyle \exists_R}}{\vdash \forall x.p(x), \exists x.(p(x) \supset q(y))}\ {\scriptstyle \forall_R} \quad \cfrac{\cfrac{\cfrac{\cfrac{q(y) \vdash q(y)}{p(x), q(y) \vdash q(y)}\ {\scriptstyle \mathsf{w_L}}}{q(y) \vdash p(x) \supset q(y)}\ {\scriptstyle \supset_R}}{q(y) \vdash \exists x.(p(x) \supset q(y))}\ {\scriptstyle \exists_R}}{\vdash \forall x.p(x), \exists x.(p(x) \supset q(y))}}{\forall x.p(x) \supset q(y) \vdash \exists x.(p(x) \supset q(y))}\ {\scriptstyle \supset_L}}{\vdash (\forall x.p(x) \supset q(y)) \supset \exists x.(p(x) \supset q(y))}\ {\scriptstyle \supset_R}
$$

and

$$
\cfrac{\cfrac{\cfrac{\cfrac{\cfrac{\cfrac{\cfrac{p(x) \vdash p(x)}{p(x) \vdash p(x), q(y)}\ {\scriptstyle \mathsf{w_R}} \quad \cfrac{q(y) \vdash q(y)}{q(y), p(x) \vdash q(y)}\ {\scriptstyle \mathsf{w_L}}}{p(x) \supset q(y), p(x) \vdash q(y)}\ {\scriptstyle \supset_L}}{p(x) \supset q(y), \forall x.p(x) \vdash q(y)}\ {\scriptstyle \forall_L}}{p(x) \supset q(y) \vdash \forall x.p(x) \supset q(y)}\ {\scriptstyle \supset_R}}{\exists x.(p(x) \supset q(y)) \vdash \forall x.p(x) \supset q(y)}\ {\scriptstyle \exists_L}}{\vdash \exists x.(p(x) \supset q(y)) \supset (\forall x.p(x) \supset q(y))}\ {\scriptstyle \supset_R} \quad .
$$

To complete the exposition of applications of rules, let's consider the cut rule.

Example 2.3. In LK the formula $\exists x.\forall y.(p(x) \supset p(y))$ can be proved this way:

$$
\cfrac{
  \cfrac{
    \cfrac{
      \cfrac{
        \cfrac{
          \cfrac{
            \cfrac{p(z) \vdash p(z)}{p(z) \vdash p(z), p(y)} \,{}_{\mathsf{W_R}}
          }{\vdash p(z), p(z) \supset p(y)} \,{}_{\supset_R}
        }{\vdash p(z), \forall y.(p(z) \supset p(y))} \,{}_{\forall_R}
      }{\vdash p(z), \exists x.\forall y.(p(x) \supset p(y))} \,{}_{\exists_R}
    }{\vdash \forall z.p(z), \exists x.\forall y.(p(x) \supset p(y))} \,{}_{\forall_R}
  \qquad
  \cfrac{
    \cfrac{
      \cfrac{
        \cfrac{
          \cfrac{
            \cfrac{p(y) \vdash p(y)}{p(x), p(y) \vdash p(y)} \,{}_{\mathsf{W_L}}
          }{p(y) \vdash p(x) \supset p(y)} \,{}_{\supset_R}
        }{\forall z.p(z) \vdash p(x) \supset p(y)} \,{}_{\forall_L}
      }{\forall z.p(z) \vdash \forall y.(p(x) \supset p(y))} \,{}_{\forall_R}
    }{\forall z.p(z) \vdash \exists x.\forall y.(p(x) \supset p(y))} \,{}_{\exists_R}
  }{
    \vdash \exists x.\forall y.(p(x) \supset p(y)), \exists x.\forall y.(p(x) \supset p(y))
  } \,{}_{\text{cut}}
}{\vdash \exists x.\forall y.(p(x) \supset p(y))} \,{}_{\mathsf{C_R}}
$$

The idea behind this proof is to use the cut in order to create two hypotheses, one for each branch the proof forks into. In the right branch we assume $\forall z.p(z)$ and in the left one we assume the contrary, i.e., $\neg\forall z.p(z)$ (note that this is the case when $\forall z.p(z)$ is at the right of the entailment symbol). The contraction rule at the bottom of the proof ensures that each branch is provided with the formula to be proved. Of course, it's easier to prove a theorem when further hypotheses are available (there is more information, in a sense): the cut rule creates such information in pairs of opposite formulae.

One should note that the cut rule is unique in the preceding sense. In fact, all other rules do not create new information. They enjoy the so called *subformula property*, which essentially means that all other rules break formulae into pieces while going up in a proof. In other words, there is no creation of new formulae, only subformulae of available formulae are used (there are some technicalities involved in the $\exists_R$ rule, but we can ignore them for now).

One should also observe that the cut rule is nothing more than a generalised modus ponens, which is the first inference rule ever appeared in logic. Systems in the sequent calculus are usually given with cut rules, because cut rules simplify matters when dealing with semantics and when relating several different systems together, especially those presented in other styles like natural deduction. In fact, one useful exercise is to try to prove that LK is indeed classical logic. No matter which way one chooses, chances are very good that the cut rule will play a major role. Of course, classical logic is a rather well settled matter, but this is not so for other logics, or for extensions of classical logic, which are potentially very interesting for automated deduction and logic programming. In all cases, the cut rule is a key element when trying to relate different viewpoints about the same logic, like for example syntax and semantics.

2.2 Cut Elimination

Gentzen's great achievement has been to show that the cut rule is not necessary in his calculus: we say that it is *admissible*. In other words, the other rules are sufficient for the completeness of the inference system. This is of course good news for automated deduction. In the example above, a logician who understands the formula to be proved can easily come up with the hypothesis $\forall z.p(z)$, but how is a computer supposed to do so? The formula used is not in fact a subformula of the formula to be proved. Since it's the only rule not enjoying the subformula property, we could say that the cut rule concentrates in itself all the 'evil'.

Given its capital importance, we state below Gentzen's theorem. The theorem actually gives us more than just the existence of cut free proofs: we could also transform a proof with cuts into a cut free one by way of a procedure (so, the theorem is constructive). This turns out to be fundamental for functional programming, but we will not talk about that in this paper.

Theorem 2.4. *For every proof in* LK *there exists a proof with the same conclusion in which there is no use of the* cut *rule.*

Example 2.5. By eliminating from the previous example cut rules according to the cut elimination algorithm you find in [1], you should obtain a much simpler proof, probably less intuitive from the semantic viewpoint:

$$
\cfrac{
  \cfrac{
    \cfrac{
      \cfrac{
        \cfrac{
          \cfrac{
            \cfrac{
              \cfrac{
                \cfrac{
                  \cfrac{ p(y) \vdash p(y) }
                       { p(y), p(x) \vdash p(y) } \; {}_{\mathsf{W_L}}
                }{ p(y) \vdash p(x) \supset p(y) } \; {}_{\supset_R}
              }{ p(y) \vdash p(z), p(x) \supset p(y) } \; {}_{\mathsf{W_R}}
            }{ \vdash p(y) \supset p(z), p(x) \supset p(y) } \; {}_{\supset_R}
          }{ \vdash \forall z.(p(y) \supset p(z)), p(x) \supset p(y) } \; {}_{\forall_R}
        }{ \vdash \exists x. \forall y.(p(x) \supset p(y)), p(x) \supset p(y) } \; {}_{\exists_R}
      }{ \vdash \exists x. \forall y.(p(x) \supset p(y)), \forall y.(p(x) \supset p(y)) } \; {}_{\forall_R}
    }{ \vdash \exists x. \forall y.(p(x) \supset p(y)), \exists x. \forall y.(p(x) \supset p(y)) } \; {}_{\exists_R}
  }{ \vdash \exists x. \forall y.(p(x) \supset p(y)) } \; {}_{\mathsf{C_R}}
}{} \;.
$$

We should remark that what happened in the previous example is not very representative of cut and cut elimination, with respect to the size of the proofs. In our example, the cut free proof is smaller than the proof with cuts above. In general, cut free proofs can be immensely bigger than proofs with cuts (there is a hyperexponential factor between them).

There is a possibility of exploiting this situation to our advantage. In fact, as we will also see here, cut free proofs correspond essentially to computations. Since proofs with cuts could prove the same theorems in much shorter ways, one could think of using cuts in order to speed up computations, or in order to make them more manageable when analysing them. This would require using cuts as sort of oracles that could divine the right thing to do to shorten a computation at certain given states. This could work by asking a human, or a very sophisticated artificial intelligence mechanism, to make a guess. We will not be dealing with these aspects in this paper, but one should keep them in mind when assessing the merits of the proof theoretic point of view on logic programming and automated deduction, because they open exciting possibilities.

As a last remark, let us notice that cut elimination is not simply a necessary feature for automated deduction, or in general for all what is related to proof construction: its use is broader. For example, a cut elimination theorem can be used to prove the consistency of a system.

Example 2.6. Prove that LK is consistent. We shall reason by contradiction. Suppose that LK is inconsistent: we can then find two proofs Π_1 and Π_2 for both $\vdash A$ and $\vdash \neg A$. We can then also build the following proof for $\vdash$:

$$
\mathsf{cut} \cfrac{
\cfrac{\Pi_1}{\vdash A}
\qquad
\mathsf{cut} \cfrac{
\cfrac{\Pi_2}{\vdash \neg A}
\qquad
{}_{\neg_L}\cfrac{A \vdash A}{\neg A, A \vdash}
}{A \vdash}
}{\vdash}.
$$

By the cut elimination theorem a proof for $\vdash$ must exist in which the cut rule is not used. But this raises a contradiction, since $\vdash$ is not an axiom, nor is the conclusion of any rule of LK other than cut.

Example 2.7. We can reduce the axiom to atomic form. In fact, every axiom $A \vdash A$ appearing in a proof can be substituted by a proof

$$
\cfrac{\Pi_A}{A \vdash A}
$$

which only uses axioms of the kind $a \vdash a$, where A is a generic formula and a is an atom. To prove this, consider a sequent of the kind $A \vdash A$ and reason by induction on the number of logical connectives appearing in A.

Base Case   If A is an atom then $\Pi_A = A \vdash A$.
Inductive Cases   If $A = B \supset C$ then

$$
\Pi_A = {}_{\supset_R}\cfrac{
{}_{\supset_L}\cfrac{
{}_{W_R}\cfrac{\cfrac{\Pi_B}{B \vdash B}}{B \vdash B, C}
\qquad
{}_{W_L}\cfrac{\cfrac{\Pi_C}{C \vdash C}}{C, B \vdash C}
}{B \supset C, B \vdash C}
}{B \supset C \vdash B \supset C}
$$

All other cases are similar:

$$
{}_{\wedge_R}\cfrac{
{}_{\wedge_{LL}}\cfrac{\cfrac{\Pi_B}{B \vdash B}}{B \wedge C \vdash B}
\qquad
{}_{\wedge_{LR}}\cfrac{\cfrac{\Pi_C}{C \vdash C}}{B \wedge C \vdash C}
}{B \wedge C \vdash B \wedge C},
\qquad
{}_{\vee_L}\cfrac{
{}_{\vee_{RL}}\cfrac{\cfrac{\Pi_B}{B \vdash B}}{B \vdash B \vee C}
\qquad
{}_{\vee_{RR}}\cfrac{\cfrac{\Pi_C}{C \vdash C}}{C \vdash B \vee C}
}{B \vee C \vdash B \vee C},
$$

$$\neg_{\mathsf{L}} \cfrac{\cfrac{\Pi_B}{B \vdash B}}{\neg B, B \vdash} \quad \neg_{\mathsf{R}} \cfrac{}{\neg B \vdash \neg B} , \qquad \forall_{\mathsf{L}} \cfrac{\cfrac{\Pi_B}{B \vdash B}}{\forall x.B \vdash B} \quad \forall_{\mathsf{R}} \cfrac{}{\forall x.B \vdash \forall x.B} , \qquad \exists_{\mathsf{R}} \cfrac{\cfrac{\Pi_B}{B \vdash B}}{B \vdash \exists x.B} \quad \exists_{\mathsf{L}} \cfrac{}{\exists x.B \vdash \exists x.B} .$$

This example vividly illustrates the internal symmetries of system LK. These same symmetries are exploited in the cut elimination procedure, but their use is much more complicated there.

From now on, we will be working with cut free systems, so, with systems where all the rules enjoy the subformula property. Normally, proof theorists deal with the problem of showing a cut elimination theorem for a given logic, so providing the logic programming language designer with a good basis to start with.

As we will see later on, Horn clauses (as well as hereditary Harrop formulas) are usually dealt with as a fragment of intuitionistic logic, rather than classical logic. We do not discuss intuitionistic logic here. We just note that intuitionistic logic is a weaker logic than classical logic, because the famous *tertium non datur* classical logic tautology $A \vee \neg A$ does not hold, together with all its consequences, of course. The reasons for restricting ourselves to intuitionistic logic are technical. For all our purposes it is enough to say that intuitionistic logic is the logic whose theorems are proved by system LK with the restriction that at most one formula always appears at the right of the entailment symbol.

We preferred not to start from intuitionistic logic for two reasons: 1) classical logic is more familiar to most people, and 2) abstract logic programming can be defined also for logics for which the one-formula-at-the-right restriction is not enforced, like linear logic. Sticking to intuitionistic logic allows for a technical simplification in the operational reading of a deductive system, as we will see later. And, of course, intuitionistic logic, although weaker than classical logic, is still more powerful than Horn clauses and hereditary Harrop logics.

3   Abstract Logic Programming

We now informally introduce the main ideas of abstract logic programming by means of an example, and move to a more precise presentation later on.

Consider *clauses* of the following form:

$$\forall \vec{x}.((b_1 \wedge \cdots \wedge b_h) \supset a),$$

where $\vec{x}$ is a sequence of variables, h can be 0, and in this case a clause is a *fact* $\forall \vec{x}.a$. A *logic programming problem* may be defined as the problem of finding a substitution σ such that

$$\mathsf{P} \vdash (a_1 \wedge \cdots \wedge a_k)\sigma$$

is provable in some formal system, where $k > 0$, P is a given collection of clauses and $a_1, \ldots, a_k$ are atoms. P is called the *program*, $(a_1 \wedge \cdots \wedge a_k)$ is the *goal* and σ is the *answer substitution*.

Let us restrict ourselves to provability in LK. Suppose that P is a multiset of clauses which contains the clause

$$\forall \vec{x}.((b_1 \wedge \cdots \wedge b_h) \supset a);$$

consider the goal $(a_1 \wedge \cdots \wedge a_k)$ and suppose that σ is a unifier of a and a_l, for some l such that $1 \leqslant l \leqslant k$. Consider the following derivation Δ, where we suppose that $h > 0$:

$$
\mathsf{\wedge_R} \cfrac{
\mathsf{\wedge_R} \cfrac{
P \vdash a_1\sigma
}{\vdots}
\quad \cdots \quad
\mathsf{\forall_L} \cfrac{
\mathsf{c_L} \cfrac{
\mathsf{\forall_L} \cfrac{
\mathsf{\supset_L} \cfrac{
\mathsf{w_R} \cfrac{
P \vdash (b_1 \wedge \cdots \wedge b_h)\sigma
}{P \vdash (b_1 \wedge \cdots \wedge b_h)\sigma, a_l\sigma}
\quad
\mathsf{w_L} \cfrac{
\mathsf{w_L} \cfrac{
a\sigma \vdash a_l\sigma
}{\vdots}
}{P, a\sigma \vdash a_l\sigma}
}{P, ((b_1 \wedge \cdots \wedge b_h) \supset a)\sigma \vdash a_l\sigma}
}{\vdots}
}{P, \forall \vec{x}.((b_1 \wedge \cdots \wedge b_h) \supset a) \vdash a_l\sigma}
}{P \vdash a_l\sigma}
\quad \cdots \quad
\mathsf{\wedge_R} \cfrac{
P \vdash a_k\sigma
}{\vdots}
}{P \vdash (a_1 \wedge \cdots \wedge a_k)\sigma}.
$$

Δ has one leaf which is an axiom $(a\sigma \vdash a_l\sigma)$; one leaf which stands for the logic programming problem $P \vdash (b_1 \wedge \cdots \wedge b_h)\sigma$ and zero or more leaves $P \vdash a_i\sigma$, for $1 \leqslant i \leqslant k$ and $i \neq l$. In the special case where $h = 0$ we consider the derivation Δ':

$$
\mathsf{\wedge_R} \cfrac{
\mathsf{\wedge_R} \cfrac{
P \vdash a_1\sigma
}{\vdots}
\quad \cdots \quad
\mathsf{\forall_L} \cfrac{
\mathsf{c_L} \cfrac{
\mathsf{\forall_L} \cfrac{
\mathsf{w_L} \cfrac{
\mathsf{w_L} \cfrac{
a\sigma \vdash a_l\sigma
}{\vdots}
}{P, a\sigma \vdash a_l\sigma}
}{\vdots}
}{P, \forall \vec{x}.a \vdash a_l\sigma}
}{P \vdash a_l\sigma}
\quad \cdots \quad
\mathsf{\wedge_R} \cfrac{
P \vdash a_k\sigma
}{\vdots}
}{P \vdash (a_1 \wedge \cdots \wedge a_k)\sigma}.
$$

For both cases we can consider a special inference rule b, which we call *backchain* and which stands for Δ or Δ':

$$
\mathsf{b} \cfrac{
P \vdash a_1\sigma \quad \cdots \quad P \vdash a_{l-1}\sigma \quad P \vdash (b_1 \wedge \cdots \wedge b_h)\sigma \quad P \vdash a_{l+1}\sigma \quad \cdots \quad P \vdash a_k\sigma
}{P \vdash (a_1 \wedge \cdots \wedge a_k)\sigma},
$$

where $P \vdash (b_1 \wedge \cdots \wedge b_h)\sigma$ may be absent if $h = 0$. The rule degenerates to an axiom when $h = 0$ and $k = 1$.

A backchain rule, when read from bottom to top, reduces one logic programming problem to zero or more logic programming problems. Please notice that every application of a backchain rule is associated to a substitution (in the case above it is σ) which allows us to use an axiom leaf. We can consider each such substitution as the answer substitution produced by the particular instance of the b rule. It is not necessarily an mgu! Of course, the 'best' choice might be an mgu, which in the first-order case is unique up to variable renaming. The composition of all answer substitutions gives us the final answer substitution to a particular logic programming problem.

We can look for proofs solving a logic programming problem that are entirely built by instances of b rules. We speak of *proof search space* for a given logic programming problem, and we mean a tree whose nodes are derivations, whose root is the logic programming problem, and such that children nodes are obtained by their fathers by adding an instance of b; every time b is applied, the associated substitution is computed and applied to the whole derivation.

Example 3.1. Consider the logic programming problem $P \vdash p(x)$, where

$$P = \{\ \forall y.(q(y) \wedge r(y) \supset p(y)),$$
$$q(1),$$
$$r(1),$$
$$r(2)\}.$$

The proof search space of proofs for this problem is shown in fig. 2. Every branch corresponds to a possible solution, where the substitution applied to the conclusion is the answer substitution (it is shown explicitly, ϵ is the empty substitution). The left and centre computations are *successful*, because a proof is found at the end; the right computation instead *fails*: there is no proof for the logic programming problem $P \vdash q(2)$.

Infinite computations may be obtained as well, as the following example shows.

Example 3.2. Consider the logic programming problem

$$P \vdash a,$$

where $P = \{a \wedge b \supset a\}$. The search space of proofs for this problem is shown in fig. 3.

So far, we did not define what a backchaining rule is, we only said that the rule transforms one logic programming problem into several ones. This takes care of an obvious intuition about the recursivity of logic programming, but it's not enough. Of course, given a formula to prove and a deductive system, like LK, there are in general several ways of reducing one logic programming problem into several others. The notions we are going to introduce address specifically the problem of choosing which rules to use.

The next, crucial, intuition, is to consider a goal as a set of instructions for organising a computation. For example, the goal $A \wedge B$, to be proven by using program P, tells the interpreter to organise the computation as the search for a

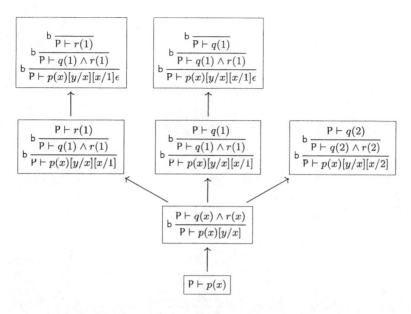

Fig. 2. Proof search space for example 3.1

proof of A and a search for a proof of B, both by using program P. This situation is exactly what the intuitionistic version of the rule $\wedge_R$ describes:

$$\wedge_R \frac{\Gamma \vdash A \quad \Gamma \vdash B}{\Gamma \vdash A \wedge B} \ .$$

However, given a program P and a goal $A \wedge B$, i.e., given a sequent $P \vdash A \wedge B$ to be proved, an interpreter based on LK has more options: it can use left rules by operating over the program P. Clearly, this does not correspond to our intuition as to how a logic programming interpreter should work.

In [7] the authors take a clear course of action:

1) They define what strategy for searching for proofs could correspond to a sensible, operational notion similar to the one adopted by Prolog; this leads to the idea of *uniform proof*, a uniform proof being a proof where the operational, sensible strategy is adopted.

2) They turn their attention to the question: when does uniform provability correspond to (normal, unrestricted) provability? For the languages and deductive systems where the two notions coincide, they speak of *abstract logic programming languages*.

We devote the next two subsections to uniform proofs and abstract logic programming languages.

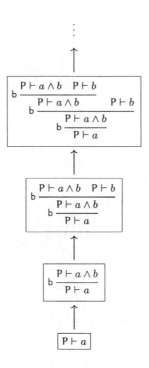

Fig. 3. Proof search space for example 3.2

3.1 Uniform Proofs

Let's now move to a more formal presentation of these ideas. We introduce a new sequent system, where structural rules have been eliminated, and their 'functionality' is included in the structure of sequents.

Sequent system MNPS, from the names of its authors Miller, Nadathur, Pfenning and Scedrov is built on sequents of the kind

$$\Gamma \vdash \Delta,$$

where Γ and Δ are sets of formulae (and not multisets as in system LK). $\top$ and $\bot$ are formulae different from atoms. Axioms and inference rules of MNPS are shown in fig. 4. In MNPS negation is obtained through $\neg A \equiv A \supset \bot$.

The reader should be able to relate the new system to LK, and then to any other presentation of classical logic. The exercise is not entirely trivial, and very useful for understanding the subtleties of the sequent calculus. However, it is not central to this tutorial.

Exercise 3.3. Prove that MNPS and LK are equivalent (consider $\top \equiv A \vee \neg A$ and $\bot \equiv A \wedge \neg A$, for example).

As we said at the end of Section 2, we are mostly interested in intuitionistic logic, i.e., the logic produced by the deductive systems we have seen so far, in

Axioms

$$a, \Gamma \vdash \Delta, a \qquad \bot, \Gamma \vdash \Delta, \bot \qquad \Gamma \vdash \Delta, \top$$

Left Rules

$$\supset_L \frac{\Gamma \vdash \Delta, A \quad B, \Gamma \vdash \Theta}{A \supset B, \Gamma \vdash \Delta, \Theta}$$

$$\wedge_L \frac{A, B, \Gamma \vdash \Delta}{A \wedge B, \Gamma \vdash \Delta}$$

$$\vee_L \frac{A, \Gamma \vdash \Delta \quad B, \Gamma \vdash \Delta}{A \vee B, \Gamma \vdash \Delta}$$

$$\forall_L \frac{A[x/t], \Gamma \vdash \Delta}{\forall x. A, \Gamma \vdash \Delta}$$

$$\exists_L \frac{A, \Gamma \vdash \Delta}{\exists x. A, \Gamma \vdash \Delta}$$

Right Rules

$$\supset_R \frac{A, \Gamma \vdash \Delta, B}{\Gamma \vdash \Delta, A \supset B}$$

$$\wedge_R \frac{\Gamma \vdash \Delta, A \quad \Gamma \vdash \Delta, B}{\Gamma \vdash \Delta, A \wedge B}$$

$$\vee_{RL} \frac{\Gamma \vdash \Delta, A}{\Gamma \vdash \Delta, A \vee B} \qquad \vee_{RR} \frac{\Gamma \vdash \Delta, B}{\Gamma \vdash \Delta, A \vee B}$$

$$\forall_R \frac{\Gamma \vdash \Delta, A}{\Gamma \vdash \Delta, \forall x. A}$$

$$\exists_R \frac{\Gamma \vdash \Delta, A[x/t]}{\Gamma \vdash \Delta, \exists x. A}$$

$$\bot_R \frac{\Gamma \vdash \Delta, \bot}{\Gamma \vdash \Delta, A} \quad \text{where } A \neq \bot$$

where in $\forall_R$ and $\exists_L$ the variable x is not free in the conclusion

Fig. 4. Sequent system MNPS

the special case when every sequent contains at most one formula at the right of the entailment symbol $\vdash$. From the operational viewpoint, this makes immediate sense, because it corresponds to always having one goal to prove.

Actually, the whole truth is more complicated than this, because, as we said, several formulae at the right of entailment just correspond to their disjunction. In the case of a disjunction, the intuitionistic restriction forces an immediate choice about which of the disjuncts the interpreter has to prove (check the rule $\vee_R$, and keep in mind that c_R is not available, neither explicitly nor implicitly). Restricting oneself to the intuitionistic case is the key to a technical simplification in the notion of uniform provability. In cases where this simplification is not desirable, like for linear logic, one can introduce a more refined notion of uniform provability [5,6].

A proof in MNPS, where each sequent has a singleton set as its right-hand side, is called an I-*proof* (intuitionistic proof).

A *uniform proof* is an I-proof in which each occurrence of a sequent whose right-hand side contains a non-atomic formula is the lower sequent of the inference rule that introduces its top-level connective.

In other words: until a goal is not reduced to atomic form, keep reducing it; when a goal is in atomic form, then you can use left inference rules.

Example 3.4. In MNPS, the formula $(a \vee b) \supset (((a \vee b) \supset \bot) \supset \bot)$ admits the following uniform proof:

$$
\cfrac{\cfrac{\cfrac{\cfrac{a \vdash a}{\vee_{RL} \cfrac{}{a \vdash a \vee b}}{\supset_{L} \cfrac{}{a, (a \vee b) \supset \bot \vdash \bot}} \quad a, \bot \vdash \bot}{\quad} \quad \cfrac{\cfrac{b \vdash b}{\vee_{RR} \cfrac{}{b \vdash a \vee b}}{\supset_{L} \cfrac{}{b, (a \vee b) \supset \bot \vdash \bot}} \quad b, \bot \vdash \bot}{\quad}}{\vee_{L} \cfrac{a \vee b, (a \vee b) \supset \bot \vdash \bot}{\supset_{R} \cfrac{a \vee b \vdash ((a \vee b) \supset \bot) \supset \bot}{\supset_{R} \cfrac{}{\vdash (a \vee b) \supset (((a \vee b) \supset \bot) \supset \bot)}}}}{}
$$

We can get back to our informal introduction of backchaining, and we can note that not only does it reduce logic programming problems to further logic programming problems, but it does so by only producing (segments of) uniform proofs.

Now that we have the notion of uniform provability, it is time to check its limits, namely, we should try to answer the question: Is uniform provability enough to prove everything we can prove in unrestricted provability? The answer is, both for classical and intuitionistic logic, no.

Example 3.5. There is no uniform proof for $\neg \forall x.p(x) \supset \exists x.\neg p(x)$. In fact, the following derivation is compulsory, if we require uniformity:

$$
\supset_{L} \cfrac{\cfrac{p(t) \vdash \forall x.p(x) \quad \bot, p(t) \vdash \bot}{\supset_{R} \cfrac{\neg \forall x.p(x), p(t) \vdash \bot}{\exists_{R} \cfrac{\neg \forall x.p(x) \vdash \neg p(t)}{\supset_{R} \cfrac{\neg \forall x.p(x) \vdash \exists x.\neg p(x)}{\vdash \neg \forall x.p(x) \supset \exists x.\neg p(x)}}}}}{}
$$

There is no proof for its left premise, being t different from x, by the proviso of the $\forall_{R}$ rule.

Example 3.6. There is no uniform proof for $(a \vee b) \supset (b \vee a)$. In fact the following derivation is compulsory if we require uniformity:

$$
\supset_{R} \cfrac{\vee_{RR} \cfrac{\vee_{L} \cfrac{a \vdash b \quad b \vdash b}{a \vee b \vdash b}}{a \vee b \vdash b \vee a}}{\vdash (a \vee b) \supset (b \vee a)}
$$

Another derivation exists, similar to this one, where the rule $\vee_{RL}$ is applied instead of $\vee_{RR}$.

Example 3.7. Let A be a generic formula; the formula $A \supset ((A \supset \bot) \supset \bot)$ doesn't always admit a uniform proof in MNPS, it may or may not have one, depending on the formula A. Example 3.4 shows a case where a uniform proof exists, for

$A = a \lor b$. If one considers $A = \forall x.(p(x) \lor q(x))$ instead, there is no way of building a uniform proof. The following derivation does not lead to a uniform proof, because the premise is not provable (and the same happens if we apply $\lor_{RR}$ instead of $\lor_{RL}$):

$$
\cfrac{
  \cfrac{
    \cfrac{
      \cfrac{
        \cfrac{
          \cfrac{\forall x.(p(x) \lor q(x)) \vdash p(x)}{\forall x.(p(x) \lor q(x)) \vdash p(x) \lor q(x)} \lor_{RL}
        }{\forall x.(p(x) \lor q(x)) \vdash \forall x.(p(x) \lor q(x))} \forall_R
        \quad
        \forall x.(p(x) \lor q(x)), \bot \vdash \bot
      }{\forall x.(p(x) \lor q(x)), \forall x.(p(x) \lor q(x)) \supset \bot \vdash \bot} \supset_L
    }{\forall x.(p(x) \lor q(x)) \vdash (\forall x.(p(x) \lor q(x)) \supset \bot) \supset \bot} \supset_R
  }{\vdash \forall x.(p(x) \lor q(x)) \supset ((\forall x.(p(x) \lor q(x)) \supset \bot) \supset \bot)} \supset_R
$$

Choosing to proceed on a different formula on the left of the entailment symbol, while building up the proof, doesn't improve the situation. Modulo applicability of $\lor_{RR}$ instead of $\lor_{RL}$, we get the following two cases:

$$
\cfrac{
  \cfrac{
    \cfrac{
      \cfrac{
        \cfrac{
          \cfrac{p(t) \lor q(t) \vdash p(x)}{p(t) \lor q(t) \vdash p(x) \lor q(x)} \lor_{RL}
        }{p(t) \lor q(t) \vdash \forall x.(p(x) \lor q(x))} \forall_R
        \quad
        p(t) \lor q(t), \bot \vdash \bot
      }{p(t) \lor q(t), \forall x.(p(x) \lor q(x)) \supset \bot \vdash \bot} \supset_L
    }{\forall x.(p(x) \lor q(x)), \forall x.(p(x) \lor q(x)) \supset \bot \vdash \bot} \forall_L
  }{\forall x.(p(x) \lor q(x)) \vdash (\forall x.(p(x) \lor q(x)) \supset \bot) \supset \bot} \supset_R
}{\vdash \forall x.(p(x) \lor q(x)) \supset ((\forall x.(p(x) \lor q(x)) \supset \bot) \supset \bot)} \supset_R
$$

where the premise is not provable, no matter which term t we choose (it cannot be $t = x$, of course), and

$$
\cfrac{
  \cfrac{
    \cfrac{
      \cfrac{
        \cfrac{p(t) \vdash \forall x.(p(x) \lor q(x)) \quad p(t), \bot \vdash \bot}{p(t), \forall x.(p(x) \lor q(x)) \supset \bot \vdash \bot} \supset_L
        \quad
        \cfrac{q(t) \vdash \forall x.(p(x) \lor q(x)) \quad q(t), \bot \vdash \bot}{q(t), \forall x.(p(x) \lor q(x)) \supset \bot \vdash \bot} \supset_L
      }{p(t) \lor q(t), \forall x.(p(x) \lor q(x)) \supset \bot \vdash \bot} \lor_L
    }{\forall x.(p(x) \lor q(x)), \forall x.(p(x) \lor q(x)) \supset \bot \vdash \bot} \forall_L
  }{\forall x.(p(x) \lor q(x)) \vdash (\forall x.(p(x) \lor q(x)) \supset \bot) \supset \bot} \supset_R
}{\vdash \forall x.(p(x) \lor q(x)) \supset ((\forall x.(p(x) \lor q(x)) \supset \bot) \supset \bot)} \supset_R
$$

where again some premises are not provable. This exhausts all possible cases for that specific A.

These examples tell us that the *language* matters as much as the deductive system as far as uniform provability goes.

3.2   Abstract Logic Programming Languages

The question is now for which languages uniform provability and (unrestricted) provability coincide. Several languages of goals and clauses can be defined (not necessarily with formulae in MNPS). Also, we could consider several intuitionistic sequent systems, different from MNPS, for which uniform provability can be contemplated. Our objective now is to define sort of a *completeness* notion which allows us to say, for a particular language, that looking for uniform proofs is equivalent to looking for proofs. Since the search for uniform proofs is computationally motivated, we have a powerful guide to assist us in the syntax-driven definition of logic programming languages.

Consider a language D of *clauses* and a language G of *goals*, both of them subsets of a language for which an entailment relation $\vdash$ is defined; let P be a finite set of clauses, called *program*; we say that $\langle D, G, \vdash \rangle$ is an *abstract logic programming language* if, whenever $P \vdash G$ is provable, then there is a uniform proof for it, for every program P and goal G.

The property of being an abstract logic programming language is usually proved by examining the *permutability relations* between pairs of inference rules in the sequent system which defines $\vdash$. For example, consider the following fragment of derivation:

$$\supset_L \frac{\Gamma \vdash A \qquad \vee_{RL} \dfrac{B, \Gamma \vdash C}{B, \Gamma \vdash C \vee D}}{A \supset B, \Gamma \vdash C \vee D} \ ;$$

it clearly cannot be part of a uniform proof. The problem can be fixed if we *permute* the $\supset_L$ and $\vee_{RL}$ rules, like this:

$$\vee_{RL} \frac{\supset_L \dfrac{\Gamma \vdash A \quad B, \Gamma \vdash C}{A \supset B, \Gamma \vdash C}}{A \supset B, \Gamma \vdash C \vee D} \ .$$

Example 3.8. Consider goals in the set G generated by the grammar:

$$G := A \mid D \supset A \mid G \vee G,$$
$$D := A \mid G \supset A \mid \forall x.D,$$

where A stands for any atom and D is the set of clauses. We want to define in MNPS a backchain rule for the language considered. Remember that a backchain rule has two properties: 1) read from bottom to top, it transforms one logic programming problem into several ones (or zero); 2) it only produces uniform proofs.

The most general case is the following:

$$b\frac{P, D \vdash G\sigma}{P \vdash G_1 \vee \cdots \vee G_h} = (\vee_{RL} \text{ or } \vee_{RR})\frac{\supset_R \frac{\forall_L \frac{\supset_L \frac{P, D \vdash G\sigma \quad P, a'\sigma, D \vdash a}{\forall_L \frac{P, (G \supset a')\sigma, D \vdash a}{\vdots}}}{P, \forall\vec{x}.(G \supset a'), D \vdash a}}{(\vee_{RL} \text{ or } \vee_{RR})\frac{P \vdash D \supset a}{\vdots}}}{P \vdash G_1 \vee \cdots \vee G_h}\ ,$$

where $a'\sigma = a$. Special cases are

$$b\frac{P \vdash G\sigma}{P \vdash G_1 \vee \cdots \vee G_h} = (\vee_{RL} \text{ or } \vee_{RR})\frac{\forall_L \frac{\supset_L \frac{P \vdash G\sigma \quad P, a'\sigma \vdash a}{\forall_L \frac{P, (G \supset a')\sigma \vdash a}{\vdots}}}{P, \forall\vec{x}.(G \supset a') \vdash a}}{(\vee_{RL} \text{ or } \vee_{RR})\frac{\vdots}{P \vdash G_1 \vee \cdots \vee G_h}}$$

and

$$b\frac{}{P \vdash G_1 \vee \cdots \vee G_h} = (\vee_{RL} \text{ or } \vee_{RR})\frac{\supset_R \frac{\forall_L \frac{\forall_L \frac{P, a'\sigma, D \vdash a}{\vdots}}{P, \forall\vec{x}.a', D \vdash a}}{P \vdash D \supset a}}{(\vee_{RL} \text{ or } \vee_{RR})\frac{\vdots}{P \vdash G_1 \vee \cdots \vee G_h}}\ ,$$

or a combination of the last two. Please observe that in the derivations above clauses $\forall\vec{x}.(G \supset a')$ at the left of the entailment can be singled out thanks to the implicit use of contraction (P is a set!).

Exercise 3.9. Consider the following languages of goals and clauses:

$$G := A \mid D \supset A \mid G \vee G,$$
$$D := A \mid G \supset A \mid \forall x.D,$$

where A are atoms. Prove that $\langle D, G, \vdash \rangle$ is an abstract logic programming language, where $\vdash$ is entailment as it is defined by (the intuitionistic fragment of) MNPS.

We now present two examples of well known languages, Horn clauses and hereditary Harrop formulas. It is proved in [7] that both admit uniform proofs and are, therefore, abstract logic programming languages with respect to uniform provability in MNPS.

Horn clauses are given by:

$$G := \top \mid A \mid G \wedge G \mid G \vee G \mid \exists x.G,$$
$$D := A \mid G \supset A \mid D \wedge D \mid \forall x.D.$$

One important limitation of Horn clauses is the inability of dealing with modules. Assume that we want to evaluate a goal, say $G_1 \wedge G_2$, in a complex program composed of several parts, say D_0, D_1 and D_2. Then, an interpreter for Horn clauses, as defined before, will need to evaluate the sequent $D_0, D_1, D_2 \vdash G_1 \wedge G_2$, or, in other words it is necessary for the entire goal to have access to all pieces of the program since the very beginning.

This is often not desirable in practice, since we might know, as programmers, that specific chunks of the program will exclusively be necessary to evaluate distinct goals, for example D_1 for G_1 and D_2 for G_2.

The language of hereditary Harrop formulas extends that of Horn clauses, in particular by providing implication in goals, thus realising a notion of module. Universal quantification in goals creates private variables for these modules.

Hereditary Harrop formulas are given by:

$$G := \top \mid A \mid G \wedge G \mid G \vee G \mid \exists x.G \mid \forall x.G \mid D \supset G,$$
$$D := A \mid G \supset A \mid D \wedge D \mid \forall x.D.$$

In this language we can better structure the information in modules, as the following example shows.

Example 3.10. An interpreter evaluates $D_0 \supset (\forall x.(D_1 \supset G_1) \wedge \forall y.(D_2 \supset G_2))$ by producing the derivation

$$\supset_R \cfrac{\wedge_R \cfrac{\forall_R \cfrac{\supset_R \cfrac{D_0, D_1 \vdash G_1}{D_0 \vdash D_1 \supset G_1}}{D_0 \vdash \forall x.(D_1 \supset G_1)} \qquad \forall_R \cfrac{\supset_R \cfrac{D_0, D_2 \vdash G_2}{D_0 \vdash D_2 \supset G_2}}{D_0 \vdash \forall y.(D_2 \supset G_2)}}{D_0 \vdash \forall x.(D_1 \supset G_1) \wedge \forall y.(D_2 \supset G_2)}}{\vdash D_0 \supset (\forall x.(D_1 \supset G_1) \wedge \forall y.(D_2 \supset G_2))} \quad .$$

The programs D_1 and D_2 are now split in two different branches of the derivation, together with the goals that are supposed to access them. Moreover, the variables x and y are private to the modules D_1 and D_2 and their respective goals G_1 and G_2, thanks to the proviso of the $\forall_R$ rule.

The theory of programming languages teaches us that these abstraction properties are very important. One can go much further than this by moving to higher orders. There we can quantify over functions and relations, thus allowing to define abstract data types in a very convenient way. It is beyond the scope of this tutorial to deal with the higher order case, it should suffice to say that the methodology shown above doesn't need any modification and carries through graciously. The reference paper is [8].

4   Conclusions

In this tutorial we have presented the proof theoretic perspective on logic programming introduced by [7]. We just stuck to the basic notions and we tried to come up with a less formal, and, hopefully, easier to understand exposition than what is already available.

Given its introductory nature, we have been forced to leave out several new exciting, recent developments, especially in connection to linear logic. Indeed, the methodology of uniform proofs and abstract logic programming lends itself naturally to applications in new logics, for new languages. Its grounds in proof theory make it especially useful for logics whose semantics are too complicated, or simply unavailable.

On the other hand, we believe that understanding this relatively new methodology in the old, familiar playground of classical logic is the best way of getting a feeling for it without having to invest too much time in its study.

References

[1] J. Gallier. Constructive logics. Part I: A tutorial on proof systems and typed λ-calculi. *Theoretical Computer Science*, 110:249–339, 1993.

[2] G. Gentzen. Investigations into logical deduction. In M. E. Szabo, editor, *The Collected Papers of Gerhard Gentzen*, pages 68–131. North-Holland, Amsterdam, 1969.

[3] D. Miller. Documentation for lambda prolog. URL:
http://lProlog/docs.htmlhttp://lProlog/docs.html.

[4] D. Miller. Overview of linear logic programming. Accepted as a chapter for a book on linear logic, edited by Thomas Ehrhard, Jean-Yves Girard, Paul Ruet, and Phil Scott. Cambridge University Press. URL:
http://papers/llp.pdfhttp://papers/llp.pdf.

[5] D. Miller. A multiple-conclusion meta-logic. In S. Abramsky, editor, *Ninth Annual IEEE Symp. on Logic in Computer Science*, pages 272–281, Paris, July 1994.

[6] D. Miller. Forum: A multiple-conclusion specification logic. *Theoretical Computer Science*, 165:201–232, 1996.

[7] D. Miller, G. Nadathur, F. Pfenning, and A. Scedrov. Uniform proofs as a foundation for logic programming. *Annals of Pure and Applied Logic*, 51:125–157, 1991.

[8] G. Nadathur and D. Miller. Higher-order Horn clauses. *Journal of the ACM*, 37(4):777–814, 1990.

Objective: In Minimum Context

Salvador Abreu[1] and Daniel Diaz[2]

[1] Universidade de Évora and CENTRIA, Portugal
spa@di.uevora.pt
[2] Université de Paris I and INRIA, France
Daniel.Diaz@univ-paris1.fr

Abstract. The current proposals for the inclusion of modules in the ISO Prolog standard are not very consensual. Since a program-structuring feature is required for a production programming language, several alternatives have been explored over the years.

In this article we recall and expand on the concepts of *Contextual Logic Programming*, a powerful and simple mechanism which addresses the general issue of modularity in Logic Programs. We claim that *unit arguments* are an essential addition to this programming model, illustrate the claim with examples and draw parallels with Object-Oriented programming.

We argue that Contextual Logic Programming is an interesting and effective tool for the development of large-scale programs built upon the Contextual Logic Programming paradigm and argue that contexts with arguments actually provide a powerful, expressive and very convenient means of structuring large applications upon a Prolog basis. We substantiate our claims with examples taken mostly from a "real world" application, Universidade de Évora's Academic Information System, which is currently being developed using the prototype implementation described in this article.

We sketch the most relevant aspects of a new implementation of Contextual Logic Programming, GNU Prolog/CX, focusing on the impact on performance of the features which were added to a regular Prolog system, highlighting the low overhead which is incurred in case these extensions are not used.

Categories: **D.2.2**–Modules and interfaces, **D.1.6**–Logic Programming, **D.1.5**–Object-oriented Programming.
General Terms: Contextual Logic Programming.

1 Introduction and Motivation

The issue of modularity in Logic Programming has long been recognized as an important and significant challenge, having spurred a large number of different proposals, for example Cabeza and Hermenegildo's proposal for Ciao Prolog[6] or, albeit with a cast towards the interaction with meta-programming issues, Hill and Lloyd's Gödel [9]. An extensive and still largely applicable overview of the issue was made by Bugliesi et al. in [5,4]. One problem mentioned in this decade-old work which hasn't yet been satisfactorily resolved is the adoption

C. Palamidessi (Ed.): ICLP 2003, LNCS 2916, pp. 128–147, 2003.

of a consensual model for a program-structuring mechanism applicable to Prolog, which simultaneously satisfies the requirements of large-scale application development while retaining Prolog's succinctness and expressivity: the proposals which impose a module system based on the hitherto-developed approaches stemming from particular implementations invariably bump into details which fail to be consensual such as: whether it should be atom or predicate-based, how the declarations fit into the general scheme of a Prolog program, what knowledge is required on the part of the programmer to effectively use the module system, just to name a few.

This issue is very present in the vendor and developer community, which is still in search of an adequate response to the modularity problem: although most implementations of Prolog provide a module system, these are sometimes subtly dissimilar, a situation which hinders the use of Prolog as a portable application implementation language, for lack of a standard covering the issue.

Some proposals which relate OO and Logic Programming depart significantly from the simple addition of predicate scoping control mechanisms, such is the case for instance in McCabe's Logic and Objects [11] or Moura's LogTalk language [15,14]. One aspect that can be pointed out about these languages, particularly the latter two, is that they require a significant amount of annotations, w.r.t. classical Prolog programs, in order to take advantage of the features they provide.

An approach which takes on the problem of modularity in a simple, close to the spirit of Prolog and yet very powerful way is Contextual Logic Programming(CxLP) [13], for which an early WAM-based implementation design was presented in [10]. Later work by Omicini et al. [16] proposed a more sophisticated approach, called CSM, based on the SICStus Prolog (version 2.1) module system, which tried hard to address the run-time efficiency aspects in a satisfactory way, although with an impact on the language itself. Not being bundled with a "vendor implementation", CxLP never attained a very significant user base.

In this article we present a new implementation of Contextual Logic Programming, for which a prototype was built: GNU Prolog/CX, based on GNU Prolog [8]. A central contribution of this work is its support for the extensive use of unit arguments.

Take a simple example: consider the issue of keeping a dictionary, represented as an incomplete Prolog term, common to a lot of predicates. A regular Prolog program would require all calls to the dictionary predicates to include the dictionary term as one of the arguments. In Contextual Logic Programming a similar effect can be achieved by designating that data structure to be an argument to a unit present in the context, for example:

```
:- unit(dict(ST)).

dict(ST).

lookup(KEY, VALUE) :- ST=[KEY=VALUE|_].
lookup(KEY, VALUE) :- ST=[_|STx], dict(STx) :> lookup(KEY, VALUE).
```

Unit dict(ST) can subsequently be included in a context, allowing for dictionary operations to simply *omit* the dictionary argument, thereby overcoming one of Prolog's most irritating features, which can arguably be considered an obstacle to the language becoming more popular: the proliferation of predicate arguments in anything other than "toy problems," as well as the lack of a language feature tying various clauses or predicates together.

GNU Prolog/CX is presently being used at Universidade de Évora to construct its second-generation integrated information system, a project which was spurred by the University's decision to simultaneously reformulate and adapt to "the Bologna principles" its 42 undergraduate study programmes, all at once, for the academic year 2003/04. This system's regular user base consists of about 8000 students, 600 faculty and 300 staff members. It is undergoing intensive development by a team of three full-time programmers and, at the time of this writing, is actually *ahead of schedule* and is already proving invaluable in assisting with the timeliness and coherence of the academic restructuring process.

The remainder of this article is structured as follows: section 2 presents our revised specification of Contextual Logic Programming. In section 3 the issue of likening Contexts and Objects is explored in some detail, while section 4 discusses some implementation issues, the options we made and their performance impact. Finally, section 5 draws some conclusions and attempts to point at unsolved issues, for further research.

2 Unit Arguments in Contextual Logic Programming

The fundamental contribution w.r.t. the previous proposals dealing with Contextual Logic Programming by Miller [12], Natali, Omicini, Porto and others [5, 7,13] is the extensive use of *unit arguments* or *parameters* as a central feature of contexts. This construct implies looking at the unit specification as a compound term, i.e. one with a main functor and subterms. The subterms are restricted to be named variables, in the unit declaration directive.

Although present in some of the early formalizations of the concept of "units as sets of clauses", parameters haven't been systematically explored in the setting of Contextual Logic Programming; we purport to do so in this article. A unit argument can be thought of as a sort of "unit global" variable, i.e. one which is shared by all clauses defined in the unit, thereby aiming to solve one of Prolog's traditionally most annoying features: the inevitable proliferation of predicate arguments, whenever a global structure is to be passed around. This sort of feature is already present in other approaches to the integration of the LP and OO paradigms, such as McCabe's Logic and Objects[11].

Consider a clause $C = H \leftarrow B$, where H is the clause head and B the body, being defined as:

$$\lambda \vec{v}.\exists \vec{w}.H \leftarrow B \qquad (1)$$

Where $\vec{v}$ is the set of variables which occur in the clause head H. $\vec{w}$ is the set all remaining variables which occur in the clause. We will subsequently omit the explicit existential quantification over $\vec{w}$ when presenting clauses: this is just notational convenience as it should remain, although implicitly.

Clause C is part of predicate p where p is the main functor of H. Predicate p is made up of the (ordered) set of clauses which have p as their head's main functor.

2.1   Unit and Unit Arguments

Arguments (parameters) for a unit u can be thought of as a unit-global substitution σ, which implicitly applies to all clauses in u.

Similarly, a unit u with parameter variables $\overrightarrow{p}$ can be described as a set of clauses, for which all variables in $\overrightarrow{p}$ are implicitly existentially quantified in all clauses in the unit. Taking this into consideration, equation (1) may now be presented as:

$$u \equiv \lambda \overrightarrow{p}.\{\lambda \overrightarrow{v_i}.H_i \leftarrow B_i\} \tag{2}$$

In other words, all clauses are augmented with variables shared with the unit identifier. During execution, these will be implicitly bound to the subterms of the head of the current context corresponding to these variables.

2.2   Context Traversal

When reducing a goal whose main functor is `pred/arity`, a Contextual Logic Programming engine will traverse the *current context* looking for the first unit which includes a definition for this predicate. This process is detailed below, in section 2.4, equation (5).

The predicate under consideration will then have its body execute in a new context, that is the suffix of the original current context which starts with the unit which contains the first definition for the predicate being invoked. This amounts to the "eager" resolution method initially mentioned in the work of Lamma et al. [10]: the new context becomes the *current context* for the selected clause and the initial current context is now designated by the *calling context*.

2.3   Context Operators

Consider that: U is a *unit descriptor*, i.e. a term whose main functor designates a unit name; C is a *context*, i.e. a list of unit descriptors; G is a Prolog goal.

There are two sets of context operators. The first three, which we'll refer to as the *basic set* consists of those which are fundamental to the specification and low-level implementation of GNU Prolog/CX. They are:

- $C :< G$, the *context switch* operation, which attempts to reduce goal G in context C, i.e. totally bypassing the current context.
- $:> C$, the *current context enquiry* operation, which unifies C with the current context.
- $:< C$, the *calling context enquiry* operation, which unifies C with the calling context.

A further set of operations involving contexts are useful in a number of situations, some of which will be addressed later in this article. These operations may be defined using the fundamental set, as follows:

- $U :> G$, the *context extension* operation, which extends the current context with unit U before attempting to reduce goal G, for which see equation (9). This operator is defined as if by the Prolog clause:

    ```
    U :> G :- :> C, [U|C] :< G.
    ```

- $:^\frown G$, the *supercontext* operation, where the suffix of the current context obtained by dropping the topmost unit is used to evaluate G. This behaves as if defined by the Prolog clause:

    ```
    :^ G :- :> [_|C], C :< G.
    ```

- $:\# G$, the *lazy call* operation, essentially the same as introduced in Lamma et al. [10] and so called because the current context doesn't change w.r.t. the calling goal, which behaves as if defined by the Prolog clause:

    ```
    :# G :- :< C, C :< G.
    ```

- $U :: G$, the *guided context traversal* operation, which behaves as if defined by the Prolog clauses:

    ```
    U :: G :- :> C, GC=[U|_], suffixchk(GC, C), GC :< G.
    ```

    Where `suffixchk/2` is a deterministic predicate where `suffixchk(SUFFIX, LIST)` succeeds if `SUFFIX` is a suffix of `LIST`.

One operation that is left out by design is that provided by the *eager call* operator, as per Lamma et al. [10], as it is implicitly used in all goals.

2.4 Operational Semantics

A GNU Prolog/CX computation is denoted by the evaluation of a *goal* in a *context*. Before stating how this process is carried out, a few definitions for a Contextual Logic Program are in order. Let:

- u denote a *unit*, i.e. a term which designates a set of predicates. A unit is said to be:
    - *simple* in which case the term is an atom.
    - *qualified* when the term is compound, i.e. has subterms.
- $\bar{u}$ denote the set of predicate symbols that are defined in unit u.
- $\gamma \equiv u_1.u_2 \cdots u_n$ is called a *context*, and is constructed as a list of units. We shall use the letters γ and δ to denote contexts. In the conditions for some rule, we may specify a context as $\gamma = u.\gamma'$.
- γ/δ is the pair formed by the *current context* and the *calling context*.
- A goal $\gamma/\delta \vdash G$ is read G *in context* γ *with calling context* δ.

- The *empty context*, denoted [] represents the set of predicates accessible from a regular Prolog program. Such predicates will be assumed to be defined in the special unit [] and will have precedence over predicates of the same name defined in other units.[1] These may resort to ISO-Prolog style module qualifiers.

Equipped with these definitions, we may now enumerate the Contextual Logic Programming rules which specify computations and apply to GNU Prolog/CX.

Prolog Goal Expansion

When a particular goal has matching clauses in the special [] unit, the *Prolog goal expansion* rule applies:

$$\frac{\gamma/\delta \vdash (G_1, G_2 \cdots G_n)\theta}{\gamma/\delta \vdash G} \begin{cases} G \in \overline{[]} \\ H \leftarrow G_1, G_2 \cdots G_n \in [] \\ \theta = \mathrm{mgu}(G, H) \end{cases} \tag{3}$$

This rule is similar to goal expansion rule (4) but for one aspect: a candidate clause for the goal was found in the *empty context*, i.e. in the set of regular Prolog clauses. The effect of applying this rule is that the goal gets replaced by the body of the clause, but without the current context being affected at all.

Whenever applicable, this rule *takes precedence over rule (4)*.

The inclusion of a rule such as this one allows for GNU Prolog/CX to easily build upon a regular Prolog implementation, preserving the semantics of all library predicates and, in particular, of meta-predicates such as `setof/3`.

Goal Expansion

When a goal has a definition in the topmost unit in the context, it will be replaced by the body of the matching clause, after unification:

$$\frac{\gamma/\delta \vdash (G_1, G_2 \cdots G_n)\theta}{\gamma/\delta \vdash G} \begin{cases} \gamma = [u, \ldots] \\ G \in \overline{u} \\ H \leftarrow G_1, G_2 \cdots G_n \in u \\ \theta = \mathrm{mgu}(G, H) \end{cases} \tag{4}$$

This rule implies that a goal G invoked in a context γ will be replaced by the body of a clause for that predicate, only if the unit u on top of the current context defines the predicate of G.

The context for each of the subgoals in the body of the clause is identical to that of the calling goal, after head unification has been performed.

Note that whenever this rule applies, the calling context δ is preserved and passed on unchanged to the clause body.

---

[1] This is a small concession to efficiency, in that regular Prolog programs should incur little or no overhead because of the CxLP engine.

Context Traversal

When neither the Prolog Goal Expansion (3) nor the Goal Expansion rule (4) apply, the context will be traversed by re-evaluating the goal in the supercontext, i.e. by dropping the top unit.

$$\frac{\gamma'/\gamma \vdash G}{\gamma/\delta \vdash G} \left\{ \begin{array}{l} \gamma = [u_1, u_2, ...u_n, ...] \\ \gamma' = [u_n, u_{n+1}, ...] \\ \forall i \in \{1 \cdots n - 1\}, G \notin \overline{u_i} \\ G \in \overline{u_n} \end{array} \right. \tag{5}$$

This process locates the first unit u_n which defines the goal's predicate. It then specifies that goal G is to be evaluated using, as *current context*, γ' which is the longest suffix of γ which starts with unit u_n and, as *calling context*, the original current context γ. The previous calling context, δ is ignored.

Context Enquiry

In order to make the context switch operation (8) useful, there needs to be an operation which fetches the current context:

$$\frac{\theta}{\gamma/\delta \vdash \; :> X} \left\{ \theta = \mathrm{mgu}(X, \gamma) \right. \tag{6}$$

This rule recovers the current context γ as a Prolog term and unifies it with term X, so that it may be used elsewhere in the program.

Calling Context Enquiry

This rule recovers the calling context as a Prolog term, to be used elsewhere in the program.

$$\frac{\theta}{\gamma/\delta \vdash \; :< X} \left\{ \theta = \mathrm{mgu}(X, \delta) \right. \tag{7}$$

This is similar to the context enquiry rule (6), except that X is unified with the current clause's calling context δ instead of the current context.

Context Switch

The purpose of this rule is to allow execution of a goal in an arbitrary context, independently of the current context.

$$\frac{\gamma'/\gamma' \vdash G}{\gamma/\delta \vdash \gamma' \; :< G} \tag{8}$$

This rule causes goal G to be executed in context γ' (both current and calling.)

Moreover, we shall present rules for the *Context Extension*, *Super Call*, the *Lazy Call* and *Guided Context Traversal* operations, even though these may be defined using the previously introduced set. We feel that these are sufficiently important in actual use that they warrant a separate discussion.

Context Extension

This rule simply prepends a single qualified unit to the current context before attempting to execute a goal.

$$\frac{\gamma'/\gamma' \vdash G}{\gamma/\delta \vdash u \ :> G} \left\{ \gamma' = [u|\gamma] \right. \tag{9}$$

Goal G will be evaluated in the new context γ', in the roles both of calling context and current context.

Super Call

The context traversal rule (5) stops as soon as the goal expansion rule (4) applies, thereby preventing units lower in the context to be candidates for the goal expansion. Sometimes it may be interesting to programatically allow a goal to be evaluated further down in the context, even though there is already a matching unit for the concerned predicate.

$$\frac{\gamma'/\gamma' \vdash G}{\gamma/\delta \vdash :\hat{} \ G} \left\{ \begin{array}{l} \gamma = [u_1, u_2 \cdots u_n] \\ \gamma' = [u_2 \cdots u_n] \end{array} \right. \tag{10}$$

This rule evaluates G in the supercontext γ' (i.e. the context obtained from the current context γ by dropping the topmost unit). The calling context for G is set identically.

Lazy Call

The *lazy call* operator is intended to behave like a regular goal expansion / context traversal (rules (4) and (5)), except that it starts with the *calling context* instead of the current context.

$$\frac{\delta/\delta \vdash G}{\gamma/\delta \vdash :\# G} \tag{11}$$

This rule evaluates G using the current clause's calling context δ both as the current and the calling contexts.

Guided Context Traversal

Sometimes it is interesting to search the context for a *specific* unit, and trigger goal expansion in the suffix of the context that starts at that point. Such is the purpose of the rule:

$$\frac{\gamma'/\gamma' \vdash G\theta}{\gamma/\delta \vdash u \ :: \ G} \left\{ \begin{array}{l} \gamma = [u_1, ...u_n, ...] \\ \gamma' = [u_n, u_{n+1}, ...] \\ \forall i \in \{1 \cdots n-1\}, \not\exists \ \sigma = \mathrm{mgu}(u, u_i) \\ \theta = \mathrm{mgu}(u, u_n) \end{array} \right. \tag{12}$$

The guided context traversal process locates the first unit u_n in the current context γ which unifies with u. It then specifies that goal G is to be evaluated using, both as *current context* and as *calling context*, γ' which is the longest suffix of γ which starts with unit u_n, after u has unified with u_n. The previous current and calling contexts are ignored. If u doesn't unify with any unit in the context, this rule *fails*.

A slightly abusive (from a formal standpoint) but convenient reading of this rule will treat parameter u specially, so that it either:

- Unifies with u_n, in which case this rule behaves exactly as stated.
- Is the *main functor* of u_n: in this situation, u is not required to unify with u_n, only to match its functor.

This rule will be especially useful for succinctly specifying particular subcontexts, as will be seen in section 3.2. Note that this rule *does not* search for which unit defines a predicate for G: this task is still left to the regular context traversal rule (5), which ought to be applicable to the resulting state.

3   Using Contexts as Objects

The integration of the Object-Oriented and Logic Programming paradigms has long been an active research area since the late 1980's; take for example McCabe's work [11]. The similarities between Contextual Logic Programming and Object-Oriented Programming have been focused several times in the literature; see for instance the work by Monteiro and Porto [13] or Bugliesi [3].

Other than the implementation-centered reports, previous work on Contextual Logic Programming focuses largely on issues such as the policy for context traversal, what the context becomes once a unit satisfying the calling goal is found, what to do when multiple units provide clauses for the same predicate, how to automatically tie several units together or how to provide encapsulation and concealment mechanisms.

To the best of our knowledge, no published work builds on the notion of context arguments and their widespread use, although Miller's initial work [12] mentions the possibility of using module variables. This feature was present as a "hack" in the first C-Prolog based implementation of Contextual Logic Programming but was a little let down, possibly for lack of an adequate formalization and the nonexistence of convincing examples. We propose to alter this situation, by addressing these issues directly.

Instead of viewing a context as an opaque execution attribute, as happens in CSM [16] for instance, we choose to regard it as a first-class entity, i.e. as a Prolog term. Not only is the context accessible from the program, but *it is intended* that it be explicitly manipulated in the course of a program's regular computation. The performance impact of this option will be succinctly analyzed in section 4: at this point we shall concentrate on the possibilities it allows from an expressiveness point of view.

3.1   Terminology

Table 1 establishes some parallels between Contextual Logic Programming (CxLP) and regular OO terminology. The most notable difference between the CxLP and OO paradigms has to do with the concept of *inheritance*: instead of being statically defined, it is completely dynamic for each context (i.e. an "object") defines its own structure and, implicitly, its behaviour wrt. messages.

Table 1. CxLP vs. OO paradigms

OO	CxLP
Class	Context skeleton
Object Instance	Context
Instance Variable	Unit argument
Class member	Unit
Method	Predicate
Message	Goal

A "context skeleton" is a list whose elements are unit designators, i.e. terms of the form FUNCTOR/ARITY where FUNCTOR is an atom and ARITY is an integer. It can be thought of as designating the structure of a specific context.

3.2   Access Methods

One fundamental feature of OO languages is that object elements are only manipulated via accessor methods, take for example the approach taken in Smalltalk, where instance variables are not visible outside the body of instance methods. Similarly and as in our approach the role of instance variable is carried out by unit parameters – which are variables of the underlying Logic Programming system, i.e. they can be either regular or constrained Logic Variables – a programming dialect has been devised which fulfills the same purpose. Consider for example the units:

```
:- unit(person(ID, NAME, BIRTH_DATE)).    :- unit(room(ID, NAME, CAPACITY)).

person(ID, NAME, BIRTH_DATE).             room(ID, NAME, CAPACITY).

id(ID).                                   id(ID).
name(NAME).                               name(NAME).
birth_date(BIRTH_DATE).                   capacity(CAPACITY).
```

Unit person/3 implicitly defines "access" predicates[2] id/1, name/1 and birth_date/1. In practice this allows for such a goal to be evaluated in a context which includes person(...), with the effect that its argument will be unified with the corresponding parameter in the context. The whole of the unit and its actual parameters may be accessed via the person/3 predicate, which unifies its arguments with the unit parameters, in an actual context. Unit room/3 is structured similarly.

Should the context include another unit which specifies arguments (and therefore access predicates) with the *same name*, as in the context C = [person(...), room(...), ...], it would seem complicated to get to unit

---

[2] These "access predicates" can be automatically generated by a preprocessor: take for instance the ISCO compiler, which can produce units for each defined class using this approach.

room/3's definition of id/1, as one would have to contract the context in order to bypass the definition provided by unit person/3. Such is the purpose for which the *Guided Context Traversal* rule (12) was introduced: we can simply evaluate the goal C :< room :: id(RID) in order to unify RID with the first argument of the first occurrence of room/3 in context C, i.e. the room's id.

3.3   Semi-static Inheritance

Sometimes it is important to ensure that one specific unit (say, u1) *specializes* the behaviour specified by another (we'll call it u2). This goal can be achieved "manually" by ensuring that contexts being built adhere to the desired structure, i.e. [u1, u2, ...]. Besides being awkward to enforce, this assumption will easily fail if we extend some context just with u1 before launching a goal.

Previous work by, namely that by Natali and Omicini [16] addressed the issue by including new directives in the unit declaration, which would enforce an explicit inheritance relation, by means of an inherits or is_a operator or the requires directive.

It is our feeling that these approaches are at odds with the nature of the Prolog language, in that they foster abundant annotations which are, essentially, alien to this programming language. To address the issue in a minimalistic way, we propose the following coding conventions, which do not rely on any mechanism other than those which have already been presented.

Consider that, for proper operation, unit registration requires units student and course to sit immediately below it in the context, registration can be coded as follows:

```
:- unit(registration(A, B)).

context([U, student(B), course(A) | CX]) :- :> [U | CX].
```

Subsequently, code wanting to use unit registration should ensure that the context is properly constructed: this is the purpose of the predicate context/1 in unit registration. Notice that it uses the :> operator to extract the current context but also the *unit arguments*, in order to unify its argument with a new term which is the desired context.

Predicate context/1 should then be used as shown in this goal:

```
registration(a, X) :> context(CX), CX :< GOAL.
```

The point is that, with this approach, a unit may specify what other units should be in the context for it to operate properly. It does so with minimal term reconstruction as the final context which the goal is applied to can share much with that provided to the context/1 goal. For this to become a standard dialect of GNU Prolog/CX it is sufficient to define the following operator:

```
U :>> GOAL :- U :> context(CX), CX :< GOAL.
```

Thus, U :>> G effectively becomes a variation on the standard context-extension goal U :> G, one which enforces the semi-static inheritance specified by the unit we're extending the context with.

Nothing prevents context/1 from being nondeterministic, thereby allowing for flexible multiple inheritance behaviors to be implemented.

3.4   Creating and Using Contexts

Consider an example loosely inspired by LDAP: objects ("records") are structured as belonging to classes in a casuistic basis, a single "key value" may be searched for, returning several instances which may be classified as belonging to distinct classes. Consider that we have an *account*, which inherits from **person** but also from other "classes": the *context* will define the structure of the complete instance and can be constructed like this:

```
person(1, 'Dan', 1970-01-01) :>
      login(diaz, foo123) :>
      email('diaz@paris.fr') :> :> C.
```

Which can be read as "unify C with the current context, after performing these extensions". After the completion of this goal, variable C will be bound to a context that is able to provide successful answer substitutions to whatever predicates are defined in the person/3, login/2 and email/1 units: this includes all access predicates, as previously introduced, as well as any other predicates defined in these units.

The term to which C is then bound can later be supplied as the context argument to a context switch operation in which the goal may be one of the access predicates. Thus, we can have the goal:

```
C :< (login(ID, _), person::name(WHO)).
```

which will succeed, binding variable ID to diaz and variable WHO to 'Dan'.

If this coding style is used in a language which provides a mechanism for persistent storage such as ISCO [2] – which presently relies on Contextual Logic Programming both for its specification and its implementation – the binding for C may be stored, retrieved and later re-used. We are presently using this approach as a means of implementing *sessions* in SIIUE's user interface, a very early version of which is described in [1].

3.5   "Virtual Methods"

A useful mechanism provided by OO languages is that of virtual methods: this allows for common behaviour to be coded once and for all in a "superclass," while allowing for subclass-specific methods to influence the outcome of the common (i.e. defined in the superclass) code.

GNU Prolog/CX retains the *lazy call* mechanism to directly address this issue, as was the case in Natali et. al's work, see for example [16]. An alternative form is achieved through a careful organization of contexts in which the pertinent calling context is included as an argument to a particular unit. Note that this approach creates circular structures, but this should not constitute a problem.

3.6   Contexts as Implicit Computations

In a setting related to the ISTO[3] language, consider a unit person(ID, NAME, BIRTH_DATE) which defines the following predicates:

- item/0 which returns, through backtracking, all instances of the person/3 database relation by instantiating unit arguments,
- delete/0 which nondeterministically removes instances of the person/3 database relation, as restricted by the unit arguments,
- insert/0 which inserts new instances into the person/3 database relation, taking the values from the unit argument.

Accessing an "object" specified by a context is always done via one of these predicates, which are to be evaluated in a context which specifies the relation (in this case person/3). Assume that there are also predicates with the same name and one argument, which represents the relevant unit with bound arguments, i.e. item/1, delete/1 and insert/1. An actual implementation of these predicates could rely on the standard Prolog built-ins clause/1, retract/1 and assertz/1 or access an external database, as is done in the ISCO compiler [2].

Consider also that we have the following general-purpose units:

```
:- unit(delete).              :- unit(insert).
item :- delete.               item :- insert.
item(X) :- delete(X).         item(X) :- insert(X).
```

These units can be prepended to the context mentioned above to signify that accessing the item/0 (or item/1) relation will map to one of the other functions: the operation which is to be applied (e.g. query, insert, delete) will then be an integral part of the context, for example:

```
person(ID, NAME, BIRTH) :> (
        read(ID),
        item -> (
            read(NNAME), read(NBIRTH),
            delete :> item,
            person(ID, NNAME, NBIRTH) :> insert :> item ))
```

This code reads a person's ID and, if it already exists, proceeds by reading and replacing the name and birth date in the corresponding tuple.

---

[3] ISTO is a development of ISCO [2], a Prolog-based mediator language which can transparently access several kinds of information sources, namely relational databases. ISTO relies on GNU Prolog/CX as its compiler's target language.

The purpose of using this stylized approach is to present the context as a complete specification for an intended ("latent") computation, leaving it up to the programmer to initiate the process by invoking the item/0 goal.

3.7 Behaviour Extension

Consider the situation where a predicate p/a defined by a context C is to be partly redefined in a unit which requires additional goals to be satisfied. For example, suppose that modifications to relation person/3 are to be logged as tuples for a new dynamic relation log(TIME, ACTION) which is to be built when new tuples for the person/3 relation are inserted or existing ones removed. Since all actions (query, insert, delete) are performed in an identical way, it is sufficient to prefix the context with a unit which redefines the "action" goal (item/1) for the insert and delete units in the intended way. A possible implementation for log is:

```
:- unit(log).
item(X) :- time(T),
           LC = [ insert, log(T, L) ],
           ( delete :: item(X) -> L=delete(X), LC :< item
           ; insert :: item(X) -> L=insert(X), LC :< item
           ; :^ item(X) ).
```

The guided traversal goals will only succeed in case there's a delete or insert unit in the context. Note the explicit construction of the LC context. For example, in order to remove a tuple X, for which the ID is less than 10, from the person/3 relation, we can write:

$$\text{ID \#< 10, person(ID, \_, \_) :> delete :> log :> item(\_).}$$

The inclusion of the log unit in the context has the effect that the removal of each tuple X is accompanied by the insertion of the term log(T, X) into the log/2 relation.

As another example, should we purport to act upon *all* tuples (e.g. as in set programming), it is sufficient to define a new unit all/0 as follows:

```
:- unit(all).
item(X) :- findall(I, :^ item(I), X).
```

Which could then be used to, say, clean up someone's financial past:

```
ID #< 10, debt(ID, _, _) :> delete :> log :> all :> item(_).
```

4 Overview of the Prototype Implementation

In order to experiment programming with contexts we have developed a first prototype inside GNU Prolog [8]. Our main goal was to have a light implementation modifying the current system as little as possible. Due to space restrictions we only give here an overview of this implementation and focus on the most important points only.

4.1   Managing Contexts

A context is simply stored as a Prolog list. Each element being either an atom (unit without arguments) or a compound term whose principal functor is the unit name and arguments are unit arguments. The drawback of this simple approach could be a little overhead when a predicate is called since the current context need to traversed (we can imagine a better data structure than a Prolog list, as done by Omicini et al. [16]). On the other hand, there are several advantages to this choice: the interface with the user code (needed by the context extension and the inquiry operations) is very simple. Also the retrieval of unit arguments is very easy. Indeed, this comes down to geting the first element of the the current context and, from this term, the associated argument. Both operations can be achieved using the built-in predicate arg/3. In fact we have enhanced the WAM with a new instruction cxt_arg_load which acts exactly as arg/3 but faster since it does not include any error checking.

The WAM must also be extended with 2 new registers to maintain the calling context (CK) and the current context (K). Initially, K and CK contain the empty context (i.e. the atom []). We decided to map these registers to 2 WAM temporaries: x(254) for CK and x(255) for K. This simplifies the compiler, reduces the number of new WAM instructions (no new instruction is needed to read/write these registers from/to WAM variables) and makes it possible to benefit from the optimizations performed by the register allocator.

Finally, note that both K and CK should be saved in choice-points and in environments. However, to avoid to penalize code which does not use contexts we do not reserve a cell in environments automatically. Instead, if a context call is needed, the value of K is saved in a permanent variable (y(...) variables in the WAM). For choice-points we also avoid to automatic allocation of an additional cell. Instead, when K or CK must be modified, its current *value* is trailed (to be restored when backtracking occurs). To avoid useless trailings (only one trailing is needed per choice-point) a time-stamp is attached to K and CK and is compared to the time-stamp of the current choice-point to detect whether the involved register has already been trailed. GNU Prolog already provides all necessary mechanisms (time-stamp on choice-points and a value-trail) since they are needed for its finite domain constraint solver.

4.2   The Context Call

The main change concerns a call to a given predicate. While such a call can be resolved statically in a classical Prolog execution, a context call needs to explore the context to resolve the call. Obviously, it is possible to consider all calls as context calls. However we introduced a little optimization: calls to built-in predicates and calls to predicates defined in the same unit are translated into classical WAM calls (which give rise to native jumps). We thus have introduced 2 new instructions: cxt_call(P/N,V) and cxt_execute(P/N,V) where P/N is the predicate to call and V is a variable specifying the context to use. Both instructions first look for a definition for P/N in the global predicate table (containing all built-in predicates and predicates not defined inside a unit). If no global definition is found, the current context is scanned until a definition is found. This process is summarized in figure 1.

```
trail value of K and CK if needed (testing their time-stamp)
K ← V
CK ← K
if there is a definition for P/N in the global table then
    branch to this definition
while K is of the form [E|K'] do    // i.e. K is not empty
    let T be the predicate table associated to <functor/arity> of E
    if there is a definition for P/N in T then
        branch to this definition
    K ← K'
end
error: P/N is an undefined predicate
```

Fig. 1. Context search procedure

4.3   Example of Code Produced

Consider the following unit:

```
:- unit(u1(A,B)).

q :- r, a :> s, t.
p(X) :- X :> q(A,B).
v :- :< C, [a|C] :< w.
```

Here is the compilation of the first clause. Note how the permanent variable y(0) is used to save K, and used to the context call of r/0 and of t/0. It is also used to extend the context with the unit a for the call to s/0.

```
predicate(q/0,3,static,private,user,[
    allocate(1),                    % environment with 1 cell to save K
    get_variable(y(0),255),         % y(1) = K (current context)
    cxt_call(r/0,y(0)),             % call r/0 with context K
    put_list(0),                    % x(0) = [
    unify_atom(a),                  %           a|
    unify_local_value(y(0)),        %             K]
    cxt_call(s/0,x(0)),             % call s/0 with context [a|K]
    put_value(y(0),0),              % x(0) = K
    deallocate,                     % remove environment
    cxt_execute(t/0,x(0))]).        % call t/0 with context K
```

The second clause shows how unit arguments are handled. Recall that cxt_arg_load is equivalent to arg/3. Note that this instruction is used to get the first element of the list (i.e. the current unit) and, from this term, all necessary unit arguments. Here is the WAM code produced:

```
predicate(p/1,5,static,private,user,[
    get_variable(x(3),0),          % x(3) = X
    cxt_arg_load(1,x(255),x(1)),   % x(1) = K (current context)
    cxt_arg_load(1,x(1),x(0)),     % x(0) = A (first unit argument)
    cxt_arg_load(2,x(1),x(1)),     % x(1) = B (second unit argument)
    put_list(2),                   % x(2) = [
    unify_local_value(x(3)),       %             X|
    unify_local_value(x(255)),     %             K]
    cxt_execute(q/2,x(2))]).       % call q/2 with context [X|K]
```

Finally, the last clause recovers the calling context and uses it to create a new context to call w/0. This gives rise to the following code:

```
predicate(v/0,7,static,private,user,[
    put_list(0),              % x(0) = [
    unify_atom(a),            %             a|
    unify_value(x(254)),      %             CK]
    cxt_execute(w/0,x(0))]).  % call w/0 with context [a|CK]
```

4.4   Evaluation of the Overhead

It this section we try to evaluate the overhead of our context implementation (i.e. when no contextual programming facility is used).

For this purpose we have compared the prototype with GNU Prolog on a set of benchmarks. However, since all benchmarks are on a single source file no context calls would be generated, due to the optimizations explained above and thus no penalty could be constated. We have then turned all optimizations off to force the compiler to generate context calls for *all* calls. This means that even recursive predicates (common in benchmarks) and built-in predicates give rise to contextual (i.e. indirect) calls. Table 2 exhibits those results on a set of classical benchmarks. We have also included the GNU Prolog

Table 2. Worst overhead evaluation

Program × 10 iter.	gprolog 1.2.18	contexts no opt.	slowdown factor
boyer	0.610	0.795	1.303
browse	0.744	1.024	1.376
cal	0.093	0.147	1.581
chat_parser	0.161	0.231	1.435
ham	0.538	0.881	1.638
nrev	0.088	0.178	2.023
poly_10	0.043	0.063	1.465
queens	0.532	0.836	1.571
queensn	2.153	3.530	1.640
reducer	0.039	0.049	1.256
sendmore	0.053	0.067	1.264
tak	0.089	0.127	1.427
zebra	0.041	0.053	1.293
pl2wam	4.600	5.800	1.260
average slowdown factor			1.466

pl2wam sub-compiler as it is a more representative example (applied to pl2wam itself). For each benchmark (including pl2wam), the execution time is the total time in seconds needed for 10 iterations. Times are measured on an Pentium4 1.7 Ghz with 512 MBytes of memory running RedHat Linux 7.2. The average slowdown factor is around 1.5 which is very encouraging taking into account the simplicity of the implementation and the lack of optimization (since the few ones implemented were turned off). Finally it is worth noticing that on a real-life application like the pl2wam compiler the slowdown factor is limited to 1.25.

4.5   Evaluation of the Contextual Logic Programming Implementation

In order to evaluate the context implementation, we follow a methodology similar to that of Denti et al. [7]: a goal is evaluated in a context which is made up of a unit which implements the goal predicate, below a variable number of "dummy" units which serve to test the overhead introduced by the context search. We use the exact same program as in [7]; the goal being used is 100,000 executions of: list :> { *dummy* :>} mem([a,b],[e,d,[f,g],h,[b,a]]), in which there are N "dummy" units in the initial context, as per [7]. The results are shown in table 3: these stem from the arithmetic mean of 10 runs on a 1GHz Pentium III running Linux.

Table 3. Varying context depth

N	Time (sec)	perf. loss	CSM perf. loss
0	0.971	0.0%	0.0%
1	0.986	1.5%	10.3%
2	1.004	3.4%	20.6%
5	1.043	7.4%	51.6%
10	1.102	13.5%	n/a
20	1.235	27.2%	n/a
50	1.595	64.3%	n/a
100	2.238	130.5%	n/a

When compared to CSM, the observed relative performance is much better in GNU Prolog/CX: even in CSM's most favorable situation (the modified WAM), there is a 50% performance hit as soon as there are 5 "dummy" units in the context. What this indicates is the effective ability to use *deep contexts* in the present implementation, as the "50% performance degradation" threshold is only reached when the context comprises about 40 dummy units. Incidentally, we observe that both implementations exhibit a performance hit which is linear on the number of dummy units, as expected.

These are a very encouraging results, as GNU Prolog is an arguably more efficient implementation than SICStus Prolog 2.1, on which CSM is based, thereby exacerbating the impact of performance-impairing extensions such as this one.

5   Conclusions and Directions for Future Work

We successfully developed a working prototype of a Contextual Logic Programming implementation on top of GNU Prolog which, while straightforward, has exhibited reasonable efficiency in different benchmarks. One goal of this work was to experiment extensively with the mechanism of unit arguments and explore its possibilities: the applications which have been developed support the claim that this construct is useful in the development of large projects with a Logic Programming language.

Several lines of work are still open and will receive attention in the near future. These include refinements to the language such as predicate concealment, implementation usability developments such as dynamically loadable units and various kinds of optimizations, both in the compiler and in the runtime support system.

References

1. Salvador Abreu. A Logic-based Information System. In Enrico Pontelli and Vitor Santos-Costa, editors, *2nd International Workshop on Practical Aspects of Declarative Languages (PADL'2000)*, volume 1753 of *Lecture Notes in Computer Science*, pages 141–153, Boston, MA, USA, January 2000. Springer-Verlag.
2. Salvador Abreu. Isco: A practical language for heterogeneous information system construction. In *Proceedings of INAP'01*, Tokyo, Japan, October 2001. INAP.
3. M. Bugliesi. A declarative view of inheritance in logic programming. In Krzysztof Apt, editor, *Proceedings of the Joint International Conference and Symposium on Logic Programming*, pages 113–127, Washington, USA, 1992. The MIT Press.
4. Michele Bugliesi, Anna Ciampolini, Evelina Lamma, and Paola Mello. Optimizing modular logic languages. *ACM Computing Surveys (CSUR)*, 30(3es):10, 1998.
5. Michele Bugliesi, Evelina Lamma, and Paola Mello. Modularity in Logic Programming. *Journal of Logic Programming*, 19/20:443–502, 1994.
6. Daniel Cabeza and Manual Hermenegildo. A New Module System for Prolog. In *Proceedings of the International Conference on Computational Logic (CL2000)*, number 1861 in LNAI, pages 131–148. Springer-Verlag, July 2000.
7. Enrico Denti, Evelina Lamma, Paola Mello, Antonio Natali, and Andrea Omicini. Techniques for implementing contexts in Logic Programming. In Evelina Lamma and Paola Mello, editors, *Extensions of Logic Programming*, volume 660 of *LNAI*, pages 339–358. Springer-Verlag, 1993. 3rd International Workshop (ELP'92), 26–28 February 1992, Bologna, Italy, Proceedings.
8. Daniel Diaz and Philippe Codognet. Design and implementation of the gnu prolog system. *Journal of Functional and Logic Programming*, 2001(6), October 2001.
9. Patricia Hill and John Lloyd. *The Goedel Programming Language*. MIT Press, Cambridge, MA, 1994. ISBN 0-262-08229-2.
10. E. Lamma, P. Mello, and A. Natali. The design of an abstract machine for efficient implementation of contexts in logic programming. In Giorgio Levi and Maurizio Martelli, editors, *Proceedings of the Sixth International Conference on Logic Programming*, pages 303–317, Lisbon, 1989. The MIT Press.
11. Francis G. McCabe. *Logic and Objects*. Prentice Hall, 1992.
12. Dale Miller. A logical analysis of modules in logic programming. *The Journal of Logic Programming*, 6(1 and 2):79–108, January/March 1989.
13. Luís Monteiro and António Porto. A Language for Contextual Logic Programming. In K.R. Apt, J.W. de Bakker, and J.J.M.M. Rutten, editors, *Logic Programming Languages: Constraints, Functions and Objects*, pages 115–147. MIT Press, 1993.
14. Paulo Moura. Logtalk web site. http://www.logtalk.org/.

15. Paulo Moura. Logtalk 2.6 Documentation. Technical Report DMI 2000/1, University of Beira Interior, Portugal, 2000.

16. Antonio Natali and Andrea Omicini. Objects with State in Contextual Logic Programming. In Maurice Bruynooghe and Jaan Penjam, editors, *Programming Language Implementation and Logic Programming*, volume 714 of *LNCS*, pages 220–234. Springer-Verlag, 1993. 5th International Symposium (PLILP'93), 25–27 August 1993, Tallinn, Estonia, Proceedings.

Handling Existential Derived Predicates in View Updating

Carles Farré, Ernest Teniente, and Toni Urpí

Universitat Politècnica de Catalunya
Mòdul C6, Jordi Girona 1-3. 08034 –Barcelona
[farre | teniente | urpi]@lsi.upc.es

Abstract. We present a method that deals effectively with existential derived predicates during view updating. Existing methods either consider all instantiations of a given existential variable or request the instantiation directly to the user. Clearly, these approaches are not appropriate since either they are not practical or rely on the user's best guess to assign the most appropriate values. On the contrary, our proposal considers only patterns of the variable instantiations that are relevant to the view update request, rather than taking into account all possible instantiations.

1 Introduction

A deductive database D is a tuple D = (EDB, IDB) where EDB is a set of facts, and IDB=DR∪IC contains a set of deductive rules DR, and a set of integrity constraints IC. The set EDB of facts is called the extensional part while IDB is the intensional part. Deductive database predicates are partitioned into base and derived (view) predicates. Derived predicates are intensionally defined by means of deductive rules and appear only in the IDB.

Consistent view updating is concerned with determining how a request to update a view can be appropriately translated into a set of base fact updates that satisfies both the requested view update and the integrity constraints of the database. Integrity constraints are handled in a consistency-maintaining way. That is, when a constraint is violated, database consistency is restored by considering additional base fact updates. In general, several possible translations exist. Then, one of the obtained translations must be selected and applied to the database.

A complete survey of previous research regarding (consistent) view updating can be found in [MT99]. The methods reviewed therein (like, for instance, [TO95, CST95, Dec96, LT97]) and more recent methods like [MT03] differ in several aspects such as the kind of databases considered, the type of updates they handle, the approach taken or their soundness and completeness results. However, none of them can manage existential derived predicates in an effective way.

An *existential derived predicate* is defined by a deductive rule that contains variables in the body that do not occur in the rule head. When an update of such a view is requested, there will be as many translations as different valid values can be assigned

C. Palamidessi (Ed.): ICLP 2003, LNCS 2916, pp. 148–162, 2003.

to the existential variables. Consider, for instance, the following database with an existential derived predicate P:

$$Q(a, b)$$
$$P(X) \leftarrow Q(X,Y) \wedge R(X,Y,Z)$$

and assume that the insertion of the IDB fact $P(a)$ is requested. Since $Q(a,b)$ is true, such a request can be satisfied by several translations of the form $\{Insert(R(a, b, val_i))\}$, one for each possible value of val_i. Moreover, the request can also be satisfied by translations of the form $\{Insert(Q(a, val_i)), Insert(R(a, val_i, val_j))\}$ for possible values of val_i different to b.

Previous view update methods handle requests that involve existentially derived predicates either by (1) considering all possible instantiations of a given existential variable or (2) requesting the instantiation directly to the user. Option (1) is clearly unpractical and requires considering finite value domains to ensure termination. On the other hand, option (2) relies on the user's best guess to assign the most appropriate values to the variables and thus it may result in dismissing some relevant translations or, even worst, failing to find any translation. In any case, the problem behind the scenes is that those methods have no criterion to determine when two different instantiations are really alternative or they are mere equivalent renamings. Our previous work in [TO95, MT03] also suffers from these drawbacks.

Note that one of the simplest kinds of database views, those that are defined just as projections of single EDB predicates, fall into the category of existential derived predicates.

In this paper we propose a new method to effectively deal with existential derived predicates during consistent view updating. To solve this problem, we propose here to extend our view updating method of [TO95] by adapting a technique that we have developed for query containment checking in [FTU03]. This technique is inspired in to the concept of *canonical databases* found in [LS93, Ull97] for query containment checking and extends it to deal with negated IDB predicates.

As a consequence, the method we propose will introduce during view updating only patterns of the variable instantiations that are *relevant* to the request, rather than the account of all possible instantiations. In this way we do not generate the whole (infinite) set of possible translations that satisfy the view update request but only a (finite) subset of them, the set of *canonical translations*. Each canonical translation defines several transactions, i.e. sets of base facts updates, that applied to the database will satisfy the requested view update. As far as we know, ours is the first method that deals with existential derived predicates in this way and, thus, it overcomes the severe limitations of previous view updating methods.

As a related work, we must mention Kakas and Michael [KM95] who have taken a similar approach for integrating Abductive Logic Programming and Constraint Logic Programming and who have discussed the application of this framework to temporal reasoning and to scheduling. In addition to the contrasts due to the different field of concern, the main drawback of [KM95] is that it is only applicable to restricted classes of logic programs where negated predicates are not considered.

This paper is structured as follows. Sections 2 and 3 review base concepts and terminology. Section 4 presents the main ideas of our method that are later formalized in section 5. Finally, section 6 presents our conclusions.

2 Base Concepts

A *deductive rule* has the form:

$$P(\bar{X}) \leftarrow R_1(\bar{X}_1) \wedge \ldots \wedge R_n(\bar{X}_n) \wedge \neg R_{n+1}(\bar{Y}_1) \wedge \ldots \wedge \neg R_m(\bar{Y}_s)$$

where p and $R_1, \ldots, R_m$ are predicate names. The atom $P(\bar{X})$ is called the *head* of the rule, and $R_1(\bar{X}_1), \ldots, R_n(\bar{X}_n), \neg R_{n+1}(\bar{Y}_1), \ldots, \neg R_m(\bar{Y}_s)$ are the positive and negative *literals* in the body of the rule. The tuples $\bar{X}, \bar{X}_1, \ldots, \bar{X}_n, \bar{Y}_1, \ldots, \bar{Y}_s$ contain *terms*, which are variables or constants. We require that every rule be *safe*, that is, every variable appearing in $\bar{X}, \bar{Y}_1, \ldots, \bar{Y}_s$ must also appear in some $\bar{X}_i$.

A set P of deductive rules is *hierarchical* if there is a partition $P = P_1 \cup \ldots \cup P_n$ such that the following condition hold for i = 1, 2, …, n: if an atom $R(\bar{T})$ occurs positively or negatively in the body of a deductive rule in P_i then the definition of *r* is contained within P_j with j < i. Throughout the paper, we suppose that IDB's are hierarchical and, thus, do not contain recursively-defined predicates.

An *integrity constraint* is a formula that every state of the database is required to satisfy. We deal with constraints in *denial* form and we associate to each integrity constraint an inconsistency predicate Icn, where n is a positive integer, and thus they have the same form as deductive rules:

$$Ic1 \leftarrow R_1(\bar{X}_1) \wedge \ldots \wedge R_n(\bar{X}_n) \wedge \neg R_{n+1}(\bar{Y}_1) \wedge \ldots \wedge \neg R_m(\bar{Y}_s)$$

where $R_1(\bar{X}_1), \ldots, R_n(\bar{X}_n), \neg R_{n+1}(\bar{Y}_1), \ldots, \neg R_m(\bar{Y}_s)$ are the (positive and negative) ordinary literals. We require also every variable appearing in $\bar{Y}_1, \ldots, \bar{Y}_s$, must also appear in some $\bar{X}_i$. An integrity constraint is violated (not satisfied), whenever its body, $R_1(\bar{X}_1) \wedge \ldots \wedge R_n(\bar{X}_n) \wedge \neg R_{n+1}(\bar{Y}_1) \wedge \ldots \wedge \neg R_m(\bar{Y}_s)$, is true on the database.

More general constraints can be transformed into denial form by applying the procedure described in [LT84].

We also assume that the database contains a distinguished derived predicate Ic defined by the n clauses: Ic ← Icn. That is, one rule for each integrity constraint Ici, i=1…n, of the database. Note that Ic will only hold in those states of the database that violate some integrity constraint and that it will not hold for those states that satisfy all constraints.

Throughout the paper, a, b, c,… are constants and 0,1,2 are skolem constants. We extend unification to allow for the possibility of a skolem constant 0 to unify with any term u.

3 The Augmented Database

Our approach is based on a set of rules that define the difference between two consecutive database states. This set of rules together with the original database form the Augmented Database which explicitly defines the insertions and deletions induced by a transaction which consists of a set of updates of the extensional database. As discussed in [TU03], reasoning about these rules will allow to reason jointly about both states involved in the transition and, thus, to reason about the effect of the updates. We shortly review here the terminology of event rules as presented in [Oli91].

The Augmented Database is strongly based on the concept of *event*. For each predicate P in the underlying language of a given deductive database D, a distinguished *insertion event predicate* ιP and a distinguished *deletion event predicate* δP are used to define the precise difference of deducible facts of consecutive states.

If P is a base predicate, ιP and δP facts represent insertions and deletions of base facts, respectively. We call them base event facts. We assume that a transaction T consists of a set of base event facts. If P is a derived predicate, ιP and δP facts represent induced insertions and induced deletions, respectively. If P is an inconsistency predicate, ιP represents a violation of the corresponding integrity constraint.

The definition of ιP and δP depends on the definition of P in D, but is independent of any transaction T and of the extensional part of D. For each derived or inconsistency predicate P, the Augmented Database contains the rules about ιP and δP, called *event rules*, which define exactly the insertions and deletions of facts about P that are induced by some transaction T:

$$\iota P(\bar{X}) \leftarrow P^n(\bar{X}) \wedge \neg P(\bar{X})$$
$$\delta P(\bar{X}) \leftarrow P(\bar{X}) \wedge \neg P^n(\bar{X})$$

where P refers to a predicate evaluated in the old state of the database, P^n refers to the predicate P evaluated in the new state of the database.

The Augmented Database also contains a set of *transition rules* associated to each predicate P which define it in the new state of the database. These transition rules define the new state of predicate P (denoted by P^n) in terms of the old state of the database and the events that occur in the transition between the old and the new state of the database. We illustrate event and transition rules by means of an example.

Example 3.1: Consider the rule $P(X) \leftrightarrow Q(X,Y) \wedge R(X,Y,Z)$. In the new state, this rule has the form rule $P^n(X) \leftrightarrow Q^n(X,Y) \wedge R^n(X,Y,Z)$. Transition rules associated to predicate $P^n(X)$ are the following:

$$P^n(X) \leftarrow Q(X,Y) \wedge \neg\delta Q(X,Y) \wedge R(X,Y) \wedge \neg\delta R(X,Y,Z)$$
$$P^n(X) \leftarrow Q(X,Y) \wedge \neg\delta Q(X,Y) \wedge \iota R(X,Y,Z)$$
$$P^n(X) \leftarrow \iota Q(X,Y) \wedge R(X,Y) \wedge \neg\delta R(X,Y,Z)$$
$$P^n(X) \leftarrow \iota Q(X,Y) \wedge \iota R(X,Y,Z)$$

Intuitively, it is not difficult to see that the first rule states that P(X) will be true in the new state of the database if Q(X,Y) and R(X,Y,Z) were true in the old state and no change of Q(X,Y) and R(X,Y,Z) is given by the transition. In a similar way, the second rule states that P(X) will be true in the new state if Q(X,Y) was true and it has not been deleted and if R(X,Y,Z) has been inserted during the transition. A similar, intuitive, interpretation can be given for the third and fourth rules.

Definition 3.1: Let D = (EDB, IDB) be a deductive database. The *augmented database* associated to D is the tuple A(D) = (EDB, IDB*), where IDB* contains the rules in DR ∪ IC and their associated simplified transition and event rules.

Example 3.2: Given the following database D = (EDB,IDB):

Q(a, b)
$P(X) \leftarrow Q(X,Y) \wedge R(X,Y,Z)$

the corresponding Augmented Database A(D) is the following:

152 C. Farré, E. Teniente, and T. Urpí

Q(a, b)

$P(X) \leftarrow Q(X,Y) \wedge R(X,Y,Z)$

$\iota P(X) \leftarrow Q(X,Y) \wedge \neg\delta Q(X,Y) \wedge \iota R(X,Y,Z) \wedge \neg P(X)$

$\iota P(X) \leftarrow \iota Q(X,Y) \wedge R(X,Y,Z) \wedge \neg\delta R(X,Y,Z) \wedge \neg P(X)$

$\iota P(X) \leftarrow \iota Q(X,Y) \wedge \iota R(X,Y,Z) \wedge \neg P(X)$

$\delta P(X) \leftarrow \delta Q(X,Y) \wedge R(X,Y,Z) \wedge \neg P^n (X)$

where P^n refers to the transition rule shown in ex. 3.1

$\delta P(X) \leftarrow Q(X,Y) \wedge \delta R(X,Y,Z) \wedge \neg P^n (X)$

4 View Updating with Existential Derived Predicates

Our approach to obtain canonical translations is based on the use of Variable Instantiation Patterns (VIPs, for short) to perform the translation of a view update request that involves existential predicates. Integrity constraints are handled in a consistency-maintaining way, i.e. when a constraint is violated it is repaired by considering additional updates.

In general, there exist several possible ways of satisfying a view update request. We aim at generating all minimal translations for a given request. A translation is *minimal* when it does not exist a subset of it which is also a translation. In general, several minimal translations may exist.

4.1 Model-Theoretic Semantics of Reference

We view our method as an extension of SLDNF-resolution [Llo87]. However, there is an important difference between both methods. When applying SLDNF-resolution, the input set of information, the logic program and the goal to attain, is closed, that is, neither new facts nor rules are added on behave of a SLDNF-resolution procedure. Instead, our method enforces the addition of new information, in terms of base events, on behave of the method, if it is considered necessary for assuring the satisfaction of a give update request. This key difference will be reflected on the semantics that founds each method.

The model-theoretic counterpart of the procedural semantics of SLDNF-resolution is Clark's completion [Llo87]. In this way, the soundness and completeness results of SLDNF-resolution are established with respect to the semantics of the completed logic programs taken as a input. In a similar way, we introduce the notion of restricted completion of the augmented database to provide a model-theoretic foundation for our method.

Let $A(D)$ be an augmented database. We define the *restricted completion* of $A(D)$, denoted by $rComp(A(D))$, as the collection of completed definitions [Llo87] of IDB predicates, EDB predicates and derived events in $A(D)$ together with an equality theory. This later one includes a set of axioms stating explicitly the meaning of the built-in predicate = introduced in the completed definitions.

Our restricted completion is practically the same as the Clark's completion of $A(D)$, $Comp(A(D))$, but without including the axioms of the form $\forall \bar{X}(\neg\iota b_i(\bar{X}))$ and $\forall \bar{X}(\neg\delta b_i(\bar{X}))$ for each base event predicate ιb_i and δb_i. Note that atoms like $\iota b_i(\bar{X})$ or $\delta b_i(\bar{X})$ only occur in the body of the insertion and/or deletion of event rules in $A(D)$.

4.2   Update Requests and Translations of an Update Request

An update request is a goal that includes the (positive and negative) base and/or derived updates to achieve. Positive event facts correspond to updates to perform, while negative events correspond to updates that must be prevented. Moreover, the order of the literals in the goal is not relevant since all of them must be satisfied.

Definition 4.1: An *update request* u is a goal containing positive and/or negative base and/or derived event facts.

For instance, the update request to insert the fact $P(a)$ is stated as $u = \leftarrow \iota P(a)$.

The classical approach to deal with (consistent) view updating is aimed to obtain extensional translations, i.e. sets of base fact updates that satisfy the request. On the contrary, the goal of our method is to draw canonical translations. A canonical translation characterizes several extensional ones since it defines a set of possible values of a set of base facts to insert and/or to delete to satisfy the update request.

Definition 4.2: *Extensional Translation.*

Let A(D) be an Augmented Database and let $u = \leftarrow L_1 \wedge \ldots \wedge L_m$ be an update request. An *extensional translation* of u is a set T of ground base events such that:

(1) $Comp(A(D) \cup T) \models \exists (L_1 \wedge \ldots \wedge L_m)$
(2) $Comp(A(D) \cup T) \not\models \iota c$

where $Comp(A(D) \cup T)$ is the Clark's completion of $A(D) \cup T$. Roughly, the first condition states that the update request is a logical consequence of the database updated according to T, while the second condition states that no integrity constraint will be violated since ιc will not be induced. Note that, as usual, we assume that no integrity constraint is violated before the update.

According to the notion of restricted completion given above, T is the set of all ground base events in M such that

(1bis) M is a model of $rComp(A(D)) \cup \{\exists (L_1 \wedge \ldots \wedge L_m)\}$
(2bis) $\iota c \notin M$

Definition 4.3: *Canonical Translation.*

Let A(D) be an Augmented Database and let u be an update request. A *canonical translation* of u consists of two different sets: a set T of base event facts whose arguments may be either constants or skolem constants and a set of inequality constraints that the skolem constants of T must satisfy.

Example 4.1: For example, the two canonical translations that satisfy $\leftarrow \iota P(a)$ in the database of Example 3.2 are:

a) $\{\iota R(a,b,0)\}$ $\qquad\qquad\qquad$ $\varnothing$
b) $\{\iota Q(a,0), \iota R(a,0,1)\}$ $\qquad\quad$ $\{0 \neq b\}$

Each canonical translation characterizes several extensional translations that are obtained by replacing the skolem constants 0 and 1 by values that satisfy the inequality constraints. All possible values that satisfy a constraints determine a different solution. For instance, a possible extensional translation that corresponds to the intensional translation b) is:

$\{\iota Q(a, c), \iota R(a, c, d)\}$

Given a deductive database D where no integrity constraint is violated, its augmented database A(D) and an update request u, our method obtains all minimal canonical translations of u. Different ways to satisfy u correspond to different solutions. If no solution is obtained, it is not possible to satisfy u by changing only the extensional database.

4.3 Obtaining Canonical Translations

Intuitively, we may describe the process we follow to obtain a canonical translation of an update request u by means of a sequence of nodes that we successively reach from the initial extended update request $u \land \neg \iota Ic$. Due to space restrictions, we illustrate our method by means of a simple example without integrity constraints.

Example 4.2: Consider again the augmented database of Example 3.2 and assume that $u = \leftarrow \iota P(a)$ (we show only event rules relevant to the update request):

$$Q(a, b)$$
$$P(X) \leftarrow Q(X,Y) \land R(X,Y,Z)$$

$$\iota P(X) \leftarrow Q(X,Y) \land \neg \delta Q(X,Y) \land \iota R(X,Y,Z) \land \neg P(X)$$
$$\iota P(X) \leftarrow \iota Q(X,Y) \land R(X,Y,Z) \land \neg \delta R(X,Y,Z) \land \neg P(X)$$
$$\iota P(X) \leftarrow \iota Q(X,Y) \land \iota R(X,Y,Z) \land \neg P(X)$$

The steps that lead to the solution a) of Example 4.1 are shown in figure 4.1, while those that lead to the solution b) are shown in figure 4.2. Each row on the figures corresponds to a node that contains the following information (columns):

1. The update request: the literals that must be satisfied. When the goal is [] it means that no literal needs to be satisfied. Here, the initial node contains only the goal $G_0 = \leftarrow \iota P(a)$ since there is no integrity constraint in this example.

2. The conditions to be enforced: the set of conditions that the constructed canonical translation is required to satisfy. Conditions are expressed in denial form and, as integrity constraints, they are violated whenever their body are evaluated as true. Initially, we always have than $F_0 = \varnothing$. Conditions to be enforced will be dynamically included in F when required to guarantee satisfaction of the update request.

3. The canonical translation T under construction. T is initially empty.

4. The conditions to be maintained: the set containing those conditions that are known to be satisfied in the current node and that must remain satisfied until the end of the process. Initial nodes have always this set empty.

5. The account of skolem constants introduced in the current and/or the ancestor nodes. Initially, such a set contains the constants appearing already in IDB^*.

6. The account of inequality constraints that the introduced skolem constants must satisfy for a canonical translation to be an extensional one.

The transition between two consecutive nodes, i.e. between an ancestor node and its successor, is a step that is performed by applying an expansion rule on a selected literal of the ancestor node. The selection of literals in the example of figures 4.1 and 4.2 is arbitrary. The selected literal in each step is underlined. In general, the only necessary criterion for selecting a literal is to avoid picking up a non-ground negative-ordinary or built-in literal. In figures 4.1 and 4.2, the steps are labeled with the name of the expansion rule that is applied. See section 5.2 for a proper formalization of these rules.

	Update request	Conditions to enforce	T	Conditions to mantain	Generated constants	Constants's constraints
	← ιP(a)	∅	∅	∅	∅	∅
1:A1						
	← Q(a,Y) ∧ ¬δQ(a,Y) ∧ ιR(a,Y,Z) ∧ ¬P(a)	∅	∅	∅	∅	∅
2:A1						
	← ¬ δQ(a,b) ∧ ιR(a,b,Z) ∧ ¬P(a)	∅	∅	∅	∅	∅
3:A5						
	← ¬ δQ(a,b) ∧ ιR(a,b,Z)	∅	∅	∅	∅	∅
4:A4						
	← ¬ δQ(a,b)	∅	{ιR(a,b,0) }	∅	{ 0 }	∅
5:A6						
	[]	←δQ(a,b)	{ιR(a,b,0) }	∅	{ 0 }	∅
6:B4						
	[]	∅	{ιR(a,b,0) }	←δQ(a,b)	{ 0 }	∅

Fig. 4.1. Obtaining the solution a) of Example 4.1

The first step unfolds the selected literal, $ιP(a)$, by substituting it with the body of its defining rule. At the second step, the selected literal is $Q(a,Y)$ which holds in the EDB for Y=b. At the third step $¬P(a)$ is selected. Since it fails for the EDB, it can be removed from G.

At the fourth step, the base event literal $ιR(a,b,Z)$ is selected. To get a successful derivation, i.e. to obtain a canonical translation, $ιR(a,b,Z)$ must be true. Hence, the method instantiates Z with a skolem constant 0 and includes the event literal in the canonical translation under construction. The procedure assigns an arbitrary constant to Z, e.g. 0, and includes an inequality constraint $Z≠k$ for each value k that satisfies $R(a,b,k)$. Note that in this case no inequality constraint is required since no fact $R(a,b,k)$ holds in the EDB.

At the fifth step, $¬δQ(a,b)$ is selected. To get success for the derivation $δQ(a,b)$ must not be true on the constructed canonical translation. This is guaranteed by adding ← $δQ(a,b)$ as a condition to be enforced.

Finally, at step 6 the selected literal is the positive EDB literal is $δQ(a,b)$ from the set of conditions to enforce. Since it matches with no event in the canonical translation under construction, the condition ← $δQ(a,b)$ is not violated at the present moment. To guarantee that it will not be violated later on, it is moved from the set of conditions to enforce to the set of conditions to maintain.

The derivation ends successfully since it reaches a node where the goal to attain is [] and the set of conditions to satisfy is empty. In other words, we can be sure that {$ιR(a,b,0)$} is a canonical translation without requiring any constraint about 0.

The steps that lead to the solution b) are illustrated in figure 4.2. The first step unfolds the selected literal, $ιP(a)$, by substituting it with the body of its defining rule. At the second step, the base event literal $\iota Q(a, Y)$ is selected. To get a successful derivation, i.e. to obtain a canonical translation, $\iota Q(a, Y)$ must be true. Hence, the method instantiates Y with a skolem constant 0 and includes the event literal in the canonical translation under construction. The procedure assigns an arbitrary constant to Y, e.g. 0, and includes an inequality constraint $0 \neq k$ for each value k that satisfies $Q(a, Y)$. Since $Q(a,b)$ holds in the EDB the inequality $0 \neq b$ is added to the constants' constraints set.

	Update request	Conditions to enforce	T	Conditions to mantain	Generated constants	Constants's constraints
	← $\iota P(a)$	∅	∅	∅	∅	∅
1:A1						
2:A4	← $\iota Q(a, Y) \wedge \iota R(a, Y, Z)$ $\wedge \neg P(a)$	∅	∅	∅	∅	∅
3:A4	← $\iota R(a, 0, Z) \wedge \neg P(a)$	∅	{ $\iota Q(a, 0)$ }	∅	{ 0 }	{ 0 ? b}
4:A5	← $\neg P(a)$	∅	{ $\iota Q(a, 0)$, $\iota R(a, 0, 1)$}	∅	{ 0, 1 }	{ 0 ? b}
	[]	∅	{ $\iota Q(a, 0)$, $\iota R(a, 0, 1)$}	∅	{ 0, 1 }	{ 0 ? b}

Fig. 4.2. Obtaining the solution b) of Example 4.1

At the third step, the base event literal $\iota R(a, 0, Z)$ is selected. Again, to get a successful derivation, $\iota R(a, 0, Z)$ must be true. Hence, the method instantiates Z with a skolem constant 1 and includes the event literal in the canonical translation under construction. Note that in this case no inequality constraint is required since no fact $R(a, 0, k)$ holds in the EDB.

Finally, at the fourth step $\neg P(a)$ is selected. Since it fails for the EDB, it can be removed from G. The derivation ends successfully since it reaches a node where the goal to attain is [] and the set of conditions to satisfy is empty. In other words, we can be sure that { $\iota Q(a, 0)$, $\iota R(a, 0, 1)$ } is a canonical translation provided that $0 \neq b$.

4.4 Variable Instantiation Patterns

Let us review more accurately how skolem constants were introduced in the derivations that are shown in figures 4.1 and 4.2. Concretely, skolem constants are introduced each time that the A4-expansion rule is applied on a positive base insertion event, as it happens in step 4 in figure 4.1 and in steps 2 and 3 in figure 4.2. In all those cases, the policy to assign skolem constants to variables was to apply the following *Variable Instantiation Pattern*: assign a distinct new skolem constant to each different variable. We refer to this pattern as the *Simple VIP*. Note that application of the Simple VIP is only explicitly manifested in the second derivation, since the one shown in figure 4.1 has just one variable to instantiate in such a way.

The application of the Simple VIP may lead to endless derivations in some cases. To illustrate this point, let us consider the following database D = (∅, IDB*):

R ← Q(X, Y)
S(X) ← Q(X, Y)
Ic ← Q(X,Y) ∧ ¬S(Y)

Note that the EDB is empty. The corresponding relevant event rules are:

ιS(X) ← ιQ(X,Y) ¬S(X)

ιIc ← Q(X,Y) ∧ ¬δQ(X,Y) ∧ δS(Y)
ιIc ← ιQ(X,Y) ∧ ¬ S(Y) ∧ ¬ ιS(Y)
ιIc ← ιQ(X,Y) ∧ δS(Y)

Assume also that in update request is ← ιR ∧ ¬ιIc. If the Simple VIP is applied, then the derivation starting from ← ιR ∧ ¬ιIc never ends. This fact can be roughly explained as follows. In order to satisfy ιR, ιQ(0,1) will be added to the translation. However, such an addition will induce ιS(1) to prevent ιIc. In turn, ιQ(1, 2) will be included in the translation to satisfy ιS(1), according to the application of the Simple VIP. Again, ιQ(1, 2) will make ιIc true if ιS(2) is not induced ... Therefore, the derivation enters in a endless loop that makes it construct the infinite translation {ιQ(0,1), ιQ(1,2), ιQ(2,3), ...}.

However, there is a trivial finite valid translation for ← ιR ∧ ¬ιIc : {ιQ(0,0)}. Consequently, to construct such a translation we need to define a new variable instantiation pattern that is an alternative to the Simple VIP: the *Reusing VIP*. According to the Reusing VIP, each time that the application of the A4-expansion rule requires to instantiate a variable either introduce a new "fresh" skolem constant or reuse one of the constants previously introduced.

The Reusing VIP will be applied whenever a IDB predicate defined as existential derived predicate negatively occurs in the body a deductive rule defining another IDB predicate, as in Ic ← Q(X,Y) ∧ ¬S(Y). Otherwise, the Simple VIP is applicable.

In some cases, independently of the applied VIP, it may happen that the application of our method leads to infinite derivations. This may happen when the database contains some axiom of infinity [BM86].

5 Formalization of Our Method

Let u be an update request on a certain database D, $A(D) = (EDB, IDB^*)$ the augmented database of D and IC a finite set of conditions expressing the integrity constraints of D. If our method performs a successful derivation from $(\leftarrow u\ IC\ \varnothing\ \varnothing\ K\ \varnothing)$ to $([]\ \varnothing\ T\ C\ K'\ R)$, where K is the set of constants appearing in $u \cup IDB^*$, then u is satisfied and $S=(T,R)$ is a canonical translation of u.

The derivations of our method start from a 6-tuple $(G_0\ F_0\ T_0\ C_0\ K_0\ R_0)$ consisting of the goal $G_0 = \leftarrow u$, the initial set of conditions to enforce $F_0 = IC$, the initial set of base events of the canonical translation $T_0 = \varnothing$, the empty set of conditions to maintain $C_0 = \varnothing$, the set K_0 of constant values appearing in $u \cup IDB^*$ and the initial account of inequality constraints that the introduced skolem constants must satisfy $R_0 = \varnothing$.

A successful derivation reaches a 6-tuple $(G_n\ F_n\ T_n\ C_n\ K_n\ R_n) = ([]\ \varnothing\ T\ C\ K'\ R)$, where the empty goal $G_n = []$ means that we have reached the goal G_0 we were looking for. The empty set $F_n = \varnothing$ means that no condition is waiting to be satisfied. $T_n = T$ is the base event part of a canonical translation that satisfies G_0 as well as F_0. $C_n = C$ is a set of conditions recorded along the derivation and that T also satisfies. $K_n = K'$ is the set of constant values appearing in $u \cup IDB^* \cup T$. R is the set of inequality constraints that T must satisfy to certainly be a translation.

On the contrary, if every "fair" derivation starting from $(\leftarrow u\ IC\ \varnothing\ \varnothing\ K\ \varnothing)$ is finite but does not reach $([]\ \varnothing\ T\ C\ K'\ R)$, it will mean that no canonical translation satisfies the goal $G_0 = \leftarrow u$ together with the set of conditions $F_0 = IC$.

5.1 Nodes, Trees, and Derivations

Let u be an update request on a certain database D, $A(D) = (EDB, IDB^*)$ the augmented database of D and IC a finite set of conditions expressing the integrity constraints of D. A *node* is a 6-tuple of the form $(G_i\ F_i\ T_i\ C_i\ K_i\ R_i)$, where G_i is a goal to attain; F_i is a set of conditions to enforce; T_i is a set of base event facts whose arguments may be either constants or skolem constants (i.e. a canonical translation under construction); C_i is a set of conditions that are currently satisfied in T_i and that must be maintained; K_i is the set of constants appearing in $CT = u \cup IDB^*$ and T_i; and R is the set of inequality constraints that the skolem constants in T must satisfy for a canonical translation to lead to a canonical one.

A *tree* is inductively defined as follows:

1. The tree consisting of the single node $(G_0\ F_0\ \varnothing\ \varnothing\ K\ \varnothing)$ is a tree.

2. Let E be a tree, and $(G_n\ F_n\ T_n\ C_n\ K_n\ R_n)$ a leaf node of E such that $G_n \neq []$ or $F_n \neq \varnothing$. Then the tree obtained from E by appending one or more descendant nodes according to an expansion rule applicable to $(G_n\ F_n\ T_n\ C_n\ K_n\ R_n)$ is again a tree.

It may happen that the application of an expansion rule on a leaf node $(G_n\ F_n\ T_n\ C_n\ K_n\ R_n)$ does not obtain any new descendant node to be appended to the tree because some necessary constraint defined on the expansion rule is not satisfied. In such a case, we say that $(G_n\ F_n\ T_n\ C_n\ K_n\ R_n)$ is a *failed* node.

Each branch in a tree is a *derivation* consisting of a (finite or infinite) sequence $(G_0\ F_0\ T_0\ C_0\ K_0\ R_0)$, $(G_1\ F_1\ T_1\ C_1\ K_1\ R_1)$, … of nodes.

A derivation is *finite* if it consists of a finite sequence of nodes; otherwise it is *infinite*. A derivation is *successful* if it is finite and its last (leaf) node has the form $([]\ \varnothing\ T_n\ C_n\ K_n\ R_n)$. That is, both the goal to attain and the set of conditions to satisfy are empty. A derivation is *failed* if it is finite and its last (leaf) node is failed.

A tree is *successful* when at least one of its branches is a successful derivation. A tree is *finitely failed* when each one of its branches is a failed derivation.

5.2 Our Expansion Rules

The eleven *expansion rules* are listed in tables 5.1 and 5.2.

For the sake of notation, if $G_i = \leftarrow L_1 \wedge \ldots \wedge L_{j-1} \wedge L_j \wedge L_{j+1} \wedge \ldots \wedge L_m$ then $G_i \backslash L_j = \leftarrow L_1 \wedge \ldots \wedge L_{j-1} \wedge L_{j+1} \wedge \ldots \wedge L_m$. If $G_i = \leftarrow L_1 \wedge \ldots \wedge L_m$ then $G_i \wedge p(\bar{X}) = \leftarrow L_1 \wedge \ldots \wedge L_m \wedge p(\bar{X})$. In addition, dnf stands for disjunctive normal form.

The application of an expansion rule on a given node $(G_i\ F_i\ T_i\ C_i\ K_i\ R_i)$ may result in none, one or several alternative (branching) descendant nodes depending on the selected literal $P(J_i) = L$. Here, J_i is either the goal G_i or any of the conditions $F_{i,j}$ in F_i. L is selected according to a safe computation rule P [Llo87], which selects negative and built-in literals only when they are fully grounded. To guarantee that such literals are selected sooner or later we require deductive rules and goals to be safe.

Once a literal is selected, some of our expansion rules may be applied. We distinguish two classes of rules: the A-rules and the B-rules. A-rules are those where the selected literal belongs to the goal G_i. Instead, B-rules correspond to those where the selected literal belongs to any of the conditions $F_{i,j}$ in F_i. Inside each class of rules, they are differentiated regarding to the type of the selected literal.

In each expansion rule, the part above the horizontal line presents the node to which the rule is applied. Below the horizontal line is the description of the resulting descendant nodes. Vertical bars separate alternatives corresponding to different descendants. Some rules like A1, B1 and B3 include also an "only if" condition that constraints the circumstances under which the expansion is possible. If such a condition is evaluated false, the node to which the rule is applied becomes a failed node. Once a substitution is applied to the set of inequality constraints (steps A2, A3, A4, B2, B4, B5, B6) it must be guaranteed that it does not induces any contradiction, i.e. no constraint of the type $a \neq a$. Finally, note that two expansion rules, A1 and B1, use the resolution principle as defined in [Llo87].

5.3 Variable Instantiation Patterns

Two different *variable instantiation patterns* are defined, VIPs for shorthand. Each of them determines how the method has to instantiate the base event facts to be added on the translation under construction. The application of a VIP in each case depends on the syntactical properties of the databases and queries considered. The two VIPs are: *Simple VIP* and *Reusing VIP*.

The method uses the *Simple VIP* in the absence of negated literals about IDB predicates defined as existential derived predicates. According to the Simple VIP, each distinct variable is bound to a distinct new skolem constant.

The method uses the *Reusing VIP* in the presence of negated literals about IDB predicates defined as existential derived predicates. According to the Reusing VIP, each distinct variable is bound either to a distinct new skolem constant or to a previously introduced constant.

A variable instantiation procedure from $(\{X_1, X_2, ..., X_n\}\ \theta_0\ K_0)$ to $(\emptyset\ \theta_n\ K_n)$ is a sequence $(\{X_1, X_2, ..., X_n\ \}\ \theta_0\ K_0), (\{X_2, ..., X_n\ \}\ \theta_1\ K_1), ..., (\emptyset\ \theta_n\ K_n)$ such that for each $0 \leq i \leq n$, θ_i is a ground substitution and K_i is a set of constants.

A variable instantiation step performs a transition from $(\bar{X}_i\ \theta_i\ K_i)$ to $(\bar{X}_{i+1}\ \theta_{i+1}\ K_{i+1})$ that instantiates the variable X_{i+1} of $\bar{X}_i$ according to one of the *VIP-rules* defined by the selected *variable instantiation pattern (VIP)*. The application of the appropriate VIP to a given class of queries and databases ensures the completeness of the Method with respect to that class. The formalization of the VIP-rules is given in table 5.3. k_{new} denotes a new skolem constant.

Table 5.1.

A1) $P(G_i) = d(\bar{X})$ is positive atom but it is not a base event:

$$(G_i\ F_i\ T_i\ C_i\ K_i\ R_i)$$

$$\overline{(G_{i+1,1}\ F_i\ T_i\ C_i\ K_i\ R_i\sigma_1)\ |\ \dots\ |\ (G_{i+1,m}\ F_i\ T_i\ C_i\ K_i\ R_i\sigma_m)}$$

only if $m \geq 1$ and each $G_{i+1,j}$ is the resolvent for G_i and some A(D) rule $d(\bar{Y}) \leftarrow M_1 \wedge \dots \wedge M_q$ in EDB∪IDB* with mgu σ_j.

A2) $P(G_i) = \delta b(\bar{X})$ is a positive base event:

$$(G_i\ F_i\ T_i\ C_i\ K_i\ R_i)$$

$$\overline{((G_i\backslash\delta b(\bar{X}))\sigma_1\ F_{i+1,1}\ T_{i+1,1}\ C_{i+1,1}\ K_i\ R_i\sigma_1)\ |\ \dots\ |\ ((G_i\backslash\delta b(\bar{X}))\sigma_m\ F_{i+1,m}\ T_{i+1,j}\ C_{i+1,m}\ K_i\ R_i\sigma_m)}$$

only if $m \geq 1$ and each σ_j is one out of m possible substitutions such that $b(\bar{X})\sigma_j \in$ EDB. $F_{i+1,j} = F_i \cup C_i$, $T_{i+1,j} = T_i \cup \{\delta b(\bar{X})\sigma_j\}$ and $C_{i+1,j} = \varnothing$ if $\delta b(\bar{X})\sigma_j \notin T_i$; otherwise $F_{i+1,j} = F_i$, $T_{i+1,j} = T_i$ and $C_{i+1,j} = C_i$.

A3) $P(G_i) = \iota b(\bar{X})$ is a positive base event:

$$(G_i\ F_i\ T_i\ C_i\ K_i\ R_i)$$

$$\overline{((G_i\backslash\iota b(\bar{X}))\sigma_1\ F_i\ T_i\ C_i\ K_i\ R_i\sigma_1)\ |\ \dots\ |\ ((G_i\backslash\iota b(\bar{X}))\sigma_m\ F_i\ T_i\ C_i\ K_i\ R_i\sigma_m)}$$

only if $m \geq 1$ and each σ_j is one out of m possible substitutions such that $\iota b(\bar{X})\sigma_j \in T_i$

A4) $P(G_i) = \iota b(\bar{X})$ is a positive base event:

$$(G_i\ F_i\ T_i\ C_i\ K_i\ R_i)$$

$$\overline{\begin{array}{l}((G_i\backslash b(\bar{X}))\sigma_1\ F_{i+1,1}\ T_{i+1,1}\ C_{i+1,1}\ K_{i+1,1}\ R_{i+1,1})\ |\ \dots\ |\ ((G_i\backslash b(\bar{X}))\sigma_1\ F_{i+1,1}\ T_{i+1,1}\ C_{i+1,1}\ K_{i+1,1}\ R_{i+1,s})\\ |\ \dots\ |\ ((G_i\backslash b(\bar{X}))\sigma_m\ F_{i+1,m}\ T_{i+1,m}\ C_{i+1,m}\ K_{i+1,m}\ R_{i+1,1})\ |\ \dots\ |\ ((G_i\backslash b(\bar{X}))\sigma_m\ F_{i+1,m}\ T_{i+1,m}\ C_{i+1,m}\\ K_{i+1,m}\ R_{i+1,s})\end{array}}$$

such that $F_{i+1,j} = F_i \cup C_i$, $T_{i+1,j} = T_i \cup \{b(\bar{X})\sigma_j\}$ and $C_{i+1,j} = \varnothing$ if $b(\bar{X})\sigma_j \notin T_i$; otherwise $F_{i+1,j} = F_i$, $T_{i+1,j} = T_i$ and $C_{i+1,j} = C_i$. Each σ_j is one out of m possible distinct ground substitutions, obtained via a variable instantiation procedure from $(vars(\bar{X}), \varnothing, K_i)$ to $(\varnothing, \sigma_j, K_{i+1,j})$ according to the appropriate variable instantiation pattern, that assigns a skolem constant from $K_{i+1,j}$ to each variable in $vars(\bar{X})$. Each $R_{i+1,k}$ is the set of inequalities appearing in a disjunct of the dnf formula that results of negating the answers to $b(\bar{X})$ in EDB∪IDB*.

A5) $P(G_i) = \neg p(\bar{X})$ is a ground negated base or derived predicate:

$$(G_i\ F_i\ T_i\ C_i\ K_i\ R_i)$$

$$\overline{(G_i\backslash\neg p(\bar{X})\ F_i\ T_i\ C_i\ K_i\ R_{i+1,1})\ |\ \dots\ |\ (G_i\backslash\neg p(\bar{X})\ F_i\ T_i\ C_i\ K_i\ R_{i+1,s})}$$

Each $R_{i+1,k}$ is the set of inequalities appearing in a disjunct of the dnf formula that results of negating the answers to $b(\bar{X})$ in EDB∪IDB*.

A6) $P(G_i) = \neg p(\bar{X})$ is a ground negated event or transition literal:

$$(G_i\ F_i\ T_i\ C_i\ K_i\ R_i)$$

$$\overline{(G_i\backslash\neg p(\bar{X})\ F_i\cup\{\leftarrow p(\bar{X})\}\ T_i\ C_i\ K_i\ R_i)}$$

Table 5.2.

B1) $P(F_{i,j}) = d(\bar{X})$ is a positive atom but it is not a base event:

$$\frac{(G_i \; \{F_{i,j}\} \cup F_i \; T_i \; C_i \; K_i \; R_i)}{(G_i \; S \cup F_i \; T_i \; C_i \; K_i \; R_i)}$$

only if $[] \notin S$.
where S is the set of all resolvents S_u for clauses in $EDB \cup IDB^*$ and $F_{i,j}$ on $d(\bar{X})$. S may be empty.

B2) $P(F_{i,j}) = b(\bar{X})$ is a positive EDB atom:

$$\frac{(G_i \; \{F_{i,j}\} \cup F_i \; T_i \; C_i \; K_i \; R_i)}{(G_i \; F_i \; T_i \; C_i \; K_i \; R_{i+1,1}) \mid \ldots \mid (G_i \; F_i \; T_i \; C_i \; K_i \; R_{i+1,s})}$$

Each $R_{i+1,k}$ is the set of inequalities appearing in a disjunct of the dnf formula that results of negating the answers to $b(\bar{X})$ in $EDB \cup IDB^*$.

B3) $P(F_{i,j}) = b(\bar{X})$ is a positive base event:

$$\frac{(G_i \; \{F_{i,j}\} \cup F_i \; T_i \; C_i \; K_i)}{(G_i \; S \cup F_i \; T_i \; C_{i+1} \; K_i)}$$

only if $[] \notin S$.
$C_{i+1} = C_i$ if $\bar{X}$ contains no variables and $b(\bar{X}) \in T_i$; otherwise, $C_{i+1} = C_i \cup \{F_{i,j}\}$
S is the set of all resolvents of clauses in T_i with $F_{i,j}$ on $b(\bar{X})$. S may be empty, meaning that $b(\bar{X})$ cannot be unified with any atom in T_i.

B4) $P(F_{i,j}) = b(\bar{X})$ is a positive base event:

$$\frac{(G_i \; \{F_{i,j}\} \cup F_i \; T_i \; C_i \; K_i \; R_i)}{(G_i \; F_i \; T_i \; C_i \cup \{F_{i,j}\} \; K_i \; R_{i+1,1}) \mid \ldots \mid (G_i \; F_i \; T_i \; C_i \cup \{F_{i,j}\} \; K_i \; R_{i+1,s})}$$

Each $R_{i+1,k}$ is the set of inequalities appearing in a disjunct of the dnf formula that results of negating the mappings of $b(\bar{X})$ in T_i.

B5) $P(F_{i,j}) = \neg p(\bar{X})$ is not an event literal:

$$\frac{(G_i \; \{F_{i,j}\} \cup F_i \; T_i \; C_i \; K_i \; R_i)}{(G_i \; F_i \; T_i \; C_i \; K_i \; R_i \sigma_1) \mid \ldots \mid (G_i \; F_i \; T_i \; C_i \; K_i \; R_i \sigma_m)}$$

Each σ_j is one out of m possible substitutions that satisfy $p(\bar{X})$ in the $EDB \cup IDB^*$.

B6) $P(F_{i,j}) = \neg p(\bar{X})$ is not an event literal:

$$\frac{(G_i \; \{F_{i,j}\} \cup F_i \; T_i \; C_i \; K_i \; R_i)}{(G_i \; \{F_{i,j} \mid \neg p(\bar{X})\} \cup F_i \; T_i \; C_i \; K_i \; R_{i+1,1}) \mid \ldots \mid (G_i \; \{F_{i,j} \mid \neg p(\bar{X})\} \cup F_i \; T_i \; C_i \; K_i \; R_{i+1,s})}$$

Each $R_{i+1,k}$ is the set of inequalities appearing in a disjunct of the dnf formula that results of negating the answers to $b(\bar{X})$ in $EDB \cup IDB^*$.

B7) $P(F_{i,j}) = \neg p(\bar{X})$ is a ground negative event or transition literal:

$$\frac{(G_i \; \{F_{i,j}\} \cup F_i \; T_i \; C_i \; K_i)}{(G_i \cup \{\leftarrow p(\bar{X})\} \; \{F_{i,j} \mid \neg p(\bar{X})\} \cup F_i \; T_i \; C_i \; K_i) \; only \; if \; F_{i,j} \mid \neg p(\bar{X}) \neq [] \mid (G_i \land p(\bar{X}) \; F_i \; T_i \; C_i \; K_i)}$$

Table 5.3. Formalization of the VIP-rules.

VIP-rule for the Simple VIP

S. $\bar{X}_{i+1} = \bar{X}_i \backslash X_{i+1}$, $\theta_{i+1} = \theta_i \cup \{X_{i+1}/k_{new}\}$ and $K_{i+1} = K_i \cup \{k_{new}\}$, where $k_{new} \notin K_i$.

VIP-rules for the Reusing VIP

R1. $\bar{X}_{i+1} = \bar{X}_i \backslash X_{i+1}$, $\theta_{i+1} = \theta_i \cup \{X_{i+1}/k\}$ and $K_{i+1} = K_i$, where $k \in K_i$.

R2. $\bar{X}_{i+1} = \bar{X}_i \backslash X_{i+1}$, $\theta_{i+1} = \theta_i \cup \{X_{i+1}/k_{new}\}$ and $K_{i+1} = K_i \cup \{k_{new}\}$, where $k_{new} \notin K_i$.

6   Conclusions and Further Work

We have presented a new method to effectively deal with existential derived predicates during view updating. Its main contribution is that of obtaining canonical translations instead of extensional ones, which has been the traditional approach followed by the up to date research in the field. A canonical translation characterizes possible values of base fact updates that satisfy an update request; while each characterized set of updates constitutes an extensional translation.

In fact, previous methods that deal with view updating either consider all instantiations of a given existential variable or request the instantiation to the user. Clearly, these approaches are not appropriate since either they are not practical or rely on the user's best guess to assign the most appropriate values. On the contrary, we approach the problem by considering only patterns of the variable instantiations that are relevant to the request rather than taking into account all possible instantiations.

As a further work, we should prove correctness and completeness of our method as well as to determine the classes of databases for which termination is guaranteed.

References

[BM86]   F.Bry, R.Manthey. "Checking Consistency of Database Constraints: a Logical Basis", VLDB, 13–20, 1986.

[CST95]   L.Console, M.L.Sapino, D.Theseider. The Role of Abduction in Database View Updating. *Journal of Intelligent Information Systems),* 4(3): 261–280, 1995.

[Dec96]   H.Decker. An Extension of SLD by Abduction and Integrity Maintenance for View Updating in Deductive Databases. *JICSLP,* 157–169, 1996.

[FTU03]   C. Farré, E. Teniente, T. Urpí. Query Containment With Negated IDB Predicates. To appear in *ADBIS,* 2003.

[KM95]   A. Kakas, A. Michael. Integrating Abductive and Constraint Logic Programming, *Proc. of the 12th ICLP ,* 399–413, Kanagawa (Japan), 1995.

[Llo87]   J.W. Lloyd. *Foundations of Logic Programming,* Springer, 1987.

[LS93]   A. Levy, Y. Sagiv. Queries Independent of Updates. In *Proceedings of the 19th International Conference on Very Large Data Bases (VLDB'93):* 171–181, 1993.

[LT97]   J.Lobo, G.Trajcevski. Minimal and Consistent Evolution in Knowledge Bases. *Journal of Applied Non-Classical Logics,* 7(1-2): 117–146, 1997.

[LT84]   J.W. Lloyd, R.W. Topor. Making Prolog more Expressive. *Journal of Logic Programming,* 1(3): 225–240, 1984.

[MT99]   E. Mayol, E. Teniente. A Survey of Current Methods for Integrity Constraint Maintenance and View Updating. *ER'99 Workshops:* 62-73, LNCS 1727, Springer, 1999.

[MT03]   E. Mayol, E. Teniente. A Review of Integrity Constraint Maintenance and View Updating Techniques. To appear in *Data & Knowledge Engineering,* 2003.

[Oli91]   A. Olivé. Integrity Checking in Deductive Databases, *Proc. of the 17th VLDB Conference,* Barcelona, 513–523, 1991.

[TO95]   E. Teniente, A. Olivé. Updating Knowledge Bases While Maintaining Their Consistency. *VLDB Journal,* 4(2): 193–241, 1995.

[TU03]   E. Teniente, T. Urpí. On the Abductive or Deductive Nature of Database Schema Validation and Update Processing Problems. *TPLP Journal,* 3(3): 287–327, 2003.

[Ull97]   J. D. Ullman. Information Integration Using Logical Views. In *Proceedings of the 6th International Conference on Database Theory (ICDT'97):* 19–40, 1997

Efficient Evaluation of Logic Programs for Querying Data Integration Systems*

Thomas Eiter[1], Michael Fink[1], Gianluigi Greco[2], and Domenico Lembo[3]

[1] Technische Universität Wien, Favoritenstraße 9-11, A-1040 Vienna, Austria
{eiter,michael}@kr.tuwien.ac.at
[2] DEIS University of Calabria, Via Pietro Bucci 41C, I-87036 Rende, Italy
ggreco@si.deis.unical.it
[3] DIS University of Roma "La Sapienza", Via Salaria 113, I-00198 Roma, Italy
lembo@dis.uniroma1.it

Abstract. Many data integration systems provide transparent access to heterogeneous data sources through a unified view of all data in terms of a global schema, which may be equipped with integrity constraints on the data. Since these constraints might be violated by the data retrieved from the sources, methods for handling such a situation are needed. To this end, recent approaches model query answering in data integration systems in terms of nonmonotonic logic programs. However, while the theoretical aspects have been deeply analyzed, there are no real implementations of this approach yet. A problem is that the reasoning tasks modeling query answering are computationally expensive in general, and that a direct evaluation on deductive database systems is infeasible for large data sets. In this paper, we investigate techniques which make user query answering by logic programs effective. We develop pruning and localization methods for the data which need to be processed in a deductive system, and a technique for the recombination of the results on a relational database engine. Experiments indicate the viability of our methods and encourage further research of this approach.

1 Introduction

Data integration is an important problem, given that more and more data are dispersed over many data sources. In a user friendly information system, a data integration system provides transparent access to the data, and relieves the user from the burden of having to identify the relevant data sources for a query, accessing each of them separately, and combining the individual results into the global view of the data.

Informally, a data integration system $\mathcal{I}$ may be viewed as system $\langle \mathcal{G}, \mathcal{S}, \mathcal{M} \rangle$ that consists of a global schema $\mathcal{G}$, which specifies the global (user) elements, a source schema $\mathcal{S}$, which describes the structure of the data sources in the system, and a mapping $\mathcal{M}$, which specifies the relationship between the sources and the global schema. There are basically two approaches for specifying the mapping [14]: the global-as-view (GAV) approach, in which global elements are defined as views over the sources, and the local-as-view (LAV), in which conversely source elements are characterized as views over the

---

* This work has been partially be supported by the European Commission FET Programme Projects IST-2002-33570 INFOMIX and IST-2001-37004 WASP.

C. Palamidessi (Ed.): ICLP 2003, LNCS 2916, pp. 163–177, 2003.

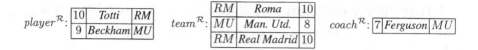

Fig. 1. Global database for the football scenario as retrieved from the sources.

global schema. In this paper, we concentrate on the GAV approach which is in general considered appropriate for practical purposes.

Usually, the global schema also contains information about constraints, Σ, such as key constraints or exclusion dependencies issued on a relational global schema. The mapping $\mathcal{M}$ is often defined by views on the sources $\mathcal{S}$, in a language which amounts to a fragment of stratified Datalog.

Example 1. As a running example, we consider a data integration system $\mathcal{I}_0 = \langle \mathcal{G}_0, \mathcal{S}_0, \mathcal{M}_0 \rangle$, referring to the context of football teams. The global schema $\mathcal{G}_0$ consists of the relation predicates $player(Pcode, Pname, Pteam)$, $team(Tcode, Tname, Tleader)$, and $coach(Ccode, Cname, Cteam)$. The associated constraints Σ_0 are that the keys of $player$, $team$, and $coach$, are the attributes $Pcode$, $Tcode$, and $Ccode$ respectively, and that a coach can neither be a player nor a team leader. The source schema $\mathcal{S}_0$ comprises the relations s_1, s_2, s_3 and s_4. Finally, the mapping $\mathcal{M}_0$ is defined by the datalog program $player(X, Y, Z) \leftarrow s_1(X, Y, Z, W); team(X, Y, Z) \leftarrow s_2(X, Y, Z); team(X, Y, Z) \leftarrow s_3(X, Y, Z); coach(X, Y, Z) \leftarrow s_4(X, Y, Z)$.   □

When the user issues a query q on the global schema, the global database is constructed by data retrieval from the sources and q is answered from it. However, the global database might be inconsistent with the constraints Σ.

Example 2. Suppose the query $q(X) \leftarrow player(X, Y, Z); q(X) \leftarrow team(V, W, X)$ is issued in our scenario, which asks for the codes of all players and team leaders. Assuming that the information content of the sources is given by the database $\mathcal{D}_0 = \{\ s_1(10, Totti, RM, 27),\ s_1(9, Beckham, MU, 28),\ s_2(RM, Roma, 10),\ s_3(MU, Man. Utd., 8)\}$, $s_3(RM, Real Madrid, 10)\}\ s_4(7, Ferguson, MU)\}$, the global database $\mathcal{R}$ in Fig. 1 is constructed from the retrieved data. It violates the key constraint on $team$, witnessed by the facts $team(RM, Roma, 10)$ and $team(RM, Real Madrid, 10)$, which coincide on $Tcode$ but differ on $Tname$.   □

To remedy this problem, the inconsistency might be eliminated by modifying the database and reasoning on the "repaired" database. The suitability of a possible repair depends on the underlying semantic assertions which are adopted for the database; in general, not a single but multiple repairs might be possible [2,6].

Recently, several approaches to formalize repair semantics by using logic programs have been proposed [3,12,4,7,5]. The common basic idea is to encode the constraints Σ of $\mathcal{G}$ into a logic program, Π, using unstratified negation or disjunction, such that the stable models of this program yield the repairs of the global database. Answering a user query, q, then amounts to cautious reasoning over the logic program Π augmented with the query, cast into rules, and the retrieved facts $\mathcal{R}$.

An attractive feature of this approach is that logic programs serve as executable logical specifications of repair, and thus allow to state repair policies in a declarative manner rather than in a procedural way. However, a drawback of this approach is that with current implementations of stable model engines, such as DLV or Smodels, the evaluation of queries over large data sets quickly becomes infeasible because of lacking scalability. This calls for suitable optimization methods that help in speeding up the evaluation of queries expressed as logic programs [5].

In this paper, we face this problem and make the following contributions:

(1) We present a basic formal model of data integration via logic programming specification, which abstracts from several proposals in the literature [3,12,4,7,5]. Results which are obtained on this model may then be inherited by the respective approaches.
(2) We foster a *localization approach* to reduce complexity, in which irrelevant rules are discarded and the retrieved data is decomposed into two parts: facts which will possibly be touched by a repair and facts which for sure will be not. The idea which is at the heart of the approach is to reduce the usage of the nonmonotonic logic program to the essential part for conflict resolution. This requires some technical conditions to be fulfilled in order to make the part "affected" by a repair small (ideally, as much as possible).
(3) We develop *techniques for recombining* the decomposed parts for query answering, which interleave logic programming and relational database engines. This is driven by the fact that database engines are geared towards efficient processing of large data sets, and thus will help to achieve scalability. To this end, we present a marking and query rewriting technique for compiling the reasoning tasks which emerge for user query evaluation into a relational database engine.

In our overall approach, the attractive features of a nonmonotonic logic programming system, such as DLV [15], can be fruitfully combined with the strengths of an efficient relational database engine. The experimental results are encouraging and show that this combination has potential for building advanced data integration systems with reasonable performance. Moreover, our main results might also be transferred to other logic programming systems (e.g., Smodels [17], possibly interfaced by XSB [20], or Dislog [19]).

For space reason, the exposition is necessarily succinct and some details are omitted. They are provided in an extended version of the paper [9].

2   Preliminaries

A *Datalog$^{\vee,\neg}$ rule* r is a clause $a_1 \vee \ldots \vee a_n \leftarrow b_1, \ldots, b_k, \neg b_{k+1}, \ldots, \neg b_{k+m}$ where $n > 0$, $k, m \geq 0$ and $a_1, \ldots, a_n, b_1, \ldots, b_{k+m}$ are function-free atoms. If $n = 1$ then r is a *Datalog$^\neg$ rule*, and if also $k + m = 0$ the rule is simply called *fact*. If $m = 0$ and $n = 1$, then r is a *plain Datalog* (or simply, a Datalog) *rule*. A *Datalog$^{\vee,\neg}$ program* $\mathcal{P}$ is a finite set of Datalog$^{\vee,\neg}$ rules; it is *plain* (or simply, a Datalog program), if all its rules are plain. A Datalog$^\neg$ program with stratified negation is denoted by *Datalog$^{\neg s}$*.

The model theoretic semantics assigns to any program $\mathcal{P}$ the set of its (disjunctive) *stable models* [11,18], denoted by $\mathrm{SM}(\mathcal{P})$. As well-known, $|\mathrm{SM}(\mathcal{P})| = 1$ for any plain and Datalog$^{\neg s}$ program $\mathcal{P}$. Given a set of facts $\mathcal{D}$, the program $\mathcal{P}$ on input $\mathcal{D}$, denoted by $\mathcal{P}[\mathcal{D}]$, is the union $\mathcal{P} \cup \mathcal{D}$. For further background, see [11,18,10].

Databases. We assume a finite, fixed database domain $\mathcal{U}$ whose elements are referenced by constants $c_1, \ldots, c_n$ under the *unique name assumption*, i.e., different constants denote different objects (we will briefly address infinite domains at the end of Section 4). A *relational schema* (or simply *schema*) $\mathcal{RS}$ is a pair $\langle \Psi, \Sigma \rangle$, where:

- Ψ is a set of relation (predicate) symbols, each with an associated arity that indicates the number of its attributes;
- Σ is a set of *integrity constraints* (ICs), i.e., a set of assertions that are intended to be satisfied by each database instance. We assume to deal with universally quantified constraints [1], i.e., first order formulas of the form:

$$\forall(\boldsymbol{x}) \bigwedge_{i=1}^{l} A_i \supset \bigvee_{j=1}^{m} B_j \vee \bigvee_{k=1}^{n} \phi_k, \tag{1}$$

where $l+m > 0, n \geq 0$, $\boldsymbol{x}$ is a list of distinct variables, $A_1, \ldots, A_l$ and $B_1, \ldots, B_m$ are positive literals, and $\phi_1, \ldots, \phi_n$ are built-in literals.

Notice that many classical constraints issued on a relational schema can be expressed in this format, as key and functional dependencies, exclusion dependencies, or inclusion dependencies of the form $\forall(\boldsymbol{x})p_1(\boldsymbol{x}) \supset p_2(\boldsymbol{x})$.

Example 3. In our ongoing example, the global schema $\mathcal{G}_0$ is the database schema $\langle \Psi_0, \Sigma_0 \rangle$, where Ψ_0 consists of the ternary relation symbols *player*, *team*, and *coach*, and Σ_0 can be formally defined as follows (quantifiers are omitted):

$$
\begin{array}{ll}
player(X, Y, Z) \wedge player(X, Y1, Z1) \supset Y{=}Y1; & player(X, Y, Z) \wedge player(X, Y1, Z1) \supset Z{=}Z1 \\
team(X, Y, Z) \wedge team(X, Y1, Z1) \supset Y{=}Y1; & team(X, Y, Z) \wedge team(X, Y1, Z1) \supset Z{=}Z1 \\
coach(X, Y, Z) \wedge coach(X, Y1, Z1) \supset Y{=}Y1; & coach(X, Y, Z) \wedge coach(X, Y1, Z1) \supset Z{=}Z1 \\
coach(X, Y, Z) \wedge player(X1, Y1, Z1) \supset X{\neq}X1; & coach(X, Y, Z) \wedge team(X1, Y1, Z1) \supset X{\neq}Z1
\end{array}
$$

The first three rows encode the key dependencies, whereas the last row models the two constraints stating that a coach cannot be a player or a team leader. □

A *database instance* (or simply *database*) $\mathcal{DB}$ for a schema $\mathcal{RS}$ is a set of facts of the form $r(t)$ where r is a relation of arity n in Ψ and t is an n-tuple of values from $\mathcal{U}$.

Given a constraint $\sigma \in \Sigma$ of the form $\forall(\boldsymbol{x})\alpha(\boldsymbol{x})$, we denote by $ground(\sigma)$ the set of all ground formulas $\alpha(\boldsymbol{x})\theta$, also called *ground constraints*, where θ is any substitution of values in $\mathcal{U}$ for $\boldsymbol{x}$; furthermore, $ground(\Sigma) = \bigcup_{\sigma \in \Sigma} ground(\sigma)$.

Given a schema $\mathcal{RS} = \langle \Psi, \Sigma \rangle$ and a database instance $\mathcal{DB}$ for $\mathcal{RS}$, we say that $\sigma^g \in ground(\Sigma)$ is *satisfied* (resp., *violated*) in $\mathcal{DB}$, if σ^g evaluates to true (resp., false) in $\mathcal{DB}$. Moreover, $\mathcal{DB}$ is *consistent* with Σ if every $\sigma \in ground(\Sigma)$ is satisfied in $\mathcal{DB}$.

3   A Logic Framework for Query Answering

In this section, we present an abstract framework for modeling query answering in data integration systems using logic programs. We first adopt a more formal description of data integration systems, and then we discuss how to compute consistent answers for a user query to a data integration system where the global database, constructed by retrieving data from the sources, might be inconsistent.

3.1 Data Integration Systems

Formally, a data integration system $\mathcal{I}$ is a triple $\langle \mathcal{G}, \mathcal{S}, \mathcal{M} \rangle$, where:

1. $\mathcal{G}$ is the *global schema*. We assume that $\mathcal{G}$ is a relational schema, i.e., $\mathcal{G} = \langle \Psi, \Sigma \rangle$.
2. $\mathcal{S}$ is the *source schema*, constituted by the schemas of the various sources that are part of the data integration system. We assume that $\mathcal{S}$ is a relational schema of the form $\mathcal{S} = \langle \Psi', \emptyset \rangle$, i.e., there are no integrity constraints on the sources.
3. $\mathcal{M}$ is the *mapping between $\mathcal{G}$ and $\mathcal{S}$*. In our framework the mapping is given by the GAV approach, i.e., each global relation in Ψ is associated with a *view*, i.e., a query, over the sources. The language used to express queries in the mapping is Datalog$^{\neg s}$.

We call any database $\mathcal{D}$ for the source schema $\mathcal{S}$ a *source database* for $\mathcal{I}$. Based on $\mathcal{D}$, it is possible to compute database instances for $\mathcal{G}$, called *global databases* for $\mathcal{I}$, according to the mapping specification. Given a data integration system $\mathcal{I} = \langle \mathcal{G}, \mathcal{S}, \mathcal{M} \rangle$ and a source database $\mathcal{D}$, the *retrieved global database*, $ret(\mathcal{I}, \mathcal{D})$, is the global database obtained by evaluating each view of the mapping $\mathcal{M}$ over $\mathcal{D}$.

Notice that $ret(\mathcal{I}, \mathcal{D})$ might be inconsistent with respect to Σ, since data stored in local and autonomous sources need in general not satisfy constraints expressed on the global schema. Hence, in case of constraint violations, we cannot conclude that $ret(\mathcal{I}, \mathcal{D})$ is a "legal" global database for $\mathcal{I}$ [14]. Following a common approach in the literature on inconsistent databases [2,12,6], we define the semantics of a data integration system $\mathcal{I}$ in terms of *repairs* of the database $ret(\mathcal{I}, \mathcal{D})$.

Repairs. Let us first consider the setting of a single database. Let $\mathcal{RS} = \langle \Psi, \Sigma \rangle$ be a relational schema, $\mathcal{DB}$ be a (possibly inconsistent) database for $\mathcal{RS}$, and $\mathcal{R}_1$ and $\mathcal{R}_2$ be two databases for $\mathcal{RS}$ consistent with Σ. We say that $\mathcal{R}_1 \leq_{\mathcal{D}} \mathcal{R}_2$ if $\triangle(\mathcal{R}_1, \mathcal{D}) \subseteq \triangle(\mathcal{R}_2, \mathcal{D})$, where $\triangle(X, Y)$ denotes the symmetric difference between sets X and Y. Furthermore, $\mathcal{R}_1 <_{\mathcal{D}} \mathcal{R}_2$ stands for $\mathcal{R}_1 \leq_{\mathcal{D}} \mathcal{R}_2 \wedge \mathcal{R}_2 \nleq_{\mathcal{D}} \mathcal{R}_1$. Then, a database $\mathcal{R}$ is a *repair for $\mathcal{DB}$ w.r.t. Σ*, if $\mathcal{R}$ is a database for $\mathcal{RS}$ consistent with Σ and $\mathcal{R}$ is *minimal* w.r.t. $\leq_{\mathcal{D}}$, i.e., there exists no database $\mathcal{R}'$ for $\mathcal{RS}$ consistent with Σ such that $\mathcal{R}' <_{\mathcal{D}} \mathcal{R}$. We refer to the set of all such repairs as $rep(\mathcal{DB})$ *wrt* Σ; when clear from the context, Σ is omitted.

Definition 1. Let $\mathcal{I} = \langle \mathcal{G}, \mathcal{S}, \mathcal{M} \rangle$ be a data integration system where $\mathcal{G} = \langle \Psi, \Sigma \rangle$, and let $\mathcal{D}$ be a source database for $\mathcal{I}$. A global database $\mathcal{R}$ for $\mathcal{I}$ is a *repair for $\mathcal{I}$ w.r.t. $\mathcal{D}$* if $\mathcal{R}$ is a repair for $ret(\mathcal{I}, \mathcal{D})$ w.r.t. Σ. The set of all repairs for $\mathcal{I}$ w.r.t. $\mathcal{D}$ is denoted by $rep_{\mathcal{I}}(\mathcal{D})$. □

Intuitively, each repair is obtained by properly adding and deleting facts from $ret_{\mathcal{I}}(\mathcal{D})$ in order to satisfy constraints in Σ, as long as we "minimize" such additions and deletions.

Note that, in the above definition we have considered the mapping $\mathcal{M}$ as *exact*, i.e., we have assumed that the data retrieved from the sources by the views of the mapping are exactly the data that satisfy the global schema, provided suitable repairing operations. Other different assumptions can be adopted on the mapping (e.g., *soundness* or *completeness* assumptions [14]). Roughly speaking, such assumptions impose some restrictions or preferences on the possibility of adding or removing facts from $ret(\mathcal{I}, \mathcal{D})$

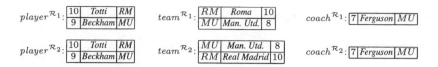

Fig. 2. Repairs of $\mathcal{I}_0$ w.r.t. $\mathcal{D}_0$.

to repair constraint violations, leading to different notions of minimality (see, e.g., [6, 8]).

We stress that dealing only with exact mappings is not an actual limitation for the techniques presented in the paper; in fact, in many practical cases, the computation of the repairs under other mapping assumptions can be modeled by means of a logic program similar to the computation of repairs under the exactness assumption.

Query. A *query* over the global schema $\mathcal{G}$ is a non-recursive Datalog$^\neg$ program that is intended to extract a set of tuples over $\mathcal{U}$; note that in real integration applications, typically a language subsumed by non-recursive Datalog is adopted. For any query $q(X_1, \ldots, X_n)$, we call the set $ans(q, \mathcal{I}, \mathcal{D}) = \{q(c_1, \ldots, c_n) \mid q(c_1, \ldots, c_n) \in SM(q[\mathcal{R}])$ for each $\mathcal{R} \in rep_{\mathcal{I}}(\mathcal{D})\}$ the *consistent answers* to q.

Example 4. Recall that in our scenario, the retrieved global database $ret(\mathcal{I}_0, \mathcal{D}_0)$ shown in Figure 1 violates the key constraint on *team*, witnessed by $team(RM, Roma, 10)$ and $team(RM, Real\,Madrid, 10)$. A repair results by removing exactly one of these facts; hence, $rep_{\mathcal{I}_0}(\mathcal{D}_0) = \{\mathcal{R}_1, \mathcal{R}_2\}$, where $\mathcal{R}_1$ and $\mathcal{R}_2$ are as shown in Figure 2. For the query $q(X) \leftarrow player(X, Y, Z)$; $q(X) \leftarrow team(V, W, X)$, we thus obtain that $ans(q, \mathcal{I}_0, \mathcal{D}_0) = \{q(8), q(9), q(10)\}$. If we consider the query $q'(Y) \leftarrow team(X, Y, Z)$, we have that $ans(q', \mathcal{I}_0, \mathcal{D}_0) = \{q'(Man.\,Utd.)\}$, while considering $q''(X, Z) \leftarrow team(X, Y, Z)$, we have that $ans(q'', \mathcal{I}_0, \mathcal{D}_0) = \{q''(RM, 10), q''(MU, 8)\}$. □

3.2 Logic Programming for Consistent Query Answering

We now describe a generic logic programming framework for computing consistent answers to queries posed to a data integration system in which inconsistency possibly arises.

According to several proposals in the literature [13,4,7,5], we provide answers to user queries by encoding the mapping assertions in $\mathcal{M}$ and the constraints in Σ in a Datalog program enriched with unstratified negation or disjunction, in such a way that the stable models of this program map to the repairs of the retrieved global database.

Definition 2. Let $\mathcal{I} = \langle \mathcal{G}, \mathcal{S}, \mathcal{M} \rangle$ be a data integration system where $\mathcal{G} = \langle \Psi, \Sigma \rangle$, $\mathcal{D}$ is a source database for $\mathcal{I}$, and q is a non-recursive Datalog$^\neg$ query over $\mathcal{G}$. Then, a *logic specification for querying* $\mathcal{I}$ is a Datalog$^{\vee, \neg}$ program $\Pi_{\mathcal{I}}(q) = \Pi_{\mathcal{M}} \cup \Pi_{\Sigma} \cup \Pi_q$ such that

1. $ret(\mathcal{I}, \mathcal{D}) \rightleftharpoons SM(\Pi_{\mathcal{M}}[\mathcal{D}])$, where $\Pi_{\mathcal{M}}$ is a Datalog$^{\neg s}$ program,
2. $rep_{\mathcal{I}}(\mathcal{D})) \rightleftharpoons SM(\Pi_{\Sigma}[ret(\mathcal{I}, \mathcal{D})])$, and

3. $ans(q, \mathcal{I}, \mathcal{D}) \rightleftharpoons \{q(t) \mid q(t) \in M$ for each $M \in \text{SM}((\Pi_q \cup \Pi_\Sigma)[ret(\mathcal{I}, \mathcal{D})])\}$,
   where Π_q is a non-recursive Datalog$^\neg$ program,

where $\rightleftharpoons$ denotes a polynomial-time computable correspondence between two sets. □

This definition establishes a connection between the semantics of $\Pi_\mathcal{I}(q)$ and the consistent answers to a query posed to $\mathcal{I}$ (Item 3) provided some syntactic transformations, which typically are simple encodings such that $\rightleftharpoons$ is a linear-time computable bijection. In particular, $\Pi_\mathcal{I}(q)$ is composed by three modules that can be hierarchically evaluated, i.e., $\Pi_\mathcal{M} \triangleright \Pi_\Sigma \triangleright \Pi_q$ [10], using Splitting Sets [16]:

• $\Pi_\mathcal{M}$ is used for retrieving data from the sources: the retrieved global database can be derived from its unique stable model (Item 1);
• Π_Σ is used for enforcing the constraints on the retrieved global database, whose repairs can be derived from the stable models of $\Pi_\Sigma[ret(\mathcal{I}, \mathcal{D})]$ (Item 2);
• finally, Π_q is used for encoding the user query q.

Our framework generalizes logic programming formalizations proposed in different integration settings, such as the ones recently proposed in [13,4,7,5]. In this respect, the precise structure of the program $\Pi_\mathcal{I}(q)$ depends on the form of the mapping, the language adopted for specifying mapping views and user queries, and the nature of constraints expressed on the global schema. We point out that, logic programming specifications proposed in the setting of a single inconsistent database [12,3] are also captured by our framework. Indeed, a single inconsistent database can be conceived as the retrieved global database of a GAV data integration system in which views of the mapping are assumed exact. The logic programs for consistently querying a single database are of the form $\Pi_\mathcal{I}(q) = \Pi_\Sigma \cup \Pi_q$.

4   Optimization of Query Answering

The source of complexity in evaluating the program $\Pi_\mathcal{I}(q)$ defined in the above section, actually lies in the conflict resolution module Π_Σ, and in the evaluation of Π_q. Indeed, $\Pi_\mathcal{M}$ is a Datalog$^{\neg s}$ program that can be evaluated in polynomial time over the source database $\mathcal{D}$ for constructing $ret(\mathcal{I}, \mathcal{D})$, whereas Π_q is a non-recursive Datalog$^\neg$ program that has to be evaluated over each repair of the retrieved global database, and Π_Σ is in general a Datalog$^{\vee, \neg}$ program whose evaluation complexity over varying databases is at the second level of the polynomial hierarchy [12]. Furthermore, also evaluating programs with lower complexity over large data sets by means of stable models solvers, such as DLV [15] or Smodels [17], quickly becomes infeasible. This calls for suitable optimization methods speeding up the evaluation (as recently stated in [5]).

Concentrating on the most relevant and computational expensive aspects of the optimization, we focus here on Π_Σ, assuming that $ret(\mathcal{I}, \mathcal{D})$ is already computed, and devise intelligent techniques for the evaluation of Π_q.

Roughly speaking, in our approach we first localize in the retrieved global database $ret(\mathcal{I}, \mathcal{D})$ the facts that are not "affected" (formally specified below) by any violation. Then, we compute the repairs by taking into account only the affected facts, and finally we recombine the repairs to provide answers to the user query. Since in practice, the size of the set of the affected facts is much smaller than the size of the retrieved global database, the computation of the stable models of Π_Σ, i.e., repairs of $ret(\mathcal{I}, \mathcal{D})$ (Item

2 in Def. 2), over the affected facts is significantly faster than the naive evaluation of $\Pi_{\mathcal{I}}(q)$ on the whole retrieved global database.

In a nutshell, our overall optimization approach comprises the following steps:

Pruning: We first eliminate from $\Pi_{\mathcal{I}}(q)$ the rules that are not relevant for computing answers to a user query q. This can be done by means of a static syntactic analysis of the program $\Pi_{\mathcal{I}}(q)$. However, this is not a crucial aspect in our technique, and due to space limits we do not provide further details on it.

Decomposition: We localize inconsistency in the retrieved global database, and compute the set of facts that are affected by repair. Finally, we compute repairs, $\mathcal{R}_1, \ldots, \mathcal{R}_n$, of this set.

Recombination: We suitably recombine the repairs $\mathcal{R}_1, \ldots, \mathcal{R}_n$ for computing the answers to q.

In the rest of this section, we describe in detail the last two steps.

4.1 Decomposition

We start with some concepts for a single database. Let $\mathcal{RS} = \langle \Psi, \Sigma \rangle$ be a relational schema. We call two facts $p_1(a_1, \ldots, a_n)$ and $p_2(b_1, \ldots, b_m)$, where $p_1, p_2 \in \Psi$ and each a_i, b_j is in the domain $\mathcal{U}$, *constraint-bounded in* $\mathcal{RS}$, if they occur in the same ground constraint $\sigma^g \in ground(\Sigma)$. Furthermore, for any $\sigma^g \in ground(\Sigma)$, we use $facts(\sigma^g)$ to denote the set of all facts $p(t)$, $p \in \Psi$, which occur in σ^g.

Let $\mathcal{DB}$ be a database for $\mathcal{RS}$. Then, the *conflict set* for $\mathcal{DB}$ w.r.t. $\mathcal{RS}$ is the set of facts $C_{\mathcal{DB}}^{\mathcal{RS}} = \{p(t) \mid \exists \sigma^g \in ground(\Sigma) \wedge p(t) \in facts(\sigma^g) \wedge \sigma^g$ is violated in $\mathcal{DB}\}$, i.e., the set of facts occurring in the constraints of $ground(\Sigma)$ that are violated in $\mathcal{DB}$.

Definition 3. Let $\mathcal{RS} = \langle \Psi, \Sigma \rangle$ be a relational schema and $\mathcal{DB}$ a database for $\mathcal{RS}$. Then, the *conflict closure* for $\mathcal{DB}$, denoted by $C_{\mathcal{DB}}^{\mathcal{RS}*}$, is the least set such that $t \in C_{\mathcal{DB}}^{\mathcal{RS}*}$ if either $t \in C_{\mathcal{DB}}^{\mathcal{RS}}$, or t is constraint-bounded in $\mathcal{RS}$ with a fact $t' \in C_{\mathcal{DB}}^{\mathcal{RS}*}$. Moreover, we call $S_{\mathcal{DB}}^{\mathcal{RS}} = \mathcal{DB} - C_{\mathcal{DB}}^{\mathcal{RS}*}$ and $A_{\mathcal{DB}}^{\mathcal{RS}} = \mathcal{DB} \cap C_{\mathcal{DB}}^{\mathcal{RS}*}$ the *safe database* and the *affected database* for $\mathcal{DB}$, respectively. $\square$

We drop the superscript $\mathcal{RS}$ if it is clear from the context. Intuitively, $C_{\mathcal{DB}}^*$ contains all facts involved in constraint violations, i.e., facts belonging to $C_{\mathcal{DB}}$, and facts which possibly must be changed in turn to avoid new inconsistency with Σ by repairing.

We now consider the following two subsets of all ground constraints.

(i) $\Sigma_{\mathcal{DB}}^A$ consists of all the ground constraints in which at least one fact from $C_{\mathcal{DB}}^*$ occurs, i.e., $\Sigma_{\mathcal{DB}}^A = \{\sigma^g \in ground(\Sigma) \mid facts(\sigma^g) \cap C_{\mathcal{DB}}^* \neq \emptyset\}$, and

(ii) $\Sigma_{\mathcal{DB}}^S$ consists of all the ground constraints in which at least one fact occurs which is not in $C_{\mathcal{DB}}^*$, i.e., $\Sigma_{\mathcal{DB}}^S = \{\sigma^g \in ground(\Sigma) \mid facts(\sigma^g) \not\subseteq C_{\mathcal{DB}}^*\}$.

We first show that $\Sigma_{\mathcal{DB}}^A$ and $\Sigma_{\mathcal{DB}}^S$ form a partitioning of $ground(\Sigma)$.

Proposition 1. (Separation) *Let* $\mathcal{RS} = \langle \Psi, \Sigma \rangle$ *be a relational schema, and let* $\mathcal{DB}$ *a database for* $\mathcal{RS}$. *Then,*

1. $\bigcup_{\sigma^g \in \Sigma_{\mathcal{DB}}^A} facts(\sigma^g) \subseteq C_{\mathcal{DB}}^*$;
2. $\bigcup_{\sigma^g \in \Sigma_{\mathcal{DB}}^S} facts(\sigma^g) \cap C_{\mathcal{DB}}^* = \emptyset$;
3. $\Sigma_{\mathcal{DB}}^A \cap \Sigma_{\mathcal{DB}}^S = \emptyset$ *and* $\Sigma_{\mathcal{DB}}^A \cup \Sigma_{\mathcal{DB}}^S = ground(\Sigma)$.

Proof. 1. All facts occurring in a ground constraint $\sigma^g \in \Sigma^A_{\mathcal{DB}}$ must belong to $C^*_{\mathcal{DB}}$. Indeed, by definition of $\Sigma^A_{\mathcal{DB}}$, σ^g contains at least one fact t in $C^*_{\mathcal{DB}}$; each other fact in σ^g is constraint-bounded in $\mathcal{RS}$ with t, and hence it also is in $C^*_{\mathcal{DB}}$.

2. Assume by contradiction that some $\sigma^g \in \Sigma^S_{\mathcal{DB}}$ with $facts(\sigma^g) \cap C^*_{\mathcal{DB}} \neq \emptyset$ exists. Then, Definition 3 implies $facts(\sigma^g) \subseteq C^*_{\mathcal{DB}}$, which contradicts $\sigma^g \in \Sigma^S_{\mathcal{DB}}$. Part 3 is straightforward from Part 1 and Part 2.   □

The separation property allows us to shed light on the structure of repairs:

Proposition 2. (Safe Database) *Let $\mathcal{RS} = \langle \Psi, \Sigma \rangle$ be a relational schema, and let $\mathcal{DB}$ be a database for $\mathcal{RS}$. Then, for each repair $\mathcal{R} \in rep(\mathcal{DB})$ w.r.t. Σ, $S_{\mathcal{DB}} = \mathcal{R} - C^*_{\mathcal{DB}}$.*

Prior to the main result of this section, we note the following lemma:

Lemma 1. *Let $\mathcal{RS} = \langle \Psi, \Sigma \rangle$ be a relational schema, and let $\mathcal{DB}$ be a database for $\mathcal{RS}$. Then, for each $S \subseteq S_{\mathcal{DB}}$, we have that*

1. *for each $\mathcal{R} \in rep(S \cup A_{\mathcal{DB}})$ w.r.t. Σ, $(\mathcal{R} \cap C^*_{\mathcal{DB}}) \in rep(A_{\mathcal{DB}})$ w.r.t. $\Sigma^A_{\mathcal{DB}}$;*
2. *for each $\mathcal{R}_a \in rep(A_{\mathcal{DB}})$ w.r.t. $\Sigma^A_{\mathcal{DB}}$, there exists some set of facts S', $S' \cap C^*_{\mathcal{DB}} = \emptyset$, such that $(\mathcal{R}_a \cup S') \in rep(S \cup C^*_{\mathcal{DB}})$ w.r.t. Σ.*

Armed with the above concepts and results, we now turn to the data integration settings in which we have to repair the retrieved global database $ret(\mathcal{I}, \mathcal{D})$. The following theorem shows that its repairs can be computed by looking only at $A_{ret(\mathcal{I},\mathcal{D})}$.

Theorem 1. (Main) *Let $\mathcal{I} = \langle \mathcal{G}, \mathcal{S}, \mathcal{M} \rangle$ be a data integration system, where $\mathcal{G} = \langle \Psi, \Sigma \rangle$, and let $\mathcal{D}$ be a source database for $\mathcal{I}$. Then,*

1. *$\forall \mathcal{R} \in rep_{\mathcal{I}}(\mathcal{D})$, $\exists \mathcal{R}' \in rep(A_{ret(\mathcal{I},\mathcal{D})})$ w.r.t. Σ such that $\mathcal{R} = \mathcal{R}' \cap C^*_{ret(\mathcal{I},\mathcal{D})} \cup S_{ret(\mathcal{I},\mathcal{D})}$;*
2. *$\forall \mathcal{R}' \in rep(A_{ret(\mathcal{I},\mathcal{D})})$, $\exists \mathcal{R} \in rep_{\mathcal{I}}(\mathcal{D})$ w.r.t. Σ such that $\mathcal{R} = \mathcal{R}' \cap C^*_{ret(\mathcal{I},\mathcal{D})} \cup S_{ret(\mathcal{I},\mathcal{D})}$.*

Proof. Recall that $ret(\mathcal{I}, \mathcal{D}) = S_{ret(\mathcal{I},\mathcal{D})} \cup A_{ret(\mathcal{I},\mathcal{D})}$ and that $rep_{\mathcal{I}}(\mathcal{D})$ coincides with $rep(ret(\mathcal{I}, \mathcal{D}))$ w.r.t. Σ. Thus, applying Lemma 1, first Part 1 for $S = S_{ret(\mathcal{I},\mathcal{D})}$ and then Part 2 for $S = \emptyset$, we obtain that for every $\mathcal{R} \in rep_{\mathcal{I}}(\mathcal{D})$, there exists some $\mathcal{R}' \in rep(A_{ret(\mathcal{I},\mathcal{D})})$ w.r.t. Σ of form $\mathcal{R}' = (\mathcal{R} \cap C^*_{ret(\mathcal{I},\mathcal{D})}) \cup S'$, where $S' \cap C^*_{ret(\mathcal{I},\mathcal{D})} = \emptyset$. Hence, $\mathcal{R}' \cap C^*_{ret(\mathcal{I},\mathcal{D})} = \mathcal{R} \cap C^*_{ret(\mathcal{I},\mathcal{D})}$. By Prop. 2, every $\mathcal{R} \in rep_{\mathcal{I}}(\mathcal{D})$ is of form $\mathcal{R} = (\mathcal{R} \cap C^*_{ret(\mathcal{I},\mathcal{D})}) \cup S_{ret(\mathcal{I},\mathcal{D})}$. Therefore, $\mathcal{R} = (\mathcal{R}' \cap C^*_{ret(\mathcal{I},\mathcal{D})}) \cup S_{ret(\mathcal{I},\mathcal{D})}$.

Similarly, applying Lemma 1, first Part 1 for $S = \emptyset$ and then Part 2 for $S = S_{ret(\mathcal{I},\mathcal{D})}$, we obtain that for every $\mathcal{R}' \in rep(A_{ret(\mathcal{I},\mathcal{D})})$ w.r.t. Σ, there exists some $\mathcal{R} \in rep_{\mathcal{I}}(\mathcal{D})$ w.r.t. Σ such that $\mathcal{R} = (\mathcal{R}' \cap C^*_{ret(\mathcal{I},\mathcal{D})}) \cup S'$, where $S' \cap C^*_{ret(\mathcal{I},\mathcal{D})} = \emptyset$. Moreover, Prop. 2 implies $S' = S_{ret(\mathcal{I},\mathcal{D})}$, which proves 2.   □

As a consequence, for computing the stable models of the retrieved global database $rep_{\mathcal{I}}(\mathcal{D})$, it is sufficient to evaluate the program Π_Σ on $A_{ret(\mathcal{I},\mathcal{D})}$, i.e., to exploit the correspondence $rep_{\mathcal{I}}(\mathcal{D}) \rightleftharpoons \mathrm{SM}(\Pi_\Sigma[A_{ret(\mathcal{I},\mathcal{D})}])$, intersect with $C^*_{ret(\mathcal{I},\mathcal{D})}$, and unite with $S_{ret(\mathcal{I},\mathcal{D})}$. Nonetheless, computing $A_{ret(\mathcal{I},\mathcal{D})}$ is expensive in general since it requires computing the closure of $C_{ret(\mathcal{I},\mathcal{D})}$. Furthermore, in repairs of $A_{ret(\mathcal{I},\mathcal{D})}$ many facts not in $C^*_{ret(\mathcal{I},\mathcal{D})}$ might be computed which are stripped off subsequently. Fortunately, in practice, for many important cases this can be avoided: repairs can be made fully local and even focused just on the immediate conflicts in the database.

Proposition 3. *Let $\mathcal{I} = \langle \mathcal{G}, \mathcal{S}, \mathcal{M} \rangle$ be a data integration system, where $\mathcal{G} = \langle \Psi, \Sigma \rangle$, and let $\mathcal{D}$ be a source database for $\mathcal{I}$. Then,*

1. *if each $\sigma \in \Sigma$ is of the form (1) with $l > 0$, then each $\mathcal{R}'$ repair of $A_{ret(\mathcal{I},\mathcal{D})}$ w.r.t. Σ satisfies $\mathcal{R}' \subseteq C^*_{ret(\mathcal{I},\mathcal{D})}$;*
2. *if each $\sigma \in \Sigma$ is of the form (1) with $m = 0$, then*
   - i) *each $\mathcal{R}'$ repair of $A_{ret(\mathcal{I},\mathcal{D})}$ w.r.t. Σ satisfies $\mathcal{R}' \subseteq C_{ret(\mathcal{I},\mathcal{D})}$,*
   - ii) *$C_{ret(\mathcal{I},\mathcal{D})} \subseteq ret(\mathcal{I}, \mathcal{D})$, and*
   - ii) *$rep(A_{ret(\mathcal{I},\mathcal{D})})$ w.r.t. Σ coincides with $rep(C_{ret(\mathcal{I},\mathcal{D})})$ w.r.t. Σ.*   □

This proposition allows us to exploit Theorem 1 in a constructive way for many significant classes of constraints, for which it implies a bijection between the repairs of the retrieved global database, $ret(\mathcal{I}, \mathcal{D})$, and the repairs of its affected part $A_{ret(\mathcal{I},\mathcal{D})}$ w.r.t. the constraints Σ. In particular, Condition 1 is satisfied by all constraints that do not unconditionally enforce inclusion of some fact in every repair, while Condition 2 is satisfied by constraints that can be repaired by just deleting facts from the database, such as key constraints, functional dependencies, and exclusion dependencies.

According to Theorem 1, in case of Condition 2 the set $rep_\mathcal{I}(\mathcal{D})$ can be obtained by simply computing the repairs of the conflicting facts, $C_{ret(\mathcal{I},\mathcal{D})}$, in place of $A_{ret(\mathcal{I},\mathcal{D})}$ and by adding $S_{ret(\mathcal{I},\mathcal{D})}$ to each repair. We also point out that the computation of the set $C_{ret(\mathcal{I},\mathcal{D})}$ can be carried out very efficiently, by means of suitable SQL statements. The following corollary formalizes the above discussion for Condition 2.

Corollary 1. *Let $\mathcal{I} = \langle \mathcal{G}, \mathcal{S}, \mathcal{M} \rangle$ be a data integration system, where $\mathcal{G} = \langle \Psi, \Sigma \rangle$, and let $\mathcal{D}$ be a source database for $\mathcal{I}$. Assume each constraint in Σ has form (1) with $m = 0$. Then, there exists a bijection $\mu : rep_\mathcal{I}(\mathcal{D}) \rightarrow rep(C_{ret(\mathcal{I},\mathcal{D})})$, such that for each $\mathcal{R} \in rep_\mathcal{I}(\mathcal{D})$, $\mathcal{R} = \mu(\mathcal{R}) \cup S_{ret(\mathcal{I},\mathcal{D})}$ (where $C_{ret(\mathcal{I},\mathcal{D})} \subseteq ret(\mathcal{I}, \mathcal{D})$).*   □

4.2   Recombination

Let us turn our attention to the evaluation of a user query q. According to the definition of consistent answers (Section 3.1), we need to evaluate q over each repair $\mathcal{R} \in rep_\mathcal{I}(\mathcal{D})$, and by Theorem 1 we can exploit the correspondence $rep_\mathcal{I}(\mathcal{D}) \rightleftharpoons SM(\Pi_\Sigma[A_{ret(\mathcal{I},\mathcal{D})}])$ for computing each such $\mathcal{R}$. More precisely, we need to recombine the repairs of $A_{ret(\mathcal{I},\mathcal{D})}$ with $S_{ret(\mathcal{I},\mathcal{D})}$ computed in the decomposition step as stated by the following theorem.

Theorem 2. *Let $\mathcal{I} = \langle \mathcal{G}, \mathcal{S}, \mathcal{M} \rangle$ be a data integration system, let $\mathcal{D}$ be a source database for $\mathcal{I}$, and let q be a query over $\mathcal{G}$. Then,*

$$ans(q, \mathcal{I}, \mathcal{D}) = \bigcap_{\mathcal{R} \in rep(A_{ret(\mathcal{I},\mathcal{D})})} \Pi_q[\mathcal{R} \cap C^*_{ret(\mathcal{I},\mathcal{D})} \cup S_{ret(\mathcal{I},\mathcal{D})}] \qquad (2)$$

Note that the number of repairs of $A_{ret(\mathcal{I},\mathcal{D})}$ is exponential in the number of violated constraints, and hence efficient computation of the intersection in (2) requires some intelligent strategy. Clearly, the overall approach is beneficial only if the recombination cost does not compensate the gain of repair localization. In the next section, we present an efficient technique for the recombination step.

$player_m{}^{ret(\mathcal{I}_0,\mathcal{D}_0)}$:

10	Totti	RM	'11'
9	Beckham	MU	'11'

$coach_m{}^{ret(\mathcal{I}_0,\mathcal{D}_0)}$:

7	Ferguson	MU	'11'

$team_m{}^{ret(\mathcal{I}_0,\mathcal{D}_0)}$:

RM	Roma	10	'10'
MU	Man. Utd.	8	'11'
RM	Real Madrid	10	'01'

Fig. 3. The retrieved global database of our running example after marking.

We close this section with briefly addressing databases over infinite domains. Here, usually a safety condition is imposed on constraints and queries in order to assure finite database instances and query results. Namely, a constraint of the form (1) is safe, if each variable occurring in some B_j or ϕ_k also occurs in some A_i, and a query $q(x)$ is safe, if each variable in x is recursively bound to some value occurring in the database. Note that important types of constraints such as key, functional and exclusion dependencies are safe. It appears that under safe constraints and queries, database repairs fully localize to the *active domain*, $AD(\mathcal{DB})$, of a database $\mathcal{DB}$, i.e., the values occurring in $\mathcal{DB}$. As for repair, the (finite or infinite) domain can thus be equivalently replaced with $AD(\mathcal{DB})$, and for query answering, by $AD(\mathcal{DB})$ plus the constants in $q(x)$. Together with further domain pruning, this may lead to considerable savings.

5 A Technique for Efficient Recombination

In this section, we describe a technique for implementing the recombination step in a way which circumvents the evaluation of Π_q on each repair of $ret(\mathcal{I},\mathcal{D})$ separately. For the sake of simplicity, we deal here with constraints of the form (1), when $l > 0$ and $m = 0$. In this case, according to Proposition 3, $rep(A_{ret(\mathcal{I},\mathcal{D})})$ coincide with $rep(C_{ret(\mathcal{I},\mathcal{D})})$, and $\mathcal{R} \subseteq C_{ret(\mathcal{I},\mathcal{D})} \subseteq ret(\mathcal{I},\mathcal{D})$ for each $\mathcal{R} \in rep(C_{ret(\mathcal{I},\mathcal{D})})$. Furthermore, thesis in Theorem 2 can be rewritten as $ans(q,\mathcal{I},\mathcal{D}) = \bigcap_{\mathcal{R} \in rep(C_{ret(\mathcal{I},\mathcal{D})})} \Pi_q[\mathcal{R} \cup S_{ret(\mathcal{I},\mathcal{D})}]$.

The basic idea of our approach is to encode all repairs into a single database over which Π_q can be evaluated by means of standard database techniques. More precisely, for each global relation r, we construct a new relation r_m by adding an auxiliary attribute *mark*. The mark value is a string $'b_1 \ldots b_n'$ of bits $b_i \in \{0, 1\}$ such that, given any tuple t, $b_i = 1$ if and only if t belongs to the i-th repair $\mathcal{R}_i \in rep(C_{ret(\mathcal{I},\mathcal{D})}) = \{\mathcal{R}_1, \ldots, \mathcal{R}_n\}$, for every $i \in \{1, \ldots, n\}$ (indexing the repairs is easy, e.g. using the order in which the deductive database system computes them). The set of all marked relations constitutes a *marked* database, denoted by $M_{ret(\mathcal{I},\mathcal{D})}$. Note that the facts in $S_{ret(\mathcal{I},\mathcal{D})}$ (the bulk of data) can be marked without any preprocessing, as they belong to every repair $\mathcal{R}_i$; hence, their mark is $'11 \ldots 1'$. For our running example, the marked database derived from the repairs in Figure 2 is shown in Figure 3.

We next show how the original query q can be reformulated in a way such that its evaluation over the marked database computes the set of consistent answers to q. Before proceeding, we point out that our recombination technique also applies in the presence of constraints of general form. In such a case, the source of complexity lies in the computation of $C^*_{ret(\mathcal{I},\mathcal{D})}$.

5.1   Query Reformulation

We next focus on non-recursive Datalog queries and provide a technique for rewriting them into SQL. The extension to non-recursive Datalog$^\neg$ queries is straightforward, and is omitted due to space limits.

Let a query $q(\boldsymbol{x})$, where $\boldsymbol{x} = X_1, \ldots X_n$, be given by the rules $q(\boldsymbol{x}) \leftarrow q_j(\boldsymbol{y}_j)$, $1 \leq j \leq n$, where each $q_j(\boldsymbol{y}_j)$ is a conjunction of atoms $p_{j,1}(\boldsymbol{y}_{j,1}), \ldots, p_{j,m}(\boldsymbol{y}_{j,m})$, where $\boldsymbol{y}_j = \bigcup_{i=1}^{m} \boldsymbol{y}_{j,i}$. Moreover, let us call each variable Y such that $Y \in \boldsymbol{y}_{j,i}$ and $Y \in \boldsymbol{y}_{j,h}$ a *join variable of* $p_{j,i}$ *and* $p_{j,h}$.

In query reformulation, we use the following functions ANDBIT and SUMBIT:

- ANDBIT is a binary function that takes as its input two bit strings $'a_1 \ldots a'_n$ and $'b_1 \ldots b'_n$ and returns $'(a_1 \wedge b_1) \ldots (a_n \wedge b_n)'$, where $\wedge$ is boolean and;
- SUMBIT is an aggregate function such that given m strings of form $'b_{i,1} \ldots b'_{i,n}$, it returns $'(b_{1,1} \vee \ldots \vee b_{m,1}) \ldots (b_{1,n} \vee \ldots \vee b_{m,n})'$, where $\vee$ is boolean or.

Then, each $q(\boldsymbol{x}) \leftarrow q_j(\boldsymbol{y}_j)$ can be translated in the SQL statement SQL_{q_j} of the form

SELECT $\mathbf{X_1}, \ldots \mathbf{X_n}, (\mathbf{p_{j,1}}.$mark ANDBIT $\ldots$ ANDBIT $\mathbf{p_{j,m}}.$mark) AS mark
FROM $\mathbf{p_1} \ldots \mathbf{p_m}$
WHERE $\mathbf{p_{j,i}}.\mathbf{Y} = \mathbf{p_{j,h}}.\mathbf{Y}$ *(for each join variable* $\mathbf{Y}$ *of* $\mathbf{p_{j,i}}$ *and* $\mathbf{p_{j,h}}, 1 \leq i, h \leq m$*)*.

In addition to the answers to $q(\boldsymbol{x}) \leftarrow q_j(\boldsymbol{y}_j)$, the statement computes the marks of the repairs in which an answer holds by applying the ANDBIT operator to the *mark* attributes of the joined relations. The results of all SQL_{q_j} can be collected into a view uq_m by the SQL statement SQL_{q_1} UNION $SQL_{q_2} \ldots$ UNION SQL_{q_n}. Finally, SQL_q is

SELECT $\mathbf{X_1}, \ldots \mathbf{X_n}$, SUMBIT(mark)
FROM uq_m
GROUP BY $\mathbf{X_1}, \ldots \mathbf{X_n}$
HAVING SUMBIT(mark) $=' 1 \ldots 1'$.

It computes query answers by considering only the facts that belong to all repairs.

Proposition 4. *Given a data integration system* $\mathcal{I} = \langle \mathcal{G}, \mathcal{S}, \mathcal{M} \rangle$, *a source database* $\mathcal{D}$ *and a query q over* $\mathcal{G}$, *the set* $ans(q, \mathcal{I}, \mathcal{D})$ *coincides with the set computed by executing* SQL_q *over the marked database* $M_{ret(\mathcal{I}, \mathcal{D})}$.

Example 5. For $q(X) \leftarrow player(X, Y, Z)$; $q(X) \leftarrow team(V, W, X)$, SQL_q is

CREATE VIEW uq_m (X, mark) AS   SELECT X, SUMBIT(mark)
SELECT $Pcode$, mark FROM $player$ FROM uq_m
UNION   GROUP BY X
SELECT $Tleader$, mark FROM $team$;   HAVING SUMBIT(mark) $=' 11'$;

It is easy to see that the answers consist of the codes *8, 9, 10*.   □

Since there may be exponentially many repairs in the number of violated constraints, the marking string can be of considerable length. In [9] we refine our technique to mark only the affected database part; the query is then rewritten using a split of each global relation r into a "safe" part and an "affected" part.

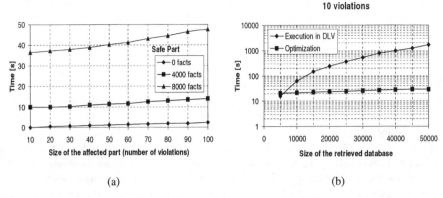

Fig. 4. (a) Execution time in DLV system w.r.t. $|A_{ret(\mathcal{I}_0, \mathcal{D}_{syn})}|$, for different sizes of $S_{ret(\mathcal{I}_0, \mathcal{D}_{syn})}$. (b) Comparison with the optimization method.

6   Experimental Results

In this section, we present experimental results obtained by means of a prototype implementation that couples the DLV deductive database system [15] with Postgresql, a relational DBMS which allows for a convenient encoding of the ANDBIT and SUMBIT operators. Notice that DLV supports disjunction, which is needed for encoding universal constraints into programs Π_Σ, since computing consistent answers in this setting is Π_2^p-complete [12]. The experiments have been carried out on a sun4u sparc SUNW ultra-5_10 with 256MB memory and processor working at 350MHz, under Solaris SUN operating system.

Football Teams. For our running example, we built a synthetic data set $\mathcal{D}_{syn}$, in which the facts in *coach* and *team* satisfy the key constraints, while facts in *player* violate it. Each violation consists of two facts that coincide on the attribute *Pcode* but differ on the attributes *Pname* or *Pteam*; note that these facts constitute $A_{ret(\mathcal{I}_0, \mathcal{D}_{syn})}$. For the query $q(X) \leftarrow player(X, Y, Z);\ q(X) \leftarrow team(V, W, X)$, we measured the execution time of the program $\Pi_{\mathcal{I}_0}(q)$ in DLV depending on $|A_{ret(\mathcal{I}_0, \mathcal{D}_{syn})}|$ for different fixed values of $|S_{ret(\mathcal{I}_0, \mathcal{D}_{syn})}|$, viz. (i) 0, (ii) 4000, and (iii) 8000. The results are shown in Fig. 4.(a).

We point out that in Case (i), in which $\Pi_{\mathcal{I}_0}(q)$ is evaluated only on the affected part, the execution time scales well to a significant number of violations. On the other hand, the evaluation of $\Pi_{\mathcal{I}_0}(q)$ on the whole database is significantly slower; in fact, a small database of 8000 facts requires up to 40 seconds for 50 violated constraints.

Figure 4.(b) shows a comparison (in log scale) between the consistent query answering by a single DLV program and the optimization approach proposed in this paper. Interestingly, for a fixed number of violations (10 in the figure) the growth of the running time of our optimization method under varying database size is negligible. In fact, a major share ($\sim$ 20 seconds) is used for computing repairs of the affected database, plus marking and storing them in Postgresql; the time for query evaluation itself is negligible. In conclusion, for small databases (up to 5000 facts), consistent query answering by straight evaluation in DLV may be considered viable; nonetheless, for larger databases, the asymptotic behavior shows that our approach outperforms a naive implementation

Further experiments are reported in [9].

We stress that the results can be significantly improved since our implementation is not optimized. Nonetheless, its advantage over the standard technique is evident.

7 Conclusion

We have described an approach to speed up the evaluation of non-monotonic logic programs modeling query answering in data integration systems. To this end, we have provided theoretical results that allow for repairing an inconsistent retrieved database by localizing the computation of repairs to its affected part. As we have shown, for important classes of constraints such as key constraints, functional dependencies, and exclusion dependencies, repairs can be restricted to the facts in the database violating the constraints, which may be only a small fragment of a large database. Furthermore, we have developed a technique for recombining such repairs to provide answers for user queries. Finally, we have experimented the viability of our approach.

We point out that our method, which is built upon repair by selection in terms of a particular preference ordering, is based on abstract properties and may be adapted to other logic programming systems as well. Furthermore, it can be generalized to other preference based repair semantics for an inconsistent database $\mathcal{DB}$. In particular, all repair semantics in which $\triangle(\mathcal{R}, \mathcal{DB}) \subset \triangle(\mathcal{R}', \mathcal{DB})$, i.e., $\mathcal{R}$ is closer to database $\mathcal{DB}$ than $\mathcal{R}'$ in terms of symmetric difference, implies that $\mathcal{R}$ is preferred to $\mathcal{R}'$ can be dealt with using our method. We point out that, for instance, cardinality-based and weighted-based repair semantics satisfy this condition.

Notice that the logic formalization of LAV systems proposed in [4,5] might be captured by our logic framework under suitable adaptations. Actually, given a source extension, several different ways of populating the global schema according to a LAV mapping may exist, and the notion of repair has to take into account a set of such global database instances. Nonetheless, analogously to our GAV framework, in [4,5] the repairs are computed from the stable models of a suitable logic program.

On the other hand, [13,7] address the repair problem in GAV systems with existentially quantified inclusion dependencies and key constraints on the global schema. They present techniques for suitably reformulating user queries in order to eliminate inclusion dependencies, which leads to a rewriting that can be evaluated on the global schema taking into account only key constraints. We point out that, provided such a reformulation, the logic specifications proposed in [13,7] perfectly fit our framework.

References

1. S. Abiteboul, R. Hull, and V. Vianu. *Foundations of Databases*. Addison Wesley, 1995.
2. M. Arenas, L. E. Bertossi, and J. Chomicki. Consistent query answers in inconsistent databases. In *Proc. 18th ACM Symposium on Principles of Database Systems (PODS-99)*, pp. 68–79, 1999.
3. M. Arenas, L. E. Bertossi, and J. Chomicki. Specifying and querying database repairs using logic programs with exceptions. In *Proc. 4th Int'l Conference on Flexible Query Answering Systems (FQAS 2000)*, pp. 27–41. Springer, 2000.
4. L. Bertossi, J. Chomicki, A. Cortes, and C. Gutierrez. Consistent answers from integrated data sources. In T. Andreasen *et al.*, editors, *Proc. 5th Int'l Conference on Flexible Query Answering Systems (FQAS 2002)*, LNCS 2522, pp. 71–85, 2002.

5. L. Bravo and L. Bertossi. Logic programming for consistently querying data integration systems. In *Proc. 18th Int'l Joint Conference on Artificial Intelligence (IJCAI 2003)*, pp. 10–15, 2003.

6. A. Calì, D. Lembo, and R. Rosati. On the decidability and complexity of query answering over inconsistent and incomplete databases. In *Proc. 22nd ACM Symposium on Principles of Database Systems (PODS-03)*, pp. 260–271, 2003.

7. A. Calì, D. Lembo, and R. Rosati. Query rewriting and answering under constraints in data integration systems. In *Proc. 18th Int'l Joint Conference on Artificial Intelligence (IJCAI 2003)*, pp. 16–21, 2003.

8. J. Chomicki and J. Marcinkowski. Minimal-change integrity maintenance using tuple deletions. Technical Report arXiv:cs.DB/0212004v1, arXiv.org, 2002.

9. T. Eiter, M. Fink, G. Greco, and D. Lembo. Efficient evaluation of logic programs for querying data integration systems. Extended Manuscript, July 2003.

10. T. Eiter, G. Gottlob, and H. Mannila. Disjunctive datalog. *ACM Trans. on Database Systems*, 22(3):364–417, 1997.

11. M. Gelfond and V. Lifschitz. The stable model semantics for logic programming. In *Proc. Fifth Logic Programming Symposium*, pp. 1070–1080. MIT Press, 1988.

12. G. Greco, S. Greco, and E. Zumpano. A logic programming approach to the integration, repairing and querying of inconsistent databases. In P. Codognet, editor, *Proc. 17th Int'l Conference on Logic Programming (ICLP 2001)*, LNCS 2237, pp. 348–364. Springer, 2001.

13. D. Lembo, M. Lenzerini, and R. Rosati. Source inconsistency and incompleteness in data integration. In *Proc. KRDB 2002*. http://ceur-ws.org/Vol-54/, 2002.

14. M. Lenzerini. Data integration: A theoretical perspective. In Lucian Popa, editor, *Proc. 21st ACM Symposium on Principles of Database Systems (PODS-02)*, pp. 233–246, 2002.

15. Nicola Leone et al. DLV homepage, since 1996.
http://www.dbai.tuwien.ac.at/proj/dlv/.

16. V. Lifschitz and H. Turner. Splitting a logic program. In Pascal Van Hentenryck, editor, *Proc. 11h Int'l Conference on Logic Programming (ICLP-94)*, pp. 23–38, 1994. MIT-Press.

17. Ilkka Niemelä et al. Smodels homepage, since 1999.
http://www.tcs.hut.fi/Software/smodels/.

18. T. Przymusinski. Stable semantics for disjunctive programs. *New Generation Computing*, 9:401–424, 1991.

19. D. Seipel. DisLog - a disjunctive deductive database prototype (system description). In F. Bry, B. Freitag, and D. Seipel, editors, *Proc. 12th Workshop on Logic Programming (WLP '97)*. LMU München, September 1997.

20. David S. Warren et al. XSB homepage, since 1997. http://xsb.sourceforge.net/.

Argumentation Databases

Shekhar Pradhan

Department of Computer Science, Vassar College
pradhan@cs.vassar.edu

Abstract. We introduce a proposal to give argumentation capacity to databases. A database is said to have argumentation capacity if it can extract from the information available to it a set of interacting arguments for and against claims and to determine the overall status of some information given all the interactions among all the arguments. We represent conflicts among arguments using a construct called a contestation, which permits us to represent various degrees of conflicts among statements. Argumentation databases as proposed here give exactly the same answers to queries as a database without argumentation capacity, but which are annotated with confidence values reflecting the degree of confidence one should have in the answer, where the degree of confidence is determined by the overall effect of all the interactions among the arguments.

1 Introduction

In this paper we describe a proposal to give argumentation capacities to any database by putting a layer of software based on logic programming techniques for knowledge representation and inferencing on top of the management system of the database without in any way modifying its data model or query answering process.

Giving an argumentation capacity to a database system means providing the system with mechanisms for extracting from the information available to the system a set of interacting arguments for and against claims, and determining how one argument affects the status of another argument, and determining the overall status of some information given all the interactions among all the arguments.

A database system augmented with an argumentation capacity returns each answer to a query annotated with a confidence value which denotes how much confidence should be placed in the answer given all the interacting and conflicting arguments that can be mined from the information available to the databases system. In any decision-making context knowing how much confidence to place in an answer to a query adds significant value to the answer. A database system without argumentation capacity will return an answer to a query without in any way taking into account information that may conflict with the answer or conflict with some information on which the answer is based. A database system with an argumentation capacity, as envisaged here, gives the system the capacity to utilize *all* the information relevant to assessing the merits of an answer to a query,

C. Palamidessi (Ed.): ICLP 2003, LNCS 2916, pp. 178–193, 2003.

where this merit is expressed as a confidence value. Thus conflicting information in a database can be viewed as a resource rather than as a threat.

Several researchers ([Lou87,Pol87,PS96a,PS97,BDKT97,Dun95,KT96]) have formalized argumentative reasoning and implemented it in computer systems. But in [Pra03] we proposed for the first time connecting the work on argumentation theory with databases. In this paper we extend the work described in [Pra03] by providing an operational semantics for argumentation databases as well an improved version of the declarative semantics described in that paper.

Outline of paper. In Section 2 we introduce basic concepts about arguments and attacks among arguments. In Section 3 we show how to represent conflicts among arguments in terms of a construct called contestations. We introduce contested annotated logic programs (CALPs) and We give a declarative semantics for CALPs. In Section 4 we give an operational semantics for CALPs. In Section 5 we introduce argumentation databases as essentially CALPs. In Section 6 we very briefly discuss some related work and some future work.

2   Preliminaries

Formalizing argumentation has recently become a very active area of research ([BDKT97,Dun95,PS96a,PS97,KT96]). Our formalization of arguments is informed by this work, but is modified to make it easier to capture argumentative reasoning in the database context.

First we define some basic concepts.

Definition 1. *An argument is a non-empty sequence*

$$\langle f_1, \ldots, f_j, \ head_1 \leftarrow body_1, \ldots, head_m \leftarrow body_m \rangle$$

where $f_1, \ldots, f_j$ are ground atoms (facts), and $head_1 \leftarrow body_1, \ldots, head_m \leftarrow body_m$ are ground rules, and for each rule $head_l \leftarrow body_l$ in the argument, $body_l \subseteq \{f_1, \ldots, f_j\} \cup \{head_n \mid n < l\}$.

If an argument contains no rules, then we assume that the argument contains only one atom. The *conclusion* of the argument is the head of the last rule in the sequence, otherwise, if the argument contains no rules, then it is the only atom in the argument.

An argument can be thought of as a specification of one way of proving the statement that is the conclusion of the argument. An argument is *minimal* if deleting a fact or a rule from the argument results in a sequence that is not a specification of a way of proving the conclusion of the original argument. For the sake of ease of exposition, and without any loss of generality, we assume that all the arguments under consideration are minimal in this sense.

Definition 2. *An argument A2 is a sub-argument of an argument A1 if A2 is a sub-sequence of A1 which satisfies the definition of an argument.*

Next we define attacks among *arguments* in terms of attacks among *statements* (i.e., literals), which we take to be a primitive relation. There are number of reasons why one statement p can be seen as attacking another statement q: because p is the negation of q, or because p provides evidence against q, or because there is a rule or policy which precludes accepting q if p is accepted, and so on.

Definition 3. *An argument $A1$ attacks an argument $A2$ iff the conclusion of $A1$ attacks the conclusion of $A2$ (direct attacks) or attacks the conclusion of a sub-argument of $A2$ (indirect attack).*

Given a set of facts $\mathcal{F}$ and a set of rules $\mathcal{R}$, we say that an argument is *successful* with respect to $\mathcal{F}$ and $\mathcal{R}$ only if the "facts" of the argument are a subset of $\mathcal{F}$ or each "fact" of the argument is a member of $\mathcal{F}$ or is the conclusion of a successful argument with respect to $\mathcal{F}$ and $\mathcal{R}$. We say that an attack by an argument A_1 against an argument A_2 is *successful* with respect to a specified set of facts and rules only if A_1 attacks A_2 and A_1 is successful. We simplify the exposition by considering only successful arguments and attacks.

To say that a statement p attacks a statement q is to say that accepting p as credible undermines the credibility of q to a certain degree. A statement q can be attacked indpendently by two statements p_1 and p_2, where the degree to which p_1 can undermine the credibility of q may be different from the degree to which p_2 can undermine the credibility of q. In terms of this idea we can define degrees of attacks among statements. In the next section we associate confidence values with statements, and the degree of an attack by a statement p by a statement q can be represented in terms of the degree to which p, if accepted as true, can reduce the confidence value of q.

Since attacks among statements are based on conflicts among statements and since conflicts are generally mutual, attacks among statements are generally mutual. However, we will not require the attack relation to be mutual. This is because it is possible that the degree to which p undermines q may be different than the degree to which q undermines p. Thus, the claim that a person has a certain symptom may undermine the claim that the person has a certain disease to a much greater degree than the degree to which the latter claim undermines the former claim. In the limiting case, we may have p undermining q (to a certain degree) without q undermining p. This can happen if p is taken as being entirely reliable for a number of possible reasons (established by entirely reliable methods, or from an entirely reliable source, or more current version of the same data as q, etc.).

In the next section we present a method of representing attacks among statements which also records the degree of the attack and which allows, in the limiting case, non-mutual attacks among statements.

3   Contestations

We represent the idea of one statement attacking another statement in terms of a construct we call a "contestation." A contestation is a claim of the form that if a certain statement p has a confidence value of at least v_1 then another statement q, which is attacked by p, has a confidence value of at most v_2. To develop this formally we need to first introduce the apparatus of statements annotated with confidence values, which is done in the subsection below.

3.1   Annotated Information

Let $\mathcal{V}$ be a set of values and $\leq$ be a partial ordering over the values. The values in $\mathcal{V}$ can be thought of as confidence values (denoted henceforth as c-values), which when associated with a statement p denotes the degree of confidence that is placed in the belief that p is true. A statement of the form $p\!:\!v$, where $v \in \mathcal{V}$, denotes that there is v degree of confidence in the truth of p.

We distinguish sharply between the truth value assigned to p and the confidence value assigned to p. The lattice of c-values can be any complete lattice. But for the sake of simplicity of exposition we assume that the lattice of c-values is $([0,1], \leq)$, where $[0,1]$ is the closed set of reals between 0 and 1.0 and the lattice of truth values is the classical *false* $<$ *true*.

Our formal treatment of c-values makes no assumption that c-values are probabilities, as the assignment of c-values need not satisfy the axioms of probability.

It will later be useful to introduce annotated rules of the form

$$a\!:\!t_0 \leftarrow b_1\!:\!t_1, \ldots, b_n\!:\!t_n$$

where $a, b_1, \ldots, b_n$ are all atoms, and each t_i is an annotation term which can be an annotation constant denoting a value from $[0,1]$, or an annotation variable which has annotation constants as its instances, or if t_i is t_0 then it can also be a function of some of the terms in $t_1, \ldots, t_n$.

Definition 4. *Let $\mathcal{I}$ be a mapping from a set of atom S to the two truth values and let $\mathcal{A}$ be a partial mapping from S to $[0,1]$. Then $\mathcal{A}$ is complete with respect to $\mathcal{I}$ if every member of S that is assigned T by $\mathcal{I}$ is assigned a c-value by $\mathcal{A}$.*

Thus an assignment of c-values by $\mathcal{A}$ to a set of atoms is complete with respect to $\mathcal{I}$ if every atom believed to be true in terms of $\mathcal{I}$ has a confidence value associated with it by $\mathcal{A}$.

By an annotated logic program we mean a set of annotated atoms, considered as unit rules, and annotated logic rules. Generalized annotated logic programs (i.e., annotated logic programs with function terms that take annotation terms as arguments) were introduced in [KS92], in which the annotations are taken to be truth values. Our treatment of annotated logic programs differs in that we take an annotation to be a confidence value which an atom can have in addition to its truth value. Thus, although syntactically there is no significant difference between the annotated logic programs of [KS92] and our annotated logic programs, semantically our treatment is different because our semantics will have to take into account both types of values at the same time.

By the *underlying* logic program of an annotated logic program we mean the annotated logic program with all its annotations removed. By a definite annotated logic program we mean an annotated program whose underlying program is a definite logic program.

Definition 5. *Let AP be a definite annotated logic program. Let P be its underlying program. Let $\mathcal{I}$ be a mapping from the Herbrand base of P to the truth values and let $\mathcal{A}$ be a partial mapping from the Herbrand base of P to $[0,1]$ which is complete with respect to $\mathcal{I}$. Then $\langle \mathcal{I}, \mathcal{A} \rangle$ is a c-interpretation of AP.*

Definition 6. *We say that a c-interpretation $\langle \mathcal{I}, \mathcal{A} \rangle$ justifies a ground annotated atom $a{:}v$ iff $\mathcal{I}(a) = T$ and $\mathcal{A}(a) \geq v$.*

$\langle \mathcal{I}, \mathcal{A} \rangle$ justifies a conjunction (disjunction) of ground annotated atoms if it justifies each (at least one) member of the conjunction (disjunction). $\langle \mathcal{I}, \mathcal{A} \rangle$ justifies a ground annotated rule just in case if it justifies the body of the rule then it justifies the head of the rule. A c-interpretation justifies a non-ground rule iff it justifies each instance of the rule with the object variables replaced by any member of the domain of discourse and the annotation variables replaced by any value in $[0,1]$.

Definition 7. *A c-interpretation of an annotated logic program is a model of the program iff it justifies every rule in the program.*

It is obvious that a c-interpretation $\langle \mathcal{I}, \mathcal{A} \rangle$ justifies a rule only if $\mathcal{I}$ is a model of the underlying rule (that is, the rule without the annotations). Thus, $\langle \mathcal{I}, \mathcal{A} \rangle$ is a model of an annotated logic program only if $\mathcal{I}$ is a model of the underlying program.

We can introduce an ordering between the models of an annotated logic program.

Definition 8. *Let $\langle \mathcal{I}_1, \mathcal{A}_1 \rangle$ and $\langle \mathcal{I}_2, \mathcal{A}_2 \rangle$ be two c-interpretations of an annotated logic program AP. Let P be the underlying logic program of AP. Then $\langle \mathcal{I}_1, \mathcal{A}_1 \rangle \preceq \langle \mathcal{I}_2, \mathcal{A}_2 \rangle$ iff for all a in the Herbrand base of P*

– *if $\mathcal{I}_1(a) = T$ then $\mathcal{I}_2(a) = T$, and $\mathcal{A}_1(a) \leq \mathcal{A}_2(a)$.*

The least models in terms of this ordering of an annotated logic program are its canonical models. It is obvious that a definite annotated logic program has a unique canonical model.

Theorem 1. *$\langle \mathcal{I}, \mathcal{A} \rangle$ is the canonical model of an annotated logic program only if $\mathcal{I}$ is the unique minimal model of its underlying program.*

Proof. Obvious.

A definite annotated logic program AP entails an annotated atom $a : v$ iff $a{:}v$ is justified by the unique canonical model of AP. It is evident that if AP entails $a{:}v$ then AP entails $a{:}v_1$, for all $v_1 \leq v$.

3.2   Contested Annotated Logic Programs

We present a construct, which we call a *contestation*, as a way of representing attacks among statements. Contestations are statements that say that if a certain statement p is accepted as true with the c-value v_1 then another statement q can be accepted as true with *at most* the c-value v_2. We write contestations formally as $p\!:\!\underline{v_1} \hookrightarrow q\!:\!\overline{v_2}$.

The expression on the left hand side of a contestation is called the *contestor* and the right hand side is called the *contested*. The annotations in a contestation are always annotation constants. In principle, the contestor in a contestation can be a conjunction of annotated atoms and the contested must always be an atom. However, a contestor which is a conjunction can always be replaced by a contestor which is a single atom without any loss of information as seen in the example below.

Example 1. The contestation $p_1\!:\!\underline{v_1} \wedge \cdots \wedge p_n\!:\!\underline{v_n} \hookrightarrow q\!:\!\overline{w}$ can be replaced by the contestation $p\!:\!\underline{min\{v_1,\ldots,v_n\}} \hookrightarrow q\!:\!\overline{w}$ and the rule $p\!:\!min\{v_1,\ldots,v_n\} \leftarrow p_1\!: v_1,\ldots,p_n\!:\!v_n$, where p is an atom that does not occur in any of the rules of the program or any of the contestations.

Definition 9. *A c-interpretation satisfies a contestation* $p\!:\!\underline{v_1} \hookrightarrow q\!:\!\overline{v_2}$ *in case if it justifies* $p\!:\!v_1$ *then it does not justify* $q\!:\!v$ *for any* $v > v_2$.

A contested annotated logic program (CALP) is an annotated logic program augmented with a set of contestations. The intended effect of adding a contestation $p\!:\!\underline{v_1} \hookrightarrow q\!:\!\overline{v_2}$ to an annotated logic program is to put a cap on the c-value of q only if $p\!:\!v_1$ can be established from the CALP. This suggests the following way of compiling contestations into rules.

The effect of adding a contestation $p\!:\!\underline{v_1} \hookrightarrow q\!:\!\overline{v_2}$ to a program with a rule $q\!:\!t_0 \leftarrow body\!:\!t_1$ can be captured by replacing the rule with the following two rules:

$$q\!:\!min(t_0, v_2) \leftarrow body\!:\!t_1, p\!:\!v_1$$
$$q\!:\!t_0 \leftarrow body\!:\!t_1, not(p\!:\!v_1)$$

The scope of *not* in the expression $not(p\!:\!v_1)$ is the annotated atom $p\!:\!v_1$, and should not be confused with $(not\ p)\!:\!v_1$. We do not use the latter expression. The second rule can be regarded as an annotated normal rule; but it is not a normal rule with annotated literals.

A c-interpretation justifies $not(p\!:\!v_1)$ iff it does not justify $p\!:\!v_1$. Thus, any c-interpretation justifies either $p\!:\!v_1$ or $not(p\!:\!v_1)$.

In this way of compiling a contestation into a rule, the second rule is understood to mean that $q\!:\!t_0$ can be inferred under the *assumption* that $p\!:\!v_1$ (the contestor) does not hold, given that $body\!:\!t_1$ can be inferred. The first rule shows the effect on the c-value of the contested if the contestor does hold.

In the general case there can be several contestations in which the same atom, possibly with different c-values, is being contested and there can be more than one rule with the same head, possibly with different c-values. The definition below specifies a method for compiling a set of contestations into an annotated definite logic program, which thereby becomes an annotated normal logic program.

Definition 10. *Let AP be an annotated definite logic program and let C be a set of contestations. Let $\mathcal{N}$ be a one-to-one mapping from AP to the set of integers which assigns a unique number to each rule in AP. Let $R = head : t_1 \leftarrow body : t_2$ be a rule in AP with $\mathcal{N}(R) = m$. $Comp_{\mathcal{N}}(R + C)$, the result of compiling the contestations into R, is as follows.*

Let $\{p_1 : \underline{w_1} \hookrightarrow head : \overline{v_1}, \ldots, p_n : \underline{w_n} \hookrightarrow head : \overline{v_n}\}$ be all the contestations in C whose contested part is the head of R. Assume, without any loss of generality, that the values $v_1, \ldots, v_n$ can be ordered numerically as $v_1 \leq \cdots \leq v_n$, and in terms of this ordering the contestations in $\{p_1 : \underline{w_1} \hookrightarrow head : \overline{v_1}, \ldots, p_n : \underline{w_n} \hookrightarrow head : \overline{v_n}\}$ can be ordered as $\langle p_1 : \underline{w_1} \hookrightarrow head : \overline{v_1}, \ldots, p_n : \underline{w_n} \hookrightarrow head : \overline{v_n} \rangle$. Then $Comp(R + C)$ contains the following set of rules.

$$m.1 :: head : min(t_1, v_1) \leftarrow body : t_2, p_1 : w_1$$
$$m.2 :: head : min(t_1, v_2) \leftarrow body : t_2, p_2 : w_2, \; not(p_1 : w_1)$$
$$\vdots$$
$$m.n :: head : min(t_1, v_n) \leftarrow body : t_2, p_n : w_n, \; not(p_1 : w_1), \ldots, not(p_{n-1} : w_{n-1})$$
$$m.(n+1) :: head : t_1 \leftarrow body : t_2, \; not(p_1 : w_1), \ldots, not(p_n : w_n)$$

$Comp_{\mathcal{N}}(AP + C) = \{Comp_{\mathcal{N}}(R + C) \mid R \in AP\}$.

In the above definition the rule numbered $m.i$ shows with what c-value the head of R can be inferred if the the body of R can be inferred and if the contestor part of the ith contestation can be inferred and none of the contestor parts of the contestations earlier in the sequence can be inferred. If $m.i < m.j$ then the c-value of the head of the rule numbered $m.i$ is less than or equal to the c-value of the head of the rule numbered $m.j$.

A model of a CALP $AP + C$ is a model of $Comp_{\mathcal{N}}(AP + C)$, i.e., a c-interpretation that justifies all the rules of $Comp_{\mathcal{N}}(AP + C)$.

In the following we shall write $Comp_{\mathcal{N}}(AP + C)$ without the subscript unless there is a reason to include the subscript.

Although it is possible to define the minimal models of $Comp(AP + C)$ as in the case of definite annotated logic programs, it is well known that minimal model theory does not provide a satisfactory semantics for programs containing negated literals. Hence, in the following we seek a different declarative semantics for compiled programs.

Below we define the c-stable models of a compiled program (a normal annotated logic program). Although not all normal annotated logic programs have c-stable models, we introduce the idea of models that are closest to being c-stable. We define the canonical models of normal annotated logic program in terms of such models.

Below we define a transformation of a normal annotated logic program into a definite annotated logic program that is based on the well-known Gelfond-Lifschitz transformation ([GL88]).

Definition 11. *Let AP be a ground annotated logic program and let C be a set of ground contestations. Let $\langle \mathcal{I}, \mathcal{A} \rangle$ be a c-interpretation of AP. Then*

$$\Pi_{\langle \mathcal{I}, \mathcal{A} \rangle}(Comp(AP + C)) = \{a : t_0 \leftarrow b_1 : t_1, \ldots, b_n : t_n \mid$$
$$a : t_0 \leftarrow b_1 : t_1, \ldots, b_n : t_n, not(c_1 : t_{n+1}), \ldots, not(c_m : t_{n+m}) \in Comp(AP + C)$$
$$\text{and } S \text{ justifies each of } not(c_1 : t_{n+1}), \ldots, not(c_m : t_{n+m})\}$$

Note that $\Pi_{\langle \mathcal{I},\mathcal{A} \rangle}(Comp(AP+\mathcal{C}))$ is an annotated definite logic program and, thus, has a unique canonical model.

$\langle \mathcal{I},\mathcal{A} \rangle$ is a c-stable model of $Comp(AP + \mathcal{C})$ iff $\langle \mathcal{I},\mathcal{A} \rangle = MM(\Pi_{\langle \mathcal{I},\mathcal{A} \rangle}(Comp(AP + \mathcal{C})))$, where $MM(\Pi_{\langle \mathcal{I},\mathcal{A} \rangle}(Comp(AP + \mathcal{C})))$ is the unique canonical model of $\Pi_{\langle \mathcal{I},\mathcal{A} \rangle}(Comp(AP + \mathcal{C}))$.

Not all CALPs have a c-stable model as shown by the following example.

Example 2. Let $AP - \{a:1; b:1; c:1\}$. Let $\mathcal{C} = \{a:\underline{0.8} \hookrightarrow b:\overline{0.3};\ b:\underline{0.7} \hookrightarrow c:\overline{0.2};\ c:\underline{0.7} \hookrightarrow a:\overline{0.1}\}$.
$Comp_{\mathcal{N}}(AP + \mathcal{C}) =$

$$1.1 :: \ a:0.1 \leftarrow c:0.7 \quad 1.2 :: \ a:1 \leftarrow not(c:0.7)$$
$$2.1 :: \ b:0.3 \leftarrow a:0.8 \quad 2.2 :: \ b:1 \leftarrow not(a:0.8)$$
$$3.1 :: \ c:0.2 \leftarrow b:0.7 \quad 3.2 :: \ c:1 \leftarrow not(b:0.7)$$

In any c-stable model of $Comp(AP+\mathcal{C})$ either $c:0.7$ is justified or $not(c:0.7)$ is justified. But if $c:0.7$ is justified then $a:0.1$ is justified (by 1.1) and no higher c-value for a would be justified. In which case $not(a:0.8)$ is justified, which implies that $b:1$ is justified (by 2.2). This implies that $c:0.2$ is justified (by 3.1) and no higher c-value for c would be justified. This contradicts the assumption that $c:0.7$ is justified.

Similar contradiction results if it is assumed that $not(c:0.7)$ is justified.

We next introduce a measure of how close a given model of $AP + \mathcal{C}$ is to being a c-stable model. This measure can be applied to even a CALP which lacks a c-stable model. We define the canonical models of $AP+\mathcal{C}$ as the models of $AP + \mathcal{C}$ which are closest to being c-stable models of $AP + \mathcal{C}$. Clearly, for a CALP having any c-stable models, these models will be its canonical models.

Definition 12. *Let AP be a ground annotated definite logic program and let $\mathcal{C}$ be a set of contestations. Let $\langle \mathcal{I}_1,\mathcal{A}_1 \rangle$ be a model of $Comp(AP + \mathcal{C})$.*

Let $\langle \mathcal{I}_2,\mathcal{A}_2 \rangle$ be the unique canonical model of $\Pi_{\langle \mathcal{I}_1,\mathcal{A}_1 \rangle}(Comp(AP + \mathcal{C}))$. Let Γ be some arbitrary sequence of the atoms that are assigned T by $\mathcal{I}$, with Γ_i being the ith member of the sequence. Then the stability measure of $\langle \mathcal{I}_1,\mathcal{A}_1 \rangle$ is

$$\langle Abs(\mathcal{A}_2(\Gamma_1) - \mathcal{A}_1(\Gamma_1)), \ldots, Abs(\mathcal{A}_2(\Gamma_n) - \mathcal{A}_1(\Gamma_n)) \rangle$$

where Abs gives the absolute value of any real.

Example 3. Let AP and $\mathcal{C}$ be as in Example 2 above. Recall that we showed in Example 2 above that this CALP has no c-stable models.

Let $\langle \mathcal{I}_1,\mathcal{A}_1 \rangle$ be the model which assigns $\langle T, 1.0 \rangle$ to a, $\langle T, 0.3 \rangle$ to b, and $\langle T, 0.6 \rangle$ to c. The unique canonical model of $\Pi_{\langle \mathcal{I}_1,\mathcal{A}_1 \rangle}(AP, \mathcal{C})$ is the model $\langle \mathcal{I}_2,\mathcal{A}_2 \rangle$ which assigns $\langle T, 1.0 \rangle$ to a, $\langle T, 0.3 \rangle$ to b, and $\langle T, 1.0 \rangle$ to c.

Let $\Gamma = \langle a, b, c \rangle$. Then the stability measure of $\langle \mathcal{I}_1,\mathcal{A}_1 \rangle$ is $\langle 0.0, 0.0, 0.4 \rangle$.

We can define an ordering among the models of a $Comp(AP + \mathcal{C})$ in terms of the stability measure of these models.

Definition 13. *Let* $\langle \mathcal{I}_1, \mathcal{A}_1 \rangle$ *and* $\langle \mathcal{I}_2, \mathcal{A}_2 \rangle$ *be two models of* $Comp(AP + C)$. *Let* S_1 *and* S_2 *be the stability measures of* $\langle \mathcal{I}_1, \mathcal{A}_1 \rangle$ *and* $\langle \mathcal{I}_2, \mathcal{A}_2 \rangle$, *respectively. Then* $\langle \mathcal{I}_1, \mathcal{A}_1 \rangle \leq \langle \mathcal{I}_2, \mathcal{A}_2 \rangle$ *iff* $S_2^i \leq S_1^i$ *for each member of the two measures, where* S_j^i *is the* i^{th} *member of* S_j.

In this ordering the c-stable models of $Comp(AP + C)$ are clearly maximal. If $Comp(AP + C)$ has no c-stable models, then strictly speaking this ordering can have no maximal elements since the property 'the number closest to a given real number' is not well defined.

In practice, however, any computing system has an actual limit to the degree of precision it can handle. Hence, in practice a CALP which has no c-stable models can still have models which are closest to being stable if the degree of precision is specified. Hence, we shall assume that for any CALP, there are models which are closest to being stable models of the CALP. Alternately, this means that the lattice $\mathcal{V}$ of c-values is a finite lattice.

Next we define the conditions under which a CALP entails an annotated atom.

Definition 14. *A CALP entails an annotated atom iff that atom is justified by each canonical model of that CALP.*

This definition of entailment is extended in the obvious way to conjunction and disjunction of annotated atoms, and to quantified annotated sentences.

In the next section we present an operational semantics for CALPs which does not require the lattice of values to be finite. This operational semantics is the basis for a query answering procedure for argumentation databases.

4   Operational Semantics

First, we extend the idea of a c-interpretation justifying an annotated atom to a set of fully ground annotated atoms (no annotation or object variables)justifying an annotated atom.

Definition 15. *A fully ground annotated atom* $a : v$ *justifies a fully ground annotated atom* $b : w$ *iff* $a = b$ *and* $v \geq w$. $a : v$ *justifies the negated atom* $not(b : w)$ *iff it does not justify* $b : w$.

A set S *of fully ground annotated atoms justifies a fully ground annotated atom* $b : w$ *iff* S *contains an atom which justifies* $b : w$. S *justifies* $not(b : w)$ *iff* S *does not justify* $b : w$.

Let $m.i :: R = a : v_0 \leftarrow b_1 : v_1, \ldots, b_n : v_n, \ not(c_1 : v_{n+1}), \ldots, not(c_m : v_{n+m})$. Assume R is fully ground. Let S be a set of ground annotated literals (with empty subscripts) such that S justifies each of $b_1 : v_1, \ldots, b_n : v_n$ and none of $c_1 : v_{n+1}, \ldots, c_m : v_{n+m}$. Then from R and S the following scripted atom can be inferred:

$$(a : v_0)_{\{m.i\}}^{not(c_1 : v_{n+1}) \wedge \cdots \wedge not(c_m : v_{n+m})}$$

We extend the above definition to scripted atoms. A scripted atom $(a : v)_u^s$ justifies $b : w$ iff $a : v$ justifies $b : w$. That is, the sub and super scripts play no role in the justification.

From R above and a set S of ground annotated atoms with possibly empty sub and super scripts, $\{(b_1:t_1)^{s_1}_{u_1}, \ldots, (b_n:t_n)^{s_n}_{u_n}\}$, such that S justifies each of $b_1:v_1, \ldots, b_n:v_n$ and none of $c_1:v_{n+1}, \ldots, c_m:v_{n+m}$, the following superscripted atom can be inferred:

$$(a:v_0)^{s_1 \wedge \cdots \wedge s_n \wedge not(c_1:v_{n+1}) \wedge \cdots \wedge not(c_m:v_{n+m})}_{\{m.i\} \,\cup\, u_1 \,\cup \cdots \cup\, u_n}$$

Based on these two ideas we define the following inference rule.

Inference Rule

Let $m.i :: R - a:t_0 \leftarrow b_1:t_1, \ldots, b_n:t_n, \ not(c_1:t_{n+1}), \ldots, not(c_m:t_{n+m})$, where the terms $t_1, \ldots, t_n$ can contain annotation variables, and t_0 is either a constant or a function of one or more of $t_1, \ldots, t_n$. Assume that R contains no object variables. Let S be a set of fully ground (no object variable or annotation variable), possibly scripted, atoms. Let δ be the c-values unifier $\{t_1 = v_1, \ldots, t_n = v_n\}$. From R, S, and δ, the atom

$$(a:(t_0\delta))^{s_1 \wedge \cdots \wedge s_n \wedge not(c_1:v_{n+1}) \wedge \cdots \wedge not(c_m:v_{n+m})}_{\{m.i\} \,\cup\, u_1 \,\cup \cdots \cup\, u_n}$$

can be inferred if each of $b_1 : (t_1\delta), \ldots, b_n : (t_n\delta)$ is justified respectively by $(b_1:v_1)^{s_1}_{u_1}, \ldots, (b_n:v_n)^{s_n}_{u_n} \in S$.

The operational semantics is based on repeated application of this inference rule on all the facts and rules in the database and the atoms so far inferred to infer an increasing set of atoms until no more new atoms can be inferred (that is, until a fix-point is reached). The inferred atoms are partitioned into those with empty superscripts (the safe knowledge) and those with the non-empty superscripts (assumption based knowledge). The assumptions (the superscripts) are evaluated in terms of the safe knowledge. The atoms whose superscripts are justified in terms of the safe knowledge are tentatively included (without the superscripts) in the safe knowledge. The subscripts are used to negotiate between two or more occurrences of the same atom with different c-values. In the negotiation step priority is given to a lower version of a rule $(m.i)$ over a higher version of the same rule $(m.(i + k))$. These priorities are used to weed out some of the atoms tentatively included in the safe knowledge set. Roughly speaking, the operational semantics is the final safe knowledge (with all the subscripts removed).

Formalization of the Operational Semantics

We define an operator Γ_{NAP} which operates on the ordered pair $\langle S, H \rangle$, where S is regarded as safe knowledge, H is regarded as knowledge based on assumptions or hypotheses, and NAP is a normal annotated program which may contain annotated unit rules. S, the safe knowledge set contains fully ground annotated atoms with empty superscripts. H, the assumption based knowledge set contains fully ground annotated atoms with non-empty superscripts which will always be a conjunction of negation of annotated atoms.

Let AP be a ground annotated program (possibly containing annotation variables) and C a set of ground contestations. Let MM be the minimal model of the definite logic program underlying AP. Let $\mathcal{N}$ be a mapping from AP to the set of integers. Let Num be the set of number labels associated with the rules of $Comp_{\mathcal{N}}(AP + C)$ by $\mathcal{N}$. Let $\mathcal{P}$ be the set of partial mappings from MM to $[0..1]$. For any such mapping, let $dom(\mathcal{P}_k)$ be the set of atoms for which $\mathcal{P}_k$ is defined. Let $\mathcal{P}_i \preceq \mathcal{P}_j$ iff $dom(\mathcal{P}_i) \subseteq dom(\mathcal{P}_j)$ and for all $a \in dom(\mathcal{P}_i)$, $\mathcal{P}_i(a) \leq \mathcal{P}_j(a)$. In this ordering the empty mapping, $\mathcal{P}_\perp$, is the least element.

Let $\mathcal{S}_i = \{a : \mathcal{P}_i(a) \mid a \in dom(\mathcal{P}_i)\}$, where $\mathcal{P}_i \in \mathcal{P}$ and $dom(\mathcal{P}_i)$ is the set of atoms for which $(\mathcal{P}_i)$ is defined. That is, $\mathcal{S}_i$ is just the set atoms for which $(\mathcal{P}_i)$ is defined, annotated with the c-values assigned to them by $(\mathcal{P}_i)$. Let $\mathcal{S}$ be the set of such sets. Formally,

$$\mathcal{S} = \{\{a : \mathcal{P}_i(a) \mid a \in dom(\mathcal{P}_i)\} \mid \mathcal{P}_i \in \mathcal{P}\}$$

We extend the ordering on the partial mappings to the sets they give rise to in the obvious way. More precisely, $\mathcal{S}_i \preceq \mathcal{S}_j$ iff $\mathcal{P}_i \preceq \mathcal{P}_j$.

Let $not\ MM$ denote the set consisting of the negation of each atom in MM. Let $CONJ$ be the set of all the conjunctive expressions that can be formed from members of $not\ MM$. Let $\mathcal{H}$ be $\{(a : t)_u^s \mid a \in MM, t \in [0 \ldots 1], s \in CONJ, u \subseteq Num\}$. That is, $\mathcal{H}$ is the set of atoms in MM annotated with a c-value and superscripted with an expression from $CONJ$ and subscripted with a subset of the numbers associated with the compiled rules.

Let $\mathcal{SH}$ be the set of ordered pairs whose first element is a member of $\mathcal{S}$ and whose second member is a subset of $\mathcal{H}$. We define an ordering over the members of $\mathcal{SH}$. $\langle \mathcal{S}_i, \mathcal{H}_j \rangle \sqsubseteq \langle \mathcal{S}_m, \mathcal{H}_n \rangle$ iff $\mathcal{S}_i \preceq \mathcal{S}_m$ and $\mathcal{H}_j \subseteq \mathcal{H}_n$, where the subscripts of members of $\mathcal{H}_j$ and $\mathcal{H}_n$ are ignored in determining whether the first set is a member of the second set.

$\mathcal{SH}, \sqsubseteq$ forms a complete lattice whose bottom element, $\perp$, is $\langle \emptyset, \emptyset \rangle$ and whose top element is the ordered pair whose first member is the set consisting of each member of MM annotated with the c-value 1.0 and whose second member is $\mathcal{H}$.

We define a monotonic operator Γ_{AP} over $\mathcal{SH}, \sqsubseteq$.

Definition 16. *Let $\mathcal{S}_n$ be a member of $\mathcal{S}$ and $\mathcal{H}_n$ be a member of $\mathcal{H}$ as defined above.*

$$\Gamma_{AP}(\langle \mathcal{S}_n, \mathcal{H}_n \rangle) = \langle \mathcal{S}', \mathcal{H}' \rangle$$

where
$\mathcal{S}' = \mathcal{S}_n \cup$
$\{(q_0 : (t_0 \delta) \mid q_0 : t_0 \leftarrow q_1 : t_1, \ldots, q_n : t_n, not(q_{n+1} : t_{n+1}), \ldots, not(q_{n+m} : t_{n+m}) \in Comp(AP + C)$ *and* $\mathcal{S}_n$ *justifies each of* $q_1 : (t_1 \delta), \ldots, q_n : (t_n \delta), not(q_{n+1} : (t_{n+1} \delta)), \ldots, not(q_{n+m} : (t_{n+m} \delta))\}$

$\mathcal{H}' = \mathcal{H} \cup$
$\{((q_0 : (t_0 \delta))_{\{m.i\} \cup u_1 \cup \cdots \cup u_n}^{not(q_{n+1} : (t_{n+1} \delta)) \wedge \cdots \wedge not(q_{n+m} : (t_{n+m} \delta))}) \mid m.i :: q_0 : t_0 \leftarrow q_1 : t_1, \ldots, q_n : t_n, not(q_{n+1} : t_{n+1}), \ldots, not(q_{n+m} : t_{n+m}) \in Comp(AP + C)$
and $\mathcal{S}_n \cup \mathcal{H}_n$ *justifies each of* $q_1 : (t_1 \delta), \ldots, q_n : (t_n \delta)$ *in terms of atoms with subscripts* $u_1, \ldots, u_n$ *and justifies none of* $q_{n+1} : (t_{n+1} \delta), \ldots, q_{n+m} : (t_{n+m} \delta)$ $\}$,
and δ is a c-unifier of the form $\{t_0 = v_0, \ldots, t_{n+m} = v_{n+m}\}$.

Clearly, Γ_{AP} is a monotonic operator since $\mathcal{S}_n$ and $\mathcal{H}_n$ are always included in the result of applying the operator to them. And since $(\mathcal{M}, \sqsubseteq)$ is a complete lattice, Γ_{AP} must have a least fixed point.

Evaluation

We evaluate the assumption set of the least fix-point in terms of the safe knowledge set of the least fix-point. This consists in determining whether the superscripts of the atoms in the assumption set are justified in terms the safe knowledge set. If all superscripts of an annotated atom are justified by the safe knowledge set, then the superscripted annotated atom is regarded as a justified atom. Otherwise it is regarded as an unjustified superscripted atom and deleted from the assumption set. Justified annotated atoms are regarded as being tentatively safe knowledge, which must be further vetted in the next step.

Negotiation

For any two atoms $(a:v_1)_{u_1}^{s_1}$ and $(a:v_2)_{u_2}^{s_2}$, both belonging to the tentatively safe knowledge set, such that $v_2 > v_1$, we need to determine whether it is $a:v_1$ or $a:v_2$ that should be included in the safe knowledge set. If $a:v_2$ is included in the final safe knowledge set (which is the operational semantics of a CALP), then implicitly so is $a:v$ for all $v \le v_2$. But the inclusion of $a:v_1$ does not guarantee that $a:v_2$ is included in the safe knowledge set if $v_2 > v_1$.

Intuitively, if both $(a:v_2)_{u_2}^{s_2}$ and $(a:v_1)_{u_1}^{s_1}$ are derived using different members of the same set of compiled rules, $Comp(R + C)$, which result from compiling a set of contestation C into a rule R, then, since $v_1 < v_2$, $(a:v_1)_{u_1}^{s_1}$ is derived using a rule from $Comp(R + C)$ with a number less than the number of the rule from which $(a:v_2)_{u_2}^{s_2}$ is derived. Given how we have set up the numbering of the compiled rules, $m.i < m.j$ (note that the ordering is entirely in terms of the second part of each number) implies that the contestation which is compiled into the rule numbered $m.i$ is more restrictive on the c-value of the head of that rule than the contestation which is compiled into the rule numbered $m.j$. A cautious approach is to assume that the most restrictive contestation holds unless otherwise shown. This can be implemented by giving higher priority to a rule numbered $m.i$ over a rule numbered $m.j$ if $i < j$. This is the approach we will use.

Definition 17. *Let u_1 and u_2 be two subscripts of annotated atoms. $u_1 \le u_2$ iff for each $m.i \in u_1$ there exists a $m.j \in u_2$ such that $i \le j$. Then,*

$$(a:v_1)_{u_1}^{s_1} \le (a:v_2)_{u_2}^{s_2} \text{ iff } u_1 \le u_2.$$

Note that as defined above there is no ordering between $m.i$ and $n.j$ if $m \ne n$.

Of the atoms tentatively included in the safe knowledge set we finally include in the safe knowledge set only those annotated atoms which are minimal in terms of this ordering.

The operational semantics of a CALP is the final safe knowledge set.

Example 4. Let AP and C be as in Example 2. In that case $NAP = Comp(AP + C)$ is

$$1.1 :: \quad a{:}0.1 \leftarrow c{:}0.7 \quad 1.2 :: \quad a{:}1 \leftarrow not(c{:}0.7)$$
$$2.1 :: \quad b{:}0.3 \leftarrow a{:}0.8 \quad 2.2 :: \quad b{:}1 \leftarrow not(a{:}0.8)$$
$$3.1 :: \quad c{:}0.2 \leftarrow b{:}0.7 \quad 3.2 :: \quad c{:}1 \leftarrow not(b{:}0.7)$$

The initial $\langle \mathcal{S}_n, \mathcal{H}_n \rangle$ is $\langle \emptyset, \emptyset \rangle$.

$$\Gamma^0_{NAP} = \langle \emptyset, \emptyset \rangle$$
$$\Gamma^1_{NAP} = \langle \emptyset, \{(a{:}1)^{not(c:0.7)}_{\{1.2\}}, \ (b{:}1)^{not(a:0.8)}_{\{2.2\}}, \ (c{:}1)^{not(b:0.7)}_{\{3.2\}} \} \rangle$$
$$\Gamma^2_{NAP} = \langle \emptyset, \{(a{:}1)^{not(c:0.7)}_{\{1.2\}}, \ (b{:}1)^{not(a0.8)}_{\{2.2\}}, \ (c{:}1)^{not(b:0.7)}_{\{3.2\}},$$
$$(a{:}0.1)^{not(b:0.7)}_{\{1.1,3.2\}}, \ (b{:}0.3)^{not(c:0.7)}_{\{2.1,1.2\}}, \ (c{:}0.2)^{not(a:0.8)}_{\{3.1,2.2\}} \} \rangle$$

Γ^2_{NAP} is a least fix-point. The safe knowledge set justifies all the superscripts. Hence $\{a{:}1_{\{1.2\}}, \ b{:}1_{\{2.2\}}, \ c{:}1_{\{3.2\}}, a{:}0.1_{\{1.1,3.2\}}, \ b{:}0.3_{\{2.1,1.2\}}, \ c{:}0.2_{\{3.1,2.2\}}\}$ are all regarded as tentative safe knowledge.

Since $1.1 < 1.2$, $2.1 < 2.2$, $3.1 < 3.2$, we get $a:0.1_{\{1.1,3.2\}} < a:1_{\{1.2\}}$, $b:0.3_{\{2.1,1.2\}} < b:1_{\{2.2\}}$, and $c:0.2_{\{3.1,2.2\}}\} < c:1_{\{3.2\}}$ Thus, $\{a{:}0.1, \ b{:}0.3, \ c{:}0.2\}$ is added to the initial safe knowledge. Thus, the final safe knowledge, which is the operational semantics of $AP + C$ is $\{a{:}0.1, \ b{:}0.3, \ c{:}0.2\}$.

The following theorem states that the operational semantics of a CALP is more cautious than the declarative semantics SEM described in the previous section.

Theorem 2. *Let AP be an annotated logic program and let C be a set of contestations. If $SEM(AP, C)$ entails $a{:}v_1$ and does not entail $a{:}v$ for any $v > v_1$ then the operational semantics of $AP + C$ entails $a : v_2$, for some $v_2 \leq v_1$ and does not entail $a{:}v$ for any $v > v_1$.*

5   Argumentation Databases

An argumentation database is a layer of software (the argumentation manager) on top of a database management system (DBMS) of the underlying database. The underlying database system can be a centralized relational database or a Datalog database or a distributed information system. The function of the argumentation manager (AM) is to annotate a c-value to each answer returned by the underlying database system to a query posed to the underlying database system. Thus, the AM generates no new answers to a query; its function is to provide for each answer a measure of how much confidence should be placed in the answer taking into account all the interacting arguments that can be mined from the information available to the argumentation database. A further condition on an argumentation database is that the AM should not lose any answers. That is, the AM should return no more or no less answers to the query than the answers returned by the underlying DBMS. We formalize this in the following requirement.

Remark 1. A fundamental requirement on any argumentation database is that it must return exactly the same answers as its underlying database system except that each answer is annotated with a c-value.

Many strategies for resolving conflicts in databases result in suppressing some information in the database ([ABC99]). Thus, these strategies can result in a different answer to a query if the strategies are employed than if they are not employed. It seems desirable that a conflict resolution strategy should be information lossless–otherwise, the user has no confidence that the particular strategy is worth using. We state below a restriction on the rules contained in the AM such that an argumentation database will satisfy the requirement in Remark 1 if the annotated rules contained in the AM satisfy this restriction.

The argumentation manager (AM) consists of the annotated rules and contestations and the capacity to do the bottom-up inferencing required to implement the operational semantics of CALPs. The facts in the underlying database are implcitly assumed to be annotated with the c-value 1.0. Thus the contestations and rules in the AM plus the facts in the underlying database implictly constitute a CALP. Hence the semantics of an argumentation database is the semantics of the CALP on which it is based.

We require that all the rules in AM are of the form

$$a_0 : min\{\mu_1, \overset{.}{.}, \mu_n\} \leftarrow b_1 : \mu_1, \overset{.}{.}, b_n : \mu_n$$

where $\mu_1, \cdots, \mu_n$ are all annotation variables. In an expanded version of this paper it will be shown that an argumentation database whose rules are restricted thus is guaranteed to satisfy the requirement in Remark1.

The AM can pose queries to the underlying database. The AM populates itself with annotated facts by annotating the tuples it receives in answer to the queries from the underlying database system. It regards these annotated tuples as safe knowledge. In the expanded version of this paper we will include the details of how this is done.

It is important to point out that the argumentation databases require no modification in the data model of the underlying database or in the query answering procedure of the underlying database.

6   Discussion and Future Work

In this paper we have introduced argumentation databases, which are databases augmented with argumentation capacity. An argumentation database gives the same answers to a query as the underlying database, but each answer is annotated with a confidence value reflecting the effect of all the interacting arguments that can be extracted from the database. In general, these arguments need not be drawn from a single database. We envisage that argumentation databases will be useful in any context where decisions have to be made on the basis of complex information drawn from many different sources, such as in security and intelligence analysis.

Our proposal for argumentation databases is based on annotated logic programming and contestations as a way of representing attack relations among arguments. Generalized annotated logic programs were introduced in [KS92]. In [KS92] the annotations represent truth values and the semantics of annotated logic programs is given in terms of these truth values. However, in our work truth values are different from the annotation values and the semantics must take into account both sorts of values.

[LS01] also associates confidence values with statements (as well as rules), where a confidence value is a tuple whose first member denotes the degree of belief in a statement and whose second member denotes the degree of doubt in that statement. Both degrees of belief and doubt are represented as a range of values. However, their work is not based on argumentation theory and does not employ the notion of attack among statements.

Databases with annotated information were introduced in [Sub94]. Contestations were introduced in [Pra96a] and [Pra96b] and further developed and applied to database theory in [Pra01]. However, in those works contestations were not annotated. Supplementing annotated logic programs with annotated constraints is introduced in [GL94]. However, in [GL94] the constraints are not used to capture conflicts in information, nor is there any interaction among the constraints. Argumentation databases were first introduced by us in [Pra03]. However, that work does not consider a model theory for CALPs which have no c-stable models; nor does it provide an operational semantics for argumentation databases which can form the basis of a query answering procedure.

The idea of attacks among arguments is discussed in all the works on argumentation cited earlier in this paper, however they do not introduce different degrees of attacks. The idea of one argument defeating another argument plays a central role in all the argumentation work cited earlier. This plays no role in our work because the fundamental requirement implies that even the conclusion of a defeated argument must be returned as an answer by an argumentation database system if it would be returned as an answer by the underlying database system.

In future work we plan to develop a query answering procedure for argumentation databases which will not affect the data model or the query answering procedure of the underlying database to which the argumentation layer is added.

References

[ABC99]   M. Arenas, L. Bertossi, and J. Chomicki. Consistent query answers in inconsistent databases. In *Proceedings of the 18th Symposium on Principles of Database Systems*, pages 68–79, 1999.

[BDKT97] A. Bonderenko, P.M. Dung, R.A. Kowalski, and F. Toni. An abstract argumentation theoretic approach to default reasoning. *Artificial Intelligence*, 93:63–101, 1997.

[Dun95]   P.M. Dung. The acceptability of arguments and its fundamental role in nonmontonic reasoning, logic programming, and n-person games. *Artificial Intelligence*, 77:321–357, 1995.

[GL94]   T. Gaasterland and J. Lobo. Qualified answers that reflect user needs and preferences. In *Proceedings of the 20th VLDB Conference*, 1994.

[GL88]   M. Gelfond and V. Lifschitz. The Stable Model Semantics for Logic Programming. In R.A. Kowalski and K.A. Bowen, editors, *Proc. 5th International Conference and Symposium on Logic Programming*, pages 1070–1080, Seattle, Washington, August 15–19 1988.

[KS92]   M. Kifer and V.S. Subrahmanian. Theory of generalized annotated logic programming and its applications. *Journal of Logic Programming*, 12:335–368, 1992.

[KT96]   R. Kowalski and F. Toni. Abstract argumentation. *Artificial Intelligence and Law*, 4:275–296, 1996.

[Lou87]   R.P. Loui. Defeat among arguments: a system of defeasible inference. *Computational Intelligence*, 2:100–106, 1987.

[LS01]   L. Lakshmanan and F. Sadri. On A Theory of Probabilistic Deductive Databases. *Theory and Practice of Logic Programming*, 1:5–42, 2001.

[Pol87]   J.L. Pollock. Defeasible reasoning. *Cognitive Science*, 11:481–518, 1987.

[Pra96a]   Shekhar Pradhan. Semantics of Normal Logic Programs and Contested Information. In *Proc. 11th IEEE Symposium on Logic in Computer Science*, 1996.

[Pra96b]   Shekhar Pradhan. Logic Programs with Contested Information. In M. Maher ed. *Proc. Joint International Conference and Symposium on Logic Programming*, MIT Press, 1996.

[Pra01]   Shekhar Pradhan. Reasoning with conflicting information in artificial intelligence and database theory. Technical Report CS-TR-4211, Dept of Computer Science, University of Maryland, College Park, Md 20742, 2001. Ph.D. dissertation.

[Pra03]   Shekhar Pradhan. Connecting Databases with Argumentation. In *Web Knowledge Management and Decision Support* ed. by Oskar Bartenstein, Ulrich Geske, Markus Hannebauer, and Osamu Yoshie. LNAI 2543, Springer Verlag, 2003.

[PS96a]   Henry Praaken and Giovanni Sartor. A system for defeasible argumentation with defeasible priorities. In *Proc. of the International Conference on Formal Aspects of Practical Reasoning*. Springer Verlag Lecture Notes in Artificial Intelligence No. 1085, 1996.

[PS97]   Henry Praaken and Giovanni Sartor. Argument-based extended logic programming with defeasible priorities. *Journal of Applied Non-classical Logics*, 7:25–75, 1997.

[Sub94]   V.S. Subrahmanian. Amalgamating knowledge bases. *ACM Transactions on Database Systems*, 19:291–331, 1994.

Order and Negation as Failure

Davy Van Nieuwenborgh* and Dirk Vermeir**

Dept. of Computer Science
Vrije Universiteit Brussel, VUB
{dvnieuwe,dvermeir}@vub.ac.be

Abstract. We equip ordered logic programs with negation as failure, using a simple generalization of the preferred answer set semantics for ordered programs. This extension supports a convenient formulation of certain problems, which is illustrated by means of an intuitive simulation of logic programming with ordered disjunction. The simulation also supports a broader application of "ordered disjunction", handling problems that would be cumbersome to express using ordered disjunction logic programs.

Interestingly, allowing negation as failure in ordered logic programs does not yield any extra computational power: the combination of negation as failure and order can be simulated using order (and true negation) alone.

1 Introduction

Non-monotonic reasoning using logic programming can be accomplished using one of several possible extensions of positive programs. The better known extension is *negation as failure* which has a long history, starting from the Clark completion [7], over stable model semantics [11] and well-founded semantics [25], to answer set programming [20]. It is well-known that adding negation as failure to programs results in a more expressive formalism. However, in the context of disjunctive logic programming [21, 19], [14] demonstrated that adding negation as failure positively in a program, i.e. in the head of the rules, yields no extra computational power to the formalism. One of the more interesting features of negation as failure in the head is that answers no longer have to be minimal w.r.t. subset inclusion (e.g. the program $\{a \vee \text{not } a \leftarrow\}$ has both $\{a\}$ and $\emptyset$ as answer sets). Indeed, such minimality turns out to be too demanding to express certain problems, e.g. in the areas of abductive logic programming [15,13] or logic programming with ordered disjunction [1,4].

Introducing (preference) order in logic programs represents another way to naturally express many "non-monotonic" problems. Many proposals [17,18,24,6,3,5,28,8,27,1] for logic programming extensions incorporate some kind of order, sometimes in a rather subtle way.

The preferred answer set semantics defined in [27], uses a partial order defined among the rules of a simple program, i.e. a non-disjunctive program containing only

---

* Supported by the FWO.
** This work was partially funded by the Information Society Technologies programme of the European Commission, Future and Emerging Technologies under the IST-2001-37004 WASP project.

C. Palamidessi (Ed.): ICLP 2003, LNCS 2916, pp. 194–208, 2003.
© Springer-Verlag Berlin Heidelberg 2003

classical negation, to prefer certain extended answer sets of the program above others, where the extended answer sets semantics naturally extends the classical one [20] to deal with inconsistencies in a program by allowing contradictory rules to defeat each other. It turns out that such an order can simulate negation as failure in both seminegative logic programs, where only rule bodies may contain negation as failure, under the stable model semantics [11], and disjunctive logic programs under the possible model semantics [23], demonstrating that order is at least as expressive as negation as failure.

Often, the introduction of order increases the expressiveness of a logic programming formalism, as illustrated by the complexity results in e.g. [16,6,3,27]. A natural question to ask then is whether combining order and negation as failure yields even more expressiveness. For the case of the ordered programs from [27], this paper will show that the answer to the above question is negative.

In this paper, we first extend the preferred answer set semantics for ordered programs to extended ordered programs, i.e. programs containing both classical negation and negation as failure combined with an order relation among the rules. Just as for disjunctive logic programming, adding negation as failure positively results in a formalism where answer sets are not anymore guaranteed to be subset minimal. Then we show, by means of a transformation, that the preferred answer set semantics for such extended ordered programs can be captured by the one for ordered programs (without negation as failure).

Despite the fact that extended ordered programs do not yield any extra computational power, they can be used profitably to express certain problems in a more intuitive and natural way. We demonstrate this by providing an elegant transformation from logic programs with ordered disjunction into extended ordered programs.

Logic programming with ordered disjunction [1] is a combination of qualitative choice logic [2] and answer set programming [20]. Instead of an order relation on the rules in a program, this formalism uses an order among the head literals of disjunctive rules. Intuitively, this relation, called ordered disjunction, ranks the conclusions in the head of rules. A lesser alternative should only be chosen if all higher ranked options could not be fulfilled.

Preferred answer sets for programs with ordered disjunction need not be subset minimal. E.g. for the program ($\times$ is used for disjunction and more preferred alternatives come first in the head of a rule)

$$a \times b \leftarrow$$
$$c \times b \leftarrow a$$
$$\neg c \leftarrow$$

both $S = \{b, \neg c\}$ and $T = \{a, b, \neg c\}$ are preferred answer sets, although $S \subset T$. Hence, a translation to a class of programs with subset minimal (preferred) answer sets is impossible unless e.g. extra atoms are introduced.

In [4] a procedure to compute the preferred answer sets of a logic program with ordered disjunction is presented. The algorithm uses two different programs: one to generate candidate answer sets and another one to test whether those candidates are preferred w.r.t. the order on the literals in the ordered disjunctions. Using our transformation into extended ordered logic programs, combined with the further translation that removes negation as failure, the algorithm to compute answer sets for ordered programs [27] can be used to do the same for logic programs with ordered disjunction.

Another advantage of translating ordered disjunction programs to ordered programs is that it becomes possible to conveniently express, using ordered programs, problems that would be cumbersome to do with ordered disjunction. As an example, suppose that, when thirsty, we prefer lemonade upon cola upon coffee upon juice, which is easily expressed using a single rule with ordered disjunction

$$lemonade \times cola \times coffee \times juice \leftarrow thirsty \ .$$

If, however, there are extra conditions attached to some of the choices, things rapidly get more complicated. E.g., suppose that we only like cola if it is warm outside and we only like coffee if we are tired. Representing these conditions needs four rules with ordered disjunctions.

$$lemonade \times juice \leftarrow thirsty, not \ warm, not \ tired$$
$$lemonade \times cola \times juice \leftarrow thirsty, warm, not \ tired$$
$$lemonade \times coffee \times juice \leftarrow thirsty, not \ warm, tired$$
$$lemonade \times cola \times coffee \times juice \leftarrow thirsty, warm, tired$$

In general, we get an exponential increase in program size; e.g. adding a similar condition on *lemonade* would result in eight rules. Using extended ordered logic programs to simulate ordered disjunction does not suffer such size increases. In fact, an extra condition only has to be added to the body of a single rule in the ordered program.

The paper is organized as follows: Section 2 generalizes simple programs with negation as failure, in both the head and body of rules. Section 3 presents the corresponding extension of ordered programs and their preferred answer set semantics. It is shown that adding negation as failure does not increase the expressiveness of ordered programs, by providing a transformation that eliminates negation as failure from such extended ordered programs. The usefulness of negation as failure in ordered programs is illustrated in Section 4 where an intuitive semantics-preserving transformation from programs with ordered disjunction to extended ordered programs is demonstrated. Conclusions and directions for further research are stated in Section 5. All proofs can be found in [26].

2   Extended Answer Sets for Extended Programs

We use the following basic definitions and notation. A *literal* is an *atom* a or a negated atom $\neg a$. An *extended literal* is a literal or a *naf-literal* of the form *not* l where l is a literal. The latter form denotes negation as failure: *not* l is interpreted as "l is not true". We use $\hat{l}$ to denote the ordinary literal underlying an extended literal, i.e. $\hat{l} = a$ if $l = not \ a$ while $\hat{l} = a$ if $l = a$, a a literal. Both notations are extended to sets so $\hat{X} = \{\hat{e} \mid e \in X\}$, with X a set of extended literals, while *not* $Y = \{not \ l \mid l \in Y\}$ for any set of (ordinary) literals Y.

For a set of literals X we use $\neg X$ to denote $\{\neg p \mid p \in X\}$ where $\neg(\neg a) \equiv a$. Also, X^+ denotes the positive part of X, i.e. $X^+ = \{a \in X \mid a$ is an atom$\}$. The *Herbrand base* of X, denoted $\mathcal{B}_X$, contains all atoms appearing in X, i.e. $\mathcal{B}_X = (X \cup \neg X)^+$. A set I of literals is *consistent* if $I \cap \neg I = \emptyset$. We use X^- to denote the literals underlying elements of X that are not ordinary literals, i.e. $X^- = \{l \mid not \ l \in X\}$. It follows that X is consistent iff the set of ordinary literals $\neg(X^-) \cup (X \backslash not \ X^-)$ is consistent.

Before studying the effects of allowing negation as failure in ordered programs, we first extend the simple logic programs introduced in [27] to support negation as failure in both the head and the body of rules.

Definition 1. *An **extended logic program** (ELP) is a countable set P of **extended rules** of the form $\alpha \leftarrow \beta$ where $\alpha \cup \beta$ is a finite set of extended literals, and $|\alpha| \leq 1$, i.e. α is a singleton or empty. If $(\alpha \cup \beta)^- = \emptyset$, i.e. all rules are free from naf-literals, P is called a **simple program** (SLP).*

We will often confuse a singleton set with its sole element, writing rules as $a \leftarrow \beta$ or $\leftarrow \beta$. The *Herbrand base* $\mathcal{B}_P$ of an ELP P contains all atoms appearing in P. An *interpretation* I of P is any consistent subset of $\mathcal{B}_P \cup \neg\mathcal{B}_P$. An interpretation I is *total* if $\mathcal{B}_P \subseteq I \cup \neg I$.

An extended literal l is true w.r.t. an interpretation I, denoted $I \models l$ if $l \in I$ in case l is ordinary, or $I \not\models a$ if $l = not\ a$ for some ordinary literal a. As usual, $I \models X$, for some set of (extended) literals X, iff $\forall l \in X \cdot I \models l$.

A rule $r = a \leftarrow \beta$ is *satisfied* by I, denoted $I \models r$, if $I \models a$, $a \neq \emptyset$, whenever $I \models \beta$, i.e. if r is *applicable* ($I \models \beta$), then it must be *applied* ($I \models \beta \cup a$).

For a simple program P, an *answer set* is a minimal interpretation I that is *closed* under the rules of P (i.e. $\forall r \in P \cdot I \models r$).

For an ELP P containing negation as failure and an interpretation I, the Gelfond-Lifschitz transformation [11] yields the *GL-reduct* program P^I that consists of those rules $(a \setminus not\ a^-) \leftarrow (\beta \setminus not\ \beta^-)$ where $a \leftarrow \beta$ is in P, $I \models not\ \beta^-$ and $I \models a^-$.

Thus, P^I is obtained from P by (a) removing all true naf-literals $not\ a$, $a \notin I$, from the bodies of rules in P, (b) removing all false naf-literals $not\ a$, $a \in I$ from the heads of rules in P, and (c) keeping in P^I only the transformed rules that are free from negation as failure. An interpretation I is then an *answer set* of P iff I is an answer set of the reduct P^I.

Another reduct w.r.t. an interpretation denotes the set of rules that are satisfied w.r.t. that interpretation.

Definition 2. *The **reduct** $P_I \subseteq P$ of an ELP P w.r.t. an interpretation I contains just the rules satisfied by I, i.e. $P_I = \{r \in P \mid I \models r\}$.*

Naturally, $P_M = P$ for any answer set M of P. Inconsistencies in ELP's are handled by considering a *defeat* relation between rules. In an *extended answer set*, all rules that are not satisfied are defeated.

Definition 3. *An extended rule $r = a \leftarrow \alpha$ is **defeated** w.r.t. an interpretation I of an ELP P iff there exists an applied **competing rule** $r' = a' \leftarrow \alpha'$ such that $\{a, a'\}$ is inconsistent. An interpretation I is an **extended answer set** of P iff I is an answer set of P_I and each unsatisfied rule from $P \setminus P_I$ is defeated w.r.t. I.*

Thus, to verify a candidate extended answer set M for a program P, one first obtains P_M by eliminating unsatisfied rules (verifying that they are defeated) and then checks that M is a minimal closure of the positive program $(P_M)^M$, obtained by applying the Gelfond-Lifschitz transformation for P_M.

Intuitively, as in [27], Definition 3 handles inconsistencies by allowing one of two contradictory rules (whose heads are inconsistent) to defeat the other.

Example 1. Consider the extended program P containing the following rules.

$$\neg a \leftarrow \qquad \neg b \leftarrow \qquad c \leftarrow$$
$$a \leftarrow not\ b \qquad b \leftarrow not\ a \qquad not\ c \leftarrow a$$

For the interpretation $I = \{a, \neg b\}$, P_I contains all rules but $\neg a \leftarrow$ and $c \leftarrow$ which are defeated (w.r.t. I) by the applied rules $a \leftarrow not\ b$ and $not\ c \leftarrow a$, respectively. I is then an extended answer set because $\{a, \neg b\}$ is an answer set of $(P_I)^I = \{\neg b \leftarrow,\ a \leftarrow\}$.

P has three more extended answer sets, namely $J = \{\neg a, b, c\}$, $K = \{\neg a, \neg b, c\}$ and $L = \{a, \neg b, c\}$. Here, $P_J = P \backslash \{\neg b \leftarrow\}$, and $(P_J)^J$ contains $\neg a \leftarrow$, $b \leftarrow$, $c \leftarrow$ and $\leftarrow a$. For K, we have that $P_K = P \setminus \{a \leftarrow not\ b,\ b \leftarrow not\ a\}$ and $(P_K)^K$ contains $\neg a \leftarrow$, $\neg b \leftarrow$, $c \leftarrow$ and $\leftarrow a$. Finally, for L, $P_L = P \setminus \{\neg a \leftarrow, not\ c \leftarrow a\}$ and $(P_L)^L$ contains $a \leftarrow$, $\neg b \leftarrow$ and $c \leftarrow$.

Adding negation as failure invalidates some properties holding for simple programs [27].

- Unlike for simple programs, extended answer sets for extended logic programs are not necessary minimal w.r.t. subset inclusion, as demonstrated by the previous example where $I \subset L$. The same holds for extended disjunctive logic programs as shown in [12].
- Every simple program that does not contain constraints (rules with an empty head) has an answer set but an extended program, e.g. $\{a \leftarrow not\ a\}$, may not have any answer set, making the semantics of Definition 3 not universal.
- If a simple program has "traditional" answer sets [20], these coincide with its extended answer sets [27]. For an extended program P, it is clear that any traditional answer set (for which $P_M = P$) is an extended answer set according to Definition 3. However, it may be that, while P has traditional answer sets, it has additional extended answer sets, as illustrated in the following example.

Example 2. Consider the following program P.

$$\neg b \leftarrow a \qquad b \leftarrow not\ b$$
$$a \leftarrow not\ b \qquad b \leftarrow not\ a$$

Clearly, $I = \{b\}$ is a traditional answer set with P^I containing $\neg b \leftarrow a$ and $b \leftarrow$ which has $\{b\}$ as a minimal answer set. Since $P_I = P$, $\{b\}$ is also an extended answer set.

However, also $J = \{a, \neg b\}$ is an extended answer set because: (1) P_J contains all rules but $b \leftarrow not\ b$; the latter rule is defeated (w.r.t. J) by the applied rule $\neg b \leftarrow a$, and (2) $(P_J)^J$ contains just $a \leftarrow$ and $\neg b \leftarrow a$ and thus J is an answer set of P_J.

Clearly, though, J is not an answer set of P. While J is not very intuitive, such sets will be eliminated by the preference relation introduced in Section 3, see Theorem 2.

Note that the program in the above example does not contain negation as failure in the head of a rule. In fact, negation as failure in the heads of rules can be removed by a construction that is similar to the one used in [14] for reducing DLP's with negation as failure in the head to DLP's without.

Definition 4. *For P an ELP, define $E(P)$ as the ELP, without negation as failure in the head, obtained from P by replacing each rule $a \leftarrow \alpha$ by (for a an ordinary literal, not_a is a new atom) by $a \leftarrow \alpha, \text{not} \neg a, \text{not} \text{ not}_a$ when a is an ordinary literal; or by $\text{not}_{\hat{a}} \leftarrow \alpha, \text{not} \hat{a}$ when a is a naf-literal.*

Note that the above definition captures our intuition about defeat: one can ignore an applicable rule $a \leftarrow \alpha$ if it is defeated by evidence for either $\neg a$ or *not a*, thus making either *not $\neg a$* or *not not_a* false and the rule $a \leftarrow \alpha, \text{not} \neg a, \text{not} \text{ not}_a$ not applicable.

The extended answer sets of P can then be retrieved from the traditional answer sets of $E(P)$.

Theorem 1. *Let P be an ELP. Then, S is an extended answer sets of P iff there is an answer set S' of $E(P)$ such that $S = S' \cap (\mathcal{B}_P \cup \neg \mathcal{B}_P)$.*

For example, let $P = \{a \leftarrow, \text{ not } a \leftarrow\}$, which has two extended answer sets $\{a\}$ and $\emptyset$. Then $E(P) = \{a \leftarrow \text{not} \neg a, \text{not} \text{ not}_a, \text{ not}_a \leftarrow \text{not } a\}$ which has two traditional answer sets $\{a\}$ and $\{\text{not}_a\}$ corresponding with $\{a\}$ and $\emptyset$.

3 Extended Ordered Programs

Adding a preference order to extended programs, or, equivalently, allowing negation as failure in ordered programs (OLPs, [27]), yields the class of *extended ordered programs*.

Definition 5. *An **extended ordered logic program** (EOLP) is a pair $\langle R, < \rangle$ where R is an extended program and $<$ is a well-founded strict[1] partial order on the rules in R.[2] If R is free from naf-literals, $\langle R, < \rangle$ is called an **ordered logic program** (OLP).*

Intuitively, $r_1 < r_2$ indicates that r_1 is more preferred than r_2. In the examples we will often represent the order implicitly using the format

$$\frac{\begin{array}{c} \cdots \\ \hline R_2 \\ \hline R_1 \\ \hline R_0 \end{array}}{}$$

where each R_i, $i \geq 0$, represents a set of rules, indicating that all rules below a line are more preferred than any of the rules above the line, i.e. $\forall i \geq 0 \cdot \forall r_i \in R_i, r_{i+1} \in R_{i+1} \cdot r_i < r_{i+1}$ or $\forall i \geq 0 \cdot R_i < R_{i+1}$ for short.

---

[1] A strict partial order $<$ on a set X is a binary relation on X that is antisymmetric, anti-reflexive and transitive. The relation $<$ is well-founded if every nonempty subset of X has a $<$-minimal element.

[2] Strictly speaking, we should allow R to be a multiset or, equivalently, have labeled rules, so that the same rule can appear in several positions in the order. For the sake of simplicity of notation, we will ignore this issue in the present paper: all results also hold for the general multiset case.

Example 3. Consider the following extended ordered logic program describing rules pertaining to a fatal shooting incident.

$$guilty \leftarrow shoot, dead, not\ self\_defense$$
$$\neg guilty \leftarrow shoot, self\_defense$$
$$self\_defense \leftarrow threatened$$
$$not\ self\_defense \leftarrow shoot, unarmed$$

$$court\_unauthorized \leftarrow normal\_court, not\ self\_defense$$
$$not\ guilty \leftarrow court\_unauthorized$$
$$not\ \neg guilty \leftarrow court\_unauthorized$$

$$unarmed \leftarrow shoot \leftarrow normal\_court \leftarrow$$
$$threatened \leftarrow dead \leftarrow$$

Here the lower (strongest) level provides the facts of the case (someone killed an unarmed person but the victim threatened the killer). The middle level represents the rules governing the handling of such a case in a normal court: if there is no self-defense, it should refer the case to a higher court and no judgment on the guilt status should be proclaimed, i.e. both *not guilty* and *not ¬guilty* should be true. The rules with the lowest preference (in the highest component) describe general criteria to determine qualifications of the case, i.e. guilt and whether a claim of self-defense can be accepted.

Definition 6. *Let* $P = \langle R, < \rangle$ *be an EOLP. For subsets* R_1 *and* R_2 *of R we define* $R_1 \sqsubseteq R_2$ *iff* $\forall r_2 \in R_2 \backslash R_1 \cdot \exists r_1 \in R_1 \backslash R_2 \cdot r_1 < r_2$. *We write* $R_1 \sqsubset R_2$ *just when* $R_1 \sqsubseteq R_2$ *and* $R_1 \neq R_2$. *For* M_1, M_2 *extended answer sets of R, we define* $M_1 \sqsubseteq M_2$ *iff* $R_{M_1} \sqsubseteq R_{M_2}$. *As usual,* $M_1 \sqsubset M_2$ *iff* $M_1 \sqsubseteq M_2$ *and* $M_1 \neq M_2$.

*An **answer set** for an EOLP P is any extended answer set of R. An answer set for P is called **preferred** if it is minimal w.r.t.* $\sqsubseteq$. *An answer set is called **proper** if it satisfies all minimal (according to* $<$) *rules in R.*

Intuitively, a reduct R_1 is preferred over a reduct R_2 if every rule r_2 which is in R_2 but not in R_1 is "countered" by a stronger rule $r_1 < r_2$ from R_1 which is not in R_2.

Note the difference between Definition 6 and other approaches such as [17], which demand that a stronger rule $r_1 \in R_1 \backslash R_2$ countering a weaker rule $r_1 < r_2 \in R_2 \backslash R_1$, must be applied and have a head that contradicts the head of r_2, thus restricting the effect of the order to "competing" rules.

In [27] it is shown that the relation $\sqsubseteq$ on reducts is a partial order.

Example 4. The program from Example 3 has three extended answer sets, all of which contain the set of facts $F = \{unarmed, shoot, dead, threatened, normal\_court\}$ asserted in the most preferred component of the program: $I_1 = F \cup \{self\_defense, \neg guilty\}$, $I_2 = F \cup \{court\_unauthorized\}$ and $I_3 = F \cup \{court\_unauthorized, guilty\}$.

The corresponding reducts are $P_{I_1} = P \backslash \{not\ self\_defense \leftarrow shoot, unarmed\}$, $P_{I_2} = P \backslash \{self\_defense \leftarrow threatened,\ guilty \leftarrow shoot, dead, not\ self\_defense\}$ and $P_{I_3} = P \backslash \{self\_defense \leftarrow threatened,\ not\ guilty \leftarrow court\_unauthorized\}$. Clearly, both $P_{I_2} \sqsubseteq P_{I_3}$, and $P_{I_1} \sqsubseteq P_{I_3}$ since both I_2 and I_1 satisfy all of the middle rules while I_3 defeats *not guilty* $\leftarrow court\_unauthorized$.

Since P_{I_1} and P_{I_2} are incomparable w.r.t. $\sqsubseteq$, it follows that both I_1 and I_2 are preferred answer sets, fitting our intuition that I_3 is unreasonable. The defense would probably argue for I_1, which clears its client, while the prosecution might assert I_2, referring the case to a higher court.

Example 5. Reconsider the program from Example 1 with the following preference relation, yielding an extended ordered program $\langle P, < \rangle$.

$$\frac{\neg a \leftarrow}{a \leftarrow not\ b} \quad \frac{\neg b \leftarrow}{b \leftarrow not\ a} \quad \frac{not\ c \leftarrow a}{c \leftarrow}$$

The reducts of the answer sets of P are $P_I = P \setminus \{c \leftarrow, \ \neg a \leftarrow\}$, $P_J = P \setminus \{\neg b \leftarrow\}$, $P_K = P \setminus \{a \leftarrow not\ b,\ b \leftarrow not\ a\}$ and $P_J = P \setminus \{\neg a \leftarrow, not\ c \leftarrow a\}$, which are ordered by $P_J \sqsubseteq P_I$, $P_J \sqsubseteq P_K$, $P_L \sqsubseteq P_I$ and $P_L \sqsubseteq P_K$, making both $J = \{\neg a, b, c\}$ and $L = \{a, \neg b, c\}$ preferred over both $I = \{a, \neg b\}$ and $K = \{\neg a, \neg b, c\}$.

An interesting interaction between defeat and negation as failure can occur when default (minimally preferred) rules of the form *not a* $\leftarrow$ are used. At first sight, such rules are useless because *not a* is true by default. However, if present, such rules can also be used to defeat others as in the following example.
Example 6.

$$\frac{not\ a \leftarrow}{a \leftarrow} \over {\leftarrow a}$$

This program has the empty set as its single preferred answer set, its reduct containing the rules *not a* $\leftarrow$ and $\leftarrow a$. Without *not a* $\leftarrow$, it would be impossible to defeat $a \leftarrow$, thus violating $\leftarrow a$ and thus the program would not have any answer sets.

Extended programs can be regarded as EOLP's with an empty order relation.
Theorem 2. *The (traditional) answer sets of an ELP P coincide with the proper preferred answer sets of the EOLP $\langle P, \emptyset \rangle$.*

As mentioned in the introduction, negation as failure can be simulated using order alone. However, from Example 1 (where $I \subset L$ are both preferred answer sets), it follows that (proper) preferred answer sets for EOLP's are not necessarily subset-minimal. On the other hand, it has been shown in [27] that (proper) preferred answer sets for ordered programs (without negation as failure) are subset minimal. Hence, simulating an EOLP with an OLP will necessarily involve the introduction of fresh atoms.

One might be tempted to employ a construction similar to the one used e.g. in [17,27] for simulating negation as failure using a two-level order. This would involve replacing extended literals of the form *not a* by fresh atoms $\mathbf{not}_a$ and adding "default" rules to introduce $\mathbf{not}_a$.

E.g. the extended program $P = \{a \leftarrow not\ b,\ b \leftarrow not\ a\}$ would be simulated by the ordered program $N(P)$

$$\frac{\mathbf{not}_a \leftarrow}{\frac{a \leftarrow \mathbf{not}_b}{\frac{\neg a \leftarrow \mathbf{not}_a}{\neg\mathbf{not}_a \leftarrow a}}} \quad \frac{\mathbf{not}_b \leftarrow}{\frac{b \leftarrow \mathbf{not}_a}{\frac{\neg b \leftarrow \mathbf{not}_b}{\neg\mathbf{not}_b \leftarrow b}}}$$

where the rules on the lowest level act as constraints, forcing one of the "default rules" in the top level to be defeated in any proper answer set of $N(P)$. The "constraint rules" also serve to indirectly introduce competition between formally unrelated atoms: in the example, we need e.g. a rule to defeat $\text{not}_a \leftarrow$, based on the acceptance of a.

This does not work, however, since it may introduce unwanted answer sets as for the program $\{a \leftarrow not\ a\}$ which would yield the OLP program

$$\frac{\begin{array}{c}\text{not}_a \leftarrow \\ \hline a \leftarrow \text{not}_a \\ \hline \neg a \leftarrow \text{not}_a \\ \neg\text{not}_a \leftarrow a \end{array}}{}$$

which has a (proper) preferred answer set $\{\text{not}_a, \neg a\}$ while the original program has no extended answer sets.

The above examples seem to point to contradictory requirements for the corresponding OLP programs: for the first example, rules implying not_a should be (indirect) competitors for a-rules while for the second example, the not_a-rule should *not* compete with the a-rule, in order not to introduce spurious answer sets.

The solution is to add not only fresh atoms for extended literals of the form *not a*, but also for ordinary literals. Thus each extended literal l will be mapped to an independent new atom $\phi(l)$. A rule $l \leftarrow \alpha$ will then be translated to $\phi(l) \leftarrow \phi(\alpha)$, which does not compete with any other such rule. Defeat between such rules is however supported indirectly by adding extra rules that encode the consequences of applying such a rule: for an original rule of the form $a \leftarrow \alpha$, a an ordinary literal, we ensure that its replacement $\phi(a) \leftarrow \phi(\alpha)$ can, when applied, indirectly defeat $\phi(\neg a)$- and $\phi(not\ a)$-rules by adding both $\neg\phi(\neg a) \leftarrow \phi(\alpha), \phi(a)$ and $\neg\phi(not\ a) \leftarrow \phi(\alpha), \phi(a)$. Similarly, for an original rule of the form *not a* $\leftarrow \alpha$, a an ordinary literal, a rule $\neg\phi(a) \leftarrow \phi(\alpha), \phi(not\ a)$ will be added along with its replacement $\phi(not\ a) \leftarrow \phi(\alpha)$. Consistency is assured by introducing a new most preferred component containing, besides translated constraints $\leftarrow \phi(\alpha)$ for the original ones, rules of the form $\leftarrow \phi(a), \phi(not\ a)$ and $\leftarrow \phi(a), \phi(\neg a)$. In addition, this new component also contains translations $a \leftarrow \phi(a)$ of the new atoms, that correspond to ordinary literals, back to their original versions.

Negation as failure can then be simulated by introducing "default" rules of the form $\phi(not\ a) \leftarrow$ in a new least preferred component.

Spurious answer sets are prevented, as these new default rules introducing $\phi(not\ a)$, which do not have defeat-enabling accompanying rules as described above, cannot be used to defeat transformed rules of the original program, but only to make them applicable. E.g. the program $\{a \leftarrow not\ a\}$ mentioned above would be translated as

$$
\begin{array}{ll}
\phi(not\ a) \leftarrow & \phi(not\ \neg a) \leftarrow \\
\hline
\phi(a) \leftarrow \phi(not\ a) & \\
\neg\phi(not\ a) \leftarrow \phi(not\ a), \phi(a) & \\
\neg\phi(\neg a) \leftarrow \phi(not\ a), \phi(a) & \\
\hline
\leftarrow \phi(a), \phi(not\ a) & a \leftarrow \phi(a) \\
\leftarrow \phi(a), \phi(\neg a) & \neg a \leftarrow \phi(\neg a) \\
\leftarrow \phi(\neg a), \phi(not\ \neg a) &
\end{array}
$$

which has no proper preferred answer sets.

Formally, for an EOLP $\langle R, < \rangle$, we define a mapping ϕ translating original extended literals by: $\phi(a) = a'$, $\phi(\neg a) = a'_\neg$, $\phi(not\ a) = not_a$ and $\phi(not\ \neg a) = not_{\neg a}$; where for each atom $a \in \mathcal{B}_R$, a', $a_\neg'$, not_a and $not_{\neg a}$ are fresh atoms. We use $\phi(X)$, X a set of extended literals, to denote $\{\phi(x) \mid x \in X\}$.

Definition 7. *Let $P = \langle R, < \rangle$ be an extended ordered logic program. The OLP version of P, denoted $N_s(P)$, is defined by $N_s(P) = \langle R_n \cup R' \cup R_c, R_c < R'_< < R_n \rangle$, where*

- $R_n = \{\phi(not\ a) \leftarrow \mid a \in \mathcal{B}_R \cup \neg\mathcal{B}_R\}$,
- R' *is obtained from R by replacing each rule*
  - $a \leftarrow \alpha$, *where a is a literal, by the rules $\phi(a) \leftarrow \phi(\alpha)$ and $\neg\phi(\neg a) \leftarrow \phi(\alpha), \phi(a)$ and $\neg\phi(not\ a) \leftarrow \phi(\alpha), \phi(a)$;*
  - $not\ a \leftarrow \alpha$ *by the rules $\phi(not\ a) \leftarrow \phi(\alpha)$ and $\neg\phi(a) \leftarrow \phi(\alpha), \phi(not\ a)$;*
- $R_c = \{\leftarrow \phi(\alpha) \in R\} \cup \{\leftarrow \phi(a), \phi(not\ a); \leftarrow \phi(a), \phi(\neg a); a \leftarrow \phi(a) \mid a \in \mathcal{B}_R \cup \neg\mathcal{B}_R\}$.

Furthermore, $R'_<$ stands for the original order on R but defined on the corresponding rules in R'.

Note that $N_s(P)$ is free from negation as failure.

Example 7. The OLP $N_s(P)$, corresponding to the EOLP of Example 5 is shown below.

$not_a \leftarrow$	$not_b \leftarrow$	$not_c \leftarrow$
$not_{\neg a} \leftarrow$	$not_{\neg b} \leftarrow$	$not_{\neg c} \leftarrow$
$a'_\neg \leftarrow$	$b'_\neg \leftarrow$	$not_c \leftarrow a'$
$\neg a' \leftarrow a'_\neg$	$\neg b' \leftarrow b'_\neg$	$\neg c' \leftarrow a', not_c$
$\neg not_{\neg a} \leftarrow a'_\neg$	$\neg not_{\neg b} \leftarrow b'_\neg$	
$a' \leftarrow not_b$	$b' \leftarrow not_a$	$c' \leftarrow$
$\neg a'_\neg \leftarrow not_b, a'$	$\neg b'_\neg \leftarrow not_a, b'$	$\neg c'_\neg \leftarrow c'$
$\neg not_a \leftarrow not_b, a'$	$\neg not_b \leftarrow not_a, b'$	$\neg not_c \leftarrow c'$
$a \leftarrow a'$	$b \leftarrow b'$	$c \leftarrow c'$
$\neg a \leftarrow a'_\neg$	$\neg b \leftarrow b'_\neg$	$\neg c \leftarrow c'_\neg$
$\leftarrow a', not_a$	$\leftarrow b', not_b$	$\leftarrow c', not_c$
$\leftarrow a'_\neg, not_{\neg a}$	$\leftarrow b'_\neg, not_{\neg b}$	$\leftarrow c'_\neg, not_{\neg c}$
$\leftarrow a', a'_\neg$	$\leftarrow b', b'_\neg$	$\leftarrow c', c'_\neg$

The OLP has two proper preferred answer sets $J' = \{\neg a, b, c, a'_\neg, b', c', \neg a', not_a,$ $\neg not_b, \neg b'_\neg, \neg not_c, \neg c'_\neg, \neg not_{\neg a}, not_{\neg b}, not_{\neg c}\}$ and $L' = \{a, \neg b, c, a', b'_\neg, c', \neg b',$ $\neg not_a, \neg a'_\neg, not_b, \neg not_c, \neg c'_\neg, not_{\neg a}, \neg not_{\neg b}, not_{\neg c}\}$, corresponding to the preferred answer sets J and L of P.

In general, we have the following correspondence.

Theorem 3. *Let $P = \langle R, < \rangle$ be an extended ordered logic program. Then, M is a preferred answer set of P iff there exists a proper preferred answer set M' of $N_s(P)$, such that $M = M' \cap (\mathcal{B}_R \cup \neg\mathcal{B}_R)$.*

Since the construction of $N_s(P)$ is polynomial, it follows that the expressiveness of EOLP is the same as for OLP, i.e. the second level of the polynomial hierarchy [27]. Consequently, order can simulate negation as failure, even if the latter is used in combination with order.

4   Ordered Disjunction and Ordered Programs

Logic programming with ordered disjunction (LPOD) [1,4] adds a new connective, called ordered disjunction, to logic programming. Using this connective, conclusions in the head of a rule are ordered according to preference. Intuitively, one tries to satisfy an applicable rule by using its most preferred, i.e. best ranked, conclusion.

Definition 8. *A* **logic program with ordered disjunction** *(LPOD) is a set of rules of the form $a_1 \times \ldots \times a_n \leftarrow \beta$, $n \geq 1$, where the a_i's are (ordinary) literals and β is a finite set of extended literals.*

An ordered disjunctive rule $a_1 \times \ldots \times a_n \leftarrow \beta$ can intuitively be read as: if β is true, then accept a_1, if possible; if not, then accept a_2, if possible; ...; if none of $a_1, \ldots, a_{n-1}$ are possible, then a_n must be accepted.

Similarly to ordered programs, the semantics for LPOD's is defined in two steps. First, answer sets for LPOD's are defined, which are then ordered by a relation that takes into account to what degree rules are satisfied. The minimal elements in this ordering are also called preferred answer sets. To avoid confusion, we will use the term "preferred LPOD answer sets" for the latter.

Answer sets for LPOD's are defined using *split programs*, a mechanism first used in [23] to define the possible model semantics for disjunctive logic programs.

Definition 9. *Let $r = a_1 \times \ldots \times a_n \leftarrow \beta$ be a LPOD rule. For $k \leq n$ we define the kth option of r as $r^k = a_k \leftarrow \beta$, not $\{a_1, \ldots, a_{k-1}\}$.*

An extended logic program P' is called a **split program** *of a LPOD P if it is obtained by replacing each rule in P by one of its options. An interpretation S is then an (LPOD)* **answer set** *of P if it is an answer set of a split program P' of P.*

Note that the split programs defined above do not contain negation as failure in the head of rules.

Example 8. The LPOD

$$b \times c \times d \leftarrow$$
$$c \times a \times d \leftarrow$$
$$\neg c \leftarrow b$$

has five answer sets, namely $S_1 = \{a, b, \neg c\}$, $S_2 = \{b, \neg c, d\}$, $S_3 = \{c\}$, $S_4 = \{a, d\}$ and $S_5 = \{d\}$.

Note that $S_5 \subset S_4$, illustrating that answer sets need not be subset-minimal. Intuitively, only S_1 and S_3 are optimal in that they correspond with a best combination of options for each of the rules.

The above intuition is formalized in the following definition of a preference relation on LPOD answer sets.

Definition 10. *Let S be an answer set of a LPOD P. Then S satisfies the rule $a_1 \times \ldots \times a_n \leftarrow \beta$*

- *to degree 1 if $S \not\models \beta$,*
- *to degree j ($1 \leq j \leq n$) if $S \models \beta$ and $j = min\{i \mid a_i \in S\}$.*

For a set of literals S, we define $S^i(P) = \{r \in P \mid deg_S(r) = i\}$, where $deg_S(r)$ is used to denote the degree to which r is satisfied w.r.t. S.

Let S_1 and S_2 be answer sets of P. Then S_1 is preferred over S_2, denoted $S_1 \sqsubset S_2$, iff there is a k such that $S_2^k(P) \subset S_1^k(P)$, and for all $j < k$, $S_1^j(P) = S_2^j(P)$. A minimal (according to $\sqsubset$) answer set is called a (LPOD) **preferred answer set** *of P.*

Example 9. In the LPOD from Example 8, both S_1 and S_3 satisfy the third rule to degree 1. In addition, S_1 satisfies the first rule to degree 1 and the second rule to degree 2, while S_3 satisfies the second rule to degree 1 and the first rule to degree 2. Thus S_1 and S_3 are incomparable w.r.t. $\sqsubset$. All other answer sets are less preferred than either S_1 or S_3: e.g. S_5 satisfies the first and second rule only to degree 3, and the third rule to degree 1, from which $S_1 \sqsubset S_5$ and $S_3 \sqsubset S_5$. It follows that S_1 and S_3 are both preferred.

The preference relation which is implicit in ordered disjunctive rules can be intuitively simulated using preference between non-disjunctive rules.

Definition 11. *The EOLP version of a LPOD P, denoted $L(P)$, is defined by $L(P) = \langle P_r \cup P_1 \cup \ldots \cup P_n \cup P_d, P_r < P_1 < \ldots < P_n < P_d \rangle$, where*

- *n is the size of the greatest ordered disjunction in P;*
- *P_r contains every non-disjunctive rule $a \leftarrow \beta \in P$, and for every ordered disjunctive rule $a_1 \times \ldots \times a_n \leftarrow \beta \in P$, P_r contains a rule $a_i \leftarrow \beta, not \{a_1, \ldots, a_n\} \setminus \{a_i\}$ for every $1 \leq i \leq n$.*
- *P_d contains $not\ a \leftarrow$ for every literal a that appears in the head of some ordered disjunctive rule;*
- *for $1 \leq k \leq n$, P_k is defined by $P_k = \{a_k \leftarrow \beta, not \{a_1, \ldots, a_{k-1}\} \mid a_1 \times \ldots \times a_m \leftarrow \beta \in P$ with $k \leq m \leq n\}$.*

Intuitively, the rules in P_r ensure that all rules in P are satisfied, while the rules in P_d allow to defeat a rule in one of the $P_1, \ldots, P_{n-1}$ in favor of a rule in a less preferred component (see also Example 6). Finally, the rules in $P_1, \ldots, P_n$ encode the intuition behind LPOD, i.e. better ranked literals in an ordered disjunction are preferred.

Example 10. The result of the transformation of the LPOD from Example 8 is shown below.

$not\ a \leftarrow$	$not\ b \leftarrow$
$not\ c \leftarrow$	$not\ d \leftarrow$
$d \leftarrow not\ b, not\ c$	$c \leftarrow not\ a, not\ d$
$c \leftarrow not\ b$	$a \leftarrow not\ c$
$b \leftarrow$	$c \leftarrow$
$b \leftarrow not\ c, not\ d$	$c \leftarrow not\ a, not\ d$
$c \leftarrow not\ b, not\ d$	$a \leftarrow not\ c, not\ d$
$d \leftarrow not\ b, not\ c$	$d \leftarrow not\ a, not\ c$
$\neg c \leftarrow b$	

This EOLP program has two proper preferred answer sets, i.e. $S_1 = \{a, b, \neg c\}$ and $S_3 = \{c\}$.

In general, the preferred LPOD answer sets for a LPOD program P coincide with the proper preferred answer sets of $L(P)$.

Theorem 4. *An interpretation S is a preferred LPOD answer set of a LPOD P iff S is a proper preferred answer set of $L(P)$.*

As mentioned in the introduction, LPOD cannot conveniently handle rules of the form $a_1\{\alpha_1\} \times \ldots \times a_n\{\alpha_n\} \leftarrow \beta$, where the $\alpha_1, \ldots, \alpha_n$ are sets of extended literals expressing extra conditions that have to be fulfilled to derive the corresponding conclusion. Intuitively, such a rule means that if β is true, then a_1 should be true if α_1 is also true and if possible; otherwise a_2 should be true if α_2 is also true and if possible; ...; otherwise a_n should be true if α_n is also true and if possible.

The example from Section 1 can then be rewritten as *lemonade* $\times$ *cola*{*warm*} $\times$ *coffee*{*tired*} $\times$ *juice* $\leftarrow$ *thirsty*. Of course, such kind of rules can be expressed in LPOD, as shown in Section 1, but the resulting programs quickly become unwieldy. On the other hand, expressing the extra condition is easily done for the EOLP version: it suffices to add each α_k to the body of the corresponding rule in P_k, $1 \leq k \leq n$, as shown below.

Example 11. Reconsider the example from Section 1 and suppose that we are thirsty, but there is no lemonade, i.e. consider the program $P = \{$*lemonade* $\times$ *cola*{*warm*} $\times$ *coffee*{*tired*} $\times$ *juice* $\leftarrow$ *thirsty*; *thirsty* $\leftarrow$; $\neg$*lemonade* $\leftarrow\}$. The EOLP version of this problem is

$$not\ juice \leftarrow$$
$$not\ coffee \leftarrow$$
$$not\ cola \leftarrow$$
$$not\ lemonade \leftarrow$$

> $juice \leftarrow thirsty, not\ coffee, not\ cola, not\ lemonade$
> $coffee \leftarrow thirsty, tired, not\ cola, not\ lemonade$
> $cola \leftarrow thirsty, warm, not\ lemonade$
> $lemonade \leftarrow thirsty$

> $lemonade \leftarrow thirsty, not\ cola, not\ coffee, not\ juice$
> $cola \leftarrow thirsty, not\ lemonade, not\ coffee, not\ juice$
> $coffee \leftarrow thirsty, not\ cola, not\ lemonade, not\ juice$
> $juice \leftarrow thirsty, not\ cola, not\ coffee, not\ lemonade$
> $thirsty \leftarrow$
> $\neg lemonade \leftarrow$

One can check that this programs has the expected proper preferred answer set $I = \{thirsty, juice, \neg lemonade\}$.

5   Conclusions and Direction for Further Research

Adding negation as failure to ordered programs provides an intuitive formalism to express certain problems. E.g. ordered disjunctive programs can be simulated using such extended ordered programs, and the simulation is actually more convenient for certain extensions of ordered disjunctive programs. Interestingly, the expressive power of extended ordered programs remains the same as for ordinary ordered programs.

Directions for further research include the practical implementation of the preferred answer set semantics for extended ordered programs, e.g. through a pre-compiler that applies the construction of Definition 7 and feeds the result to an OLP evaluation algorithm as described in [27]. Alternatively, a direct interpretation of EOLP programs may turn out to be more efficient.

In addition, there are some promising application areas for EOLP. E.g. diagnostic problems [22,9] have a natural representation as extended ordered programs where constraints of the form $o \leftarrow not\ o$ represent observations, slightly less preferred rules model the normal operation and the weakest rules describe the fault model. The proper preferred answer set semantics will then return an explanation for the observations that minimizes recourse to the fault model, which naturally coincides with our intuition of a "best" explanation.

References

1. G. Brewka. Logic programming with ordered disjunction. In *Proc. of the 18th AAAI Conf.*, pages 100–105. AAAI Press, 2002.
2. G. Brewka, S. Benferhat, and D. Le Berre. Qualitative choice logic. In *Proc. of the 8th Intl. Conf. on Knowledge Representation and Reasoning*, pages 158–169. Morgan Kaufmann, 2002.
3. Gerhard Brewka and Thomas Eiter. Preferred answer sets for extended logic programs. *Artificial Intelligence*, 109(1-2):297–356, 1999.
4. Gerhard Brewka, Ilkka Niemela, and Tommi Syrjanen. Implementing ordered disjunction using answer set solvers for normal programs. In Flesca et al. [10], pages 444–455.
5. Francesco Buccafurri, Wolfgang Faber, and Nicola Leone. Disjunctive logic programs with inheritance. In Danny De Schreye, editor, *Proc. of the Intl. Conf. on Logic Programming*, pages 79–93. MIT Press, 1999.
6. Francesco Buccafurri, Nicola Leone, and Pasquale Rullo. Disjunctive ordered logic: Semantics and expressiveness. In A. et al. Cohn, editor, *Proc. of the 6th Intl. Conf. on Principles of Knowledge Representation and Reasoning*, pages 418–431. Morgan Kaufmann, 1998.
7. Keith L. Clark. Negation as failure. In H. Gallaire and J. Minker, editors, *Logic and Data Bases*, pages 293–322. Plemum Press, 1978.
8. Marina De Vos and Dirk Vermeir. Dynamically ordered probabilistic choice logic programming. In Sanjiv Kapoor and Sanjiva Prasad, editors, *Foundations of 20th Software Technology and Theoretical Computer Science, 20th Conference, Proceedings*, volume 1974 of *LNCS*, pages 227–239. Springer Verlag, 2000.
9. Thomas Eiter, Georg Gottlob, and Nicola Leone. Abduction from logic programs: Semantics and complexity. *Theoretical Computer Science*, 189(1-2):129–177, 1997.
10. Sergio Flesca, Sergio Greco, Nicola Leone, and Giovambattista Ianni, editors. *Logic in Artificial Intelligence*, volume 2424 of *LNAI*. Springer Verlag, 2002.
11. Michael Gelfond and Vladimir Lifschitz. The stable model semantics for logic programming. In R. et al. Kowalski, editor, *Proc. of the 5th Intl. Conf. on Logic Programming*, pages 1070–1080. The MIT Press, 1988.
12. Katsumi Inoue and Chiaki Sakama. On positive occurrences of negation as failure. In J. at al. Doyle, editor, *Proc. of the 4th Intl. Conf. on Principles of Knowledge Representation and Reasoning*, pages 293–304. Morgan Kaufmann, 1994.
13. Katsumi Inoue and Chiaki Sakama. A fixpoint characterization of abductive logic programs. *Journal of Logic Programming*, 27(2):107–136, 1996.

14. Katsumi Inoue and Chiaki Sakama. Negation as failure in the head. *Journal of Logic Programming*, 35(1):39–78, 1998.
15. A. C. Kakas, R. A. Kowalski, and F. Toni. Abductive logic programming. *Journal of Logic and Computation*, 2(6):719–770, 1992.
16. Robert A. Kowalski and Fariba Sadri. Logic programs with exceptions. In David H. D. Warren and Peter Szeredi, editors, *Proc. of the 7th Intl. Conf. on Logic Programming*, pages 598–613. The MIT Press, 1990.
17. E. Laenens and D. Vermeir. A fixpoint semantics of ordered logic. *Journal of Logic and Computation*, 1(2):159–185, 1990.
18. Els Laenens and Dirk Vermeir. Assumption-free semantics for ordered logic programs: On the relationship between well-founded and stable partial models. *Journal of Logic and Computation*, 2(2):133–172, 1992.
19. Nicola Leone, Pasquale Rullo, and Francesco Scarcello. Disjunctive stable models: Unfounded sets, fixpoint semantics, and computation. *Information and Computation*, 135(2):69–112, 1997.
20. Vladimir Lifschitz. Answer set programming and plan generation. *Journal of Artificial Intelligence*, 138(1-2):39–54, 2002.
21. Teodor C. Przymusinski. Stable semantics for disjunctive programs. *New Generation Computing*, 9(3-4):401–424, 1991.
22. Raymond Reiter. A theory of diagnosis from first principles. *Artificial Intelligence*, 32(1):57–95, 1987.
23. Chiaki Sakama and Katsumi Inoue. An alternative approach to the semantics of disjunctive logic programs and deductive databases. *Journal of Automated Reasoning*, 13(1):145–172, 1994.
24. Chiaki Sakama and Katsumi Inoue. Representing priorities in logic programs. In Michael J. Maher, editor, *Proc. of the Intl. Conf. on Logic Programming*, pages 82–96. MIT Press, 1996.
25. Allen van Gelder, Kenneth A. Ross, and John S. Schlipf. Unfounded sets and well-founded semantics for general logic programs. In *Proc. of the 7th PODS Symposium*, pages 221–230. ACM Press, 1988.
26. Davy Van Nieuwenborgh and Dirk Vermeir. Order and negation as failure. Technical report, Vrije Universiteit Brussel, Dept. of Computer Science, 2003.
27. Davy Van Nieuwenborgh and Dirk Vermeir. Preferred answer sets for ordered logic programs. In Flesca et al. [10], pages 432–443.
28. Kewen Wang, Lizhu Zhou, and Fangzhen Lin. Alternating fixpoint theory for logic programs with priority. In John W. Lloyd et al., editor, *Computational Logic*, volume 1861 of *LNCS*, pages 164–178. Springer, 2000.

Computing Minimal Models, Stable Models, and Answer Sets

Zbigniew Lonc[1] and Mirosław Truszczyński[2]

[1] Faculty of Mathematics and Information Science, Warsaw University of Technology,
00-661 Warsaw, Poland
[2] Department of Computer Science, University of Kentucky,
Lexington, KY 40506-0046, USA

Abstract. We propose and study algorithms for computing minimal models, stable models and answer sets of 2- and 3-CNF theories, and normal and disjunctive 2- and 3-programs. We are especially interested in algorithms with *non-trivial worst-case performance bounds*. We show that one can find all minimal models of 2-CNF theories and all answer sets of disjunctive 2-programs in time $O(m1.4422..^n)$ (n is the number of atoms in an input theory or program and m is its size). Our main results concern computing stable models of normal 3-programs, minimal models of 3-CNF theories and answer sets of disjunctive 3-programs. We design algorithms that run in time $O(m1.6701..^n)$, in the case of the first problem, and in time $O(mn^2 2.2720..^n)$, in the case of the latter two. All these bounds improve by exponential factors the best algorithms known previously. We also obtain closely related upper bounds on the number of minimal models, stable models and answer sets a 2- or 3-theory or program may have.

1 Introduction

Our goal in this paper is to propose and study algorithms for computing *minimal* models of CNF theories, *stable* models of normal logic programs and *answer sets* of disjunctive logic programs. We are especially interested in algorithms for which we can derive *non-trivial worst-case performance bounds*. Our work builds on studies of algorithms to compute models of propositional CNF theories [8] and improves on our earlier study of algorithms to compute stable models [10].

Propositional logic with the minimal-model semantics (propositional circumscription) [13,9], logic programming with stable-model semantics [6] and disjunctive logic programming with the answer-set semantics [7] are among the most commonly studied and broadly used knowledge representation formalisms (we refer the reader to [12,2] for a detailed treatment of these logics and additional pointers to literature). Recently, they have been receiving much attention due to their applications in *answer-set programming* (ASP) — an emerging declarative programming paradigm. Fast algorithms to compute minimal models, stable models and answer sets are essential for the computational effectiveness of propositional circumscription, logic programming and disjunctive logic programming as answer-set programming systems.

C. Palamidessi (Ed.): ICLP 2003, LNCS 2916, pp. 209–223, 2003.

These computational tasks can be solved by a "brute-force" straightforward search. We will now briefly describe this approach. Here and throughout the paper, by $At(T)$ or $At(P)$ we denote the set of atoms occurring in a theory T or a program P. We represent models of propositional theories, stable models of normal logic programs and answer sets of disjunctive logic programs as sets of atoms that are true in these models and answer sets. Finally, we use n to denote the number of atoms of an input theory or program, and m to denote its *size*, that is, the total number of atom occurrences in the theory or program[1].

We can compute all minimal models of a CNF theory T in time $O(m3^n)$. Indeed, to check whether a set $M \subseteq At(T)$ is a minimal model of T, it is enough to verify that M is a model of T and that none of its subsets is. Each such test can be accomplished in $O(m)$ steps. Thus, if $|M| = i$, we can verify whether M is a minimal model of T in time $O(m2^i)$. Checking all sets of cardinality i requires $O(\binom{n}{i}m2^n)$ steps and checking all sets — $O(\sum_{i=0}^{n} \binom{n}{i}m2^n) = O(m3^n)$.

Next, we note that to determine whether a set of atoms M is an answer set of a disjunctive logic program P we need to verify whether M is a minimal model of the *reduct of P with respect to M* [7] or, equivalently, whether M is a minimal model of the propositional theory that corresponds to the reduct. Thus, a similar argument as before demonstrates that also answer sets of a finite propositional disjunctive logic program P can be computed in time $O(m3^n)$.

In the case of stable models we can do better. The task of verifying whether a set of atoms M is a stable model of a finite propositional logic program P can be accomplished in time $O(m)$. Consequently, one can compute all stable models of P in $O(m2^n)$ steps, using an exhaustive search through all subsets of $At(P)$.

We refer to these straightforward algorithms and to the corresponding worst-case performance bounds of $O(m3^n)$ and $O(m2^n)$ as *trivial*. A fundamental question, and the main topic of interest in this paper, is whether there are algorithms for the three computational problems discussed here with better worst-case performance bounds.

We note that researchers proposed several algorithms to compute minimal models of propositional CNF theories [1,14], stable models of logic programs [17] and answer sets of disjunctive logic programs [5]. Some implementations based on these algorithms, for instance, *smodels* [17] and *dlv* [5] perform very well in practice. However, so far very little is known about the worst-case performance of these implementations.

In this paper, we study the three computational problems discussed earlier. We focus our considerations on *t-CNF theories* and *t-programs*, that is, theories and programs, respectively, consisting of clauses containing no more than t literals. Despite restricted syntax, t-CNF theories and t-programs are of significant interest and appear frequently as encodings of problems in planning, model checking, computer-aided verification, circuit design and combinatorics. To encode a problem by means of a propositional (disjunctive) logic program we often proceed in a two-step process. We first develop an encoding of this

---

[1] Throughout the paper, even when we do not mention explicitly an input theory or program, we consistently write n for its number of atoms and m for its size.

problem as a program in the syntax of (disjunctive) DATALOG with negation [11,15,5]. In the next step, we *ground* this program and obtain its propositional counterpart also representing the problem in question. It is clear that programs obtained by grounding finite (disjunctive) DATALOG-with-negation programs are t-programs, for some fixed and usually small t that depends only on the problem specification and not on a particular problem instance. In fact, in most cases programs obtained by grounding and some subsequent straightforward simplifications become (disjunctive) 2- or 3-programs.

In our earlier work, we studied the problem of computing stable models of normal t programs [10]. We presented an algorithm to compute all stable models of a normal 2-program in time $O(m3^{n/3}) = O(m1.4422..^n)$ and showed its asymptotic optimality. We proposed a similar algorithm for the class of normal 3-programs and proved that its running time is $O(m1.7071..^n)$.

We improve here on our results from [10] and extend them to the problems of computing minimal models of CNF theories and answer sets of disjunctive logic programs. Since 2- and 3-CNF theories and 2- and 3-programs appear frequently in applications and since our results are strongest in the case of these two classes, we limit our discussion here to 2- and 3-theories and programs only.

Our results are as follows. We show that one can find all minimal models of 2-CNF theories and all answer sets of disjunctive 2-programs in time $O(m1.4422..^n)$, generalizing a similar result we obtained earlier for computing stable models of normal 2-programs. Our main results concern computing stable models of normal 3-programs, minimal models of 3-CNF theories and answer sets of disjunctive 3-programs. We design algorithms that run in time $O(m1.6701..^n)$, for the first problem, and in time $O(mn^2 2.2720..^n)$, for the latter two. These bounds improve by exponential factors the best algorithms known previously. We also obtain closely related upper bounds on the number of minimal models, stable models and answer sets a 2- or 3-theory or program may have.

2   Lower Bounds

In this section, we present lower bounds on the running time of algorithms for computing *all* minimal models, stable models or answer sets. We obtain them by constructing theories and programs for which the total size of output is large, and use this quantity to derive a lower bound on the exponential factor in our running time estimates. Due to space limitations, we present here only the results, leaving out details of the constructions. In what follows, we use the notation $\mu_t = \binom{2t-1}{t}^{1/2t-1}$.

Theorem 1. *Let t be an integer, $t \geq 2$. There are positive constants d_t, D_t and D_t' such that for every $n \geq 2t-1$ there is a t-CNF theory T (normal t-program P and disjunctive t-program P, respectively) with n atoms and such that*

1. *The size m of T (P, respectively) satisfies $m \leq d_t n$*
2. *The number of minimal models of T (stable models of P or answer sets of P, respectively) is at least $D_t \mu_t^n$ and the sum of their cardinalities is at least $D_t' n \mu_t^n$.*

Corollary 1. *Let t be an integer, $t \geq 2$.*

1. *Every algorithm computing all minimal models of t-CNF theories (stable models of normal t-programs, answer sets of disjunctive t-programs, respectively) requires in the worst case at least $\Omega(m\mu_t^n)$ steps*
2. *Let $0 < \alpha < \mu_t$. There is no polynomial f and no algorithm for computing all minimal models of t-CNF theories (stable models of normal t-programs, answer sets of disjunctive t-programs, respectively) with worst-case performance of $O(f(m)\alpha^n)$.*

For $t = 2$ and 3, the lower bound given by Corollary 1 specializes to $\Omega(m1.4422..^n)$ and $\Omega(m1.5848..^n)$, respectively.

3   Main Results

We will now present and discuss the main results of our paper. We start by stating two theorems that deal with minimal models of 2-CNF theories and answer sets of disjunctive 2-programs. They extend the results we obtained in [10] for the case of stable models of normal 2-programs.

Theorem 2. *There are algorithms to compute all minimal models of 2-CNF theories, stable models of normal 2-programs and answer sets of disjunctive 2-programs, respectively, that run in time $O(m3^{n/3}) = O(m1.4422..^n)$.*

Theorem 3. *Every 2-CNF theory (every normal 2-program and every disjunctive 2-program, respectively) has at most $3^{n/3} = 1.4422..^n$ minimal models (stable models, answer-sets, respectively).*

It follows from Theorem 1 and Corollary 1 that these results are asymptotically optimal.

Next, we present results concerning the case of 3-CNF theories and normal and disjunctive 3-programs. These results constitute the main contribution of our paper. First, we derive upper estimates on the number of minimal models, stable models and answer sets. In fact, we obtain the same upper bound in all three cases. It improves the bound on the number of stable models of normal 3-programs from [10] and it is the first non-trivial bound on the number of minimal models of 3-CNF theories and answer sets of disjunctive programs.

Theorem 4. *Every 3-CNF theory T (every normal 3-program P and every disjunctive 3-program P, respectively) has at most $1.6701..^n$ minimal models (stable models, answer-sets, respectively).*

For 2-CNF theories and 2-programs, the common bound on the number of minimal models, stable models and answer sets, appeared also as an exponential factor in formulas estimating the running time of algorithms to compute the corresponding objects. In contrast, we find that there is a difference in how fast we can compute stable models of normal 3-programs as opposed to minimal models of 3-CNF theories and answer sets of disjunctive 3-programs. The reason is that the problem to check whether a set of atoms is a stable model of a normal program is in P, while the problems of deciding whether a set of atoms is a minimal model of a 3-CNF theory or an answer set of a disjunctive 3-program are co-NP complete [3,4]. Our next result concerns computing stable models of normal 3-programs. It gives an exponential improvement on the corresponding result from [10].

Theorem 5. *There is an algorithm to compute stable models of normal 3-programs that runs in time* $O(m1.6701^n)$

Since checking whether a set of atoms is a minimal model of a 3-CNF theory or an answer set of a disjunctive 3-program is NP-hard, our results concerning computing minimal models and answer sets are weaker. Nevertheless, in each case they provide an exponential improvement over the trivial bound of $O(m3^n)$.

Theorem 6. *There is an algorithm to compute minimal models of 3-CNF theories and answer sets of disjunctive 3-programs, respectively, that runs in time* $O(mn^2 2.2720..^n)$.

4   Outlines of Algorithms and Proofs

Due to space limitations, we will not discuss here proofs of Theorems 2 and 3. One can prove these results by modifying arguments we developed in [10] for the case of stable models of normal 2-programs. We will however sketch proofs of Theorems 4, 5 and 6, as they require several new techniques.

Let T be a CNF theory. By $Lit(T)$ we denote the set of all literals built of atoms in $At(T)$. For a set of literals $L \subseteq Lit(T)$, we define:

$$L^+ = \{a \in At(T) : a \in L\} \quad \text{and} \quad L^- = \{a \in At(T) : \neg a \in L\}.$$

We also define $L_0 = L^+ \cup L^-$. A set of literals L is *consistent* if $L^+ \cap L^- = \emptyset$. A set of atoms $M \subseteq At(T)$ is *consistent* with a set of literals $L \subseteq Lit(T)$, if $L^+ \subseteq M$ and $L^- \cap M = \emptyset$.

Let T be a CNF theory and let $L \subseteq Lit(T)$ be a set of literals. By T_L we denote the theory obtained from T by removing:

1. every clause c that contains a literal $\ell \in L$ (intuitively, eliminate every clause that is subsumed by a literal in L)
2. all occurrences of literals built of atoms in L_0 that remain after performing step (1) (intuitively, resolve the remaining clauses with literals in L).

We note that it may happen that T_L contains empty clauses (is contradictory) or is empty (is a tautology). The theory T_L has the following important property.

Proposition 1. *Let T be a CNF theory and let $L \subseteq Lit(T)$. If $X \subseteq At(T)$ is a minimal model of T consistent with L, then $X \setminus L^+$ is a minimal model of T_L.*

$min^+(T, S, L)$
% T and S are CNF theories, L is a set of literals
% T, S and L satisfy the preconditions: $L \subseteq Lit(T)$, and $S = T_L$
(0) **if** S does not contain an empty clause **then**
(1)   **if** $S = \emptyset$ **then**
(2) $M := L^+$; **output**(M)
(3)   **else**
(4) $\mathcal{A} := complete(S)$;
(5)   **for every** $A \in \mathcal{A}$ **do**
(6) $SA := S_A$;
(7) $min^+(T, SA, L \cup A)$
(8)   **end of for**
(9)   **end of else**
(10) **end of** min^+.

Fig. 1. Algorithm min^+

We will now describe an algorithm min^+, from which we will subsequently derive algorithms for all three computational tasks that we study here. The input parameters of min^+ are: CNF theories T and S, and a set of literals L. We will require that $L \subseteq Lit(T)$ and $S = T_L$. We will refer to these two conditions as the *preconditions* for min^+. The output of the algorithm $min^+(T, S, L)$ is a family $\mathcal{M}_L^+(T)$ of sets containing all minimal models of T that are consistent with L. The input parameter S is determined by the two other parameters T and L (through the preconditions on T, S and L). We choose to specify it explicitly as that simplifies the description and the analysis of the algorithm.

A key concept that we need is that of a *complete* collection. Let T be a CNF theory. A non-empty collection $\mathcal{A}$ of non-empty subsets of $Lit(T)$ is *complete* for T if every minimal model of T is consistent with at least one set $A \in \mathcal{A}$. The collection $\mathcal{A} = \{\{a\}, \{\neg a\}\}$, where a is an atom of T, is a simple example of a complete collection for T.

In the description of the algorithm min^+ given in Figure 1, we assume that *complete* is a procedure computing, for an input CNF theory T, a complete collection of sets of literals.

Since $L_0 \cap A_0 = \emptyset$ and $S = T_L$, $SA = S_A = (T_L)_A = T_{L \cup A}$. Moreover, $L \cup A \subseteq Lit(T)$. Thus, T, SA and $L \cup A$ satisfy the preconditions for the algorithm min^+ and the recursive calls in line (7) are legal. Moreover, since $A \neq \emptyset$ and $A \subseteq Lit(T_L)$, we have $|At(T_L)| > |At(T_{L \cup A})|$ and, so, the algorithm terminates.

Proposition 2. *Let T be a CNF theory and let $L \subseteq Lit(T)$ be a set of literals. If X is a minimal model of T consistent with L, then X is among the sets returned by $min^+(T, T_L, L)$.*

Proof: We prove the assertion, proceeding by induction on $|At(T_L)|$. Let us assume that $|At(T_L)| = 0$ and that X is a minimal model of T. By Proposition 1, $X \setminus L^+$ is a minimal model of T_L. In particular, T_L contains no empty clause.

Since $|At(T_L)| = 0$, $T_L = \emptyset$. Consequently, $X \setminus L^+ = \emptyset$ (as $X \setminus L^+$ is a minimal model of T_L). It follows that, $X \subseteq L^+$. Furthermore, since X is consistent with L, $L^+ \subseteq X$. Thus, $X = L^+$. Finally, since T_L is empty, the program enters line (2) and outputs X since, as we already showed, $X = L^+$.

For the inductive step, let us assume that $|At(T_L)| > 0$ and that X is a minimal model of T consistent with L. By Proposition 1, $X \setminus L^+$ is a minimal model of T_L. Since $\mathcal{A}$, computed in line (4), is a complete collection for T_L, there is $A \in \mathcal{A}$ such that $X \setminus L^+$ is consistent with A. Clearly, $L_0 \cap A_0 = \emptyset$. Thus, X is consistent with $L \cup A$. By the induction hypothesis (as we noted, the parameters T, SA and $L \cup A$ satisfy the preconditions for the algorithm min^+ and $|At(T_L)| > |At(T_{L \cup A})|$), the call $min^+(T, SA, L \cup A)$, within loop (5), returns the set X.   □

Corollary 2. *Let T be a CNF theory. The family $\mathcal{M}_\emptyset^+(T)$ of sets that are returned by $min^+(T, T, \emptyset)$ contains all minimal models of T.*

Typically, algorithms for computing stable models and answer sets of logic programs, and minimal models of CNF theories search over a binary tree: at each branch point they select a variable and consider for it both truth assignments. The search tree traversed by our algorithm is not necessarily binary. At each branch point, the search splits into as many different paths as there are elements in the complete family returned by the procedure *complete*. While algorithms searching over binary trees can be derived from our template by designing the procedure *complete* to return collections consisting of at most two sets, the class of algorithms specified by our template is broader.

We will now study the performance of the algorithm min^+. First, for a CNF theory S we define a tree $\mathcal{T}_S$ inductively as follows. If S contains an empty clause or if S is empty, $\mathcal{T}_S$ consists of a single node labeled with S. Otherwise, let $\mathcal{A}$ be a complete family computed by the procedure *complete(S)*. To construct tree $\mathcal{T}_S$, we create a node and label it with S. Next, we connect this node to roots of the trees $\mathcal{T}_{S_A}$, where $A \in \mathcal{A}$. Since the theories S_A have fewer atoms than S, the definition is well founded. We denote the set of leaves of the tree $\mathcal{T}_S$ by $L(\mathcal{T}_S)$.

One can show that for every CNF theory T and for every set of literals $L \subseteq Lit(T)$, the tree $\mathcal{T}_S$, where $S = T_L$, is precisely the tree of recursive calls to the procedure min^+ made by the top-level call $min^+(T, S, L)$. In particular, the tree $\mathcal{T}_T$ describes the execution of the call $min^+(T, T, \emptyset)$. Since only those recursive calls that correspond to leaves of $\mathcal{T}_T$ produce output, Corollary 2 implies the following result.

Proposition 3. *Let T be a CNF theory. The number of minimal models of T is at most $|L(\mathcal{T}_T)|$.*

We use the tree $\mathcal{T}_T$ to estimate not only the number of minimal models of a CNF theory T but also the running time of the algorithm min^+. We say that an implementation of the procedure *complete* is *splitting* if for every theory T, such that $|At(T)| \geq 2$, it returns a complete family with at least two elements. We can show the following result.

Theorem 7. *Let us assume that there is a splitting implementation of the algorithm complete that runs in time $O(t(m))$, where t is an integer function such that $t(m) = \Omega(m)$. Then, for every CNF theory T, the algorithm min^+ runs in $O(|L(\mathcal{T}_T)|t(m))$ steps in the worst case.*

The specific bounds on $|L(\mathcal{T}_T)|$ and hence, on the number of minimal models of a CNF theory T and on the running time of the algorithm min^+ depend on the procedure *complete*. For 3-CNF theories we have the following results.

Theorem 8. *There is a splitting implementation of the procedure complete such that $t(m) = O(m)$ and for every 3-CNF theory T, $|L(\mathcal{T}_T)| \leq 1.6701..^n$.*

Corollary 3. *There is an implementation of the algorithm min^+ that, for 3-CNF theories, runs in time $O(m1.6701..^n)$.*

Corollary 3 is a direct consequence of Theorems 7 and 8. The proof of Theorem 7 is routine and we omit it. We will outline a proof of Theorem 8 in Section 5. In the remainder of this section, we will show that Theorem 8 and Corollary 3 imply our main results concerning minimal models of 3-CNF theories, stable models of normal 3-programs and answer sets of disjunctive 3-programs (Theorems 4, 5 and 6).

We start with the problem of computing minimal models of a CNF theory T. Let us assume that we have an algorithm *test_min* which, for a given CNF theory T and a set of atoms $M \subseteq At(T)$ returns the boolean value **true** if M is a minimal model of T, and returns **false**, otherwise.

We now modify the algorithm min^+ by replacing each occurrence of the command **output**(M) (line (2)), which outputs a set M, with the command

if *test_min*(T, M) then **output**(M).

We denote the resulting algorithm by *min_mod* (we assume the same preconditions on *min_mod* as in the case of min^+). Since all minimal models of T that are consistent with L belong to $\mathcal{M}_L^+(T)$ (the output of $min^+(T, S, L)$), it is clear that the algorithm *min_mod*(T, S, L) returns all minimal models of T.

Computation of stable models and answer sets of logic programs follows a similar pattern. First, let us recall that we can associate with a disjunctive logic program P (therefore, also with every normal logic program P) its propositional counterpart, a CNF theory $T(P)$ consisting of clauses of P but interpreted in propositional logic and rewritten into CNF. Specifically, to obtain $T(P)$ we replace each disjunctive program clause

$$c_1 \vee \ldots \vee c_p \leftarrow a_1, \ldots, a_r, \mathbf{not}(b_1), \ldots, \mathbf{not}(b_s)$$

in P with a CNF clause

$$\neg a_1 \vee \ldots \vee \neg a_r \vee b_1 \vee \ldots \vee b_s \vee c_1 \vee \ldots \vee c_p.$$

It is well known that stable models (answer sets) of (disjunctive) logic program P are minimal models of $T(P)$ [12].

Let us assume that $test\_stb(P, M)$ and $test\_anset(P, M)$ are algorithms to check whether a set of atoms M is a stable model and an answer set, respectively, of a program P.

To compute stable models of a logic program P that are consistent with a set of literals L, we first compute the CNF theory $T(P)$. Next, we run on the triple $T(P)$, $T(P)_L$ and L, the algorithm min^+ modified similarly as before (we note that the triple $(T(P), T(P)_L, L)$ satisfies its preconditions). Namely, we replace the command **output**(M) (line (2)), which outputs a set M, with the command

if $test\_stb(P, M)$ **then output**(M).

The effect of the change is that we output only those sets in $\mathcal{M}_L^+(T(P))$, which are stable models of P. Since every stable model of P is a minimal model of $T(P)$, it is also an element of $\mathcal{M}_L^+(T(P))$. Thus, this modified algorithm, we will refer to it as stb_mod, indeed outputs all stable models of P and nothing else.

To design an algorithm to compute answer sets, we will refer to it as ans_set, we proceed in the same way. The only difference is that we use the algorithm $test\_anset$ in place of $test\_stb$ to decide whether to output a set.

Let t_1 be an integer function such that the worst-case running time of the algorithm min^+ is $O(t_1(n, m))$. Similarly, Let t_2 be an integer function such that the worst-case running time of the algorithm $test\_min$ ($test\_stb$ or $test\_anset$, depending on the problem) is $O(t_2(n, m))$. The following observation is evident.

Proposition 4. *The running time of the algorithms min_mod, stb_mod and ans_set (in the worst case) is $O(t_1(n, m) + \gamma t_2(n, m))$, where $\gamma = |L(\mathcal{T}_T)|$ or $|L(\mathcal{T}_{T(P)})|$, depending on the problem.*

Proofs of Theorems 4 and 5. Stable models (answer sets, respectively) of a normal (disjunctive, respectively) program P are minimal models of a CNF theory $T(P)$. Thus, Theorem 4 follows from Proposition 3 and Theorem 8. One can check in time $O(m)$ whether a set of atoms $M \subseteq At(P)$ is a stable model of a normal logic program P. Thus, Theorem 5 follows from Proposition 4, Theorem 8 and Corollary 3. □

We will now prove Theorem 6. We focus on the case of minimal models of 3-CNF theories. The argument in the case of answer sets of disjunctive 3-programs is similar. We start with a simple result on testing minimality.

Proposition 5. *Let p be an integer function and t an integer such that $t \geq 2$. If there is an algorithm that decides in time $O(p(n, m))$ whether a t-CNF theory T is satisfiable, then there is an algorithm that decides in time $O(|M|p(|M|, m + 1) + m)$ whether a set $M \subseteq At(T)$ is a minimal model of a t-CNF theory T.*

Proof: Let $M = \{a_1, \ldots, a_k\}$. We define $L = \{\neg x : x \in At(T) \setminus M\}$ and observe that M is a minimal model of T if and only if M is a model of T and none of t-CNF theories $T_L \cup \{\neg a_i\}$, $i = 1, \ldots, k$, is satisfiable. □

There is an algorithm to decide satisfiability of 3-CNF theories that runs in time $O(m1.4756..^n)$ [16]. Thus, by Proposition 5, there is an an algorithm to

decide whether a set $M \subseteq At(T)$ is a minimal model of a 3-CNF theory T that
runs in time $O(|M|m1.4756..^{|M|})$. We denote this algorithm $test\_min$.

Proof of Theorem 6. Let β be a real number such that $0.6 < \beta < 1$ (we will
specify β later). To estimate the running time of the algorithm min^+, we split
$\mathcal{M}_L^+(T)$ into two parts:

$$\mathcal{M}_1 = \{M \in \mathcal{M}_L^+(T): |M| \geq \beta n\} \text{ and } \mathcal{M}_2 = \{M \in \mathcal{M}_L^+(T): |M| < \beta n\}.$$

Clearly, the total time t_{min} needed to execute all calls to $test\_min$ throughout
the execution of min^+ is:

$$t_{min} = \sum_{M \in \mathcal{M}_1} m|M|(1.4756..)^{|M|} + \sum_{M \in \mathcal{M}_2} m|M|(1.4756..)^{|M|}.$$

We have

$$\sum_{M \in \mathcal{M}_1} m|M|(1.4756..)^{|M|} \leq \sum_{i \geq \beta n} m\binom{n}{i}i(1.4756..)^i$$

$$\leq \beta mn^2 \binom{n}{\lceil \beta n \rceil}(1.4756..)^{\lceil \beta n \rceil}.$$

This last inequality follows from that fact that for every i, $i \geq 0.6n$,

$$m\binom{n}{i}i(1.4756..)^i \geq m\binom{n}{i+1}(i+1)(1.4756..)^{i+1},$$

and from the observation that the number of terms in the sum is less than n.

To estimate the second term, we note that $|\mathcal{M}_2| \leq |\mathcal{M}_L^+(T)|$ and, for every
$M \in \mathcal{M}_2$, $|M| < \beta n$. Thus,

$$\sum_{M \in \mathcal{M}_2} m|M|(1.4756..)^{|M|} \leq (\beta mn)(1.6701..)^n(1.4756..)^{\beta n}.$$

Let us choose β so that $1.6701..^n = \binom{n}{\lceil \beta n \rceil}$. For this β, we obtain that $t_{min} = O(mn^2(1.6701..(1.4756..)^\beta)^n)$. One can verify that $\beta = 0.7907..$. It follows that
the complexity of our algorithm is $O(mn^2 2.2720..^n)$, which completes the proof
of Theorem 6.   □

5   Algorithm *Complete* and a Proof of Theorem 8

Our approach exploits a method to estimate the number of leaves in a search
tree proposed in [8]. We outline here this method adapted to our needs. Let $\mathcal{T}$
be a rooted tree and let, as before, $L(\mathcal{T})$ be the set of leaves in $\mathcal{T}$. For a node x
in $\mathcal{T}$, we denote by $C(x)$ the set of *directed* edges that link x with its children.
For a leaf w of $\mathcal{T}$, we denote by $P(w)$ the set of *directed* edges on the unique
path from the root of $\mathcal{T}$ to the leaf w. The following observation was shown in
[8].

Proposition 6. [8] *Let p be a function assigning positive real numbers to edges of a rooted tree $\mathcal{T}$ such that for every internal node x in $\mathcal{T}$, $\sum_{e \in C(x)} p(e) = 1$. Then, $|L(\mathcal{T})| \leq \max_{w \in L(\mathcal{T})} (\prod_{e \in P(w)} p(e))^{-1}$.*

To estimate the number of leaves in our search tree $\mathcal{T}_T$, we associate with every 3-CNF theory T a certain measure μ of its complexity, which approximates the number of leaves in the tree $\mathcal{T}_T$. We define $\mu(T) = n(T) - \alpha c(T)$, where $n(T) = |At(T)|$, $c(T)$ is the maximum number of 2-clauses in T with pairwise disjoint sets of atoms, and α is a constant such that $0 \leq \alpha \leq 1$ (we will specify α later). Clearly, for every 3-CNF theory T, $\mu(T) \geq 0$.

This definition reflects the following intuition. The number of leaves in the tree $\mathcal{T}_T$ grows when the number of atoms in T grows. On the other hand, if T has a large number of 2-clauses, the number of leaves in $\mathcal{T}_T$ is usually smaller than in the case when T has few 2-clauses (and the same number of atoms).

For a directed edge $e = (T', T'')$ in the tree $\mathcal{T}_T$ (we recall that vertices of $\mathcal{T}_T$ are CNF theories), we define $\Delta(e) = \mu(T') - \mu(T'')$ and make an assumption (which we will verify later) that $\Delta(e) \geq 0$. Clearly, for every leaf $W \in L(\mathcal{T}_T)$,

$$\sum_{e \in P(W)} \Delta(e) = \mu(T) - \mu(W) \leq \mu(T) \leq n(T). \tag{1}$$

Next, for every internal node S of the tree $\mathcal{T}_T$, by τ_S we denote the unique positive real number τ satisfying the equation

$$\sum_{e \in C(S)} \tau^{-\Delta(e)} = 1 \tag{2}$$

and we define τ_0 to be the largest of these roots. One can verify that for each internal node S, $\tau_S \geq 1$. Thus, $\tau_0 \geq 1$, too.

Finally, for every edge $e = (S, S')$ in the tree $\mathcal{T}_T$, we define $p(e) = \tau_S^{-\Delta(e)}$. Since $\Delta(e) \geq 0$, $p(e)^{-1} = \tau_S^{\Delta(e)} \leq \tau_0^{\Delta(e)}$.

Let $W \in L(\mathcal{T}_T)$. We now have (the last inequality in the chain follows by (1))

$$(\prod_{e \in P(W)} p(e))^{-1} \leq \prod_{e \in P(W)} \tau_0^{\Delta(e)} = \tau_0^{\sum_{e \in P(W)} \Delta(e)} \leq \tau_0^{n(T)}.$$

By the definition, the function p satisfies the assumptions of Proposition 6. Thus (we recall that by our convention, $n(T) = n$),

$$|L(\mathcal{T}_T)| \leq \tau_0^n. \tag{3}$$

When designing the procedure *complete*, our goal is then to make sure that the value τ_0 be as small as possible. To this end, we consider several cases that reflect different structural properties of a 3-CNF theory S. In each of the cases we compute the numbers $\Delta(e)$, where $e = (S, S_A)$ and A is an element of the complete family produced by running the procedure *complete* on input S. Next we find the positive root τ_S of the equation (2).

To get the best upper bound for the number $|L(T)|$ of leaves in $\mathcal{T}_T$ (see inequality (3)), we choose the value of α so that the maximum of the solutions of the equation (2) over all cases considered in the definition of the procedure *complete* is as small as possible. This optimal value turns out to be $\alpha = 0.1950\ldots$ Moreover, for this choice of α we can also show that for each edge $e = (S, S_A)$ in the tree $\mathcal{T}_T$, $\Delta(e) \geq 0$ thus, verifying an earlier assumption.

There are many cases in our specification of the procedure *complete*. Due to space limitations, we discuss only two of them here — those that actually determine the optimal value of α.

Case 1. We assume that the theory S has no 2-clauses and there are four clauses in S of the form $a \vee \beta_i \vee \gamma_i$, $i = 1, 2, 3, 4$, where a is an atom and $\beta_1, \ldots, \beta_4, \gamma_1, \ldots, \gamma_4$ are literals with pairwise distinct atoms different from a.

In this case the procedure *complete* outputs the family $\mathcal{A} = \{\{a\}, \{\neg a\}\}$. The set of atoms of $S_{\{\neg a\}}$ is $At(S) - \{a\}$ so $n(S_{\{\neg a\}}) = n(S) - 1$. In addition, $c(S) = 0$ and, since $S_{\{\neg a\}}$ contains at least four 2-clauses $\beta_i \vee \gamma_i$, $i = 1, 2, 3, 4$, with pairwise different atoms, $c(S_{\{\neg a\}}) \geq 4$. Let $e_{\{\neg a\}} = (S, S_{\{\neg a\}})$. We have

$$\Delta(e_{\{\neg a\}}) = \mu(S) - \mu(S_{\{\neg a\}}) = n(S) - n(S_{\{\neg a\}}) - \alpha(c(S) - c(S_{\{\neg a\}})) \geq 1 + 4\alpha.$$

Similarly, we can show that $\Delta(e_{\{a\}}) \geq 1$, where $e_{\{a\}} = (S, S_{\{a\}})$.

Thus, the positive root of the equation (2) is in this case not larger than the positive root τ of the equation $\tau^{-1} + \tau^{-1-4\alpha} = 1$, where $\alpha = 0.1950\ldots$ (indeed, the function $\phi(\tau, t_1, \ldots, t_k) = \sum_{i=1}^{k} \frac{1}{\tau^{t_i}}$ is decreasing for $\tau \geq 1$ and $t_1, \ldots, t_k \geq 0$). This root is $\tau = 1.6701\ldots$

Case 2. We assume that no two 2-clauses of the theory S have a common atom. Moreover there are five 2-clauses $a_i \vee b_i$, $i = 1, 2, 3, 4, 5$, and two 3-clauses $a_1 \vee a_2 \vee a_3$, $a_1 \vee a_4 \vee a_5$ in S, where $a_1, \ldots, a_5, b_1, \ldots, b_5$ are pairwise different atoms.

The following family

$$\mathcal{A}' = \{\{a_1\}, \{\neg a_1, a_2, a_4\}, \{\neg a_1, a_2, \neg a_4\}, \{\neg a_1, \neg a_2, a_4\}, \{\neg a_1, \neg a_2, \neg a_4\}\}$$

is complete. We observe that every model consistent with $\neg a_i$ is consistent with b_i because the clause $a_i \vee b_i$ has to be satisfied. Moreover, every model consistent with $\neg a_1$ and $\neg a_2$ (respectively $\neg a_1$ and $\neg a_4$) has to be consistent with a_3 (respectively a_5) because the clause $a_1 \vee a_2 \vee a_3$ (respectively $a_1 \vee a_4 \vee a_5$) has to be satisfied. These observations show that also the family

$$\mathcal{A} = \{\{a_1\}, \{\neg a_1, a_2, a_4, b_1\}, \{\neg a_1, a_2, \neg a_4, b_1, b_4, a_5\}, \{\neg a_1, \neg a_2, a_4, b_1, b_2, a_3\},$$
$$\{\neg a_1, \neg a_2, \neg a_4, b_1, b_2, b_4, a_3, a_5\}\}$$

is complete.

For every $A \in \mathcal{A}$, the theory S_A contains all 2-clauses of S except for those which have an atom or its negation in A. Since no two 2-clauses in S have a common atom, the only clauses which are in S but not in S_A are of the form $a_i \vee b_i$. For example, for $A = \{\neg a_1, a_2, \neg a_4, b_1, b_4, a_5\}$, S_A has the same 2-clauses as S, except for $a_1 \vee b_1$, $a_2 \vee b_2$, $a_4 \vee b_4$, and $a_5 \vee b_5$, which are not in S_A. Thus, for this particular A, $c(S_A) = c(S) - 4$. Proceeding similarly for all the sets $A \in \mathcal{A}$, we get

$$c(S_A) = \begin{cases} c(S) - 1, \text{ if } A = \{a_1\}; \\ c(S) - 3, \text{ if } A = \{\neg a_1, a_2, a_4, b_1\}; \\ c(S) - 4, \text{ if } A = \{\neg a_1, a_2, \neg a_4, b_1, b_4, a_5\}; \\ c(S) - 4, \text{ if } A = \{\neg a_1, \neg a_2, a_4, b_1, b_2, a_3\}; \\ c(S) - 5, \text{ if } A = \{\neg a_1, \neg a_2, \neg a_4, b_1, b_2, b_4, a_3, a_5\}. \end{cases}$$

Clearly, $\Delta(S_A) = \mu(S) - \mu(S_A) = |A| - \alpha(c(S) - c(S_A))$. Consequently,

$$\Delta(S_A) = \begin{cases} 1 - \alpha, \text{ if } A = \{a_1\}; \\ 4 - 3\alpha, \text{ if } A = \{\neg a_1, a_2, a_4, b_1\}; \\ 6 - 4\alpha, \text{ if } A = \{\neg a_1, a_2, \neg a_4, b_1, b_4, a_5\}; \\ 6 - 4\alpha, \text{ if } A = \{\neg a_1, \neg a_2, a_4, b_1, b_2, a_3\}; \\ 8 - 5\alpha, \text{ if } A = \{\neg a_1, \neg a_2, \neg a_4, b_1, b_2, b_4, a_3, a_5\}. \end{cases}$$

Thus, the equation (2) in this case reduces to $\tau^{-1+\alpha} + \tau^{-4+3\alpha} + 2\tau^{-6+4\alpha} + \tau^{-8+5\alpha} = 1$. Its positive solution (assuming $\alpha = 0.1950..$) is $\tau = 1.6701..$.

In all remaining cases the solutions of the equations (2) are smaller than $1.6701..$ so, $\tau_0 = 1.6701..$. Thus, by the inequality (3), the bound on $|L(\mathcal{T}_T)|$ follows.

Given a 3-CNF theory T, one can recognize in time $O(m)$ which case in the procedure *complete* applies (clearly each of the cases we discussed here can be recognized in time $O(m)$ and all other cases are described in similar terms). Thus, our procedure *complete* can be implemented to run in time $t(m) = O(m)$. Moreover, in each case, one can produce the appropriate complete collection also in time $O(m)$. Lastly, one can design all the cases so that the procedure *complete* is splitting (again, this is evident for the two cases discussed here). These observations complete the proof of Theorem 8.   □

6   Discussion

The algorithms we presented in the case of 2-CNF theories, and normal and disjunctive 2-programs have worst-case performance of $O(m1.4422..^n)$. The algorithm we designed for computing stable models of normal 3-programs runs in time $O(m1.6701..^n)$. Finally, our algorithms for computing minimal models of 3-CNF theories and answer sets of disjunctive logic programs run in time $O(mn^2 2.2720..^n)$. All these bounds improve by exponential factors over the corresponding straightforward ones.

The key question is whether still better algorithms are possible. In this context, we note that our algorithms developed for the case of 2-CNF theories and 2-programs are optimal, as long as we are interested in *all* minimal models, stable models and answer sets, respectively. However, we can compute a *single* minimal model of a CNF theory T or decide that T is unsatisfiable in *polynomial* time, using Proposition 5 and a well known fact that deciding satisfiability of 2-CNF theories is in P. In contrast, deciding whether a normal 2-program has a stable model and whether a disjunctive 2-program has an answer set is NP-complete. Thus, it is unlikely that there are polynomial-time algorithms to compute a single stable model (answer set) of a (disjunctive) 2-program or decide that none exist. Whether our bound of $O(m1.4422..^n)$ can be improved by an exponential factor if we are interested in computing a single stable model or a single answer set, rather than all of them, is an open problem.

The worst-case behavior of our algorithms designed for the case of 3-CNF theories and 3-programs does not match the lower bound of $O(n1.5848..^n)$ implied by Corollary 1. Thus, there is still room for improvement, even when we want to compute *all* minimal models, stable models and answer sets. In fact, we conjecture that exponentially faster algorithms exist.

In the case of 3-CNF theories, one can show, again using Proposition 5 and the algorithm from [16], that there is a simple algorithm to compute *one* minimal model of a 3-CNF theory or determine that it is unsatisfiable, running in time $O(p(m,n)1.4756..^n)$, where p is a polynomial. This is a significantly lower bound than $O(mn^2 2.2720..^n)$ that we obtained for computing *all* minimal models. We do not know however, whether the bound $O(p(m,n)1.4756..^n)$ is optimal. Furthermore, we do not known whether an exponential improvement over the bound of $O(mn^2 2.2720..^n)$ is possible if we want to compute a single answer set of a disjunctive 3-program or determine that none exists. Similarly, we do not know whether one can compute a single stable model of a 3-program or determine that none exists in time exponentially lower than $O(m1.6701..^n)$.

In some cases, our bound in Theorem 6 can be improved. Let $\mathcal{F}$ be the class of all CNF theories consisting of clauses of the form $a_1 \vee \ldots \vee a_p$ or $a \vee \neg b$, where $a_1, \ldots, a_p$, a and b are atoms. Similarly, let $\mathcal{G}$ be the class of all disjunctive programs with clauses of the form $a_1 \vee \ldots \vee a_p \leftarrow \mathbf{not}(b_1), \ldots, \mathbf{not}(b_r)$ or $a \leftarrow b, \mathbf{not}(b_1), \ldots, \mathbf{not}(b_r)$, where $a_1, \ldots, a_p, b_1, \ldots, b_r$, a and b are atoms. Checking whether a set M is a minimal model of a theory from $\mathcal{F}$ or an answer set of a program from $\mathcal{G}$ is in P (can be solved in linear time). Thus, using Proposition 4, one can show the following result.

Theorem 9. *There is an algorithm to compute minimal models of 3-CNF theories in $\mathcal{F}$ (answer sets of disjunctive 3-programs in $\mathcal{G}$, respectively), that runs in time $O(m1.6701..^n)$.*

Finally, we stress that our intention in this work was to better understand the complexity of problems to compute stable models of programs, minimal models of CNF theories and answer sets of disjunctive programs. Whether our theoretical results and algorithmic techniques we developed here will have any significant practical implications is a question for future research.

Acknowledgments. This research was supported by the National Science Foundation under Grant No. 0097278.

References

1. R. Ben-Eliyahu and L. Palopoli. Reasoning with minimal models: Efficient algorithms and applications. In *Proceedings of KR'94*, San Francisco, CA, 1994. Morgan Kaufmann.
2. G. Brewka, J. Dix, and K. Konolige. *Nonmonotonic Reasoning, An Overview.* CSLI Publications, 1997.
3. M. Cadoli and M. Lenzerini. The complexity of propositional closed world reasoning and circumscription. *Journal of Computer and System Sciences*, 48:255–310, 1994. Shorter version in the Proceedings of AAAI-90.
4. T. Eiter and G. Gottlob. On the computational cost of disjunctive logic programming: propositional case. *Annals of Mathematics and Artificial Intelligence*, 15(3-4):289–323, 1995.
5. Thomas Eiter, Wolfgang Faber, Nicola Leone, and Gerald Pfeifer. Declarative problem-solving in DLV. In Jack Minker, editor, *Logic-Based Artificial Intelligence*, pages 79–103. Kluwer Academic Publishers, Dordrecht, 2000.
6. M. Gelfond and V. Lifschitz. The stable semantics for logic programs. In R. Kowalski and K. Bowen, editors, *Proceedings of the 5th International Conference on Logic Programming*, pages 1070–1080. MIT Press, 1988.
7. M. Gelfond and V. Lifschitz. Classical negation in logic programs and disjunctive databases. *New Generation Computing*, 9:365–385, 1991.
8. O. Kullmann. New methods for 3-SAT decision and worst-case analysis. *Theoretical Computer Science*, pages 1–72, 1999.
9. V. Lifschitz. Circumscriptive theories: a logic-based framework for knowledge representation. *Journal of Philosophical Logic*, 17(4):391–441, 1988.
10. Z. Lonc and M. Truszczyński. Computing stable models: worst-case performance estimates. *Theory and Practice of Logic Programming*, 2003. To appear.
11. V.W. Marek and M. Truszczyński. Stable models and an alternative logic programming paradigm. In K.R. Apt, W. Marek, M. Truszczyński, and D.S. Warren, editors, *The Logic Programming Paradigm: a 25-Year Perspective*, pages 375–398. Springer Verlag, 1999.
12. W. Marek and M. Truszczyński. *Nonmonotonic Logic; Context-Dependent Reasoning.* Springer-Verlag, Berlin, 1993.
13. J. McCarthy. Circumscription — a form of non-monotonic reasoning. *Artificial Intelligence*, 13(1-2):27–39, 1980.
14. I. Niemelä. A tableau calculus for minimal model reasoning. In *Proceedings of the Fifth Workshop on Theorem Proving with Analytic Tableaux and Related Methods*, Lecture Notes in Computer Science, pages 278–294. Springer-Verlag, 1996.
15. I. Niemelä. Logic programming with stable model semantics as a constraint programming paradigm. *Annals of Mathematics and Artificial Intelligence*, 25(3-4):241–273, 1999.
16. R. Rodošek. A new approach on solving 3-satisfiability. In *Proc. 3rd Int. Conf. on AI and Symbolic Math. Comput.*, pages 197–212. Springer-Verlag, 1996. LNCS 1138.
17. P. Simons, I. Niemelä, and T. Soininen. Extending and implementing the stable model semantics. *Artificial Intelligence*, 138:181–234, 2002.

Uniform Equivalence of Logic Programs under the Stable Model Semantics *

Thomas Eiter and Michael Fink

Institut für Informationssysteme, Abt. Wissensbasierte Systeme,
Technische Universität Wien
Favoritenstraße 9-11, A-1040 Vienna, Austria
{eiter,michael}@kr.tuwien.ac.at

Abstract. In recent research on nonmonotonic logic programming, repeatedly strong equivalence of logic programs P and Q has been considered, which holds if the programs $P \cup R$ and $Q \cup R$ have the same stable models for any other program R. This property strengthens equivalence of P and Q with respect to stable models (which is the particular case for $R = \emptyset$), and has an application in program optimization. In this paper, we consider the more liberal notion of uniform equivalence, in which R ranges only over the sets of facts rather than all sets of rules. This notion, which is well-known, is particularly useful for assessing whether programs P and Q are equivalent as components in a logic program which is modularly structured. We provide semantical characterizations of uniform equivalence for disjunctive logic programs and some restricted classes, and analyze the computational cost of uniform equivalence in the propositional (ground) case. Our results, which naturally extend to answer set semantics, complement the results on strong equivalence of logic programs and pave the way for optimizations in answer set solvers as a tool for input-based problem solving.

Keywords: uniform equivalence, strong equivalence, stable models, answer set semantics, computational complexity, program optimization.

1 Introduction

In the last years, logic programming with non-monotonic negation, and in particular stable semantics, as a problem solving tool has received increasing attention, which led to application in several fields. To a great deal, this is due to the availability of several advanced implementations of the stable semantics such as smodels [18], DLV [11], or ASSAT [15]. In turn, the desire of more efficient stable models solvers has raised the need for sophisticated optimization methods by which logic programs can be simplified and processed more efficiently. In this direction, properties of logic programs under the stable semantics have been investigated which may aid in optimization.

A particular useful such property is *strong equivalence* [12,23]: Two logic programs P_1 and P_2 are strongly equivalent, if by adding any set of rules R to both P_1 and P_2,

* This work was partially supported by the Austrian Science Fund (FWF) Project Z29-N04, and the European Commission projects FET-2001-37004 WASP and IST-2001-33570 INFOMIX.

the resulting programs $P_1 \cup R$ and $P_2 \cup R$ are equivalent under the stable semantics, i.e., have the same set of stable models. Thus, if a program P contains a subprogram Q which is strongly equivalent to a program Q', then we may replace Q by Q', in particular if the resulting program is simpler to evaluate than the original one.

However, strong equivalence is a very restrictive concept. As for optimization, it is not very sensitive to a modular structure of logic programs which naturally emerges by splitting them into layered *components* that receive input from lower layers by facts and in turn output facts to a higher layer [13,5], nor to the usage of the same logic program to compute solutions over varying inputs given as sets of facts.

In this paper, we study the more liberal notion of *uniform equivalence* [22,16], which is better suited in this respect: Two logic programs P_1 and P_2 are uniformly equivalent, if by adding any set of *facts* F to both P_1 and P_2, the resulting programs $P_1 \cup F$ and $P_2 \cup F$ have the same set of stable models. Thus, a component C within a program P may be (offline) replaced by a uniformly equivalent set of rules C', provided the global component structure of the program is not affected (a simple syntactic check).

That strong equivalence and uniform equivalence are different concepts is illustrated by the following simple example.

Example 1. Let $P = \{a \vee b\}$ and $Q = \{a \leftarrow not\, b;\ b \leftarrow not\, a\}$. Then P and Q are not strongly equivalent, since $P \cup \{a \leftarrow b;\ b \leftarrow a\}$ has the stable model $\{a, b\}$, which is not a stable model of $Q \cup \{a \leftarrow b;\ b \leftarrow a\}$. However, it can be seen that P and Q are uniformly equivalent.

Moreover, this holds even for programs without disjunction.

Example 2. Let $P = \{a \leftarrow not\, b;\ a \leftarrow b\}$ and $Q = \{a \leftarrow not\, c;\ a \leftarrow c\}$. Then, it is easily verified that P and Q are uniformly equivalent. However, they are not strongly equivalent: For $P \cup \{b \leftarrow a\}$ and $Q \cup \{b \leftarrow a\}$, we have that $S = \{a, b\}$ is a stable model of $Q \cup \{b \leftarrow a\}$ but not of $P \cup \{b \leftarrow a\}$.

While strong equivalence of logic programs under stable semantics has been considered in a number of papers [3,4,14,12,19,23,24], to our knowledge uniform equivalence of has not been considered. Sagiv [22] has studied the property in the context of definite Horn datalog programs, where he showed decidability of uniform equivalence testing, which contrasts with the undecidability of equivalence testing for datalog programs. Maher [16] considered the property for definite general Horn programs, and reported undecidability. Moreover, both [22,16] showed that uniform equivalence coincides for the respective programs with Herbrand logical equivalence.

In this paper we focus on propositional logic programs (to which general programs reduce). Our main contributions are briefly summarized as follows.

• We provide characterizations of uniform equivalence of logic programs. In particular, we use the concept of strong-equivalence models (SE-models) [23,24] and thus give characterizations which appeal to classical models and the Gelfond-Lifschitz reduct [9, 10]. Our characterizations of uniform equivalence will elucidate the differences between strong and uniform equivalence in the examples above such that they immediately become apparent.

• For the finitary case, we provide a simple and appealing characterization of a logic program with respect to uniform equivalence in terms of its *uniform equivalence models* (*UE models*), which is a special class of SE-models. The associated notion of consequence can be fruitfully used to determine redundancies under uniform equivalence.

- We consider restricted subclasses, in particular positive programs, head-cycle free programs [1], and Horn programs, and consider the relationship between uniform and strong equivalence on them.
- We analyze the computational complexity of deciding uniform equivalence of two given programs P and Q. We show that the problem is Π_2^P-complete in the general propositional case, and thus harder than deciding strong equivalence of P and Q, which is in coNP [19,24]. However, the complexity of testing uniform equivalence decreases on important fragments; in particular, it is coNP-complete for positive and head-cycle free programs, while it is polynomial for Horn programs. In the nonground case, the complexity increases by an exponential for function-free programs.
- Finally, we address extensions to extended and to nested logic programs.

Our results complement the results on strong equivalence of logic programs, and pave the way for optimization of logic programs under stable negation by exploiting uniform equivalence. For space reasons, some proofs are omitted here (see [6] for an extended version).

2   Preliminaries

We deal with disjunctive logic programs, which allow the use of default negation *not* in rules. A rule r is a triple $\langle H(r), B^+(r), B^-(r) \rangle$, where $H(r) = \{A_1, \ldots, A_l\}$, $B^+(r) = \{A_{l+1}, \ldots, A_m\}$, $B^-(r) = \{A_{m+1}, \ldots, A_n\}$, where $0 \leq l \leq m \leq n$ and $A_i, 1 \leq i \leq n$, are atoms from a first-order language. Throughout, we use the traditional representation of a rule as an expression of the form

$$A_1 \vee \ldots \vee A_l \leftarrow A_{l+1}, \ldots, A_m, not\ A_{m+1}, \ldots, not\ A_n.$$

We call $H(r)$ the *head* of r, and $B(r) = \{A_{l+1}, \ldots, A_m, not\ A_{m+1}, \ldots, not\ A_n\}$ the *body* of r. If $H(r) = \emptyset$, then r is a *constraint*. As usual, r is a *fact* if $B(r) = \emptyset$, which is also represented by $H(r)$ if it is nonempty, and by $\bot$ (falsity) otherwise. A rule r is *normal* (or non-disjunctive), if $l \leq 1$; *definite*, if $l = 1$; and *positive*, if $n = m$. A rule is *Horn* if it is normal and positive.

A *disjunctive logic program* (DLP) P is a (possibly infinite) set of rules. A program P is a *normal logic program* (NLP) (resp., definite, positive, or Horn), if all rules in P are normal (resp., definite, positive, or Horn). Furthermore, a program P is *head-cycle free* (HCF) [1], if its dependency graph (which is defined as usual) has no directed cycle that contains two atoms belonging to the head of the same rule. *In the rest of this paper, we focus on propositional programs over a set of atoms $\mathcal{A}$ – programs with variables reduce to their ground (propositional) versions as usual.*

We recall the stable model semantics for $DLPs$ [10,21], which generalizes the stable model semantics for $NLPs$ [9]. An *interpretation* I, viewed as subset of $\mathcal{A}$, models the head of a rule r, denoted $I \models H(r)$, iff $A \in I$ for some $A \in H(r)$. It models $B(r)$, i.e., $I \models B(r)$ iff (i) each $A \in B^+(r)$ is true in I, i.e., $A \in I$, and (ii) each $A \in B^-(p)$ is false in I, i.e., $A \notin I$. Furthermore, I models rule r, iff $I \models H(r)$ whenever $I \models B(r)$, and $I \models P$, for a program P, iff $I \models r$, for all $r \in P$.

The *reduct* of a rule r *relative to* a set of atoms I, denoted r^I, is the positive rule r' such that $H(r') = H(r)$ and $B^+(r') = B^+(r)$ if $I \cap B^-(r) = \emptyset$, and is void otherwise. The

Gelfond-Lifschitz reduct P^I, of a program P, is $P^I = \{r^I \mid r \in P \text{ and } I \cap B^-(r) = \emptyset\}$. An interpretation I is a *stable model* of a program P iff I is a minimal model (under inclusion $\subseteq$) of P^I. By $\mathcal{SM}(P)$ we denote the set of all stable models of P.

Equivalences. Several notions for equivalence of logic programs have been considered, cf. [12,16,22]. Under stable semantics, two *DLPs* P and Q are regarded as equivalent, denoted $P \equiv Q$, iff $\mathcal{SM}(P) = \mathcal{SM}(Q)$.

The more restrictive forms of strong equivalence [12] and uniform equivalence [22, 16] are as follows.

Definition 1. *Let P and Q be two DLPs, Then*

(i) *P and Q are strongly equivalent, denoted $P \equiv^s Q$, iff for any rule set R, the programs $P \cup R$ and $Q \cup R$ are equivalent, i.e., $P \cup R \equiv Q \cup R$.*

(ii) *P and Q are uniformly equivalent, denoted $P \equiv^u Q$, iff for any set of non-disjunctive facts F, the programs $P \cup F$ and $Q \cup F$ are equivalent, i.e., $P \cup F \equiv Q \cup F$.*

One of the main results of [12] is a semantical characterization of strong equivalence in terms of the non-classical logic HT. For characterizing strong equivalence in logic programming terms, Turner introduced the following notion of SE-models [23,24]:

Definition 2. *Let P be a DLP, and let X, Y be sets of atoms such that $X \subseteq Y$. The pair (X, Y) is an SE-model of P, if $Y \models P$ and $X \models P^Y$. By $SE(P)$ we denote the set of all SE-models of P.*

Strong equivalence can be characterized as follows.

Proposition 1 ([23,24]). *For every DLPs P and Q, $P \equiv^s Q$ iff $SE(P) = SE(Q)$.*

Example 3. Reconsider $P = \{a \leftarrow not\, b;\ a \leftarrow b\}$ and $Q = \{a \leftarrow not\, c;\ a \leftarrow c\}$. Recall that $P \equiv^u Q$. However, $P \not\equiv^s Q$, as $(\emptyset, \{a, b\})$ is in $SE(P)$ but not in $SE(Q)$.

3   Characterizations of Uniform Equivalence

After the preliminary definitions, we now turn to the issue of characterizing uniform equivalence between logic programs in model-theoretic terms. As restated above, strong equivalence can be captured by the notion of SE-model (equivalently, HT-model [12]) for a logic program. The weaker notion of uniform equivalence can be characterized in terms of SE-models as well, by imposing further conditions.

We start with a seminal lemma, which allows us to derive simple characterizations of uniform equivalence.

Lemma 1. *Two DLPs P and Q are uniformly equivalent, i.e. $P \equiv^u Q$, iff for every SE-model (X, Y), such that (X, Y) is an SE-model of exactly one of the programs P and Q, it holds that (i) $Y \models P \cup Q$, and (ii) there exists an SE-model (M, Y), $X \subset M \subset Y$, of the other program.*

Proof. For the only-if direction, suppose $P \equiv^u Q$. If Y neither models P, nor Q, then (X, Y) is not an SE-model of any of the programs P and Q. Without loss of generality, assume $Y \models P$ and $Y \not\models Q$. Then, since in this case $Y \models P^Y$ and no strict subset of Y models $P \cup Y$, $Y \in \mathcal{SM}(P \cup Y)$, while $Y \notin \mathcal{SM}(Q \cup Y)$. This contradicts our assumption $P \equiv^u Q$. Hence, item (i) must hold.

To show (ii), assume first that (X, Y) is an SE-model of P but not of Q. In view of (i), it is clear that $X \subset Y$ must hold. Suppose now that for every set M, $X \subset M \subset Y$, it holds that (M, Y) is not an SE-model of Q. Then, since no subset of X models $Q^Y \cup X$, (Y, Y) is the only SE-model of $Q \cup X$ of form $(\cdot, Y)$. Thus, $Y \in \mathcal{SM}(Q \cup X)$ in this case, while $Y \notin \mathcal{SM}(P \cup X)$ ($X \models P^Y$ implies $X \models (P \cup X)^Y$, so (X, Y) is an SE-model of $P \cup X$). However, this contradicts $P \equiv^u Q$. Thus, it follows that for some M such that $X \subset M \subset Y$, (X, Y) is an SE-model of Q. The argument in the case where (X, Y) is an SE-model of Q but not of P is analogous. This proves item (ii).

For the if direction, assume that (i) and (ii) hold for every SE-model (X, Y) which is an SE-model of exactly one of P and Q. Suppose that there exist sets of atoms A and X, such that w.l.o.g., $X \in \mathcal{SM}(P \cup A) \setminus \mathcal{SM}(Q \cup A)$. Since $X \in \mathcal{SM}(P \cup A)$, we have that $A \subseteq X$, and, moreover, $X \models P$. Consequently, (X, X) is an SE-model of P. Since $X \notin \mathcal{SM}(Q \cup A)$, either $X \not\models (Q \cup A)^X$, or there exists $X' \subset X$ such that $X' \models (Q \cup A)^X$.

Let us first assume $X \not\models (Q \cup A)^X$, then, since $(Q \cup A)^X = Q^X \cup A$ and $A \subseteq X$, it follows that $X \not\models Q^X$. This implies $X \not\models Q$ and hence, (X, X) is not an SE-model of Q. Thus, (X, X) is an SE-model of exactly one program, P, but (X, X) violates (i) since $X \not\models Q$; this is a contradiction.

It follows that $X \models (Q \cup A)^X$ must hold, and that there must exist $X' \subset X$ such that $X' \models (Q \cup A)^X = Q^X \cup A$. So we can conclude $X \models Q$ and that (X', X) is an SE-model of Q but not of P. To see the latter, note that $A \subseteq X'$ must hold. So if (X', X) were an SE-model of P, then it would also be an SE-model of $P \cup A$, contradicting the assumption that $X \in \mathcal{SM}(P \cup A)$. Again we get an SE-model, (X', X), of exactly one of the programs, Q in this case. Hence, according to (ii), there exists an SE-model (M, X) of P, $X' \subset M \subset X$. However, because of $A \subset X'$, it follows that (M, X) is also an SE-model of $P \cup A$, contradicting our assumption that $X \in \mathcal{SM}(P \cup A)$.

This proves that, given (i) and (ii) for every SE-model (X, Y) such that (X, Y) is an SE-model of exactly one of P and Q, no sets of atoms A and X exists such that X is a stable model of exactly one of $P \cup A$ and $Q \cup A$. That is, $P \equiv^u Q$ holds.   □

From Lemma 1 we immediately obtain the following characterization of uniform equivalence between logic programs.

Theorem 1. *Two DLPs, P and Q are uniformly equivalent, $P \equiv^u Q$, iff*

(i) (X, X) *is an SE-model of P iff it is an SE-model of Q, and*

(ii) (X, Y), *where $X \subset Y$, is an SE-model of P (respectively Q) iff there exists a set M, such that $X \subseteq M \subset Y$, and (M, Y) is an SE-model of Q (respectively P).*

Example 4. Reconsider the programs $P = \{a \vee b\}$ and $Q = \{a \leftarrow not\, b;\ b \leftarrow not\, a\}$. By Theorem 1, we can easily verify that P and Q are uniformly equivalent: Their SE-models differ only in $(\emptyset, \{a, b\})$, which is an SE-model of Q but not of P. Thus, items (i) and (ii) clearly hold for all other SE-models. Moreover, $(\{a\}, \{a, b\})$ is an SE-model of P, and thus item (ii) also holds for $(\emptyset, \{a, b\})$.

Note that P and Q are strongly equivalent after adding the constraint $\leftarrow a, b$, which enforces exclusive disjunction. Uniform equivalence does not require such an addition.

Example 5. Let P and Q as in the previous example. Since $SE(R \cup S) = SE(R) \cap SE(S)$ for any programs P and S, the pair $(\emptyset, \{a, b\})$ is no longer an SE-model of $Q \cup \{c : \leftarrow a, b\}$ (because $\{a, b\} \not\models c$). Hence, $P \cup \{c\} \equiv^s Q \cup \{c\}$.

For finite programs, we can derive from Theorem 1 the following characterization of uniform equivalence.

Theorem 2. *Two finite DLPs P and Q are uniformly equivalent, i.e., $P \equiv^u Q$, iff the following conditions hold:*

(i) (X, X) is an SE-model of P iff it is an SE-model of Q for every X, and
(ii) for every SE-model $(X, Y) \in SE(P) \cup SE(Q)$ such that $X \subset Y$, there exists an SE-model $(M, Y) \in SE(P) \cap SE(Q)$ ($=SE(P \cup Q)$) such that $X \subseteq M \subset Y$.

Proof. Since (i) holds by virtue of Theorem 1, we only need to show (ii). Assume (X, Y), where $X \subset Y$, is in $SE(P) \cup SE(Q)$.

If $(X, Y) \in SE(P) \cap SE(Q)$, then the statement holds. Otherwise, by virtue of Theorem 1, there exists (M_1, Y), $X \subseteq M_1 \subset Y$, such that (M_1, Y) is in $SE(P) \cup SE(Q)$. By repeating this argument, we obtain a chain of SE-models $(X, Y) = (M_0, Y)$, $(M_1, Y), \ldots, (M_i, Y), \ldots$ such that $(M_i, Y) \in SE(P) \cup SE(Q)$ and $M_i \subseteq M_{i+1}$, for all $i \geq 0$. Furthermore, we may choose M_1 such that M_1 coincides with Y on all atoms which do not occur in $P \cup Q$ (and hence all M_i, $i \geq 1$, do so). Since P and Q are finite, it follows that $M_i = M_{i+1}$ must hold for some $i \geq 0$ and hence $(M_i, Y) \in SE(P) \cap SE(Q)$ must hold. This proves the result. $\qquad\square$

Note that the previous theorem remains valid even if only one of P and Q is finite.

In the light of this result, we can capture uniform equivalence of finite programs by the notion of UE-model defined as follows.

Definition 3 (UE-model). *Let P be a DLP. Then, any $(X, Y) \in SE(P)$ is a uniform equivalence (UE) model of P, if for every $(X', Y) \in SE(P)$ it holds that $X \subset X'$ implies $X' = Y$. By $UE(P)$ we denote the set of all UE-models of P.*

That is, the UE-models comprise all SE-models of a *DLP* which correspond to classical models of P (for $Y = X$), plus all its maximal 'non-classical' SE-models, i.e., $UE(P) = \{(X, X) \in SE(P)\} \cup \max_{\geq}\{(X, Y) \in SE(P) \mid X \subset Y\}$, where $(X', Y') \geq (X, Y) \Leftrightarrow Y' = Y \land X \subseteq X'$.

By means of UE-models, we then can characterize uniform equivalence of finite logic programs by the following simple condition.

Theorem 3. *Two finite DLPs P and Q are uniformly equivalent, i.e., $P \equiv^u Q$, if and only if $UE(P) = UE(Q)$.*

Proof. By Theorem 2 we have to show that Conditions (i) $(X, X) \models P \Leftrightarrow (X, X) \models Q$ and (ii) $(X, Y) \models P \land X \subset Y \Rightarrow \exists M, X \subseteq M \subset Y : (M, Y) \models P \cup Q$ hold iff $UE(P) = UE(Q)$.

For the if direction assume $UE(P) = UE(Q)$. Then (i) holds by definition of UE-models. Now let (X, Y) be an SE-model of P, such that $X \subset Y$. There are two possibilities: If (X, Y) is maximal, then $(X, Y) \in UE(Q)$ as well and thus (ii) holds ($M = X$); otherwise, (X, Y) is not maximal, which means that there exists some

$(X', Y) \in UE(P)$ such that $X \subset X' \subset Y$, and since $UE(P) = UE(Q)$ Condition
(ii) holds again ($M = X'$).

For the only-if direction let $P \equiv^u Q$. Then by Condition (i) $UE(P)$ and $UE(Q)$
coincide on models (X, X). Assume w.l.o.g. that (X, Y), $X \subset Y$, is in $UE(P)$, but not
in $UE(Q)$. By (ii) there exists (M, Y), $X \subseteq M \subset Y$, which is an SE-model of both
P and Q. Since $X \subset M$ contradicts $(X, Y) \in UE(P)$, let $M = X$, i.e., (X, Y) is an
SE-model of Q as well, but it is not in $UE(Q)$. Hence, there exists $(X', Y) \in UE(Q)$,
$X \subset X' \subset Y$ and by (ii) there exists (M', Y), $X' \subseteq M \subset Y$, which is an SE-model
of P. This again contradicts $(X, Y) \in UE(P)$. Hence, $UE(P) = UE(Q)$.   □

This result shows that UE-models capture the notion of uniform equivalence, in the
same manner as SE-models capture strong equivalence. That is, the essence of a program
P with respect to uniform equivalence is expressed by a semantic condition on P alone.

Example 6. Each SE-model of the program $P = \{a \lor b\}$ satisfies the condition of an
UE-model, and thus $UE(P) = SE(P)$. The program $Q = \{a \leftarrow not\, b;\ b \leftarrow not\, a\}$
has the additional SE-model $(\{\}, \{a, b\})$, and all of its SE-models except this one are
UE-models of Q. Thus, $UE(P) = UE(Q) = \{(\{a\}, \{a\}), (\{b\}, \{b\}), (\{a\}, \{a, b\}),$
$(\{b\}, \{a, b\}), (\{a, b\}, \{a, b\})\}$.

Note that the strong equivalence between P and Q fails because $(\emptyset, \{a, b\})$ is not
an SE-model of P. This SE-model is enforced by the intersection property $((X_1, Y)$
and (X_2, Y) in $SE(P)$ implies $(X_1 \cap X_2, Y) \in SE(P)$) which the Horn program
Q^Y enjoys, which however is not satisfied by the disjunctive program P^Y $(=P)$. The
maximality condition of UE-models eliminates this intersection property.

Example 7. Reconsider $P = \{a \leftarrow not\, b;\ a \leftarrow b\}$, which has classical models $\{a\} \cup Y$,
$Y \subseteq \{b, c\}$. Its UE-models are of form $(\{a\} \cup X, \{a\} \cup Y)$ where $X \in \{Y, Y \setminus \{b\}, Y \setminus$
$\{c\}\}$. Note that the atoms b and c have symmetric roles in $UE(P)$. Consequently, the
program obtained by exchanging the roles of b and c, $Q = \{a \leftarrow not\, c;\ a \leftarrow c\}$ has the
same UE models. Hence, P and Q are uniformly equivalent.

Like Theorem 2, also Theorem 3 remains valid if only one of P and Q is finite.
However, the following example shows that it fails if both P and Q are infinite.

Example 8. Consider the programs P and Q over $\mathcal{A} = \{a\} \cup \{b_i \mid i \geq 1\}$, defined by

$$P = \{a \leftarrow ,\ b_i \leftarrow \mid i \geq 1\}, \text{ and } Q = \{a \leftarrow not\, a,\ b_i \leftarrow b_{i+1},\ b_i \leftarrow a \mid i \geq 1\}.$$

Both P and Q have the single classical model $M = \{a, b_i \mid i \geq 1\}$. Furthermore, P
has no "incomplete" SE-model (X, Y) such that $X \subset Y$, while Q has the incomplete
SE-models (X_i, M), where $X_i = \{b_1, \ldots, b_i\}$ for $i \geq 0$. Both P and Q have the
same maximal incomplete SE-models (namely none), and hence they have the same
UE-models.

However, $P \not\equiv^u Q$, since e.g. P has a stable model while Q has obviously not. Note
that this is caught by our Theorem 1, item (ii): for (X_0, M), which is an SE-model of Q
but not of P, we cannot find an SE-model (X, M) of P between (X_0, M) and (M, M).

Based on UE-models, we define an associated notion of consequence under *uniform
equivalence*. Recall that (X, Y) models a rule r iff $Y \models r$ and $X \models r^Y$.

Definition 4 (UE-consequence). *A rule, r, is an* UE-consequence *of a program P, denoted* $P \models_u r$, *if* $(X, Y) \models r$ *for all* $(X, Y) \in UE(P)$.

Clearly, $P \models_u r$ for all $r \in P$, and $\emptyset \models r$ iff r is a classical tautology. The next result shows that a program remains invariant under addition of UE-consequences.

Proposition 2. *For any finite program P and rule r, if* $P \models_u r$ *then* $P \cup \{r\} \equiv^u P$.

From this proposition, we obtain an alternative characterization of uniform equivalence in terms of UE-consequence. As usual, we write $P \models_u R$ for any set of rules R if $P \models_u r$ for all $r \in R$.

Theorem 4. *Let P and Q be any finite DLPs. Then* $P \equiv^u Q$ *iff* $P \models_u Q$ *and* $Q \models_u P$. *Proof.* For the if-direction, we apply Prop. 2 repeatedly and obtain $P \equiv^u P \cup Q \equiv^u Q$. For the only-if direction, we have $UE(P) = UE(Q)$ if $P \equiv^u Q$ by Theorem 3, and thus P and Q have the same UE-consequences. Since $(X, Y) \models P$ (resp. $(X, Y) \models Q$), for all $(X, Y) \in UE(P)$ (resp. $(X, Y) \in UE(Q)$), it follows $Q \models_u P$ and $P \models_u Q$. □

We note that with respect to uniform equivalence, every program P has a canonical normal form, P^*, given by its UE-consequences, i.e., $P^* = \{r \mid P \models_u r\}$.

Clearly, $P \subseteq P^*$ holds for every program P, and P^* has exponential size. Applying optimization methods which build on UE-consequence, P resp. P^* may be transformed into smaller uniform equivalent programs; we leave this for further study.

As for the relationship of UE-consequence to classical consequence and cautious consequence under stable semantics, we note the following hierarchy. Let $\models_c$ denote consequence from the stable models, i.e., $P \models_c r$ iff $M \models r$ for every $M \in \mathcal{SM}(P)$.

Proposition 3. *For any finite program P and rule r, (i)* $P \models_u r$ *implies* $P \cup A \models_c r$, *for each set of facts A; (ii)* $P \cup A \models_c r$, *for each set of facts A, implies* $P \models_c r$; *and (iii)* $P \models_c r$ *implies* $P \models r$.

This hierarchy is strict, i.e., none of the implications holds in the converse direction. (For (i), note that $\{a \leftarrow not\, a\} \models_c a$ but $\{a \leftarrow not\, a\} \not\models_u a$, since the UE-model $(\emptyset, \{a\})$ violates a.)

We next present a semantic characterization in terms of UE-models, under which UE-and classical consequence and thus all four notions of consequence coincide.

Lemma 2. *Let P be a finite DLP. Suppose that* $(X, Y) \in UE(P)$ *implies* $X \models P$ *(i.e., X is a model of P). Then,* $P \models r$ *implies* $P \models_u r$, *for every rule r.*

Lemma 3. *Let P be a finite DLP. Then,* $P \models_u r$ *implies* $P \models r$, *for every rule r.*

Theorem 5. *Let P be any finite DLP. Then the following conditions are equivalent:*

(i) $P \models_u r$ *iff* $P \models r$, *for every rule r.*
(ii) For every $(X, Y) \in UE(P)$, *it holds that* $X \models P$.

Proof. $(ii) \Rightarrow (i)$ Follows immediately from Lemmas 2 and 3.
$(i) \Rightarrow (ii)$ Suppose $P \models_u r$ iff $P \models r$, for every rule r, but there exists some UE-model (X, Y) of P such that $X \not\models P$. Hence $X \not\models r$ for some rule $r \in P$. Let r' be the rule which results from r by shifting the negative literals to the head, i.e., $H(r') = H(r) \cup B^-(r)$, $B^+(r') = B^+(r)$, and $B^-(r') = \emptyset$. Then, $X \not\models r'$. On the other hand, $r \in P$ implies $(X, Y) \models r$. Hence, $Y \models r$ and thus $Y \models r'$. Moreover, $B^-(r') = \emptyset$ implies that $r' \in P^Y$, and hence $X \models r'$. This is a contradiction. It follows that $X \models P$ for each UE-model (X, Y) of P. □

An immediate corollary to this result is that for finite positive programs, the notion of UE-consequence collapses with classical consequence, and hence uniform equivalence of finite positive programs amounts to classical equivalence. We shall obtain these results as corollaries of more general results in the next section, though.

4   Restricted Classes of Programs

After discussing uniform equivalence of general propositional programs, let us now consider two prominent subclasses of programs, namely positive and head-cycle free programs.

4.1   Positive Programs

While for programs with negation, strong equivalence and uniform equivalence are different, the notions coincide for positive programs, as shown next.

Proposition 4. *Let P and Q be positive DLPs. Then $P \equiv^u Q$ iff $P \equiv^s Q$.*

Proof. The if-direction is immediate as $P \equiv^s Q$ implies $P \equiv^u Q$.

For the only-if-direction, we show that if P and Q are not strongly equivalent then P and Q are not uniformly equivalent. To start with, observe that $P^X = P$ holds for any positive program P and any set of literals X.

W.l.o.g., let (X, Y) be an SE-model of P but not of Q. By definition of SE-model we have $X \models P^Y$, i.e. $X \models P$. On the other hand, since (X, Y) is not SE-model of Q, either (*i*) $X \not\models Q^Y$, i.e., $X \not\models Q$, or (*ii*) $Y \not\models Q$.

(*i*) Consider the programs $P_X = P \cup X$ and $Q_X = Q \cup X$. Clearly, $X \models P_X$ and for each $X' \subset X$, $X' \not\models P_X = P_X^X$. Hence, X is an answer set of P_X. On the other hand, $X \not\models Q$ and thus $X \not\models Q_X$. Hence, X cannot be an answer set of Q_X.

(*ii*) Consider the programs $P_Y = P \cup Y$ and $Q_Y = Q \cup Y$. Clearly, $Y \models P_Y$ and for each $Y' \subset Y$, $Y' \not\models P_Y = P_Y^Y$. Hence, Y is an answer set of P_Y. On the other hand, $Y \not\models Q$ and thus $Y \not\models Q_Y$. Hence, Y cannot be an answer set of Q_Y.

In any case we must conclude that P and Q are not uniformly equivalent.   □

As known and easy to see from the main results of [12,23,24], on the class of positive programs classical equivalence and strong equivalence coincide. By combining this and the previous result, we obtain

Theorem 6. *Let P and Q be positive DLPs. Then $P \equiv^u Q$ if and only if $P \models Q$ and $Q \models P$, i.e., P and Q have the same set of classical models.*

Note that Sagiv [22] showed that uniform equivalence of datalog programs Π and Π' is equivalent to equivalence of Π' and Π over Herbrand models; this implies the above result for definite Horn programs. Maher [16] showed a generalization of Sagiv's result for definite Horn logic programs with function symbols.

Example 9. Consider the positive programs $P = \{a \vee b; \ c \leftarrow a; \ c \leftarrow b\}$ and $Q = \{a \vee b; \ c\}$. Their classical models are $\{a, c\}$, $\{b, c\}$, and $\{a, b, c\}$. Hence, P and Q are uniformly equivalent, and even strongly equivalent (due to Prop. 4).

4.2 Head-Cycle Free Programs

The class of head-cycle free programs generalizes the class of NLPs by permitting a restricted form of disjunction. Still, it is capable of expressing nondeterminism such as a guess for the value of an atom a, which does not occur in the head of any other rule.

As shown by Ben-Eliyahu and Dechter, each head-cycle free program can be rewritten to an NLP, obtained by shifting atoms from the head to the body, which has the same stable models. More formally, let us define the following notation:

Definition 5. *For any rule r, let $r^{\rightarrow} = \{r' \mid H(r') = \{a\}, a \in H(r), B^+(r') = B^+(r), B^-(r') = B^-(r) \cup H(r) \setminus \{a\}\}$ if $H(r) \neq \emptyset$ and $r^{\rightarrow} = \{r\}$ otherwise. For any DLP P, let $P^{\rightarrow} = \bigcup_{r \in P} r^{\rightarrow}$.*

It is well-known that for any head-cycle free program P, it holds that $P \equiv P^{\rightarrow}$ (cf. [1]). This result can be strengthened to uniform equivalence.

Theorem 7. *For any head-cycle free program P, it holds that $P \equiv^u P^{\rightarrow}$.*

Proof. For any set of facts A, it holds that $(P \cup A)^{\rightarrow} = P^{\rightarrow} \cup A$ and that this program is head-cycle free. Thus, $P \cup A \equiv (P \cup A)^{\rightarrow} \equiv P^{\rightarrow} \cup A$. Hence, $P \equiv^u P^{\rightarrow}$.   □

We emphasize that a similar result for strong equivalence fails, as shown by the canonical counterexample in Example 1. Moreover, the program $P = \{a \vee b \leftarrow .\}$ is not strongly equivalent to any NLP. Thus, we can not conclude without further consideration that a simple disjunctive "guessing clause" like the one in P (such that a and b do not occur in other rule heads) can be replaced in a more complex program by the unstratified clauses $a \leftarrow not\ b$ and $b \leftarrow not\ a$; addition of a further constraint $\leftarrow a, b$ is required. However, we can conclude this under uniform equivalence taking standard program splitting results into account [13,5].

We close this section with the following result, which provides a characterization of arbitrary programs which are strongly equivalent to their shift variant.

Theorem 8. *Let P be any DLP. Then, $P \equiv^s P^{\rightarrow}$ if and only if for every disjunctive rule $r \in P$ it holds that $P^{\rightarrow}$ has no SE-model (X, Y) such that (i) $|H(r) \cap Y| \geq 2$ and (ii) $X \cap H(r) = \emptyset$ and $X \models B^+(r)$, i.e., X violates the reduced rule r^Y.*

Example 10. Reconsider $P = \{a \vee b \leftarrow\}$. Then $P^{\rightarrow} = \{a \leftarrow not\ b, b \leftarrow not\ a\}$ has the SE-model $(\emptyset, \{a, b\})$, which satisfies the conditions (i) and (ii) for $r : a \vee b \leftarrow$. Note that also the extended program $P' = \{a \vee b \leftarrow, a \leftarrow b, b \leftarrow a\}$ is not strongly equivalent to its shifted program $P'^{\rightarrow}$. Indeed, $(\emptyset, \{a, b\})$ is also an SE-model of $P'^{\rightarrow}$. Furthermore, P is also not uniformly equivalent to $P'^{\rightarrow}$, since $(\emptyset, \{a, b\})$ is moreover a UE-model of $P'^{\rightarrow}$, but P has the single SE-model (and thus UE-model) $(\{a, b\}, \{a, b\})$.

5 Complexity

In this section, we address the computational complexity of uniform equivalence. While our main interest is with the problem of deciding uniform equivalence between two given programs, we also consider the related problems of UE-model checking and UE-consequence.

For UE-model checking, we have the following result. Let $\|\alpha\|$ denote the size of an object α.

Theorem 9. *Given a pair of sets (X, Y) and a program P, deciding whether $(X, Y) \in UE(P)$ is (i) coNP-complete in general, and (ii) feasible in polynomial time with respect to $\|P\| + \|X\| + \|Y\|$, if P is head-cycle free. Hardness in case (i) holds even for positive programs.*

Corollary 1. *UE-model checking for Horn programs is polynomial.*

We now consider the problem of our main interest, namely deciding uniform equivalence. By the previous theorem, the following upper bound on the complexity of this problem is obtained.

Lemma 4. *Given two DLPs P and Q, deciding whether $P \equiv^u Q$ is in the class Π_2^P.*

Recall that $\Pi_2^P = \text{coNP}^{\text{NP}}$ is the class of problems such that the complementary problem is nondeterministically decidable in polynomial time with the help of an NP oracle (i.e., in $\Sigma_2^P = \text{NP}^{\text{NP}}$).

Proof. To show that two *DLPs* P and Q are not uniformly equivalent, we can by Theorem 3 guess an SE-model (X, Y) such that (X, Y) is an UE-model of exactly on of the programs P and Q. By Theorem 9, the guess for (X, Y) can be verified in polynomial time with the help of an NP oracle. This proves Π_2^P-membership of $P \equiv^u Q$. $\square$

This upper bound has a complementary lower bound proved in the following result.

Theorem 10. *Given two DLPs P and Q, deciding $P \equiv^u Q$ is Π_2^P-complete.*

Proof. (Sketch) Membership in Π_2^P has already been established in Lemma 4. To show Π_2^P-hardness, we provide a polynomial reduction of evaluating a quantified Boolean formula (QBF) from a fragment which is known Π_2^P-complete to deciding uniform equivalence of two *DLPs* P and Q.

Consider a $QBF_{2,\exists}$ F of form $F = \exists X \forall Y \bigvee_{i=1}^{i=l} D_i$, where each D_i is a conjunct of at most three literals over the boolean variables in $X \cup Y$, $X = \{x_i \mid 1 \leq i \leq n\}$ and $Y = \{y_i \mid 1 \leq i \leq m\}$. Deciding whether a given such F is true is well-known to be Σ_2^P-complete; thus deciding whether F is false is Π_2^P-complete.

W.l.o.g., we assume that each D_i contains some literal over Y. Now let P and Q be the following programs:

$$
\begin{aligned}
P = \{ \; & x_i \vee x_i' \leftarrow . & & 1 \leq i \leq n; \\
& y_i \vee y_i' \leftarrow y_j. & & 1 \leq i \neq j \leq m; \\
& y_i \vee y_i' \leftarrow y_j'. & & 1 \leq i \neq j \leq m; \\
& w_0 \leftarrow x_i, x_i'. & & 1 \leq i \leq n; \quad w_1 \leftarrow y_i, y_i'. \quad 1 \leq i \leq m; \\
& x_i \leftarrow w_0. & & 1 \leq i \leq n; \quad w_1 \leftarrow D_i^*. \quad\;\; 1 \leq i \leq l; \\
& x_i' \leftarrow w_0. & & 1 \leq i \leq n; \quad y_i \leftarrow w_1. \quad\;\;\; 1 \leq i \leq m; \\
& y_i \leftarrow w_0. & & 1 \leq i \leq m; \quad y_i' \leftarrow w_1. \quad\;\;\; 1 \leq i \leq m; \\
& y_i' \leftarrow w_0. & & 1 \leq i \leq m; \quad w_1 \leftarrow not\, w_1. \\
& w_1 \leftarrow w_0. & & \qquad\qquad\qquad\qquad\qquad\qquad\qquad \},
\end{aligned}
$$

and $Q = P \cup \{y_1 \vee y_1' \leftarrow .\}$,

where D_i^* results from D_i by replacing literals $\neg x_i$ and $\neg y_i$ by x_i' and y_i', respectively.

Informally, the disjunctive clauses with x_i and x_i' in the head resp. y_i and y_i' serve for selecting a truth assignment to the variable x_i (resp., y_i). The atom w_0 serves for handling a spoiled assignment to some x_i, which occurs if both x_i and x_i' are true, and enforces the maximal interpretation as the unique model of P, by the rules with w_0 in the body. Similarly, w_1 recognizes a spoiled assignment to some variable y_i or that some disjunct D_j of the QBF is true, and enforces for all atoms y_i, y'_i and w_1 the unique value true. However, for P the selection of a truth assignment is conditional to the truth of any atom y_i or y'_i, while for Q it is mandatory by the additional rule $y_1 \vee y'_1 \leftarrow$. This difference leads to a suite of candidate SE-models (A_χ, M_χ) of P which do not satisfy Q, where χ corresponds to a truth assignment to X and all atoms not in $X \cup X'$ are false, such that (A_χ, M_χ) violates uniform equivalence of P and Q via (ii) just if there is no way to make all D_j false by some assignment μ to Y. These candidate models for spoiling uniform equivalence are eliminated iff formula F evaluates to false. Since P and Q are obviously constructible in polynomial time, our result follows.   □

The previous result shows that deciding uniform equivalence of $DLPs$ P and Q is more complex than deciding strong equivalence, which is in coNP [19,24]. Thus, the more liberal notion of uniform equivalence comes at higher computational cost in general. However, for important classes of programs, it has the same complexity

Theorem 11. *Let P and Q be DLPs without simultaneous negation and head-cycles (i.e., each program is either positive or head-cycle free). Then, deciding $P \equiv^u Q$ is* coNP- *complete, where* coNP-*hardness holds if P is either positive or a NLP, and Q is Horn.*

Note that Sagiv showed [22] that deciding $P \equiv^u Q$ for given definite Horn programs P and Q is polynomial. This clearly generalizes to arbitrary Horn programs. We further remark that for $NLPs$ deciding strong equivalence is also coNP-hard.

Finally, we complement the results on uniform equivalence and UE-model checking with briefly addressing the complexity of UE-consequence.

Theorem 12. *Given a DLP P and a rule r, deciding $P \models_u r$ is (i) Π_2^P-complete in general, (ii)* coNP-*complete if P is either positive or head-cycle free, and (iii) polynomial if P is Horn.*

Proof. (Sketch) The complementary problem, $P \not\models_u r$, is in Σ_2^P for general P and in NP for head-cycle free P, since a guess for a UE-model (X, Y) of P which violates r can, by Theorem 9 be verified with a call to a NP-oracle resp. in polynomial time. In case of a positive P, by Theorem 5, $P \models_u r$ iff $P \models r$, which is in coNP for general P and polynomial for Horn P. The hardness results can be obtained by adapting the constructions in hardness proofs of previous results.   □

We conclude this section with some remarks on the complexity of programs with variables. For such programs, in case of a given finite Herbrand universe the complexity of equivalence checking increases by an exponential. Intuitively, this is explained by the exponential size of the ground instance of a program over the universe. Note that Lin reported [14], without a full proof, that checking strong equivalence for programs in this setting is in coNP, and thus has the same complexity as in the propositional case; however, this is not correct. Unsurprisingly, uniform equivalence of logic programs over an arbitrary Herbrand universe is undecidable according to Maher [16].

6   Extensions

Our results easily carry over to extended logic programs, i.e., programs where classical (also called strong) negation is allowed as well. If the inconsistent answer set is disregarded, i.e., an inconsistent program has no models, then, as usual, the extension can be semantically captured by representing strongly negated atoms $\neg A$ by a positive atom A' and adding constraints $\leftarrow A, A'$, for every atom A, to any program.

Furthermore, since the proofs of our main results are generic in the use of reducts, they can be easily generalized to nested logic programs considered in [12,23,24,19], i.e., we get the same characterizations and the same complexity (Π_2^P).

However, if in the extended setting the inconsistent answer set is taken into account, then the given definitions have to be slightly modified such that the characterizations of uniform equivalence capture the extended case properly. The same holds true for the characterization of strong equivalence by SE-models as illustrated by the following example. Note that the redefinition of $\equiv^u$ and $\equiv^s$ is straightforward.

Let $Lit_{\mathcal{A}} = \{A, \neg A \mid A \in \mathcal{A}\}$ denote the set of all literals using strong negation over $\mathcal{A}$.

Example 11. Consider the extended logic programs $P = \{a \vee b \leftarrow ; \neg a \leftarrow a; \neg b \leftarrow b\}$ and $Q = \{a \leftarrow not\, b; b \leftarrow not\, a; \neg a \leftarrow a; \neg b \leftarrow b\}$. They both have no SE-model; hence, by the criterion of Prop. 1, $P \equiv^s Q$ would hold, which implies $P \equiv^u Q$ and $P \equiv Q$. However, P has the inconsistent answer set $Lit_{\mathcal{A}}$, while Q has no answer set. Thus formally, P and Q are not even equivalent if $Lit_{\mathcal{A}}$ is admitted as answer set.

Since [23,12,24] made no distinction between no answer set and inconsistent answer set, we start adapting the definition of SE-models.

Definition 6. *A pair (X, Y), $X \subseteq Y \subseteq Lit_{\mathcal{A}}$, is an SEE-model of an extended DLP P, if each of X and Y is either consistent or equals $Lit_{\mathcal{A}}$ and $Y \models P \wedge X \models P^Y$.*

From previous characterizations we get more general characterizations in terms of SEE-models for extended programs.

Theorem 13. *Two extended DLPs P and Q are*

- *strongly equivalent iff they have the same SEE-models, and*
- *uniformly equivalent iff*
  - *(i) (X, X) is an SEE-model of P iff it is an SEE-model of Q, and*
  - *(ii) (X, Y), $X \subset Y$, is an SEE-model of P (resp. Q) iff there exists a set M, such that $X \subseteq M \subset Y$, and (M, Y) is an SEE-model of Q (resp. P).*

For positive programs, uniform and strong equivalence coincide also in the extended case.

Theorem 14. *Let P and Q be positive, extended DLPs. Then $P \equiv^s Q$ iff $P \equiv^u Q$.*

As a consequence of previous complexity results, checking $P \equiv^u Q$ (resp. $P \equiv^s Q$) for extended logic programs, P and Q, is Π_2^P-hard (resp. coNP-hard).

However, not all properties do carry over. As Example 11 reveals, in general a head-cycle free extended DLP P is no longer equivalent, and hence not uniformly equivalent, to its shift $P^{\leftarrow}$. However, under the condition below $P \equiv^u P^{\leftarrow}$ holds as well. Call any DLP contradiction-free, if $Lit_{\mathcal{A}}$ is not an answer set of it.

Proposition 5. *Let P be a head-cycle free and contradiction-free extended DLP. Then $P \equiv^u P^\leftarrow$ iff for each $A \subseteq Lit_A$, the program $P \cup A$ is contradiction-free if the program $\{r \in P \mid |H(r)| \leq 1\} \cup A$ is contradiction-free.*

As shown in [6], "$A \subseteq Lit_A$" can be equivalently replaced by "$A \subseteq Lit_A$ such that $D_H(P) \not\subseteq A$," where $D_H(P) = \{L \mid L \in H(r), |H(r)| > 1, r \in P\}$.

We finally note that Pearce and Valverde have given, inspired by our work, a generalization of our results on UE-models to equilibrium logic [20].

7 Conclusion

Uniform equivalence of logic programs, which has been considered earlier for datalog and general Horn logic programs [22,16], under stable semantics is an interesting concept which can be exploited for program optimization. We have presented characterizations of uniform equivalence in terms of Turner's SE-models [23,24] (equivalently, HT models [12]), and we have analyzed the computational cost for testing uniform equivalence and related problems.

While we have presented a number of results, there are several issues which remain to be considered. We have found a simple and appealing characterization of uniform equivalence in terms of UE-models for finitary programs, which single out from the SE-models certain maximal models. However, in case of infinite programs, such maximal models need not exist. It thus would be interesting to see whether also in this case uniform equivalence can be captured by a set of SE-models, or whether a completely novel notion of model (like SE-model for strong equivalence) is needed. Researching this issue is part of our ongoing work.

Another direction of research is to investigate the usage of uniform equivalence for program replacement and program rewriting in optimization. To this end, in follow-up works [7,8] we analyzed compliances with current optimization techniques and gave characterizations of programs possessing equivalent programs belonging to syntactic subclasses of disjunctive logic programs under both, uniform and strong equivalence. Furthermore we gave encodings of our characterizations in answer-set programming and investigated the computational complexity of program simplification and determining semantical equivalence.

Acknowledgments. We thank the anonymous referees for their valuable comments.

References

1. R. Ben-Eliyahu and R. Dechter. Propositional semantics for disjunctive logic programs. *Annals of Mathematics and Artificial Intelligence*, 12:53–87, 1994.
2. R. Ben-Eliyahu and L. Palopoli. Reasoning with minimal models: Efficient algorithms and applications. In *Proc. KR'94*, pp. 39–50, 1994.
3. P. Cabalar. A three-valued characterization for strong equivalence of logic programs. In *Proc. AAAI '02*, pp. 106–111, 2002.
4. D. J. de Jongh and L. Hendriks. Characterizations of strongly equivalent logic programs in intermediate logics. *Theory and Practice of Logic Programming*, 3(3):259–270, 2003.

5. T. Eiter, G. Gottlob, and H. Mannila. Disjunctive datalog. *ACM TODS*, 22(3):364–417, 1997.
6. T. Eiter and M. Fink. Uniform equivalence of logic programs under the stable model semantics. Tech. Rep. INFSYS RR-1843-03-08, Inst. für Informationssysteme, TU Wien, 2003.
7. T. Eiter, M. Fink, H. Tompits, and S. Woltran. Simplifying logic programs under uniform and strong equivalence. Manuscript, submitted, July 2003.
8. T. Eiter, M. Fink, H. Tompits, and S. Woltran. Eliminating disjunction from propositional logic programs under stable model preservation. Manuscript, submitted, August 2003.
9. M. Gelfond and V. Lifschitz. The stable model semantics for logic programming. In *Logic Programming: Proc. Fifth Int'l Conference and Symposium*, pp. 1070–1080, 1988.
10. M. Gelfond and V. Lifschitz. Classical negation in logic programs and disjunctive databases. *New Generation Computing*, 9:365–385, 1991.
11. N. Leone, G. Pfeifer, W. Faber, T. Eiter, G. Gottlob, C. Koch, C. Mateis, S. Perri, and F. Scarcello. The DLV system for knowledge representation and reasoning. Tech. Rep. INFSYS RR-1843-02-14, Inst. für Informationssysteme, TU Wien, 2002.
12. V. Lifschitz, D. Pearce, and A. Valverde. Strongly equivalent logic programs. *ACM Trans. on Computational Logic*, 2(4):526–541, 2001.
13. V. Lifschitz and H. Turner. Splitting a logic program. In *Proc. ICLP-94*, pp. 23–38, 1994.
14. F. Lin. Reducing strong equivalence of logic programs to entailment in classical propositional logic. In *Proc. KR-2002*, pp. 170–176, 2002.
15. F. Lin and Y. Zhao. ASSAT: Computing answer sets of a logic program by SAT solvers. In *Proc. AAAI-2002*, pp. 112–117, 2002.
16. M. J. Maher. Equivalences of logic programs. In Minker [17], pp. 627–658.
17. J. Minker, editor. *Foundations of Deductive Databases and Logic Programming*. Morgan Kaufmann, 1988.
18. I. Niemelä, P. Simons, and T. Syrjänen. Smodels: A system for answer set programming. In *Proc. 8th Int'l Workshop on Non-Monotonic Reasoning (NMR'2000)*, 2000.
19. D. Pearce, H. Tompits, and S. Woltran. Encodings for equilibrium logic and logic programs with nested expressions. In *Proc. EPIA 2001*, LNCS 2258, pp. 306–320, 2001.
20. D. Pearce and A. Valverde. Some types of equivalence for logic programs and equilibrium logic. In *Proc. Joint Conf. Declarative Programming (APPIA-GULP-PRODE)*, 2003.
21. T. Przymusinski. Stable semantics for disjunctive programs. *New Generation Computing*, 9:401–424, 1991.
22. Y. Sagiv. Optimizing datalog programs. In Minker [17], pp. 659–698.
23. H. Turner. Strong equivalence for logic programs and default theories (made easy). In *Proc. LPNMR-01*, LNCS 2173, pp. 81–92, 2001.
24. H. Turner. Strong equivalence made easy: nested expressions and weight constraints. *Theory and Practice of Logic Programming*, 3(4-5):609–622, 2003.

Answer Set Programming Phase Transition: A Study on Randomly Generated Programs

Yuting Zhao and Fangzhen Lin

Department of Computer Science
Hong Kong University of Science and Technology
Clear Water Bay, Kowloon, Hong Kong
{yzhao,flin}@cs.ust.hk

Abstract. We study the following problems on some classes of randomly generated logic programs under the answer set semantics: the existence of an answer set and the hardness of finding one answer set, if any.
Firstly in logic programs with 3 or more literals in the rules, for the first problem, despite the non-monotonicity of the answer set semantics, we observe a phase transition occurring on some particular critical values of L/N, where L and N are the number of rules and atoms in a program, respectively. More specifically, the probability of having an answer set drops from near 1 to near 0 abruptly and monotonically when the ratio increases from 0 to ∞. For the second problem, we find that for all three of the systems that we have tested: Smodels, DLV, and ASSAT, the problem of finding one answer set becomes much harder when the ratio falls into a certain region. Our experiments also show that a logic program without answer sets is much harder to compute than those with. This suggests that the most effective strategies for improving the performance of ASP systems should be those that can detect the non-existence of answer sets early on. In a class of logic program with 2 or 3 literals in the rules, we observe an interesting non-monotonicity on the probability of existing answer sets, which coincides with the non-monotonicity of the answer set semantics.

1 Introduction

Answer Set Programming (ASP) is a general declarative knowledge representation paradigm which supports non-monotonic reasoning. One problem with it is that computing answer sets is computationally expensive; it has been shown that the problem of deciding whether a program has an answer set is NP-complete[12]. There are, however, some practical systems that show encouraging results on some typical application problems [15,4,11]. It will be interesting to investigate where the hard problems are in the space of the ASP problem.

It has been shown that many NP-hard problems often involve a phase transition. These include SAT, TSP (traveling salesman problem), and graph coloring *etc.*[10,2,7]. For instance, studies in [2] indicate that many NP-hard problems have difficult instances occurring around some particular critical values of some

C. Palamidessi (Ed.): ICLP 2003, LNCS 2916, pp. 239–253, 2003.

"order parameter". Interestingly these critical values also separate the problem space into two regions, one that is under-constrained and a solution is relatively easy to find, the other that is over-constrained and relatively easy to prove there is no solution.

In this paper, we study the phase transition phenomenon in randomly generated logic programs with answer set semantics. While the existence of an answer set of a logic program is an NP-complete problem, it differs from problems like SAT in that answer set semantics is non-monotonic. If a problem has no answer, then adding some rules to the program may yield an answer set. Because of this, one could imagine that for logic programs the phase transition phenomenon could be different.

We use the *fixed body length model* to refer to a class of logic programs whose rules have a fixed body length, and the *mixed body length model* to a class of logic programs whose rules have a mixed body length.

Specifically, we concentrate the following two problems on randomly generated logic programs: the existence of an answer set and the hardness of finding one answer set, if any.

In the 3^+-*LP*, a class of logic programs whose rules have not less than 3 literals, *i.e.*, more than and including 2 literals in its body, we investigate both the fixed body length model and the mixed body length model. For the first problem, despite the non-monotonicity of the answer set semantics, we observe a phase transition occurring on some particular critical values of L/N, where L and N are the number of rules and atoms in a program, respectively. More specifically, the probability of having an answer set drops from near 1 to near 0 abruptly and monotonically when the ratio increases from 0 to ∞. For the second problem, we found that the problem of finding one answer set becomes much harder when the ratio falls into a certain region, so called "hard-job-region", for all three of the systems that we have tested: Smodels [15], DLV [4], and ASSAT [11]. The first two are considered state-of-the-art specific ASP systems, the last one is a SAT-based system implemented by ourselves. Our experiments also show that a logic program without answer sets is much harder to compute than those with. This idea is mainly supported by two consistent observations in the experiments[1]. This suggests that the most effective strategies for improving the performance of ASP systems should be those that can detect the non-existence of answer sets early on.

The answer set semantics and propositional satisfiable semantics are closely related. We introduce two approaches to measure the hardness of the ASP problem in terms of SAT. With these terms, we explore *2-3-LP*, a class of logic programs in which each program is a mixture of 2-literal rules and 3-literal rules, 50% to 50%, and finally we evaluate the hard-job-region although it does not show any obvious easy-hard-easy pattern in early experiment. More interesting; the 2-3-LP shows an obvious non-monotonicity on the probability of having answer sets, which coincides with the non-monotonicity of the answer set semantics.

---

[1] More details are given in the section Conclusion.

This paper is organized as follows. Firstly, we introduce some preliminaries in section 2, and the random ASP problem in section 3. In the following two sections, we show experimental results in the fixed body length model and the mixed body length model respectively. In section 6, we introduce the approaches to measure the hardness of ASP in terms of SAT. In section 7, we explore the 2-3-LP class. Finally, a conclusion is given in section 8.

2   Preliminaries

2.1   Definite Logic Program

We assume that A is a set of propositional symbols. Each element of A is called an *atom*. Atoms will also be called *positive literals*; a *negative literal* is an atom preceded by a negation symbol, '¬' in the propositional logic, or 'not' in the logic programming. A *literal* is a positive literal or a negative literal. A *clause* is a disjunction of literals.

A *definite logic program* is a set of *rules* of the form:

$$q \leftarrow l_1, \cdots, l_n. \tag{1}$$

where $q, l_1, \cdots, l_n$ are atoms, $n \geq 0$.

A definite logic program without variables and negative literals has a unique minimal model [16]. The minimal model M of logic program P can be derived by using the immediate consequence operator:

$$T_P(M) = \{ q \mid q \leftarrow l_1, \cdots, l_n \in P \text{ and } \{l_1, \cdots, l_n\} \subseteq M\} \tag{2}$$

where $q, l_1, \cdots, l_n$ are atoms, $n \geq 0$.

2.2   Normal Logic Program

A *normal logic program* is a finite set consisting of *rules* of the form:

$$p \leftarrow p_1, ..., p_k, \text{not } q_1, ..., \text{not } q_m, \tag{3}$$

and *constraints* of the form:

$$\leftarrow p_1, ..., p_k, \text{not } q_1, ..., \text{not } q_m, \tag{4}$$

where $p, p_1, ..., p_k, q_1, ..., q_m$ are atoms, $k \geq 0, m \geq 0$. We call the left of $\leftarrow$ the *head* of the rule, the right the *body*. Usually we say a rule is *k-length*, if the body has exactly $(k-1)$ different literals.

2.3   Stable Model Semantics and Answer Set Semantics

To define the answer sets of a logic program with constraints, we first define the *stable models* [6] of a logic program that does not have any constraint. Given a logic program P without constraints, and a set M of atoms, the *Gelfond-Lifschitz transformation* of P on M, written P^M, is obtained from P as follows:

- For each negative literal 'not q' in the body of any rule in P, if $q \notin M$, then delete this negative literal.
- In the resulting set of rules, delete all those that still contain a negative literal in their bodies.

Clearly for any M, P^M is a set of rules without any negative literal. This means that there is a unique minimal model of P^M, which can be derived by using the T_P operator in section 2.1. In the following, we shall denote this set by $Cons(P^M)$. Now a set M is a stable model [6] of P iff $M = Cons(P^M)$.

In general, given a logic program P with constraints, a set of atoms M is the *answer set* if it is a stable model of the program resulted from deleting all the constraints in P, and it satisfies all the constraints in P.

Something interesting in answer set programming is its capability of non-monotonic reasoning: adding more rules to a logic program may force us to retract some of the previous conclusions, which were obtained using fewer rules. For example, consider the logic program $G = \{p \leftarrow \text{not } q \}$, it has an answer set $\{p\}$, and accordingly gets a conclusion p, but if we add another rule $q \leftarrow \text{not } r$, it retracts its previous conclusion and gets a new answer set $\{q\}$ and a new conclusion q. Additionally, if a logic program is inconsistent (having no answer set), adding some new rule may turn it into consistent. For instance, consider a logic program $G = \{p \leftarrow \text{not } p.\}$, it has no answer set, but if we add one rule $p \leftarrow \text{not } q$, it becomes consistent and gets an answer set $\{p\}$.

2.4   Completion Semantics

Given a logic program P, its completion, written $Comp(P)$, is the union of the constraints in P and the Clark's completion [3] of the set of rules in P, that is, it consists of the following sentences:

- For any atom p, let $p \leftarrow G_1, \cdots, p \leftarrow G_n$ be all the rules about p in P, then formula '$p \leftrightarrow G_1 \vee \cdots \vee G_n$' is in $Comp(P)$. In particular, if $n = 0$, then formula '$p \leftrightarrow False$' is included in $Comp(P)$.
- If $\leftarrow G$ is a constraint in P, then formula '$\neg G$' is in $Comp(P)$.

3   Random ASP Problem

In the experiments, we calculate the ratio of logic programs that have answer sets in an ASP class X, and denote it by $pro(X)$:

$$pro(X) = \frac{A}{B},$$

where B is the total number of instances (programs) drawn from the ASP class X, and A is the number of programs having answer set.

In this paper, all experiments were done on Sun Ultra 5 machines with 256M memory running Solaris. The reported times are in CPU seconds as reported by Unix "time" command. Rather than using the number of recursive calls as in some works on SAT phase transition [13,7], here we use the *mean* CPU time to measure the performance, because currently we do not have a fundamental ASP procedure like what the Davis-Putnam procedure acts as in SAT. In order to get rid of the noise brought by a certain ASP system, we use 3 different ASP systems in the experiments, and use the CPU time on the same machine to measure the hardness of the problem and compare the performance of disparate algorithms.

The ASP systems used in the experiment are, two specialized ASP systems: Smodels 2.27[2], and DLV April 12th, 2002 version[3], and a SAT-based ASP solver, ASSAT 2.0[4] working with SAT solver Chaff2[5]. Actually, as the generated programs are ground programs, lparse[6] is only used for Smodels and ASSAT to convert the format of input files from text format to digital. Another SAT solver SATO 3.2.1[7] is used to evaluate the hardness in a term of SAT.

3.1   Randomly Generated Logic Program

Firstly we consider the fixed body length model. By *k-LP(N,L)* we denote the class of logic programs that have exactly L rules, N atoms, and whose rules have a length of k, *i.e.* , have exactly $(k-1)$ literals in its body.

Let $A = \{a_1, a_2, ..., a_N\}$ be a set of atoms, we generate random logic programs in class k-LP(N,L) ($2 \le k \le N$) with the following procedure:

Procedure 1 Repeat the following steps until results L rules:

1. Generate the head: randomly select an atom from A as the head,
2. Generate the body: randomly select $(k-1)$ different elements from A as the body, and negate each with the probability 0.5,
3. If this rule is already in the program, skip it and go to step 1; else add it in the program.

We denote, by *k-LP(N)*, the class of logic programs of k-length rules that have N variables:

$$k\text{-}LP(N) = \bigcup_{L \ge 0} k\text{-}LP(N, L).$$

Notice that according to Procedure 1, there are no duplicate rules in a logic program, and no duplicate literals in the body of any rule. Therefore for a finite

---

[2] Smodels: http://saturn.tcs.hut.fi/Software/smodels/

[3] DLV: http://www.dbai.tuwien.ac.at/proj/dlv/

[4] ASSAT: http://assat.cs.ust.hk/

[5] mchaff: http://www.ee.princeton.edu/~chaff/software.php

[6] lparse: http://www.tcs.hut.fi/Software/smodels/src/lparse-1.0.11.tar.gz

[7] SATO: http://www.intellektik.informatik.tu-darmstadt.de/SATLIB/Solvers/

number of atoms N, the number of all possible rules cannot be infinite. In general, this hold for the mixed body length model as well. In this paper we use δ to denote the number of all possible distinct rules of a class of logic programs. For instance, for k-LP(N) ($2 \leq k \leq N$),

$$\delta \ = \ N2^{k-1}C_N^{k-1}.$$

3.2   On the Existence of Answer Sets

Assume P is the largest program in k-LP(N) ($2 \leq k \leq N$) *i.e.* , it contains all possible rules. Let A be the set of atoms in P. Consider $p \in A$ and its completion:

$$p \leftrightarrow G_1 \vee \cdots \vee G_t,$$

where $G_i = g_1^i \wedge \ldots \wedge g_{k-1}^i$ $(1 \leq i \leq t)$. The right of '$\leftrightarrow$' must be a tautology, since it contains all possible conjunctions with $(k - 1)$ literals. Then we have $p = True$. So the only model of the completion of P is A. It is known that an answer set of a logic program must be a model of its completion [5]. By checking A on P, obviously A is not an answer set of P, because every rule remained after the Gelfond-Lifschitz transformation is involved in positive loops [1,11]. Actually, every atom $p \in P$ is a tautology head, but together they lead to no answer set. So we have,

Proposition 1.

$$pro(k\text{-}LP(N, \delta)) = 0,$$

where $2 \leq k \leq N$.

Theoretically, an empty logic program has a unique answer set, ϕ. So in any class k-LP(N), we have,

Proposition 2.

$$pro(k\text{-}LP(N, 0)) = 1,$$

where $1 \leq k \leq N$.

4   Experiments on the Fixed Body Length Model

4.1   3-LP(150)

Figure-1 summarizes our experimental data for class 3-LP(150). For this class we have tested 3 thousand random problems at each point from $L/N = 0.5$ to 12 with an increment of 0.5. In Figure-1 the black dash curve is *pro*, the probability of existence of an answer set. At the very beginning, the probability drops rapidly from 1, which is guaranteed by Proposition-2, as the ratio L/N increases from 0. Then at about $(2, 0.27)$, the decrease of the probability slows down. The curve reaches close to 0 near $L/N = 12$. Unlike the SAT phase transition, it seems that

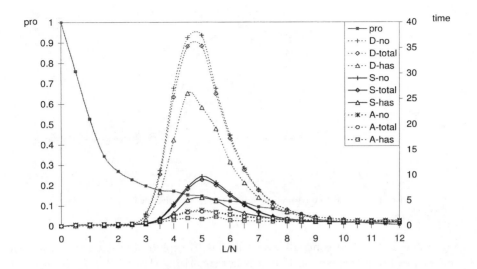

Fig. 1. 3-LP(150).

Legends: *pro – the probability; L – number of rules; N – number of atoms; A-total/has/no – time costs by ASSAT, specifically, A-total – total time cost, A-has – time cost for instances with solution, A-no – time cost for instances without solution; Similarly, S-total/has/no – time costs by Smodels; D-total/has/no – time cost by DLV.*

the ASP transition does not have the "highly satisfiable" phase in where most of the instances have solutions. This would likely be called "half phase transition".

Figure-1 also shows a typical "easy-hard-easy" pattern in problem difficulty for 3-LP(150). The right y-axis gives the mean CPU time reported by ASP systems, and the three ASP systems show the same hard job region being around $L/N = 5$. It is reasonable to assume the hard job region is not caused by ASP solvers since the three ASP systems used in the experiment are implemented by totally different approaches. The hard job region separates the space of 3-LP problems into two regions, the one with a small value of the ratio L/N is under-constrained, the other with a large value of the ratio L/N is over-constrained, and problems in both regions are easy to compute. Programs in the hard job region are likely to be difficult to compute.

From Figure-1, the hard job region lies in the low probability area – between 0.2 to 0.1. It seems that programs without answer sets are much more difficult to compute than those with. This is very different from that observed in other systems. For example, in 3-SAT the hard job region occurs at the "50% satisfiable" point, where the problems are finely balanced between being solvable and unsolvable[7]. As a monotonic system, SAT never retracts any local (or previous) conclusions. So if a local contradiction is found in SAT, then one can immediately conclude that this problem has no model – it is inconsistent. For ASP, an non-monotonic system, one can not conclude that a problem is inconsistent sim-

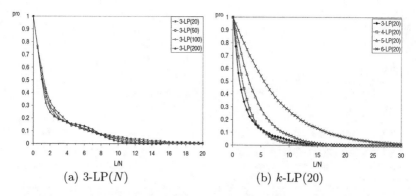

Fig. 2. Probability of having answer sets in 3-LP(N) and k-LP(20).

ply because of a local contradiction – he has to explore more search space with more time. From this perspective, it is not surprising that the hard job region of ASP occurs in the low probability area instead of at the "50% satisfiable" point.

In the experiments we collect three kinds of data: (i)-*total*: average time cost on all instances both having or not having a solution, (ii)-*has*: average time cost on those instances having a solution, and (iii)-*no*: average time cost on those instances not having a solution. Figure-1 also shows that, even in the hard job region, programs without a solution are always harder than those with solutions, for any of the three ASP systems. For example, in the figure the peak of the curve for DLV of (ii) is just 26 seconds, while that of (iii) is more than 38 seconds.

We also have a comparison of the performance among the three ASP systems: ASSAT performed best. It solved the hardest job ($L/N = 5$) in 3 seconds on average, while Smodels and DLV spent 10 and 38 seconds respectively.

4.2   On the Probability of Having Answer Set in k-LP(N)

For 3-LP(N), we observe similar transition patterns for different values of N as shown in Figure-2(a). We have tested 10 thousand random 3-LP problems at each point from $L/N = 0.5$ to 20 in steps of 0.5, for $N = 20$, 50, 100, 200, respectively. In Figure-2 (a) the four curves are similar, at the beginning the curve drops fast, then at about $L/N = 2$, where the curves reached $0.2 \sim 0.3$, the dropping becomes slower, after two crossovers at $(4, 0.18)$ and $(8.5, 0.06)$, the curves reach close to 0 near by $L/N = 15$. The difference between these curves is that, at the beginning the curve for a larger N drops faster.

We note that the hard job regions always occur between the two crossovers. Similar to SAT phase transition, to verify the existence of the crossovers in ASP and clarify the relationship between the crossovers and the hard-job-region should be interesting.

We also compare the transition patterns in different k-LP classes. Figure-2(b) gives the comparison of the probability in 4 different classes: 3-LP(20), 4-LP(20), 5-LP(20), and 6-LP(20). We have tested 10 thousand random problems at each

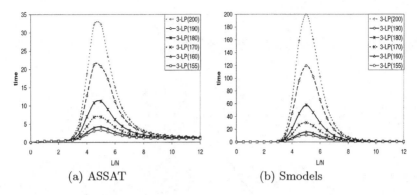

(a) ASSAT   (b) Smodels

Fig. 3. Performance of ASSAT and Smodels on the hard job region of 3-LP(N).

point, from $L/N = 0.5$ to 30. Figure-2(b) shows that they have similar curves of probability. We note that a small k maps to a steep curve, which means it goes rapidly to the region without an answer set as the number of rules increases.

4.3   On the Hard Job Region in 3-LP(N)

Figure-3 gives the description of the hard-job-region on a varying N in 3-LP. Figure-3 (a) gives the performances (in total time cost) of ASSAT, while Figure-3 (b) that of Smodels. It shows that, for $N = 155, 160, 170, 180, 190, 200$, the hard-job-regions are around $L/N = 5$. This suggests that in the same k-LP class the hard-job-regions are the same.

We also note that ASSAT is much faster than Smodels for the LP that we experimented with.

5   The Mixed Body Length Model

Now we consider the mixed body length model. Similar to the mixed SAT model in [7], in this model the length of rules is following a probability distribution ϕ on the positive integers,

$$\sum_{k>0} \phi(k) = 1.$$

For example, if $\phi(l_1) = 1/3$ and $\phi(l_2) = 2/3$, then rules in l_1-length appear with probability $1/3$ and in l_2-length with probability $2/3$. We use $LP_\phi(N, L)$ to denote the class logic programs in the mixed body length model.

It is easy to see that Proposition-1 and 2 hold for the mixed body length model as well. Actually, the previous fixed body length model is a special case of the mixed body length model:

$$LP_\phi(N, L) = k\text{-}LP(N, L), \quad if \ \phi(k) = 1.$$

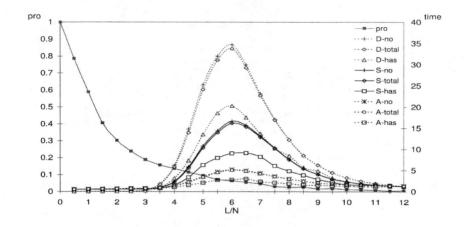

Fig. 4. 3-4-LP(100).

Legends: *As same as Figure-1.*

In this paper, we also use a simple way to denote some class of logic program in the mixed body length model. For example, for a probability distribution ϕ_1, $\phi_1(3) = \phi_1(4) = 1/2$, we would like to denote $LP_{\phi_1}(N, L)$ by 3-4-$LP(N, L)$; for ϕ_2, $\phi_2(2) = 1/3$ and $\phi_2(3) = 2/3$, we denote $LP_{\phi_2}(N, L)$ by 2-3-3-$LP(N, L)$. Accordingly, we have 3-4-$LP(N)$ and 2-3-3-$LP(N)$.

5.1   3-4-LP(100)

Figure-4 summarizes our experimental data for class 3-4-LP(100). We have tested 4 thousand random problems at each point from $L/N = 0.5$ to 12 with an increment of 0.5. In Figure-4, the x-axis is the ratio L/N, the left y-axis is the probability, the right y-axis is the time cost in seconds. The dash curve is *pro*, the probability of existence of an answer sets. Figure-4 shows that the hard-job-region of 3-4-LP(100) is around $L/N = 6$.

Experiments on the mixed body length model verify the consistency of features in the phase transition as we have observed in the fixed body length model.

6   ASP Phase Transition and SAT Phase Transition

The answer set semantics and propositional satisfiable semantics are closely related. Following the definition of a stable model [6], one naive strategy to compute the answer sets of a logic program is, to convert a logic program into a set of clauses directly [8], and check every propositional model of it. If a model is stable under the Gelfond-Lifschitz transformation, then it is a stable model.

---

[8] Every rule is converted to its equivalent logic implication.

People would seldom like to adopt this strategy to get stable models because it is not effective – little heuristic is used and the search space is very huge. However this could be one approach for measuring the hardness of an ASP problem in terms of SAT.

As shown in [5,1,11], stable models are hidden in the models of the completion of a logic program. So the hardness of computing the satisfiability of the completion is well related to the hardness of the original ASP problem. This could be another approach for measuring the hardness of an ASP problem in terms of SAT.

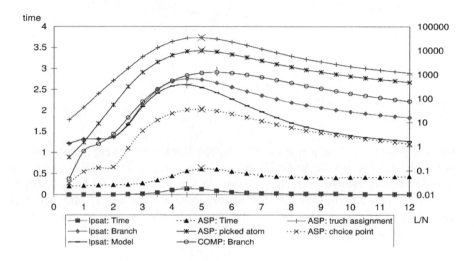

Fig. 5. ASP vs SAT : 3-LP(100).

Given a logic program P, we denote by $lpsat(P)$ [9] the set of clauses given by the above naive translation, and by $COMP(P)$ the completion of the program. In general, the number of branches for a set of clauses represents the hardness of computing satisfiability.

In the experiment, SATO is used as the SAT solver, and Smodels as the ASP solver. For Smodels, we collect the "time cost", "number of picked atoms", "number of choice points", and the "number of truth assignments". For SATO, we collect the "time cost in computing all propositional models", "number of branches" and the "number of models" for $lpsat(P)$, and only the "number of branches" for $COMP(P)$.

Figure-5 summarizes the experimental data. It shows that, the hardness of the three kinds of problems are quite similar, and the locations of the hardest job are very close. In Figure-5, the x-axis is the ratio L/N of the original ASP problem,

---

[9] This is a special SAT problem, every clause contain at least one positive literal. Therefore the set of clauses is always satisfiable.

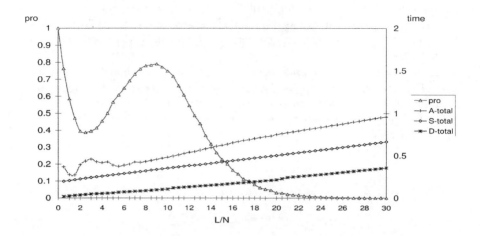

Fig. 6. 2-3-LP(100).

Legends: *Similar to Figure-1.*

the left y-axis is the time cost in seconds, the right y-axis is the number of the other parameters in a log scale. This figure shows that, the peaks of curves for $lpsat(P)$ are all located at $L/N = 4.5$, for ASP at $L/N = 5$, and for $COMP(P)$ at $L/N = 5.5$. The position of the hardest jobs of $lpsat$ and $COMP$ are very close to that of the ASP. So $lpsat$ and $COMP$ could be used to evaluate the hardness of ASP, if necessary.

7   2-3-LP

2-literal logic program is a kind of special logic program whose rules have only one literal in their bodies. 2-3-LP is a class of logic programs in which half of the rules have 2 literals, and half have 3. It is well-known that ASP is an non-monotonic reasoning system. In Figure-6 we observe an obvious non-monotonic transition in 2-3-LP.

For $N = 100$, we have tested 5 thousand random 2-3-LP problems at each point from $L/N = 0.5$ to 30 with an increment of 0.5. In Figure-6, the x-axis is the ratio L/N, the left y-axis is the probability, the right y-axis is the time cost in seconds, the dash curve *pro* is the probability of having answer sets. The Figure-6 shows that, the probability drops down very fast at the beginning of the increase of L/N, when it decreases to about 0.4, the curve makes a jump-up, and the probability can even rise back to almost 0.8 at $L/N = 9$, then the probability drops down again and reaches almost 0 at last. Figure-6 also gives the average total-time costs. Among the three ASP systems, DLV performs the best here.

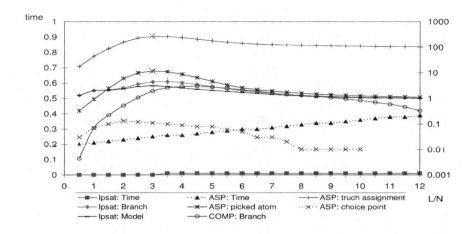

Fig. 7. ASP vs SAT: 2-3-LP(100).

In some other domains[10], Monasson *et al.* [14] and Walsh [17] have argued that there is a smooth interpolation from the P to the NP problem. We also note that the computation of problems in this class seems to be linear hard, as reported by all three of the ASP systems, although the problem of deciding whether a 2-literal logic program has an answer set is NP-complete [9]. We believe to clarify the interpolation in ASP, if it exists, should be an interesting future work.

Although it does not show the hard-job-region clearly in Figure-6, we would like to evaluate the potential hard-job-region by the approach introduced in Section-6. Figure-7 shows the hard-job-region should be in $L/N = 3 \sim 4.5$, at where the curve of the probability starts to rise as shown in Figure-6.

8   Conclusions

We have investigated two problems on randomly generated logic programs under the answer set semantics: the existence of an answer set and the hardness of finding one answer set, if any.

In the 3^{+}-LP class, we investigate both the fixed body length model, and the mixed body length model. For the first problem, despite the non-monotonicity of the answer set semantics, we observe a phase transition occurring on some particular critical values of L/N, where L and N are the number of rules and atoms in a program, respectively. For the second problem, we found a "easy-hard-easy" pattern in the space of the problem: a certain region is hard for all of the three ASP systems we have tested: Smodels, DLV, and ASSAT. Our experiments also show that a logic program without answer sets is much harder to compute

---

[10] Such as SAT, coloring, XOR SAT etc.

than those with. This idea is mainly supported by two consistent observations in the experiments. The first one is, the hard-job-region always lies in the region of lower probability of having answer sets. Its probability is always less than 0.2 in the experiments that a logic program in the hard-job-region has an answer set. The second one is, even in the hard-job-region, the logic programs without answer sets consume much more time in the computation than those with. This suggests that the most effective strategies for improving the performance of ASP systems should be those that can detect the non-existence of answer sets early on.

The answer set semantics and propositional satisfiable semantics are closely related. We introduce two approaches to measure the hardness of ASP problem in terms of SAT. With these approaches, we explore the 2-3-LP, which does not show obvious easy-hard-easy pattern in our early experiment, and finally evaluate the hard-job-region of the 2-3-LP. More interesting, the 2-3-LP problem shows an obvious non-monotonicity on the probability of having answer sets, which coincides with the non-monotonicity of the answer set semantics.

Although fruitful theoretical and experimental works reveal the phase transition phenomena in AI domains [10,2,7], few work is related to ASP. In 1999, Giannella and Schlipf [8] shows that in 3-LP there is a particular region where Smodels requires a large number of recursive calls. That work originally aimed at investigating two pruning strategies for Smodels on those hard problems. It did not further investigate the phase transition and explore the "easy-hard-easy" pattern in ASP.

As we note in the experiments in this paper, different ASP system perform differently on randomly generated logic programs. This suggests that the randomly generated logic programs could be used as a benchmark to test the effectiveness of ASP systems. To test more ASP systems on randomly generated logic programs could be interesting.

Based on this paper, one work would be to investigate more space of the ASP problem and produce the ASP "phase diagrams", as suggested in [2], to "aid in hard problem identification and for prediction of solution existence probability". Other future work would be to investigate the interpolation and the relationship between the crossovers and the hard-job-region, if they exist.

Acknowledgement. We would like to thank Patrik Simons, the author of Smodels, for explaining the the output data of Smodels in detail, and the authors of SAT solvers, Hantao Zhang of SATO, and Matthew Moskewicz of mchaff, for the help on the features of their SAT solvers. We are also grateful to Michael Gelfond and Mirek Truszczynski for private talks at a very early stage of this research, and to the anonymous reviews of this paper for their useful comments. This work was supported in part by the RGC of HKSAR under grant CERG HKUST 6061/00E.

References

1. Yulia Babovich, Esra Erdem, and Vladimir Lifschitz. Fages' theorem and answer set programming. In *Proc. of NMR-2000*, 2000.
2. Peter Cheeseman, Bob Kanefsky, and William M. Taylor. Where the Really Hard Problems Are. In *Proceedings of the Twelfth International Joint Conference on Artificial Intelligence, IJCAI-91, Sydney, Australia*, pages 331–337, 1991.
3. Keith L. Clark. Negation as failure. In H. Gallaire and J. Minker, editors, *Logics and Databases*, pages 293–322. Plenum Press, New York, 1978.
4. Thomas Eiter, Nicola Leone, Cristinel Mateis, Gerald Pfeifer, and Francesco Scarcello. A deductive system for non-monotonic reasoning. In Ulrich Furbach Jurgen Dix and Anil Nerode, editors, *Proceedings of the 4th International Conference on Logic Programming and Nonmonotonic Reasoning (LPNMR'97)*, pages 364–375, Berlin, 1997. Springer.
5. Franois Fages. Consistency of clark's completion and existence of stable of stable models. *Journal of Methods of Logic in Computer Science*, 1:51–60, 1994.
6. Michael Gelfond and Vladimir Lifschitz. The stable model semantics for logic programming. In *Proc. Fifth International Conference and Symposium on Logic Programming*, pages 1070–1080, 1988.
7. Ian P. Gent and Toby Walsh. The SAT phase transition. In *Proceedings of the Eleventh European Conference on Artificial Intelligence (ECAI'94)*, pages 105–109, 1994.
8. Chris. Giannella and John Schlipf. An empirical study of the 4-valued kripke kleene semantics and 4-valued well-founded semantics in random propositional logic programs. *Annals of Mathematics and Artificial Intelligence*, 25(3,4):275–309, 1999.
9. Guan-Shieng Huang, Xiumei Jia, Churn-Jung Liau, and Jia-Huai You. Two-literal logic programs and satisfiability representation of stable models: A comparison. In *Proceedings 15th Canadian Conference on AI*. Springer, 2002.
10. Bernardo A. Huberman and Tad Hogg. Phase transitions in artificial intelligence systems. *Artificial Intelligence*, 33:155–171, 1987.
11. Fangzhen Lin and Yuting Zhao. Assat: Computing answer sets of a logic program by sat solvers. In *Proceedings of the 18th National Conference on Artificial Intelligence (AAAI-2002), AAAI Press, Menlo Park, CA.*, 2002.
12. Victor W. Marek and Miroslaw Truszczynski. Autoepistemic logic. *Journal of the ACM*, (38):588–619, 1991.
13. David G. Mitchell, Bart Selman, and Hector J. Levesque. Hard and easy distributions for SAT problems. In Paul Rosenbloom and Peter Szolovits, editors, *Proceedings of the Tenth National Conference on Artificial Intelligence*, pages 459–465, Menlo Park, California, 1992. AAAI Press.
14. Remi Monasson, Riccardo Zecchina, Scott Kirkpatrick, Bart Selman, and Lidror Troyansky. (2+p)- sat: Relation of typical-case complexity to the nature of the phase transition. *Random Structures And Algorithms*, 15:414–435, 1999.
15. Ilkka Niemela and Patrik Simons. Efficient implementation of the well-founded and stable model semantics. In *Joint International Conference and Symposium on Logic Programming*, pages 289–303, 1996.
16. Maarten H. van Emden and Robert A. Kowalski. The semantics of predicate logic as a programming language. *JACM*, 23:733–742, 1976.
17. Toby Walsh. The interface between p and np: Col, xor, nae, 1-in-k, and horn sat. In *Proceedings of AAAI-2002*, 2002.

Termination Analysis with Types Is More Accurate

Vitaly Lagoon[1], Fred Mesnard[2], and Peter J. Stuckey[1]

[1] Department of Computer Science and Software Engineering
The University of Melbourne, Vic. 3010, Australia
{lagoon,pjs}@cs.mu.oz.au

[2] IREMIA
Université de La Réunion, France
fred@univ-reunion.fr

Abstract. In this paper we show how we can use size and groundness analyses lifted to regular and (polymorphic) Hindley/Milner typed programs to determine more accurate termination of (type correct) programs. Type information for programs may be either inferred automatically or declared by the programmer. The analysis of the typed logic programs is able to completely reuse a framework for termination analysis of untyped logic programs by using abstract compilation of the type abstraction. We show that our typed termination analysis is uniformly more accurate than untyped termination analysis for regularly typed programs, and demonstrate how it is able to prove termination of programs which the untyped analysis can not.

1 Introduction

Logic programming languages are increasingly typed languages. While Mycroft and O'Keefe [22] showed how to include Hindley/Milner types in logic programs, Prolog has never really made use of types. But new logic programming languages such as Gödel [16], Mercury [24] and HAL [13] include strong types as an important part of the language. On the other hand new techniques for inferring types of Prolog programs [10,12] are increasingly in use. In this paper we investigate the impact of types on universal left termination analysis of logic programs.

The following example shows why termination analysis of typed programs can give better accuracy than untyped analysis. We use Mercury [24] syntax for type definitions and declarations.

```
:- type list(T) ---> [] ; [T|list(T)].
:- type erk ---> a ; b(erk) ; c.
:- pred g(list(erk)).
g(W) :- X = [[a],[R]], Y = [[S,c],[]],
        append(X,Y,Z), Z = [U|V], append(U,U,W).
:- pred append(list(T),list(T),list(T)).
append(A, B, C) :- A = [], B = C.
append(A, B, C) :- A = [D|E], C = [D|F], append(E,B,F).
```

C. Palamidessi (Ed.): ICLP 2003, LNCS 2916, pp. 254–268, 2003.

The goal g(W) cannot be proven to universally terminate if we use the term size norm (because the term size of X is unknown), nor will it terminate if we use the list size norm (because the list size of U is unknown). On the other hand, the typed termination analysis we present proves that g(W) is always terminating. Typed termination analysis can determine that the list skeleton of U is fixed, and hence the goal terminates. Note that this relies on polymorphic size analysis.

Our approach maps the original program to a *type separated program* where each subtype is considered separately. Each variable is split into size components for each type. For example X is split into three variables XLL (which corresponds to the type list(list(erk))), XL (list(erk)) and XE (erk).

Each primitive constraint is mapped to its size effect on each subtype separately. The size of a term for a subtype is the number of subterms of that term that match that type. For example the term $t = $[[a],[R]] has 3 subterms, t, [[R]], and [], matching type list(list(erk)), and four matching list(erk), while the number of erk subterms is one more than those in R.

Each call is mapped to calls where a variable is replaced by its (typed) components. Difficulties arise for polymorphic calls where the call has a more specific type than the predicate called. This is overcome by calling the predicate once for each subtype that maps to the type parameter. The code below is the (simplified) type separated program for the program above. Note how call append(X,Y,Z) maps to two calls to the typed append, one where type parameter T is matched to list(erk) and one where it is matched to erk.

```
g(WE,WL)  :- XLL = 3, XL = 4, XE = 1 + RE, YLL = 3, YL = 4, YE = SE + 1,
             append(XLL,XL,YLL,YL,ZLL,ZL), append(XLL,XE,XLL,YE,ZLL,ZE),
             ZLL = 1 + VLL, ZL = UL + VL, ZE = UE + VE,
             append(UL,UE,UL,UE,WL,WE).
append(AL,AT,BL,BT,CL,CT) :- AL = 1, AT = 0, BL = CL, BT = CT.
append(AL,AT,BL,BT,CL,CT) :- AL = 1 + EL, AT = D + ET,
             CL = 1 + FL, CT = D + FT, append(EL,ET,BL,BT,FL,FT).
```

We can perform typed size analysis for the original program using this program. Similarly typed rigidity analysis simply interprets + as ∧ and constants as *true*. Surprisingly the *untyped* termination analysis of this program gives the correct termination information for the original program, and more accurate information than same untyped analysis on the original program.

The contributions of this paper are:

– We provide a correct termination analysis for regular and polymorphic Hindley/Milner typed programs.
– We show that for regular typed programs the results are uniformly more accurate than the untyped analysis (assuming no widening is required).
– We give an implementation of typed termination analysis and experiments showing the accuracy benefits.

Due to space considerations the proofs for theorems on typed analysis are omitted, they can be found in [18].

Types have long been advocated as a means to improve logic programming termination analysis, e.g. [4,19]. De Schreye *et al.*, e.g. [9], were among the first to study the use of inferred *typed norms* in their works on automatic termination analysis. They pointed out that measuring the same term differently with respect to types complicates the analysis. Another solution to this problem is proposed in [14], by copying each parameter for each norm in each predicate, where norms are either given by the user or based on inferred regular types. In contrast to our proposal, these works did not address the issues related to polymorphic types. Ironically, termination analyses for Mercury (e.g. [25]) are currently untyped.

The closest work to ours is that of Bruynooghe *et al.* [7,26,5]. The typed termination analysis framework of [26] is similar to the approach defined herein, but the size and rigidity relations for a procedure are considered separated for subtype. This makes the analysis information uniformly less accurate than the approach herein, it also means that the approach is not guaranteed to be more accurate than an untyped analysis even for regular typed programs (the same counterexample as in Example 8). The approach of [26] cannot be applied to all polymorphically typed programs (e.g. the call in Example 7), while the extension in [5] to arbitrary polymorphically typed programs can give incorrect analysis results (e.g. for Example 8) although this can be corrected (see [6]). There are no experiments reported in [7,26,5].

The next section recalls types for logic programming. Section 3 presents the typed analysis with correctness and accuracy results. Section 4 describes our experiments and concludes.

2   Preliminaries

In the following we assume a familiarity with the standard definitions and notation for (constraint) logic programs as described in [17], and with the framework of abstract interpretation [8]. In particular, we assume familiarity with semantics $T_P \uparrow \omega$ and $S_P \uparrow \omega$ defined by the least fixpoints of the immediate consequence operator T_P and the non-ground consequence operation S_P. We assume *terms* are made up using tree constructors with arities from a set Σ_{tree} and (Herbrand) variables $\mathcal{V}_{tree}$.

We assume the rules of the program are in *canonical form*. That is, procedure calls and rule heads are normalized such that parameters are distinct variables, and unifications are broken into sequences of simple constraints of the form $x = y$ or $x = f(y_1, \ldots, y_n)$ where $x, y_1, \ldots, y_n$ are distinct variables. In addition, the heads of each rule for predicate p/n are required to be identical atoms $p(x_{p1}, \ldots, x_{pn})$, and every variable not appearing in the head of a rule is required to appear in exactly one rule. It is straightforward to convert any logic program to an equivalent program in this form.

2.1   Typed Logic Programs

The techniques of abstract compilation of typed analyses presented in this work are applied to *typed logic programs*. A typed logic program is a logic program where each program variable x is associated with its respective *type description* type(x). We shall be interested in two forms of typed programs: *regular typed programs*, where type(x) is a (monomorphic) deterministic regular type, and *Hindley/Milner typed programs* where type(x) is a (polymorphic) Hindley/Milner type. The types can be either prescribed by the programmer or inferred by some type inference algorithm (e.g. [21,11]).

Both kinds of types are defined using the same language of types. We adopt the Mercury syntax of *type definitions* [21].

Type expressions (or *types*) $\tau \in$ Type are constructed using *type constructors* Σ_{type} and *type parameters* $\mathcal{V}_{type}$. Each type constructor $g/n \in \Sigma_{type}$ must have a unique definition.

Definition 1. *A type definition for $g/n \in \Sigma_{type}$ is of the form*

:- type $g(\nu_1, \ldots, \nu_n)$ ---> $f_1(\tau_1^1, \ldots, \tau_{m_1}^1)$; $\cdots$; $f_k(\tau_1^k, \ldots, \tau_{m_k}^k)$.

where $\nu_1, \ldots, \nu_n$ are distinct type parameters (in $\mathcal{V}_{type}$), $\{f_1/m_1, \ldots, f_k/m_k\} \subseteq \Sigma_{tree}$ are distinct tree constructor/arity pairs, and $\tau_1^1, \ldots, \tau_{m_k}^k$ are type expressions in Type involving at most parameters $\nu_1, \ldots, \nu_n$.

Note that we allow the same tree constructor to appear in multiple type definitions (unlike strict Hindley/Milner types).

Example 1. Example type definitions are given below:

```
:- type list(T) ---> [] ; [T|list(T)].¹
:- type nest(T) ---> e(T) ; n(list(nest(T))).
:- type list2(T) ---> [] ; [T|list2(T)].
```

Note how [] is overloaded as part of list and list2.

Type definitions define deterministic regular tree grammars in an obvious way. Formally, a grammar $\mathcal{G}(\tau)$ corresponding to the type τ is a tuple $\mathcal{G}(\tau) = \langle \tau, N(\tau), \Delta(\tau) \rangle$, where τ is the start symbol, and $N(\tau)$ and $\Delta(\tau)$ are respectively the sets of *non-terminals* and *productions*.

If $\tau \in \mathcal{V}_{type}$ is a type parameter, then $N(\tau) = \{\tau\}$ and $\Delta(\tau) = \emptyset$. Otherwise $\tau = \sigma(g(\nu_1, \ldots, \nu_n))$ for some type substitution σ on $\{\nu_1 \ldots, \nu_n\}$ and the type definition for g/n is :

:- type $g(\nu_1, \ldots, \nu_n)$ ---> $f_1(\tau_1^1, \ldots, \tau_{m_1}^1)$; $\cdots$; $f_k(\tau_1^k, \ldots, \tau_{m_k}^k)$.

The sets $N(\tau)$ and $\Delta(\tau)$ are defined respectively as the least sets satisfying:

$$N(\tau) = \tau \cup \bigcup_{\substack{i=1\ldots k \\ j=1\ldots m_i}} N(\sigma(\tau_j^i))$$

$$\Delta(\tau) = \left\{ \begin{array}{c} \tau \to \sigma(f_1(\tau_1^1, \ldots, \tau_{m_1}^1)) \\ \vdots \\ \tau \to \sigma(f_k(\tau_1^k, \ldots, \tau_{m_k}^k)) \end{array} \right\} \cup \bigcup_{\substack{i=1\ldots k \\ j=1\ldots m_i}} \Delta(\sigma(\tau_j^i))$$

---

¹ We write the list constructor [|] in the usual Prolog notation.

We assume that type definitions are such that the grammar for any type is *finite*, thus disallowing definitions like :- `type g(T) ---> a ; b(g(list(T)))`. This is a common restriction, although see [23] for the use of such types.

Example 2. The productions for the grammar of `list2(nest(erk))` are

```
list2(nest(erk)) → [] ; [ nest(erk) | list2(nest(erk)) ]
nest(erk)        → e(erk) ; n(list(nest(erk)))
list(nest(erk))  → [] ; [ nest(erk) | list(nest(erk)) ]
erk              → a ; b(erk) ; c
```

while for `list(U)` they are `list(U)` → `[]` ; `[ U | list(U) ]`

For a canonical program P we can lift **type** to act on predicates p/n since the unique head of rules for p/n defines its unique type. If $p(x_{p1}, \ldots, x_{pn})$ is the head of rules for p/n in P, then $\mathsf{type}(p/n) = p(\mathsf{type}(x_{p1}), \ldots, \mathsf{type}(x_{pn}))$. We sometimes use Mercury syntax to illustrate predicate types, for example for **append** in the introduction.

A basic assumption for this paper is that the programs we analyze are well-typed. In practice this means that type-correctness of a program must be verified by a type checker before the typed analysis can be performed. A ground term t is *well-typed* for ground type τ if $t \in \mathcal{L}(\tau)$, that is the term is in the language of the grammar of type τ. A non-ground term t is well-typed for τ if there is a grounding substitution θ such that $\theta(t)$ is well-typed for τ. An atom $p(t_1, \ldots, t_n)$ is *well-typed* if there is a substitution θ such that each $\theta(t_i)$ is well-typed for type $\mathsf{type}(x_{pi})$ for $1 \leq i \leq n$.

We assume the program is well-typed in one of two senses. Either $\mathsf{type}(x)$ is always a regular type, and every atom occurring in a derivation for a well-typed atom is well-typed. Or $\mathsf{type}(x)$ is always a Hindley/Milner type and the program is Hindley/Milner type correct [22].

We will be interested in discovering sizes and rigidities of terms for each possible subtype. Define the multiset of nodes of term t of type τ which match a particular subtype $\tau' \in N(\tau)$, written as $\{\!\{ t : \tau \}\!\}_{\tau'}$.

$$\{\!\{ f(t_1, \ldots, t_n) : \tau \}\!\}_\tau = \{f\} \uplus \{\!\{ t_1 : \tau_1 \}\!\}_\tau \uplus \cdots \uplus \{\!\{ t_n : \tau_n \}\!\}_\tau$$
$$\text{where } \tau \to f(\tau_1, \ldots, \tau_n) \in \Delta(\tau)$$
$$\{\!\{ f(t_1, \ldots, t_n) : \tau \}\!\}_{\tau'} = \{\!\{ t_1 : \tau_1 \}\!\}_{\tau'} \uplus \cdots \uplus \{\!\{ t_n : \tau_n \}\!\}_{\tau'}$$
$$\text{where } \tau \neq \tau', \tau \to f(\tau_1, \ldots, \tau_n) \in \Delta(\tau)$$
$$\{\!\{ v : \tau \}\!\}_{\tau'} = \{v\} \text{ where } v \in \mathcal{V}_{tree}$$
$$\{\!\{ t : \tau \}\!\}_{\tau'} = \emptyset \text{ otherwise}$$

where $\uplus$ denotes multiset union. We can compute size (number of matching non-variable nodes) and rigidity (there exist no matching variable nodes) for subtypes from these multiset expressions.

$$size(t : \tau, \tau') = |\{\!\{ t : \tau \}\!\}_{\tau'} - \mathcal{V}_{tree}|$$
$$rigid(t : \tau, \tau') = (\{\!\{ t : \tau \}\!\}_{\tau'} \cap \mathcal{V}_{tree} = \emptyset)$$

Example 3. For this and later examples we use shorthands l for list, n for nest, $l2$ for list2 and e for erk. Consider the term $t \equiv [n([X|Y]), Z]$, the table shows the multisets of nodes, and size and rigidities for each subtype when t is of type $l2(n(e))$.

τ	$\{\!\!\{t : l2(n(e))\}\!\!\}_\tau$	$size(t : l2(n(e)), \tau)$	$rigid(t : l2(n(e)), \tau)$
$l2(n(e))$	$\{[], [], []\}$	3	*true*
$l(n(e))$	$\{[], Y, Z\}$	1	*false*
$n(e)$	$\{n, Y, Z\}$	1	*false*
e	$\{X, Y, Z\}$	0	*false*

We shall extend our notion of type expressions by introducing two new type construction mechanisms: type intersection, and (named) renaming. These will not be available to the programmer, but used to construct intermediate types for the translation process.

The first is for building the intersections of two types. The type expression $\langle \tau_1 \cap \tau_2 \rangle$ defines the intersection of types τ_1 and τ_2, a type with grammar as follows. $\Delta(\langle \tau_1 \cap \tau_2 \rangle)$ contains rules

$$\langle \tau_1 \cap \tau_2 \rangle \to f(\langle \tau_{11} \cap \tau_{21} \rangle, \dots, \langle \tau_{1n} \cap \tau_{2n} \rangle) \text{ where } \tau_1 \to f(\tau_{11}, \dots, \tau_{1n}) \in \Delta(\tau_1)$$
$$\tau_2 \to f(\tau_{21}, \dots, \tau_{2n}) \in \Delta(\tau_2)$$

together with rules from $\Delta(\langle \tau_{1i} \cap \tau_{2i} \rangle), 1 \le i \le n$. $N(\langle \tau_1 \cap \tau_2 \rangle)$ is given by the types $\langle \tau_1' \cap \tau_2' \rangle$ where $\tau_1' \in N(\tau_1)$ and $\tau_2' \in N(\tau_2)$ that occur anywhere in $\Delta(\langle \tau_1 \cap \tau_2 \rangle)$ (not just on the left hand side). The start symbol is $\langle \tau_1 \cap \tau_2 \rangle$.

The renamed type expression $name.\tau$ where $name \in \mathcal{V}_{tree} \cup \{copy_i \mid i \ge 1\}$ and τ is a type expression, builds a new type which is identical to τ but with different non-terminals. The type $name.\tau$ is defined by the grammar as $\langle name.\tau, \{name.\tau' \mid \tau' \in N(\tau)\}, \Delta \rangle$ where

$$\Delta = \{name.\tau \to f(name.\tau_1, \dots name.\tau_n) \mid \tau \to f(\tau_1, \dots \tau_n) \in \Delta(\tau)\}.$$

3 Typed Termination Analysis

We assume the reader is familiar with the untyped termination analysis approach of [20] on how to compute classes of queries for which universal left termination of a pure untyped logic program is guaranteed.

Our approach to typed termination analysis simply maps the typed logic program to an untyped CLP(N) program which represents the size relationships of the original program. We call this the *type separated program*. The *untyped* analysis of this program gives us the termination results for the original typed program.

3.1 The Type Separated Program

The type separated program type(P) arising from a type program P and a correct typing type is defined as follows. Each rule is mapped to a rule, by mapping each of the literals of the rule to a sequence of literals.

Variables. Each variable $v \in V_{tree}$ with type $\mathsf{type}(v)$ is mapped to a set of typed variables of the form $v.\tau$ where τ is a type. Define $\overline{v : \tau}$ to be the sequence of variables $v.\tau', \tau' \in N(\tau)$ in lexicographic order. The order will be important in order to map calls correctly.

Heads. Each head atom $\overline{p(x_{p1}, \dots, x_{pn})}$ is directly translated to an atom $p(\overline{x_{p1} : \mathsf{type}(x_{p1})}, \dots, \overline{x_{pn} : \mathsf{type}(x_{pn})})$. For example, the head atom $q(Z)$ where $\mathsf{type}(Z) = n(e)$ is mapped to the fact $q(Z.e, Z.l(n(e)), Z.n(e))$.

Primitive constraints. The primitive constraint $v_1 = v_2$ is mapped to a conjunction of constraints defined as follows. First we build the named instances of the types for v_1 and v_2. Let $\tau_1 = v_1.\mathsf{type}(v_1)$ and $\tau_2 = v_2.\mathsf{type}(v_2)$

Consider $N(\langle \tau_1 \cap \tau_2 \rangle)$ as edges in a bipartite graph with nodes $N(\tau_1)$ and $N(\tau_2)$. Then we can separate these nodes into connected components. For each connected component U we create an equation

$$\Sigma\{x \mid x \in U \cap N(\tau_1)\} = \Sigma\{y \mid y \in U \cap N(\tau_2)\}$$

The intuition is that for the unification to succeed v_1 and v_2 must take a value in the intersection type. And each node in v_1 of type τ_1' can only appear in v_2 as type τ_2' if $\langle \tau_1' \cap \tau_2' \rangle \in N(\langle \tau_1 \cap \tau_2 \rangle)$. Hence the size equation must hold.

Example 4. Consider $X = Y$ where $\mathsf{type}(X) = l(n(e))$ and $\mathsf{type}(Y) = l2(n(e))$. Then $N(\langle X.\mathsf{type}(X) \cap Y.\mathsf{type}(Y) \rangle)$ contains $\{\langle X.l2(n(e)) \cap Y.l(n(e)) \rangle, \langle X.n(e) \cap Y.n(e) \rangle, \langle X.e \cap Y.e \rangle, \langle X.l(n(e)) \cap Y.l(n(e)) \rangle\}$. The connected components are $\{X.l(n(e)), X.l2(n(e)), Y.l(n(e))\}$, $\{X.n(e), Y.n(e)\}$ and $\{X.e, Y.e\}$. The resulting equations are

$$X.l2(n(e)) + X.l(n(e)) = Y.l(n(e)), \quad X.n(e) = Y.n(e), \quad X.e = Y.e$$

The sum of sizes of the two kinds of list nodes in X must equal the size of the single kind in Y.

Treatment of the equation $v_0 = f(v_1, \dots, v_n)$ is similar. First we create the type τ_2 for the right hand side defined by $\langle 1, \{1\} \cup \cup_{i=1}^{n} N(v_i.\mathsf{type}(v_i)), \Delta \rangle$ where $\Delta = \{1 \rightarrow f(v_1.\mathsf{type}(v_1), \dots, v_n.\mathsf{type}(v_n))\} \cup \cup_{i=1}^{n} \Delta(v_i.\mathsf{type}(v_i))$. The remainder is as for the equation $v_1 = v_2$, where $\tau_1 = v_1.\mathsf{type}(v_1)$. Note the (ab)use of 1 as a type name so that the same equation creation as above holds. The 1 represents the size contribution of the functor f.

Example 5. Consider the equation $A = [D|E]$, where $\mathsf{type}(A) = \mathsf{type}(E) = l(T)$ and $\mathsf{type}(D) = T$. The new type τ_2 consists of rules $1 \rightarrow [D.T|E.l(T)]$, $E.l(T) \rightarrow []$, and $E.l(T) \rightarrow [E.T|E.l(T)]$. The grammar intersection of τ_2 and $A.l(T)$ gives pairs $\{\langle A.l(T) \cap 1 \rangle, \langle A.T \cap D.T \rangle, \langle A.l(T) \cap E.l(T) \rangle, \langle A.T \cap E.T \rangle\}$. The connected components are $\{A.l(T), 1, E.l(T)\}$ and $\{A.T, D.T, E.T\}$. The resulting equations are $A.l(T) = 1 + E.l(T)$ and $A.T = D.T + E.T$.

The equation $A = []$ leads to connected components of the intersection grammar as $\{A.l(T), 1\}$ and $\{A.T\}$. The resulting equations are $A.l(T) = 1$, $A.T = 0$.

Monomorphic calls. For a procedure with monomorphic type we translate a body atom $p(v_1, \ldots, v_n)$ as follows. Let $\mathsf{type}(p/n) = p(\tau_1, \ldots, \tau_n)$. Construct new variables $v'_1, \ldots, v'_n$ where $\mathsf{type}(v'_i) = \tau_i$. We translate the call by the translation of each $v_i = v'_i$ followed by the call $p(\overline{v'_1 : \tau_1}, \ldots, \overline{v'_n : \tau_n})$. This maintains the invariant that each p atom has arguments arising from the exact type declared for p/n.

Note if $\mathsf{type}(v_i) = \tau_i$ already we can omit the equations resulting from $v_i = v'_i$ and use $\overline{v_i : \tau_i}$ instead of $v'_i : \tau_i$

Example 6. Consider the atom $p(X)$ where $\mathsf{type}(X) = l(n(e))$ and $\mathsf{type}(p/1) = p(l2(n(e)))$, then we create new variable Y of type $l2(n(e))$ and build the equations resulting from $X = Y$ as defined in Example 4 above and the atom $p(Y.e, Y.l(n(e)), Y.l2(n(e)), Y.n(e))$.

Polymorphic calls. Handling of polymorphic calls is more complex. The main complexity arises since we must create a new variable whose type *grammar* is an instance of the grammar of the polymorphically typed call. We then will use a call to the polymorphic code for each subtype which matches the type parameter arguments.

Given the program is Hindley/Milner type correct we know that for body atom $p(v_1, \ldots, v_n)$, we have that $\mathsf{type}(p/n) = p(\tau_1, \ldots, \tau_n)$ and there exists type substitution σ such that $\mathsf{type}(v_i) = \sigma(\tau_i), 1 \leq i \leq n$. Let $\nu_j \in \mathcal{V}_{type}, 1 \leq j \leq m$ be the type parameters in $\mathsf{type}(p/n)$. For each type parameter ν_j we create a new type $S_j = copy_j.\sigma(\nu_j))$. Define $\sigma' = \{\nu_j \mapsto S_j \mid 1 \leq j \leq m\}$. We create new variables v'_i where $\mathsf{type}(v'_i) = \sigma'(\tau_i)$. And add the equations resulting from $v_i = v'_i$.

The final step is to add calls to the type separated predicate p. For each combination of $S'_j \in N(S_j)$ for all $1 \leq j \leq m$ we add the call

$$p(\overline{v'_1 : \tau_1}, \ldots, \overline{v'_n : \tau_n})$$

except that the type variable ν_j is replaced by $copy_j.\sigma(\nu_j)$ in all variable names except where it appears as ν_j (e.g. $v'_i.\nu_j$) where it is replaced by S'_j. Note the construction of the vectors of variables is completed before the type name substitution, to ensure that the lexicographic order agrees with the definition of p in the type separated program.

Example 7. Consider a call $p(X)$ where $\mathsf{type}(X) = l(n(e))$ and $\mathsf{type}(p/1) = p(l(T))$. Then $\sigma = \{T \mapsto n(e)\}$. We create a type $copy_1.n(e)$. Let Y be a new variable where $\mathsf{type}(Y) = l(copy_1.n(e))$. We then create the equations resulting from $X = Y$ (which are analogous to those from Example 4). The unsubstituted call is $p(Y.l(T), Y.T)$. We create a copy for each $\tau' \in N(copy_1.n(e))$. The resulting translation is the last 4 lines of the program shown in Figure 1 (where $copy_1$ is written as c for brevity).

The copying of types avoids confusing $Y.l(copy_1.n(e))$ which represents the list nodes in the outer skeleton of the list Y, with $Y.copy_1.l(n(e))$ which represents the list nodes appearing inside nests in Y.

```
q(Z.e,Z.l(n(e)),Z.n(e))  :- Z.n(e)=1+X.n(e), Z.l(n(e))=X.l(n(e)), Z.e=X.e,
      X.l(n(e)=Y.l(c.n(e))+Y.c.l(n(e)), X.n(e)=Y.c.n(e), X.e=Y.c.e,
      p(Y.l(c.n(e)), Y.c.l(n(e))),
      p(Y.l(c.n(e)), Y.c.n(e)),
      p(Y.l(c.n(e)), Y.c.e).
```

Fig. 1. Type separated rule for `q(Z) :- Z = n(X), p(X)`.

The type separated program just translates each rule in P into the corresponding rule in $\mathsf{type}(P)$. The translation of the rule `q(Z) :- Z = n(X), p(X)` where $\mathsf{type}(Z) = n(e)$ and $\mathsf{type}(X) = l(n(e))$ and $\mathsf{type}(p/1) = l(T)$ is shown in Figure 1.

Note that the type separated program can be significantly larger than the original program, but only by a factor equal to the largest number of non-terminals in a type multiplied by the largest number of type parameters appearing in a single predicate type.

3.2   Typed Analysis

The key theorems of this paper are that the untyped analyses of the type separated program are correct with respect to the typed original program. The size analysis computes an approximation of the answer semantics of $\mathsf{type}(P)$ using the abstract domain Size [15].

Theorem 1. *([18] Theorem 23) Analysis using Size of the type separated program $\mathsf{type}(P)$ is correct with respect to type correct program P.*

Let $post_p^{\mathcal{N}}(\overline{x_{p1}}_{\mathsf{type}}, \dots, \overline{x_{pn}}_{\mathsf{type}}) \iff C$ be the result of the size analysis of $\mathsf{type}(P)$, then for any well-typed atom $p(t_1, \dots, t_n) \in T_P \uparrow \omega$ we have that $\{x_{pi}.\tau \mapsto size(t_i : \mathsf{type}(x_{pi}), \tau) \mid 1 \leq i \leq n, \tau \in N(\mathsf{type}(x_{pi}))\}$ is a solution of C.

Rigidity analysis translates the $+$ of the type separated program as $\wedge$ and replaces all the numbers by *true*, it then computes an approximation of this CLP(B) program using the abstract domain Pos [2].

Theorem 2. *([18] Theorem 17) Rigidity analysis using Pos of the type separated program $\mathsf{type}(P)$ is correct with respect to type correct program P.*

Let $post_p^{\mathcal{B}}(\overline{x_{p1}}_{\mathsf{type}}, \dots, \overline{x_{pn}}_{\mathsf{type}}) \iff C$ be the result of the rigidity analysis of $\mathsf{type}(P)$, then for any well-typed atom $p(t_1, \dots, t_n) \in S_P \uparrow \omega$ we have that $\{x_{pi}.\tau \mapsto rigid(t_i : \mathsf{type}(x_{pi}), \tau) \mid 1 \leq i \leq n, \tau \in N(\mathsf{type}(x_{pi}))\}$ is a solution of C.

3.3   Accuracy of Typed Analysis

The typed analysis is generally much more accurate than the untyped analysis. We can show that for regular typed programs the typed analysis is uniformly more accurate than the untyped analysis.

Theorem 3. *([18] Theorem 18)*
For any regular typed program P, let $post_p^B(\overline{x_{p1}}_{type}, \ldots, \overline{x_{pn}}_{type}) \Longleftrightarrow C_{type}$ be the result of the Pos rigidity analysis of type(P), and $post_p^B(x_{p1}, \ldots x_{pn}) \Longleftrightarrow C$ be the result of the untyped Pos rigidity (groundness) analysis of P. Then

$$(C_{type} \wedge \bigwedge_{i=1}^{n} x_{pi} \leftrightarrow (\wedge_{\tau \in N(type(x_{pi}))} x_{pi}.\tau)) \quad \rightarrow \quad C$$

The same result holds for typed term size analysis, provided no widening operation is used. Since the widening operation for Size is *non-monotonic* more accurate information from the typed analysis is not guaranteed to lead to more accurate results after widening.

Theorem 4. *([18] Theorem 24)*
For any regular typed program P, let $post_p^N(\overline{x_{p1}}_{type}, \ldots, \overline{x_{pn}}_{type}) \Longleftrightarrow C_{type}$ be the result of the Size analysis of type(P) assuming no widening operations were used, and $post_p^N(x_{p1}, \ldots x_{pn}) \Longleftrightarrow C$ be the result of the untyped Size analysis of P. Then

$$(C_{type} \wedge \bigwedge_{i=1}^{n} x_{pi} = (\Sigma_{\tau \in N(type(x_{pi}))} x_{pi}.\tau)) \quad \rightarrow \quad C$$

The accuracy results do not extend to polymorphic analysis, even for rigidity analysis.

Example 8. Consider the following simple program with two possible type declarations for p, the first polymorphic and the second monomorphic.

```
:- type pair(U,V) ---> U-V.
:- type foo ---> d ; e ; f.
:- pred p(list(T),list(T)).
:- pred p(list(pair(erk,foo)),list(pair(erk,foo))).
p(A,B) :- A = [].
p(A,B) :- B = [].
```

The rigidity analysis of the predicate p/2 obtains the respective answers (for brevity we use *lpef* for *list(pair(erk, foo))*, *pef* for *pair(erk, foo)*)

$(A.list(T) \wedge A.T) \vee (B.list(T) \wedge B.T)$
$(A.lpef \wedge A.pef \wedge A.erk \wedge A.foo) \vee (B.lpef \wedge B.pef \wedge B.erk \wedge B.foo)$

The analysis of a call to polymorphically typed p where $T = pef$ gives 3 copies of the answer for p conjoined. This is the answer

$((A.lpef \wedge A.pef) \vee (B.lpef \wedge B.pef)) \wedge ((A.lpef \wedge A.erk) \vee (B.lpef \wedge B.erk)) \wedge$
$((A.lpef \wedge A.foo) \vee (B.lpef \wedge B.foo))$

This is less accurate than the answer using the monomorphic type, and in fact less accurate than the untyped groundness analysis result $A \vee B$ when mapped back to these variables.

If the original program P does not have any (type) polymorphic recursive procedures, we can monomorphise the program and analyze this program. Of course then we make no reuse of the analysis of polymorphic code, and the monomorphisation could cause an exponential increase in code size.

In practice the widening operation and the possible inaccuracy resulting from the handling of polymorphic calls do not seem to occur for real programs. In the empirical results in Section 4 the (polymorphic) typed analysis is never less accurate than the untyped analysis.

We conjecture that the typed size analysis is also uniformly more accurate than (untyped) list size analysis for regular typed programs (when widening is not used). The proof techniques of [18] do not apply to this case, but the type separated program contains all the constraints in the CLP(N) program used for list size analysis.

3.4   Level Mappings

We need to show that the type separated program is also correct for the computation of level mappings. This is obvious for monomorphic programs since the size analysis is correct. For polymorphic programs we need to justify the level mappings for each instance used. The result follows from the following theorem that shows that the level mapping never depends on arguments which have parameter types.

Theorem 5. *If there exists a level mapping for a polymorphically typed predicate p, then there exists a level mapping with zero coefficients for the arguments which have type $\tau \in \mathcal{V}_{type}$.*

Proof. (Sketch) It is easy to show that the size constraints C arising in the type separated program for an argument of parameter type $\nu \in \mathcal{V}_{type}$ are such, if θ is a solution of C then $\theta' = \{v.\nu \mapsto 0 \mid \nu \in \mathcal{V}_{type}\} \cup \{v.\tau \mapsto \theta(v.\tau) \mid \tau \notin \mathcal{V}_{type}\}$ is also a solution of C'. This is because no function symbols can appear in positions relating to the parameter type. Suppose $\bar{a}$ is a level mapping for some binary clause $p(x_1, \ldots, x_k)\text{:-}C, p(y_1, \ldots, y_k)$, Then $\bar{a} \cdot \theta(\bar{x}) > \bar{a} \cdot \theta(\bar{y})$ for every solution θ of C. But since θ' is also a solution we have that $\bar{a}'$ is also a correct level mapping, where $a_i' = a_i$ except for arguments i of parameter type where $a_i' = 0$.

Bruynooghe et al [5] prove a weaker version of this theorem that shows that if there is a level mapping for a monomorphic instance of a polymorphic typed procedure, then there is a level mapping for the polymorphic typed procedure.

The above result also means that the direct termination analysis on the type separated program will not remove possible termination proofs. In the set of binary unfoldings corresponding to the program the first instance of a recursive predicate will compute the appropriate level mapping, and later instances can safely use the same level mapping since they do not differ on arguments whose type is not a type parameter.

3.5   Termination Conditions

The final result is that the termination conditions computed from the type separated program are correct for the original typed program.

Theorem 6. *The typed termination conditions computed from* type(P) *are correct.*

   Let ϕ_p be a termination condition for $p(\overline{x_{p1}}_{\text{type}}, \ldots, \overline{x_{pn}}_{\text{type}})$ in type(P). *Then if $p(t_1, \ldots, t_n)$ is an atom such that $\{x_{pi}.\tau \mapsto rigid(t_i : \text{type} x_{pi}, \tau) \mid 1 \leq i \leq n, \tau \in N(\text{type}(x_{pi}))\}$ is a solution of ϕ_p, then this goal terminates.*

Proof. (Sketch) Since the analysis results are correct, and the duplication of calls for polymorphic calls does not change the termination problem, the termination conditions computed are correct.

4   Experiments and Conclusion

We implemented the translation to the type separated program as a source to source transformation for Prolog programs with Mercury style type definitions and declarations. We then passed the resulting CLP(N) programs to the *untyped* termination analyzer of [20]. The typed termination results are simply read from the results of the untyped analysis of type(P).

   In the first experiment we considered (pure Prolog + arithmetic) programs from the first 10 chapters of the book [1], avoiding some almost repeats. We rewrote question in order to avoid the 90 anonymous variables in one clause (which made the untyped and typed analysis run out of memory). We manually added polymorphic Hindley/Milner types to these programs and checked well-typedness. We analyzed left termination of the resulting type separated programs for the first predicate in each program, except query, where we used the query ?- map(L), color_map(L,[r,g,b]) from page 138 of the text.

   Table 1 compares the typed analysis, and untyped analysis using term size and list size. For each procedure we show the termination condition for each analysis, and give a ✓ or = to show when the typed termination is more or equally accurate compared to the untyped analysis. The termination conditions use notation $||\_||_{ls}$, $||\_||_{ts}$, and $||\_||_{bt}$ to represent list size, term size, and binary tree size (number of nodes) metrics respectively. For the predicate color_map(X,Y), Y is a list of colors and X is a list of regions. A region is a tuple of three elements: a country, a color, and a list of neighbors. The metric $||X||_{24}$ requires that X is a finite list of regions, each having a finite list of neighbors.

   The total analysis time for all programs in Table 1 for the two untyped analyses took 0.5 seconds each. The total typed analysis took 5.0 seconds. We ran the cTI termination analyzer, written in SICStus Prolog 3.10.1 using the PPL library [3], a timeout of 3 seconds for each strongly connected component, allowing 4 iterations before widening on an Intel 686, 2.4 GHz, 512 Mb, Linux 2.4.

Table 1. Some programs from Apt's book.

Page#	Query	type-size	term-size		list-size	
114	`sunny`	$true$	$true$	$=$	$true$	$=$
115	`neighbour(X,Y)`	$true$	$true$	$=$	$true$	$=$
118	`num(X)`	$\|X\|_{ts}$	$\|X\|_{ts}$	$=$	$false$	✓
120	`sum(X,Y,Z)`	$\|Y\|_{ts} \vee \|Z\|_{ts}$	$\|Y\|_{ts} \vee \|Z\|_{ts}$	$=$	$false$	✓
122	`mult(X,Y,Z)`	$\|X\|_{ts} \wedge \|Y\|_{ts}$	$\|X\|_{ts} \wedge \|Y\|_{ts}$	$=$	$false$	✓
122	`less(X,Y)`	$\|X\|_{ts} \vee \|Y\|_{ts}$	$\|X\|_{ts} \vee \|Y\|_{ts}$	$=$	$false$	✓
124	`list(X)`	$\|X\|_{ls}$	$\|X\|_{ts}$	✓	$\|X\|_{ls}$	$=$
125	`len(X,Y)`	$\|X\|_{ls} \vee \|Y\|_{ts}$	$\|X\|_{ts} \vee \|Y\|_{ts}$	✓	$\|X\|_{ls}$	✓
126	`member(X,Y)`	$\|Y\|_{ls}$	$\|Y\|_{ts}$	✓	$\|Y\|_{ls}$	$=$
127	`subset(X,Y)`	$\|X\|_{ls} \wedge \|Y\|_{ls}$	$\|X\|_{ts} \wedge \|Y\|_{ts}$	✓	$\|X\|_{ls} \wedge \|Y\|_{ls}$	$=$
127	`app(X,Y,Z)`	$\|X\|_{ls} \vee \|Z\|_{ls}$	$\|X\|_{ts} \vee \|Z\|_{ts}$	✓	$\|X\|_{ls} \vee \|Z\|_{ls}$	$=$
129	`select(X,Y,Z)`	$\|X\|_{ls} \vee \|Z\|_{ls}$	$\|X\|_{ts} \vee \|Z\|_{ts}$	✓	$\|X\|_{ls} \vee \|Z\|_{ls}$	$=$
130	`perm(X,Y)`	$\|X\|_{ls}$	$\|X\|_{ts}$	✓	$\|X\|_{ls}$	$=$
131	`perm1(X,Y)`	$\|X\|_{ls}$	$\|X\|_{ts}$	✓	$\|X\|_{ls}$	$=$
131	`prefix(X,Y)`	$\|X\|_{ls} \vee \|Y\|_{ls}$	$\|X\|_{ts} \vee \|Y\|_{ts}$	✓	$\|X\|_{ls} \vee \|Y\|_{ls}$	$=$
132	`suffix(X,Y)`	$\|Y\|_{ls}$	$\|Y\|_{ts}$	✓	$\|Y\|_{ls}$	$=$
132	`sublist(X,Y)`	$\|Y\|_{ls}$	$\|Y\|_{ts}$	✓	$\|Y\|_{ls}$	$=$
133	`reverse(X,Y)`	$\|X\|_{ls}$	$\|X\|_{ts}$	✓	$\|X\|_{ls}$	$=$
133	`reverse1(X,Y)`	$\|X\|_{ls}$	$\|X\|_{ts}$	✓	$\|X\|_{ls}$	$=$
135	`palindrome(X)`	$\|X\|_{ls}$	$\|X\|_{ts}$	✓	$\|X\|_{ls}$	$=$
136	`question(X)`	$true$	$\|X\|_{ts}$	✓	$true$	$=$
137	`color_map(X,Y)`	$\|X\|_{24} \wedge \|Y\|_{ls}$	$\|X\|_{ts} \wedge \|Y\|_{ts}$	✓	$false$	✓
138	`query`	$true$	$false$	✓	$false$	✓
139	`bin_tree(X)`	$\|X\|_{bt}$	$\|X\|_{ts}$	✓	$false$	✓
139	`tree_member(X,Y)`	$\|Y\|_{bt}$	$\|Y\|_{ts}$	✓	$false$	✓
140	`in_order(X,Y)`	$\|X\|_{bt}$	$\|X\|_{ts}$	✓	$false$	✓
140	`front(X,Y)`	$\|X\|_{bt}$	$\|X\|_{ts}$	✓	$false$	✓
238	`max(X,Y,Z)`	$true$	$true$	$=$	$true$	$=$
240	`ordered(X)`	$\|X\|_{ls}$	$\|X\|_{ts}$	✓	$\|X\|_{ls}$	$=$
241	`ss(X,Y)`	$\|X\|_{ls}$	$\|X\|_{ts}$	✓	$\|X\|_{ls}$	$=$
241	`qs(X,Y)`	$\|X\|_{ls}$	$\|X\|_{ts}$	✓	$\|X\|_{ls}$	$=$
242	`ms(X,Y)`	$\|X\|_{ls}$	$false$	✓	$\|X\|_{ls}$	$=$
247	`search_tree(X)`	$\|X\|_{bt}$	$\|X\|_{ts}$	✓	$false$	✓
247	`in(X,Y)`	$\|Y\|_{bt}$	$\|Y\|_{ts}$	✓	$false$	✓
248	`minimum(X,Y)`	$\|X\|_{bt}$	$\|X\|_{ts}$	✓	$false$	✓
249	`insert(X,Y,Z)`	$\|Y\|_{bt} \vee \|Z\|_{bt}$	$\|Y\|_{ts} \vee \|Z\|_{ts}$	✓	$false$	✓
249	`delete(X,Y,Z)`	$\|Y\|_{bt} \vee \|Z\|_{bt}$	$\|Y\|_{ts} \vee \|Z\|_{ts}$	✓	$false$	✓
253	`len1(X,Y)`	$\|X\|_{ls}$	$\|X\|_{ts}$	✓	$\|X\|_{ls}$	$=$

The current implementation is fairly naive, as the type separated program introduces many new variables which perform no useful role, and could be eliminated. We believe a slightly specialized termination analyzer for typed programs could remove a significant part of this overhead.

Table 2. Some logic programs from the literature.

Ref.	Query	type-size	term-size		list-size		reg-size
[19]	flatten_ length(X,Y,Z)	$\|X\|_{lls} \vee$ $(\|X\|_{ls} \wedge \|Y\|_{ls}) \vee$ $(\|Y\|_{ls} \wedge \|Z\|_{ts})$	$\|X\|_{ts} \vee$ $(\|Y\|_{ts} \wedge$ $\|Z\|_{ts})$	✓	$\|X\|_{ls} \wedge$ $\|Y\|_{ls}$	✓	$\|X\|_{lls} \vee$ $(\|X\|_{ls} \wedge \|Y\|_{ts}) \vee$ $(\|Y\|_{ls} \wedge \|Z\|_{ts})$
[26]	flatten(X,Y)	$\|X\|_{lls} \vee$ $(\|X\|_{ls} \wedge \|Y\|_{ls})$	$\|X\|_{ts}$	✓	$\|X\|_{ls} \wedge$ $\|Y\|_{ls}$	✓	$\|X\|_{lls} \vee$ $(\|X\|_{ls} \wedge \|Y\|_{ls})$
[14]	p(X)	$\|X\|_{ts}$	false	✓	false	✓	false
[14]	factor(X,Y)	$\|X\|_{ts}$	false	✓	false	✓	false
[14]	t(X)	$\|X\|_{ts}$	false	✓	false	✓	false
Sect. 1	g(X)	true	false	✓	$\|X\|_{ls}$	✓	$\|X\|_{ts}$

In Table 2, our second experiment, we selected six programs from the literature, including our first example of Section 1. First, we manually added polymorphic Hindley/Milner types and checked well-typedness. The termination condition $\|X\|_{lls}$ is true when X denotes a finite list of elements, each of which is also a finite list. The accuracy of the typed analysis is striking, although it should be noted that the last four examples were synthesized for this purpose.

Next, we applied bottom-up inference of regular types [11] to the *untyped* programs. To construct the type separated program we used the inferred regular types. The results are shown in the last column of Table 2. In some cases we significantly improve the termination conditions for an *untyped* program without needing any user-added type information. Total analysis times for this set of examples are 0.5 seconds for each of the typed analyses, and 0.1 seconds for each of the untyped analyses.

In summary, typed termination analysis seems in practice to be uniformly more accurate than the untyped analysis, and even a naive implementation is reasonably efficient. There are many further questions to pursue. One promising direction is a hybrid analyzer that first uses untyped analysis and refines to typed analysis where untyped analysis is not able to prove termination.

References

1. K. R. Apt. *From Logic Programming to Prolog*. Prentice Hall, 1997.
2. T. Armstrong, K. Marriott, P. Schachte, and H. Søndergaard. Two classes of Boolean functions for dependency analysis. *Science of Computer Programming*, 31(1):3–45, 1998.
3. R. Bagnara, E. Ricci, E. Zaffanella, and P. M. Hill. Possibly not closed convex polyhedra and the Parma Polyhedra Library. *SAS*, LNCS 2477:213–229, 2002.
4. A. Bossi, N. Cocco, and M. Fabris. Typed norms. *ESOP*, LNCS 582:73–92, 1992.
5. M. Bruynooghe, M. Codish, S. Genaim, and W. Vanhoof. Reuse of results in termination analysis of typed logic programs. *SAS*, LNCS 2477:477–492, 2002.
6. M. Bruynooghe, M. Codish, S. Genaim, and W. Vanhoof. A note on the reuse of results in termination analysis of typed logic programs. Forthcoming TR, Dpt CS, K.U. Leuven, 2003.

7. M. Bruynooghe, W. Vanhoof, and M. Codish. Pos(T) : Analyzing dependencies in typed logic programs. *PSI*, LNCS 2244:406–420, 2001.

8. P. Cousot and R. Cousot. Abstract Interpretation: A Unified Lattice Model for Static Analysis of Programs by Construction or Approximation of Fixpoints. *POPL*, 238–252, 1977.

9. S. Decorte, D. De Schreye, and M. Fabris. Exploiting the power of typed norms in automatic inference of interargument relations. TR 246, Dpt CS, , K.U.Leuven, 1997.

10. F. Fages and E. Coquery. Typing constraint logic programs. *Theory and Practice of Logic Programming*, 1(6):751–777, 2001.

11. J. Gallagher and A. de Waal. Fast and precise regular approximations of logic programs. *ICLP*, pages 599–613. MIT Press, 1994.

12. J. Gallagher and G. Puebla. Abstract interpretation over non-deterministic finite tree automata for set-based analysis of logic programs. *SAS*, LNCS 2257:243–261, 2002.

13. M. García de la Banda, B. Demoen, K. Marriott, and P.J. Stuckey. To the Gates of HAL: A HAL tutorial. LNCS, 2441:47–66, 2002.

14. S. Genaim, M. Codish, J. Gallagher, and V. Lagoon. Combining norms to prove termination. *VMCAI*, LNCS 2294:126–138, 2002.

15. N. Halbwachs. *Détermination Automatique de Relations Linéaires Vérifiées par les Variables d'un Programme*. PhD thesis, USM de Grenoble, France, 1979.

16. P. Hill and J. Lloyd. *The Gödel Language*. MIT Press, 1994.

17. J. Jaffar, M. Maher, K. Marriott, and P.J. Stuckey. The semantics of constraint logic programs. *Journal of Logic Programming*, 37(1–3):1–46, 1998.

18. V. Lagoon and P. J. Stuckey. Polymorphic analysis of typed logic programs. TR, Dpt CSSE, University of Melbourne, Australia, 2003. www.cs.mu.oz.au/~pjs/papers/poly-tr.ps

19. J. Martin, A. King, and P. Soper. Typed norms for typed logic programs. *LOPSTR*, LNCS 1207:224–238, 1996.

20. F. Mesnard and U. Neumerkel. Applying static analysis techniques for inferring termination conditions of logic programs. *SAS*, LNCS 2126:93–110, 2001.

21. R. Milner. A theory of type polymorphism in programming. *Journal of Computer and System Sciences*, 17:348–375, 1978.

22. A. Mycroft and R. A. O'Keefe. A Polymorphic Type System for Prolog. *Artificial Intelligence*, 23:295–307, 1984.

23. C. Okasaki. *Purely Functional Data Structures*. Cambridge University Press, 1998.

24. Z. Somogyi, F. Henderson, and T. Conway. The execution algorithm of Mercury, an efficient purely declarative logic programming language. *Journal of Logic Programming*, 29(1–3):17–64, 1996.

25. C. Speirs, Z. Somogyi, and H. Søndergaard. Termination analysis for Mercury. *SAS*, LNCS 1302:160–171, 1997.

26. W. Vanhoof and M. Bruynooghe. When size does matter. *LOPSTR*, LNCS 2372:129–147, 2002.

A Propagation Tracer for GNU-Prolog: From Formal Definition to Efficient Implementation[*]

Ludovic Langevine[1], Mireille Ducassé[2], and Pierre Deransart[1]

[1] INRIA Rocquencourt, {ludovic.langevine, pierre.deransart}@inria.fr
[2] IRISA/INSA de Rennes, mireille.ducasse@irisa.fr

Abstract. Tracers give some insight of program executions: with an execution trace a programmer can debug and tune programs. Traces can also be used by analysis tools, for example to produce statistics or build graphical views of program behaviors. Constraint propagation tracers are especially needed because constraint propagation problems are particularly hard to debug. Yet, there is no satisfactory tracer for CLP(FD) systems. Some do not provide enough information, others are very inefficient. The tracer formally described in this article provides more complete information than existing propagation tracers. Benchmarks show that its implementation is efficient. Its formal specification is useful both to implement the tracer and to understand the produced trace. It is designed to cover many debugging needs.

1 Introduction

Constraint problems are particularly hard to debug: problems may have a huge number of variables and constraints, the resolution generates a dramatic number of events and uses a large variety of specific algorithms. Several debugging tools have already been developed for constraint programming over finite domain, for instance, Grace [15], the Oz Explorer [17], the Oz Constraint Investigator [16], the DiSCiPl tools [6], the Christmas Tree visualizer [2] or CLPGUI [9]. Despite their very interesting functionalities these tools have two major drawbacks: a specific solver instrumentation is often needed and they are implemented on a specific platform. The work to port them from one platform to another may require a tremendous effort. From an industrial point of view, one would like to easily implement new debugging tools without modifying the solver. From a research point of view, one would like to experiment with different tools on different platforms without too much re-engineering effort.

The previous drawbacks are all the more daunting since most of the tool functionalities do not depend on solver peculiarities. They use quite the same kind of basic information collected in the course of the program execution. This basic information can be taken out from a generic trace generated by a "traditional" tracer. Furthermore, this tracer can be configured dynamically to feed

[*] This work has been partially supported by the French RNTL project OADymPPaC, http://contraintes.inria.fr/OADymPPaC/

C. Palamidessi (Ed.): ICLP 2003, LNCS 2916, pp. 269–283, 2003.

a specific tool. Thus, a traditional tracer, that provides a rich enough trace, is a powerful back-end to new debugging tools. Graphical and application specific tools can be built on top of the tracer while the difficult task of instrumenting the solver is made only once.

Yet, there is no satisfactory such tracer for finite domain constraint solvers. The only two that we are aware of are, firstly, the tracing facilities of Ilog Solver [11] and, secondly, the prototype tracer for the finite domain (FD) solver of Sicstus Prolog [1]. We show in the following that the first one provides a too limited amount of information at each execution step. The second one requires to store the whole execution, this is much too inefficient for real program debugging.

This paper presents a tracer embedded in GNU-Prolog, an open source Prolog compiler with a finite domain solver developed by Diaz et al. [7]. Its main novelty is to trace events related to the constraint propagation in a systematic and efficient way. Our tracer has a formal specification. It provides more complete information than existing tracers. Furthermore, benchmarks show that this specification can be implemented in an efficient way.

The benefits of the formal specification are threefold. Firstly, the formal specification defines in a rigorous way *what* has to be implemented in the tracer. A direct consequence is that, when implementing the tracer, we could concentrate on *how* to do it efficiently. Secondly, the formal specification tells the users how to interpret the produced trace. Users, indeed, often complain, that they do not know the meaning of a portion of trace. With the transition rules of the formal specification, they can understand what they see. Thirdly, debugging tools that use the produced traces can be built on solid bases. Tool developers know exactly on which information they can count and what this information corresponds to.

The contribution of this paper is thus to formally describe a propagation tracer for CLP(FD) and to show that it is efficiently implemented. To our best knowledge it is the first time that a tracer is implemented according to such a rigorous methodology.

In the following, Section 2 presents the formal specification. Section 3 gives a short trace example. Section 4 gives a sketch of the implementation of the tracer. Section 5 provides experimental results showing the efficiency of the tracer. Section 6 discusses related work.

2   A Formal Trace Model for GNU-Prolog

In this section, we present the formalization of a trace model for the GNU-Prolog system. It is a refinement and a major revision, validated by implementation, of the preliminary model presented in [4].

Throughout its description, the trace model is compared to the actual behavior of GNU-Prolog. Since GNU-Prolog has no complete formal operational semantics, the correspondence is presented informally. Our references are two comprehensive implementation descriptions by Diaz and Codognet [3,8] and the current source distribution of GNU-Prolog [7], that has been instrumented to implement the tracer.

A trace is a sequence of trace events which can be formalized as instances of a finite set of event-types. An event-type corresponds to a transition from some execution state to another. The trace model primarily formalizes the notion of execution state (the *observed state*). Thus each event-type can be specified by a rule which characterizes a possible state transition.

The observed state consists of two parts: the solver state and the search-tree state. In the remaining of this section, we describe in detail the components of the solver state, we present the search-tree, we then give all the rules that describe the events. Events are divided into two classes: control and propagation. Control events are related to the management of variables and constraints, as well as the management of the search. Propagation events are related to the filtering of domains and the awakening of constraints.

2.1   Solver State

Before we define the solver state, we must make a remark about the constraints. GNU-Prolog is based on the so-called "RISC approach" [3] which consists in translating at compile-time all primitive constraints into simpler agents of the form X **in** r (indexicals), which constrains the domain of X according to an expression r. Moreover, some user-level constraints are split into several primitive constraints and then into indexicals. For example, the constraint fd_all_different generates a set of primitive constraints which are binary disequalities and each binary disequality generates two indexicals. Therefore there are several possible abstraction levels at which a constraint can be observed in GNU-Prolog. We initially proposed to observe constraints at the level of indexicals: the trace was close to the solver implementation but too far from user's concerns. We therefore now propose to observe constraints at the level of primitive constraints. Indexicals are rather seen as *propagators* (as defined by Müller [16], an agent that ensures the propagation of a first-class constraint). The actions of an indexical are seen as actions of the corresponding primitive constraint.

Definition 1. *(Solver State) A solver state is a 9-tuple:*
$\mathbb{S} = (\mathcal{C}, \mathcal{V}, \mathcal{D}, A, E, R, S, F, Q)$ *where: $\mathcal{C}$ is the set of already declared constraints; $\mathcal{V}$ is the set of already declared finite-domain variables; $\mathcal{D}$ is the function that assigns a domain to each variable in $\mathcal{V}$; A is the set containing the active constraint if there exists any; E is the set of entailed constraints; R is the set of unsatisfiable (or rejected) constraints (at most one). S is the set of sleeping constraints; F is the set containing the current domain update to propagate; Q is the set of achieved reductions to propagate (the propagation "queue").*   □

The FD solver of GNU-Prolog mainly handles FD variables and constraints. Constraints, in $\mathcal{C}$, are goals that call constraint primitives. FD variables, in $\mathcal{V}$, are logical variables that are involved in a constraint goal. The set of variables involved in a constraint c is denoted by $\mathbf{var}(c)$. Each FD variable x gets a finite domain D_x, namely a set of possible positive integer values. $\mathcal{D}$ is a set of pairs variable/domain (a function from $\mathcal{V}$ to $\mathcal{P}(\mathbb{N})$).

A, E, R and S describe all the possible states of a constraint during the propagation stage: active, entailed, rejected or sleeping. The set A (active constraint) contains at most one constraint: the constraint under examination. The set E of *entailed* constraints consists of primitive constraints that can not perform any further propagation, such as $x \neq 5$ (as soon as 5 is no longer in D_x, the constraint is entailed). The set of *rejected* constraints R has at most one element: the constraint whose satisfiability check has just failed. S is the set of *sleeping* constraints, namely constraints that may still lead to further domain reduction. The *store of constraints* σ is the set of constraints of $\mathbb{S}$, defined as: $\sigma = A \cup E \cup R \cup S$.

Constraint propagation is driven by the *domain updates* (modifications of domains) previously performed. The set of possible domain updates of D_x is $U_x = \{\min_x, \max_x, \text{minmax}_x, \text{dom}_x, \text{val}_x\}$ (resp.: update of the lower bound, of the upper bound, of one of the bounds, any update of the domain, instantiation of the variable). For each variable x, for each domain update, the implementation maintains a list of the constraints that may be impacted by this update. These lists are modeled by the predicate $dependence(c, u)$: the awakening of the constraint c depends on the domain update u.

F contains the current domain update to propagate. One of the dependent constraints can be put in A and reductions can be achieved.

Q is the propagation queue, it contains the domain updates which are still to be propagated.

Initially, all the sets are empty.

When a constraint c is entailed by the domains in $\mathcal{D}$, $entailed(c, \mathcal{D})$ holds. When the constraint c is considered as unsatisfiable by the domains in $\mathcal{D}$, $rejected(c, \mathcal{D})$ holds. When a constraint has no further reduction to perform $no\_reduction(c)$ holds.

2.2   Search-Tree

The control of the execution may be represented by a depth-first traversal of a search-tree [5]. This tree can be formalized by a set of ordered labels $\mathcal{L}$ and a function Σ which associates to each label a solver state. There are three kinds of nodes, characterized by three predicates: failure leaves ($failure(\mathbb{S})$), solution leaves ($solution(\mathbb{S})$), and choice-point nodes ($choice\text{-}point(\mathbb{S})$). Solutions correspond to the toplevel successes. Failures correspond to inconsistent solver states. Choice-points correspond to solver states that can be restored during the remaining of the execution.

The last visited node is called *current node* and its label is denoted by $\mathcal{N}$. A notion of *depth* is associated to the search-tree: the depth of the root is 1, and the depth is increased by one between a node and its children. The depth is formalized by the function δ which associates to a node label l the depth $\delta(l)$. Therefore, the state of the search-tree is a quadruple: $(\mathcal{L}, \Sigma, \delta, \mathcal{N})$.

$$\text{new variable} \quad \frac{x \notin \mathcal{V}}{\mathcal{V} \leftarrow \mathcal{V} \cup \{x\}, \quad \mathcal{D} \leftarrow \mathcal{D} \cup \{(x, D_x)\}} \quad \{D_x : \text{initial domain of } x\}$$

$$\text{new constraint} \quad \frac{c \notin \mathcal{C} \ \wedge \ \mathbf{var}(c) \subseteq \mathcal{V}}{\mathcal{C} \leftarrow \mathcal{C} \cup \{c\}}$$

$$\text{post} \quad \frac{c \in \mathcal{C} \ \wedge \ c \notin \sigma \ \wedge \ A = \emptyset}{A \leftarrow \{c\}, \quad F \leftarrow \emptyset}$$

$$\text{new child} \quad \frac{choice\text{-}point(\mathbb{S}) \ \wedge \ l \notin \mathcal{L}}{\mathcal{L} \leftarrow \mathcal{L} \cup \{l\}, \Sigma \leftarrow \Sigma \cup \{(l, \mathbb{S})\}, \delta \leftarrow \delta \cup \{(l, \delta(\mathcal{N}) + 1)\}, \mathcal{N} \leftarrow l}$$

$$\text{jump to} \quad \frac{l \in \mathrm{dom}(\Sigma) \ \wedge \ choice\text{-}point(\Sigma(l))}{\mathcal{N} \leftarrow l, \mathbb{S} \leftarrow \Sigma(l)}$$

$$\text{solution} \quad \frac{solution(\mathbb{S}) \ \wedge \ l \notin \mathcal{L}}{\mathcal{L} \leftarrow \mathcal{L} \cup \{l\}, \Sigma \leftarrow \Sigma \cup \{(l, \mathbb{S})\}, \delta \leftarrow \delta \cup \{(l, \delta(\mathcal{N}) + 1)\}, \mathcal{N} \leftarrow l}$$

$$\text{failure} \quad \frac{failure(\mathbb{S}) \ \wedge \ l \notin \mathcal{L}}{\mathcal{L} \leftarrow \mathcal{L} \cup \{l\}, \Sigma \leftarrow \Sigma \cup \{(l, \mathbb{S})\}, \delta \leftarrow \delta \cup \{(l, \delta(\mathcal{N}) + 1)\}, \mathcal{N} \leftarrow l}$$

Fig. 1. GNU-Prolog Trace Model: Control Event-Types

2.3   Control Events

The rules of Fig. 1 describe the control event-types of the trace model. They are related to the handling of the constraint store and the search. The conditions on the top of each rule specify what the event guarantees about the current observed state. These conditions are not checked by the tracer but are ensured by the behavior of GNU-Prolog. The bottom part specifies all the changes of the observed state that are reflected by the event. In most of the rules, only the changes are noted, the unchanged items are not reproduced. Additional notations are defined on the right-hand side of some rules. Rule new variable specifies that a new FD variable x is introduced in $\mathcal{V}$ and that its initial domain is D_x. Rule new constraint specifies that the solver introduces a new constraint c in $\mathcal{C}$ when all variables involved in c are already defined. The rule post introduced a declared constraint into the store as the active one. There is no domain update to propagate yet ($F = \emptyset$).

The following four rules describe the construction of the search-tree. Rule new child specifies that the current solver state corresponds to a new node of the search-tree which is candidate as choice-point, i.e. the solver may jump back to this state later. This state is recorded in Σ, with a new label l. This node becomes the current node and the depth is increased. Jumping from the current solver state to a previous choice-point is specified by the rule jump to: a former node l becomes the current node and the corresponding solver state is restored. This models the backtracking to the last pending choice-point. Finally, two rules are used to declare the leaves of the search-tree. solution specifies that the current solver state is a solution (a toplevel success). failure specifies that the current state is inconsistent. In GNU-Prolog, an inconsistent state may be due to a failed satisfiability check or to the fact that no clause head is unifiable with the current goal. In both cases the corresponding state satisfies the *failure* condition.

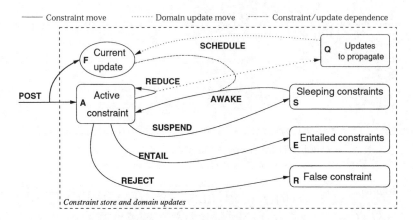

Fig. 2. Illustration of the Transition Described by the Propagation Rules

reduce $\dfrac{A = \{c\} \ \wedge \ x \in \mathbf{var}(c) \ \wedge \Delta_x^c \neq \emptyset \wedge R = \emptyset}{D_x \leftarrow D_x - \Delta_x^c, \quad Q \leftarrow Q \cup \bar{u}}$ $\left\{ \begin{array}{l} \Delta_x^c \text{ subset of } D_x \text{ to remove} \\ \bar{u} \subseteq U_x \end{array} \right.$

suspend $\dfrac{A = \{c\} \wedge no\_reduction(c, \mathcal{D}) \wedge R = \emptyset}{A \leftarrow \emptyset, \quad S \leftarrow S \cup \{c\}}$

entail $\dfrac{A = \{c\} \ \wedge \ entailed(c, \mathcal{D}) \wedge R = \emptyset}{A \leftarrow \emptyset, \quad E \leftarrow E \cup \{c\}}$

reject $\dfrac{A = \{c\} \ \wedge \ rejected(c, \mathcal{D}) \wedge R = \emptyset}{A \leftarrow \emptyset, \quad R \leftarrow \{c\}}$

awake $\dfrac{A = \emptyset \ \wedge \ F = \{u\} \wedge c \in S \ \wedge \ dependence(c, u) \ \wedge \ R = \emptyset}{A \leftarrow \{c\}}$

schedule $\dfrac{A = \emptyset \wedge \ u \in Q \ \wedge \ R = \emptyset}{F \leftarrow \{u\}, \quad Q \leftarrow Q - \{u\}}$

Fig. 3. GNU-Prolog Trace Model: Propagation Event-Types

2.4   Propagation Events

The propagation process is a sequence of constraint awakenings: a *sleeping* constraint is activated by a scheduled update to make more domain reductions. In GNU-Prolog, the propagation is scheduled by a queue of variables. When the domain of a variable is reduced, the variable is put in the queue and some of its dependency lists are marked for awakening. For instance, when the lower bound of variable X is increased, X is put in the queue (if it was not already in) and the lists min, minmax and dom are marked: the depending constraints will be awaked later. This queue is modeled here by the set of domain updates Q.

The propagation can be described by state transition rules acting in the structured solver state, as illustrated by Fig. 2. These transitions rules are formalized in Fig. 3. A, S, E, R, Q and F are parts of the current solver state $\mathbb{S}$ previously defined. The active constraint in A can reduce some domains. Rule reduce specifies that the solver reduces the domain of a variable involved in the active constraint. A single domain is reduced in this step. $\bar{u}$ is a set of domain updates that characterize the reduction, for example if $x \in \{2, 3, 5\}$ and $\Delta_x^c = \{2\}$, then $\bar{u} = \{\min_x, \text{minmax}_x, \text{dom}_x\}$. Δ_x^c is computed by one of the filtering algorithm of c. Each domain reduction generates new domain updates that are recorded in Q. When the active constraint cannot reduce any more domain, it is suspended in S (rule suspend). An active constraint that is true is said to be *entailed* and put in E (rule entail). An active constraint that is unsatisfiable is said to be *rejected* and put in R by the reject rule. Domain updates in Q are waiting to be propagated by sleeping constraints in S. The domain updates are processed in turn by the schedule rule and put in F: all the constraints in S that depend on the scheduled domain update in F are awaken in turn (rule awake). Those awakenings may lead to new domain reductions. It is worth noticing that once there is a rejected constraint ($R \neq \emptyset$), no propagation rule can be applied anymore.

2.5   Event Attributes

Each event has common and specific attributes. The common attributes are: port (event-type), namely the name of the applied transition rule, a chronological event number, the depth in the search-tree of the current node $\delta(\mathcal{N})$, the solver state $\mathbb{S}$. The specific attributes depend on the port. Using the notations of Fig. 1 the specific attributes for the port new variable are x and D_x, for the ports new constraint and post c, for the ports related to the search-tree the only specific attribute is the label l. Using the notations of Fig. 3, the specific attributes for the port reduce are c, x, Δ_x and $\bar{u}$. For the ports suspend, entail and reject there is a single specific attribute c. For the port awake, they are c and u, and only u for the port schedule.

3   A Trace Example

Figure 4 presents the trace of a toy program: `fd_element(I, [2,5,7],A)`, `(A#=I ; A#=2)` where the first constraint specifies that A is in $\{2, 5, 7\}$ and I is the index of the value of A in this list. Moreover A is either equal to I or equal to 2. The first alternative is obviously infeasible. The tracer is able to provide, at each event, the full state of the FD solver (e.g. the domains or the store). The presented trace is thus a selection of data that seem relevant to understand the execution. This is the *default trace*. The default trace is displayed as follows. Each numbered row is an event. The leftmost number is the chronological number, followed by the depth in the search-tree and the port. Most of the specific attributes follow (all the attributes detailed in Section 2.5, except $\bar{u}$ for reduce and u for awake). In this trace, the variable number n is denoted by vn and the constraint number n is denoted by cn.

The trace begins with the creation of the root (new child, node number 0), two variables corresponding to I and A are created with the maximum domain (full range of 28-bit unsigned integers) then the first constraint is created and posted: `fd_element` (c1, events 4 and 5). This constraint makes two domain

```
 1[1]newChild node(0)              15[2]schedule dom(v2)
 2[1]newVariable v1[0-268435455]   16[2]awake c1
 3[1]newVariable v2[0-268435455]   17[2]reject c1
 4[1]newConstraint c1              18[3]failure node(2)
    fd_element([v1,[2,5,7],v2])    19[2]jumpTo node(1)
 5[1]post c1                       20[2]newConstraint c7
 6[1]reduce c1 v1                     assign([v2,2])
   delta=[0,4-268435455]           21[2]post c7
 7[1]reduce c1 v2                  22[2]reduce c7 v2 delta=[5,7]
   delta=[0-1,3-4,6,8-268435455]   23[2]entail c7
 8[1]suspend c1                    24[2]schedule dom(v2)
 9[2]newChild node(1)              25[2]awake c1
10[2]newConstraint c4              26[2]reduce c1 v1 delta=[2-3]
    x_eq_y([v2,v1])                27[2]suspend c1
11[2]post c4                       28[2]schedule dom(v1)
12[2]reduce c4 v2 delta=[5,7]      29[2]awake c1
13[2]reduce c4 v1 delta=[1,3]      30[2]suspend c1
14[2]suspend c4                    31[3]solution node(3)
```

Fig. 4. A Trace for `fd_element(I,[2,5,7],A)`, `(A#=I ; A#=2)`. *a-b* means *from a to b* and *a,b* means *a and b*

reductions: the domain of the first variable (I) becomes $\{1, 2, 3\}$ and the domain of A becomes $\{2, 5, 7\}$. After these reductions, the constraint is suspended and a choice-point is recorded (event 9). Events 10 to 17 post the next constraint, A#=I (c4), the store becomes inconsistent (17: reject). The resulting failure leads to the backtracking to the last pending choice-point (18 and 19). Events 20 and 21 create and post the constraint A#=2 (c7): the domain of variable 2 is ground. This domain update is scheduled (24) and awakes the constraint 1 (25) that instantiates the first variable to 1. The unique solution is then reached: A=2,I=1. Since there is no pending choice-point, the execution ends.

4   Implementation

A solver is based on complex and optimized mechanisms. Embedding a tracer into a solver means modifying the source code of the solver: its mechanisms have to be instrumented in order to trace the execution. To be efficient, the tracer is lazy: while no data is needed, most of the work of the tracer is avoided. This section gives a sketch of the implementation of the tracer into GNU-Prolog. The implementation of the GNU-Prolog platform is detailed in [8].

A GNU-Prolog program is compiled into WAM and, then, into byte-code or C code, depending on the compilation mode. The C code is then compiled into a native binary. The target file is linked to a C library that is the FD solver. The top-level loop of GNU-Prolog is written in GNU-Prolog and compiled through this native compilation scheme. The implementation of the tracer has modified three components of GNU-Prolog: the solver library, the WAM engine and the

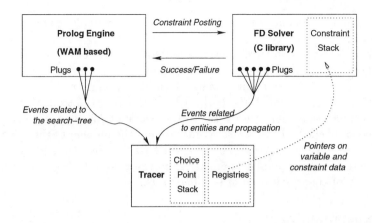

Fig. 5. General Structure of the GNU-Prolog Tracer

toplevel loop. Some new built-ins have also been implemented to activate the tracer and to configure the trace to be generated.

The structure of the tracer and its components are shown in Figure 5. The two parts of GNU-Prolog that are mainly relevant here are the Prolog engine and the FD solver. The Prolog engine drives the execution. When a goal which is a constraint is called, it is sent to the FD solver (*constraint posting*). The solver performs all the suitable domain reductions and leads the constraint propagation. At the end of the propagation stage, the solver returns either *true* (the constraint has been successfully posted) or *false* (a failure occurred). In the first case, the Prolog engine continues the execution, in the second case it backtracks to the last pending choice point.

The trace events are encoded by some *plugs* in the Prolog engine (trace events related to the search tree) and in the FD Solver library (trace events related to the variables, constraints, and constraint propagation). Roughly speaking, a plug is some lines of code (e.g. a function call) inserted at a particular point of the program to instrument. The plugs update the data of the tracer and trigger the generation of the trace.

All the variables and constraints (the FD *entities*) are stored by the solver in a *constraint stack*. Several types of data coexist in this stack: domains, constraint environments, dependency lists. The solver manipulates pointers on those data (pointers on variables, pointers on constraints). The debugging process needs to associate a unique identifier to each entity: a variable number to each FD variable and a constraint number to each constraint. The tracer needs a simple and efficient process to retrieve the unique identifier of an entity whose pointer is known and proceed through the set of all the variables or the set of all the constraints and access to the corresponding data in the constraint stack. Therefore, the tracer maintains two tables called *registries* (see Figure 5): the first one is dedicated to the FD variables, the second one is dedicated to the constraints. Those tables record, for each entity, its unique identifier, a pointer to its data in the constraint stack and some debugging data (for example, the initial bounds of a variable).

To handle the search-tree, the tracer maintains a stack of choice-points: each choice-point is given a number (the node number in a left-to-right pre-order traversal of the search-tree) and a value of the WAM register CS (pointer on the top of the constraint stack). On backtracking, the WAM untrails the content of the constraint stack and restores the former value of CS. The tracer seeks this CS value in its choice-point stack in order to find the number of the choice-point the solver has just jumped to. The two registries are then cleaned by removing all the entities whose pointer is greater than the restored CS. This ensures the consistency of the tracer data after a backtracking.

5 Experimental Results

This section assesses the performance of the tracer. It compares execution times of programs run by GNU-Prolog and by several configurations of the tracer.

5.1 Methodology of the Experiments

When tracing a program, some time is spent in the program execution (T_{prog}), some time is spent in the basic mechanisms of the tracer (Δ_{tracer}), some time is spent in the generation of the requested attributes X (Δ_{genX}), and some time is spent in the output of the trace (Δ_{output}). Hence, if we call T the execution time of a traced program, we have: $T = T_{prog} + \Delta_{tracer} + \Delta_{genX} + \Delta_{output}$

The generation of the requested attributes consists of retrieving relevant data in the own data of the tracer and in the state of the solver, then processing them to get the requested attributes. Then the events can be output into a file or an inter-process communication.

The display of the traced information takes a time which can be very large compared to the time taken by the rest of the mechanisms. Furthermore, one can conjecture that when some output is requested, the time taken by the display itself does not matter to users because they see something happening. For users, the annoying slowdowns are the ones which occur in hidden parts. Therefore, in the following we want to assess the cost of $\Delta_{tracer} + \Delta_{genX}$. Δ_{output} depends on the output mean and on the debugging tool, which are out of the scope of this paper: in our experiments, the output of the trace is disabled, ensuring $\Delta_{output} = 0$.

The time Δ_{genX} depends on the attributes the tracer is configured to give for each port. In these experiments, we consider two different traces. The first one is the default trace presented in Section 3 restricted to the events related to the search tree: new child, jump to, solution and failure ($\Delta_{genTree}$). The second one is the full default trace ($\Delta_{genDefault}$). We compare Δ_{tracer} and Δ_{genX}, against T_{prog}. We will therefore compute the following ratios:

$$R_{tracer} = \frac{T_{prog} + \Delta_{tracer}}{T_{prog}}, R_{genTree} = \frac{T_{prog} + \Delta_{tracer} + \Delta_{genTree}}{T_{prog}},$$
$$\text{and } R_{genDefault} = \frac{T_{prog} + \Delta_{tracer} + \Delta_{genDefault}}{T_{prog}}$$

Time Measurement.   The measurements result of experiments run on a PC (400MHz Pentium II, 512Kb of cache, 384Mb of RAM) under GNU/Linux 2.2.17 using GNU-Prolog1.2.16 (last stable release). The tracer is an instrumentation of the source code of this very same version and has been compiled in the same conditions by `gcc-2.95.2`. The execution times have been measured with the GNU-Prolog `statistics` predicate. The measured executions consist of a batch of executions such that each measured time is at least 20 s. The command accuracy is 1 ms. The measured time includes both *user* and *system* times. Each experiment has been done five times and the deviation was smaller than 1 %.

Benchmark programs.   8 benchmark programs[1] were used. Half of them are part of CSPLib, a benchmark library by Gent and Walsh [10]: the computation of the magic sequence of size 100;   the perfect square packing problem with 24 squares (a 2D-placement problem);   the computation of an optimal 8-marks golomb ruler;   the instance <5, 4, 4> of the social golfer (a classical problem for studying symmetry).   These four programs have been chosen among the whole library for their significant execution time and for the variety of constraints they involve (arithmetic, reified and symbolic). Four other programs have been added to cover more specific aspects of the solver mechanisms: Van Hentenryck's bridge problem; two instances of the n-queens problem (all the solutions for $n = 14$ and the first one for $n = 256$), two highly backtracking computations; the proof that $1 \leq x, y \leq 70000000, x < y \wedge y < x$ is infeasible. The interest of the latter is the long stage of propagation involving one of the simplest and optimized constraints GNU-Prolog provides: bound consistency for a strict inequality. Therefore, this program represents the worst case for the propagation instrumentation.

The 8 traced programs are listed in Table 1. They are sorted by increasing number of trace events. The first column gives the name of the program. The second column gives the type of computation: *1st sol.* means breaking the execution after the first solution, *all sol.* means finding all the solutions, *optim.* means finding the best solution. The further columns are statistics about the trace of each computation: the number of trace events, the number of FD variables and constraints involved (including the constraints added by the search procedure). "% prop." denotes the percentage of events that describes the propagation engine behavior (*awake* selection of a constraint in the propagation queue and *schedule* selection of a constraint list). "% red." denotes the percentage of events that describe domain reduction. These two types of events are the fine-grained description of the computation. The last column is the average time of execution per event (in nanoseconds), $\varepsilon = \frac{T_{prog}}{\text{Nb. evt.}}$.

The benchmark programs have executions large enough for the measurements to be meaningful. Indeed, they range from less than 200,000 events to about 400 millions events. Furthermore, they represent a wide range of CLP(FD) programs. They are of quite different nature (2 *optim.*, 3 *1st sol.* and 3 *all sol.*). The number of variables and constraints that they manage is quite different, respectively from 2 to 35654, and from 4 to over 5 millions. The percentage of propagation events

---

[1] The source code of this benchmark suite is available on the web [14].

Table 1. Characterization of the Traced Programs

Program	Type	Nb. evt.	Nb. var.	Nb. cstr.	% prop.	% red.	ε (ns)
bridge	optim.	$0.2 \cdot 10^6$	46	9513	64%	14%	413
queens(256)	1st sol.	$0.8 \cdot 10^6$	256	99981	54%	8%	1003
magic(100)	all sol.	$3.2 \cdot 10^6$	15485	15781	87%	11%	266
square(24)	1st sol.	$4.2 \cdot 10^6$	35654	38642	86%	10%	363
golomb(8)	optim.	$39 \cdot 10^6$	36	127152	85%	13%	228
golfer(5,4,4)	1st sol.	$63 \cdot 10^6$	4640	96916	80%	19%	326
propag	all sol.	$280 \cdot 10^6$	2	4	75%	25%	79
queens(14)	all sol.	$399 \cdot 10^6$	14	5726185	82%	11%	198

Table 2. Cost of the trace mechanisms on benchmarks (deviation smaller than 1 %).

Program	Type	Nb. evts	T_{prog} (ms)	R_{tracer}	$R_{genTree}$	$R_{genDefault}$
bridge	optim.	$0.2 \cdot 10^6$	81	1.27	1.27	2.95
queens(256)	1st sol.	$0.8 \cdot 10^6$	793	1.12	1.12	3.06
magic(100)	all sol.	$3 \cdot 10^6$	860	1.05	1.06	4.62
square(24)	1st sol.	$4 \cdot 10^6$	1526	1.07	1.08	3.94
golomb(8)	optim.	$39 \cdot 10^6$	8872	1.04	1.04	7.36
golfer(5,4,4)	1st sol.	$63 \cdot 10^6$	20634	1.03	1.03	4.31
propag	all sol.	$280 \cdot 10^6$	22252	1.07	1.07	6.96
queens(14)	all sol.	$399 \cdot 10^6$	78940	1.07	1.07	5.19

varies from 54 % to 87 %. The percentage of reduction events varies from 8% to 25%. The last column shows that ε is between 198 and 413ns per event for most of the suite. The two remarkable exceptions are *propag* ($\varepsilon = 79$ns) and *queens(256)* ($\varepsilon = 1003$ns). The low ε is due to the efficiency of the propagation stage for the constraints involved in this computation. The large ε is due to a lower proportion of "fine-grained" events.

Measuring T_x. The measure of T_{prog} is the execution time of the program run by GNU-Prolog. The measure of T_{tracer} is the execution time of the program run by the tracer in the following configuration: the tracer is first activated from the top-level, then the generated trace is tuned to trace nothing, so as to the tracer creates and maintains its own data but does not compute any additional attributes. The measure of T_{genX} is the same as T_{tracer} but the tracer is configured before each execution to generate a subset X of the trace (here, the default trace or the search-tree trace).

5.2   Results

Table 2 gives the results of the measurements. The first three columns recall information from Table 1. The fourth column gives the durations of executions without any tracing mechanism.

The fifth column gives the ratio $R_{tracer} = \frac{T_{tracer}}{T_{prog}}$, which measures the overhead of the basic trace mechanism, namely the maintenance of the internal tracer data. This overhead is less than 30% in the worst case and, in most of the traced programs, less than 10%. It is worth noticing that the worst overhead is actually for the smallest execution. In that particular case, the overhead is 21ms, which should not be noticed by users. For the very large executions the overhead is very stable, and 10% is quite bearable. For example, for the longest execution (queens(14)), the overhead is less than 6 seconds for an untraced execution of 1 min 30 s. The results for R_{tracer} are very positive, they mean that the basic mechanisms of the tracer can be systematically activated. Users will hardly notice the overhead. Therefore, while developing programs, users can directly work in "traced" mode, they do not need to switch from untraced to traced environments. This is a great comfort.

The sixth column gives the ratio $R_{genTree} = \frac{T_{genTree}}{T_{prog}}$ which measures the overhead due to the generation of the search-tree trace. One can notice that this overhead is equal, with less than 1.10^{-2} difference, to R_{tracer}. This is consistent with the fact that the basic trace mechanism already handles all the data necessary to the generation of the search-tree. These results are again very positive. Not only can users always activate the tracing mechanism, they can also get a basic trace for a marginal cost.

The seventh column gives the ratio $R_{genDefault} = \frac{T_{genDefault}}{T_{prog}}$. It measures the overhead due to the generation of the default trace which gives detailed information about propagation. Here the overhead is between 2.95 and 7.36. For six of the programs the ratio is around 5 or less. For two programs the ratio is around 7. For program "propag", this result is not really a surprise as the program exhibits a very large proportion of reduce events, which are quite costly to build. For "golomb(8)", more specific measures have shown that half of this overhead is due to the computation of "Δ_x^c". The filtering algorithms of most of the constraints involved in this program compute a bit field containing the values to keep: Δ_x is computed by a set difference between D_x and the domain to keep. Among the four ways to reduce a domain GNU-Prolog uses, this one is the most expensive to instrument. Even with a factor of 7, these performances are comparable to other debuggers known to be efficient enough. For example the ML tracer of Tolmach and Appel [19] is said to have an average slowdown of 3. Our average is closer to 5 but the trace model of Tolmach and Appel has far less details than ours. For executions of size equivalent to those of our measurements, the Mercury tracer by Somogyi and Henderson [18], regularly used by Mercury developers, has an overhead from 2 to 15, with an average of 7 [12].

Our tracer can be dynamically configured in order to produce only some events and some attributes. Since the basic trace has a marginal cost, there is always a configuration of the tracer which will produce more interesting information at a cost acceptable by a given user for a given program.

6   Related Work

Two event-oriented tracers have already been implemented into real solvers, Ilog Solver and Sicstus. Ilog Solver provides some tracing facilities as a class of its solver library [11]. It is fully dedicated to Ilog Solver. The Ilog Christmas Tree [2] is built by processing an XML trace produced by the debugger. This tracer is generic: it can be specialized to feed a specific tool. This specialization requires, however, a good understanding of the solver behavior and cannot be modified during the execution. Moreover, the amount of data available at each event is very limited compared to the full state the GNU-Prolog tracer can provide. For instance, the set of constraints and variables cannot be inspected. In the GNU-Prolog tracer, the whole state of the solver can be accessed at any event upon request. Moreover, the formal specification is sufficient to understand the trace: no further knowledge of the GNU-Prolog implementation is needed.

A tracer for the FD solver of Sicstus Prolog has been prototyped by Ågren et al [1]. Its main quality is the explanations it provides about the domain narrowing. This helpful information needs a difficult and costly instrumentation of Sicstus constraints: only a few ones have actually been instrumented. It is still a prototype and no performance results are available. Some tuning of the trace display seems possible but the tracer is based on a complete storage of the trace and a postmortem investigation: this approach is impractical with real-sized executions. The lazy generation of the trace our tracer implements leads to the same kind of trace data in a more efficient and practical way.

Some debugging tools enable the user to interact with the execution states. User acts on the current state of the execution to drive the search-tree exploration (Oz Explorer [17]), to add new constraints on a partial solution (CLPGUI [9]), to recompute a former state (both) or to cancel some constraints chosen thanks to failure explanations (PaLM [13]). Those features are really helpful but go much beyond the scope of this paper. We are considering the connection of the GNU-Prolog tracer to the existing CLPGUI interface.

7   Conclusion

We have presented a propagation tracer for GNU-Prolog. It shows that fine-grained tracing of a propagation-based solver is possible. Moreover, such a tracer can be efficient. The tracer has been presented with a default trace, with a small number of useful attributes. It allows to display many more information without slowing down. In fact it has been designed to be connected to a trace analyzer [12] which selects only the attributes needed by a specific use. Therefore the number and the size of the attributes of the trace model impact the performances only in proportion to their actual use.

The specification of the tracer is a refinement of the general trace model presented in [4]. On the one hand this ensures that many debugging needs will be covered by the trace. On the other hand, the same trace can be implemented on several different FD platforms. This approach has been developed in the context of the OADymPPaC project. The generic trace is produced with a concrete format based on an XML DTD. Several debugging tools can be thus connected to the generic tracer as long as they use this format to input the data. The GNU-Prolog tracer has a module to output the trace in this format.

The GNU-Prolog version including the tracer is known as *Codeine*. Codeine and its documentation can be downloaded on the web [14].

Acknowledgments. The authors would like to thank their OADymPPaC partners for fruitful discussions, and the anonymous referees for their helpful comments. Special thanks also to Sylvain Soliman for his careful proofreading.

References

1. M. Ågren, T. Szeredi, N. Beldiceanu, and M. Carlsson. Tracing and explaining execution of clp(fd) programs. In *Proc. of WLPE'02*, 2002. CoRR:cs.SE/0207047.
2. C. Bracchi, C. Gefflot, and F. Paulin. Combining propagation information and search-tree visualization using opl studio. In *Proc. of WLPE'01*, Cyprus, 2001.
3. P. Codognet and D. Diaz. Compiling constraints in clp(FD). *Journal of Logic Programming*, 27(3):185–226, June 1996.
4. P. Deransart, M. Ducassé, and L. Langevine. A generic trace model for finite domain solvers. In B. O'Sullivan, editor, *Proc. of UICS'02*, Ithaca (USA), 2002.
5. P. Deransart, A. Ed-Dbali, and L. Cervoni. *Prolog, The Standard; Reference Manual*. Springer Verlag, April 1996.
6. P. Deransart, M. Hermenegildo, and J. Małuszyński, editors. *Analysis and Visualisation Tools for Constraint Programming*. Springer, 2000. LNCS 1870.
7. D. Diaz. GNU prolog, a free prolog compiler with constraint solving over finite domains, 2003. http://gprolog.sourceforge.net/ Distributed under the GNU GPL.
8. D. Diaz and P. Codognet. Design and implementation of the gnu prolog system. *Journal of Functional and Logic Programming*, 6–10, 2001.
9. F. Fages. Clpgui: a generic graphical user interface for constraint logic programming over finite domains. In *Proc. of WLPE'02*, 2002. CoRR:cs.SE/0207048.
10. I.P. Gent and T. Walsh. CSPLib: a benchmark library for constraints, 1999. http://csplib.cs.strath.ac.uk/. A presentation appears in the Proc. of CP-99.
11. Ilog. SOLVER 5.1 reference manual, 2001.
12. E. Jahier and M. Ducassé. Generic program monitoring by trace analysis. *Theory and Practice of Logic Programming*, 2002.
13. N. Jussien and V. Barichard. The palm system: explanation-based constraint programming. In *Proc. of TRICS'00*, pages 118–133, Singapore, September 2000.
14. L. Langevine. Codeine, a propagation tracer for GNU-Prolog, 2003. http://contraintes.inria.fr/~langevin/codeine.
15. M. Meier. Debugging constraint programs. In U. Montanari and F. Rossi, editors, *Proc. of CP 1995*, number 976 in LNCS. Springer Verlag, 1995.
16. T. Müller. Practical investigation of constraints with graph views. In *Proc. of CP 2000*, number 1894 in LNCS. Springer-Verlag, 2000.
17. C. Schulte. Oz Explorer: A Visual Constraint Programming Tool. In *Proc. of ICLP'97*, pages 286–300, Leuven, Belgium, June 1997. The MIT Press.
18. Z. Somogyi and F. Henderson. The implementation technology of the Mercury debugger. In *Proc. of WLPE'99*, volume 30(4). Elsevier, ENTCS, 1999.
19. A. Tolmach and A.W. Appel. A debugger for Standard ML. *Journal of Functional Programming*, 5(2):155–200, April 1995.

Intensional Sets in CLP

A. Dovier[1], E. Pontelli[2], and G. Rossi[3]

[1] Univ. di Udine, Dip. di Matematica e Informatica. dovier@dimi.uniud.it
[2] New Mexico State University, Dept. Computer Science. epontell@cs.nmsu.edu
[3] Univ. di Parma, Dip. di Matematica. gianfr@prmat.math.unipr.it

Abstract. We propose a parametric introduction of intensionally defined sets into any $CLP(\mathcal{D})$ language. The result is a language
$CLP(\{\mathcal{D}\})$, where constraints over sets of elements of $\mathcal{D}$ and over sets
of sets of elements, and so on, can be expressed. The semantics of
$CLP(\{\mathcal{D}\})$ is based on the semantics of logic programs with aggregates
and the semantics of CLP over sets. We investigate the problem of constraint resolution in $CLP(\{\mathcal{D}\})$ and propose algorithms for constraints
simplification.

Keywords. *Constraint Logic Programming, Sets, Aggregates.*

1   Introduction

The literature is rich of proposals aimed at developing declarative programming
frameworks that incorporate different types of *set-based primitives* (e.g., [13,2,5,
6,1]). These frameworks provide a high level of data abstraction, where complex
algorithms can be encoded in a natural fashion, by directly using the popular
language of set theory. These features make this type of languages particularly
effective for modeling and rapid prototyping of algorithms.

A recognized downside of most of the existing languages embedding sets is the
focus on extensional set constructions [6,13,15,11] and/or the severe restrictions
imposed on the use of *intensional set constructions* [2,20]. *Intensionally* defined
sets (a.k.a. *intensional sets*) are collections of elements where the membership is
decided by properties instead of enumeration. There is significant evidence that
the ability to handle general intensional sets can drastically simplify the development of solutions to complex problems, leading to more convenient languages
and compact programs—e.g., [16] suggests that encodings of traditionally hard
problems in this type of notations are more compact that SAT encodings.

In this work we propose a parametric introduction of intensionally defined
sets into any $CLP(\mathcal{D})$ language—e.g., $\mathcal{D}$ can be $\mathbb{FD}$ for Finite Domains or $\mathbb{R}$ for
Real numbers. Given a language $CLP(\mathcal{D})$ and its interpretation domain D, we
define the domain $\mathcal{U}_D$, which is used to construct an intuitive interpretation for
intensional sets and set-based constraints (Section 3). We define a new language,
$CLP(\{\mathcal{D}\})$, where $\mathcal{D}$-constraints can be expressed, as well as arbitrarily nested
extensional and intensional sets of elements over $\mathcal{D}$ and constraints over these
entities. In this new framework the declarative style of constraint-based programming is enhanced by the availability of well-known set-based constructors. The

C. Palamidessi (Ed.): ICLP 2003, LNCS 2916, pp. 284–299, 2003.
© Springer-Verlag Berlin Heidelberg 2003

development of a semantics for $CLP(\{\mathcal{D}\})$ introduces problems analogous to those studied in the context of logic programming with aggregates. In Section 2 we explain the relationships between aggregates and intensional sets.

The semantic characterization of $CLP(\{\mathcal{D}\})$ (Section 4) is provided as a generalization of Gelfond and Lifschitz stable model semantics; this allows us to provide a semantics to a larger class of programs than various previously proposed schemes (e.g., [2,9])—in particular those relying on the use of stratification. E.g., a simple program such as

$$q(1). \qquad q(Z) \leftarrow Y = \{X \;:\; p(X)\} \wedge Z \in Y.$$
$$p(2). \qquad p(Z) \leftarrow Y = \{X \;:\; q(X)\} \wedge Z \in Y.$$

has the stable model $I = \{q(1), q(2), p(1), p(2)\}$, in spite of not being stratified.

In Section 5 we build on our previous research on constraint solving in presence of sets [6] to provide an incomplete solver for constraints of $CLP(\{\mathcal{D}\})$. The proposed solver simplifies constraints to a solved form. In particular, the main goal is to eliminate occurrences of intensional sets from the constraints *without* explicit enumeration of the sets. Some constraints between intensional sets are easily seen to be undecidable (e.g., $\{X : p(X)\} = \{X : q(X)\}$); this prevents us from developing a parametric and *complete* constraint solver. To address this issue we subdivide the constraint solving process in two phases. The first phase (*propagation*) consists of rewriting rules, that take advantage of the semantics of set operation to avoid the explicit computation of intensional sets. The second phase (*labeling*) forces the removal of intensional sets—via translation to formulae containing negation and/or explicit collection of solutions. The intuition is that, while propagation is transparently performed whenever possible, labeling should be explicitly requested—being a potentially unsafe and expensive step.

2 Related Work

A number of proposals have been made to support the introduction of aggregate functions in deductive databases and logic programming. Among them we discuss [14,21,19,18,4], where an *aggregate subgoal* is a constraint of the form

$$E = \mathbb{F}(\{\!\!| \; e[\bar{X}, \bar{Y}, \bar{Z}] \;:\; (\exists \bar{Z})\, p[\bar{X}, \bar{Y}, \bar{Z}] \; |\!\!\}) \tag{1}$$

whose intuitive semantics is: given values for the variables $\bar{Y}$ (grouping variables), collect in a multiset all the expressions involving $\bar{X}$ such that there are values for the variables $\bar{Z}$ (local variables) for which $p[\bar{X}, \bar{Y}, \bar{Z}]$ holds. The function $\mathbb{F}$ is finally applied to this multiset. The constraint aggregate (1) is written as: $E = \mathbb{F}e[\bar{X}, \bar{Y}, \bar{Z}] : p[\bar{X}, \bar{Y}, \bar{Z}]$ in [18], and as: group_by($p[\bar{X}, \bar{Y}, \bar{Z}], [\bar{Y}], E = \mathbb{F}(e[\bar{X}, \bar{Y}, \bar{Z}])$) in [14].

In this paper we consider a particular function $\mathbb{F}$: $\mathbb{F}(S)$ returns the set of all elements in the multiset S—i.e., it removes multiple occurrences of the same element. On one hand, this may appear as a simplification—there is no need to compute possibly complex functions. On the other hand, this leads to a number of complications. In particular, sets have to be introduced as first-class citizens of the language and, hence, they must be properly dealt with.

The work [18] provides a minimal model semantics for *monotonic* programs, i.e., programs for which the T_P operator is monotonic. However, monotonicity is in general undecidable, and the syntactic restrictions they impose to ensure it are rather strong. For instance, the program:

$$r(0). \quad r(1). \quad p(1, E) \leftarrow E = \text{MIN}\{X : r(X)\}.$$
$$s(1). \qquad\qquad p(1, E) \leftarrow E = \text{MIN}\{X : s(X)\}.$$

is not accepted—the argument of a predicate defined in terms of an aggregate is required to depend functionally on the other arguments (cost-consistency). Moreover, $\mathbb{F}$ can be only a simple function of the elements of the aggregate (such as SUM, MIN, MAX).

In [14] the authors introduce aggregate subgoals and they investigate both the 3-valued Well-Founded Semantics and the 2-valued Stable Model Semantics for programs containing aggregations. In [19] the authors investigate the problem of checking satisfiability for programs with aggregate subgoals when the function $\mathbb{F}$ is a simple *SQL aggregate function*. The well-founded and stable model semantics for logic programs with aggregates has been extended through the use of approximation theory in [4].

The work that comes closer in spirit to what we propose here is [21], where Van Gelder provides a treatment of aggregates based on the capability of expressing a collection (findall) of answers to a predicate. The idea is that the function $\mathcal{F}$ can be easily programmed on top of this aggregate capability. Similarly to [5, 2], Van Gelder shows how to program findall using negation. The definition of set-grouping can exploit the following intended semantics of intensional sets [8]:

$$\begin{aligned} E = \{X : p(X)\} &\leftrightarrow \forall X(X \in E \rightarrow p(X)) \land \forall X(p(X) \rightarrow X \in E) \\ &\leftrightarrow \forall X(X \in E \rightarrow p(X)) \land \neg \exists X(X \notin E \land p(X)). \end{aligned} \tag{2}$$

The first subformula can be computed (for finite sets) using a recursively defined predicate—this corresponds to what authors have called *restricted universal quantification* [6,15]—while the second subformula can be expressed as a negated predicate, whose single clause definition has $X \notin E \land p(X)$ as its body. Semantics is therefore reduced to the semantics of Prolog programs with negation. In [21] well-founded semantics is employed to handle negation in this framework, while in [8] a general form of constructive negation is used. This approach is very general. Nevertheless, the direct transformation approach used to handle aggregations via negation has drawbacks. Semantic characterization of negation in logic programming is fairly involved and it is not clear how it reflects on the corresponding meaning attributed to the aggregate constructs. Furthermore, if the desire is to allow a general use of sets as first-class citizens of the language, then one needs to explore the interactions between sets and negation—which are not straightforward [7]. Moreover, investigating the semantics of aggregation through translation to other constructs hampers the development of implementation techniques directly targeted to aggregation—especially implementations based on constraint solving and delaying techniques.

Our investigation builds on the existing work dedicated to the development of a *CLP* language over sets. The language $CLP(\mathcal{SET})$ [6] is an instance of the *CLP* framework, whose constraint domain is that of *hereditarily finite sets*. The language $CLP(\mathcal{SET})$ allows sets to be *nested* and *partially specified*, e.g., set elements can contain unbound variables and sets can be only partially enumerated. $CLP(\mathcal{SET})$ provides a collection of primitive constraint predicates sufficient to cover all the basic set-theoretic operations. In [6] we presented a complete constraint solver capable of deciding the satisfiability of arbitrary conjunctions of these primitive set constraints. Intensional sets are allowed, but they are rewritten [8] according to the technique sketched in formula (2). Moreover, $CLP(\mathcal{SET})$ does not interoperate with other constraints solvers.

3   Syntax

Following the notation of [12], let $\mathcal{D}$ be an arbitrary constraint domain and $\mathcal{C}_\mathcal{D}$ be the class of *admissible constraints* for $\mathcal{D}$. We assume that $\mathcal{C}_\mathcal{D}$ is closed under negation. The language we propose has a signature $\Sigma = \langle \Pi_\mathcal{S}, \Pi_\mathcal{D}, \Pi_\mathcal{P}, \mathcal{F}, \mathcal{V} \rangle$ ($\mathcal{S}$ stands for *Set*, $\mathcal{D}$ for *Domain*, and $\mathcal{P}$ for *Program*). Intuitively, $\Pi_\mathcal{S}$ provides constraint predicates to handle sets, $\Pi_\mathcal{D}$ provides the constraint predicates inherited from the underlying constraint domain $\mathcal{D}$, while $\Pi_\mathcal{P}$ contains the user-defined predicates. In particular, we assume that $\Pi_\mathcal{S}$ contains $\in, \cup_3, \cap_3, \subseteq, \|$ (these are the basic set predicates used in [6]). We also assume that $=$ is present in $\Pi_\mathcal{S} \cap \Pi_\mathcal{D}$. Furthermore, $\mathcal{F} = \mathcal{F}_\mathcal{S} \cup \mathcal{F}_\mathcal{D} \cup \mathcal{F}_\mathcal{P}$, where $\mathcal{F}_\mathcal{S}$ contains function symbols used to create set terms, $\mathcal{F}_\mathcal{D}$ contains the function symbols provided by the language of $\mathcal{D}$, and $\mathcal{F}_\mathcal{P}$ contains free function symbols. In particular $\emptyset$ and the binary set-constructor $\{\cdot \,|\, \cdot\}$ [6] are expected to be in $\mathcal{F}_\mathcal{S}$. The term $\{s \,|\, t\}$ denotes the set $\{s\} \cup t$. $\mathcal{F}$ and $\Pi_\mathcal{S}$ allow us to write terms and constraints regarding extensionally defined finite sets, such as $\emptyset, \{a, b\}, \{\emptyset, \{a, b\}\}$. The set $\mathcal{V}$ contains a countable number of variables, separated in the three sorts D, P, and S, described below.

Definition 1. *We allow three sorts* D, P, *and* S *for terms.*

- *For* $\mathcal{X} \in \{\mathcal{D}, \mathcal{P}, \mathcal{S}\}$, *constant symbols from* $\mathcal{F}_\mathcal{X}$ *are terms of sort* X.
- *We assume that function symbols from* $\mathcal{F}_\mathcal{D}$ *of arity n have the sort* $\mathsf{D}^n \longrightarrow \mathsf{D}$.
- *The sort of* $\{\cdot \,|\, \cdot\}$ *is* $(\mathsf{D} \cup \mathsf{P} \cup \mathsf{S}) \times \mathsf{S} \longrightarrow \mathsf{S}$.
- *The sort of a function symbol from* $\mathcal{F}_\mathcal{P}$ *of arity n is:* $(\mathsf{D} \cup \mathsf{P} \cup \mathsf{S})^n \longrightarrow \mathsf{P}$.

Definition 2. *Atoms are defined as follows:*

- *If* $p \in \Pi_\mathcal{P}$ *with arity n and* $t_1, \ldots, t_n$ *are terms (of any sort), then* $p(t_1, \ldots, t_n)$ *is a* $\mathcal{P}$-atom.
- *If* $p \in \Pi_\mathcal{D}$ *with arity n and* $t_1, \ldots, t_n$ *are terms of sort* D, *then* $p(t_1, \ldots, t_n)$ *is a domain constraint atom (or simply a* $\mathcal{D}$-atom*).*
- *If* $p \in \Pi_\mathcal{S}$ *with arity n and* $t_1, \ldots, t_n$ *are terms of sort* S, *then* $p(t_1, \ldots, t_n)$ *is a* $\mathcal{SET}$-constraint atom. *The only exception is represented by the symbol* $\in$: *if t is a term of any sort and s is a term of sort* S, *then* $t \in s$ *is a* $\mathcal{SET}$-constraint atom, *as well.*

- If $E \in \mathcal{V}$, $t_1, \ldots, t_n$ are terms and $p \in \Pi_{\mathcal{P}}$ with arity n, then $\{X : p(t_1, \ldots, t_n)\}$ is an intesional set and $E = \{X : p(t_1, \ldots, t_n)\}$ is an aggregate constraint atom. The sort of E is S.

A $\mathcal{S}$-atom is either an $\mathcal{SET}$-constraint or an aggregate constraint atom.

Observe that the aggregate constraint atom is exactly the constraint aggregate (1) where $\mathbb{F}$ is the function that removes duplicates from a multiset and the expression e is simply X. It is immediate to see that limiting our attention to this form of aggregation does not lead to any loss of generality. In particular, the variables indicated with $\bar{Y}$ in (1) can appear as arguments of $p(t_1 \ldots, t_n)$, while the local (existentially quantified) variables can be directly placed within the program rules defining p.

Definition 3. A $\mathcal{D}$-admissible constraint is any formula belonging to the class of constraints $\mathcal{C}_{\mathcal{D}}$.

A $\mathcal{S}$-admissible constraint is a propositional combination of $\mathcal{S}$-atoms. For the sake of simplicity we do not allow the use of negation applied to aggregate constraint atoms. Let us denote with $\mathcal{C}_{\mathcal{S}}$ the class of $\mathcal{S}$-admissible constraints.

A $\{\mathcal{D}\}$-admissible constraint is an arbitrary propositional composition of $\mathcal{D}$-admissible and $\mathcal{S}$-admissible constraints. We will denote with $\mathcal{C}_{\{\mathcal{D}\}}$ the class of all $\{\mathcal{D}\}$-admissible constraints.

Example 1. Assume that $\mathcal{D} = \mathbb{FD}$ is the constraint domain for *finite domain constraints*. Thus, constraints such as X in $1..5, Y$ in $2..4, X < Y$ belong to $\mathcal{C}_{\mathcal{D}}$. An example of $\{D\}$-admissible constraint is:

$$A \text{ in } 1..2, B \text{ in } 2..3, E = \{X : p(A, X, B)\}, K = \{A, E\}.$$

Definition 4. A $CLP(\{\mathcal{D}\})$ rule is a formula $H \leftarrow c_{\mathcal{S}}, c_{\mathcal{D}} | B_1, \ldots, B_n$ where

- $c_{\mathcal{D}}$ is a $\mathcal{D}$-admissible constraint,
- $c_{\mathcal{S}}$ is a $\mathcal{S}$-admissible constraint, and
- H is a $\mathcal{P}$-atom and $B_1, \ldots, B_n$ are $\mathcal{P}$-literals (i.e., positive or negated $\mathcal{P}$-atoms).

A $CLP(\{\mathcal{D}\})$ program P is a finite collection of $CLP(\{\mathcal{D}\})$ rules.

Example 2. Assume again that $\mathcal{D} = \mathbb{FD}$. The following is a $CLP(\{\mathcal{D}\})$ program:

$p(A, X, B) \leftarrow A < X, X < B.$
$\quad q(K) \leftarrow A \text{ in } 1..2, B \text{ in } 2..3, E = \{X : p(A, X, B)\}, K = \{A, E\} | p(A, Z, B).$

Let us observe that even if we accept any propositional combination, in our examples we will deal with conjunctions of $\{\mathcal{D}\}$-atomic constraints or negated atomic $\{\mathcal{D}\}$-constraints. Disjunctions can be removed by introducing new rules.

4   Semantics

In this section we provide the semantics for the language $CLP(\{\mathcal{D}\})$. In particular, we propose an interpretation of the aggregate constraint atoms based on a variation of stable model semantics [10]. A three-valued well-founded semantics can be also derived from the ideas provided in [21].

Let $\mathcal{D}$ be the initial domain constraint, D its interpretation domain, and I_D its interpretation function. We define the domain $\mathcal{U}_D = \bigcup_{i \geq 0} \mathcal{U}_i$ where:

$$\left\{ \begin{array}{l} \mathcal{U}_0 = D \\ \mathcal{U}_{i+1} = \mathcal{U}_i \cup \wp(\mathcal{U}_i) \cup \\ \qquad \{ c_{f(a_1,\ldots,a_n)} : a_1 \in \mathcal{U}_i, \ldots, a_n \in \mathcal{U}_i, f \in \mathcal{F}_\mathcal{P} \} \end{array} \right.$$

where for all f and $a_1, \ldots, a_n$, $c_{f(a_1,\ldots,a_n)}$ is a new object in the domain, different from all other objects. Observe that the Herbrand universe for $\mathcal{F}_\mathcal{P}$ and D are both contained in $\mathcal{U}_D$.

We will use the following partial order on $\mathcal{U}_D$: given two elements $a, b \in \mathcal{U}_D$: $a \leq b$ if and only if (1) $a, b \in D$ and $a = b$, or (2) a and b are sets and $a \subseteq b$, or (3) $a = c_{f(a_1,\ldots,a_n)}$ and $b = c_{g(b_1,\ldots,b_n)}$ and $f \equiv g, a_1 \leq b_1, \ldots, a_n \leq b_n$.

Stable model semantics for logic programs is defined for *ground* programs. In a *CLP* context, the notion of grounding has to be properly modified to accommodate for the properties of the selected interpretation domain.

Definition 5. *(Pre-interpretation) Let t be a term and $\sigma : vars(t) \mapsto \mathcal{U}_D$ be a valuation function that maps variables of sort D to elements in D, variables of sort S to elements in $\mathcal{U}_D \setminus \mathcal{U}_0$, and variables of sort P to elements in $\mathcal{U}_D$. Furthermore, let R be the map that associates to each element $f \in \mathcal{F}_P$ of arity k a k-ary function from $\mathcal{U}_D{}^k$ to $\mathcal{U}_D$. R is called the base of the pre-interpretation. The pre-interpretation $t^{R,\sigma}$ of a term t w.r.t. R, σ is defined as follows:*

- *If t is a variable, then $t^{R,\sigma}$ is $\sigma(t)$.*
- *If t is a constant of sort D, then $t^{R,\sigma} = t^\mathcal{D}$ (i.e., the standard interpretation of the constant in the constraint domain $\mathcal{D}$).*
- *If t is $f(t_1,\ldots,t_k)$ and $f \in \mathcal{F}_D$, then $t^{R,\sigma} = f^\mathcal{D}(t_1^{R,\sigma}, \ldots, t_k^{R,\sigma})$, where $f^\mathcal{D}$ is the standard interpretation of f in $\mathcal{D}$.*
- *If t is $f(t_1,\ldots,t_k)$ and $f \in \mathcal{F}_S$, then $t^{R,\sigma} = f^\mathcal{S}(t_1^{R,\sigma}, \ldots, t_k^{R,\sigma})$, where $f^\mathcal{S}$ is the standard set-theoretic interpretation of f. In particular,*
  * *If t is $\emptyset$, then $t^{R,\sigma}$ is the empty set.*
  * *If t is $\{a \mid b\}$, then $t^{R,\sigma}$ is the set $\{a^{R,\sigma}\} \cup b^{R,\sigma}$.*
- *If t is a constant in $\mathcal{F}_P$ then $t^{R,\sigma}$ is simply t^R.*
- *If t is $f(t_1,\ldots,t_k)$ and $f \in \mathcal{F}_P$ then $t^{R,\sigma} = f^R(t_1^{R,\sigma}, \ldots, t_k^{R,\sigma})$.*

In the rest of this discussion we will assume that the base R is fixed and in particular, that it interprets $f \in \mathcal{F}_P$ using the $c_{f(\cdot,\ldots,\cdot)}$ introduced in $\mathcal{U}_D$.

Definition 6. *(Grounding) Given an atom A and a pre-interpretation R, σ for the terms in A (where σ is defined for all variables in A), we define the notion of grounding of A w.r.t. R, σ as follows:*

- If $A = p(t_1, \ldots, t_n)$ is a $\mathcal{D}$-constraint atom, the grounding of $p(t_1, \ldots, t_n)$ w.r.t. R, σ is true if $\mathcal{D} \models p(t_1^{R,\sigma}, \ldots, t_n^{R,\sigma})$, false otherwise.
- If $A = p(t_1, \ldots, t_n)$ is a $\mathcal{SET}$-constraint atom, then the grounding of the atom w.r.t. R, σ is the atom true if $p^{\mathcal{U}_D}(t_1^{R,\sigma}, \ldots, t_n^{R,\sigma})$ is true (where $p^{\mathcal{U}_D}$ is the traditional set-theoretic interpretation of the predicate p on the domain $\mathcal{U}_D$), the atom false otherwise. In particular, given R and σ:
  - $\cup_3(s_1, s_2, s_3)$ is pre-interpreted as $s_3^{R,\sigma} = s_1^{R,\sigma} \cup s_2^{R,\sigma}$
  - $s \in t$ is pre-interpreted as $s^{R,\sigma} \in t^{R,\sigma}$
  - $s \subseteq t$ is pre-interpreted as $s^{R,\sigma} \subseteq t^{R,\sigma}$
  - $s || t$ is pre-interpreted as $s^{R,\sigma} \cap t^{R,\sigma} = \emptyset$
  - $\cap_3(s_1, s_2, s_3)$ is pre-interpreted as $s_3^{R,\sigma} = s_1^{R,\sigma} \cap s_2^{R,\sigma}$
- If $A = p(t_1, \ldots, t_n)$ is a $\mathcal{P}$-atom, then its grounding w.r.t. R, σ is the object $p(t_1^{R,\sigma}, \ldots, t_n^{R,\sigma})$.
- If A is an atom of the form $E = \{X : B\}$ and $B[X/X']$ is B with X renamed to X' (X' a new variable), then its grounding w.r.t. R, σ is the equality $E^{R,\sigma} = \{X' : B[X/X']^{R,\sigma}\}$.

Given an atom A and a pre-interpretation base R, a grounding of A w.r.t. R is a grounding of A w.r.t. R, σ for an arbitrary σ such that R, σ is a pre-interpretation for A. The notion of grounding can be extended to rules and to programs.

Let $I_D = \langle D, (\cdot)^D \rangle$ be the standard interpretation for the constraint domain $\mathcal{D}$.

Definition 7. An interpretation I is a pair $\langle \mathcal{U}_D, (\cdot)^I \rangle$, where the interpretation function $(\cdot)^I$ is defined as follows:

- I coincides with I_D on the interpretation of atoms built using $\mathcal{F}_D$ and Π_D.
- $\in, \subseteq, \cup_3$, and the other symbols in Π_S are interpreted in $\mathcal{U}_D$ according to their standard set-theoretical meaning.
- $=$ is interpreted as the identity over $\mathcal{U}_D$.
- $(\cdot)^I$ interprets each predicate symbol in Π_P as a predicate over $\mathcal{U}_D$.
- for each grounding R, σ of $E = \{X : B\}$, $(\cdot)^I$ interprets $(E = \{X : B\})^{R,\sigma}$ to true if $E^{R,\sigma}$ is equal to the set $\{X' : (B[X/X']^{R,\sigma})^I\}$ (where X' is a new variable), to false otherwise.

If the variable X does not occur in B, then the semantics of $\{X : B\}$ is the empty set if there is no σ s.t. $(B^{R,\sigma})^I$ is true; it is the universe $\mathcal{U}_D$ otherwise.

Example 3. Let A in 1..2 and B in 2..3 be two $\mathbb{FD}$ variables, R be an arbitrary base and $\sigma = \{A/2, B/3, E/\{2\}\}$ be a valuation function. The pre-interpretation $t^{R,\sigma}$ of the term $t \equiv \{X : p(A, X, B)\}$ is $\{2\} = \{X' : p(2, X', 3)\}$.

Let I and J be two interpretations on $\mathcal{U}_D$. We say that $I \preceq J$ if for each atom $P \equiv p(t_1, \ldots, t_n)$ and for each grounding R, σ of P there exists a an atom $Q \equiv p(s_1, \ldots, s_n)$ and a grounding R, θ of Q such that $(P^{R,\sigma})^I \rightarrow (Q^{R,\theta})^J$ and $(t_i^{R,\sigma})^I \leq (s_i^{R,\theta})^J$ for $i = 1, \ldots, n$. Given an atom P and a grounding R, σ of P, we define an interpretation I to be a *model* of $P^{R,\sigma}$ if $(P^{R,\sigma})^I$ is true. We denote this fact with $I \models P^{R,\sigma}$. Similarly, we can extend the definition of $\models$ to conjunctions of atoms. We define an interpretation I to be a *model* of a grounded rule $head \leftarrow c_{\mathcal{S}}, c_{\mathcal{D}} \mid body$ if $I \models c_{\mathcal{S}} \wedge c_{\mathcal{D}} \wedge body$ implies $I \models head$. I is a model of a rule if it is a model of each grounding of the rule.

Example 4. A model for the $CLP(\{\mathbb{FD}\})$ program of the Example 2 is
$$I = \{p(a, b, c) \; : \; a, b, c \in \mathsf{inf..sup}, a < b < c\} \cup \{q(\{1, \{2\}\})\}.$$
In this case D is the set of integer numbers between inf and sup.

4.1 Stable Model Semantics

Let P be a $CLP(\{\mathcal{D}\})$ program and let I be an interpretation (built on the pre-interpretation base R). Let P' contain all possible R, σ groundings of the rules in P. Following the principle used in [10], we define the intensional stable model transformation $G(P, I)$. The transformation is achieved in two steps, i.e., $G(P, I) = G_{set}(G_{neg}(P, I), I)$. The first transformation, G_{neg} is defined as follows: for each rule in P'
$$head \leftarrow c_{\mathcal{S}}, c_{\mathcal{D}} \mid A_1, \ldots, A_n, \neg B_1, \ldots, \neg B_m$$
if for all B_i, $1 \leq i \leq m$ we have that $I \models \neg B_i$, then the rule grounding
$$head \leftarrow c_{\mathcal{S}}, c_{\mathcal{D}} \mid A_1, \ldots, A_n$$
is added to $G_{neg}(P, I)$ (otherwise the rule is erased). Observe that $G_{neg}(P, I)$ is the grounding of a program without negation.

The transformation G_{set} is defined as follows; for each rule $head \leftarrow c_{\mathcal{S}}, c_{\mathcal{D}} \mid A_1, \ldots, A_n$ in $G_{neg}(P, I)$ (i.e., a grounding of a program rule without negation), if for all atoms A in $c_{\mathcal{S}}$ it holds that $I \models A$ then the rule
$$head \leftarrow c_{\mathcal{D}} \mid A_1, \ldots, A_n$$
is added to $G_{set}(G_{neg}(P, I), I)$ (otherwise the rule is erased). $G_{set}(G_{neg}(P, I), I)$ is the grounding of a program with neither negation nor set atoms.

Definition 8. *I is a* stable model *of P if I is the least $\mathcal{U}_D$-model of the program $G_{set}(G_{neg}(P, I), I)$.*

Example 5. Consider the program: $r(1). p(X) \leftarrow X = \{Y : r(Y)\}.$ and let us consider $G_{set}(P, I)$ for $I = \{r(1), p(\{1\})\}$. With $X = \emptyset$ the constraint aggregate becomes: $\emptyset = \{1\}$ which is an atom false in its interpretation in $\mathcal{U}_D$. This grounding is removed. The only true grounded clause is: $p(\{1\}) \leftarrow \{1\} = \{Y : r(Y)\}$. Thus, $G_{set}(G_{neg}(P, I), I) = \{r(1), p(\{1\})\}$. I is a stable model of P.

Proposition 1. *Let P be a $CLP(\{\mathcal{D}\})$ program.*

1. if I be a stable model of P, then I is a model of P.

2. if I is the unique stable model of P, then I is the $\preceq$-minimal model of P.

We cannot claim minimality in general. Consider:

$$
\begin{array}{lll}
r(1). & q(1). & \\
r(2). & q(2) \leftarrow Z = \{X : r(X)\}, p(Z). & p(Y) \leftarrow Y = \{X : q(X)\}.
\end{array}
$$

This program has two stable models: $I_1 = \{q(1), q(2), p(\{1, 2\}), r(1), r(2)\}$ and $I_2 = \{q(1), p(1), r(1), r(2)\}$. Observe that $I_1 \preceq I_2$. The fact that non-minimal models can be stable models is a common problem in the use of stable model semantics for handling of aggregates (without restrictions on aggregations) [14]. Similar problems are present for the limited set aggregations described in [17].

Example 6. Consider the program

$$r(1). \qquad\qquad p(X) \leftarrow q(X), s(X).$$
$$s(\{1\}). \qquad\qquad q(X) \leftarrow X = \{Y : r(Y)\}.$$

This program has the unique stable model: $\{r(1), s(\{1\}), q(\{1\}), p(\{1\})\}$.

Example 7. Simple recursive constructions may lead to infinite intensional sets. For example, consider the program

$$p(1). \qquad\qquad p(X) \leftarrow X = \{Y\}, p(Y).$$
$$q(X) \leftarrow X = \{Y : p(Y)\}.$$

The stable model contains: $\{p(1), p(\{1\}), p(\{\{1\}\}), \dots\}$. Additionally, it should contain $q(\{1, \{1\}, \{\{1\}\}, \dots\})$.

Example 8. Intensional definitions may also lead to situations that cannot be justified according to our treatment of intensional sets. E.g., the program
$$p(a). \qquad\qquad p(S) \leftarrow S = \{X : p(X)\}.$$
does not admit any stable model.

5   Constraint Solver

A $\{\mathcal{D}\}$-constraint (Def. 3) is a propositional combination of $\mathcal{D}$ and $\mathcal{S}$ constraints. In the language $CLP(\{\mathcal{D}\})$ we recognize different classes of constraints:

- $\mathcal{D}$-*constraints.* We assume that this class is decidable, and we denote with $\mathcal{SAT}_{\mathcal{D}}$ the procedure used to solve this class of constraints.
- *Extensional* $\mathcal{S}$-*constraints.* these are $\mathcal{S}$-constraints that do not involve any occurrence of intensional sets. This class of constraints is decidable and it corresponds to the class of constraints supported by the language $CLP(\mathcal{SET})$. In [6] an effective procedure to solve constraints in this class is proposed—we denote with $SAT_{\mathcal{SET}}$ such procedure. Traditional equality and disequality constraints between terms of the sort P are also treated in this procedure.
- *Intensional* $\mathcal{S}$-*constraints.* These are $\mathcal{S}$-constraints that contain occurrences of intensional sets (aggregate constraints). A procedure to handle this type of constraints is described in Sect. 5.1; we refer to this procedure as $SAT_{\mathcal{S}}$.

In order to accomplish the goal of resolving constraints in $CLP(\{\mathcal{D}\})$, we develop a constraint solver, called $\mathsf{Solve}_{\{\mathcal{D}\}}$. This solver repeatedly simplifies the constraint until no further simplifications are possible. The overall structure is shown in Fig. 1. Since constraint solvers can be non-deterministic, with

Solve$_{\{\mathcal{D}\}}(C)$:
repeat
    select c **in** C;
    if c *is a* $\mathcal{D}$*-constraint* **then** $c' = SAT_{\mathcal{D}}(c)$;
    if c *is an Extensional* $\mathcal{S}$*-constraint* **then** $c' = SAT_{\mathcal{SET}}(c)$;
    if c *is an Intensional* $\mathcal{S}$*-constraint* **then** $c' = SAT_{\mathcal{S}}(c)$;
    replace c **by** c' **in** C;
until *no rewriting is possible;*

Fig. 1. Overall structure of Solve$_{\{\mathcal{D}\}}$

$c' = SAT_{\mathcal{X}}(c)$ we mean *one* of the possible non-deterministic solutions returned. Thus, Solve$_{\{\mathcal{D}\}}(C)$ is a non-deterministic procedure. In addition, for a program P we also introduce another function, called Solvegoal$_P$. The predicate Solvegoal$_P$ applied to a $\mathcal{P}$-atom or formula means that the solving of its argument is delayed at the end of the constraint solving and it will be done by the general (constraint) resolution procedure. Let us observe that the non-deterministic result c of Solve$_{\{\mathcal{D}\}}(C)$ is the conjunction of a constraint with possibly some atoms Solvegoal$_P(G)$. At this time, the only requirement we impose is that: Solvegoal$_P(G) \Leftrightarrow G$. The intuition is that the Solvegoal$_P$ will encode the language mechanisms required to support the explicit removal of intensional sets—e.g., through the use of negation (as in Sect. 2).

In this section we develop constraint solvers for intensional constraints, showing the generality of some rewriting rules (propagation) and the difficulties introduced by other rewriting rules (labeling). We also discuss the cooperation between the three solvers. We allow intensional terms to occur freely as terms in programs—it is simple to transform a program into the flat form of Def. 4.

5.1   Propagation Procedures

In this subsection we present some rewriting rules for $\mathcal{S}$-constraints of $CLP(\{\mathcal{D}\})$ that can be easily implemented starting from any initial domain $\mathcal{D}$; these rules allow us to deal finitely with intensional sets (without any restriction on the finiteness of the intensional sets). The application of these rewriting rules to a $\mathcal{S}$-constraint C leads to a disjunction of constraints that is equisatisfiable to C. However, the rewriting rules are incomplete, since constraints obtained might be unsatisfiable, but unsatisfiability could be not detected right away. Thus, the behavior is not dissimilar from that of incomplete constraint solvers used in other CLP systems—e.g., arc and bound consistency employed in $\mathbb{FD}$-solvers (e.g., in SICStus Prolog) are insufficient to detect unsatisfiability of a constraint such as

$$X \text{ in } 1..2, Y \text{ in } 1..2, Z \text{ in } 1..2, X \neq Y, X \neq Z, Y \neq Z.$$

A complete constraint solver can be called into play by the user with a procedure analogous to the labeling used in $CLP(\mathbb{FD})$. We discuss this enhanced capability in the following subsection 5.2.

Some propagation rewriting rules are presented in Fig. 2. These rules are meant to complement the rewriting rules that have been proposed in our previous works to handle constraints over *extensionally defined sets*—due to lack of space we omit reproducing these rewriting rules [6,3]. We give only the rewriting rules for some of the predicates involved, in particular for those assumed primitive in [6] and $\subseteq$. No rules are needed for ψ_3 since the unique rule in [6] applies to intensional sets as well.

All the propagation rules presented in Fig. 2 do not actually compute the intensional sets—i.e., they do not force the explicit enumeration of the elements of the intensional set; thus, they can work without any assumption on the finiteness of these sets. Moreover, they do not introduce negation, but negated constraint literals that are treated as constraints—this can be seen, for example, in case $=$-2 in Fig. 2. In addition, some of the propagation rules are non-deterministic—see, for example, the case $\neq$-3. The presence of non-determinism leads to a family of formulas (consisting of constraints and $\mathsf{Solvegoal}_P$ atoms) that are returned at the end of the processing, whose disjunction is equisatisfiable to the initial constraint C. In the rewriting rules we also omit the explicit description of the steps used to verify violation of the sorts of the predicates (with the exception, for the sake of clarity, of the $=$-1 and $\neq$-1 cases).

We use some syntactic sugars in the rewriting rules. We make use of the notation $\{X : \varphi_1 \vee \varphi_2\}$ to represent $\{X : p(\bar{Y})\}$, where $\{\bar{Y}\} = FV(\varphi_1) \cup FV(\varphi_2)$ and p is defined as: $p(\bar{Y}) \leftarrow \varphi_1$. $p(\bar{Y}) \leftarrow \varphi_2$. Another syntactic sugar is $\mathsf{less}(X, Y, Z)$, defined as

$$\forall X, Y, Z (\mathsf{less}(X, Y, Z) \leftrightarrow Y = \{X \mid Z\} \wedge X \notin Z).$$

namely, Z is the set Y without the element X. Further rewriting rules for propagation can be easily defined; for instance,

$$\cap_3(\{X : \varphi_1\}, \{X : \varphi_2\}, s) \mapsto s = \{X : \varphi_1 \wedge \varphi_2\}$$

Other rewriting rules can be considered if we accept the use of negation. Negation is allowed in $CLP(\{\mathcal{D}\})$ programs. However, it is clear that it might introduce new problems. In particular, it introduces requirements on the capabilities of the $\mathcal{D}$ constraint solver to handle more difficult constraints. Observe that the rules in Fig. 3 produce a negated version of the property employed to construct the intensional set. It is important to observe that the interaction between the constraint solvers may actually facilitate the handling of negated constraints—e.g., by grounding its argument and thus making it easier to solve. Although the rules for $\notin$- and $\|$-constraints make use of negation, the intensional sets (that could be infinite) do not need to be explicitly generated (using the process described in equation (2) of Sect. 2).

Correctness and completeness of the rewriting rules are immediate consequences of the semantics of the set-based operators involved. These results can be formally proved in the theory *Set* [6], a minimal set theory that deals with $\emptyset, \{\cdot \mid \cdot\}, =, \in, \cup_3, \|$ (and also with $\cap_3$ and $\subseteq$, that can be easily defined in terms of the previous ones). The theory has to be extended by adding the well-known *comprehension scheme* of the ZF set theory

$$\forall s \forall y (y \in \{X \in s : \varphi[X]\} \leftrightarrow (y \in s \wedge \varphi[X/y])) \text{ for any f.o.f. } \varphi.$$

Condition '$X \in s$'—introduced by Zermelo in 1908—is used to overcome Russell's famous paradox (pick φ as $X \notin X$). In the syntax for intensional sets this condition is not required. We assume that $X \in \mathcal{U}_D$.

	=-constraints
=-1.	$\left.\begin{array}{l}\{X\,:\,\varphi\}=t\\ \mathsf{sort}(t)\neq\mathsf{S}\end{array}\right\}\mapsto\mathtt{false}$
=-2.	$\{X\,:\,\varphi\}=\{t\,\vert\,s\}\}\mapsto\begin{array}{l}(i)\;t\in\{X\,:\,\varphi\}\wedge\{X\,:\,(\varphi\wedge X\neq t)\}=s\\ (ii)\;t\in\{X\,:\,\varphi\}\wedge\{X\,:\,\varphi\}=s\end{array}$

	$\neq$-constraints
$\neq$-1.	$\left.\begin{array}{l}\{X\,:\,\varphi\}\neq t\\ \mathsf{sort}(t)\neq\mathsf{S}\end{array}\right\}\mapsto\mathtt{true}$
$\neq$-2.	$\{X\,:\,\varphi\}\neq\emptyset\mapsto\mathsf{Solvegoal}_P(\exists X\psi)$
$\neq$-3.	$\{X\,:\,\varphi_1\}\neq\{X\,:\,\varphi_2\}\mapsto\begin{array}{l}(i)\;Z\in\{X\,:\,\varphi_1\}\wedge Z\notin\{X\,:\,\varphi_2\}\\ (ii)\;Z\in\{X\,:\,\varphi_2\}\wedge Z\notin\{X\,:\,\varphi_1\}\end{array}$
$\neq$-4.	$\{X\,:\,\varphi\}\neq\{s\,\vert\,t\}\mapsto\begin{array}{l}(i)\;Z\in\{X\,:\,\varphi\}\wedge Z\notin\{s\,\vert\,t\}\\ (ii)\;Z\in\{s\,\vert\,t\}\wedge Z\notin\{X\,:\,\varphi\}\end{array}$

	$\in$-constraints
$\in$-1.	$t\in\{X\,:\,\varphi\}\mapsto\mathsf{Solvegoal}_P(\varphi[X/t])$

	$\cup_3$-constraints
$\cup_3$-1.	$\cup_3(\{X\,:\,\varphi\},\emptyset,s)\mapsto s=\{X\,:\,\varphi\}$
$\cup_3$-2.	$\cup_3(\{X\,:\,\varphi\},s,\emptyset)\mapsto\emptyset=\{X\,:\,\varphi\}\wedge\emptyset=s$
$\cup_3$-3.	$\cup_3(\{s\,\vert\,t\},r,\{X\,:\,\varphi\})\mapsto\begin{array}{l}s\in\{X\,:\,\varphi\}\wedge\mathsf{less}(s,\{s\,\vert\,t\},N)\wedge\\ \cup_3(N,r,\{X\,:\,\varphi\wedge X\neq s\})\end{array}$
$\cup_3$-4.	$\cup_3(\{X\,:\,\varphi_1\},\{X\,:\,\varphi_2\},s)\mapsto s=\{X\,:\,\varphi_1\vee\varphi_2\}$
$\cup_3$-5.	$\cup_3(\{X\,:\,\varphi_1\},r,\{X\,:\,\varphi_2\})\mapsto\begin{array}{l}r\subseteq\{X\,:\,\varphi_2\}\wedge\{X\,:\,\varphi_1\}\subseteq\{X\,:\,\varphi_2\}\wedge\\ \{X\,:\,\varphi_2\}\subseteq\{X\,:\,\varphi_1\vee X\in r\}\end{array}$
$\cup_3$-6.	$\cup_3(\{X\,:\,\varphi\},r,\{s\,\vert\,t\})\mapsto$ $\mathsf{less}(s,\{s\,\vert\,t\},N)\wedge$ $(i)\;s\in\{X\,:\,\varphi\}\wedge s\notin r\wedge\cup_3(\{X\,:\,\varphi\wedge X\neq s\},r,N)$ $(ii)\;s\in\{X\,:\,\varphi\}\wedge\mathsf{less}(s,r,N_1)\wedge\cup_3(\{X\,:\,\varphi\wedge X\neq s\},N_1,N)$ $(iii)\;s\notin\{X\,:\,\varphi\}\wedge\mathsf{less}(s,r,N_1)\wedge\cup_3(\{X\,:\,\varphi\},N_1,N)$

	$\|$-constraints
$\|$-1.	$\emptyset\|\{X\,:\,\varphi\}\mapsto\mathtt{true}$

	$\nparallel$-constraints
$\nparallel$-1.	$\emptyset\nparallel\{X\,:\,\varphi\}\mapsto\mathtt{false}$
$\nparallel$-2.	$\{X\,:\,\varphi\}\nparallel\{s\,\vert\,t\}\mapsto\begin{array}{l}(i)\;\mathsf{Solvegoal}_P(\varphi[X/s])\\ (ii)\;\mathsf{less}(s,\{s\,\vert\,t\},N)\wedge\{X\,:\,\varphi\}\nparallel N\end{array}$
$\nparallel$-3.	$\{X\,:\,\varphi\}\nparallel\{X\,:\,\psi\}\mapsto\mathsf{Solvegoal}_P(\exists X(\varphi\wedge\psi))$

	$\subseteq$-constraints
$\subseteq$-1.	$\emptyset\subseteq\{X\,:\,\varphi\}\mapsto\mathtt{true}$
$\subseteq$-2.	$\{X\,:\,\varphi\}\subseteq\emptyset\mapsto\emptyset=\{X\,:\,\varphi\}$
$\subseteq$-3.	$\{s\,\vert\,t\}\subseteq\{X\,:\,\varphi\}\mapsto s\in\{X\,:\,\varphi\}\wedge t\subseteq\{X\,:\,\varphi\}$
$\subseteq$-4.	$\{X\,:\,\varphi\}\subseteq\{s\,\vert\,t\}\mapsto\begin{array}{l}(i)\;s\in\{X\,:\,\varphi\}\wedge\mathsf{less}(s,\{s\,\vert\,t\},N)\wedge\\ \quad\{X\,:\,\varphi\wedge X\neq s\}\subseteq N\\ (ii)\;s\notin\{X\,:\,\varphi\}\wedge\mathsf{less}(s,\{s\,\vert\,t\},N)\wedge\\ \quad\{X\,:\,\varphi\}\subseteq N\end{array}$

Fig. 2. Propagation Rewriting Rules

With $c \in \mathsf{Solve}_{\{\mathcal{D}\}}(C)$ we mean one of the possible non-deterministic solutions returned by $\mathsf{Solve}_{\{\mathcal{D}\}}(C)$. Each of them is a conjunction of $\{\mathcal{D}\}$-constraints and $\mathsf{Solvegoal}_P$ atoms. In the second result, the introduction of negation requires to call into play the completion $\mathsf{comp}(P)$ of a program P.

Proposition 2. *(Non-negative Simplification) Let $\mathcal{C}_\mathcal{D}$ be a decidable class of $\mathcal{D}$-constraints; let $\mathsf{Solve}_{\{\mathcal{D}\}}$ be defined as in Fig. 1, with $SAT_\mathcal{S}$ composed of the rules in Fig. 2. Let C be a $CLP(\{\mathcal{D}\})$ constraint and P be a $CLP(\{\mathcal{D}\})$ program. Then $Set, \mathcal{D}, P \models \left(C \Leftrightarrow \bigvee_{c \in \mathsf{Solve}_{\{\mathcal{D}\}}(C)} c \right)$.*

Proposition 3. *(Negative Simplification) Let $\mathcal{C}_\mathcal{D}$ be a decidable class of $\mathcal{D}$-constraints; let $\mathsf{Solve}_{\{\mathcal{D}\}}$ be defined as in Fig. 1, with $SAT_\mathcal{S}$ composed of the rules in Fig. 2–3. Let C be a $CLP(\{\mathcal{D}\})$ constraint and P be a $CLP(\{\mathcal{D}\})$ program. Then $Set, \mathcal{D}, \mathsf{comp}(P) \models \left(C \Leftrightarrow \bigvee_{c \in \mathsf{Solve}_{\{\mathcal{D}\}}(C)} c \right)$.*

$\not\in$-constraints		
$\not\in$-1.	$t \notin \{X \ : \ \varphi\} \mapsto \mathsf{Solvegoal}_P(\neg\varphi[X/t])$	
‖-constraints		
‖-2. $\{X \ : \ \varphi\} \, \| \, \{X \ : \ \psi\} \mapsto$	$\mathsf{Solvegoal}_P\left(\exists X(\varphi \wedge \neg\psi) \vee \exists X(\neg\varphi \wedge \psi)) \right) \vee$ $\{X \ : \ \varphi\} = \emptyset \wedge \{X \ : \ \psi\} = \emptyset$	
‖-3.	$\{X \ : \ \varphi\} \, \| \, \{s \mid t\} \mapsto \mathsf{Solvegoal}_P(\neg\varphi[X/s]) \wedge \mathsf{less}(s, \{s \mid t\}, N) \wedge \{X \ : \ \varphi\} \, \| \, N$	

Fig. 3. Propagation with negation

5.2   Labeling

As mentioned in the previous subsection, the propagation rules allow us, given an original constraint C, to determine a disjunction of constraints that is equi-satisfiable to C. Each constraint belonging to the disjunction is "simpler" than C—e.g., it may contain fewer occurrences of intensional constraints. On the other hand, these rewriting rules do not constitute a complete solver—in particular, there is no guarantee that unsatisfiable constraints are reduced to `false` and tautologies are reduced to `true`. This situation makes the rewriting procedure weaker than, e.g., the procedures used in $CLP(\mathcal{SET})$, where each set constraint can be always reduced to `false` or to a satisfiable constraint in solved form.

In order to approximate a similar behavior in the context of $CLP(\{\mathcal{D}\})$ it is necessary to force the removal of intensional sets from the constraint. This process can be seen as a sort of *labeling* of the variables in the constraint. More in detail, intensional sets must be expanded (and, possibly, $\mathcal{D}$-constraints may have to be subjected to a similar transformation). We show in Fig. 4 how the labeling can be accomplished in the various cases left. See also the formula (2) for computing a single intensional sets. Observe that the right-hand side of the transformation can be encoded either through the use of negation or by introducing an explicit construct to collect solutions to a goal (e.g., `findall`). The additional rewriting rules satisfy the following properties:

- the new rules cannot guarantee completeness, as the problem we are trying to solve is undecidable in general (e.g., intensional sets build on properties with an infinite number of solutions);
- the rules rely on the ability to handle negated computations.

=-constraints	
=-3. $\{X : \varphi\} = \emptyset$	$\mapsto$ Solvegoal$_P(\neg(\exists X \varphi))$
=-4. $\{X : \varphi_1\} = \{X : \varphi_2\}$	$\mapsto$ Solvegoal$_P(\forall X(\varphi_1 \leftrightarrow \varphi_2))$

$\subseteq$-constraints	
$\subseteq$-5. $\{X : \varphi_1\} \subseteq \{X : \varphi_2\}$	$\mapsto$ Solvegoal$_P(\forall X(\varphi_1 \rightarrow \varphi_2))$

Fig. 4. Labeling using negation

5.3   Further Considerations

Negation handling in this context deserves special attention. Negation as failure in the context of a language with sets has been studied only for programs that are stratified and meet restrictive allowedness requirements to avoid floundering [2]. Constructive negation in the context of Constraint Logic Programming with Sets has been studied in [8]. However, the class of programs that can be dealt with successfully does not enlarge significantly the class of those that can be dealt with negation as failure and stratification.

We are currently investigating how these mechanisms can be employed in the context of *Answer Set Programming (ASP)* [16]. For instance, the negative reductions required in $\not\subseteq$-1 and $||$-2 of Fig. 3 can be encoded as ASP rules:

$\not\subseteq$-1.	$\leftarrow \varphi[t].$	
$||$-2.	$p_1 \mid p_2 \mid p_3 \leftarrow$	
	$q_1 \leftarrow dom_\varphi(X), dom_\psi(X), \varphi, not\ \psi.$	
	$q_2 \leftarrow dom_\varphi(X), dom_\psi(X), \psi, not\ \varphi.$	
	$\leftarrow p_1, not\ q_1.$	$\leftarrow p_2, not\ q_2.$
	$\leftarrow p_3, q_1.$	$\leftarrow p_3, q_2.$

where p_1, p_2, p_3, q_1, q_2 are brand new atoms. The predicates dom_φ and dom_ψ are domain predicates as required by smodels [17]. Similar constructions can be employed to handle rules =-3, =-4, and $\subseteq$-5:

=-3.	$p \leftarrow dom_\varphi(X), \varphi.$
	$\leftarrow p.$
=-4.	$\leftarrow \varphi_1, not\ \varphi_2.$
	$\leftarrow \varphi_2, not\ \varphi_1.$
$\subseteq$-5.	$\leftarrow \varphi_1, not\ \varphi_2.$

6   Conclusions

In this paper we presented preliminary ideas on how to extend any $CLP(\mathcal{D})$ language with set-based primitives and constraints. The novelty of the framework is not only the presence of intensional sets but the ability to develop (extensional and intensional) sets on top of arbitrary constraint domains $\mathcal{D}$. We developed a syntactic and semantics specification of the new language (called $CLP(\{\mathcal{D}\})$). We also developed rewriting algorithms to simplify constraints containing intensional sets—possibly relying on the use of negation.

In the immediate future we plan to effectively implement the technique at least for some largely used constraint domains, such as finite domain constraint. A preliminary result in this direction is [3] where the $CLP(\mathcal{SET})$ constraint solver is integrated with the $CLP(\mathbb{FD})$ constraint solver of SICStus Prolog. In this preliminary work intensional set constraints are allowed but currently solved via explicit enumeration.

Acknowledgments.   The work is partially supported by MIUR projects: *Automatic Aggregate—and number—Reasoning for Computing* and *Constraint-based Verification of Reactive systems* and NSF grants EIA-0220590, EIA-0130887, CCR-9875279, and CCR-9820852.

References

1. P. Arenas-Sánchez and M. Rodríguez-Artalejo. A General Framework for Lazy Funct'l Logic Programming with Algebraic Polymorphic Types. *TPLP*, 2(1), 2001.
2. C. Beeri, S. Naqvi, O. Shmueli, and S. Tsur. Set Constructors in a Logic Database Language. *Journal of Logic Programming*, 10(3):181–232, 1991.
3. A. Dal Palù, A. Dovier, E. Pontelli, and G. Rossi. Integrating Finite Domain Constraints and CLP with Sets. In *PPDP'03*, pp. 219–229. ACM Press, 2003.
4. M. Denecker et al. Ultimate well-founded and stable semantics for logic programs with aggregates. In *ICLP*, pp. 212–226. Springer, 2001.
5. A. Dovier, E. G. Omodeo, E. Pontelli, and G. Rossi. {log}: A Logic Programming Language with Finite Sets. In *ICLP*, pages 111–124. MIT Press, 1991.
6. A. Dovier, C. Piazza, E. Pontelli, and G. Rossi. Sets and Constraint Logic Programming. *ACM TOPLAS*, 22(5):861–931, 2000.
7. A. Dovier, E. Pontelli, and G. Rossi. A Necessary Condition for Constructive Negation in Constraint Logic Programming. *IPL*, 74(3-4):146–156, 2000.
8. A. Dovier, E. Pontelli, and G. Rossi. Constructive Negation and Constraint Logic Programming with Sets. *New Generation Computing*, 19(3):209–255, 2001.
9. M. Gelfond. Representing Knowledge in A-Prolog. In *Computational Logic: Logic Programming and Beyond*, pages 413–451. Springer Verlag, 2002.
10. M. Gelfond and V. Lifschitz. The stable model semantics for logic programming. In *JICSLP*, pages 1070–1080. MIT Press, 1988.
11. C. Gervet. Interval Propagation to Reason about Sets: Definition and Implementation of a Practical Language. *Constraints*, 1:191–246, 1997.
12. J. Jaffar and M. J. Maher. Constraint Logic Programming: A Survey. *Journal of Logic Programming*, 19–20:503–581, 1994.

13. B. Jayaraman. Implementation of Subset-Equational Programs. *Journal of Logic Programming*, 12(4):299–324, 1992.
14. D. B. Kemp and P. J. Stuckey. Semantics of Logic Programs with Aggregates. In *ILPS*, pages 387–401. MIT Press, 1991.
15. G. M. Kuper. Logic Programming with Sets. *JCSS*, 41(1):66–75, 1990.
16. V. W. Marek and M. Truszczyński. Stable Models and an Alternative Logic Programming Paradigm. In *The Logic Programming Paradigm*. Springer Verlag, 1999.
17. I. Niemela and P. Simons. Extending Smodels with Cardinality and Weight Constraints. In *Logic-Based Artificial Intelligence*, pp. 491–521. Kluwer, 2000.
18. K. A. Ross and Y. Sagiv. Monotonic Aggregation in Deductive Databases. *Journal of Computer ans System Science*, 54:79–97, 1997.
19. K. A. Ross, D. Srivastava, P. J. Stuckey, and S. Sudarshan. Foundations of aggregation constraints. *Theoretical Computer Science*, 193(1–2):149–179, 1998.
20. J. T. Schwartz, R. B. K. Dewar, E. Dubinsky, and E. Schonberg. *Programming with Sets: an Introduction to SETL*. Springer, 1986.
21. A. Van Gelder. The Well-Founded Semantics of Aggregation. In *11th Principles of Database Systems*, pages 127–138. ACM Press, 1992.

Implementing Constraint Propagation by Composition of Reductions*

Laurent Granvilliers and Eric Monfroy

IRIN – University of Nantes – France
2, rue de la Houssinière – BP 92208 – F-44322 Nantes cedex 3
{granvilliers,monfroy}@irin.univ-nantes.fr

Abstract. Constraint propagation is a general algorithmic approach for pruning the search space of a constraint satisfaction problem. In a uniform way, K. R. Apt [1] has defined computation as an iteration of reduction functions over a domain. In [2], he has also demonstrated the need for integrating static properties of reduction functions (commutativity and semi-commutativity) to design specialized algorithms such as AC3 and DAC. We introduce here a set of operators for modeling compositions of reduction functions in an iteration framework. Two of the major goals are to tackle parallel computations, and to manage dynamic behaviors such as slow convergences in numerical computations. An object-oriented software architecture is described using the Unified Modeling Language.

Keywords: Constraint propagation, chaotic iteration, dynamic strategy, composition, software architecture, design pattern.

1 Introduction

A Constraint Satisfaction Problem (CSP) is defined by a set of variables with their associated domains, and a set of constraints. Solving a CSP consists in finding assignments of variables that satisfy the constraints. Since this problem is NP-hard in general, preprocessing techniques have been implemented to prune domains before backtracking, such as filtering algorithms based on local consistency properties of subsets of constraints [25,17]. Constraint propagation is a generic term for these techniques.

Recently, K. R. Apt [1] has proposed a unified framework for constraint propagation. The solving process is defined as a chaotic iteration [6], which is an iteration of reduction functions over domains. Under well-chosen properties of domains (partial and well-founded ordering) and functions (monotonicity, contractance), iteration-based algorithms are shown to be terminating and confluent. In [2], further refinements have been devised in order to tackle propagation strategies based on additional properties of functions: an example is the arc-consistency algorithm AC3 that requires idempotence and commutativity of reduction functions. Hence, specializations of component functions of the generic

---

* This work has been supported by the IST project COCONUT of the European FP5 Programme.

C. Palamidessi (Ed.): ICLP 2003, LNCS 2916, pp. 300–314, 2003.

iteration algorithm have been implemented to tune the order of applications of functions in order to realize specific strategies.

In this paper, we propose a general algorithmic approach to tackle strategies that can be dynamically tuned with respect to the current state of constraint propagation. This objective led us to define the notion of composition operator. Basically, a composition operator models a sub-sequence of an iteration, in which the ordering of application of reduction functions is described by means of combinators for sequential, parallel or fixed-point computations. An iteration is then defined as a sequence of application of composition operators. The "good" properties of chaotic iterations, namely termination and confluence, are preserved. A generic iteration algorithm is easily defined, each step of it being an application of a new composition operator. This way, strategies are smoothly integrated in the model.

Composition operators are used to design and to implement well-known and efficient strategies: scheduling of constraints with respect to priorities in the finite domain solver Choco [14], cycle breaking to handle slow convergence arising in interval narrowing [16], efficient heuristics for interval narrowing [24], and distributed or parallel computations [19,11]. Essentially, these strategies take into account global information during propagation in order to tune the ordering of application of subsets of reduction functions. In this sense, the composition-based approach improves the chaotic iteration framework, in which only one function is applied at each step.

This general framework provides a good level of abstraction for designing an object-oriented architecture for constraint propagation. Composition can be handled by the Composite design pattern [8], which supports inheritance between elementary and compound reduction functions. The propagation mechanism uses the Listener pattern, which makes the connection between domain modifications and reinvocation of reduction functions. The generic propagation algorithm is implemented by the Strategy pattern, which allows one to parameterize parts of algorithms. Doing so, specific strategies are embedded in components that can be plugged in the generic algorithm, as proposed in [21,12]. We have implemented a prototype library. One of the main features is that solvers (reduction functions) are separated from constraints. This approach decreases the coupling of components. Furthermore, this is a good basis for cooperative strategies, in which different solvers may process the same constraints. We believe that this approach can be easily implemented in object-oriented systems like ILOG Solver [22].

The outline of this paper is the following. The constraint propagation framework is introduced in Section 2. Our new framework based on composition operators is described in Section 3. We conclude in Section 4.

2   Local Consistency Techniques

Let $\mathbb{S}$ be a nonempty set and let $\mathbb{D}$ be a subset of the powerset of $\mathbb{S}$, such that $(\mathbb{D}, \subseteq)$ is a well-founded partially ordered set in which every nonempty finite subset has a greatest lower bound. The ordering $\subseteq$ is set inclusion, the meet operation is set intersection, and $(\mathbb{D}, \subseteq)$ is called the computation domain. In practice, $\mathbb{S}$ may represent the set of integers, and $\mathbb{D}$ the set of ranges of integers.

Let $\mathcal{V} = \{x_1, \ldots, x_n\}$ be a finite set of variables taking their values in $\mathbb{S}$. Each variable x_i is associated with a domain of possible values $D_i \in \mathbb{D}$. A p-ary constraint $c(x_{i_1}, \ldots, x_{i_p})$ is defined as a subset of $\mathbb{S}^p$. Let $\text{Var}(c)$ denote the set of variables $\{x_{i_1}, \ldots, x_{i_p}\}$. Constraints are extended to $\mathbb{S}^n$ as follows.

$$c^+ = \{(a_1, \ldots, a_n) \in \mathbb{S}^n \mid (a_{i_1}, \ldots, a_{i_p}) \in c\}$$

In the following, the same notation will be used to denote a constraint c and its extension c^+. The i-th projection of c is defined as the set

$$\pi_i(c) = \{a_i \in \mathbb{S} \mid \exists (a_1, \ldots, a_{i-1}, a_{i+1}, \ldots, a_n) \in \mathbb{S}^{n-1} : (a_1, \ldots, a_n) \in c\}.$$

A Constraint Satisfaction Problem (CSP) is a tuple $\mathcal{P} = (\mathcal{V}, \mathcal{C}, D)$ where $D = (D_1, \ldots, D_n)$ is the vector of variable domains and $\mathcal{C} = \{c_1, \ldots, c_m\}$ is a finite set of constraints. The search space is the Cartesian product $D_1 \times \cdots \times D_n \subseteq \mathbb{S}^n$. A solution of $\mathcal{P}$ is an assignement of variables (a tuple from the search space) such that all the constraints are satisfied.

2.1 Local Consistency

The general technique for solving CSPs is a process of trials and errors called backtracking. A backtracking algorithm creates a search tree whose nodes contain partial assignements of the set of variables. In order to accelerate backtracking, pruning methods of the search space such as local consistency techniques have been proposed.

Different levels of consistency have been defined. The strongest level corresponds to the notion of global consistency: a CSP is globally consistent if each domain D_i for $i = 1, \ldots, n$ corresponds to the i-th projection of the solution set of the CSP. In general, weaker properties are implemented, such as instances of k-consistency [7] for discrete domains or kB-consistency [15] for continuous domains. In practice, the most often used ones are arc-consistency [17] or related approximations [4].

Definition 1 (arc-consistency). *Let c be a constraint and let $i \in \{1, \ldots, n\}$ be a natural. The i-th projection of c is arc-consistent if*

$$D_i = \pi_i(c \cap D_1 \times \cdots \times D_n).$$

In other words, for all $a_i \in D_i$ and for all $j \in \{1, \ldots, i-1, i+1, \ldots, n\}$, there exists $a_j \in D_j$ such that $(a_1, \ldots, a_n) \in c$. The tuple $(a_1, \ldots, a_{i-1}, a_{i+1}, \ldots, a_n)$ is called a value support of a_i w.r.t. c.

Domain filtering consists in removing locally inconsistent values from domains. More precisely, given a variable x_i and a constraint c_j, all values from D_i having no support w.r.t. c_j can be eliminated. The `AC3revise` function implements filterings for arc-consistency, as follows.

$$\texttt{AC3revise}(c_j, i, D) = (D_1, \ldots, D_{i-1}, \pi_i(c_j \cap D_1 \times \cdots \times D_n), D_{i+1}, \ldots, D_n)$$

Given a CSP, filterings can be applied over constraint projections until a fixed-point is reached, using a constraint propagation algorithm. The resulting CSP is said to be maximally arc-consistent: the output domains are the greatest arc-consistent domains included in the input domains. Several constraint propagation strategies have been proposed, such as AC3 [17] and AC4-like algorithms [5] using data structures for support memorizations. Since AC4 cannot be extended to continuous domains in a tractable manner, only AC3 is implemented for numeric CSPs (numeric constraints and interval domains).

2.2   Constraint Propagation

Several abstract models of local consistency techniques have been defined, for instance in [20,3]. In the following, we use the chaotic iteration formalism [2]. In this framework, domain reductions are seen as applications of monotonic functions (called reduction functions) on variable domains.

Definition 2 (reduction function). *Consider a function f on $\mathbb{D}^n$.*

- *f is contracting if $\forall D \in \mathbb{D}^n$, $f(D) \subseteq D$;*
- *f is monotonic if $\forall D, D' \in \mathbb{D}^n$, $D \subseteq D' \Rightarrow f(D) \subseteq f(D')$.*

A reduction function is a contracting and monotonic function on $\mathbb{D}^n$.

For instance, given some variable x_i occurring in constraint c_j, the function

$$\texttt{AC3revise}[i,j] : \ D \mapsto \texttt{AC3revise}(c_j, i, D)$$

is a reduction function, which can be used to narrow down the i-th component of D. Observe that this operator is also idempotent (two consecutive applications are useless). In the lattice theory, such operators are called closures. In the following, we consider a finite set of reduction functions $F = \{f_1, \ldots, f_k\}$ on $\mathbb{D}^n$.

Definition 3 (Iteration). *Given an element $D \in \mathbb{D}^n$, an iteration of F over D is an infinite sequence of values $D^0, D^1, \ldots$ defined inductively by:*

$$D^0 := D$$
$$D^i := f_{j_i}(D^{i-1}) \quad i \geqslant 1$$

where j_i is an element of $[1, \ldots, k]$. A sequence $D^0 \supseteq D^1 \supseteq \cdots$ of elements from $\mathbb{D}^n$ stabilizes at E if for some $j \geqslant 0$, we have $D^i = E$ for $i \geqslant j$.

In this framework, the following stabilization lemma holds.

Lemma 1. *Suppose that an iteration of F over D stabilizes at a common fixed-point E of the functions from F. Then, $E = (\cap_{i=1}^k f_i) \uparrow \omega(D)$ is the greatest common fixed-point of the functions from F that is included in D.*

Proof. See [2]. It follows from the monotonicity of the reduction functions.

Table 1. Generic Constraint Propagation Algorithm

function GI $(F = \{f_1, \ldots, f_k\}, D = (D_1, \ldots, D_n))$: $\mathbb{D}^n$
begin
   $G := F$
   while $G \neq \varnothing$ **do**
      choose $g \in G$
      $G := G - \{g\}$
      $G := G \cup \text{update}(G, g, D)$
      $D := g(D)$
   od
   return D
end

    where for all G, g, D the set of functions $\text{update}\,(G, g, D)$ is such that
    A. $\{f \in F - G \mid f(D) = D \ \wedge \ f(g(D)) \neq g(D)\} \subseteq \text{update}\,(G, g, D)$
    B. $g(D) = D$ implies that $\text{update}\,(G, g, D) = \varnothing$
    C. $g(g(D)) \neq g(D)$ implies that $g \in \text{update}\,(G, g, D)$

The generic iteration algorithm defined in [2] is given in Table 1. The input is a set of reduction functions and a tuple of domains. The loop invariant states that the current domain is a fixed-point of every function not in the propagation set G. The correctness of GI is stated by Theorem 1.

Theorem 1. *Every execution of* GI *terminates and computes in* D *the greatest common fixed-point of the functions from* F.

Proof. See [2]. It follows from the monotonicity and contractance of the reduction functions, and the well-foundedness of the computation domain.

Given a CSP $(\mathcal{V}, D, \mathcal{C})$, AC3-like algorithms for arc-consistency corresponds to GI(F, D) where the set of reduction functions is defined by

$$F = \{\text{AC3revise}[i, j] \mid \exists x_i \in \mathcal{V}, \ \exists c_j \in \mathcal{C}, \ x_i \in \text{Var}(c_j)\}.$$

A consequence of this definition of AC3 is that maximal consistency corresponds to the computation of some greatest fixed-point.

2.3   Some Constraint Propagation Strategies

AC3-like algorithms are heavily used to tackle discrete or continuous CSPs. In the following, we describe specific strategies improving the standard strategy where the choose function of the GI algorithm just considers a queue of reduction functions. They are not only based on static properties of reduction functions, but on dynamic behaviours of the propagation algorithm.

Priorities. Choco is a constraint programming system for finite domains [14]. The core algorithm is constraint propagation, whose main feature is to process constraints according to the complexity in time of their associated reduction algorithms. A fixed-point of the set of reduction functions is computed as a sequence of layered fixed-points of subsets of reduction functions. The application of functions of a given priority requires that all the functions having higher priorities are asleep.

The solving engine of Numerica [24] is based on constraint propagation for interval domains using box-consistency [4], which is a safe approximation of arc-consistency. The strategy applies first reduction functions for box-consistency, and then an algorithm from linear algebra which takes as input a relaxation of the CSP.

Acceleration of Interval Narrowing. Constraint propagation with interval domains (interval narrowing) is inefficient if slow convergence happens. A slow convergence corresponds to a cycle of reduction functions $f_i \ldots f_j \ldots f_i$ such that each application only deletes a small part of a domain. This problem is often due to singularities or points of tangency associated with nonlinear constraints. O. Lhomme et al. [16] have devised an efficient strategy based on cycle detection and simplification. The aim is to locally select and apply the best reduction functions while delaying some active functions supposed to slow the computation.

Distributed/Parallel Scheme. Parallel processing of numerical problems via interval constraints has been proposed as a general framework for high-performance numerical computation in [13]. A basic strategy consists in creating a partition of the propagation structure $G = G_1 \cup \cdots \cup G_k$, k depending on the number of processors. Then iterations are performed componentwise on processors. Nevertheless, it has been observed that the classical notion of parallel speed-up is not a correct measure of success for such algorithms. This is due to a parallel decoupling phenomenon: convergence may be faster when two interval contractions are applied in sequence than in parallel. As a consequence, a parallel version of Lhomme's strategy has been proposed in [11]. Essentially, parallelism is only used to select the best functions.

Distributed constraint propagation [19] operationally consists in distributing reduction functions among sites, performing local computations, and then accumulating and intersecting new domains.

3   Composition-Based Constraint Propagation

In the following, we describe a new chaotic iteration framework based on composition of reduction functions. Then we show how to implement well-known strategies hardcoded in constraint solvers. An object-oriented software architecture is then introduced.

3.1   Framework

Consider a finite set of functions $F = \{f_1, \ldots, f_k\}$ on $\mathbb{D}^n$. We introduce a set of composition operations on F as follows.

$$
\begin{array}{lll}
\text{Sequence:} & F^\circ & \text{denotes the function} \quad \mathrm{D} \mapsto f_1 f_2 \ldots f_k(\mathrm{D}) \\
\text{Closure:} & F^\omega & \text{\textemdash} \qquad\qquad\qquad\quad \mathrm{D} \mapsto (\cap_{i=1}^k f_i) \!\uparrow\! \omega(\mathrm{D}) \\
\text{Decoupling:} & F^\cap & \text{\textemdash} \qquad\qquad\qquad\quad \mathrm{D} \mapsto f_1(\mathrm{D}) \cap \cdots \cap f_k(\mathrm{D})
\end{array}
$$

Note that F is supposed to be ordered since the sequence operation is not commutative. This assumption is no longer necessary for the closure and decoupling operations since the intersection operation is commutative. There are several motivations for introducing such operations in a generic propagation framework:

- The sequence operation fixes the order of application of the reduction functions. It can be used for computing directional arc-consistency based on the semi-commutativity property, for modeling priorities of solvers, and for implementing heuristics or knowledge of solvers about their relative efficiencies.
- The closure operation allows us to make a closure from a non idempotent function, and to describe multi-level algorithms which compute fixed-points of different solvers.
- The decoupling operation is essentially used to model parallel computations, enforcing different functions over the same domain, and then computing the intersection using a fold reduction step.

The notion of composition operator models a function (a complex solver) built from composition operations.

Definition 4 (Composition operator). *Let $F = \{f_1, \ldots, f_k\}$ be a finite set of reduction functions. A composition operator on F is a function $\mathbb{D}^n \to \mathbb{D}^n$ defined by induction as follows. Suppose that Φ is a finite set of composition operators on F.*

$$
\begin{array}{lll}
\text{Atomic:} & f_i & \text{is a composition operator} \quad (i = 1, \ldots, k) \\
\text{Sequence:} & \Phi^\circ & \text{is a composition operator} \\
\text{Closure:} & \Phi^\omega & \text{\textemdash} \\
\text{Decoupling:} & \Phi^\cap & \text{\textemdash}
\end{array}
$$

The generator $\mathsf{Gen}(\phi)$ of a composition operator ϕ on F is the subset of functions from F that are "involved" in ϕ. It is defined inductively as follows.

- $\mathsf{Gen}(\phi) = \{\phi\}$ *if ϕ is an atomic operator from F*
- $\mathsf{Gen}(\phi) = \mathsf{Gen}(\phi_1) \cup \cdots \cup \mathsf{Gen}(\phi_k)$ *if $\phi = \{\phi_1, \ldots, \phi_k\}^\star$ for $\star \in \{\circ, \omega, \cap\}$*

Lemma 2 states that a composition operator is also a reduction function.

Lemma 2. *Consider a finite set of reduction functions $F = \{f_1, \ldots, f_k\}$. Then, every composition operator on F is (i) contracting, and (ii) monotonic.*

Proof. The proof is done by induction. Every atomic operator is contracting and monotonic by definition of a reduction function. Now consider a set $\Phi = \{\phi_1, \ldots, \phi_k\}$ of contracting and monotonic composition operators.

(i) By hypothesis the composition operators from Φ are contracting. Then it is immediate to prove the contractance of Φ°, Φ^ω, and $\Phi^\cap$.

(ii) Given $X, Y \in \mathbb{D}^n$ suppose that $X \subseteq Y$.
- *Since every ϕ_i is supposed to be monotonic, then, we have $\phi_k(X) \subseteq \phi_k(Y)$, and then, $\phi_{k-1}\phi_k(X) \subseteq \phi_{k-1}\phi_k(Y)$, and so on. It follows that Φ° is monotonic.*
- *In order to prove the monotonicity of Φ^ω, we consider the function $\varphi : \cap_{i=1}^k \phi_i$. Then, we prove that φ is monotonic (third item). It follows that $\varphi \uparrow \omega(X) \subseteq \varphi \uparrow \omega(Y)$. Then it is immediate to prove by a double inclusion that the set of fixed-points of φ coincides with the set of common fixed-points of the functions from Φ. As a consequence, we have $\varphi \uparrow \omega \equiv \Phi^\omega$, that completes the proof.*
- *For $i = 1, \ldots, k$, we have $\phi_i(X) \subseteq \phi_i(Y)$ by monotonicity of ϕ_i. It follows that $\cap_{i=1}^k \phi_i(X) \subseteq \cap_{i=1}^k \phi_i(Y)$, that ends the proof.*

Lemma 3 states that a fixed-point of a composition operator is a common fixed-point of the functions from its generator. The key idea is that the application of a composition operator implies that each reduction function in its generator is applied at least once. This property can be used to tune the update phase of iteration algorithms. Computing a fixed-point of a composition operator implies that all the functions from the generator become useless.

Lemma 3. *Consider a finite set of reduction functions F and a composition operator ϕ on F. Then, E is a fixed-point of ϕ if and only if E is a common fixed-point of the functions from $\mathtt{Gen}(\phi)$.*

Proof. We prove by induction the equivalence $\phi(E) = E \Leftrightarrow \forall f \in \mathtt{Gen}(\phi)\; f(E) = E$. It obviously holds for an atomic operator ϕ. Now consider a set of composition operators $\Phi = \{\phi_1, \ldots, \phi_k\}$ on F and assume that the equivalence holds for each $\phi_1, \ldots, \phi_k$. If we have $\phi \equiv \Phi^\star$ for $\star \in \{\circ, \omega, \cap\}$, then it follows:

$$\phi(E) = E \Leftrightarrow \forall i \in \{1, \ldots, k\}\; \phi_i(E) = E \qquad \text{(immediate result)}$$
$$\Leftrightarrow \forall i \in \{1, \ldots, k\}\; \forall f \in \mathtt{Gen}(\phi_i)\; f(E) = E \text{ (induction hypothesis)}$$

Considering $\mathtt{Gen}(\phi) = \cup_i \mathtt{Gen}(\phi_i)$ completes the proof.

Now the notion of iteration is slightly extended to deal with composition operators instead of reduction functions.

Definition 5 (Iteration). *Consider a finite set of reduction functions F, and a finite set $\Phi = \{\phi_1, \ldots, \phi_k\}$ of composition operators on F. Given an element $D \in \mathbb{D}^n$, an iteration of Φ over D is an infinite sequence of values $D^0, D^1, \ldots$ defined inductively by:*

$$D^0 := D$$
$$D^i := \phi_{j_i}(D^{i-1}) \quad i \geqslant 1$$

where j_i is an element of $[1, \ldots, k]$.

Lemma 1 (Apt's stabilization lemma) remains valid, that follows from the monotonicity of the composition operators (Lemma 2). Moreover, we have the following, essential result.

Lemma 4. *If an iteration on $\Phi = \{\phi_1, \ldots, \phi_k\}$ over D stabilizes at a common fixed-point E of the functions from Φ, and $F = \cup_i \text{Gen}(\phi_i)$, then $E = F^\omega(D)$.*

Proof. We first prove that E is a common fixed-point of the functions from F. By hypothesis E is a fixed-point of each $\phi_i \in \Phi$. By Lemma 3, it follows that $f(E) = E$ for each $f \in \text{Gen}(\phi_i)$. The proof is completed since, by hypothesis, the set of generators covers F.

We prove now that E is the greatest common fixed-point of the functions from F. Consider a common fixed-point E' of the functions from F. It suffices to prove that E' is included in every element from the iteration, namely $D^0, D^1, \ldots$ It obviously holds for $i = 0$. Suppose now it holds for i, i.e., $E' \subseteq D^i$, and assume that $D^{i+1} = \phi_j(D^i)$ for some $j \in [1, \ldots, k]$. By monotonicity of ϕ_j, we have $\phi_j(E') \subseteq \phi_j(D^i)$. By Lemma 3, we have $\phi_j(E') = E'$, that completes the proof.

Table 2. Generic Iteration Algorithm based on Composition Operators

function CompoundGI $(F = \{f_1, \ldots, f_k\}, D = (D_1, \ldots, D_n))$: $\mathbb{D}^n$
begin
   $G := F$
   while $G \neq \varnothing$ **do**
      $\phi :=$ **create a composition operator on a nonempty subset of** G
      $G := G - \text{Gen}(\phi)$
      $G := G \cup \text{update}(G, \phi, D)$
      $D := \phi(D)$
   od
   return D
end

where for all G, ϕ, D the set of functions $\text{update}(G, \phi, D)$ is such that
A. $\text{upA} := \{f \in F - G \mid f(D) = D \wedge f\phi(D) \neq \phi(D)\} \subseteq \text{update}(G, \phi, D)$
B. $\text{upB} := \phi(D) = D$ implies that $\text{update}(G, \phi, D) = \varnothing$
C. $\text{upC} := \{f \in \text{Gen}(\phi) \mid f\phi(D) \neq \phi(D)\} \subseteq \text{update}(G, \phi, D)$

We describe in Table 2 the generic iteration algorithm CompoundGI, which is based on composition operators on a finite set of reduction functions F. Note that the set of composition operators is not fixed, since each operator is dynamically created from the set G of active reduction functions, and it is applied only once. Theorem 2 proves the correctness of CompoundGI with respect to F.

Theorem 2. *Every execution of* CompoundGI *terminates and computes in D the greatest common fixed-point of the functions from F.*

Proof. The proof is a direct adaptation of Apt's [2]. To prove termination, it suffices to prove that the pair $(\mathrm{D}, \#G)$ strictly decreases in some sense at each iteration of the `while` loop, and to note that the ordering $\subseteq$ is well-founded.

The correctness is implied by the invariant of the `while` loop: $f \in F - G$ implies $f(\mathrm{D}) = \mathrm{D}$. It follows that the final domain is a common fixed-point of the functions from F (since $G = \varnothing$). The second part of the proof of Lemma 4 ensures that it is the greatest one included in the initial domain.

The following corollary concerns the update after an application of a closure operator in algorithm `CompoundGI`.

Corollary 1. *Consider operator ϕ that is applied in algorithm* `CompoundGI`. *If ϕ is idempotent, then assumption C is reduced to* "`upC := ` $\varnothing$".

Proof. See Apt [2].

3.2   Implementation of Strategies

In the following, we show how the strategies described in Section 2.3 can be implemented using composition operators. Furthermore new strategies are easily designed, for instance a strategy that decreases updating costs.

Priorities. Implementing the propagation engine of Choco using Algorithm `CompoundGI` can be done by considering priorities of reduction functions. Composition operators are dynamically generated as follows:

$$\phi := \{g \in G \mid priority(g) = \alpha\}^{\omega} \quad \text{s.t.} \quad \alpha = \min(\{priority(g) \mid g \in G\})$$

The composition is a closure of the set of active reduction functions with the greatest priority (the computationally less expensive functions). Note that Corollary 1 applies for the `update` function.

We propose a second operational model improving the one of Choco. The corresponding algorithm implements a sequence of closures, each closure processing the set of functions of a given priority. Priorities are ordered in increasing ordering.

$$\phi := (G_1^{\omega} \cup \cdots \cup G_p^{\omega})^{\circ} \quad \text{s.t.} \quad \begin{cases} G_1, \ldots, G_p \text{ is a partition of } G \\ \forall i \in [1, \ldots, p], \forall g \in G_i, priority(g) = \alpha_i \\ \alpha_p < \alpha_{p-1} < \cdots < \alpha_1 \end{cases}$$

There are two differences with respect to the first method. First, a function with low priority can be applied even if another function with high priority is active. Second, there is no update between closures since they are embedded in a sequence operator. We have first observed that this strategy decreases costs for updating propagation structures. In particular, a gain of one half has been observed for interval-based consistencies [10]. Another reason for improvement may be that efficient functions, even if they are computationally expensive, are not too much delayed (diversification).

Acceleration of Interval Narrowing. The aim is to break cycles in iterations from which are extracted the best functions, and independent functions to be delayed. In [16], this strategy has been shown to be very efficient for handling slow convergences. Two reductions functions f and g are independent if $\forall D \in \mathbb{D}^n$, $fg(D) = gf(D)$ and $gf(D) = g(D) \cap f(D)$. Given a cycle, that is a set of functions $G' = \{f_{i_1}, \ldots, f_{i_k}\} \subseteq G$ such that the sequence $f_{i_1}, \ldots, f_{i_k}$ has been computed several times consecutively, the solving process using `CompoundGI` consists in creating two sets of functions:

- The set G'_1 of best functions. For each variable whose domain can be modified by a function from G', the function that reduced it the most is added in G'_1.
- The set G'_2 of independent functions. All the functions from $G' - G'_1$ which are independent from all the functions from G'_1 are added in G'_2.

Doing so the strategy is the following:

$$\phi := \left(G'^{\,\omega}_1 \cup G'^{\,\circ}_2\right)^{\circ}$$

The best functions are applied until a fixed-point is reached. Then the delayed functions are applied using a sequence operator. Note that cycle detection needs memorizing the iteration.

Parallel Scheme. The decoupling operator can be used to implement parallel constraint propagation. A basic strategy is to create a partition of the propagation structure $G = G_1 \cup \cdots \cup G_k$, k depending on the number of processors, and to consider operator ϕ to be applied in Algorithm `CompoundGI`:

$$\phi := G^{\circ}_1 \cap \cdots \cap G^{\circ}_k$$

Moreover, if one wants to perform more local computations before synchronization and communication, a closure can be computed on each processor as follows:

$$\phi := G^{\omega}_1 \cap \cdots \cap G^{\omega}_k$$

3.3   Software Architecture

The composition-based framework can be implemented using design patterns [8]. A design pattern handles a general design problem in object-oriented software within a particular context. More precisely, this is a recurring structure of communicating objects. Recall that in class diagrams of UML rectangles may represent classes and arrows ended by white triangle model inheritance relations. Abstract classes, of which one method cannot be implemented, are written in italic. Plus and minus symbols represent public and private accesses.

The proposed architecture in the UML syntax is depicted in Figure 1. The abstract classes `Function` and `Composition` respectively implement reduction functions and composition operators. Every function has a priority, which may represent some inverse of the complexity in time, and is associated to a vector of constraints from which it has been created. Every composition operator (composite object) has a nonempty vector of reduction functions. Furthermore, this class inherits from `Function`, which just corresponds to the definition by induction of composition operators. The other classes are concrete since they all implement the reduction algorithm (method `algoReduce`). Specific functions represent atomic functions such as `AC3revise`. Classes derived from the composition operator class define the specific composition strategies.

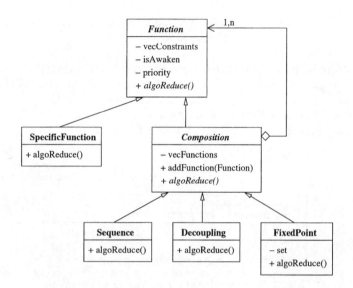

Fig. 1. UML Diagram of Classes using the Composite Design Pattern

The fixed-point reduction algorithm is of interest since it allows one to illustrate the message passing procedure between variables and reduction functions. When the `algoReduce` method is called, all the reduction functions from the base class attribute `vecFunctions` are declared awaken, and then added in the propagation set (in general, a queue). The rest of the algorithm is a while loop until either the propagation set becomes empty, or a reduction fails. An iteration of the loop consists in extracting a reduction function from the propagation set and applying it. Updating the set needs managing a dependency relation between variable events such as domain modifications, and reduction functions. In practice, a reduction function has to be reinvoked if the domain of a variable of an associated constraint is modified, and consequently propagation structures have to be updated.

The Listener pattern helps implementing event-based relations between objects. The structure of the dependency relation is illustrated in Figure 2. Every variable manages a set of listeners, here reduction functions. Every domain listener has to be declared to variables using the `onDomain` method. Specific functions have the responsibility to call `onDomain` on all the variables they depend on. Finally, listeners are notified by the `whenDomain` method each time a modification of domain happens.

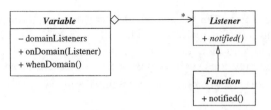

Fig. 2. Listeners of Variable Domain Events

When a reduction function f is notified, then there are two effects. First, f becomes awaken. Second, f is added in structures of more general algorithms, for instance in sets of closure composition operators ϕ such that $f \in \text{Gen}(\phi)$. For this purpose, it suffices that f knows the set of such functions ϕ. This way, the message passing between objects is shown in Figure 3.

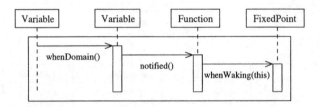

Fig. 3. Sequence Diagram of Waking of Functions

In this architecture, Algorithm `CompoundGI` is a kind of composition operator implementing a fixed-point strategy. More precisely, it can be derived from the class `FixedPoint`, provided that the choice of a function in the propagation set is replaced with the creation of a composition operator at each iteration of the loop. In pattern terms, we have to use the Strategy pattern in order to abstract some parts of the fixed-point algorithm (choice and update). We describe in Table 3 the implementation of the composition operation modeling the second strategy of Choco.

To conclude, it is worth noting that there is a low coupling between components. Composition operators take as input a set of reduction functions and some code for creating compositions, and uses a dependency relation variables–functions. Reduction functions have to be generated by specific components before propagation. This part of the architecture is not described there due to a lack of space.

4 Conclusion

A set of composition operations of reduction functions is introduced to design dynamic constraint propagation strategies. Apt's iteration model is slightly modified while preserving the semantics. Several well-known strategies using priorities

Table 3. Pseudo-code for the Composition Operation of Choco

```
function ComposeChoco (G = {g₁,...,gₖ}): reduction function
begin
    φ := new instance of Sequence
    while G ≠ ∅ do
        α := max({priority(g) | g ∈ G})
        ψ := new instance of FixedPoint
        for each g ∈ G do
            if priority(g) = α then
                ψ := addFunction(g)
                G := G - {g}
            fi
        od
        φ := addFunction(ψ)
    od
    return φ
end
```

of constraints, heuristics on the order of application of functions, and parallelism are modeled using a single iteration algorithm. A generic object-oriented model of constraint propagation, integrating composition operators, has been designed. This work may be extended in many ways.

The set of composition operators is (intentionally) reduced to sequence, closure, and decoupling operators. One may desire additional operators to model sequences of fixed length, quasi closures with a notion of precision, or conditional strategies with respect to dynamic criteria. We believe that their integration in our framework is feasible.

Composition operators implement propagation strategies for handling conjunctions of functions. We believe that this framework can be extended to process quantified constraints [23]. Quantifiers and connectives may be represented as forms of compositions to which are associated specific reduction algorithms.

Properties such as redundancy and strongness are important for efficient compositions [18,9]. Further research may integrate these properties in the framework, which will make update functions explicit.

Acknowledgments. Gerson Sunyé is gratefully acknowledged for fruitul discussions on these topics.

References

1. K. R. Apt. The Essence of Constraint Propagation. *Theoretical Computer Science*, 221(1-2):179–210, 1999.
2. K. R. Apt. The Role of Commutativity in Constraint Propagation Algorithms. *ACM TOPLAS*, 22(6):1002–1036, 2000.
3. F. Benhamou. Heterogeneous Constraint Solving. In *Proceedings of ALP*, volume 1139 of *LNCS*, pages 62–76. Springer, 1996.

4. F. Benhamou, D. McAllester, and P. Van Hentenryck. CLP(Intervals) Revisited. In *Proceedings of ILPS*, pages 124–138. MIT Press, 1994.

5. C. Bessière. Arc-Consistency and Arc-Consistency Again. *Artificial Intelligence*, 65:179–190, 1994.

6. D. Chazan and W. Miranker. Chaotic Relaxation. *Linear Algebra and its Applications*, 2:199–222, 1969.

7. E. C. Freuder. Synthesizing Constraint Expressions. *CACM*, 21(11):958–966, 1978.

8. E. Gamma, R. Helm, R. Johnson, and J. Vlissides. *Design Patterns: Elements of Reusable Object-Oriented Software*. Addison Wesley, 1994.

9. R. Gennari. Arc Consistency Algorithms via Iterations of Subsumed Functions. In *Proceedings of CL*, volume 1861 of *LNCS*, pages 358–372. Springer, 2000.

10. L. Granvilliers. On the Combination of Interval Constraint Solvers. *Reliable Computing*, 7(6):467–483, 2001.

11. L. Granvilliers and G. Hains. A Conservative Scheme for Parallel Interval Narrowing. *Information Processing Letters*, 74:141–146, 2000.

12. L. Granvilliers and E. Monfroy. Declarative Modelling of Constraint Propagation Strategies. In *Proceedings of ADVIS*, volume 1909 of *LNAI*, pages 201–215. Springer, 2000.

13. G. Hains and M. H. van Emden. Towards high-quality, high-speed numerical computation. In *Proceedings of PACRIM*. IEEE Computer Society, 1997.

14. F. Laburthe and the OCRE project team. CHOCO: implementing a CP kernel. In *Proceedings of TRICS*, 2000.

15. O. Lhomme. Consistency Techniques for Numeric CSPs. In *Proceedings of IJCAI*, pages 232–238. Morgan Kaufman, 1993.

16. O. Lhomme, A. Gotlieb, and M. Rueher. Dynamic Optimization of Interval Narrowing Algorithms. *Journal of Logic Programming*, 37(1–2):165–183, 1998.

17. A. K. Mackworth. Consistency in Networks of Relations. *Artificial Intelligence*, 8(1):99–118, 1977.

18. E. Monfroy. Using Weaker Functions for Constraint Propagation over Real Numbers. In *Proceedings of ACM SAC*, pages 553–559. ACM Press, 1999.

19. E. Monfroy and J.-H. Réty. Chaotic Iteration for Distributed Constraint Propagation. In *Proceedings of ACM SAC*, pages 19–24. ACM Press, 1999.

20. A. S. Narin'yani. Subdefinite models and operations with subdefinite values. *Preprint, USSR academy of sciences, Siberian Division*, 400, 1982.

21. K. B. K. Ng, C. W. Choi, M. Henz, and T. Mueller. GIFT: A Generic Interface for Reusing Filtering Algorithms. In *Proceedings of TRICS*, 2000.

22. J.-F. Puget and M. Leconte. Beyond the Glass Box: Constraints as Objects. In *Proceedings of ILPS*, pages 513–527. MIT Press, 1995.

23. S. Ratschan. Continuous First-Order Constraint Satisfaction. In *Proceedings of AISC*, volume 2385 of *LNCS*, pages 181–195. Springer, 2002.

24. P. Van Hentenryck, L. Michel, and Y. Deville. *Numerica: a Modeling Language for Global Optimization*. MIT Press, 1997.

25. D. L. Waltz. Generating Semantic Descriptions from Drawings of Scenes with Shadows. In P. H. Winston, editor, *The Psychology of Computer Vision*. McGraw Hill, 1975.

Forward versus Backward Verification of Logic Programs

Andy King and Lunjin Lu

[1] Computing Laboratory, University of Kent, Canterbury, CT2 7NF, UK
[2] Department of Computer Science, Oakland University, Rochester, MI 48309, USA

Abstract. One recent development in logic programming has been the application of abstract interpretation to verify the partial correctness of a logic program with respect to a given set of assertions. One approach to verification is to apply forward analysis that starts with an initial goal and traces the execution in the direction of the control-flow to approximate the program state at each program point. This is often enough to verify that the assertions hold. The dual approach is to apply backward analysis to propagate properties of the allowable states against the control-flow to infer queries for which the program will not violate any assertion. This paper is a systematic comparison of these two approaches to verification. The paper reports some equivalence results that relate the relative power of various forward and backward analysis frameworks.

1 Introduction

Recently there has been growing awareness that abstract interpretation has an important rôle in both the verification and debugging of logic programs [6,20, 26]. In this context, the programmer is typically equipped with an annotation language in which she/he can encode properties of the program state at various program points [26]. One approach to verification is to trace the program state in the direction of control-flow from an initial goal, using abstract interpretation to finitely represent and track the state. The program is deemed to be correct if all the assertions are satisfied whenever they are encountered; otherwise the program is potentially buggy. This is how forward analysis can be applied in logic program verification. The dual approach is to trace execution against the control-flow to infer those queries which ensure that the assertions are satisfied should they be encountered during execution [17,23]. If the class of initial queries does not conform to those expected by the programmer, then the program is potentially buggy. This is how backward analysis can be applied in verification.

This paper is an examination and comparison of these two opposing approaches to verification. Specifically the paper compares forward analysis [3, 10,14,21,27] to the backward analysis of [17] which uses the relative pseudo-complement operator [13] to trace information (weakest pre-conditions) against the control-flow. Every condensing domain possesses a pseudo-complement operator and it is always possible to synthesise a condensing domain from an arbitrary (downward-closed) domain by applying Heyting completion [13]. Examples

C. Palamidessi (Ed.): ICLP 2003, LNCS 2916, pp. 315–330, 2003.

of condensing domains include the class of positive Boolean functions, the relational type domain of [4], directional types [1,13] and the two variable per inequality power domain presented in section 6 of this paper. This paper arose from a study of how the domain operations that arise in backward analysis effect precision. In fact, the equivalence results reported in this paper flow from the following practical, albeit technical, questions (annotated Q1, Q2 and Q3).

The backward analysis framework of [17] is parameterised by an abstract domain that is required to be condensing. Fixing the domain $\langle D, \trianglelefteq \rangle$, fixes the join $\oplus$ and meet $\otimes$ operations that are used to model the merging of computation paths and the conjunction of constraints. Fixing D also fixes the relative pseudo-complement. The pseudo-complement of d_1 relative to d_2, denoted $d_1 \Rightarrow d_2$, delivers the weakest element of D whose conjunction with d_1 implies d_2, or more exactly, $d_1 \Rightarrow d_2 = \oplus \{d \in D \mid d \otimes d_1 \trianglelefteq d_2\}$. The rôle of pseudo-complement is that if d_2 expresses a set of requirements that must hold after a constraint is added to the store, and d_1 models the constraint itself, then $d_1 \Rightarrow d_2$ expresses the requirements that must hold on the store before the constraint. In addition to these operations that are fixed by D, backward analysis employs an unusual operator $\forall_x : D \to D$, dubbed universal projection, that complements standard projection $\exists_x : D \to D$, hereafter named existential projection, in that $\forall_x(d) \trianglelefteq d \trianglelefteq \exists_x(d)$. Both projections are monotonic, both eliminate a variable x from a given abstraction d and both are used to restrain the size of abstractions; the fundamental difference is in the direction of approximation. The correctness of backward analysis relies on the property $\forall_x(d) \trianglelefteq d$. Defining $\forall_x(d) = \bot$ (the strongest abstraction) for all $d \in D$ is sufficient for correctness but the resulting analysis is useless in that the class of queries inferred by the analysis is empty.

Q1. This leads to the question of how to define $\forall_x$ so the precision of the resulting analysis compares favourably with that of forward analysis?

This paper reports that if $\langle D, \forall_x, D, \exists_x \rangle$ is a Galois connection, then a surprising equivalence is established between forward and backward analysis so that the power of backward analysis exactly matches that of forward analysis for verification. On the practical side, it means that backward analysis need not be applied, if forward analysis cannot verify that a given query satisfies the assertions. Conversely, if an initial query is not inferred by backward analysis, then it follows that forward analysis cannot infer that the query satisfies the assertions.

Another issue relates to the fixpoint engines that are used in forward analysis. Since these engines vary in complexity, another question relates to which engine in the precision and tractability continuum is best suited to verification.

Q2. This begs the question of whether a polyvariant analysis (that maintains a set of call and answer patterns for each predicate) has any precision advantage over a monovariant analysis (that records a single call and answer pattern pair for each predicate) for the task of verification?

The answer to this question is negative for condensing domains provided that $\exists_x$ is additive, that is, $\exists_x(\oplus E) = \oplus \{\exists_x(d) \mid d \in E\}$ whenever $E \subseteq D$.

Since one way of constructing a condensing domain, is to lift a base domain $\langle D, \trianglelefteq \rangle$ to its power domain $\langle D', \trianglelefteq' \rangle$, then the answer to Q1 raises the question of what properties are required of D for $\langle D', \forall'_x, D', \exists'_x \rangle$ to be Galois connection to thereby guarantee equivalence between the frameworks.

Q3. Specifically if $\forall'_x$ and $\exists'_x$ are synthesised from $\forall_x$ and $\exists_x$ (in the natural way) then what does this require of D?

This paper shows that the only way to satisfy the Galois connection on D' is to engineer $\forall_x$ and $\exists_x$ so that $\langle D, \forall_x, D, \exists_x \rangle$ is also a Galois connection.

The paper is structured as follows. Section 2 presents an operational semantics for verification. Sections 3, 4 and 5 compare top-down, condensing and backward framework for the task of verification. Section 6 discuses the rôle of power domains and section 7 the related work. Finally section 8 concludes.

2   Operational Semantics

To precisely spell out the relationship between various forward and backward analysis frameworks, a formal language is required to specify both the operational semantics and the frameworks themselves. This section, and the proceeding section, introduces this necessary formalism.

Let Con be a set of constraints that is pre-ordered by entailment $\models$ and includes equational constraints of the form $\boldsymbol{x} = \boldsymbol{y}$ where $\boldsymbol{x}$ and $\boldsymbol{y}$ are tuples of variables. The set of order-ideals of Con is defined $Ord = \{C \subseteq Con \mid C = \downarrow(C)\}$ where $\downarrow(C) = \{c \in Con \mid \exists c' \in C.c \models c'\}$. The basic semantic domain is the complete lattice $\langle Ord, \subseteq, \cup, \cap, Con, \emptyset \rangle$. To observe violations of assertions, Ord is augmented with a new top element $\top$ to obtain $\widehat{Ord} = Ord \cup \{\top\}$. The ordering $\subseteq$ extends to $\widehat{Ord}$ by $C \subseteq \top$ for all $C \in \widehat{Ord}$ and the operators $\cup$ and $\cap$ extend analogously. It is useful, however, to define a variant of $\cap$, denoted $\widehat{\cap}$, that ensures that $\top$ can never be annulled. This is defined $C \widehat{\cap} \top = \top \widehat{\cap} C = \top$ for all $C \in \widehat{Ord}$ and $C_1 \widehat{\cap} C_2 = C_1 \cap C_2$ for all $C_1, C_2 \in Ord$.

The verification problem is formulated in terms of an additional (abstract) domain $\langle D, \trianglelefteq, \oplus, \otimes, \top, \bot \rangle$ equipped with an abstraction map $\alpha : Ord \to D$ and a concretisation map $\gamma : D \to Ord$ that interpret elements of D. A constraint logic program is annotated with assertions over D and a program is deemed to be correct if the assertions are satisfied whenever they are reached. The problem is to decide whether a given program is correct for some input. For brevity, programs are expressed (concurrent constraint style) using $\mathsf{ask}(d)$ where $d \in D$ to distinguish an assertion from a conventional store write that is denoted $\mathsf{tell}(c)$ where $c \in Con$. In what follows, P denotes a program and A an agent, that is, $P ::= \epsilon \mid p(\boldsymbol{x}) \leftarrow A \mid P.P'$ and $A ::= \mathsf{ask}(d) \mid \mathsf{tell}(c) \mid A_1, A_2 \mid \sum_{i=1}^{n} A_i \mid p(\boldsymbol{x})$. Due to the presence of an explicit choice operator predicates can be assumed to be defined with exactly one definition of the form $p(\boldsymbol{x}) \leftarrow A$ without any loss of generality. Let Age_P denote the set of agents in a program P that is closed under renaming and let $Poly_P$ denote the function space $Age_P \to \widehat{Ord} \to \widehat{Ord}$. The ordering $\subseteq$ over $\widehat{Ord}$ lifts $Poly_P$ point-wise by $f_1 \sqsubseteq f_2$ iff $f_1[\![A]\!](C) \subseteq f_2[\![A]\!](C)$ for all $A \in Age_P$ and $C \in \widehat{Ord}$. In fact $\langle Poly_P, \sqsubseteq, \sqcup, \sqcap \rangle$ is a complete lattice where $f_1 \sqcup f_2 = \lambda A.\lambda d.(f_1[\![A]\!](d) \cup f_2[\![A]\!](d))$ and $\sqcap$ is defined analogously.

Definition 1 (operational semantics). The operator $\mathcal{F}_P : Poly_P \to Poly_P$ is defined $\mathcal{F}_P(f) = f'$ where $f, f' \in Poly_P$ and:

$$f'[\![\mathsf{ask}(d)]\!] = \lambda C.\text{if } \alpha(C) \trianglelefteq d \text{ then } C \text{ else } \top$$
$$f'[\![\mathsf{tell}(c)]\!] = \lambda C.\!\downarrow\!(\{c\})\widehat{\cap}C$$
$$f'[\![A_1, A_2]\!] = \lambda C.f[\![A_2]\!](f[\![A_1]\!](C))$$
$$f'[\![\textstyle\sum_{i=1}^{n} A_i]\!] = \lambda C.\cup_{i=1}^{n} f[\![A_i]\!](C)$$
$$f'[\![p(\boldsymbol{x})]\!] = \lambda C.\cup\{f[\![A]\!](\!\downarrow\!(\{\boldsymbol{x} = \boldsymbol{y}\})\widehat{\cap}C) \mid p(\boldsymbol{y}) \leftarrow A \ll_{p(\boldsymbol{x}),C} P\}$$

Note that the composition operator , is sequential thus control is left-to-right. Note too that choice occurs both explicitly within the construct $\sum_{i=1}^{n} A_i$ and implicitly within renaming. The notation $p(\boldsymbol{y}) \leftarrow A \ll_{p(\boldsymbol{x}),C} P$ indicates that $p(\boldsymbol{y}) \leftarrow A$ is a renaming of a definition in P such that $var(p(\boldsymbol{y}) \leftarrow A) \cap (var(p(\boldsymbol{x})) \cup var(C)) = \emptyset$ where $var(o)$ is the set of variables in the object o. Since $\mathcal{F}_P$ is monotonic and $Poly_P$ is a complete lattice, $\mathsf{lfp}(\mathcal{F}_P)$ exists and the verification problem can be formally stated as the problem of characterising the following set of atomic queries:

Definition 2. $\mathcal{F}[\![P]\!] = \{\langle p(\boldsymbol{x}), C \rangle \mid \mathsf{lfp}(\mathcal{F}_P)[\![p(\boldsymbol{x})]\!](C) \neq \top\}$

3 Verification with a Top-Down Framework

An analysis for approximating $\mathcal{F}[\![P]\!]$ can be constructed by mimicking concrete operations over Ord with abstract operations over D and applying the projection operator $\exists_x : D \to D$ to finitely bound the number of variables. The operator $\exists_x$ is assumed to comply with the rules $d \trianglelefteq \exists_x(d)$, $\exists_x(d_1) \trianglelefteq \exists_x(d_2)$ if $d_1 \trianglelefteq d_2$, $\exists_x(\exists_y(d)) = \exists_y(\exists_x(d))$ and $\exists_x(d_1) \otimes \exists_x(d_2) = \exists_x(d_1 \otimes \exists_x(d_2))$. The last rule is useful within itself as well as implying that $\exists_x$ is idempotent, that is, $\exists_x(\exists_x(d)) = \exists_x(d)$. Finally, $\exists_x$ is also required to eliminate a variable, hence $x \notin var(\exists_x(d))$. For brevity, let $\exists_o(d) = (\exists_{x_1} \ldots \exists_{x_n})(d)$ where $var(o) = \{x_1, \ldots, x_n\}$ and let $\overline{\exists}_o(d) = \exists_{var(d)\backslash var(o)}(d)$. D is assumed to contain elements of the form $\boldsymbol{x} = \boldsymbol{y}$ to model argument passing. To express renaming, let $\rho_{\boldsymbol{x},\boldsymbol{y}}(d) = \exists_x((\boldsymbol{x} = \boldsymbol{y}) \otimes d)$. Suppose that $\langle \widehat{D}, \trianglelefteq \rangle$ is augmented with $\top$ in a similar fashion to $\langle \widehat{Ord}, \subseteq \rangle$. To trace violations of assertions, a variant of $\otimes$, denoted $\widehat{\otimes}$, is defined such that $d\widehat{\otimes}\top = \top\widehat{\otimes}d = \top$ for all $d \in \widehat{D}$ and $d_1\widehat{\otimes}d_2 = d_1 \otimes d_2$ for all $d_1, d_2 \in D$.

The semantic equations for a polyvariant, top-down framework are given overleaf. The map $\mathcal{F}_P^D$ operates over $Poly_P^D \to Poly_P^D$ where $Poly_P^D = Age_P \to \widehat{D} \to \widehat{D}$. Thus if $f \in Poly_P^D$, f associates each agent A with a map between input (the call pattern) and output (the answer pattern). The ordering $\trianglelefteq$ over $\widehat{D}$ induces an ordering on $Poly_P^D$ by $f_1 \trianglelefteq f_2$ iff $f_1[\![A]\!](d) \trianglelefteq f_2[\![A]\!](d)$ for all $d \in \widehat{D}$ and $A \in Age_P$. Moreover $\langle Poly_P^D, \trianglelefteq, \oplus, \otimes \rangle$ is a complete lattice where $f_1 \circledast f_2 = \lambda A.\lambda d.(f_1[\![A]\!](d) \circledast f_2[\![A]\!](d))$ and $\circledast \in \{\oplus, \otimes\}$.

Definition 3 (top-down framework). The operator $\mathcal{F}_P^D : Poly_P^D \to Poly_P^D$ is defined $\mathcal{F}_P^D(f) = f'$ such that:

$$f'[\![\mathsf{ask}(d')]\!] = \lambda d.\text{if } d \trianglelefteq d' \text{ then } d \text{ else } \top$$
$$f'[\![\mathsf{tell}(c)]\!] = \lambda d.\alpha(\downarrow(\{c\}))\widehat{\otimes}d$$
$$f'[\![A_1, A_2]\!] = \lambda d.f[\![A_2]\!](f[\![A_1]\!](d))$$
$$f'[\![\textstyle\sum_{i=1}^n A_i]\!] = \lambda d.\oplus_{i=1}^n f[\![A_i]\!](d)$$
$$f'[\![p(\boldsymbol{x})]\!] = \lambda d.\rho_{\boldsymbol{y},\boldsymbol{x}}(\bar{\exists}_{\boldsymbol{y}}(f[\![A]\!](\rho_{\boldsymbol{x},\boldsymbol{y}}(\bar{\exists}_{\boldsymbol{x}}(d))))))\widehat{\otimes}d \text{ where } p(\boldsymbol{y}) \leftarrow A \ll_{p(\boldsymbol{x})} P$$

Note how the use of projection eliminates the requirement for considering each definition renaming separately. The functional defined in the semantics can be interpreted as a formalisation of the top-down framework of Bruynooghe [3] that is widely used in analysis and specialisation because of its precision and polyvariance (different calls to the same predicate are analysed separately). Since $\mathcal{F}_P^D$ is monotonic and $Poly_P^D$ is a complete lattice, $\mathsf{lfp}(\mathcal{F}_P^D)$ exists. However, efficient implementations of the Bruynooghe framework, such as GENA [10], PLAI [14] and GAIA [21], only compute $\mathsf{lfp}(\mathcal{F}_P^D)$ in a partial query-directed fashion. The verification problem can be tackled in the abstract setting by characterising the following set of atomic queries:

Definition 4. $\mathcal{F}^D[\![P]\!] = \{\langle p(\boldsymbol{x}), C\rangle \mid \mathsf{lfp}(\mathcal{F}_P^D)[\![p(\boldsymbol{x})]\!](\alpha(C)) \neq \top\}$

The following proposition states this is a safe, albeit possibly imprecise, strategy for solving the verification problem. The proof is straightforward.

Proposition 1. $\mathcal{F}^D[\![P]\!] \subseteq \mathcal{F}[\![P]\!]$

Observe that Age_P is finite (modulo renaming) since P is finite. Therefore a computable analysis can be constructed by appropriately factoring out renaming provided that D is finite. The proof for the following lemma is straightforward.

Lemma 1. If $d_1 \trianglelefteq d_2$ then $\mathsf{lfp}(\mathcal{F}_P^D)[\![A]\!](d_1) \trianglelefteq \mathsf{lfp}(\mathcal{F}_P^D)[\![A]\!](d_2)$.

4   Verification with Condensing Domain

It has long been realised that if an abstract domain is condensing [16,19], then a goal-dependent analysis can be performed in a goal-independent way without incurring a loss in precision. Langen observed that if a compound goal (the body of a clause) returns an answer pattern of d when invoked with a call pattern of $\top$, then the compound goal will return an answer pattern of $d \wedge d'$ when invoked with a call pattern of d' [19][Lemma 9]. Jacobs and Langen exploited this to factor out repeated computation in a polyvariant, top-down framework [16, 19]. Other condensing frameworks were monovariant [27]; first computing one success pattern for each predicate with a goal-independent analysis then, second, deriving one call pattern for each predicate in a goal-dependent fashion as directed by an initial query. Quite apart from their efficiency, monovariant condensing frameworks are attractive because of their simplicity and modularity [27] and therefore it is interesting to compare a monovariant, condensing framework against a polyvariant, top-down framework for the purposes of verification.

Semantic equations for a monovariant condensing framework are given below. Success and call patterns are calculated by $\mathcal{S}_P^D$ and $\mathcal{C}_P^D$ respectively. Both maps operate over the function space $Mono_P^D = Age_P \to D$ where each $f \in Mono_P^D$ assigns a domain element to each agent of P. The ordering $\trianglelefteq$ over D induces a point-wise ordering on $Mono_P^D$ by $f_1 \trianglelefteq f_2$ iff $f_1[\![A]\!] \trianglelefteq f_2[\![A]\!]$ for all $A \in Age_P$. More-over $f_1 \circledast f_2 = \lambda A.(f_1[\![A]\!] \circledast f_2[\![A]\!])$ where $\circledast \in \{\oplus, \otimes\}$. In fact $\langle Mono_P^D, \trianglelefteq, \oplus, \otimes \rangle$ is a complete lattice with $\lambda A.\bot$ and $\lambda A.\top$ for bottom and top.

Definition 5 (condensing framework). The operators $\mathcal{S}_P^D : Mono_P^D \to Mono_P^D$ and $\mathcal{C}_P^D : Mono_P^D \to Mono_P^D$ are defined $\mathcal{S}_P^D(f) = f'$ and $\mathcal{C}_P^D(g) = g'$ such that:

$$
\begin{aligned}
&f'[\![\mathsf{ask}(d)]\!] = \top \\
&f'[\![\mathsf{tell}(c)]\!] = \alpha(\downarrow(\{c\})) \\
&f'[\![A_1, A_2]\!] = f[\![A_1]\!] \otimes f[\![A_2]\!] \\
&f'[\![\textstyle\sum_{i=1}^n A_i]\!] = \oplus_{i=1}^n f[\![A_i]\!] \\
&f'[\![p(\boldsymbol{x})]\!] = \rho_{\boldsymbol{y},\boldsymbol{x}}(\bar{\exists}_{\boldsymbol{y}}(f[\![A]\!]))
\end{aligned}
\qquad
\begin{aligned}
&g'[\![A_1]\!] = g[\![A_1, A_2]\!] \\
&g'[\![A_2]\!] = g[\![A_1, A_2]\!] \otimes \mathsf{lfp}(\mathcal{S}_P^D)[\![A_1]\!] \\
&g'[\![A_i]\!] = g[\![\textstyle\sum_{i=1}^n A_i]\!] \\
&g'[\![A]\!] = \rho_{\boldsymbol{x},\boldsymbol{y}}(\bar{\exists}_{\boldsymbol{x}}(g[\![p(\boldsymbol{x})]\!]))
\end{aligned}
$$

where $p(\boldsymbol{y}) \leftarrow A \ll_{p(\boldsymbol{x})} P$

The equations of $\mathcal{C}_P^D$ detail how to propagate the call pattern for an agent to its sub-agents; equations are not required for $\mathsf{ask}(d)$ and $\mathsf{tell}(c)$ since they do not invoke sub-agents. The verification problem can be formalised in this setting as the problem of computing the class of atomic queries that lead to call patterns which do not violate the $\mathsf{ask}(d)$ assertions.

Definition 6. $\mathcal{C}^D[\![P]\!] = \left\{ \langle p(\boldsymbol{x}), C \rangle \;\middle|\; \begin{array}{l} f \in \mathsf{fp}(\mathcal{C}_P^D) \wedge \alpha(C) \trianglelefteq f[\![p(\boldsymbol{x})]\!] \wedge \\ \forall\, \mathsf{ask}(d) \in Age_P. f[\![\mathsf{ask}(d)]\!] \trianglelefteq d \end{array} \right\}$

More exactly, to verify the correctness of a concrete atomic query $\langle p(\boldsymbol{x}), C \rangle$, it is sufficient to find a fixpoint $f \in \mathsf{fp}(\mathcal{C}_P^D)$ (any fixpoint) with a call to $p(\boldsymbol{x})$ that is not stronger than $\alpha(C)$ yet with a call for each $\mathsf{ask}(d)$ agent that is not weaker than d. Since $\mathcal{C}_P^D$ is continuous such a fixpoint, if one exists, can be computed by assigning $g_0 = \lambda A.(\text{if } A = p(\boldsymbol{x}) \text{ then } \alpha(C) \text{ else } \bot)$ and calculating $g_{i+1} = \mathcal{C}_P^D(g_i)$. Then $g = \oplus_i g_i$ is the least fixpoint of $\mathcal{C}_P^D$ such that $\alpha(C) \trianglelefteq g[\![p(\boldsymbol{x})]\!]$. Computation can be aborted if $g_i[\![\mathsf{ask}(d)]\!] \ntrianglelefteq d$ for some $\mathsf{ask}(d) \in Age_P$ since then no fixpoint of $\mathcal{C}_P^D$ can satisfy both the $p(\boldsymbol{x})$ and $\mathsf{ask}(d)$ requirements and hence verify $\langle p(\boldsymbol{x}), C \rangle$. The following lemmas explain how $\mathsf{lfp}(\mathcal{S}_P^D)$ can characterise $\mathsf{lfp}(\mathcal{F}_P^D)$.

Lemma 2. If $\mathsf{lfp}(\mathcal{F}_P^D)[\![A]\!](d) \neq \top$ then $\mathsf{lfp}(\mathcal{F}_P^D)[\![A]\!](d) \trianglelefteq d \otimes \mathsf{lfp}(\mathcal{S}_P^D)[\![A]\!]$.

Lemma 3. If D is a complete Heyting algebra (cHa) then $d \otimes \mathsf{lfp}(\mathcal{S}_P^D)[\![A]\!] \trianglelefteq \mathsf{lfp}(\mathcal{F}_P^D)[\![A]\!](d)$.

A domain D is a cHa if it is (completely) meet-distributive, that is, $d \otimes (\oplus_{i \in I} d_i) = \oplus_{i \in I}(d \otimes d_i)$ whenever $d \in D$ and $\{d_i \mid i \in I\} \subseteq D$ where I is some index set

[2][Chapter IX, Theorem 15]. Lemmas 2 and 3 are closely related to Theorem 8.2 of [13] which can be interpreted as stating $\mathsf{lfp}(\mathcal{F}_P^D)[\![A]\!](d) = d \otimes \mathsf{lfp}(\mathcal{F}_P^D)[\![A]\!](\top)$ for a program P without $\mathsf{ask}(d)$ agents. Theorem 8.2 does not stipulate any requirements on existential projection since the semantics of [13] does not apply this operator. Theorem 1 and theorem 2 (with its corollary) flow from the lemmas and state conditions on the domain operations for a monovariant, condensing framework to match the verification power of a polyvariant, top-down framework.

Theorem 1 (precision). If D is a cHa and $\exists_x$ is additive then $\mathcal{F}^D[\![P]\!] \subset \mathcal{C}^D[\![P]\!]$.

Theorem 2. $\mathcal{C}^D[\![P]\!] \subseteq \mathcal{F}^D[\![P]\!]$.

Corollary 1 (correctness). $\mathcal{C}^D[\![P]\!] \subseteq \mathcal{F}[\![P]\!]$.

Proof. By theorem 2, $\mathcal{C}^D[\![P]\!] \subseteq \mathcal{F}^D[\![P]\!]$ and by proposition 1, $\mathcal{F}^D[\![P]\!] \subseteq \mathcal{F}[\![P]\!]$.

The correctness of the program depends only on those calls that actually arise in a derivation from the initial query. The functional $\mathcal{F}_P^D$ that defines the top-down framework, on the other hand, maps an arbitrary call pattern to its answer pattern. Thus the domain is augmented with $\top$ to record whether any of the call patterns that occur in a derivation violate any of the assertions. This domain element is not required in the condensing approach because all the calls that arise in a derivation are merged and recorded. This approach to verification, however, is only guaranteed to be as precise as the top-down scheme if D is a cHa and $\exists_x$ is additive. The following example illustrates one domain which satisfies these properties that has been widely applied in verification.

Example 1. Let $Term$ denote the set of terms and $\wp^{\downarrow}(Term)$ denote the set of term sets that are closed under instantiation. Let $\Pi \subseteq \wp^{\downarrow}(Term)$ denote a finite set of primitive types and suppose $Term \in \Pi$. To enrich Π with dependencies, let $Type_X = \{x \subseteq \pi \mid x \in X \wedge \pi \in \Pi\} \cup \{\tau_1 \circledast \tau_2 \mid \circledast \in \{\wedge, \vee, \rightarrow\} \wedge \tau_1, \tau_2 \in Type_X\}$. The construction is completed by augmenting $Type_X$ with a bottom element $\perp$. A mapping $\theta : X \rightarrow \Pi$ assigns a truth value to each $\tau \in Type_X$ as follows: $\theta(\perp)$ is always false, $\theta(x \subseteq \pi) \iff \theta(x) \subseteq \pi$ and $\theta(\tau_1 \circledast \tau_2) \iff \theta(\tau_1) \circledast \theta(\tau_2)$. Then $\langle Type_X, \models, \vee, \wedge \rangle$ is a complete lattice where $\tau_1 \models \tau_2$ iff $\theta(\tau_1) \rightarrow \theta(\tau_2)$ holds for all $\theta : X \rightarrow \Pi$. In fact it can be shown that this lattice is a cHa. The concretisation map $\gamma_{Type} : Type_X \rightarrow \wp(Eqn)$ is defined $\gamma_{Type}(f) = \{E \in Eqn \mid \alpha(\sigma) \models f \wedge \sigma \in mgu(E)\}$ where

$$\alpha(\sigma) = \bigwedge \left\{ y \subseteq \pi \leftrightarrow \wedge_{i=1}^n y_i \subseteq \pi_i \,\middle|\, \begin{array}{l} y \in dom(\sigma) \,\wedge\, var(\sigma(y)) = \{y_i\}_{i=1}^n \,\wedge \\ \kappa \in var(\sigma(y)) \rightarrow Term \qquad\qquad \wedge \\ \kappa(\sigma(y)) \in \pi \iff \wedge_{i=1}^n \kappa(y_i) \in \pi_i \end{array} \right\}$$

Moreover, the abstraction map $\alpha_{Type} : \wp(Eqn) \rightarrow Type_X$ is defined as $\alpha_{Type}(S) = \wedge\{f \in Type_X \mid S \subseteq \gamma_{Type}(f)\}$. $Type_X$ includes types of the form

$(\wedge_{i=1}^n x_i \subseteq \pi_i) \rightarrow (\wedge_{i=1}^n x_i \subseteq \pi_i')$ where $\pi_i, \pi_i' \in \Pi$ that can capture the input and output types of an n-ary predicate [13] in a similar fashion to directional types [1] that are used in type checking and verification. Finally define $\exists_x(\tau) = \vee\{\{x \mapsto \pi\}(\tau) \mid \pi \in \Pi\}$ and let $\pi \in \Pi$, $\{\tau_i \mid i \in I\} \subseteq Type_X$ where I is some index set. Observe that $\{x \mapsto \pi\}(\vee_{i \in I} \tau_i) = \vee_{i \in I}\{x \mapsto \pi\}\tau_i$. It follows that $\exists_x$ is additive, hence the condensing framework is applicable.

5   Verification with a Backward Framework

The semantic equations for (a reformulation of) the backward analysis framework of [17] are given below. The key idea in $\mathcal{B}_P^D$ is embedded in the semantic equation for sequenced agents A_1, A_2. The problem is to find the weakest $d \in D$ (which describes the largest set of states) which guarantees that the agent A_1, A_2 will not violate an assertion. The problem, in fact, is to compute such a d given $d_1, d_2 \in D$ which ensures that A_1 and A_2 will not violate their assertions. One observation that underpins backward analysis is that $d \otimes \mathsf{lfp}(\mathcal{S}_P^D)[\![A_1]\!]$ describes that state immediately before the execution of A_2, hence A_2 will not violate an assertion if $d \otimes \mathsf{lfp}(\mathcal{S}_P^D)[\![A_1]\!] \trianglelefteq d_2$. This will hold if $d = d_1 \otimes (\mathsf{lfp}(\mathcal{S}_P^D)[\![A_1]\!] \Rightarrow d_2)$ where $\Rightarrow$ denotes the pseudo-complement in D (which exists whenever D is a cHa). Because $d \trianglelefteq d_1$, it follows that A_1 must satisfy its assertions. Since $d \models (\mathsf{lfp}(\mathcal{S}_P^D)[\![A_1]\!] \Rightarrow d_2)$ it follows from the axioms of a cHa [29], that $d \otimes \mathsf{lfp}(\mathcal{S}_P^D)[\![A_1]\!] \trianglelefteq d_2$, hence A_2 cannot violate an assertion either. The insight behind the $\Rightarrow$ application comes by using the axioms of a cHa to rewrite $d = d_1 \otimes (\mathsf{lfp}(\mathcal{S}_P^D)[\![A_1]\!] \Rightarrow d_2)$ as $d = d_1 \otimes ((d_1 \otimes \mathsf{lfp}(\mathcal{S}_P^D)[\![A_1]\!]) \Rightarrow d_2)$. Then $(d_1 \otimes \mathsf{lfp}(\mathcal{S}_P^D)[\![A_1]\!]) \Rightarrow d_2$ is the *weakest* element of D whose meet with $d_1 \otimes \mathsf{lfp}(\mathcal{S}_P^D)[\![A_1]\!]$ implies d_2. Thus d is the *weakest* element of D which ensures that A_1 and A_2 satisfy their assertions. The question is, of course, whether this tactic for propagating requirements leads to a useful approach to verification.

Definition 7 (backward framework). The operator $\mathcal{B}_P^D : Mono_P^D \rightarrow Mono_P^D$ is defined $\mathcal{B}_P^D(f) = f'$ such that:

$$f'[\![\mathsf{ask}(d)]\!] = d$$
$$f'[\![\mathsf{tell}(c)]\!] = \top$$
$$f'[\![A_1, A_2]\!] = f[\![A_1]\!] \otimes (\mathsf{lfp}(\mathcal{S}_P^D)[\![A_1]\!] \Rightarrow f[\![A_2]\!])$$
$$f'[\![\textstyle\sum_{i=1}^n A_i]\!] = \otimes_{i=1}^n f[\![A_i]\!]$$
$$f'[\![p(x)]\!] = \rho_{y,x}(\overline{\forall}_y(f[\![A]\!])) \text{ where } p(y) \leftarrow A \ll_{p(x)} P$$

Universal projection $\forall_x(d) \trianglelefteq d$ is required to satisfy $\forall_x(d) \trianglelefteq d$ for all $d \in D$ for reasons of correctness [17]. This is because of the way it is used to propagate requirements over procedure boundaries; if d describes a set of states for which an agent A does not violate an assertion, then so does $\forall_x(d)$ since it represents a subset of those states. The $\overline{\forall}$ operator is defined in an analogous fashion to $\overline{\exists}$. Like $\mathcal{C}_P^D$, $\mathcal{B}_P^D$ requires $\mathsf{lfp}(\mathcal{S}_P^D)$ to be pre-computed. Like $\mathcal{C}_P^D$, the map $\mathcal{B}_P^D$ operates over $Mono_P^D$ and hence is monovariant. Unlike $\mathcal{C}_P^D$, repeated application yields a decreasing sequence. In fact $\mathcal{B}_P^D$ is co-continuous, thus the sequence

$f_0 = \top$, $f_{i+1} = \mathcal{B}_P^D(f_i)$ converges onto the greatest fixpoint of $\mathcal{B}_P^D$, that is, $\mathsf{gfp}(\mathcal{B}_P^D) = \otimes_i f_i$. The following definition states how $\mathsf{gfp}(\mathcal{B}_P^D)$ can be interpreted for the purposes of verification.

Definition 8. $\mathcal{B}^D[\![P]\!] = \{\langle p(\boldsymbol{x}), C \rangle \mid \alpha(C) \trianglelefteq \mathsf{gfp}(\mathcal{B}_P^D)[\![p(\boldsymbol{x})]\!]\}$

The following theorems and corollary state conditions under which this backward approach to verification coincides with forward verification. These equivalence results rest crucially, and perhaps surprisingly, on the relationship between the projection operators used within forward and backward analysis.

Theorem 3 (precision). If D is a cHa and $\langle D, \forall_x, D, \exists_x \rangle$ is a Galois connection, then $\mathcal{F}^D[\![P]\!] \subseteq \mathcal{B}^D[\![P]\!]$

Theorem 4. If D is a cHa, $\exists_X(\bot) = \bot$ and $\langle D, \forall_x, D, \exists_x \rangle$ is a Galois connection, then $\mathcal{B}^D[\![P]\!] \subseteq \mathcal{F}^D[\![P]\!]$.

Corollary 2 (correctness). If D is a cHa, $\exists_X(\bot) = \bot$ and $\langle D, \forall_x, D, \exists_x \rangle$ is a Galois connection, then $\mathcal{B}^D[\![P]\!] \subseteq \mathcal{F}[\![P]\!]$

The proofs of these theorems (see the technical report version of this paper [18]) rely on properties that flow from the Galois connection. The proof of theorem 3 relies on two properties of universal quantification – the monotonicity of $\forall_x$ and the property that $d = \forall_x(d)$ whenever $d = \exists_x(d)$. Since $\exists_x(d) = \exists_x(\exists_x(d))$ the latter property ensures that $\exists_x(d) = \forall_x(\exists_x(d))$ and since $d \trianglelefteq \exists_x(d)$ it follows that $d \trianglelefteq \forall_x(\exists_x(d))$, that is, that $\forall_x \circ \exists_x$ is extensive. On the other hand, the proof of theorem 4 relies on the property that $\forall_x(d) \trianglelefteq d$. From this it follows that $\exists_x(\forall_x(d)) = \forall_x(d) \trianglelefteq d$, that is, that $\exists_x \circ \forall_x$ is reductive. The monotonicity of $\forall_x$ combined with the monotonicity of $\exists_x$ and the extensive and reductive properties of $\forall_x \circ \exists_x$ and $\exists_x \circ \forall_x$, implies that $\langle D, \forall_x, D, \exists_x \rangle$ is a Galois connection [7]. Thus the Galois connection requirement cannot be relaxed. Interestingly, the direction of approximation in $\forall_x$ and $\exists_x$ suggests the existance of a Galois connection: the adjoint of an upper closure operator ($\exists_x$) is a lower closure operator ($\forall_x$). Curiously, $\exists_X(\bot) = \bot$ is required to guarantee that $\forall_x$ eliminates the variable x for each $x \in X$; specifically $\exists_X(\bot) = \bot$ ensures $x \notin var(\forall_x(d))$.

A Galois connection gives a systematic way of synthesising $\forall_x$ from $\exists_x$, that is, $\forall_x(d) = \oplus\{d' \in D \mid \exists_x(d') \trianglelefteq d\}$ [7,17]. It also ensures that $\exists_x$ is additive [7], thereby satisfying the condensing requirement. The equivalence it induces, also provides a simple tactic to establishing safety which avoids arguments that involve both state abstraction and reversed information flow [17]. In fact Hughes and Launchbury [15] argue that ideally the direction of an analysis should be reversed without reference to the concrete semantics. Indeed, the equivalence between backward and forward analysis, means that the correctness of backward analysis follows immediately from that of forward analysis. The following examples illustrate some domains for which $\langle D, \forall_x, D, \exists_x \rangle$ is a Galois connection.

Example 2. Let $Bool_X$ denote the Boolean functions over a set of variables X. The domain Pos_X is defined by $Pos_X = \{\bot\} \cup \{f \in Bool_X \mid (\wedge X) \models f\}$. The lattice $\langle Pos_X, \models, \vee, \wedge, 1, \bot \rangle$ is finite. Each element of Pos_X is interpreted as a set of equation sets by the concretisation map $\gamma_{Pos} : Pos_X \rightarrow \wp(Eqn)$ where $\gamma_{Pos}(f) = \{E \in Eqn \mid \alpha(\theta) \models f \wedge \theta \in mgu(E)\}$ and $\alpha(\theta) = \wedge\{y \leftrightarrow \wedge var(\theta(y)) \mid y \in dom(\theta)\}$. The abstraction map $\alpha_{Pos} : \wp(Eqn) \rightarrow Pos_X$ is defined as $\alpha_{Pos}(S) = \wedge\{f \in Pos_X \mid S \subseteq \gamma_{Pos}(f)\}$. In forward analysis, existential projection is conventionally defined by Schröder elimination as $\exists_x(f) = f[x \mapsto 1] \vee f[x \mapsto 0]$. To obtain a Galois connection, define universal projection by $\forall_x(f) = f'$ if $f' \in Pos$ otherwise $\forall_x(f) = \bot$ where $f' = f[x \mapsto 0] \wedge f[x \mapsto 1]$. Although $f[x \mapsto 0] \vee f[x \mapsto 1] \in Pos_X$ for any $f \in Pos_X$, $f[x \mapsto 0] \wedge f[x \mapsto 1] \notin Pos_X$ for some $f \in Pos$. Consider, for instance, $f = (x \leftarrow y)$. Note that $f \models \exists_x(f) = \forall_x(\exists_x(f))$, hence $\forall_x \circ \exists_x$ is extensive. Moreover, if $\forall_x(f) = \bot$ then $\exists_x(\forall_x(f)) = \bot \models f$. Otherwise $f \models \forall_x(f) = \exists_x(\forall_x(f))$. Thus $\exists_x \circ \forall_x$ is reductive. Since $\exists_x$ and $\forall_x$ are monotonic, $\langle Pos_X, \forall_x, Pos_X, \exists_x \rangle$ is a Galois connection. The pseudo-complement $\Rightarrow$ is $\rightarrow$ for Pos_X.

Example 3. The Galois connection property does not uniquely define the existential and projection operators for a given domain. For example, for Pos_X consider $\exists_x(f) = 1$ and $\forall_x(f) = \bot$. Then $f \models 1 = \exists_x(\forall_x(f))$ and $\forall_x(\exists_x(f)) = \bot \models f$, and $\langle Pos_X, \forall_x, Pos_X, \exists_x \rangle$ is again a Galois connection.

Example 4. An intriguing non-example for Pos_X is obtained by defining:

$$\exists_x(f) = \begin{cases} f \text{ if } x \notin var(f) \\ 1 \text{ otherwise} \end{cases} \qquad \forall_x(f) = \begin{cases} f \text{ if } x \notin var(f) \\ \bot \text{ otherwise} \end{cases}$$

Now compare a forward analysis that uses $\exists_x$ against a backward analysis that applies both $\exists_x$ and $\forall_x$ for a program P that consists of two definitions $p(x) \leftarrow \mathsf{ask}(x \vee y)$ and $q(x) \leftarrow \mathsf{ask}(x)$. Then $\mathsf{lfp}(\mathcal{F}_P^D)[\![p(x)]\!](x) = x \neq \top$ however $\mathsf{gfp}(\mathcal{B}_P^D)[\![p(x)]\!] = \bot$. Dually $\mathsf{lfp}(\mathcal{F}_P^D)[\![q(x)]\!](x \wedge y) = \top$ whereas $\mathsf{gfp}(\mathcal{B}_P^D)[\![q(x)]\!] = x$. Since Pos_X is a cHa, by theorems 3 and 4 it follows that $\langle Pos_X, \forall_x, Pos_X, \exists_x \rangle$ is not a Galois connection although $\forall_x \circ \exists_x$ is extensive and $\exists_x \circ \forall_x$ is reductive. In fact equivalence is lost because neither $\exists_x$ nor $\forall_x$ are monotonic as is witnessed by $\exists_x(x \wedge y) = 1 \not\models y = \exists_x(y)$ and $\forall_x(y) = y \not\models \bot = \exists_x(x \vee y)$.

6   Verification with a Power Domain

One classic way [7] of enriching an abstract domain is to apply a power domain construction in which the elements of the new domain correspond to sets of elements in the old domain. The rational for this construction is usually to improve the precision of join that is required to merge abstractions arising along different computational paths. However, as originally pointed out in [19], it also provides a mechanism for synthesising a domain that is condensing. This approach is useful if the Heyting completion [13] of a domain is unknown. Thus consider a power domain constructed from an abstract domain $\langle D, \unlhd, \oplus, \otimes \rangle$ that is a complete lattice. The ordering $\unlhd$ over D lifts to sets $S_1, S_2 \subseteq D$ by $S_1 \unlhd S_2$ if and only if for all $d_1 \in S_1$ there exists $d_2 \in S_2$ such that $d_1 \unlhd d_2$.

Proposition 2. Let $\langle D, \unlhd \rangle$ be a poset that satisfies the ascending chain condition. Let $S_1, S_2 \subseteq S \subseteq D$ such that $S \unlhd S_1$ and $S \unlhd S_2$. Then $S \unlhd S_1 \cap S_2$.

The force of proposition 2, is that it ensures that the following operator is well-defined (at least for domains that satisfy the ascending chain condition):

Definition 9. The map $\varrho : \wp(D) \to \wp(D)$ is defined $\varrho(S) = \cap \{S' \subseteq S \mid S \unlhd S'\}$.

For domains that satisfy the ascending chain condition – the focus of our study – this operator ϱ computes the most compact representation of a set of abstractions S. This provides a normal form that enables a power domain to be constructed without recourse to equivalence class manipulation. The power domain is then the complete lattice $\langle \varrho(\wp(D)), \unlhd, \oplus, \otimes \rangle$ where $\oplus$ and $\otimes$ are defined as $S_1 \oplus S_2 = \varrho(S_1 \cup S_2)$ and $S_1 \otimes S_2 = \varrho(\{d_1 \otimes d_2 \mid d_1 \in S_1 \wedge d_2 \in S_2\})$. To observe that $\langle \varrho(\wp(D)), \unlhd, \oplus, \otimes \rangle$ is a cHa, let $S \in \varrho(\wp(D))$ and $\{S_i \mid i \in I\} \subseteq \varrho(\wp(D))$ for some index set I. It follows from the definitions of $\otimes$ and $\oplus$ that $S \otimes (\oplus_{i \in I} S_i) = \varrho(\{d \otimes d_i \mid d \in S \wedge d_i \in S_i \wedge i \in I\}) = \oplus_{i \in I}(S \otimes S_i)$ and this equivalence is enough to verify that the power domain a cHa [2][Chapter IX, Theorem 15].

The projection operators lift to the power domain in a natural way by $\exists_x(S) = \varrho(\{\exists_x(d) \mid d \in S\})$ and similarly $\forall_x(S) = \varrho(\{\forall_x(d) \mid d \in S\})$. For equivalence between the three semantics to hold, $\langle \varrho(\wp(D)), \forall_x, \varrho(\wp(D)), \exists_x \rangle$ is required to be a Galois connection. The following proposition asserts that the only way to ensure this property, is to engineer $\forall_x : D \to D$ and $\exists_x : D \to D$ so that $\langle D, \forall_x, D, \exists_x \rangle$ is a Galois connection.

Theorem 5. $\langle \varrho(\wp(D)), \forall_x, \varrho(\wp(D)), \exists_x \rangle$ is a Galois connection if and only if $\langle D, \forall_x, D, \exists_x \rangle$ is a Galois connection.

Example 5. Consider the construction of a power domain for capturing numeric relationships between variables such that $\langle \varrho(\wp(D)), \forall_x, \varrho(\wp(D)), \exists_x \rangle$ is a Galois connection. Specifically consider Lin_X, the set of finite sets of equations of the form $ax + by < 0$ and $ax + by \leq 0$ where $a, b \in \{-1, 0, 1\}$ and $x, y \in X$ – a domain that arises in termination verification [22]. A mapping $\theta : X \to \mathbb{R}$ assigns a truth value to each $E \in Lin_X$ by $\theta(E) = \wedge_{e \in E} \theta(e)$ and $\theta(ax + by \circledast 0) \iff a\theta(x) + b\theta(y) \circledast 0$ where $\circledast \in \{<, \leq\}$. Then $E_1 \models E_2$ iff $\theta(E_1) \to \theta(E_2)$ holds for all $\theta : X \to \mathbb{R}$. Let $\bot = \{0 < 0\}$ and observe that $\theta(\bot)$ is false for all $\theta : X \to \mathbb{R}$. To construct $\oplus$ and $\otimes$, an operator $cl : Lin_X \to Lin_X$ is introduced to compute the entire set of equations entailed by a given equation set E (unless $E \models \bot$). Specifically $cl(E) = \cup\{E' \in Lin_X \mid E \models E'\}$ if $E \not\models \bot$ otherwise $cl(E) = \bot$. Then $\langle cl(Lin_X), \models, \oplus, \otimes \rangle$ is a finite lattice with a bottom element $\bot$ where $E_1 \oplus E_2 = E_1 \cap E_2$ if $E_1 \neq \bot$ and $E_2 \neq \bot$ whereas $E_1 \oplus E_2 = E_1$ if $E_2 = \bot$ and $E_1 \oplus E_2 = E_2$ if $E_1 = \bot$. Moreover $E_1 \otimes E_2 = cl(E_1 \cup E_2)$. By applying Floyd-Warshall shortest-path algorithms $cl(E)$ can be computed in $O(X^3)$ time [25]. To specify $\exists_x$ and $\forall_x$, the concept of a free variable is formalised as $FV(E) = \cup_{e \in E} FV(e)$ where $FV(ax + by \circledast 0) = \{x \mid a \neq 0\} \cup \{y \mid b \neq 0\}$. Then $\exists_x(E) = cl(\{e \in E \mid x \notin FV(e)\})$ and $\forall_x(E) = E$ if $x \notin FV(E)$ otherwise $\forall_x(E) = \bot$. Since $\exists_x \circ \forall_x(E) \models E \models \forall_x \circ \exists_x(E)$ and $\exists_x$ and $\forall_x$ are both monotonic, it follows that $\langle cl(Lin_X), \forall_x, cl(Lin_X), \exists_x \rangle$ is a Galois insertion. Moreover, when $\exists_x$ and $\forall_x$ are lifted to $\varrho(\wp(cl(Lin_X)))$, as specified above, then theorem 5 ensures that $\langle \varrho(\wp(cl(Lin_X)), \forall_x, \varrho(\wp(cl(Lin_X)), \exists_x \rangle$ is also a Galois connection. This guarantees that the semantics have equal power for verification.

If a cHa is constructed via a power domain, although the pseudo-complement is guaranteed to exist, it may not be clear how to compute $S_1 \Rightarrow S_1$ so that the backward framework can be applied in verification. However, for a given cHa $\langle L, \sqcup, \sqcap \rangle$, from the axioms of Heyting algebras it follows that $(\sqcup_{i \in I} a_i) \Rightarrow b = \sqcap_{i \in I}(a_i \Rightarrow b)$ where $\{a_i \mid i \in I\} \subseteq L$ for an index set I and $b \in L$. Moreover, it can be shown that $b \Rightarrow (\sqcup_{i \in I} a_i) = \sqcup_{i \in I}(b \Rightarrow a_i)$. These properties enable strength reduction to be applied in the calculation of $S_1 \Rightarrow S_2$ for $S_1, S_2 \in \varrho(\wp(D))$. Specifically $S_1 \Rightarrow S_2 = \otimes\{\{d_1\} \Rightarrow S_2 \mid d_1 \in S_1\}$ and $S_1 \Rightarrow S_2 = \oplus\{S_1 \Rightarrow \{d_2\} \mid d_2 \in S_2\}$. Thus, in a similar fashion to $\forall_x$ and $\exists_x$, it is enough to define an procedure for computing $\{d_1\} \Rightarrow \{d_2\}$ over $d_1, d_2 \in D$, and then lift the operator to full $\varrho(\wp(D))$. This construction scheme is illustrated below.

Example 6. Returning to example 5, it is thus sufficient to construct an operation $\rightrightarrows: Lin_X^2 \rightarrow \wp(Lin_X)$ such that $E_1 \rightrightarrows E_2 = \{E_1\} \Rightarrow \{E_2\}$ if $E_1, E_2 \in cl(Lin_X)$. To aid the construction, define $\neg(ax + by < 0) = (-a)x + (-b)y \leq 0$ and $\neg(ax + by \leq 0) = (-a)x + (-b)y < 0$. Suppose $E_2 = \{e_1, \ldots, e_n\}$. Then $E_1 \rightrightarrows E_2 = \varrho(\{cl(\cup_{i=1}^n \{\neg e'_i\}) \mid e'_i \in cl(E_1 \cup \{\neg e_i\})\})$. The following proposition asserts the correctness of this construction.

Proposition 3. Let $E_1, E_2 \in cl(Lin_X)$. Then $E_1 \rightrightarrows E_2 = \{E_1\} \Rightarrow \{E_2\}$.

Example 7. To illustrate an application of $E_1 \rightrightarrows E_2$ consider

$$E_1 = \{x - y \leq 0, -x + y \leq 0\} \qquad \text{and} \qquad E_2 = \{y - z \leq 0, y < 0\}$$

so that $E_1, E_2 \in cl(Lin_X)$ as required. Let $e_1 = y - z \leq 0$ and $e_2 = y < 0$, hence $\neg e_1 = -y + z < 0$ and $\neg e_2 = -y \leq 0$. Then

$$cl(E_1 \cup \{\neg e_1\}) = \{x - y \leq 0, -x + y \leq 0, -y + z < 0, -x + z < 0\}$$
$$cl(E_1 \cup \{\neg e_2\}) = \{x - y \leq 0, -x + y \leq 0, -y \leq 0, -x \leq 0\}$$

and therefore $E_1 \rightrightarrows E_2 = \{\{-x + y < 0\}, \{x - y < 0\}, \{y - z \leq 0, y < 0\}, \{y - z \leq 0, x < 0\}, \{x - z \leq 0, y < 0\}, \{x - z \leq 0, x < 0\}\}$. Observe that $\{\neg e_1\} \in E_1 \rightrightarrows E_2$ for all $e_1 \in E_1$ and that $E_2 \in E_1 \rightrightarrows E_2$. By lifting $\{E_1\} \Rightarrow \{E_2\}$ to arbitrary $S_1 \Rightarrow S_2$, the power domain construction is complete, thereby enabling any of the verification frameworks to be applied.

7   Related Work

This paper compares various fixpoint frameworks for the task of verification. However, if assertions are given for each predicate, for instance, to specify properties of computed answers as in [8], then the verification problem reduces to checking a pre-fixpoint [6] and iteration can be avoided altogether. This check merely requires the assertion language to possess a decidable entailment test and therefore these languages can be particularly expressive [30]. If the assertion language coincides with an abstract domain, then properties can be automatically inferred relaxing the requirement to systematically annotate each predicate.

Schachte compares the precision of a goal-independent analysis for abstract success patterns against the concrete success patterns [28] and likewise compares a goal-dependent analysis for abstract call patterns (derived using a condensing framework) relative to the concrete call patterns [27]. Optimality theorems for the goal-independent [28][Theorem 15] and goal-dependent analysis [27][Theorem 3.13] state that these analyses derive abstractions that exactly match those obtained by applying the abstraction map to the concrete patterns. These results hold for condensing domains equipped with an abstraction map α that satisfies the relation $\alpha(C_1) \barwedge \alpha(C_2) = \alpha(\{c_1 \wedge c_2 \mid c_1 \in C_1 \wedge c_2 \in C_2\} \setminus \{false\})$ where $\barwedge$ is the abstract conjunction operator. Interestingly, whether these results are applicable critically depends on how α handles sets of unsolvable constraints. For instance, for the domain Pos_X consider $C_1 = \{E_1\}$ and $C_2 = \{E_2\}$ with the equation sets $E_1 = \{x = a\}$ and $E_1 = \{x = b\}$. Then $\alpha_{Pos}(\{E_1\}) \barwedge \alpha_{Pos}(\{E_2\}) = x \wedge x = x$, however $\alpha_{Pos}(\{E_1 \cup E_2\} \setminus \{false\}) \models \alpha_{Pos}(\{E_1 \cup E_2\}) = false$ since $\{E_1 \cup E_2\} \setminus \{false\} \subseteq \{E_1 \cup E_2\}$ and $E_1 \cup E_2$ is unsolvable. Although comparing abstract with concrete is a laudable goal, our work merely compares one abstract framework against another and thereby relaxing the requirement on α.

One alternative approach to analysis that is more in tune with the needs of verification is to structure the analysis around the assertions themselves and only perform the computation necessary for verifying the assertions, thereby analysing the program on demand. A method for constructing such an demand-driven analysis is presented in [9] for dataflow analyses with distributive flow functions. These demand-driven algorithms propagate assertion requirements backward against the control-flow until they are satisfied. Interestingly, reversing the binding mechanism between actual and formal arguments is analogous to calculating universal projection. However, the reverse binding operator of [9] is incorrect (for copy constant propagation) – the direction of approximation in parameter passing needs to be revised to return the strongest abstraction and thereby simulate universal projection. In fact, incredibly, the same Galois connection requirement for correctness and precision appears also to be necessary in the demand-driven analysis of imperative programs.

Termination checking is the problem of verifying that a logic program left-terminates for a given query whereas termination inference is the problem of inferring initial queries under which a logic program left-terminates [24]. It has been observed [12] that the "missing link" between termination inference and termination checking is the backward analysis of [17]. Indeed, Genaim and Codish

[12] reconstruct the method of [24] in terms of existing black-box components that, according to [12], simplifies the formal justification and implementation of a termination inference analyser. First, the termination engine of [5] is used to compute a set of binary clauses which describe possible loops in the program with size relations. Second, Boolean functions are inferred for each predicate that describes moding conditions sufficient for each loop to only be executed a finite number of times. Third, the backward analysis of [17] is applied to infer initial modes that guarantee termination. The technical report version of [12] addresses the intriguing question of whether termination checking can verify all queries that can be inferred by termination inference and dually whether termination inference can infer all the queries that be verified with termination checking. The technical report presents a theorem that basically says that a termination checker reports that a program terminates for a mode if and only if the mode is deduced by a termination inference engine. The proof makes two assumptions about backward analysis named BA_1 and BA_2, and focuses on comparing the CHK and INF procedures that arise in termination analysis [12]. BA_1 is a precision assumption on backward analysis relating backward to forward analysis driven from input mode for a predicate q. Specifically, if backward analysis is applied to a program which is annotated with the call modes derived by the forward analysis, then the input mode inferred for q by backward analysis is not stronger than the mode of q used to initial the forward analysis. Note that this assumption relies, among other things, on the precision of universal projection.

Future work will examine the relation precision of differential methods [11].

8   Conclusions

This paper has provided a systematic comparison of the relative power of three different abstract interpretation frameworks for the problem of logic program verification. Conditions on the abstract domain operations have been derived which detail when these frameworks possess equivalent power. The paper also explains how power domains can satisfy the requirements for equivalence.

Acknowledgments. We thank Roberto Giacobazzi for his insightful comments on the relationship between existential and universal projection that motivated this work. We also thank John Gallagher, Samir Genaim, Peter Schachte for their comments and NSF grant CCR-0131862 for partly funding this work.

References

1. A. Aiken and T. K. Lakshman. Directional Type Checking of Logic Programs. In *Static Analysis Symposium*, volume 864 of *LNCS*, pages 43–60. Springer, 1994.
2. G. Birkhoff. *Lattice Theory*. AMS Press, 1967.
3. M. Bruynooghe. A Practical Framework for the Abstract Interpretation of Logic Programs. *The Journal of Logic Programming*, 10(1/2/3&4):91–124, 1991.

4. M. Codish and V. Lagoon. Type Dependencies for Logic Programs using ACI-unification. *Theoretical Computer Science*, 238:131–159, 2000.
5. M. Codish and C. Taboch. A Semantic Basis for the Termination Analysis of Logic Programs. *The Journal of Logic Programming*, 41(1):103–123, 1999.
6. M. Comini, R. Gori, G. Levi, and P. Volpe. Abstract Interpretation based Verification of Logic Programs. *Electronic Notes of Theoretical Computer Science*, 30(1), 1999.
7. P. Cousot and R. Cousot. Abstract Interpretation and Application to Logic Programs. *The Journal of Logic Programming*, 13(2–3):103–179, 1992.
8. W. Drabent and J. Małuszyński. Inductive Assertion Method for Logic Programs. *Theoretical Computer Science*, 59(1).133–155, 1988.
9. E. Duesterwald, R. Gupta, and M. L. Soffa. Demand-driven Computation of Interprocedural Data Flow. In *Principles of Programming Languages*, pages 37–48. ACM, 1995.
10. C. Fecht and H. Seidl. A Faster Solver for General Systems of Equations. *Science of Computer Programming*, 35(2–3):137–162, 1999.
11. M. García de la Banda, K. Marriott, P. J. Stuckey, and H. Søndergaard. Differential Methods in Logic Program Analysis. *The Journal of Logic Programming*, 35(1):1–37, 1998.
12. S. Genaim and M. Codish. Inferring Termination Conditions for Logic Programs using Backwards Analysis. In *International Conference on Logic for Programming, Artificial Intelligence and Reasoning*, volume 2250 of *LNAI*, pages 681–690. Springer, 2001. Technical report version available at http://www.cs.bgu.ac.il/~mcodish/Papers/Pages/lpar01.html.
13. R. Giacobazzi and F. Scozzari. A Logical Model for Relational Abstract Domains. *ACM Transactions on Programming Languages and Systems*, 20(5):1067–1109, 1998.
14. M. Hermenegildo, G. Puebla, K. Marriott, and P. Stuckey. Incremental analysis of constraint logic programs. *ACM Transactions on Programming Languages and Systems*, 22(2):187–223, 2000.
15. R. J. M. Hughes and J. Launchbury. Reversing Abstract Interpretations. *Science of Computer Programming*, 22(3):307–326, 1994.
16. D. Jacobs and A. Langen. Static Analysis of Logic Programs for Independent And-Parallelism. *The Journal of Logic Programming*, 13(1/2/3&4):291–314, 1992.
17. A. King and L. Lu. A Backward Analysis for Constraint Logic Programs. *Theory and Practice of Logic Programming*, 2(4–5):517–547, 2002.
18. A. King and L. Lu. Forward versus Backward Verification of Logic Programs. Technical Report 5-03, Computing Laboratory, University of Kent, April 2003.
19. A. Langen. *Advanced Techniques for Approximating Variable Aliasing in Logic Programs*. PhD thesis, Computer Science Department, University of Southern California, Los Angeles, 1991.
20. B. Le Charlier, C. Leclére, S. Rossi, and A. Cortesi. Automatic Verification of Prolog Programs. *The Journal of Logic Programming*, 39(1–3):3–42, 1999.
21. B. Le Charlier and P. Van Hentenryck. Experimental Evaluation of a Generic Abstract Interpretation Algorithm for Prolog. *ACM Transactions on Programming Languages and Systems*, 16(1):35–101, 1994.
22. N. Lindenstrauss and Y. Sagiv. Automatic Termination Analysis of Logic Programs. In *International Conference on Logic Programming*, pages 63–77. MIT Press, 1997.
23. L. Lu and A. King. Backward Type Inference Generalises Type Checking. In *Static Analysis Symposium*, volume 2477 of *LNCS*, pages 85–101. Springer, 2002.

24. F. Mesnard and S. Ruggieri. On Proving Left Termination of Constraint Logic Programs. *ACM Transactions on Computational Logic*, 4(2):207–259, 2003.
25. A. Miné. The Octagon Abstract Domain. In *Eighth Working Conference on Reverse Engineering*, pages 310–319. IEEE Computer Society, 2001.
26. G. Puebla, F. Bueno, and M. Hermenegildo. An Assertion Language for Constraint Logic Programs. In *Analysis and Visualization Tools for Constraint Programming*, volume 1870 of *LNCS*, pages 23–61. Springer, 2000.
27. P. Schachte. *Precise and Efficient Static Analysis of Logic Programs*. PhD thesis, Department of Computer Science, University of Melbourne, 1999.
28. P. Schachte. Precise Goal-independent Abstract Interpretation of Constraint Logic Programs. *Theoretical Computer Science*, 293(3):557–577, 2003.
29. D. van Dalen. *Logic and Structure*. Springer, 1997.
30. P. Volpe. A First-Order Language for Expressing Aliasing and Type Properties of Logic Programs. *Science of Computer Programming*, 39(1):125–148, 2001.

Native Preemptive Threads in SWI-Prolog

Jan Wielemaker

Social Science Informatics (SWI),
University of Amsterdam,
Roetersstraat 15, 1018 WB Amsterdam, The Netherlands,
jan@swi.psy.uva.nl

Abstract. Concurrency is an attractive property of a language to exploit multi-CPU hardware or perform multiple tasks concurrently. In recent years we see Prolog systems experimenting with multiple threads only sharing the database. Such systems are relatively easy to build and remain very close to standard Prolog while providing valuable extra functionality. This article describes the introduction of multiple threads in SWI-Prolog exploiting OS-native threading. We discuss the extra primitives available to the Prolog programmer as well as implementation issues. We explored speedup on multi-processor hardware and speed degradation when executing a single task.

1 Introduction

There are two approaches to concurrency in the Prolog community, implicit fine-grained parallelism where tasks share Prolog variables and systems (see Sect. 7) in which Prolog engines only share the database (clauses) and run otherwise completely independent. Programming these *multi-threaded* systems is very close to programming single-threaded Prolog systems, turning these systems into an attractive platform for tasks where concurrency is desirable:

Network servers/agents. These systems must be able to pay attention to multiple clients. Threading allows multiple, generally almost independent, tasks to make progress at the same time and can improve overall performance when exploiting multiple CPUs (SMP) or if the tasks are I/O bound. Section 4.1 provides an example.

Embedding in multi-threaded servers. Concurrent network-service infrastructures such as CORBA or .NET that embed Prolog can profit from multi-threaded Prolog retaining their overall concurrent behaviour, which is lost if request must be serialized to a single Prolog instance that is responsible for a significant part of the server's work.

Background processing in interactive systems. Responsiveness and usefulness of interactive applications can be improved if background processing deals with tasks such as spell-checking and syntax-highlighting. Implementation as a foreground process either harms response-time or is complicated by interaction with the GUI event-handling.

C. Palamidessi (Ed.): ICLP 2003, LNCS 2916, pp. 331–345, 2003.

CPU intensive tasks. On SMP systems CPU intensive tasks that can easily be split into independent subtasks can profit from a multi-threaded implementation. Section 6.2 describes an experiment.

In multi-threaded Prolog we must add primitives for threads to communicate and synchronise their activities. Our choices are based on the requirement to cooperate smoothly with multi-threaded foreign language code as well as the desire to keep it simple for the Prolog programmer.

Our implementation is based to the POSIX thread (pthread) API [2] for its portability and clean design. On Windows we use a mixture of pthread-win32[1] and the native Win32 thread-API.

This paper explores the loss of performance of single-threaded Prolog code executing in a multi-threaded environment. It also explores the consequences of introducing threads in an originally single-threaded implementation of the Prolog language including difficult areas such as atom garbage-collection.

In Sect. 2 we summary our requirements for multi-threaded Prolog. Next we describe what constitutes a thread and what primitives are used to make threads communicate and synchronise. In Sect. 4 we summarise our new primitives. Section 5 describes implementation experience, followed by performance analysis in Sect. 6 and an overview of related work in Sect. 7.

2 Requirements

Smooth cooperation with (threaded) foreign code. Prolog applications operating in the real world often require substantial amounts of 'foreign' code for interaction with the outside world: window-system interface, interfaces to dedicated devices and networks. Prolog threads must be able to call arbitrary foreign code without blocking the other (Prolog-) threads and foreign code must be able to create, use and destroy Prolog engines.

Simple for the Prolog programmer. We want to introduce few and easy to use primitives to the Prolog programmer.

Robust during development. We want to be as robust as feasible during interactive use and the test-edit-reload development cycle. In particular this implies the use of synchronisation elements that will not easily create deadlocks when used incorrectly.

3 What Is a Prolog Thread?

A Prolog thread is an OS-native thread running a Prolog *engine*, consisting of a set of stacks and the required state to accommodate the engine. After being started from a *goal* it proves this goal just like a normal Prolog implementation. Figure 1 illustrates the architecture. As each engine has its own stacks, Prolog terms can only be transferred between threads by copying. Both dynamic predicates and FIFO queues of Prolog terms can be used to transfer Prolog terms between threads.

---

[1] http://sources.redhat.com/pthreads-win32/

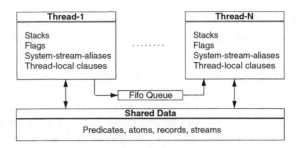

Fig. 1. Multiple Prolog engines sharing the same database. Flags and the system-defined stream aliases such as `current_input` are copied from the creating thread. Clauses are normally shared, except for thread-local clauses discussed below in Sect. 3.1.

3.1   Predicates

By default, all predicates, both static and dynamic, are shared between all threads. Changes to static predicates only influence the test-edit-reload cycle, which is discussed in Sect. 5. For dynamic predicates we kept the 'logical update semantics' as defined by the ISO standard [6]. This implies that a goal uses the predicate with the clause set as found when the goal was started, regardless of whether clauses are asserted or retracted by the calling thread or another thread. The implementation ensures consistency of the predicate as seen from Prolog's perspective. Consistency as required by the application such as clause order and consistency with other dynamic predicates must be ensured using *synchronisation* as discussed in Sect. 3.2.

Thread-local predicates are dynamic predicates that have a different set of clauses in each thread. Modifications to such predicates using **assert/1** or **retract/1** are only visible from the thread that performs the modification. In addition, such predicates start with an empty clause set and clauses remaining when the thread dies are automatically removed. Like the related POSIX thread-specific data primitive, thread-local predicates simplifies making code designed for single-threaded use *thread-safe*.

3.2   Synchronisation

The most difficult aspect of multi-threaded programming is the need to *synchronise* the concurrently executing threads: ensure they use proper protocols to exchange data and maintain invariants of *shared-data* in dynamic predicates. POSIX threads offer three mechanisms to organise this:

A mutex is a **Mut**ual **Ex**clusive device. At most one thread can 'hold' a mutex. By associating a mutex to data it can be assured only one thread has access to this data at any time, allowing it to maintain the invariants.

A condition variable is an object that can be used to wait for a certain *condition*. For example, if data is not in a state where a thread can start using it it can wait on a condition variable associated with this data. If another thread updates the data it *signals* the condition variable, telling the waiting thread something has changed and it may re-examine the condition.

As [2] explains in chapter 4, the commonly used thread cooperating techniques can be realised using the above two primitives. These primitives however are not very attractive to the Prolog user because great care is required to use them in the proper order and complete all steps of the protocol. Failure to do so may lead to data corruption or all threads waiting for an event to happen that never will (deadlock). Non-determinism, exceptions and the interactive development-cycle supported by Prolog complicate this further.

Our primary synchronisation primitive is a FIFO (first-in-first-out) queue of Prolog terms. This approach has been used successfully in similar projects and languages, see Sect. 7. Queues (also called *channels* or *ports*) are well understood, easy to understand by non-experts in multi-threading, can safely handle abnormal execution paths (backtracking and exceptions) and can naturally represent serialised flow of data (*pipeline*). Next to the FIFO queues we support goals guarded by a mutex by means of **with_mutex**(*Mutex, Goal*) as defined in Sect. 4.2.

3.3   I/O and Debugging

Support for multi-threaded I/O is rather primitive. I/O streams are global objects that may be created, accessed and closed from any thread knowing their handle. All I/O predicates lock a mutex associated with the stream, providing elementary consistency.

Stream alias names for the system streams (e.g. `user_input`) are thread-specific, where a new thread inherits the bindings from its creator. Local system stream aliases allow us to re-bind the user streams and provide separate interaction consoles for each thread as implemented by **attach_console/0**. The console is realised using a clone of the normal SWI-Prolog console on Windows or an instance of the `xterm` application in Unix. The predicate **interactor/0** creates a thread, attaches a console and runs the Prolog toplevel.

Using **thread_signal/2**, a primitive similar to **thread_push_goal/2** in Qu-Prolog and described in Sect. 4.2, the user can attach a console to any thread as well as start the debugger in any thread as illustrated in Fig. 2.

4   Managing Threads from Prolog

An important requirement is to make threads easy for the programmer, especially for the task we are primarily targeting at, interacting with the outside world. First we start with an example, followed by a partial description of the Prolog API and the consequences for the foreign language interface.

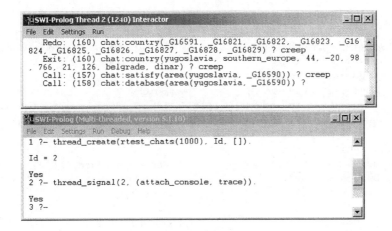

Fig. 2. Attach a console and start the debugger in another thread.

4.1   A Short Example

Before describing the details, we present the implementation of a simple network service in Fig. 3. We will not discuss the details of all built-in and library predicates used in this example. The thread-related predicates are discussed in more detail in Sect. 4.2 while all details can be found in [13]. Our service handles a single TCP/IP request per connection, using a specified number of 'worker threads' and a single 'accept-thread'. The accept-thread executes **acceptor/2**, accepting connection requests and adding them to the queue for the workers. The workers execute **worker/1**, getting the accepted socket from the queue, read the request and execute **process/2** to compute a reply and write this to the output stream. After this, the worker returns to the queue for the next request.

The advantages of this implementation over a traditional single-threaded Prolog implementation are evident. Our server exploits SMP hardware and will show much more predictable response times, especially if there is a large distribution in the time required by **process/1**. In addition, we can easily improve on it with more monitoring components. For example, **acceptor/2** could immediately respond with an estimated reply time, and commands can be provided to examine and control activity of the workers. Using multi-threaded code, such improvements do not affect the implementation of **process/2**, keeping this simple and reusable.

4.2   Prolog Primitives

This section discusses the built-in predicates we have added to Prolog. The description of the API is incomplete to keep it concise. A full description is in [13].

thread_create(*:Goal, -Id, +Options*)
    Create a thread which starts executing *Goal*. *Id* is unified with the thread-

:- use_module(library(socket)).
 	
make_server(Port, Workers) :-
    create_socket(Port, S),
    message_queue_create(Q),
    forall(between(1, Workers, _),
        thread_create(worker(Q), _, [])),
    thread_create(acceptor(S, Q), _, []).
 	
create_socket(Port, Socket) :-
    tcp_socket(Socket),
    tcp_bind(Socket, Port),
    tcp_listen(Socket, 5).
	acceptor(Socket, Q) :-
	    tcp_accept(Socket, Client, _Peer),
	    thread_send_message(Q, Client),
	    acceptor(Socket, Q).
	
	worker(Q) :-
	    thread_get_message(Q, Client),
	    tcp_open_socket(Client, In, Out),
	    read(In, Command),
	    close(In),
	    process(Command, Out),
	    close(Out),
	    worker(Q).
	
	process(hello, Out) :-
	    format(Out, 'Hello world!~n', []).

Fig. 3. Implementation of a multi-threaded server. Threading primitives are set in bold. The left column builds the server. The top-right runs the *acceptor* thread, while the bottom-right contains the code for a *worker* of the crew.

identifier. The **thread_create/3** call returns immediately. *Goal* can succeed at most once.

The new Prolog engine runs independently. If the thread is *attached*, any thread can wait for its completion using **thread_join/2**. Otherwise all resources are reclaimed silently on completion.

thread_join(*+Id, -Result*)

Wait for the thread *Id* to finish and unify *Result* with the completion status, which is one of **true, false** or **exception**(*Term*).

message_queue_create(*-Queue*)

Create a FIFO message queue (*channel*). Message queues can be read from multiple threads. Each thread has a message queue (*port*) attached as it is created.

thread_send_message(*+QueueOrThread, +Term*)

Add a copy of term to the given queue or default queue of the thread. Return immediately.[2]

thread_get_message(*[+Queue], ?Term*)

Get a message from the given queue (*channel*) or default queue if *Queue* is omitted (*port*). The first message that unifies with *Term* is removed from the queue and returned. If multiple threads are waiting, only one will be given the term. If the queue has no matching terms, execution of the calling thread is suspended.

---

[2] For a memory-efficient realisation of the pipeline model it may be desirable to suspend if the queue exceeds a certain length, waiting for the consumers to drain the queue.

with_mutex(+*Name, :Goal***)**

Execute *Goal* as **once/1** while holding the named mutex. *Name* is an atom. Explicit use of mutex objects is used to serialise access to code that is not designed for multi-threaded operation as well as coordinate access to shared dynamic predicates. The example below updates **address/2**. Without a mutex another thread may see no address for *Id* if it executes just between the **retractall/1** and **assert/1**.

```
set_address(Id, Address) :-
        with_mutex(address, (retractall(address(Id, _)),
                             assert(address(Id, Address)))).
```

thread_signal(+*Thread, :Goal***)**

Make *Thread* execute *Goal* on the first opportunity. 'First opportunity' is defined to be the next pass through the call-port or foreign code calling PL_handle_signals(). The latter mechanism is used to make threads handle signals during blocking I/O, etc. This primitive is intended for 'manager' threads to control their work-crew as illustrated in Fig. 4 and for the developer to abort or trace a thread (Fig. 2).

Worker	Manager

worker(Queue) :-
    thread_get_message(Queue, Work),
    catch(do_work(Work),   **stop**,
cleanup),
    worker(Queue).
	. . .
	    thread_signal(Worker,
	throw(stop)),
	    . . .

Fig. 4. Stopping a worker using **thread_signal/2**. Bold fragments show the relevant parts of the code.

4.3   Accessing Prolog Threads from C

Integration with C-code has always been one of the main design goals of SWI-Prolog. With Prolog threads, flexible embedding in multi-threaded environments becomes feasible. The system provides two sets of primitives, one for long living external threads that want to use Prolog often and one to facilitate environments with many or short living threads that have to do some infrequent work in Prolog.

The API PL_thread_attach_engine() creates a Prolog engine and makes it available to the thread for running queries. The engine may be destroyed explicitely using PL_thread_destroy_engine() or it will be destroyed automatically when the underlying POSIX thread terminates. This method is not very suitable for many threads that infrequently require Prolog as creating and destroying

Prolog engines is an expensive operation and engines require significant memory resources.

Alternatively, foreign code can create one or more Prolog engines using PL_create_engine() and attach an engine using PL_set_engine(). Setting and releasing an engine is a fast operation and the system can realise a suitable pool of engines to balance concurrency and memory requirements. A demo implementation is available.[3]

5   Implementation Issues

We tried to minimise the changes required to turn the single-engine and single-threaded SWI-Prolog system into a multi-threaded version. For the first implementation we split all global data into three sets: data that is initialised when Prolog is initialised and never changes afterwards, data that is used for shared data-structures, such as atoms, predicates, modules, etc. and finally data that is only used by a single engine such as the stacks and virtual machine registers. Each set is stored in a single C-structure, using thread-specific data (Sect. 3.2) to access the engine data in the multi-threaded version. Update to shared data was serialised using mutexes.

A prototype using this straight-forward transition was realised in only two weeks, but it ran slowly due to too heavy use of pthread_getspecific() and too many mutex synchronisation points. In the second phase, fetching the current engine using pthread_getspecific() was reduced by caching this information inside functions that use it multiple times and passing it as an extra variable to commonly used small functions as identified using the gprof [8] profiling tool. Mutex contention was analysed and reduced from some critical places:

All predicates used reference counting to clean up deleted clauses after **retract/1** for dynamic or (re-)consult/1 for static code. Dynamic clauses require synchronisation to make changes visible and cleanup erased clauses, but static code can do without this. Reclaiming dead clauses from static code as a result of the test-edit-reconsult cycle is left to a garbage collector that operates similarly to the atom garbage collection described in Sect. 5.1.

Permanent heap allocation uses a pool of free memory chunks associated with the thread's engine. This allows threads to allocate and free permanent memory without synchronisation.

5.1   Garbage Collection

Stack garbage collection is not affected by threading and continues concurrently. This allows for threads under real-time constraints by writing them such that they do not perform garbage collections, while other threads can use garbage collection.

---

[3] http://gollem.swi.psy.uva.nl/twiki/pl/bin/view/Development/
MultiThreadEmbed

Atom garbage collection is more complicated because atoms are shared global resources. Atoms referenced from global data such as clauses and records use reference counting, while atoms reachable from the stacks are marked during the marking phase of the atom garbage collector. With multiple threads this implies that all threads have to mark their atoms before the collector can reclaim unused atoms. The pseudo code below illustrates the signal-based implementation used on Unix systems.

```
atom_gc()
{ mark_atoms_on_stacks();              // mark my own atoms
  foreach(thread except self)          // ask the other threads
  { pthread_kill(thread, SIG_ATOM_GC);
    signalled++;
  }
  while(signalled-- > 0)               // wait until all is done
    sem_wait(atom_semaphore);
  collect_unmarked_atoms();
}
```

A thread receiving SIG_ATOM_GC calls mark_atoms_on_stacks() and signals the atom_semaphore semaphore when done. The mark_atoms_on_stacks() function is designed such that it is safe to call it asynchronously. Uninitialised variables on the Prolog stacks may be interpreted incorrectly as an atom, but such mistakes are infrequent and can be corrected in a later run of the garbage collector. The atom garbage collector holds the *atom* mutex, preventing threads to create atoms or increment the reference count. The marking phase is executed in parallel.

Windows does not provides asynchronous signals and synchronous (cooperative) marking of referenced atoms is not acceptable because the invoking thread as well as any thread that wishes to create an atom must block until atom GC has completed. Therefore the thread that runs the atom garbage collector uses SuspendThread() and ResumeThread() to stop and restart each thread in turn while it marks the atoms of the suspended thread.

Atom-GC and GC interaction. SWI-Prolog uses a sliding garbage collector [1]. During the execution of GC, it is very hard to mark atoms. Therefore during atom-GC, GC cannot start. Because atom-GC is such a harmful activity, we should avoid it being blocked by a normal GC. Therefore the system keeps track of the number of threads executing GC. If a GC is running atom-GC is delayed until no thread executes GC.

6   Performance Evaluation

Our aim was to use the multi-threaded version as default release version, something which is only acceptable if its performance running a normal non-threaded program is close to the performance of the single-threaded version, which is investigated in Sect. 6.1. In Sect. 6.2 we studied the speedup on SMP systems by splitting a large task into subtasks that are distributed over a pool of threads.

6.1   Comparing Multi-threaded to Single Threaded Version

We used the benchmark suite by Fernando Pereira[4] for comparing the single
threaded to the multi threaded version on a range of benchmarks addressing
very specific parts of the Prolog implementation. We normalised the iterations
of each test to make it run for approx. one second, after which we executed the
34 tests in 5 different settings, described here in the left-to-right order used in
Fig. 5. All test were run on a 550Mhz Crusoe machine running SuSE Linux 7.3
and Windows 2000.

Bar	Threading	OS	Comments
1	Single	Linux	Our *base-case*.
2	Single	Linux	With extra variable. See below.
3	Multi	Linux	Normal release version.
4	Single	Windows	Compiled for these tests.
5	Multi	Windows	Normal release version.

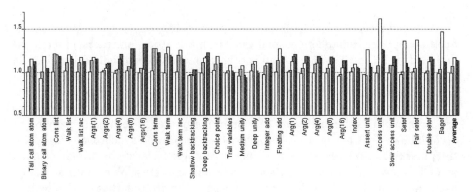

Fig. 5. Performance comparison between single and multi-threaded versions. The Y-
axis shows the time to complete the benchmark in seconds.

Figure 5 indicates there is no significant difference on any of the tests between
the single- and multi-threaded version on Windows 2000. It does show significant
differences on Linux, where the single-threaded version is considerably faster
and the multi-threaded version performs overall slightly worse and a few tests
that perform much less. The poorly performing tests all require frequent mutex
synchronisation due to the use of dynamic predicates or, for tests using **setof/3**,
locking atoms in the result table.

The state of the virtual machine in the single threaded version is stored
in a global structure, while it is accessible through a pointer passed between
functions in the multi threaded version. To explain the differences on Linux
we first compiled a version that passes a pointer to the virtual machine state

---

[4] http://www-2.cs.cmu.edu/afs/cs/project/ai-repository/ai/lang/prolog/
code/bench/pereira.txt

but is otherwise identical to the single threaded version. This version (2nd bar) exhibits behaviour very similar to the multi-threaded (3th bar) version on many of the tests, except for the tests that require heavy synchronisation. We conclude that the extra variable and argument in many functions is responsible for the difference and the difference does not show up in the Windows version due to inferior optimisation of MSVC 5 compared to gcc 2.95.[5] We also conclude that Microsoft *critical sections* used in the Windows version are considerably faster than the glibc implementation of the more general POSIX mutex objects.

Finally we give the cumulative results of a few other platforms and compilers. Dual AMD-Athlon, SuSE 8.1, gcc 3.1: -19%; Single UltraSPARC, Solaris 5.7, gcc 2.95: -7%; Single Intel PIII, SuSE 8.2, gcc 3.2: -19%. Solaris performs better on the mutex-intensive tests.

6.2   A Case Study: Speedup on SMP Systems

This section describes the results of multi-threading the Inductive Logic Programming system Aleph [11], developed by Ashwin Srinivasan at the Oxford University Computing Laboratory. Inductive Logic Programming (ILP) is a branch of machine learning that synthesises logic programs using other logic programs as input.

The main algorithm in Aleph relies on searching a space of possible general clauses for the one that scores best with respect to the input logic programs. Given any one example from the input, a lattice of plausible single-clauses ordered by generality is bound from above by the clause with true as the body ($\top$), and bound from below by a long (up to hundreds of literals) clause known as the most-specific-clause (or bottom) ($\bot$) [10].

Many strategies are possible for searching this often huge lattice. Randomised local search [12] is one form implemented in Aleph. Here a node in the lattice is selected at random as a starting location to *(re)-start* the search. A finite number of *moves* (e.g. radially from the starting node) are made from the start node. The best scoring node is recorded, and another node is selected at random to restart the search. The best scoring node from all restarts is returned.

As each restart in a randomised local search of the lattice is independent, the search can be multi-threaded in a straight forward manner using the worker-crew model, with each worker handling moves from a random start point and returning the best clauses as depicted in Fig. 6. We exploited the thread-local predicates described Sect. 3.1 to make the working memory of the search kept in dynamic predicates local to each worker.

Experimental results and discussion. An exploratory study was performed to study the speedup resulting from using multiple threads on an SMP machine. We realised a work-crew model implementation for randomised local search in

---

[5] This could be verified by compiling Prolog using GCC on Windows. This test has not been performed.

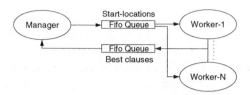

Fig. 6. Concurrent Aleph. A manager schedules start points for a crew of workers. Each worker computes the best clause from the neighbourhood of the start point, delivers it to the manager and continues with the next start-point.

Aleph version 4. As the task is completely CPU bound we expected optimal results if the number of threads equals the number of utilised processors.[6] The task consisted of 16 random restarts, each making 10 *moves* using the *carcinogenesis* [9] data set.[7] This task was carried out using a work-crew of 1, 2, 4, 8 and 16 workers scheduled on an equal number of CPUs. Figure 7 shows the result.

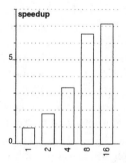

Fig. 7. Speedup with an increasing number of CPUs defined as elapsed time using one CPU divided by elapsed time using N CPUs. The task consisted of 16 *restarts* of 10 *moves*. The values are averaged over 30 runs. The study was performed on a Sun Fire 6800 with 24 UltraSPARC III 900 MHz Processors, 48 GB of shared memory, utilising up to 16 processors. Each processor had 2 GB of memory.

Finally, we used Aleph to assess performance using many threads per CPU. These results indicate the penalty of splitting a single-threaded design into a multi-threaded one. The results are shown in Fig. 8.

---

[6] We forgot to reserve a CPU for the manager. As it has very little work to do we do not expect results with an additional CPU for the manager to differ significantly with our results.

[7] ftp://ftp.comlab.ox.ac.uk/pub/Packages/ILP/Datasets/carcinogenesis/ progol/carcinogenesis.tar.Z

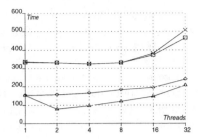

Fig. 8. CPU- and elapsed time running Aleph concurrent on two architectures. The top two graphs are executed on a single CPU Intel PIII/733 Mhz, SuSE 8.2. The bottom two graphs are executed on a dual Athlon 1600+, SuSE 8.1. The X and triangle marked graps represent elapsed time.

7   Related Work

This section provides an incomplete overview of other Prolog implementations providing multi-threading where threads only share the database. Many implementations use message queues (called *port* if the queue is an integral part of the thread or *channel* if they can be used by multiple threads).

SICStus-MT. [7] describes a prototype implementation of a multi-threaded version of SICStus Prolog based on the idea to have multiple Prolog engines only sharing the database. They used a proprietary preemptive scheduler for the prototype and therefore cannot support SMP hardware and have trouble with clean handling of blocking system-calls. The programmer interface is similar to ours, but they do not provide queues (channels) with multiple readers, nor additional synchronisation primitives.

CIAO Prolog [8] [4] provides preemptive threading based on POSIX threads. The referenced article also gives a good overview of concurrency approaches in Prolog and related languages. Their design objectives are similar, though they stress the ability to backtrack between threads as well as Linda-like [3] blackboard architectures. Threads that succeed non-deterministically can be restarted to produce an alternative solution and instead of queues they use 'concurrent' predicates where execution suspends if there is no alternative clause and is resumed after another thread asserts a new clause.

Qu-Prolog [9] provides threads using its own scheduler. Thread creation is similar in nature to the interface described in this article. Thread communication is, like ours, based on exchanging terms through a queue attached to each thread. For atomic operations it provides **thread_atomic_goal/1** which freezes all threads.

---

[8] http://clip.dia.fi.upm.es/Software/Ciao/
[9] http://www.svrc.uq.edu.au/Software/QuPrologHome.html

This operation is nearly impossible to realise on POSIX threads. Qu-Prolog supports **thread_signal/2** under the name **thread_push_goal/2**. For synchronisation it provides **thread_wait/1** to wait for arbitrary changes to the database.

Multi-prolog [5] is logic programming instantiation of the Linda blackboard architecture. It adds primitives to 'put' and 'get' both passive Prolog literals and active Prolog atoms (threads) to the blackboard. It is beyond the scope of this article to discuss the merits of message queues vs. a blackboard.

8   Issues and Future Work

Concurrency running static Prolog code is very good. Performance however degrades quickly on SMP systems when using primitives that require synchronisation. The most important issues are:

Dynamic predicates harm concurrency. Dynamic predicates require mutex synchronisation on assert, retract, entry and exit. Heavy use of dynamic code can harm efficiency significantly. Thread-local dynamic code can avoid expensive synchronisation.

Atoms harm concurrency. Atom handling in the current implementation has serious flaws. Creating an atom, creating a reference to an atom from **assert/1** or **recorda/1** as well as erasing records and clauses referencing atoms require locking the atom table. Even worse, atom garbage collection affects all running threads, harming threads under tight real-time constraints.

Meta-calling harms concurrency. Meta-calling requires synchronised mapping from module and functor to predicate.

Mutex synchronisation. POSIX mutexes are stand-alone entities and thus not related to the data they protect through any formal mechanism. This also holds for our Prolog-level mutexes. Alternatively a lock could be attached to the object it protects (i.e. a dynamic predicate). We have not adopted this model as we regard the use of explicit mutex objects restricted to special cases.

9   Conclusions

We have demonstrated the feasibility of supporting preemptive multi-threading using portable (POSIX) thread primitives in an existing Prolog system developed for single-threading. Concurrently running static Prolog code performs comparable to the single-threaded version and scales well on SMP hardware. Threaded Prolog using a shared database is relatively easy to implement while providing valuable functionality for server, interactive and CPU-intensive applications.

Built on the POSIX thread API, the system has been confirmed to run unmodified on six Unix dialects. The MacOS X and MS-Windows versions required special attention due to the partial support for POSIX semaphores in MacOS X and the lack of asynchronous signals in MS-Windows.

Acknowledgements. SWI-Prolog is a Free Software project which, by nature, profits heavily from user feedback and participation. We would like to express our gratitude to Sergey Tikhonov for his courage to test and help debug early versions of the implementation. The work reported in Sect. 6.2 was performed jointly with Ashwin Srinivasan and Steve Moyle at the Oxford University Computing Laboratory. We gratefully acknowledge the Oxford Supercomputing Centre for the use of their system, and in particular Fred Youhanaie for his patient guidance and support. Anjo Anjewierden has provided extensive comments on earlier versions of this article.

References

1. Karen Appleby, Mats Carlsson, Seif Haridi, and Dan Sahlin. Garbage collection for Prolog based on WAM. *Communications of the ACM*, 31(6): 719–741, 1988.
2. David R. Butenhof. *Programming with POSIX threads*. Addison-Wesley, Reading, MA, USA, 1997.
3. Nicholas Carriero and David Gelernter. Linda in context. *Communications of the ACM*, 32(4):444–458, April 1989.
4. Manuel Carro and Manuel V. Hermenegildo. Concurrency in Prolog using threads and a shared database. In *International Conference on Logic Programming*, pages 320–334, 1999.
5. Koen de Bosschere and Jean-Marie Jacquet. Multi-Prolog: Definition, operational semantics and implementation. In David S. Warren, editor, *Proceedings of the Tenth International Conference on Logic Programming*, pages 299–313, Budapest, Hungary, 1993. The MIT Press.
6. P. Deransart, A. Ed-Dbali, and L. Cervoni. *Prolog: The Standard*. Springer-Verlag, New York, 1996.
7. Jesper Eskilson and Mats Carlsson. SICStus MT—a multithreaded execution environment for SICStus Prolog. In C. Palamidessi, H. Glaser, and K. Meinke, editors, *Programming Languages: Implementations, Logics, and Programs*, volume 1490 of *Lecture Notes in Computer Science*, pages 36–53. Springer-Verlag, 1998.
8. Susan L. Graham, Peter B. Kessler, and Marshall K. McKusick. gprof: a call graph execution profiler. In *SIGPLAN Symposium on Compiler Construction*, pages 120–126, 1982.
9. R.D. King and A. Srinivasan. Prediction of rodent carcinogenicity bioassays from molecular structure using inductive logic programming. *Environmental Health Perspectives*, 104(5):1031–1040, 1996.
10. S. Muggleton. Inverse entailment and Progol. *New Generation Computing, Special issue on Inductive Logic Programming*, 13(3-4):245–286, 1995.
11. A. Srinivasan. *The Aleph Manual*, 2003.
12. F. Železný, A. Srinivasan, and D. Page. Lattice-search runtime distributions may be heavy-tailed. In S. Matwin and C. Sammut, editors, *Proceedings of the 12th International Conference on Inductive Logic Programming*, volume 2583 of *Lecture Notes in Artificial Intelligence*, pages 333–345. Springer-Verlag, 2003.
13. J. Wielemaker. *SWI-Prolog 5.1: Reference Manual*. SWI, University of Amsterdam, Roetersstraat 15, 1018 WB Amsterdam, The Netherlands, 1997–2003. E-mail: jan@swi.psy.uva.nl.

Flow Java: Declarative Concurrency for Java

Frej Drejhammar[1,2], Christian Schulte[1], Per Brand[2], and Seif Haridi[1,2]

[1] Institute for Microelectronics and Information Technology
KTH - Royal Institute of Technology
Electrum 229, SE-16440 Kista, Sweden
{frej,schulte}@imit.kth.se
[2] SICS - Swedish Institute of Computer Science
Box 1263, SE-16429 Kista, Sweden
{perbrand,seif}@sics.se

Abstract. Logic variables pioneered by (concurrent) logic and concurrent constraint programming are powerful mechanisms for automatically synchronizing concurrent computations. They support a declarative model of concurrency that avoids explicitly suspending and resuming computations. This paper presents *Flow Java* which conservatively extends Java with single assignment variables and futures as variants of logic variables. The extension is conservative with respect to object-orientation, types, parameter passing, and concurrency in Java. Futures support secure concurrent abstractions and are essential for seamless integration of single assignment variables into Java. We show how Flow Java supports the construction of simple and concise concurrent programming abstractions. We present how to moderately extend compilation and the runtime architecture of an existing Java implementation for Flow Java. Evaluation using standard Java benchmarks shows that in most cases the overhead is between 10% and 40%. For some pathological cases the runtime increases by up to 75%.

1 Introduction

Concurrent, distributed, and parallel programs fundamentally rely on simple, powerful, and hopefully even automatic mechanisms for synchronizing concurrent computations on shared data. Powerful programming abstractions for automatic synchronization are logic variables and futures (as read-only variants of logic variables). Logic variables for concurrent programming have been pioneered in the area of concurrent logic programming [19], concurrent constraint programming [17,16,20], and distributed programming [11].

This paper presents Flow Java which conservatively extends Java with variants of logic variables referred to as *single assignment variables*. By *synchronization variables* we refer to both single assignment variables and futures. Synchronization variables provide a declarative concurrent programming model allowing the programmer to focus on *what* needs to be synchronized among concurrent computations [24]. This is in contrast to synchronized methods in Java where explicit actions to suspend and resume computations are required. Moreover, a

C. Palamidessi (Ed.): ICLP 2003, LNCS 2916, pp. 346–360, 2003.
© Springer-Verlag Berlin Heidelberg 2003

programmer is always faced with the complexities of shared mutable state in a concurrent setting (even if not necessary). Synchronization variables in particular support the organization of concurrent computations in a dataflow style.

Flow Java. Flow Java is a conservative extension of Java with respect to types, object-orientation, parameter passing, and concurrency. Flow Java programs without synchronization variables compute as their Java counterpart and Flow Java classes integrate seamlessly with Java classes. As a consequence, Flow Java programs can take advantage of the wealth of available Java libraries.

Single assignment variables in Flow Java are typed and can only be bound to objects of compatible types. Type-compatible single assignment variables can be aliased allowing easy construction of powerful concurrency abstractions such as barriers. Statements automatically synchronize on variables being bound.

To achieve security as well as seamless integration, futures serve as read-only variants of single assignment variables. Futures share the synchronization behavior of single assignment variables but can only be bound through their associated single assignment variables. Futures are used in a novel way to achieve conservative argument passing essential for seamless integration. Passing a single assignment variable to a method not expecting a single assignment variable automatically passes the associated future instead.

Implementation. Flow Java is implemented by a moderate extension (less than 1200 lines) to the GNU GCJ Java compiler and the libjava runtime environment. Source code for Flow Java is available from www.sics.se/~frej/flow_java. The implementation slightly extends the memory layout of objects to accommodate for single assignment variables and is independent of native code or bytecode compilation. Binding and aliasing are implemented using common implementation techniques from logic programming systems. These techniques reuse the functionality for synchronized methods in Java to implement automatic synchronization. We present important optimizations that help reducing the cost incurred by single assignment variables and automatic synchronization.

Evaluation of Flow Java on standard Java benchmarks shows that synchronization variables incur an overhead between 10% and 40%. For some pathological cases runtime increases by up to 75%. Some rare cases currently show an excessive slowdown of up to two orders of magnitude. This slowdown is due to problems in the underlying optimizer and not related to the extensions for Flow Java. Evaluation uses native code obtained by compiling Flow Java programs.

Contributions. The general contribution of this paper is the design, implementation, and evaluation of an extension to Java that makes logic programming technology for concurrent programming available in a widely used programming language. More specifically, it contributes the new insight that futures as read-only variants of logic variables are essential for seamless integration of logic variables. Additionally, the paper contributes techniques for integrating logic variables and futures in implementations based on objects with a predefined concurrency model.

Structure of the Paper. The next section introduces Flow Java by presenting its features as well as showing concurrency abstractions programmed from these features. The implementation of Flow Java is discussed in Section 3 followed by its evaluation in Section 4. Flow Java is related to other approaches in Section 5. The paper concludes and presents concrete plans for future work in Section 6.

2   Flow Java

This section introduces Flow Java and presents some concurrent programming abstractions. The first section introduces single assignment variables, followed by futures in Section 2.2. The next section discusses aliasing of single assignment variables. Finally, Section 2.4 details types for synchronization variables. We assume some basic knowledge on Java as for example available from [2,8].

2.1   Single Assignment Variables

Single assignment variables in Flow Java are typed and serve as place holders for objects. They are introduced with the type modifier `single`. For example,

```
single Object s;
```

introduces s as a single assignment variable of type `Object`.

Initially, a single assignment variable is *unbound* which means that it contains no object. A single assignment variable of type t can be bound to any object of type t. Types for single assignment variables are detailed in Section 2.4. Binding a single assignment variable to an object o makes it indistinguishable from o. After binding, the variable is *bound* or *determined*.

Restricting single assignment variables to objects is essential for a simple implementation, as will become clear in Section 3. This decision, however, follows closely the philosophy of Java to restrict the status of non-object data structures such as integers or floats. For example, explicit synchronization in Java is only available for objects. Additionally, Java offers predefined classes for these restricted data structures (for example, the class `Integer` storing an `int`) which can be used together with single assignment variables.

Binding. Flow Java uses `@=` to bind a single assignment variable to an object. For example,

```
Object o = new Object();
s @= o;
```

binds s to the newly created object o. This makes s equivalent to o in any subsequent computation.

The attempt to bind an already determined single assignment variable x to an object o raises an exception if x is bound to an object different from o. Otherwise, the binding operation does nothing. Binding two single assignment variables is discussed in Section 2.3. Note that the notion of equality used is concerned with the identity of objects only (token equality).

Synchronization. Statements that access the content of a yet undetermined single assignment variable automatically suspend the executing thread. These statements are: field access and update, method invocation, and type conversion (to be discussed later). Suspension for synchronization variables has the same properties as explicit synchronization in Java through `wait()` and `notify()`.

For example, assume a class C with method `m()` and that c refers to a single assignment variable of type C. The method invocation `c.m()` suspends its executing thread, if c is not determined. As soon as some other thread binds c, execution continues and the method m is executed for c.

Example: Spawning concurrent computations with results. This examples shows an abstraction for concurrently computing a result that is needed only much later and where synchronization on its availability is automatic. A typical application is network access where concurrency hides network latency.

The following Flow Java fragment spawns a computation in a new thread returning the computation's result in a single-assignment variable:

```
1    class Spawn implements Runnable {
         private single Object result;
         private Spawn(single Object r) {
             result = r;
5        }
         public void run() {
             result @= computation();
         }
     }
10
     public static void main (String[] args) {
         single Object r;
         new Thread(new Spawn(r)).start();
         System.out.println(r);
15   }
```

Spawn defines a constructor which takes a single assignment variable and stores it in the field `result`. The method `run` binds the single assignment variable to the result of some method `computation` (omitted here). The `run` method is invoked when creating a thread as in the method `main`. After thread creation, r refers to the result of the spawned computation. Execution of `println` automatically suspends until r becomes bound.

A similar abstraction in plain Java requires roughly twice the lines of code which uses explicit synchronization for both storing and retrieving the result. Additionally, usage requires awareness that the result is wrapped by an object. This is in contrast to Flow Java, where the result is transparently available.

2.2   Futures

The abstraction presented above is easily compromised. The main thread can, unintentionally or maliciously, bind the result, thus raising an unexpected exception in the producer of the result. To this end, Flow Java offers *futures* as secure and read-only variants of single assignment variables.

A single assignment variable x has an associated future f. The future is bound, if and only if the associated variable is bound. If x becomes bound to object o, f also becomes bound to o. Operations suspending on single assignment variables also suspend on futures.

The future associated with a single assignment variable is obtained by converting the type from **single** t to t. This can be done by an explicit type conversion, but in most cases this is performed implicitly. A typical example for implicit conversion is calling a method not expecting a single assignment variable as its argument. Implicit conversion to a future is essential for seamless integration of single assignment variables. Conversion guarantees that any method can be called, in particular methods in predefined Java libraries. The methods will execute with futures and execution will automatically suspend and resume depending on whether the future is determined.

Example: Secure spawning. The design flaw in the previous example is rectified by using a future to pass the result of the spawned computation. The following addition of a class-method (static method) to **Spawn** achieves this:

```
1    public static Object spawn() {
         single Object r;
         new Thread(new Spawn(r)).start();
         return r;
5    }
```

As **spawn** is not declared to return a single assignment variable, the result is automatically converted to a future.

2.3   Aliasing

Single assignment variables in Flow Java can be aliased (made equal) while still being unbound. Aliasing two single assignment variables x and y is done by x @= y. Binding either x or y to an object o, binds both x and y to o. Aliasing single assignment variables also aliases their associated futures.

Flow Java extends the equality test == such that x == y immediately returns true, if x and y are two aliased single assignment variables. Otherwise, the equality test suspends until both x and y become determined or aliased.

Example: Barriers. A frequent task in multi-threaded programs is to create several threads and wait on their termination. This is usually achieved by an abstraction called barrier. A barrier can be implemented in Flow Java by giving each thread two single assignment variables *left* and *right*. Before a thread terminates, it aliases the two variables. The main thread, assuming it spawns n threads, creates $n + 1$ single assignment variables $v_0, \ldots, v_n$. It then initializes *left* and *right* as follows: $left_i = v_i$ and $right_i = v_{i+1}$ where i $(0 \le i < n)$ is the index of the thread, thus sharing the variables pairwise among the threads.

The main thread then waits for v_0 to be aliased to v_n as this indicates that all threads have terminated.

In Flow Java the described algorithm has the following implementation:

```
1    class Barrier implements Runnable {
         private single Object left;
         private single Object right;
         private Barrier(single Object l, single Object r) {
5            left = l; right = r;
         }
         public void run() {
             computation();
             left @= right;
10       }
         public static void spawn(int n) {
             single Object first; single Object prev = first;
             for(int i = 0; i < n; i++) {
                 single Object t;
15               new Thread(new Barrier(prev, t)).start();
                 prev = t;
             }
             first == prev;
         }
20   }
```

The `left` and `right` variables are stored in the instance when it is created with the constructor on line 4. The actual computation is done in `run()` on line 8 and finishes by aliasing `left` to `right` on the next line.

The main function `spawn()` creates the threads and waits until they have completed. Each loop iteration creates a new single assignment variable t and a thread running the computation. The final check suspends until all threads have terminated and hence all variables have been aliased. This technique is often referred to as *short circuit* [16].

The previous example shows that variable aliasing can be useful for concurrent programs. Let us consider a design variant of Flow Java without variable aliasing. Then, binding would need to suspend until at least one of the two single assignment variables (or futures) is determined. Hence, an object would be passed as a token through binding resulting in more threads being suspended in contrast to early termination with aliasing. Early termination is beneficial and might even be essential as resources become available to other concurrent computations. This is in particular true as threads are costly in Java.

2.4 Types

Variables of type t in Java can refer to any object of a type which is a subtype of t. To be fully compatible with Java's type system, single assignment variables follow this design. A single assignment variable of type t can be bound to an object of type t' provided that t' is a subtype of t.

Aliasing. The same holds true for aliasing of variables. Aliasing two single assignment variables x and x' with types t and t' respectively, restricts the type of both variables as follows: the type is restricted to t, if t is a subtype of t'; it is restricted to t', if t' is a subtype of t. Note that there is no need for type intersection as Java only supports subtypes created by single inheritance.

Type conversions. Type conversion can also convert the type of a single assignment variable by converting to a type including the `single` type modifier. Widening type conversions immediately proceed. A narrowing type conversion proceeds and modifies the type of the single assignment variable.

A widening type conversion on a future also immediately proceeds. A narrowing type conversion on a future will instead suspend until the associated variable becomes determined. This is in accordance with the idea that futures are read only, including their type.

3   Implementation

The Flow Java implementation is based on the GNU `GCJ` Java compiler and the `libjava` runtime environment. They provide a virtual machine and the ability to compile Java source code and byte code to native code.

The `GCJ/libjava` implementation uses a memory layout similar to C++. An object reference points to a memory area containing the object fields and a pointer, called *vptr*, to a virtual method table, called *vtab*. The *vtab* contains pointers to object methods and a pointer to the object class. The memory layout is the same for classes loaded from byte code and native code. Instances of interpreted classes store pointers in their *vtab* to wrapper methods which are byte code interpreters. The byte code interpreters are instantiated with byte code for the methods.

To implement Flow Java, extensions to the runtime system as well as to the compiler are needed. These extensions implement the illusion of transparent binding and make method invocations and field accesses suspendable.

The extensions described in this section can easily be implemented in any Java runtime environment using a memory layout similar to the layout described below. The extensions are not limited to Java, they can equally well be applied to other object-oriented languages such as C#.

3.1   Runtime System Extensions

The runtime system does not distinguish between single assignment variables and futures as this distinction is maintained by the compiler. In the runtime system all synchronization variables are represented as *synchronization objects.*

Object representation. To support synchronization objects, a redirection-pointer field (*rptr*) is added to all objects. Standard Java objects have their *rptr* pointing to the object itself. Synchronization objects are allocated as two-field objects containing the *rptr* and the *vptr*. Initially, the *rptr* is set to a sentinel UNB (for unbound). Figure 1 shows an unbound synchronization object.

The reason for using the sentinel UNB instead of a null pointer to represent an undetermined synchronization object is that a null pointer would make an undetermined synchronization object indistinguishable from a synchronization object bound to `null` (being a valid object reference in Java).

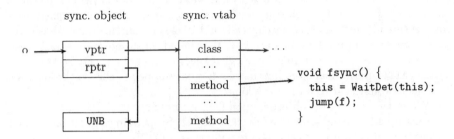

Fig. 1. An unbound synchronization object in Flow Java.

Binding. When a synchronization object becomes determined, its *rptr* is set to point to the object to which it is bound, as shown in Fig. 2. This scheme is similar to the forwarding pointer scheme used in the WAM [4]. To guarantee atomicity the per object lock provided by the standard Java runtime system is acquired before the *rptr* is changed.

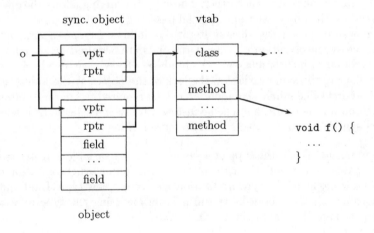

Fig. 2. A bound synchronization object in Flow Java.

The *vptr* field of a synchronization object is initialized to a synchronization *vtab* containing a synchronization wrapper for each of its methods. A wrapper waits for the synchronization object to become determined using a runtime primitive. When the object has been determined, the object reference pushed on the stack as part of the method invocation is replaced with the determined object. The invocation is continued by dispatching to the corresponding method in the standard *vtab*. This supports transparent redirection of method invocations without a performance penalty when synchronization objects are not used.

Suspension. Suspension is handled by the wait() and notifyAll() methods implemented by all Java objects. Calling wait() suspends the currently executing thread until another thread calls notifyAll() on the same object. To guarantee that no notifications are lost, the thread must acquire the lock associated with the object before calling wait() and notifyAll(). For wait() and notifyAll() to work as intended they cannot be wrapped in the synchronization *vtab* as it would lead to an infinite loop.

When the *rptr* of an object is modified, its notifyAll() method is called to wake up all threads suspended on that object. Suspending operations always follow the *rptr* chain to its end before calling wait().

Aliasing. Aliasing of synchronization objects is implemented by allowing a synchronization object's *rptr*-field to point to another synchronization object. The aliasing operation updates the *rptr* of the synchronization object at the higher address to point to the object at the lower address. The ordering allows the efficient implementation of the equality operators == and !=. They follow the *rptrs* in order to determine reference equality. They suspend until either both arguments have been determined or aliased to each other. As suspension is implemented by the wait() and notifyAll() methods, care must be taken to only suspend on one object at a time but still guarantee the reception of a notification if the objects are aliased to each other. The explicit ordering allows the operators to suspend on the object at the higher address.

To guarantee atomicity, aliasing iteratively follows the *rptr*-chains until the locks of the synchronization objects at the ends are acquired or an determined object is found (which is analogous to binding). To prevent deadlock between threads aliasing the same variables, the lock of the object at the lowest address is acquired first. The minimal amount of locking required to guarantee atomicity is the reason for choosing this scheme instead of Taylor's scheme [21], where all involved synchronization objects would require locking.

Type conversion. When the type of a synchronization variable is restricted by a narrowing type conversion, the *vptr* of the corresponding synchronization object is updated to point to the synchronization *vtab* of the new type. Bind and alias operations are checked for validity during runtime using the type information provided through the class reference in the *vtab*.

The primitives following *rptr* chains implement path compression by updating the *rptr* of the first synchronization object to the last object in the chain.

3.2   Compiler Extensions

The compiler is responsible for generating a call to a constructor which initializes single assignment variables to undetermined synchronization objects. The initialization is done each time a single assignment variable enters scope.

When a reference is dereferenced to access a field, the compiler wraps the reference in a call to a runtime primitive. The primitive suspends the currently executing thread, if the reference is undetermined or returns a reference to the object to which it is bound. This behavior is correct but unnecessarily strict as not all accesses need to be wrapped. This is further elaborated in Sect. 3.3.

The bind/alias operator, @=, is translated into a call to runtime primitives implementing bind or alias depending on the type of the right-hand argument. The reference equality operators == and != are also implemented as calls to runtime primitives described above.

Widening conversions are handled exactly as in standard Java. For narrowing conversions, the reference undergoing conversion is wrapped in a call to a runtime primitive. The primitive suspends the currently executing thread until the reference becomes determined.

3.3   Optimizations

Dereferencing all references by a call to a runtime primitive (named `WaitDet`) is correct but not needed in many cases. For example, when accessing the fields of `this` (the self object), `this` is always determined when executing a member method.

A second optimization critical for the performance of the Flow Java implementation is to optimize `WaitDet` for the non-suspending case. This is done by annotating the conditionals in the primitive with GCC-specific macros for telling the optimizer the most probable execution path.

A third optimization avoids repeated calls to `WaitDet` within a basic block, if a reference is known to be constant inside the block. For example:

```
1    class Vec {
2      int x, y;
3      public void add(Vec v) {
4        x += v.x; y += v.y;
5      }
6    }
```

Inside `add(Vec v)` the `v` is constant and can therefore be transformed into:

```
1    public void add(Vec v) {
2      v = WaitDet(v);
3      x += v.x; y += v.y;
4    }
```

thereby avoiding one call to `WaitDet`. This optimization has previously been described in the context of PARLOG in [9]. It is implemented by exploiting the common subexpression elimination in GCC by marking `WaitDet` as a pure function (its output only depends on its input). Evaluation shows that this optimization yields a performance improvement of 10% to 40% for real programs.

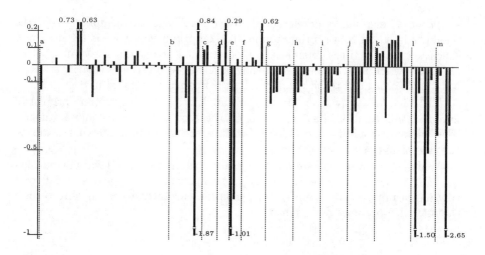

Fig. 3. The relative performance of Flow Java compared to Java.

4   Evaluation

This section answers two questions: How large is the overhead for programs not using the Flow Java extensions? How does a program using Flow Java features perform compared to a similar program implemented in plain Java?

Benchmarks used. To determine the performance impact of the Flow Java extensions we used the Java Grande benchmark suite [7]. The suite has been run using both the Flow Java compiler and the standard Java compiler. The suite has been run 20 times where the standard deviation is less than 2%.

We use two benchmarks to measure the performance of a Flow Java program compared to a program in standard Java implementing the same functionality. The first benchmark, *Spawn*, is based on the `Spawn` abstraction described in Sect. 2.2. The second benchmark (*Producer-Consumer*) is based on a on-demand producer-consumer scenario, where a producer and a consumer thread communicate over a stream. The two benchmarks have been run using the same methodology as above.

All benchmarks have been run on a standard PC with a 1.7GHz Pentium 4 and 512MB main memory running Linux 2.4.21.

Java Grande benchmark suite. Figure 3 shows the results of running the Java Grande benchmark suite. A value of 1.0 means that the Flow Java program is twice as fast (100% speedup), whereas a value of −1.0 means that the Flow Java program is twice as slow as the plain Java program. A solid line indicates the performance of one benchmark, a dotted lines separates groups of benchmarks. The groups are as follows: (a) arithmetic and math operations, (b) assignment operations, (c) casts, (d) exceptions, (e) loops, (f) method invocation, (g-j) creation of arrays with 1, 2, 4, 8, 16, 32, 64 and 128 elements of different types ((g) int,

(h) long, (i) float, (j) Object), (k) instance (object) creation, (l) small computing kernels, and (m) real applications.

The large slow-downs apparent in groups (b) and (e) are due to a problem in the current implementation of Flow Java. In some cases, the optimizer makes a wrong decision for conditional jumps in loops. Running hand-edited assembler code removes the slowdown for (e) and reduces it to 40% for (b).

Disregarding the previously described problem, the Flow Java extensions show very little impact on arithmetic, conversion, loops and method invocation (groups (a), (c), (e), (f)). This is as expected, since the underlying mechanisms are the same in Flow Java.

The overhead due to the extra redirection pointer in each object instance is noticeable for object creation. It penalizes allocation of small objects with as much as 40%, but is typically around 15%. For larger objects the performance is comparable to plain Java (groups (g), (h), (i), (j), each group creating successively larger arrays, (k) creates single instances, and (d) creates exceptions). These effects are probably due to particularities of the memory allocator.

What is very apparent is the overhead incurred by the check that a reference is determined before actually dereferencing it (Sect. 3.2). The check involves a call as opposed to a pointer dereference with constant offset in plain Java. The overhead is noticeable for real applications in the Java Grande benchmarks ((l) and (m) in the figure). The slowdown ranges between 75% to 45% for programs in which member methods make frequent accesses to instance variables of other objects. The two very large slow-downs in (l) and (m) are due to the previously described optimizer problem as well as the penalty for allocating small objects.

Flow Java versus plain Java. Performance of a Flow Java program is comparable to a plain Java program implementing similar abstractions (*Spawn* and *Producer-Consumer* benchmarks). The Flow Java version of *Spawn* performs slightly worse than the traditional implementation (by 2%), whereas the Flow Java *Producer-Consumer* is slightly faster (by 6%).

5   Related Work

The design of Flow Java has been inspired by concurrent logic programming [19] and concurrent constraint programming [17,16,20]. The main difference is that Flow Java does not support terms or constraints, in order to be a conservative extension of Java. On the other hand, Flow Java extends the above models by futures and types. The closest relative to Flow Java is Oz [20,15,24], offering single assignment variables as well as futures. The main difference is that Oz is based on a constraint store as opposed to objects with mutable fields and has a language specific concurrency model. As Oz lacks a type system, conversion from single assignment variables to futures is explicit.

Another closely related approach is Alice [1] which extends Standard ML by single assignment variables without aliasing (called promises) and futures. Access to futures is by an explicit operation on promises but without automatic type conversion. Alice and Flow Java share the property that futures are not manifest in the type system.

The approach to extend an existing programming language with either single assignment variables or futures is not new. Multilisp is an extension of Lisp which supports futures and threads for parallel programming [10]. Here, futures and thread creation are combined into a single primitive similar to the spawn abstraction in Section 2.2. Multilisp is dynamically typed and does not offer single assignment variables and in particular no aliasing. Another related approach is Id with its I-structures [3]. I-structures are arrays of dataflow variables similar to single assignment variables without aliasing. A field in an I-structure can be assigned only once and access to a not yet assigned field will block.

Thornley extends Ada as a typed language with single assignment variables [22]. The extension supports a special type for single assignment variables but no futures and hence also no automatic conversion. The work does not address to which extent it is a conservative extension to Ada, even though it reuses the Ada concurrency model. It does neither support aliasing nor binding of an already bound single assignment variable to the same object. A more radical approach by the same author is [23]. It allows only single assignment variables and hence is not any longer a conservative extension to Ada.

Chandy and Kesselman describe CC++ in [6] as an extension of C++ by typed single assignment variables without aliasing together with a primitive for thread creation. CC++ does not provide futures. Calling a method not being designed to deal with single assignment variables suspends the call. This yields a much more restricted concurrency model.

The approach to extend Java (and also C#) by new models for concurrency has received some attention recently. Decaf [18] is a confluent concurrent variant of Java which also uses logic variables as its concurrency mechanism. It does not support futures and changes Java considerably, hence requiring a complete reimplementation. Hilderink, Bakkers, et al. describe a Java-based package for CSP-style channel communication in [13]. An extension to C# using Chords is described in [5], where the system is implemented by translation to C# without Chords. While the two latter approaches use models for concurrent programming different from synchronization variables, they share the motivation to ease concurrent programming in Java or C# with Flow Java.

6   Conclusion and Future Work

Flow Java minimally extends Java by single assignment variables and futures which yield a declarative programming model of concurrency. Single assignment variables and futures in Flow Java are compatible with the object-oriented design of Java, its type system, and its model of concurrency. Futures are essential for both security as well as seamless integration.

The implementation of Flow Java is obtained by small extensions to the GCJ implementation of Java. The extensions for synchronized variables are straightforward and only make few assumptions on how objects are represented. Java's concurrency model provides the necessary support for automatic synchronization. The implementation is shown to be not only moderate in the amount of modifications required, also the efficiency penalty incurred is moderate.

Flow Java is but a first step in the development of a platform for high-level and efficient distributed and parallel programming. We will add distribution support similar to the support available in Oz [12] to Flow Java based on language-independent distribution middleware [14]. Our goal is to make these powerful abstractions available in a widely used language such as Java while being based on a high-level and declarative model of concurrent programming. Additionally, we plan to investigate how to implement Flow Java by extending other Java implementations.

Acknowledgments. We are grateful to Joe Armstrong, Guido Tack, and the anonymous reviewers for giving helpful comments on the paper. This work has been partially funded by the Swedish Vinnova PPC (Peer to Peer Computing, project 2001-06045) project.

References

1. Alice Team. The Alice system. Programming Systems Lab, Universität des Saarlandes. Available from www.ps.uni-sb.de/alice/.
2. Ken Arnold and James Gosling. *The Java Programming Language*. The Java Series. Addison-Wesley, Reading, MA, USA, 1996.
3. Arvind, Rishiyur S. Nikhil, and Keshav K. Pingali. I-structures: data structures for parallel computing. *ACM Transactions on Programming Languages and Systems*, 11(4):598–632, 1989.
4. Hassan Aït-Kaci. *Warren's Abstract Machine: A Tutorial Reconstruction*. Logic Programming Series. The MIT Press, Cambridge, MA, USA, 1991.
5. Nick Benton, Luca Cardelli, and Cédric Fournet. Modern concurrency abstractions for C#. In Boris Magnusson, editor, *ECOOP 2002 - Object-Oriented Programming, 16th European Conference*, volume 2374 of *Lecture Notes in Computer Science*, pages 415–440, Málaga, Spain, June 2002. Springer-Verlag.
6. K. Mani Chandy and Carl Kesselman. CC++: A declarative concurrent object-oriented programming notation. In Gul Agha, Peter Wegner, and Aki Yonezawa, editors, *Research Directions in Concurrent Object-Oriented Programming*. The MIT Press, Cambridge, MA, USA, 1993.
7. Edinburgh Parallel Computing Centre (EPCC). The Java Grande forum benchmark suite. Available from www.epcc.ed.ac.uk/javagrande.
8. James Gosling, Bill Joy, and Guy Steele. *The Java Programming Language Specification*. The Java Series. Addison-Wesley, Reading, MA, USA, 1996.
9. Steve Gregory. *Parallel Logic Programming in PARLOG*. International Series in Logic Programming. Addison-Wesley, Reading, MA, USA, 1987.
10. Robert H. Halstead, Jr. Multilisp: A language for concurrent symbolic computation. *ACM Transactions on Programming Languages and Systems*, 7(4):501–538, October 1985.
11. Seif Haridi, Peter Van Roy, Per Brand, Michael Mehl, Ralf Scheidhauer, and Gert Smolka. Efficient logic variables for distributed computing. *ACM Transactions on Programming Languages and Systems*, 21(3):569–626, May 1999.
12. Seif Haridi, Peter Van Roy, Per Brand, and Christian Schulte. Programming languages for distributed applications. *New Generation Computing*, 16(3):223–261, 1998.

13. Gerald Hilderink, André Bakkers, and Jan Broenink. A distributed real-time Java system based on CSP. In *3rd International Symposium on Object-Oriented Real-Time Distributed Computing (ISORC 2000)*, Newport Beach, CA, USA, March 2000. IEEE Computer Society.

14. Erik Klintskog, Zacharias El Banna, and Per Brand. A generic middleware for intra-language transparent distribution. SICS Technical Report T2003:01, Swedish Institute of Computer Science, January 2003. ISSN 1100-3154.

15. Michael Mehl, Christian Schulte, and Gert Smolka. Futures and by-need synchronization for Oz. Draft, Programming Systems Lab, Universität des Saarlandes, May 1998.

16. Vijay A. Saraswat. *Concurrent Constraint Programming*. ACM Doctoral Dissertation Awards: Logic Programming. The MIT Press, Cambridge, MA, USA, 1993.

17. Vijay A. Saraswat and Martin Rinard. Concurrent constraint programming. In *Proceedings of the 7th Annual ACM Symposium on Principles of Programming Languages*, pages 232-245, San Francisco, CA, USA, January 1990. ACM Press.

18. Tobias Sargeant. Decaf: Confluent concurrent programming in Java. Master's thesis, School of Computer Science and Software Engineering, Faculty of Information Technology, Monash University, Melbourne, Australia, May 2000.

19. Ehud Shapiro. The family of concurrent logic programming languages. *ACM Computing Surveys*, 21(3):413-510, 1989.

20. Gert Smolka. The Oz programming model. In Jan van Leeuwen, editor, *Computer Science Today*, volume 1000 of *Lecture Notes in Computer Science*, pages 324-343. Springer-Verlag, Berlin, 1995.

21. Andrew Taylor. Parma - bridging the performance gap between imperative and logic programming. *The Journal of Logic Programming*, 1-3(29):5-16, 1996.

22. John Thornley. Integrating parallel dataflow programming with the Ada tasking model. In *Proceedings of the conference on TRI-Ada '94*, pages 417-428. ACM Press, 1994.

23. John Thornley. Declarative Ada: parallel dataflow programming in a familiar context. In *Proceedings of the 1995 ACM 23rd annual conference on Computer science*, pages 73-80. ACM Press, 1995.

24. Peter Van Roy and Seif Haridi. *Concepts, Techniques, and Models of Computer Programming*. The MIT Press, Cambridge, MA, USA, 2003. Forthcoming.

On the Complexity of Dependent
And-Parallelism in Logic Programming*

Y. Wu, E. Pontelli, and D. Ranjan

Department of Computer Science
New Mexico State University
{yawu,epontell,dranjan}@cs.nmsu.edu

Abstract. We present results concerning the computational complexity of the key execution mechanisms required to handle Dependent And-Parallel executions in logic programming. We develop formal abstractions of the problems in terms of dynamic trees, design efficient data structures, and present some lower bound results. This work is part of a larger effort to understand, formalize, and study the complexity-theoretic and algorithmic issues in parallel implementations of logic programming.

1 Introduction

An interesting property of logic programming (LP) languages is that they are highly amenable for automatic parallelization—i.e., parallelism can be automatically extracted from logic programs by the compiler or the runtime system, without requiring any effort from the programmer [8]. However, the efficient implementation of a parallel LP system poses many interesting and challenging problems. Several solutions have been proposed for these problems and parallel implementations have been realized in the past. However, the formal study of the computational properties of the various operations involved in the parallel execution of a logic program is still a largely unexplored field.

The problem of developing a parallel implementation of a LP language can be abstracted as the process of maintaining and manipulating a dynamic tree. The operational semantics of the logic language determine how this tree is built and what operations on the tree are of interest. As the execution proceeds according to the operational semantics, this tree grows and shrinks. In a parallel implementation, different parts of the computation tree can grow and shrink *in parallel*. Various operations are needed during parallel execution to guarantee the correct behavior—e.g., left-to-right ordering of nodes, detection of particular ancestors. Although properties of dynamic data structures have been studied extensively, the specific structures used in parallel LP have only been formally investigated recently. We have started a comprehensive study of these problems [11] and obtained results related to or-parallelism [10].

* Research partially supported by NSF grants EIA-0220590, EIA-0130887, CCR-9875279, CCR-9820852, CCR-9900320

C. Palamidessi (Ed.): ICLP 2003, LNCS 2916, pp. 361–376, 2003.

In this paper we extend our previous efforts and discuss the basic operations that are required to *manage shared variables and side effects* in *dependent and-parallel (DAP)* LP systems. We derive upper bounds and lower bounds for the time complexity for both problems (shared variables and side-effects management). The results presented are important because: (i) they provide a formal framework for the comparison of existing execution models for and-parallel LP; (ii) they prove some lower bounds that provide formal justifications for the limitations experimentally encountered in existing systems [13,9]; (iii) they provide hints for the development of novel and more efficient solutions; (iv) they represent the first formal proof of conjectures presented in a variety of previous works [13,8,11]. This last aspect is very important, as it provides for the first time formal evidence that some difficulties encountered in implementing DAP [13,9] are inherent to the problem and hence unavoidable. These complexity results provide insights into the computational nature of DAP and have already guided the development of novel execution mechanisms [8,9].

Issues in And-Parallel Execution of Prolog Programs: We focus on the most general form of and-parallelism, called DAP [9,13]. Various parallel implementations of Prolog have been proposed and realized [8]. Most of the inefficiencies in the existing proposals arise from the need to guarantee Prolog semantics during parallel execution. Preserving Prolog semantics requires various operations (e.g., access to common variables) to be ordered correctly; this creates dependences between the concurrent executions. Only executions that respect such dependences can be accepted. Given a goal $B_1, \ldots, B_n$, multiple subgoals can be concurrently reduced during an and-parallel execution. The and-parallel execution can be visualized using an *and-tree*. The root of the and-tree is labeled with the initial goal. If a node contains $B_1, \ldots, B_n$, then it will have n children: the ith child is labeled with the body of the clause used to solve B_i.

The main problem in the implementation of ANDP is how to efficiently manage the *unifiers* produced by the concurrent reduction of different subgoals. Two subgoals B_i and B_j ($1 \leq i < j \leq n$) in the goal $B_1, \ldots, B_n$ should agree in the bindings for all the variables in $vars(B_i) \cap vars(B_j)$—such variables are termed *dependent* (or *shared*) variables in parallel LP terminology. In sequential Prolog execution, usually, B_i, the goal to the left, binds the shared variables and B_j works with the bindings produced by B_i. During ANDP execution, however, B_i and B_j may produce a conflicting binding for a dependent variable. In and-parallel execution, when B_j is started, the common variables will be unbound. B_j may attempt to instantiate one of these variables first, violating sequential Prolog semantics. The key problem is to ensure that bindings to common variables are made *in the same order* as in a sequential execution. This requirement is stronger compared to simply requiring that Prolog semantics be preserved. If a parallel system satisfies this stronger requirement, we say that it *preserves strong Prolog semantics* [9]. Preserving strong Prolog semantics is important for an ANDP system, as otherwise large amounts of redundant computation may be performed [8,13,6]. Maintaining strong Prolog semantics is the most commonly used *decidable approximation* to the problem of guaranteeing Prolog semantics [9]. There are two ways to achieve this: *curative* schemes and *preventive* schemes.

Curative schemes: These schemes [15,6] impose no special action when binding a shared variable unless a *conflict* occurs—i.e., an attempt to bind a variable which has already a different value. Whenever a conflict occurs, a *validation* step is required, to verify whether the conflict is legitimate (i.e., it would have occurred during a sequential execution) or it is due to an incorrect sequence of bindings. An illegal sequence of bindings will have to be handled by undoing the incorrect computation and redoing it with a correct binding installed. The validation step is performed by comparing the goal which has created the binding with the goal which is attempting another binding; the leftmost of the two is the one who is allowed to create the binding. If the existing binding was generated by the rightmost of the two goals, then an illegal situation has occurred.

Preventive schemes: These schemes handle the requirement of preserving strong Prolog semantics by assigning *producer* or *consumer* status to each subgoal that shares a given dependent variable [13,8]. The leftmost subgoal that has access to the dependent variable is designated as the producer subgoal while all others are consumers. A consumer subgoal is not allowed to bind the dependent variable, it is only allowed to read its binding. If a consumer subgoal attempts to bind an unbound dependent variable, it has to suspend until the producer goal binds it first. If the producer subgoal terminates without binding the dependent variable, then the producer "status" is transferred to the leftmost active consumer of that variable. A major problem in ANDP implementations is to dynamically keep track of the leftmost active subgoal that shares each variable.

Pointer Machines: The computational model used for our complexity study is the pointer machine model [2]. A *Pure Pointer Machine (PPM)* consists of a finite but expandable collection of *records* and a finite collection of *registers* (each can store a pointer). Each record is uniquely identified through an address. Each record is composed of a finite, constant collection of named fields, each capable of storing a pointer. The PPM instructions allow to move addresses between registers and records, create new records, and perform conditional jumps. In terms of analysis of complexity, it is assumed that each instruction has a unit cost. Differently from RAM, the PPM makes the cost of arithmetic operations explicit. The *Arithmetic Pointer Machine (APM)* model is an extension of the PPM that allows numbers to be stored in the records and that allows constant time arithmetic for $O(\lg n)$-size integers. Further details on the structure of PPMs and APMs can be found in [2].

2 Problem Abstraction

2.1 Background, Notations, and Definitions

A tree $\mathcal{T} = \langle V, E \rangle$ is a connected, rooted, and acyclic graph. Without loss of generality we will focus exclusively on binary trees. Additionally, we consider *labeled trees*, i.e., trees which have a label attached to each node. Labels are drawn from a label set Γ. For a node v in the tree, we denote with $left(v)$

($right(v)$) the left (right) child of v in the tree. If v does not have a left (right) child, then $left(v)$ ($right(v)$) has value $\bot$. We assume that the following operations are available for manipulating the structure of trees: *(a) create_tree(ℓ)*, used to create a tree containing a single node labeled $\ell \in \Gamma$; *(b) expand(u, ℓ_1, ℓ_2)*: given a leaf of the tree u, the operation creates two children of u (labeled ℓ_1 and ℓ_2); *(c) remove(u)*: given a leaf u in the tree, the operation removes it from the tree.

For two nodes u and v in $\mathcal{T}$, we write $u \preceq v$ if u is an ancestor of v. We will often refer to the notion of *leftmost branch*. Given a node u, *left_branch(u)* contains all the nodes (including u) that belong to the leftmost branch of the subtree rooted in u. For any node u, the elements of *left_branch(u)* constitute a total order with respect to $\preceq$. The notion of leftmost branch allows us to define another relation between nodes, indicated by $\lhd$. Intuitively, given two nodes u, v, we say that $u \lhd v$ if v is a node in the leftmost branch of the subtree rooted at u. Formally, $u \lhd v \Leftrightarrow v \in \textit{left\_branch}(u)$. $\lhd$ is a partial order but not a total order. Given a node v, let $\mu(v) = min_{\preceq}\{u \in V | u \lhd v\}$. $\mu(v)$ is the highest node u in the tree such that v is in the leftmost branch of the subtree rooted at u. $\mu(v)$ is also known in the LP community as the *subroot node* of v.

The nearest common ancestor of two nodes u, v is a common ancestor of u and v that is furthest from the root: $nca(u, v) = max_{\preceq}\{w \in V | w \preceq u \textit{ and } w \preceq v\}$.

2.2   Abstracting And-Parallelism

A DAP execution model is characterized by three basic mechanisms [13,8]:

- *Goals management:* this involves managing the subgoals that are created during program execution. This includes the mechanisms required to start, schedule, and terminate the execution of the parallel subgoals.

- *Variables management:* this includes all those mechanisms which are used to handle variables shared between and-parallel subgoals—i.e., *(i)* binding shared variables and retrieving the value of shared variables, and *(ii)* validating the binding to a shared variable—i.e., ensuring that the creation of a binding does not lead to a violation of strong Prolog Semantics.

- *Backward execution:* mechanisms to support backtracking.

Goals management is abstracted in terms of operations on the dynamic tree representing the execution of a program. During parallel execution, nodes are added and deleted from the and-tree. The execution steps can be expressed using the tree operations described in the previous section. Each and-parallel computation is described by a branch in the tree. The tip of each branch represents the current "execution point" of that computation. Whenever a computation (currently located at a certain leaf u of the tree) activates a new and-parallel execution, then an *expand* operation is executed to expand u with the new branches created. Whenever an and-parallel computation either terminates or fails, the node which represents the current "point" of such computation is removed from the tree. This corresponds to using a *remove* operation. Note that an and-parallel conjunction (node v of the tree) terminates only when all the and-parallel subgoals (which are represented by the children of v) have been completed—i.e., only when v has itself turned into a leaf. This justifies the assumption that the *remove* operation is applied to leaves. Thus, management of goals can be directly abstracted as a correct sequence of *create, expand, remove* operations. In this paper we focus on the management of goals and variables management; analysis of the mechanisms for backward execution [13,8] are left for future work.

Let us focus then on the management of goals and shared variables. Informally, each node may create a variable, try to bind a variable, or alias two variables to each other. In our abstraction, variables are represented as attributes drawn from a family Γ. The management of shared variables requires:

- *variable creation*: for our purposes, we can assume that creation is implicit within the *expand* operation. If a shared variable X is introduced in a given goal (represented by node u), then we assume that X is an attribute that has been associated with u when the *expand* operation which generated u was performed. Given a variable X, let us denote with $node(X)$ the node representing the goal that introduced the variable X.

- *binding*: assign a value to the variable X;

- *aliasing*: given two variables X and Y, alias one to the other. Once two variables are aliased, they will reference the same value. We will denote the fact that X and Y have been aliased using the notation $X \simeq Y$. The relation $\simeq$ is an equivalence relation. Given a variable X, we identify with $alias(X)$ the set of all variables which are aliased to X, i.e., $alias(X) = \{Y : X \simeq Y\}$.

Aliasing of variables, in general, does not create an immediate problem for and-parallel computations. On the other hand, the binding of an aliased variable does create a problem. If two variables X and Y are aliased, and later an attempt to bind one of them is made, then the binding should be allowed only if it satisfies the binding requirements for *both* variables. In our abstraction we introduce an operation, *alias*, which is used to denote the execution of an aliasing between two variables: $alias(u, X, Y)$ which indicates that at node u in the tree we have performed an aliasing between the variables X and Y. According to Prolog semantics, the aliasing will be valid only in the subtree which is rooted in u.

Abstracting Curative Schemes: As described earlier, a curative scheme is characterized by the need of *validating* variable bindings whenever a conflict occurs. This can be easily abstracted as a simple operation on the nodes of the tree: $left\_of(u, v)$ which verifies whether the node u is to the left of the node v in the tree. If u is the node in which we are detecting a conflict and v is the node which has generated the binding for the variable of interest, then the conflict is legitimate only if $left\_of(u, v)$ is false. Otherwise a curative action has to be taken. Performing a curative action implies undoing the execution which has caused the conflict. This undoing of the computation can be expressed by a sequence of operations which contains: *(a)* a sufficient number of *remove* operations to remove all the nodes present in the subtree rooted in v; *(b)* repetition of all the operations which have lead to the construction of the subtree rooted in v. In order to more faithfully model the behavior of curative schemes, we place the following assumptions on the $left\_of(x, y)$ operation: if either x is an ancestor of y or y is an ancestor of x, then the operation gracefully succeeds—this denotes a failure in the execution, but the failure is legitimate since the binding is created in the same branch as the point of conflict. To summarize, we have the following data structure problem ($\mathcal{ANDP}^{\mathcal{C}}$): *"The $\mathcal{ANDP}^{\mathcal{C}}$ problem consists of supporting the following operations in a dynamic tree: create, expand, remove, and left_of."*

The complete abstraction of the problem would also require supporting the *alias* operation. This operation can be abstracted as solving the union-find problem [14]. Formal study of the issues involving *alias* are left for future study.

Abstracting Preventive Schemes: In the context of the Preventive Schemes, the binding condition can be expressed as follows: a binding for variable X taking place in a node u of the tree can be safely performed (w.r.t., strong Prolog semantics) iff the node u lies on the leftmost branch of each node in $alias(X)$. Equivalently, $\forall Y \in alias(X)$ $(u \trianglelefteq node(Y))$. In the following we will denote with *verify_leftmost*(u, v) the operation which given nodes u and v verifies that u is in the leftmost branch in the subtree rooted in v. Given a variable X for which a binding is attempted at node u, to bind X we need to:

- identify in $alias(X)$ the "oldest" variable, Z, in the set (X is older than Y if $node(X)$ is an ancestor of $node(Y)$). This is necessary to determine the reference node for the leftmost test.
- verify whether the leaf node u is in the leftmost branch with respect to the node identified in the previous step (*verify_leftmost*$(u, node(Z))$).

As stated before, we will not deal with aliasing in this paper but concern ourselves with supporting the operation *verify_leftmost* which, given a node u and a node v, returns true iff u is the leftmost leaf in the subtree rooted at v. To summarize, we have the following new data structure problem, called $\mathcal{ANDP}^{\mathcal{P}}$: *"The problem $\mathcal{ANDP}^{\mathcal{P}}$ consists of supporting the following operation on dynamic tree structures: create, expand, remove, and verify_leftmost."* Depending on the type of preventive scheme, the node u could be always a leaf or not.

Abstracting Order-Sensitive Predicates: Let us consider the problem of correct ordering of side-effects in ANDP. Whenever a branch encounters a side-effect, it must check if it can execute it. This check requires verifying that the branch containing the side-effect is currently the leftmost active computation in the tree. If u is the current leaf of the branch where the side-effect is encountered, its computation is allowed to continue only if $\mu(u) =$ root. Thus, checking if a side-effect can be executed requires the ability to perform *find_subroot*(u) which, given a leaf u, computes the node $\mu(u)$. We let $\mathcal{SE}$ denote the problem of supporting the operations *create, expand, remove,* and *find_subroot* for a dynamic tree.

3   Results for the $\mathcal{SE}$ Problem

Several schemes to manage side effect in parallel LP have been presented (see, e.g., [8]), but none is optimal. We present an optimal scheme to solve the $\mathcal{SE}$ problem. We prove the following result for the $\mathcal{SE}$ problem:

Theorem: *The $\mathcal{SE}$ problem can be solved with the worst case time complexity of $O(1)$ per operation.*

This result has provided an effective solution for side-effects in the PALS system [18]. The construction of a solution to the above problem can be developed in two steps, *frontier identification* and *identification of the subroot nodes*.

The first step consists of developing an explicit representation of the frontier of the tree—as a doubly-linked list of nodes. Thanks to the fact that all the operations that modify the structure of the tree operate on the leaves, it is possible to efficiently maintain this doubly-linked list. The way that each operation modifies the list is very "localized". We can state the following result:

Lemma: *The frontier of a tree created via create_tree, expand, and remove, can be maintained as a doubly-linked list with $\Theta(1)$ time per operation.*

The missing operation is *find_subroot*, which computes the node $\mu(u)$ for each leaf u of the tree. The previous data structure can be augmented to support this operation in constant time. The result is based on the following lemma:

Lemma: *Let u and v be two different leaves. The value of $\mu(v)$ changes when u is removed from the tree iff u is the left child of a node w and $\mu(v)$ is the right child of w. If u and v are two distinct leaves in a binary tree, then $\mu(u) \neq \mu(v)$.*
Corollary: *The removal of a leaf will affect the μ of at most one leaf.*

The representation of each node is modified by adding an additional pointer, named sub. If u is a leaf in the tree, then $sub(u)$ contains a pointer to the node $\mu(u)$. When a node w is expanded by appending two children (in order, u and v) to it, the subroot nodes for the two new leaves can be determined as follows:

- $sub(u) = sub(w)$. In fact, u represents a node which is on the same left branch as w, and as such it must have the same μ node.
- $sub(v) = v$. In fact the parent of the node for v is w, which has a left child. Thus such right child is not leftmost for any subtree rooted at a higher node.

During the removal of a leaf u, three cases may occur. If u is the only child of its parent, then copy the value of sub of the leaf to the sub field of the parent. If u is the right child of a node v, which has also a left child, then the removal of u will not modify any μ (previous lemma). If u is the left child of v, and v has a right branch, then the removal of u can affect the μ of at most one leaf. Let w be the leaf which follows u in the frontier, then set $\mu(w) = \mu(u)$. It is straightforward to see that in every possible case, the cost of maintaining the sub field is constant. The availability of the sub field allows us to implement (in $\Theta(1)$ time) the find_subroot operation to compute $\mu(u)$: find_subroot$(u) = sub(u)$.

4 Results for the $\mathcal{ANDP^C}$ Problem

Lower Bound Time Complexity: The $\mathcal{ANDP^C}$ problem has a single operation worst case time complexity $\Omega(\lg\lg n)$, where n is the number of nodes in the tree. This result can be easily proved by reducing the $\mathcal{TP}$ problem [12] to the $\mathcal{ANDP^C}$. The $\mathcal{TP}$ is the problem of maintaining a data structure with two operations: *insert*(x)—that inserts the element x at the end of a list—and *precedes*(x, y) that verifies whether x precedes y in the list (i.e., x was inserted earlier than y). This problem has been proved to have a single operation worst case time complexity $\Omega(\lg\lg n)$ (and a matching upper bound has been provided in [12]) on PPMs. The reduction can be realized as follows. Each $insert(x)$ operation is performed as $expand(last, x, \_)$, where $last$ keeps track of the last element inserted and $\_$ is a dummy node. The elements of the list compose the left spine of the tree. Each $precedes(x, y)$ is equivalent to $left\text{-}of(x, y)$ in the tree.

A Matching Upper Bound Time Complexity: A matching upper bound for the $\mathcal{ANDP}^{\mathcal{C}}$ problem can be obtained by making use of the efficient nearest common ancestor algorithm for PPMs presented in [5]. This algorithm provides the ability to perform the $expand$, $remove$ operations in constant time, and compute nearest-common ancestor queries for any pair of nodes in the tree in single operation worst case time complexity $O(\lg \lg n)$. Each $left\text{-}of(x, y)$ query can be performed as follows. Let $z = nca(x, y)$ and let l_z and r_z be respectively the left and right child of z. Then, $left\text{-}of(x, y)$ is true iff l_z is an ancestor of x—this can be checked by testing whether $l_z = nca(l_z, x)$.

Observe that the $\mathcal{ANDP}^{\mathcal{C}}$ problem can be solved in constant time on RAM, since constant time solutions for the nearest common ancestor problem have been proposed on RAMs. The problem can be solved in amortized $O(1)$ time on APMs by maintaining a generalized linked list representing the in-order traversal of the tree; each $left\text{-}of$ query corresponds to a precedence test in such list. It has been shown that it is possible to maintain generalized linked lists on APMs with amortized time complexity $O(1)$ [16].

5   Results for the $\mathcal{ANDP}^{\mathcal{P}}$ Problem

The crux of the $\mathcal{ANDP}^{\mathcal{P}}$ problem is verification of "leftness" in a dynamically changing tree. We systematically study variants of such problem.

The $\mathcal{GLL}$ Problem

The Global Left Leaf problem ($\mathcal{GLL}$), calls for supporting following operations: *(i) create, expand, remove* to manipulate the structure of the tree; *(ii) global_left_leaf(v)*. The operation returns *true* iff the leaf v is the leftmost leaf in the tree. For a leaf node v: $global\_left\_leaf(v)$ iff $verify\_leftmost(v, root(T))$ where $root(T)$ is the root of the tree T. The $\mathcal{GLL}$ problem can be solved in $O(1)$ time per operation on PPMs by simply maintaining the frontier of the tree as a double-linked list, and by keeping an explicit pointer to the first node of the frontier. The $\mathcal{SE}$ problem can be seen as a generalized version of $\mathcal{GLL}$.

The $\mathcal{GLB}$ Problem

The Global Leftmost Branch ($\mathcal{GLB}$) problem requires the following operations:

- *create, expand, remove* to manipulate the structure of the tree;
- *on_leftmost_path(v)* where v is an *arbitrary node* in the tree. The operation returns *true* if the node v lies on the leftmost branch of the tree.

We present two PPM solutions to this problem, one with an $O(1)$ amortized time complexity per operation (but $\Omega(n)$ single operation time complexity), the other with a $O(\lg \lg n)$ worst-case time per operation.

An Amortized Constant Time Solution: We represent the tree using a standard pointer-based representation. In addition a single bit is attached to each node of the tree. The bit is set to 1 if the node is on the leftmost path of the tree, 0 otherwise. The bit can be easily set to the correct value when nodes are inserted in the tree using the *expand* operation: if the parent has the bit set to 1, then the left child also gets a bit set to 1 otherwise it is set to 0. The right child always receives the bit 0 upon creation. When a *remove* operation is performed, we have two possible cases: *(1)* if the removed leaf has a bit 0, or it has bit 1 but has no right sibling, then no changes are required; *(2)* if the removed leaf u has a bit 1, and it has a right sibling v, then the bits of all the nodes lying in the leftmost branch of the tree rooted at v are set to 1. It is important to observe the following property: the bit of each node in the tree can be turned from 0 to 1 at most once; furthermore, a node with a bit set to 1 is never changed to 0.

Given this data structure, the *on_leftmost_path* test can be performed in worst case time $O(1)$ by simply checking the status of the bit. The *expand* operation also requires $O(1)$ time. The time complexity of the *remove* operation is $\Omega(n)$ in the worst case. However, a simple argument using the accounting method allows us to conclude that an arbitrary sequence of *expand*, *remove*, and *on_leftmost_path* operations can be performed in amortized $O(1)$ time.

An $O(\lg \lg n)$ Solution: We now present a solution with a better worst-case time complexity per operation. As mentioned earlier it is easy to maintain in $O(1)$ time a pointer to the leftmost leaf in the tree. Let us denote with ℓ the leftmost leaf of the tree. The following observation can be used to solve our problem:

$$on\_leftmost\_path(v) \text{ iff } is\_ancestor(v, \ell)$$

where $is\_ancestor(x, y)$ is an operation that returns true if node x is an ancestor of node y in the tree. Using the scheme presented in [5] to handle ancestor problems on PPMs, it is possible to design a PPM data structure where *expand* and *remove* can be performed with $O(1)$ amortized time complexity and *is_ancestor* queries are performed with $O(\lg \lg n)$ worst case time complexity, where n is the number of *expand* operations performed. It is also possible to solve the problem on RAM in time $O(1)$ per operation. However we don't know if this problem can be solved in worst case $O(1)$ time on PPMs or APMs.

Verifying Local Leftmostness
We can have different formulations of the general problem of verifying leftmostness of a node with respect to another node. In all the cases we are considering trees that are manipulated using the operations *create*, *expand*, and *remove*. The formulations differ in the generality allowed for the arguments of *verify_leftmost*:

1. *verify_leftmost*(u, v), u a leaf in the tree and v an ancestor of u, returns *true* iff u lies in the leftmost branch in the subtree rooted in v.
2. *verify_leftmost*(u, v), u a leaf in the tree and v an arbitrary node, returns *true* iff u lies in the leftmost branch in the subtree rooted in v.
3. *verify_leftmost*(u, v), u an arbitrary node in the tree and v an ancestor of u, returns *true* iff u lies in the leftmost branch in the subtree rooted in v.
4. *verify_leftmost*(u, v), u, v arbitrary nodes in the tree, returns *true* iff u lies in the leftmost branch in the subtree rooted in v.

Problem (1) is the simplest, while problem (4) is the hardest—and the one representing the most general case of $\mathcal{AND}\mathcal{DP}^{\mathcal{P}}$. We investigate all the cases as they gracefully lead to the solution of the most general case.

Problem (1): The problem can be solved as follows:

- Use the standard $O(1)$ method for inserting and removing nodes.
- Use the solution to the $\mathcal{SE}$ problem, to keep track of subroot of each leaf.
- Maintain a pointer to a node in a temporal precedence list representing the height of the node in the tree. Insertion of new nodes in the tree may require the addition of a new element in such temporal precedence list (whenever the first node of a new level in the tree is created); in [12] we have shown that this can be performed in amortized $O(1)$ time.
- *verify_leftmost*(u, v) can be solved as follows: *(1)* from the leaf u, access the corresponding subroot node $sub(u)$; *(2)* compare (using the *precede* operation of $\mathcal{TP}$) the heights of $sub(u)$ and v. If v precedes $sub(u)$ then return *false* else return *true*. The test requires time $O(\lg \lg n)$ [12].

The problem can be solved in time $O(1)$ if constant-time comparisons between $\lg n$-bit integers are allowed—as in the APMs and RAMs. The exact complexity of this problem on PPMs is unknown. In particular, we don't know if an $O(1)$ worst-case time per operation solution is possible on PPM's.

Problem (2): In this case the operation guarantees that one node is a leaf, but there is no knowledge regarding whether the other node is an ancestor. The operation *verify_leftmost*(u, v) can be executed as follows: *(i)* first check if v is an ancestor of u—this test can be done in time $O(\lg \lg n)$ using the solution to the nearest-common ancestor problem on pure pointer machines [5]; *(ii)* if the v is an ancestor of u, then the solution for the Problem (1) can be used; otherwise immediately return false. The problem can be solved in $O(1)$ time on RAM, since the nearest common ancestor can be computed in constant time [4]. However it is not clear whether an $O(1)$ solution exists on APMs. Moreover, it is not clear whether amortized $O(1)$ solutions exist on either APM or PPM.

Problem (4): In the most general case, the two nodes compared can be both internal nodes and we do not knowledge of whether they lie on the same branch in the tree. In this case, we can show that the problem has an $\Omega(\lg \lg n)$ worst-case time complexity. This can be again obtained via reduction of the temporal precedence problem. We can develop a tree composed of a single left spine; each **insert** operation expands the leftmost leaf of the tree. Each **precedes** operation can be accomplished by applying the **verify_leftmost** operation on the parents of the two leaves representing the list elements.

Problem (3): The problem is the same as Problem (4), with the difference that we know in advance that one node is an ancestor of the other. This provides us with solutions with the same complexity as those proposed for Problem (4). However, because the lower bound for the previous problem depends on determining the "ancestorness", such bound cannot be applied to this problem.

Solutions to the Problem (4)

We begin by observing that the general leftness verification can be done efficiently if one could maintain the subroot nodes for all nodes (not only the leaves) in the tree

---
Algorithm VERIFY_LEFTMOST (u, v)
   $s_1 \leftarrow$ SUBROOT(u)
   $s_2 \leftarrow$ SUBROOT(v)
   return $(s_1 = s_2$ AND height$(v) <$ height$(u))$;

Fig. 1. Verifying Leftmostness

efficiently. More precisely, the ability to determine SUBROOT(v) for any node v allows the solution in Fig. 1 for verifying leftness. The time complexity of this algorithm is the sum of time of the procedure *subroot* and time used to compare heights. In general, the set of nodes in a dynamic tree can be partitioned into disjoint subsets of nodes with each nodes in each subset having the same subroot node. The nodes of each subset actually form a path in the tree each of which terminates in a leaf (see Fig. 2). It is easy to relate the problem to the Union-Find Problem [14,3] and the Marked-Ancestor Problem [1].

Relationship to the Union-Find Problem: A solution to the problem can be obtained by using the solution to the *union-find* problem [14]. We maintain the disjoint paths with the same subroot nodes as disjoint sets, with the subroot nodes as the representatives. Each time we perform an *expand*, we create a new set that contains only the right child, we create a set that contains the left child, which is immediately unioned to the set containing its parent. When a *remove* is performed, if the removed node does not have a right sibling, then nothing needs to be done. If the removed node u has a right sibling w, then we need to union the set containing w and the set containing the parent of u (Fig. 2). In order to perform *verify_leftmost*(u, v), we need to verify that *find*(u) is equal to *find*(v) and the node v is closer to the root than u.

The union-find problem can be solved optimally on an APM in amortized time $O(m\alpha(m, n))$ where m is the total number of operations performed, and n is the total number of elements in the tree. Comparison of the heights of the nodes can be done in constant time on an APM. To analyze the complexity of this scheme on PPM, let us denote with e the number of *expand* operations, with d the number of *remove* operations, and with q the number of *verify_leftmost* queries performed. Let $m = d + e + q$. Each *expand* operation requires creation of two singleton sets, and union of one of these sets with another existing set—this can be done in constant time. Each *remove* operation requires one union operation; the union using the union-by-rank heuristic can be performed in $O(\lg \lg \lg n)$ time on a PPM. Each *verify_leftmost* operation requires two find operations and one *precedes* operation (for height comparison). This can be done in $O(\lg \lg n)$ time. This solution can be implemented on a PPM in amortized time $O(m\alpha(m, e) + d \lg \lg \lg e + q \lg \lg e)$. The solution proposed in [3] provides also a PPM solution to the problem with a worst-case time complexity of $O(\lg n / \lg \lg n)$ per operation.

Adjacent Union-Find Problem: The type of union-find operations that are required to support the computation of subroot nodes for each node in the tree are actually very specialized. Each union operation is performed when a node with a right sibling is removed from the tree; in that case the union links the set

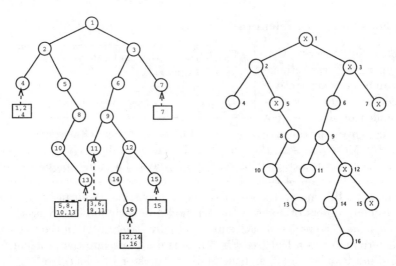

Fig. 2. Subroots as Union-Find

Fig. 3. Subroots as marked ancestors

associated to the right sibling with the set associated to its parent. This can be seen as an instance of the *adjacent union-find* problem investigated in [17]—a union-find problem where elements are arranged in a list and only sets that are adjacent in the list are allowed to be united. The problem has been shown to be solvable in worst-case time complexity $O(\lg\lg n)$ on a pointer machine with arithmetic (APM); the corresponding solution on a PPM requires $O(\lg n \lg\lg n)$. *Marked Ancestor:* Another problem that is strongly related to the one at hand is the Marked Ancestor problem [1]. The problem assumes the presence of a tree structure, where each node can either marked or unmarked. The operations available are mark(v)—used to mark the node v—unmark(v)—used to remove the mark from node v—and firstmarked(v)—used to retrieve the nearest marked ancestor of node v. The results in [1] provides optimal solutions for the marked ancestor problem (on RAM), with worst-case time complexity $\Theta(\lg n / \lg\lg n)$ per operation. A simplified version of the problem, the *decreased marked ancestor problem*, allows only the unmark and firstmarked operations; this problem can be solved in amortized constant time (on RAM) and with worst case $O(\lg\lg n)$ per unmark and $O(\lg n / \lg\lg n)$ per firstmarked.

Our problem can be seen as an instance of the decreasing marked ancestor problem (see Fig. 3). We start from the same tree structure as in $\mathcal{ANDP}^{\mathcal{P}}$ problem; initially the only marked nodes are those that are subroot nodes of at least on node in the tree—i.e., the root as well as any other node who has an immediate sibling to its left (during each *expand* the right child will be marked). Each time a *remove(v)* operation is required, the following steps are performed: *(i)* if the node v has a right sibling, then the right sibling is unmarked; *(ii)* otherwise no nodes are changed. It is then easy to see that Each SUBROOT operation is simply a corresponding firstmarked operation. This provides us with a solution for our problem with worst-case time complexity $O(\lg n / \lg\lg n)$ per operation, and amortized time complexity $O(1)$—both on RAM. These results do not provide us with a significantly better complexity on pointer machines.

Improved Algorithms for the Static $\mathcal{ANDP}^{\mathcal{P}}$ Problem

In the static version of the problem all the *expand* operations are performed prior to the *remove* and *verify_leftmost* operations. We provide a solution to the static $ANDP^P$ problem in worst-case time $O((\lg\lg n)^2)$ per operation on PPMs. Results, similar in spirit to this investigation, have been obtained by Gabow and Tarjan [7] for the Union-Find Problem. Our algorithm relies on the following key observation (the proof is omitted for lack of space):

Theorem: *Let T be a tree where only subroot nodes are marked, and L be the preorder traversal of T. For every node v, the subroot node is the nearest marked node to the left (marked predecessor) of v in L.*

Hence solving the static version of the problem can be simplified to maintaining a list of nodes, some of which are marked, supporting the operations *unmark* and *find-marked-predecessor*. Notice that this is a special case of the Marked-Ancestor Problem as it is the Marked-Ancestor problem on a linear tree.

A $O(\lg n \lg\lg\lg n/\lg\lg n)$ **solution:** Let L be the pre-order traversal of T. Let T' be a complete k-ary tree with the nodes of L as leaves. T' has height $\lceil\lg_k n\rceil$. In T' mark a node if any of its descendants is marked. This requires time $O(T') = O(L)$. The procedure in Fig. 4 finds the marked predecessor of u in L using T'.

To assist in this computation, for every internal node, we maintain a pointer to the rightmost marked child and a pointer to the leftmost marked child respectively, as well as double-linked list of all marked children. The loop in step 3 requires at most $\lg_k n$ precedence tests in the worst-case (one for each tree level). With the help of the data structure in Temporal Precedence Problem [12], the precedence comparison can be done in $\lg\lg k$ time. Line 6 requires time $O(k)$ as one can walk left starting from

---

Algorithm Find-Marked-Predecessor(u)
1. $v' \leftarrow u$;
2. $v \leftarrow parent(u)$;
3. **while** ((leftmost marked child of v does not precede v'))
4. $v' \leftarrow v$;
5. $v \leftarrow parent(v)$;
6. $w \leftarrow$ rightmost marked child of v that is to the left of v'
7. **while** (w is not a leaf)
8. $w \leftarrow$ rightmost marked child of w;
9. **return** w

Fig. 4. Improved Marked Predecessor

---

v' until a marked sibling is found. The loop in line 7 requires time at most $\lg_k n$. Hence the total time required by Find-Marked-Predecessor is bounded by $\lg\lg k \lg_k n + k + \lg_k n$. The *unmark($u$)* operation is performed as follows: unmark the node u; if u is either the leftmost or the rightmost marked child of its parent, update this information. If u is the only marked child of its parent, then repeat the unmarking procedure on the parent of u. The total time for unmark in the worst-case is $O(\lg_k n)$. Choosing $k = \lg n/\lg\lg n$, the time complexity of Find-Marked-Predecessor is $O(\lg n \lg\lg\lg n/\lg\lg n)$; the time complexity of *unmark* is $O(\lg n/(\lg\lg n))$.

An $O((\lg\lg n)^2)$ **Solution:** The idea here is to note that in line 6 of the Find-Marked-Predecessor procedure above, we are actually finding the marked predecessor of v' in the list of children of v. Hence, naturally one could recursively organize the children of a node as a tree. We use a $\sqrt{n}$-ary tree with height 2 (Fig.

Algorithm Find-Marked-Predecessor(u,ℓ)
0. **if** ($\ell = \lg\lg n$) **then** use direct list search;
1. **if** (marked(u)) **then return**(u);
2. $v \leftarrow parent(u, \ell)$;
3. **if** ((leftmost marked child of v precedes u)) **then**
4.   **return**(Find-Marked-Predecessor($u,\ell+1$));
5. $w \leftarrow$ Find-Marked-Predecessor(v,ℓ);
6. **return** rightmost marked child w;

Fig. 5. Final Algorithm

---

6). The $\sqrt{n}$-ary tree has $\sqrt{n}$ subtrees in which each has size $\sqrt{n}$. We recursively maintain a similar structure for each subtree—thus, the $\sqrt{n}$ children of a node are themselves organized in a $\sqrt[4]{n}$-ary tree, etc. The number of levels at which we can repeat the recursive construction is bounded by $O(\lg\lg n)$. We have to maintain the tree structure information for each level. This can be done efficiently using the scheme developed to efficiently solve the $\mathcal{TP}$ problem, described in [12]. The algorithm below finds the marked predecessor of node u at level ℓ of the recursive tree structure. To find the marked predecessor of u in L we shall call Find-Marked-Predecessor(u,0)—see Fig. 5.

Note that a node may have different parents at different recursive levels (see Fig. 6)—in the algorithm $parent(u,\ell)$ denotes the parent of u at level ℓ. Note also that a node may have children only in one of the recursive levels. With this scheme the worst-case time $T(n)$ required by the Find-Marked-Predecessor operation satisfies the recurrence: $T(n) = O(\lg\lg\sqrt{n}) + T(\sqrt{n})$, where n is the number of nodes in the

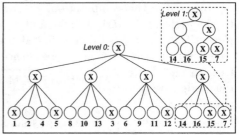

Fig. 6. A 16 node $\sqrt{n}$-ary tree with height 2

list L. The solution of this recurrence is $T(n) = \Theta((\lg\lg n)^2)$. The *unmark* operation takes time $O(1)$ per level of nesting. Hence the total required time $O(\lg\lg n)$.

On an APM (and hence on RAM), our scheme requires only $O(\lg\lg n)$ for both operations as the precedes now requires $O(1)$ time and the recurrence for $T(n)$ becomes: $T(n) = T(\sqrt{n}) + O(1)$. An $O(\lg\lg n)$ scheme to solve this problem on RAM machines also follows from [17]. However, directly translated that scheme will require $O(\lg n \lg\lg n)$ time on PPMs.

Further Considerations: At this time we do not have any results concerning lower bound time complexity for all cases of $\mathcal{ANDP^P}$. The problem has efficient amortized solutions—as mentioned earlier, the use of specialized union-find methodologies provide $O(1)$ amortized solutions [7]. On the other hand, both union-find as well as the decreasing marked ancestor problem have been shown to have lower bound time complexity of $\Omega(\lg n/\lg\lg n)$ per operation.

It is our conjecture that the problem has a lower bound time complexity of at least $\Omega(\lg\lg n)$. The solution proposed for $\mathcal{ANDP}^{\mathcal{P}}$ problem is for a static case (after all *expand* are peformed); it is easy to generalize the solution to obtain a dynamic version where *expand* requires $O((\lg\lg n)^2)$ amortized time. We are investigating fully dynamic solutions with the same worst-case time complexity.

6   Conclusion

We presented a formal abstraction of the problem of handling goals and dependent variables during ANDP execution of logic programs, based on the two standard methods considered in the literature (preventive and curative). We developed efficient data structures for solving the abstract versions of these problems. We also proved some results pertaining to the inherent complexity of these problems. Interestingly, these theoretical results confirm some empirically motivated conjectures of researchers working on and-parallelism [8], e.g., it is impossible to implement a constant time curative and preventive solutions to the and-parallel problem. Some of the data structures proposed suggest that it is theoretically possible to improve over existing execution models—e.g., none of the curative schemes accomplishes the fast conflict detection described in this paper. Furthermore, some of the solutions provided have already been applied in the design of more efficient schemes—this is the case of the solution to the $\mathcal{SE}$ problem (that has inspired the current side-effect handling scheme used in PALS [18]) and some of the original results from the study presented in this paper have contributed to the design of the ANDP mechanisms used in ACE [9].

We have also identified a number of open problems. For some of the problems, currently we do not have matching upper and lower bounds. Regarding the $\mathcal{ANDP}^{\mathcal{P}}$ problem, we conjecture the problem to have a single operation worst case time complexity of $\Omega(\lg\lg n)$. However, proving this result will require the use of techniques significantly different than those used to prove the lower bounds for related problems (e.g., the $\mathcal{TP}$ problem [12]). The lower bound proofs for these problems are based on building a special sequence of operations, leading to a configuration where, no matter what data structure is used, it is impossible to answer the queries efficiently. Such lower bound proofs do not exist for our problems. In particular, for the fully dynamic $\mathcal{ANDP}^{\mathcal{P}}$ problem, if the sequence of operations was known in advance, then one can always build in linear time a suitable data structure to answer the queries in $O(1)$ time.

References

1. S. Alstrup et al. Marked Ancestor Problems. In *FOCS*, pages 534–544, 1998.
2. A.M. Ben-Amram and Z. Galil. On Pointers versus Addresses. *JACM*, 39(3), 1992.
3. N. Blum. On the single-operation worst-case time complexity of the disjoint set union problem. *SIAM Journal on Computing*, 15(4):1021–1024, 1986.
4. R. Cole and R. Hariharan. Dynamic LCA Queries on Trees. *SODA*, ACM, 1999.
5. A. Dal Palù et al. An Optimal Algorithm for NCA on PPMs. *SWAT*, 2002.
6. N. Drakos. Unrestricted And-Parallel Execution of Logic Programs with Dependency Directed Backtracking. *IJCAI*, pages 157–162, 1989. Morgan Kaufmann.

7. H.N. Gabow and R.E. Tarjan. A Linear-time Algorithm for a Special Case of Disjoint Set Union. *Journal of Computer and System Sciences*, 30:209–221, 1985.
8. G. Gupta et al. Parallel Execution of Prolog Programs. *TOPLAS*, 23(4), 2001.
9. E. Pontelli et al. Implementation Mechanisms for DAP. *ICLP*, 1997. MIT Press.
10. E. Pontelli et al. An Optimal Data Structure to Handle Dynamic Environments in Non-Deterministic Computations. *Computer Languages*, 28(2), 2002.
11. E. Pontelli, D. Ranjan, and G. Gupta. On the Complexity of Parallel Implementation of Logic Programs. *FSTTCS*, pages 123–137, 1997. Springer Verlag.
12. D. Ranjan et al. The Temporal Precedence Problem. *Algorithmica*, 28, 2000.
13. K. Shen. Exploiting Dependent And-parallelism in Prolog. *JICSLP*, MIT, 1992.
14. R.E. Tarjan. A Class of Algorithms which Require Nonlinear Time to Maintain Disjoint Sets. *Journal of Computer and System Sciences*, 2(18):110–127, 1979.
15. H. Tebra. Optimistic And-Parallelism in Prolog. *PARLE*, 1987. Springer Verlag.
16. A. Tsakalidis. Maintaining Order in a Generalized Linked List. *ACTA Informatica*, 21:101–112, 1984.
17. P. van Emde Boas et al. Design and Implementation of an Efficient Priority Queue. *Mathematical Systems Theory*, 10, 1977.
18. K. Villaverde et al. A Methodology for Order-sensitive Execution of Non-deterministic Languages on Beowulf Platforms. *Euro-Par*, Springer, 2003.

Higher-Order Substitution Tree Indexing

Brigitte Pientka*

Department of Computer Science
Carnegie Mellon University
bp@cs.cmu.edu

Abstract. We present a higher-order term indexing strategy based on substitution trees. The strategy is based in linear higher-order patterns where computationally expensive parts are delayed. Insertion of terms into the index is based on computing the most specific linear generalization of two linear higher-order patterns. Retrieving terms is based on matching two linear higher-order patterns. This indexing structure is implemented as part of the Twelf system to speed-up the execution of the tabled higher-logic programming interpreter. Experimental results show substantial performance improvements, between 100% and over 800%.

1 Introduction

Efficient term indexing techniques have resulted in dramatic speed improvements in all major first-order logic programming and theorem proving systems and have been crucial to their success. Over the last years, different indexing techniques have been proposed for first-order terms (see [19] for a survey). However, indexing techniques for higher-order terms are missing thereby severely hampering the performance of higher-order reasoning systems such as Twelf [13], λProlog [8] or Isabelle [11].

In this paper, we present a higher-order term indexing technique based on substitution trees. Substitution tree indexing [3] is highly successful in the first-order setting and allows the sharing of common sub-expressions via substitutions. Given the following terms,pred (h (g a)) (g b) a (term 1), pred (h (g b)) (g b) a (term 2))and the term (3) pred (h (g c)) (g b) c , we compute their most specific common generalization, which is pred (h (g *1)) (g b) *2 where *1

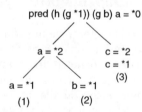

Fig. 1. Substitution tree

and *2 are placeholders. We then obtain the first term, by substituting a for the placeholders *1 and *2. The second term is recovered by substituting b for *1 and a for *2. Finally, the third term is obtained by substituting c for *1 and *2. The common structure of these three terms can be shared by storing substitutions in a tree (see Figure 1). To obtain the first term, we compose the substitutions in the left-most branch. Similarly, composing all the substitutions in the right-most branch yields the third term.

* This work has been partially supported by NSF Grant CCR-9988281 *"Logical and Meta-Logical Frameworks"* and by a *Siebel Scholarship*.

C. Palamidessi (Ed.): ICLP 2003, LNCS 2916, pp. 377–391, 2003.
© Springer-Verlag Berlin Heidelberg 2003

Extending this idea to the higher-order setting poses several challenges: First, building a substitution tree relies on computing the most specific generalization of two terms. However in the higher-order setting, the most specific generalization of two terms does not exist in general. Second, retrieving all terms, which unify or match, needs to be efficient – but higher-order unification is undecidable in general. Although decidable fragments, called higher-order patterns [7, 12], exist, algorithms based on them may not be efficient enough in practice [17]. Hence it is not obvious that they are a suitable basis for higher-order term indexing techniques.

In this paper, we present substitution tree indexing for higher-order terms based on linear higher-order patterns [17]. Linear higher-order patterns refine the notion of higher-order patterns further and factor out any computationally expensive parts. As shown in [17], many terms encountered fall into this fragment and linear higher-order pattern unification performs well in practice. In this paper, we give algorithms for computing the most specific generalization of two linear higher-order patterns, for inserting and retrieving terms from the index. This indexing structure is implemented as part of the Twelf system [13] to speed-up the execution of the tabled logic programming interpreter [15]. Experimental results show substantial performance improvements.

The paper is organized as follows: First, we give a theoretical framework for the dependently-typed lambda calculus. In Section 3, we present the general idea of higher-order substitution trees. In Section 4, we give algorithms for computing the most specific generalization of two terms and inserting terms into the index. Retrieval is discussed in Section 5. In Section 6, we present some experimental results comparing the tabled higher-order logic programming interpreter with and without indexing.

2   Dependently Typed Lambda Calculus

In this section, we introduce a conservative extension of LF [5] where we have existential variables as first-class objects [17]. We distinguish between ordinary variables denoted by x and existential variables denoted by u. c and a are constants, which are declared in a signature. In the presentation, we suppress some routine details such as signatures. Although we use the dependently typed lambda-calculus, the presented indexing techniques can be easily adopted for the simply-typed case.

$$
\begin{array}{rrl}
\text{Kinds} & K &::= \text{type} \mid \Pi x{:}A.\,K \\
\text{Families } A, B, C &::= a \mid A\,M \mid \Pi x{:}A_1.\,A_2 \\
\text{Objects} & M, N &::= c \mid x \mid u[\sigma] \mid \lambda x{:}A.\,M \mid M_1\,M_2 \\
\text{Substitutions} & \sigma, \tau &::= \cdot \mid \sigma, M/x \\
\text{Contexts} & \Gamma, \Psi &::= \cdot \mid \Gamma, x{:}A \\
\text{Modal Contexts} & \Delta &::= \cdot \mid \Delta, u{::}(\Psi \vdash A)
\end{array}
$$

Existential variable u are viewed as modal variables of type A in the context Ψ and are declared in a modal context Δ, while ordinary variables are declared in the context Γ. Note that the substitution σ is part of the syntax of existential variables. The principal judgments are listed below. As usual, we omit similar judgments on types and kinds and all judgments concerning definitional equality.

$\Delta; \Gamma \vdash M : A$ Object M has type A

$\Delta \vdash \theta : \Delta'$ Modal substitution θ matches Δ'

$\Delta; \Gamma \vdash \sigma : \Psi$ Substitution σ matches context Ψ

$\vdash \Delta$ mctx Δ is a valid modal context

$\Lambda \vdash \Psi$ ctx Ψ is a valid context

We will tacitly rename bound variables, and maintain that contexts and substitutions declare no variable more than once. Note that substitutions σ are defined only on ordinary variables x and not existential variables u. We write id_Γ for the identity substitution $(x_1/x_1, \dots, x_n/x_n)$ for a context $\Gamma = (\cdot, x_1{:}A_1, \dots, x_n{:}A_n)$. We will use π for a substitution which may permute the variables, i.e $\pi = (x_{\Phi(1)}/x_1, \dots, x_{\Phi(n)}/x_n)$ where Φ is a total permutation defined on the elements from a context $\Gamma = (\cdot, x_1{:}A_1, \dots, x_n{:}A_n)$. We only consider well-typed substitutions, so π must respect possible dependencies in its domain. We also streamline the calculus slightly by always substituting simultaneously for all ordinary variables. This is not essential, but saves some tedium in relating simultaneous and iterated substitution. Moreover, it is also closer to the actual implementation where we use de Bruijn indices and postpone explicit substitutions. Our convention is that substitutions as defined operations on expressions are written in prefix notation $[\sigma]P$ for an object, family, kind, or substitution P. These operations are capture-avoiding as usual. Moreover, we always assume that all free variables in P are declared in σ. Ordinary substitutions are defined in a standard manner, and we omit the details for the sake of brevity (for a more detailed account see [17]). Substitutions that are part of the syntax are written in postfix notation, $u[\sigma]$. Note that such explicit substitutions occur only for existential variables u defined in Δ. Substitutions θ are defined on existential variables. We write θ for a simultaneous substitution $[\![M_1/u_1, \dots, M_n/u_n]\!]$ where $u_1, \dots, u_n$ are distinct existential variables. The new operation of substitution is compositional, but two interesting situations arise: when a variable u is encountered, and when we substitute into a λ-abstraction (or a dependent type Π respectively).

Substitutions

$$[\![\theta]\!](\cdot) = \cdot$$
$$[\![\theta]\!](\sigma, N/y) = ([\![\theta]\!]\sigma, [\![\theta]\!]N/y)$$

Objects

$$[\![\theta]\!]c = c$$
$$[\![\theta]\!]x = x$$
$$[\![\theta_1, M/u, \theta_2]\!](u[\sigma]) = [\![\theta_1, M/u, \theta_2]\!]\sigma]M$$
$$[\![\theta]\!](N_1\, N_2) = ([\![\theta]\!]N_1)\,([\![\theta]\!]N_2)$$
$$[\![\theta]\!](\lambda y{:}A.\, N) = \lambda y{:}[\![\theta]\!]A.\, [\![\theta]\!]N$$

We remark that the rule for substitution into a λ-abstraction does not require a side condition. This is because the object M is defined in a different context, which is accounted for by the explicit substitution stored at occurrences of u.

Finally, consider the case of substituting into a closure, which is the critical case of this definition.

$$[\![\theta_1, M/u, \theta_2]\!](u[\sigma]) = [\![[\![\theta_1, M/u, \theta_2]\!]\sigma]\!]M$$

This is clearly well-founded, because σ is a subexpression (so $[\![\theta_1, M/u, \theta_2]\!]\sigma$ will terminate) and application of an ordinary substitution is defined without reference to the new form of substitution. The modal substitutions are compositional and the usual substitution properties hold (see [16] for a detailed discussion). We write id_Δ for the identity modal substitution $(u_1[\mathrm{id}_{\Psi_1}]/u_1, \ldots, u_n[\mathrm{id}_{\Psi_n}]/u_n)$ for a modal context $\Delta = (u_1::\Psi_1\vdash A_1, \ldots, u_n::\Psi_n\vdash A_n)$. The typing rules are given below.

Modal substitutions

$$\overline{\Delta \vdash (\cdot) : (\cdot)}$$

$$\frac{\Delta \vdash \theta : \Delta' \quad \Delta; [\![\theta]\!]\Psi \vdash M : [\![\theta]\!]A}{\Delta \vdash (\theta, M/u) : (\Delta', u::\Psi\vdash A)}$$

Ordinary substitutions

$$\overline{\Delta; \Gamma \vdash (\cdot) : (\cdot)}$$

$$\frac{\Delta; \Gamma \vdash \sigma : \Psi \quad \Delta; \Gamma \vdash M : [\sigma]A}{\Delta; \Gamma \vdash (\sigma, M/x) : (\Psi, x:A)}$$

Objects

$$\overline{\Delta; \Gamma, x:A, \Gamma' \vdash x : A}$$

$$\frac{\Delta, u::(\Psi\vdash A), \Delta'; \Gamma \vdash \sigma : \Psi}{\Delta, u::(\Psi\vdash A), \Delta'; \Gamma \vdash u[\sigma] : [\sigma]A}$$

$$\frac{\Delta; \Gamma, x:A_1 \vdash M : A_2}{\Delta; \Gamma \vdash \lambda x:A_1.. M : \Pi x:A_1. A_2}$$

$$\frac{\Delta; \Gamma \vdash M_1 : \Pi x:A_2. A_1 \quad \Delta; \Gamma \vdash M_2 : A_2}{\Delta; \Gamma \vdash M_1 M_2 : [\mathrm{id}_\Gamma, M_2/x]A_1}$$

Modal Context

$$\overline{\vdash (\cdot) \text{ mctx}}$$

$$\frac{\vdash \Delta \text{ mctx} \quad \Delta \vdash \Psi \text{ ctx} \quad \Delta; \Psi \vdash A : \text{type}}{\vdash (\Delta, u::(\Psi\vdash A)) \text{ mctx}}$$

Ordinary Context

$$\overline{\Delta \vdash (\cdot) \text{ ctx}}$$

$$\frac{\Delta \vdash \Psi \text{ ctx} \quad \Delta; \Psi \vdash A : \text{type}}{\Delta \vdash (\Psi, x:A) \text{ ctx}}$$

We only consider objects in $\beta\eta$-normal form and require that all terms which are not functions must be of atomic type. In particular, existential variables must also be of atomic type. This is accomplished by a technique called *lowering*. Lowering replaces a variable $u::(\Psi\vdash\Pi x:A_1. A_2)$ by a new variable $u'::(\Psi, x:A_1\vdash A_2)$. This process is repeated until all existential variables have a type of the form $\Psi \vdash b N_1 \ldots N_k$. For a more detailed account we refer the reader to [17,9,16]. Here, we just present the refined grammar for objects:

$$\text{Normal Objects } U ::= \lambda x. U \mid u[\sigma] \mid H U_1 \ldots U_n$$

The head H is either a constant c or a variable x. Note that type labels on λ-abstraction may be omitted for canonical forms. To illustrate the notation, we give a sample signature together with a set of terms we want to index. We define a type family exp for expressions and a predicate pred which takes in three arguments, where each argument is an expression. In addition, we give constants a, b, c and constructors f, g, h for building expressions of this small language.

exp: type.	pred: exp -> exp -> exp -> type.
a: exp.	h: exp -> exp.
b: exp.	g: exp -> exp.
c: exp.	f: (exp -> exp) -> exp.

Next, we give four examples of the predicate pred:

$$\cdot; \cdot \vdash \text{pred } (\text{h } (\text{g b})) \ (\text{g b}) \ \text{a} \qquad (1)$$
$$\cdot; \cdot \vdash \text{pred } (\text{h } (\text{g b})) \ (\text{g b}) \ \text{b} \qquad (2)$$
$$v:: \cdot \vdash \text{exp}; \cdot \vdash \text{pred } (\text{h } (\text{h b})) \ (\text{g b}) \ (\text{f } \lambda x.v[\cdot]) \qquad (3)$$
$$u::x:\text{exp}\vdash\text{exp}; \cdot \vdash \text{pred } (\text{h } (\text{h c})) \ (\text{g b}) \ (\text{f } \lambda x.u[x/x]) \ (4)$$

The first two predicates do not refer to any existential variables, while predicate (3) and (4) contain existential variables v and u respectively which are bound in the modal context. Note that all terms are well-typed in the context $\Delta = u::x:\text{exp}\vdash\text{exp}, v:: \cdot \vdash\text{exp}$ by weakening. Using these examples, we will briefly highlight some of the subtle issues concerning the interplay of bound and existential variables. The third predicate (3) refers to the existential variable v. Note that v is associated with the empty substitution, although it occurs in the context of a bound variable x. This means that any instantiation we find for v is not allowed to depend on the bound variable x. In contrast, predicate (4) refers to an existential variable u, which is associated with the identity substitution. This means that any instantiation we find for u may depend on the bound variable x. We come back to this point in Section 3.1.

3 Higher-Order Substitution Trees

We start by giving the general idea of higher-order substitution tree. To build a higher-order substitution tree, we proceed in two steps: First, we standardize the terms and convert terms into linear higher-order patterns. Second, we represent terms as a sequence of substitutions, which are stored in a tree.

3.1 Standardization: Linear Higher-Order Pattern

To get the maximum structure sharing across different indexed terms it is important to use variables in a consistent manner. In first-order term indexing we therefore standardize the term before inserting a term into an index. In addition, first-order term indexing strategies often employ linearization. When converting the term into standard form every occurrence of an existential variable is represented as a distinct standardized existential variable. Together with the linear term, we then also store variable definitions, which establish the equality between these two variables. One of the reasons for using linearization is efficiency. Non-linear terms may have multiple occurrences of the same existential variable and therefore requiring to check whether different substitutions for the same variable are consistent. Since such consistency checks can be potentially expensive and may lead to performance degradation, most first-order indexing techniques rely on a post-processing step to carry out the consistency checks.

To design a higher-order indexing technique, we will extend this notion of linearization and standardization. We will require that terms are linear higher-order patterns. Higher-order patterns [7,12] are terms where every existential variable must be applied to *some* distinct bound variables. Linear higher-order patterns [17] impose some further restrictions on the structure of terms: First, all existential variables must occur only once. This allows us to delay any expensive consistency checks. Second, all existential variables must be applied to *all* distinct bound variables. This eliminates any computationally expensive checks involving bound variables. This observation to restrict higher-order patterns even further to patterns where existential variables must be applied to all bound variables has also been made by Hanus and Prehofer [4] in the context of higher-order functional logic programming. While Hanus and Prehofer syntactically disallow terms which are not fully applied, we translate any term into a linear higher-order pattern together with some variable definitions. Any consistency checks are delayed after linear higher-order pattern unification has succeeded. As was shown in [17], performance of unification is improved substantially by this technique.

To illustrate, let us consider the previous term pred (h (g b)) (g b) (f $\lambda x.v[\cdot]$). The existential variable $v[\cdot]$ occurs only once, but is not applied to all distinct bound variables, since v is not allowed to depend on the bound variable x. Therefore $v[\cdot]$ is a higher-order pattern, but it is not linear. We can enforce that every existential variable occurs only once and is applied to *all* bound variables, by translating it into a linear higher-order pattern:

$$\text{pred (h (g b)) (g b) (f } \lambda x.u[x/x])$$

together with a variable definition,

$$\forall x{:}\text{exp}.u[x/x] \stackrel{D}{=} v[.]$$

where u is a new existential variable which is applied to the bound variable x. Similarly to first-order standardization and linearization, linearization in the higher-order case remains quite straightforward and can be done by traversing the term once. The main difference is that the postponed variable definitions may be more complex.

Variable Definitions $D ::= \text{true} \mid u[\text{id}_\Psi] \stackrel{D}{=} U \mid D_1 \wedge D_2 \mid \forall x{:}A.D$

3.2   Higher-Order Substitution Trees: An Example

In this section, we show the substitution tree for the set of terms given earlier. In each node, we store a set of substitutions, which we write here as $U = i$ where

U is a linear higher-order pattern and i is an internal existential variable and i will always be applied to all bound variables it may depend on. Therefore it will always be associated with the identity substitution id.

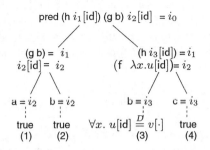

Note that variable definitions are stored at the leafs. By composing the substitutions in the right-most branch for example we get

$$[\![c/i_3]\!][\![f\ \lambda x.\ u[\mathsf{id}]/i_2, (\mathsf{h}\ i_3[\mathsf{id}])/i_1]\!][\![\mathsf{pred}\ (\mathsf{h}\ i_1[\mathsf{id}])\ (\mathsf{g\ b})\ i_2[\mathsf{id}]/i_0]\!]i_0[\mathsf{id}]$$

which represents the term (4) $\mathsf{pred}\ (\mathsf{h}\ (\mathsf{h\ c}))\ (\mathsf{g\ b})\ (\mathsf{f}\ \lambda x.\ u[\mathsf{id}])$. Note that in the implementation we can omit the identity substitution $i_2[\mathsf{id}]/i_2$ and maintain as an invariant that the substitutions in each node can be extended appropriately. This will simplify the theoretical treatment slightly.

In the following development we will distinguish between internal existential variables i which are defined in the modal context Σ and "global" existential variables u and v which are defined in the modal context Δ. A higher-order substitution tree is an ordered tree and is defined as follows:

1. A tree is a leaf node with substitution ρ such that $\Delta \vdash (\mathsf{id}_\Delta, \rho) : (\Delta, \Sigma)$.
2. A tree is a node with substitution ρ such that $(\Delta, \Sigma) \vdash (\mathsf{id}_\Delta, \rho) : (\Delta, \Sigma')$ and children nodes $N_1, \ldots, N_n$ where each child Node N_i has a substitution ρ_i such that $(\Delta, \Sigma_i) \vdash (\mathsf{id}_\Delta, \rho_i) : (\Delta, \Sigma)$.

For every path from the top node ρ_0 where $(\Delta, \Sigma_1) \vdash (\mathsf{id}_\Delta, \rho_0) : (\Delta, \Sigma_0)$ to the leaf node ρ_n, we have $\Delta \vdash [\![id_\Delta, \rho_n]\!]([\![id_\Delta, \rho_{n-1}]\!] \ldots (\mathsf{id}_\Delta, \rho_0)) : (\Delta, \Sigma_0)$. In other words, there are no internal existential variables left after we compose all the substitutions ρ_n up to ρ_0. Note that there are no typing dependencies among the variables in Σ and they can be arbitrarily re-ordered. Moreover, it is convenient to consider the extended modal substitution $(\mathsf{id}_\Delta, \rho_i)$ in the theory although in an implementation, we do not need to carry around explicitly the modal substitution id_Δ, but can always assume that any substitution ρ_i can be extended appropriately.

4   Insertion into Index

Insertion of a term U into the index is viewed as insertion of the substitution U/i_0. Assuming that U has type A in a modal context Δ and a bound variable context Γ, U/i_0 is a modal substitution such that $\Delta \vdash U/i_0 : i::(\Gamma\vdash A)$. We will call the modal substitution which is going to be inserted into the index ρ.

The insertion process works by following down a path in the tree that is *compatible* with the modal substitution ρ. To formally define insertion, we show how to compute the most specific linear generalization (msg) of two modal substitutions and describe the most specific linear generalization of two terms. We start by giving the judgments for computing the msg of two modal substitutions and the msg of two linear higher-order patterns.

$$(\Delta, \Sigma_1) \vdash \rho_1 \sqcup \rho_2 : \Sigma_2 \Longrightarrow \rho/(\Sigma, \theta_1, \theta_2) \qquad \rho \text{ is the msg of } \rho_1 \text{ and } \rho_2$$
$$(\Delta, \Sigma); \Gamma \vdash L_1 \sqcup L_2 : A \Longrightarrow L/(\Sigma', \theta_1, \theta_2) \; L \text{ is the msg of } L_1 \text{ and } L_2$$

If $(\Delta, \Sigma_1) \vdash (\mathrm{id}_\Delta, \rho_1) : (\Delta, \Sigma_2)$ and $(\Delta, \Sigma_1) \vdash (\mathrm{id}_\Delta, \rho_2) : (\Delta, \Sigma_2)$ then ρ is the msg of ρ_1 and ρ_2. Moreover, ρ is a modal substitution such that $[\![\mathrm{id}_\Delta, \theta_1]\!]\rho$ is syntactically equal to ρ_1 and $[\![\mathrm{id}_\Delta, \theta_2]\!]\rho$ is syntactically equal to ρ_2. We think of ρ_1 as the modal substitution which is already in the index, while the modal substitution ρ_2 is to be inserted. The result of the msg are the modal substitution θ_1 and θ_2, where $\Delta, \Sigma_1 \vdash \theta_1 : \Sigma$ and $\Delta, \Sigma_1 \vdash \theta_2 : \Sigma$. In other words, θ_1 (resp. θ_2) only replaces internal existential variables in Σ.

If the terms L_1 and L_2 have type A in modal context (Δ, Σ) and bound variable context Γ, then L is the most specific generalization of L_1 and L_2 such that $[\![\mathrm{id}_\Delta, \theta_1]\!]L$ is syntactically equal to L_1 and $[\![\mathrm{id}_\Delta, \theta_2]\!]L$ is syntactically equal to L_2. Moreover, θ_1 and θ_2 are modal substitutions which map existential variables from Σ' to the modal context (Δ, Σ). We think of L_1 as an object which is already in the index and L_2 is the object to be inserted. First, we give the rules for computing the most specific generalization of two modal substitutions.

$$\overline{(\Delta, \Sigma) \vdash \cdot : \cdots \Longrightarrow \cdot/(\cdot, \cdot, \cdot)}$$

$$\frac{(\Delta, \Sigma_1) \vdash \rho_1 \sqcup \rho_2 : \Sigma_2 \Longrightarrow \rho/(\Sigma, \theta_1, \theta_2) \quad (\Delta, \Sigma_1); \Gamma \vdash L_1 \sqcup L_2 : \tau \Longrightarrow L/(\Sigma', \theta_1', \theta_2')}{(\Delta, \Sigma_1) \vdash (\rho_1, L_1/i) \sqcup (\rho_2, L_2/i) : (\Sigma_2, i::(\Gamma\vdash\tau)) \Longrightarrow (\rho, L/i)/((\Sigma, \Sigma'), (\theta_1, \theta_1'), (\theta_2, \theta_2'))}$$

Note, that we are allowed to just combine the modal substitutions θ_1 (θ_2 resp.) and θ_1' (θ_2' resp.) since we require that they refer to distinct existential variables and all the existential variables occur uniquely. Computing the most specific generalization of two modal substitutions relies on finding the most specific generalization of two objects.

$$\frac{(\Delta, \Sigma); \Gamma, x{:}A_1 \vdash L_1 \sqcup L_2 : A_2 \Longrightarrow L/(\Sigma', \theta_1, \theta_2)}{(\Delta, \Sigma); \Gamma \vdash \lambda x.L_1 \sqcup \lambda x.L_2 : A_1 \to A_2 \Longrightarrow \lambda x.L/(\Sigma', \theta_1, \theta_2)}$$

$$\frac{u::(\Psi\vdash a) \in \Delta}{(\Delta, \Sigma); \Gamma \vdash u[\pi] \sqcup u[\pi] : a \Longrightarrow u[\pi]/(\cdot, \cdot, \cdot)} \; (*)$$

$$\frac{u::\Psi\vdash a \in (\Delta, \Sigma) \quad i \text{ must be new}}{(\Delta, \Sigma); \Gamma \vdash u[\pi] \sqcup L : a \Longrightarrow i[\mathrm{id}_\Gamma]/(i::\Gamma\vdash a, u[\pi]/i, L/i)} \; (1a)$$

$$\frac{i::\Gamma \vdash a \in (\Delta, \Sigma)}{(\Delta, \Sigma); \Gamma \vdash i[\mathrm{id}_\Gamma] \sqcup L : a \Longrightarrow i[\mathrm{id}_\Gamma]/(i::\Gamma\vdash a, \ i[\mathrm{id}_\Gamma]/i, \ L/i)} \quad (1b)$$

$$\frac{u::(\Psi \vdash a) \in \Delta}{(\Delta, \Sigma); \Gamma \vdash L \sqcup u[\pi] : a \Longrightarrow i[\mathrm{id}_\Gamma]/(i::\Gamma\vdash a, \ L/i, \ u[\pi]/i)} \quad (2)$$

$$\frac{\begin{array}{c} (\Delta, \Sigma); \Gamma \vdash L_1' \sqcup L_1'' : A_1 \Longrightarrow L_1/(\Sigma_1, \theta_1', \theta_1'') \\ \vdots \\ (\Delta, \Sigma); \Gamma \vdash L_n' \sqcup L_n'' : A_n \Longrightarrow L_n/(\Sigma_n, \theta_n', \theta_n'') \\ L = H \ L_1 \ldots L_n \quad \Sigma = (\Sigma_1, \ldots \Sigma_n) \quad \theta_1 = (\theta_1', \ldots, \theta_n') \quad \theta_2 = (\theta_1'', \ldots, \theta_n'') \end{array}}{(\Delta, \Sigma); \Gamma \vdash H \ L_1'' \ldots L_n'' \sqcup H \ L_1' \ldots L_n' : a \Longrightarrow L/(\Sigma, \theta_1, \theta_2)} \quad (3a)$$

$$\frac{H_1 \neq H_2 \quad i \text{ must be new} \quad \theta_1 = (H_1 \ L_1' \ldots L_n'/i) \quad \theta_2 = (H_2 \ L_1'' \ldots L_n''/i)}{(\Delta, \Sigma); \Gamma \vdash H_1 \ L_1' \ldots L_n' \sqcup H_2 \ L_1'' \ldots L_n'' : a \Longrightarrow i[\mathrm{id}_\Gamma]/((i::\Gamma\vdash a), \theta_1, \theta_2)} \quad (3b)$$

Note in the rule for lambda, we do not need to worry about capture, since existential variables and bound variables are defined in different context. Rule (*) treats the case where both terms are existential variables. Note that we require that both existential variables must be the same and their associated substitutions must also be equal. In rule (1) and (2), we just create the substitution $u[\pi]/i$. In general, we would need to create $[\mathrm{id}_\Gamma]^{-1} (u[\pi])$, but since we know that π is a permutation substitution, we know that $[\mathrm{id}_\Gamma]^{-1} (\pi)$ exists. In addition the inverse substitution of the identity is the identity. Note that we distinguish between the internal existential variables i and the "global" existential variables u in the rules (1a) and (1b). The key distinction is that we pick a new internal existential variable i in rule (1a) while we re-use the internal existential variable i in rule (1b). This is important for maintaining the invariant that any child of $(\Delta, \Sigma_2) \vdash (\mathrm{id}_\Delta, \rho) : (\Delta, \Sigma_1)$ has the form $(\Delta, \Sigma_3) \vdash (\mathrm{id}_\Delta, \rho') : (\Delta, \Sigma_2)$.

In rule (3a) and (3b) we distinguish two cases. If H_1 and H_2 are not equal, then we generate a new internal existential variable $i[\mathrm{id}_\Gamma]$ together with the substitutions $H_1 \ L_1' \ldots L_n'/i$ and $H_2 \ L_1'' \ldots L_n''/i$. Otherwise, we compute the most specific generalization for each L_i' and L_i'' and combine all the substitutions together. This is allowed since we require that all existential variables occur uniquely, and hence there are no dependencies among Σ_i.

To insert a new substitution ρ_2 into the substitution tree N where node N has the substitution $\Delta, \Sigma \vdash \rho : \Sigma'$, we proceed in two steps. First, we inspect all the children N_i of a parent node N, where N_i contains a modal substitution $\Delta, \Sigma_i \vdash \rho_i : \Sigma$ and check if ρ_i is compatible with ρ_2. This compatibility check has three possible result.

1. $(\Delta, \Sigma_i) \vdash \rho_i \sqcup \rho_2 : \Sigma \Longrightarrow \mathrm{id}_\Sigma/(\Sigma, \rho_i, \rho_2)$
   This means ρ_i and ρ_2 are not compatible. As a result we create a new leaf with substitution ρ_2 and add it to the children of N.
2. $(\Delta, \Sigma_i) \vdash \rho_i \sqcup \rho_2 : \Sigma \Longrightarrow \rho_1/(\Sigma_i, \mathrm{id}_{\Sigma_i}, \theta_2)$
   In this case $[\![\mathrm{id}_\Delta, \theta_2]\!]\rho_2$ is syntactically equivalent to ρ_i. This means ρ_2 is an instance of ρ_i and we will continue to insert θ_2 into the children C_i of the node N_i.
3. $(\Delta, \Sigma_i) \vdash \rho_i \sqcup \rho_2 : \Sigma \Longrightarrow \rho'/(\Sigma'', \theta_1, \theta_2)$
   ρ_i and ρ_2 are compatible and ρ' is more general than ρ_i and ρ_2. Then we

replace node N_i with a new node with the substitution ρ' and two children, where the first child contains substitution θ_1 and has children C_i and the second child has the substitution θ_2 with no children.

We illustrate this process by an example. Assume we have the following two modal substitutions:

$$\rho_1 = [\![(g\ a)/i_1,\ f\ (\lambda x.u[\mathsf{id}])/i_2,\ (h\ c)/i_3]\!]$$
$$\rho_2 = [\![(g\ b)/i_1,\ c/i_2,\ (h\ a)/i_3]\!]$$

Then, the most specific linear common generalization of the substitution is computed as follows. We compute the most specific linear generalization for each element. Hence the resulting most specific common substitution ρ of ρ_1 and ρ_2 is $[\![(g\ i_4[\mathsf{id}])/i_1,\ i_2[\mathsf{id}]/i_2,\ (h\ i_5[\mathsf{id}])/i_3]\!]$. In addition, ρ_1 will be split into the most specific common substitution ρ and the substitution $\theta_1 = [\![a/i_4,\ f\ (\lambda x.u[\mathsf{id}])/i_2,\ c/i_5]\!]$, s.t. $[\![\theta_1]\!]\rho = \rho_1$. Similarly ρ_2 will be split into ρ and the substitution $\theta_2 = [\![b/i_4,\ c/i_2,\ a/i_5]\!]$, s.t. $[\![\theta_2]\!]\rho = \rho_2$. Next, we illustrates the process of inserting the terms (1) to (4) from page 381 into a higher-order substitution tree. As mentioned earlier in the implementation we do not explicitly carry around the identity substitution $i_2[\mathsf{id}]/i_2$ and we will omit them in this figure.

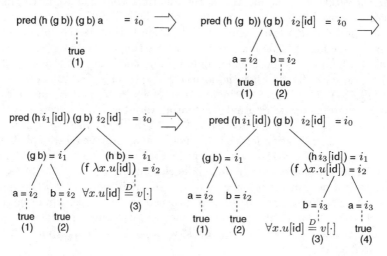

5   Retrieval

In general, we can retrieve all terms from the index which satisfy some property (e.g unifiability, instance, variant). One advantage of substitution trees is that all these retrieval operations can be implemented with only small changes. We adapt here the assignment for linear higher-order patterns described in [17] to check whether the term L_2 is an instance of the term L_1. The principal judgment for normal objects is defined as follows:

$$(\Delta, \Sigma); \Gamma \vdash L_1 \doteq L_2 \ /(\theta, \rho) \ L_2 \text{ is an instance of } L_1$$

Again we assume that L_1 and L_2 must be well-typed in the modal context Δ, Σ and the bound variable context Γ. Let Δ_1 be the existential variables in L_1. Then θ is a substitution for the existential variables in Δ_1 and ρ is the substitution for the internal existential variables in Σ then $[\![\theta, \rho]\!]L_1$ is syntactically equal to L_2.

$$\frac{(\Delta, \Sigma); \Gamma, x{:}A \vdash L_1 \doteq L_2 \ / \ (\theta, \rho)}{(\Delta, \Sigma); \Gamma \vdash \lambda x{:}A.L_1 \doteq \lambda x{:}A.L_2 \ / \ (\theta, \rho)} \ lam$$

$$\frac{}{(\Delta, \Sigma); \Gamma \vdash i[\mathrm{id}_\Gamma] \doteq L \ / \ (\cdot, (L/i))} \ exL1 \qquad \frac{u{::}\Psi \vdash a \in \Delta}{(\Delta, \Sigma); \Gamma \vdash u[\pi] \doteq L \ / \ (([\pi]^{-1} \, L/u), \cdot)} \ exL2$$

$$(\Delta, \Sigma); \Gamma \vdash L_1' \doteq L_1'' \ / \ (\theta_1, \rho_1)$$

$$\vdots$$

$$\frac{(\Delta, \Sigma); \Gamma \vdash L_n' \doteq L_n'' \ / \ (\theta_n, \rho_n)}{(\Delta, \Sigma); \Gamma \vdash H L_1' \ldots L_n' \doteq H L_1'' \ldots L_n'' \ / \ ((\theta_1, \ldots, \theta_n), (\rho_1 \ldots \rho_n))} \ app$$

Note that we need not worry about capture in the rule for lambda expressions since existential variables and bound variables are defined in different contexts. In the rule *app*, we are allowed to union the two substitutions θ_1 and θ_2, as the linearity requirement ensures that the domains of both substitutions are disjoint. Note that the case for matching an existential variable $u[\pi]$ with another term L is simpler and more efficient than in the general higher-order pattern case. In particular, it does not require a traversal of L (see rules *exL1* and *exL2*). Since the inverse of the substitution π can be computed directly and will be total, we know $[\pi]^{-1} L$ exists and can simply generate a substitution $[\pi]^{-1} L/u$. The algorithm can be easily specialized to retrieve variances by requiring in the *exL2* rule that L must be $u[\pi]$. To check unifiability we need to add the dual rule to *exL2* where we unify L with an existential variable $u[\pi]$. The only complication is that L may contain internal existential variables which are defined later on the path in the substitution tree.

This instance algorithm for terms can be straightforwardly extended to instances of substitutions. Let $\rho' = [\![U_1/i_k, \ldots, U_n/i_n]\!]$ be associated with node N' and $\rho'' = [\![V_1/i_k, \ldots, V_n/i_n]\!]$, then we match each U_k against V_k and the final result is $\theta = [\![\theta_1, \ldots, \theta_n]\!]$ and $\rho = [\![\rho_1, \ldots, \rho_n]\!]$. In the next step, we continue to retrieve all children C' of node N' such that ρ is an instance of C'.

6   Experimental Results

In this section, we discuss examples from three different applications which use the tabled logic programming engine in Twelf [14,15]. Here we focus on an evaluation of the indexing technique. All experiments are done on a machine with the following specifications: 1.60GHz Intel Pentium Processor, 256 MB RAM. We are using SML of New Jersey 110.0.3 under Linux Red Hat 7.1. Times are measured in seconds. All the examples use variant checking as a retrieval mechanism. Although we have implemented subsumption checking, we did not observe substantial performance improvements using subsumption. A similar observation has been made for tabling in the first-order logic programming engine XSB [18]. Potentially subsumption checking becomes more important in theorem proving, as the experience in the first-order setting shows.

6.1   Parsing of First-Order Formulae

Parsing and recognition algorithms for grammars are excellent examples for tabled evaluation, since we often want to mix right and left recursion (see also [20]). In this example, we adapted ideas from Warren [20] to implement a parser for first-order formulas using higher-order abstract syntax.

#tok	noindex	index	speed-up
20	0.13	0.07	85%
58	2.61	1.25	108%
117	10.44	5.12	103%
178	32.20	13.56	137%
235	75.57	26.08	190%

The first column denotes the number of tokens which are parsed. This example illustrates that indexing can lead to speed-ups to over 190%. In fact, the more tokens need to be parsed and the longer the tabled logic programming engine runs, the larger the benefits of indexing. The table grows up to over 4000 elements in this example. This indicates that indexing prevents to some extent program degradation due to large tables and longer run-times.

6.2   Refinement Type-Checker

In this section, we discuss experiments with a bi-directional type-checking algorithm for a small functional language with intersection types which has been developed by Davies and Pfenning [1]. We use an implementation of the bi-directional type-checker in *Elf* by Pfenning. The type-checker is executable with the original logic programming interpreter, which performs a depth-first search. However, redundant computation may severely hamper its performance as there are several derivations for proving that a program has a specified type.

We give several examples which are grouped in three categories. In the first category, we are interested in finding the first answer to a type checking problem and once we have found the answer execution stops. The second category contains example programs which are not well-typed and the implemented type-checker rejects these programs as not well-typed. The third category are examples where we are interested in finding all answer to the type-checking problem.

First answer

example	noindex	index	speed-up
sub1	3.19	0.46	593%
sub2	4.22	0.55	663%
sub3	5.87	0.63	832%
mult	7.78	0.89	774%
square1	9.08	0.99	817%
square2	9.02	0.98	820%

Not provable

example	noindex	index	speed-up
multNP1	2.38	0.38	526%
multNP2	2.66	0.51	422%
plusNP1	1.02	0.24	325%
plusNP2	6.48	0.85	662%
squareNP1	9.29	1.09	752%
squareNP2	9.26	1.18	685%

All answers

example	noindex	index	speed-up
sub1	6.88	0.71	869%
sub2	3.72	0.48	675%
sub3	4.99	0.59	746%
mult	9.06	0.98	824%
square1	10.37	1.11	834%
square2	10.30	1.08	854%

As the results demonstrate indexing leads to substantial improvements by over 800%. Table sizes are not as large as in the parsing example, however we accessed the table often.

6.3 Evaluating Mini-ML Expression via Reduction

In the third experiment we use an implementation which evaluates expressions of a small functional language via reduction. The reduction rules are highly non-deterministic containing reflexivity and transitivity rules.

example	noindex	index	speed-up
mult1	10.86	6.26	73%
mult2	39.13	18.31	114%
addminus1	54.31	14.42	277%
addminus2	57.34	15.66	266%
addminus3	55.23	25.45	117%
addminus4	144.73	56.63	155%
minusadd1	1339.16	462.83	189%

As the results demonstrate, performance is improved by up to 277%. Table size was around 500 entries in the table. The limiting factor in this example is not necessarily the table size but the large number of suspended goals which is over 6000. This may be the reason why the speed-up is not as large as in the refinement type-checking example.

7 Related Work and Conclusion

We have presented a term indexing technique, called higher-order substitution trees for dependently-typed terms which may contain λ-abstraction. This indexing technique is based on linear higher-order patterns. We only know of two other attempts to design and implement a higher-order term indexing technique. L. Klein [6] developed in his master's thesis a higher-order term indexing technique for simply typed terms where algorithms are based on a fragment of Huet's higher-order unification algorithm, the simplification rules. Since the most specific generalization of two higher-order terms does not exist in general, he suggests to maximally decompose a term into its atomic subterms. This approach result in larger substitution trees and stores redundant substitutions. In addition, he does not use explicit substitutions leading to further redundancy in the representation of terms. As no linearity criteria is exploited, the consistency checks are necessary.

Necula and Rahul briefly discuss the use of automata driven indexing for higher-order terms in [10]. Their approach is restricted to a fragment of LF and essentially ignores all higher-order features when maintaining the index, and return an imperfect set of candidates where full higher-order unification on the original term is used to filter out the ones which are in fact unifiable in a post-processing step. Their approach is also based on Huet's unification algorithm, which is highly nondeterministic. Although, they have achieved substantial speed-up for their application in proof-carrying code, it is not as general as the technique we have presented here.

So far, we have implemented and successfully used higher-order substitution trees in the context of higher-order tabled logic programming. Another interesting use is in indexing the actual higher-order logic program. While the table is a dynamically built index, indexing of program clauses can be done statically. Although the general idea of substitution trees is also applicable in this setting there are several important optimizations, such as unification factoring [2], we plan do adapt to the higher-order setting in the future.

Acknowledgments. This work could not have been accomplished without the insights, persistence and critical feedback of my advisor Frank Pfenning.

References

1. Rowan Davies and Frank Pfenning. Intersection types and computational effects. In *Proceedings of the International Conference on Functional Programming (ICFP 2000), Montreal, Canada*, pages 198–208. ACM Press, 2000.
2. Steve Dawson, C. R. Ramakrishnan, Steve Skiena, and Terrance Swift. Principles and practice of unification factoring. *ACM Transactions on Programming Languages and Systems*, 18(6):528–563, 1995.
3. Peter Graf. Substitution tree indexing. In *Proceedings of the 6th International Conference on Rewriting Techniques and Applications, Kaiserslautern, Germany,* Lecture Notes in Computer Science (LNCS) 914, pages 117–131. Springer-Verlag, 1995.
4. Michael Hanus and Christian Prehofer. Higher-order narrowing with definitional trees. *Journal of Functional Programming*, 9(1):33–75, 1999.
5. Robert Harper, Furio Honsell, and Gordon Plotkin. A framework for defining logics. *Journal of the Association for Computing Machinery*, 40(1):143–184, January 1993.

6. Lars Klein. Indexing für Terme höherer Stufe. Diplomarbeit, FB 14, Universität des Saarlandes, Saarbrücken, Germany, 1997.

7. Dale Miller. Unification of simply typed lambda-terms as logic programming. In *Eighth International Logic Programming Conference*, pages 255–269, Paris, France, June 1991. MIT Press.

8. Gopalan Nadathur and Dale Miller. An overview of λProlog. In Kenneth A. Bowen and Robert A. Kowalski, editors, *Fifth International Logic Programming Conference*, pages 810–827, Seattle, Washington, August 1988. MIT Press.

9. Aleksander Nanevski, Brigitte Pientka, and Frank Pfenning. A modal foundation for meta-variables. In *2nd ACM SIGPLAN Workshop on Mechanized Reasoning about Languages with variable binding (Merlin), Uppsala, Sweden*. to appear, August 2003.

10. G. Necula and S. Rahul. Oracle-based checking of untrusted software. In *28th ACM Symposium on Principles of Programming Languages (POPL'01)*, pages 142–154, 2001.

11. Lawrence C. Paulson. Natural deduction as higher-order resolution. *Journal of Logic Programming*, 3:237–258, 1986.

12. Frank Pfenning. Unification and anti-unification in the Calculus of Constructions. In *Sixth Annual IEEE Symposium on Logic in Computer Science*, pages 74–85, Amsterdam, The Netherlands, July 1991.

13. Frank Pfenning and Carsten Schürmann. System description: Twelf — a meta-logical framework for deductive systems. In H. Ganzinger, editor, *Proceedings of the 16th International Conference on Automated Deduction (CADE-16)*, pages 202–206, Trento, Italy, July 1999. Springer-Verlag Lecture Notes in Artificial Intelligence (LNAI) 1632.

14. Brigitte Pientka. Memoization-based proof search in LF: an experimental evaluation of a prototype. In *Third International Workshop on Logical Frameworks and Meta-Languages (LFM'02), Copenhagen, Denmark*, Electronic Notes in Theoretical Computer Science (ENTCS), 2002.

15. Brigitte Pientka. A proof-theoretic foundation for tabled higher-order logic programming. In P. Stuckey, editor, *18th International Conference on Logic Programming, Copenhagen, Denmark*, Lecture Notes in Computer Science (LNCS), 2401, pages 271–286. Springer-Verlag, 2002.

16. Brigitte Pientka. *Tabled higher-order logic programming*. PhD thesis, Department of Computer Sciences, Carnegie Mellon University, 2003. forthcoming.

17. Brigitte Pientka and Frank Pfennning. Optimizing higher-order pattern unification. In F. Baader, editor, *19th International Conference on Automated Deduction, Miami, USA*, Lecture Notes in Artificial Intelligence (LNAI) 2741, pages 473–487. Springer-Verlag, July 2003.

18. I. V. Ramakrishnan, P. Rao, K. Sagonas, T. Swift, and D. Warren. Efficient access mechanisms for tabled logic programs. *Journal of Logic Programming*, 38(1):31–54, Jan 1999.

19. I. V. Ramakrishnan, R. Sekar, and A. Voronkov. Term indexing. In Alan Robinson and Andrei Voronkov, editors, *Handbook of Automated Reasoning*, volume 2, pages 1853–1962. Elsevier Science Publishers B.V., 2001.

20. David S. Warren. *Programming in tabled logic programming*. draft available from http://www.cs.sunysb.edu/w̄arren/xsbbook/book.html, 1999.

Incremental Evaluation of Tabled Logic Programs*

Diptikalyan Saha and C.R. Ramakrishnan

Department of Computer Science,
State University of New York at Stony Brook
Stony Brook, New York, 11794-4400, U.S.A.
{dsaha, cram}@cs.sunysb.edu

Abstract. Tabling has emerged as an important evaluation technique in logic programming. Currently, changes to a program (due to addition/deletion of rules/facts) after query evaluation compromise the completeness and soundness of the answers in the tables. This paper presents incremental algorithms for maintaining the freshness of tables upon addition or deletion of facts. Our algorithms improve on existing materialized view maintenance algorithms and can be easily extended to handle changes to rules as well. We describe an implementation of our algorithms in the XSB tabled logic programming system. Preliminary experimental results indicate that our incremental algorithms are efficient. Our implementation represents a first step towards building a practical system for incremental evaluation of tabled logic programs.

1 Introduction

Tabled resolution [19,1,3] removes some of the best-known shortcomings of Prolog's evaluation strategy, especially its susceptibility to infinite looping. The XSB system [20] has become a stable platform for evaluating tabled logic programs, and several alternative implementations are emerging [4,22,9]. The added power of tabling has been crucial to the construction of many applications— such as practical program analysis and verification systems (e.g., [5,14]), object-oriented knowledge bases (e.g. Flora-2 [21]) and ontology management systems— by encoding them at a high level as logic programs.

Tabled resolution-based systems evaluate programs by memoizing subgoals (referred to as *calls*) and their provable instances (referred to as *answers*) in a set of tables. Traditionally, the systems keep all calls in a *call table*. For each subgoal in the call table, its provable instances are kept in an *answer table*. During resolution, if a subgoal is present in the call table, then it is resolved against the answers recorded in the corresponding answer table; otherwise the subgoal is entered in the call table, and its answers, computed by resolving the subgoal against program clauses, are also entered in the answer table.

* This research was supported in part by NSF grants EIA-9705998, CCR-9876242, IIS-0072927, CCR-0205376, CCR-0311512, and ONR grant N000140110967. We would like to thank Luis Castro for his extensive help with the implementation of our techniques in XSB.

C. Palamidessi (Ed.): ICLP 2003, LNCS 2916, pp. 392–406, 2003.

```
1:   reach(X,Y) :- edge(X,Y).
2:   reach(X,Y) :- reach(X,Z), edge(Z,Y).
```

```
edge(0,1).
edge(0,2).
edge(1,1).
edge(1,2).
```

```
edge(0,1).
edge(0,2).
edge(1,1).
edge(1,2).
edge(2,3).
```

(a)   (b)   (c)

Fig. 1. Example reachability program (a) and two edge/2 relations (b & c).

The Problem: The answers in the tables represent conclusions that can be inferred from the set of facts and rules in the program. *When the program changes (either by addition or deletion of facts/rules), the tables become stale:* they may not have all the answers or the answers in the tables may be incorrect.

For instance, consider the evaluation of query reach(0,X) over the program in Figure 1(a) using the definition of edge/2 relation in Figure 1(b). Tabled evaluation will create an answer table for reach(0,X) with {X=1, X=2} as the answers. Subsequent invocation of reach(0,Y) will simply resolve the subgoal against the answers in the table, returning {Y=1, Y=2} as answers.

Now let a new tuple edge(2,3) be added to the edge/2 relation. Note that the answer table for call reach(0,X) contains only answers {X=1, X=2} and hence is stale. Invocation of, say reach(0,Z), will return only answers Z=1 and Z=2, and miss the answer Z=3. The problem becomes worse if tuples can be deleted. If the tuple edge(0,1) is deleted from the edge/2 relation, the query reach(0,Z) will still return answers Z=1 and Z=2, even though reach(0,1) is no longer true!

Tabling systems currently provide no mechanism to refresh the tables after a change to the program. In fact, in the applications we have built so far, we remove all affected tables after an update to the program and then reissue the query. This approach is clearly wasteful, especially if the changes to the program are small. For instance, in the above example, after the addition of edge(2,3), the subgoal reach(0,Z) and its answer table must be removed and recomputed, deriving answers {Z=1, Z=2, Z=3}, in effect *rederiving* answers Z=1 and Z=2.

The above example illustrates the need to incrementally maintain the "freshness" of the tables. We address this problem in this paper. This problem, considered as the *materialized view maintenance problem,* has been extensively studied in the deductive database community (see, e.g. [8,12] for extensive surveys in this area). Most existing solutions have been derived in the context of bottom-up (semi-naive) evaluation; we address this problem in the context of top-down tabled evaluation. See Section 5 for further discussion on the related work.

Our Solution: In this paper we first consider definite logic programs where all non-tabled[1] user-defined predicates are defined by facts. We consider recursive rules but permit only additions and deletions of facts and rules in a program. We subsequently describe straightforward extensions that remove these restrictions.

---

[1] Systems such as XSB permit a programmer to mark specific predicates as *tabled;* calls and answers involving other predicates (called *non-tabled* predicates) are not stored in the table.

Handling Addition: Top-down goal-oriented evaluation systems (such as those based on the SLGWAM) inherently process answers incrementally. A subgoal that causes answers to be added to the tables is called a producer, and a subgoal which is resolved against answers already in the tables is called a consumer. The evaluation engine maintains auxiliary data structures to ensure that no consumer sees an answer more than once: e.g. environments to produce and consume answers and control structures linking answer producers to answer consumers. These data structures are torn down when all answers to a call have been derived, an operation that is crucial to memory efficiency of top-down evaluators. Retaining these after query evaluation to support incremental additions imposes unacceptable overheads; e.g., the space usage for evaluating left-recursive reachability queries increases by 2-6 times.

An alternative, similar to the approach used in prior works such as [7], is to generate rules to capture the new answers due to addition of facts. For instance, the changes to the reach/2 relation can be computed by evaluating the predicate reach'/2 defined as follows (where the additions to edge/2 are given by the edge'/2 relation):

```
reach'(X,Y) :- edge'(X,Y).
reach'(X,Y) :- reach'(X,Z), edge(Z,Y).
reach'(X,Y) :- (reach(X,Z); reach'(X,Z)), edge'(Z,Y).
```

Direct tabled evaluation of the auxiliary rules will lead to two distinct tables for reach and reach'. Consequently, the same answer may be stored in both the tables, and the two tables must be merged after the incremental evaluation. In Section 2 we describe a data structure that enables the two predicates to share the same table, eliminating most of the overheads of incremental evaluation.

Handling Deletion: Deletion of facts in a program pose a more complicated problem, especially in the presence of recursive rules. Algorithms that incrementally maintain recursive views typically follow the two-phase delete-rederive approach best exemplified by the *DRed* algorithm [7]. The first phase deletes *all* answers which can be derived from the deleted facts. For instance, consider the answers to reach(0,X) after the deletion of edge(0,1) from Figure 1(c). Using DRed, we will delete the answers reach(0,1), reach(0,2), and reach(0,3) since all of them can be derived using edge(0,1). The second phase rederives answers deleted in the first phase that have alternative derivations not involving the deleted facts. Continuing with our example, we will now rederive reach(0,2) (due to edge(0,2)) and consequently reach(0,3). It must be noted that the MCI algorithm for incremental model checking [17] follows a strikingly similar approach (see Section 5).

The delete-rederive algorithms have relatively high overheads. As the above example illustrates, these algorithms hastily delete a number of answers in the first phase, only to rederive many of them (with considerable additional effort) in the second phase.

Our technique handles the deletion of facts as well as rules but achieves considerable savings compared to the delete/redeive algorithms by carefully controlling the deletion of answers in the first phase. Note that, in the above example, `reach(0,2)` need not even be considered for deletion since it has an alternative derivation (due to `edge(0,2)`) when `reach(0,1)` is deleted. We keep a succinct representation of all possible derivations of an answer by keeping a set of *supports* for the answer. Informally, a support for an answer is a set of atoms such that there is a rule $\alpha :- \beta_1, \ldots \beta_n$ where the answer is an instance of α and the support is an instance of $\{\beta_1, \ldots, \beta_n\}$. For instance, the supports for answer `reach(0,2)` are $\{$`edge(0,2)`$\}$ and $\{$`reach(0,1)`, `edge(1,2)`$\}$.

The following key observation permits the use of support sets to control the first phase. An answer α is valid whenever there is a valid support s such that s does not depend on α, and a support is valid whenever all answers in it are valid. However, short of maintaining strongly connected components, there is no efficient mechanism to determine the interdependencies between supports and answers. But it turns out that the first support that adds an answer to the table will always be independent of the answer. We use this as a heuristic to control the propagation of deletions. In the above example, deletion of `reach(0,1)` does not delete `reach(0,2)` since the latter is supported by $\{$`edge(0,2)`$\}$. Consequently, `reach(0,3)` is also retained without additional work.

Support sets are also central to the efficiency of the rederivation phase where we attempt to rederive each answer deleted in the first phase. Using support sets, an answer can be rederived by simply checking the validity of supports (analogous to proof checking) instead of launching a full-fledged proof search.

We have implemented our incremental techniques in the XSB tabling engine. Preliminary experiments with our implementation indicate that our support-based technique is superior to standard delete-rederive techniques. Furthermore, the overheads for generating and maintaining supports are negligible compared to the benefits. Our implementation also indicates the ease of deployment, efficiency, and practicality of our techniques.

Summary: We present, to the best of our knowledge, the first techniques for incremental evaluation of tabled logic programs. We describe efficient data structures and algorithms for incremental maintenance of tables in the presence of addition (see Section 2) and deletion (see Section 3) of rules/facts. We also describe how to handle non-tabled predicates and stratified negation. We present preliminary experimental results which show the effectiveness of our techniques (see Section 4). We compare of our work with previous works in incremental view maintenance in Section 5. Further research problems are sketched in Section 6.

2 Addition

Preliminaries: The XSB system uses trie-based data structures for storing terms in call and answer tables [15]. Tries permit efficient lookup and one-pass check-insert operations. However, tries do not maintain the terms in the order of insertion. When resolving answers against an incomplete table (where new answers may be added), XSB maintains and uses an *answer list*, which links leaf nodes in the trie in their order of insertion. When a table is complete, which means no new answers can be added to the table with respect to a given set of facts, answer resolution is done by backtracking through the trie top-down; the answer list is no longer needed and is deleted.

Incremental Evaluation after Additions: Let P be a definite logic program and γ be a query. We denote the answers to γ with respect to P by $ans_P(\gamma)$. Let δ_p be a set of facts and rules added to the program P. The problem of incremental evaluation of query γ then is one of computing the smallest set Δ of answers such that $ans_{P \cup \delta_p}(\gamma) = \Delta \cup ans_P(\gamma)$. That is, Δ is the set of *new* answers for γ.

Given a definite logic program P and an added program δ_p we derive a transformed program P' used for incremental evaluation as follows. For each predicate p/n defined in the program $P \cup \delta_p$, we introduce an incremental predicate p'/n. If γ is an atom with p at its root, we denote by γ' the atom obtained by replacing the p in γ by p'. The transformed program P' is such that $ans_P(\gamma) \cup ans_{P'}(\gamma') = ans_{P \cup \delta_p}(\gamma)$.

First of all, P' contains all the clauses in P. For each fact α in δ_p we add α' to P'. For every clause of the form $\gamma :- \beta_1, \beta_2, \ldots \beta_n$ in the program $P \cup \delta_p$, we add the clause $\gamma' :- (\beta_1; \beta'_1), \ldots, (\beta_{i-1}; \beta'_{i-1}), \beta'_i, \beta_{i+1}, \ldots, \beta_n$ for each $i \in [1, n]$. The i-th clause computes new answers of γ due to new answers of β_i. The incremental predicate **reach'** defined in the introduction is derived from the original definition of **reach** by the above transformation. The transformation is a straightforward application of finite differencing [13], and its variants have been widely used for materialized view maintenance [7,10].

Direct evaluation of the transformed program has two sources of inefficiency. Firstly, the new answers of a query γ are actually added as answers to the new query γ'; consequently, we must merge the two answer tables after the incremental evaluation is complete. Secondly, to ensure that γ' computes only the new answers, each derived answer must be first checked against answers to the original query γ (e.g. using the goal $\neg\gamma$ [18]), causing an extra table lookup.

We overcome these problems by sharing the call table entry and the answer tables between the incremental goal and the original goal, although the calls access the answer table in different ways. Let γ be an original goal and γ' be its incremental counterpart. The first call to γ' creates a new subgoal frame. Answers to γ' are computed by program clause resolution, are added to the answer table of γ, and also kept in a separate answer list. Subsequent calls to γ' consume from this answer list (even after completion of γ')— exactly the same way answers are currently consumed from incomplete tables.

In order to prevent answers to γ' from being accessed when backtracking through the answers of γ, we mark all the newly added answers as "deleted". This exploits the current implementation of tries in XSB which provides a flag to mark terms as deleted without physically removing them. This flag is used in XSB for maintaining dynamic asserted data using tries. Finally, when the incremental evaluation is complete, we reset the deleted flag of all answers in the answer list of γ', thereby adding these answers to γ. Figure 2 shows the states

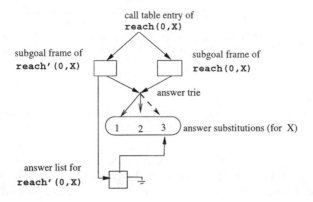

Fig. 2. Example of the data structure to maintain tables for incremental predicates.

of the answer tables of `reach(0,X)` and its incremental version `reach'(0,X)`, just before the completion of the incremental evaluation.

Discussion: The data structure described above enables us to incrementally evaluate queries without changing any other part of the tabling engine. Moreover, in contrast to bottom-up techniques, we refresh a table only on demand when a query is made. Note, though, that we maintain only two versions of answers, and hence cannot maintain tables with varying "staleness". For instance, if γ_1 and γ_2 are two queries, when γ_1 is incrementally evaluated after changes to facts, observe that γ_1 has consumed all the new facts while γ_2 has not. However, since after this evaluation we merge all new answers with the old, γ_2 will remain stale. A promising approach for solving this problem is to associate timestamps with the added facts and answers, and drive the incremental computation based on the timestamps. With the time-stamp based solution, we can maintain multiple versions of tables within the same data structure and hence handle tables with different degrees of staleness. This is a topic of future research.

3   Deletion

Let P be a definite logic program, γ be a query and δ_p be a set of facts F and set of rules R_d to be deleted from the program. For notational purposes, we assume that every rule is associated with an unique identifier (e.g see Figure 1(a)). Following the notation used in Section 2, the problem of incremental evaluation of query γ after the deletion is that of computing a set Δ of answers such that $ans_{P-\delta_p}(\gamma) = ans_P(\gamma) - \Delta$. We develop an algorithm to efficiently compute the set Δ in this section and describe its implementation in terms of tabling data structures.

Formulation: Clearly, the only answers that can be in Δ are those that depend on δ_p. The algorithms based on the delete-rederive approach [7,17] first over-

```
edge(0,1)
edge(0,2)
edge(1,1)
edge(1,2)
```
(a)

Answer	Supports
reach(0,1)	$\langle 1, \{ \texttt{edge(0,1)} \} \rangle$, $\langle 2, \{ \texttt{reach(0,1)}, \texttt{edge(1,1)} \} \rangle$
reach(0,2)	$\langle 1, \{ \texttt{edge(0,2)} \} \rangle$, $\langle 2, \{ \texttt{reach(0,1)}, \texttt{edge(1,2)} \} \rangle$

(b)

Fig. 3. Example edge relation (a); and supports for answers to query reach(0,X) over that relation (b).

approximate Δ by the set of <u>all</u> answers that depend on δ_p. We use a better approximation based on the notion of *support* for an answer defined below.

Definition 1 (Support) *Let P be a program, and let T be a set of answer tables obtained when evaluating a query γ over P. A tuple $s = \langle k, \{ \beta_1, \beta_2, \ldots, \beta_n \} \rangle$ is called a support of an answer α of γ if there exists a clause k of the form $\alpha' :- \beta_1', \beta_2', \ldots, \beta_n'$ and a substitution θ, such that $\alpha' \theta = \alpha$, and for all $i \in [1, n]$ $\beta_i' \theta = \beta_i$ and β_i is an instance of an answer in T or a fact in P.*

For instance, consider the query reach(0,X) over the reachability program in Figure 1(a) and edge/2 relation in Figure 3(a).

Note that each support for an answer represents one step in some derivation of that answer. We can construct a derivation of an answer by picking a support and constructing derivations for all the atoms in that support. However, the choice of support picked at each step is crucial to the construction of a valid (i.e. finite) derivation. For instance, picking the support $\langle 2, \{ \texttt{reach(0,1)}, \texttt{edge(1,1)} \} \rangle$ each time to derive reach(0,1) will not lead to a finite derivation; for finiteness we must eventually pick the support $\langle 1, \{ \texttt{edge(0,1)} \} \rangle$. The key to quickly determining whether an answer is still derivable is to distinguish supports which can be selected without regard to the history and yet build finite derivations. This is done using the notion of a primary support, defined below.

Definition 2 (Primary Support) *Let $\alpha :- \beta_1, \beta_2 \ldots, \beta_n$ be the instance of a rule k that is used by tabled resolution to derive the answer α for the first time. Then $\langle k, \{ \beta_1, \beta_2 \ldots, \beta_n \} \rangle$ is called the primary support of α, and is denoted by $ps(\alpha)$.*

In Figure 3(b) the first support listed for each answer is its primary support. We use primary supports to (over)approximate the set Δ of answers to be deleted as follows.

Definition 3 (Candidates for Deletion) *Let P be a program, γ be a query, and A be the answers computed during the evaluation of γ. Let $ps(\alpha) = \langle k, S \rangle$ be the primary support $\alpha \in A$. The set of candidates for deletion due to the deletion of the program δ_p from P, denoted by $\Gamma(P, \delta_p)$ is the smallest set such that $\alpha \in \Gamma(P, \delta_p)$ whenever $\exists \beta \in S$ such that $\beta \in F \cup \Gamma(P, \delta_p)$ or rule $k \in R_d$.*

It is easy to establish that the set of candidates for deletion overapproximates the set of deleted answers. Formally,

Proposition 1. *The set of answers for a query γ over a program P, $ans_P(\gamma)$ is such that $ans_P(\gamma) - ans_{P-\delta_p}(\gamma) \subseteq \Gamma(P, \delta_p)$.*

Traditional delete-rederive algorithms such as [7,17] use a coarser approximation. Also the effect of deletion of rules is not addressed in any view maintenance literature. The answers they delete in the first phase, which we denote by $\Gamma^\sharp$, can be characterized as follows. The set $\Gamma^\sharp$ which is the smallest set such that $\alpha \in \Gamma^\sharp(P, \delta_p)$ if there is some support $s = \langle k, S \rangle$ of α such that $\exists \beta \in S$ and $\beta \in \delta_p \cup \Gamma^\sharp(P, \delta_p)$. It can be easily shown that $\Gamma(P, \delta_p) \subseteq \Gamma^\sharp(P, \delta_p)$. Note that the coarser approximation has a cascading effect: an answer marked incorrectly as a candidate, in turn, leads to (incorrect) marking of other answers. Our approximation reduces such propagation and hence is considerably less coarse. Note that the notion of primary support is not specific to tabled evaluation and can be easily extended to any least fixed point computation.

Although only primary supports are used to obtain candidates for deletion, we still keep the set of all supports for an answer. First of all, note that due to the approximation, some candidates for deletion may be still derivable. We check this in the second *rederivation* phase. Traditional algorithms in the view maintenance literature pose rederivation in terms of rule evaluation. In contrast, we avoid the proof search using an algorithm based on keeping counts and the set of all supports with each answer. Secondly, when a primary support is removed in incremental evaluation but the answer is still valid, we need to identify the new primary support; the new support can be easily generated from the set of all supports. Lastly, we can improve our approximation by finding all supports of an answer which are not dependent on the answer itself and falsify the answer when all such supports are falsified. Below we describe the data structures and algorithms for computing the candidates for deletion and for rederiving answers.

Data Structures: Supports for an answer are maintained using a bipartite graph, called the support graph. Its vertices are partitioned into two sets: *or-nodes* and *and-nodes*. Every or-node in a support graph corresponds to an answer, a fact or a rule and every and-node corresponds to a support.

Edges in the support graph are placed as follows. Whenever s is a support for answer α, we place an edge from s to α. These edges define the 'support of' relationship. The edges are represented by an attribute *support_of* of and-nodes such that $s.support\_of = \alpha$. Whenever a support s contains a fact or an answer or a rule β, we place an edge from β to s. These edges define the 'part of' relationship. These edges are represented by a (set-valued) attribute *part_of* of or-nodes such that $s \in \beta.part\_of$. At first the direction of edges may appear to be counter-intuitive. However, it coincides with the flow of information in our algorithm: we propagate deletion and rederivation from an or-node β to all and-nodes s that contain β; and from an and-node s to or-nodes α for which s is a support. For illustration, Figure 4 shows the support graph for answers to query reach(0,X) for the support sets listed in Figure 3(a).

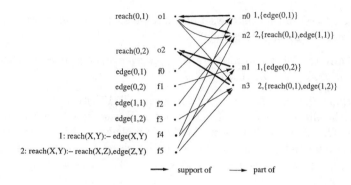

Fig. 4. Support graph for answers to query `reach(0,X)`.

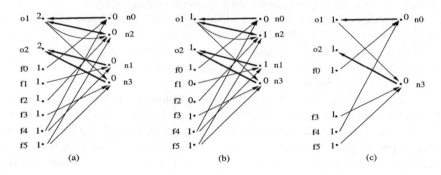

Fig. 5. Counts in support graph: at start (a); after deletion (b); after rederivation (c).

We also maintain the following additional attributes with each or-node o: (i) *supportlist*: the list of all supports of o; (ii) *answer*: the answer corresponding to o; and (iii) *primary_support*: the primary support of o.

In the rederivation phase, we need to check if candidates for deletion identified in the first phase have alternative derivations. We do so efficiently by maintaining counts with each node in the support graph. The meaning of the counts is different for or-nodes and and-nodes. For an or-node representing an answer α, its count denotes the number of supports that α must lose before it becomes false. For example, in Figure 5(a) the count of or-node $o1$ and $o2$ is 2. The count of an or-node representing true fact or a rule is initially 1; it is decreased by 1 when the fact or the rule is deleted. For an and-node representing a support s, its count denotes the number of false answers and facts in s; in other words, the count is the number of answers that must become true before the support itself becomes true. An and-node's count enables us to quickly determine the truth value of a support without evaluating its constituents.

In Figure 5(a) the count of and-nodes $n0$, $n1$, $n2$ and $n3$ are all zero. Whenever an or-node o becomes false, we increment the count of all and-nodes

```
delete:                                      rederive:
 1.   foreach unprocessed o ∈ dlist           1.   /* 1. Find the basis for rederivation. */
 2.      foreach s in o.part_of               2.   rlist := {};
 3.         s.count + +;                       3.   foreach o ∈ dlist
 4.         if (s.count = 1) then              4.      if (o.count > 0) then
 5.            /* s just became false */       5.         o.leaf_node.deleted := false;
 6.            o' := s.support_of;             6.         rlist := rlist + {o};
 7.            o'.count − −;                    7.         let s ∈ o.supportlist
 8.            if (o'.primary_support = s) then 8.            such that s.count = 0;
 9.               o'.leaf_node.deleted := true; 9.         o.primary_support := s;
10.               dlist := dlist + {o'};      10.   /* 2. Propagate rederived answers. */
                                             11.   foreach unprocessed o ∈ rlist
                                             12.      foreach s ∈ o.part_of
                                             13.         s.count − −;
                                             14.         if (s.count = 0) then
                                             15.            o' := s.support_of;
                                             16.            o'.count + +;
                                             17.            if (o'.count = 1) then
                                             18.               o'.primary_support := s;
                                             19.               o'.leaf_node.deleted := false;
                                             20.               rlist := rlist + {o'};
```

Fig. 6. Algorithm for incremental evaluation after deletion.

that contain o (given by $o.part\_of$). Similarly, when an and-node s becomes false, we decrement the count of the or-node that is supported by s (given by $s.support\_of$).

The Algorithm: The algorithm for incremental evaluation after deletion of facts is shown Figure 6 and has two phases as described below.

Deletion Phase: The algorithm starts in the deletion phase, with the variable *dlist* initialized to the set of or-nodes corresponding to the deleted facts and rules. When the phase ends, the variable *dlist* represents the candidates for deletion (Γ in Definition 3). We explain the algorithm by using the support graph in Figure 5(a) as an example. Consider the deletion of two facts edge(0,2) (or-node $f1$) and edge(1,1) (or-node $f2$). We enter the deletion phase with *dlist* set to $\{f1, f2\}$. Observe from Figure 5(a) that $f1.part\_of = \{n1\}$; hence we increment $n1.count$ to 1. Now, $n1.support\_of$ is the or-node $o2$, and $o2.count$ is decremented to 1. Moreover, $n1$ is the primary support $o2$. So $o2$ is a candidate for deletion and is added to *dlist*.

We then process or-node $f2$. We increment $n2.count$ to 1. Since $n2.support\_of$ is the or-node $o1$, we decrement $o1.count$. However, $n2$ is not the primary support of $o1$, and hence nothing is added to *dlist*. Finally we pick the unprocessed node $o2$, but since $o2.part\_of$ is empty, the processing ends. It must be noted that traditional delete-rederive algorithms would have picked both $o1$ and $o2$ as candidates for deletion. In contrast, we have been able to approximate the set of deleted answers better, and not even consider $o1$ as a candidate for deletion.

Rederivation Phase: The rederivation phase, invoked with the set of candidates for deletion in *dlist*, proceeds in two steps. In the first step we determine, among all nodes in *dlist*, those that have alternative supports. In the second step we propagate the rederived answers through the support graph. We explain the rederivation phase by continuing our earlier example.

In Figure 5(b), after the deletion phase, *dlist* contains $\{f1, f2, o2\}$. Among these the counts of $f1$ and $f2$ (which correspond to the deleted facts) are zero and hence lead only to trivial processing. The count of $o2$ is 1 indicating that it is actually true. Hence we add $o2$ to *rlist*; its support $n3$ has a zero count indicating that it is valid. Hence we make $n3$ as the primary support of $o2$. We begin the second step with *rlist* set to $\{o2\}$. Note that $o2$ is not a part of any support in the graph and hence the processing ends.

Discussion: Supports for an answer are constructed based on the rule that generated the answer. In our implementation, when inserting an answer in a table we determine its supports by using the consumer choice points and other structures used to generate the answer. Hence the construction of the support graph does not increase the time complexity of query evaluation. However, the space requirements for the support graph typically exceed that of the answer tables. For instance, the number of answers for query reach(X,Y) is $O(n^2)$ where n is the number of vertices in the graph. For each answer, there may be up to n supports, and hence the support graph has $O(n^3)$ nodes.

4 Experimental Results

We implemented our incremental algorithms by modifying XSB (version 2.5). In the following we present results of our preliminary experiments designed to measure (i) the effectiveness of our techniques, (ii) their overheads, (iii) the effect of repeated incremental evaluation, and (iv) the effectiveness of using supports to control deletion. All measurements were made on an Intel Xeon 1.7GHz machine with 2GB RAM running RedHat Linux 7.2. For nonincremental evaluation, we used the standard release of XSB version 2.5. We used left-recursive reachability and same generation predicates over trees and complete graphs as benchmarks.

Effectiveness: Figures 7(a) compare the incremental and non-incremental evaluation time of one query after the *addition* of a set of facts to the edge relations. The figures do not include the times for evaluating the initial query. Observe that when the size of addition is small (less than 5% of the total size of the edge relation), incremental evaluation is 20–60 times faster than nonincremental evaluation. Moreover, as the size of the addition increases, incremental evaluation time approaches that of nonincremental evaluation, but remains lower even when the size of addition is over 90% of the original edge relation.

Figure 7(b) compares the times of one query after the *deletion* of a set of facts from the edge relation. Incremental deletion on this benchmark takes very little time (less than 0.1s for all deletion set sizes) and far outperforms its nonincremental counterpart. The two are comparable only when the input graph becomes very small due to deletion of a large number of edges.

Overheads: We find that the initial query evaluation time for incremental evaluation is at most 8% greater than that for nonincremental evaluation. How-

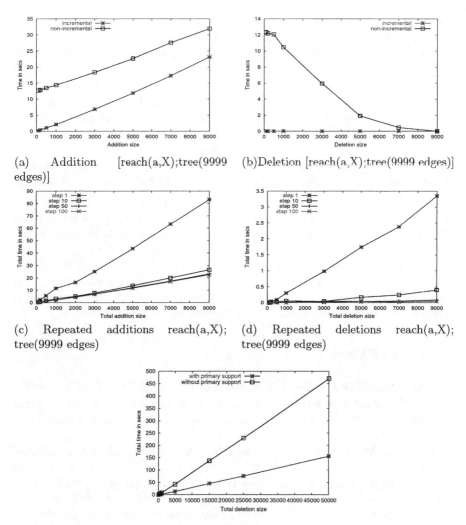

(a)   Addition   [reach(a,X);tree(9999 edges)]

(b)Deletion [reach(a,X);tree(9999 edges)]

(c)   Repeated   additions   reach(a,X); tree(9999 edges)

(d)   Repeated   deletions   reach(a,X); tree(9999 edges)

(e) Deletions with and without primary support [reach(a,X);complete graph(89700 edges);step 1]

Fig. 7. Experimental results

ever, since the support graph size may be much larger than the answer set size, we do observe significant memory overheads. Memory overheads range from a factor of 1.9 (49MB incremental vs. 26MB nonincremental) for same generation queries over binary trees, to as much as 131 (2.5MB incremental vs. 19KB nonincremental) for reachability over complete graphs. Note that the space overhead is due to the support graph alone, and is incurred only if we handle deletions.

Effect of repeated evaluation: We now compare the performance of the incremental engine for sequences of query evaluations and changes (additions/

deletions) such that the changes are interspersed between evaluations. In all the runs, the total number of changes is the same; the number of changes between two query evaluations is the step size of the run. For instance, a run with step size 10 means that after every 10 changes we issue an incremental query to refresh the table. Figure 7(c) and (d) show the total evaluation times for additions and deletions, respectively, for runs with different step sizes. Observe from the figure that batching changes together (i.e. querying infrequently, and hence allowing tables to go stale) usually takes less time than maintaining the tables fresh all the time (i.e. step size 1). Nevertheless, consistently maintaining freshness is only only 3 to 5 times slower than refreshing the table only after all changes are done. This reflects the low overheads for incremental query evaluation.

Role of support-based control of deletion: Finally, we compare the effectiveness of selecting the candidate answers for deletion based on primary supports. Figure 7(e) compares the performance of the incremental engine with control based on primary support turned off, with that of the full algorithm. Both versions used support graphs for rederivation. We measured the performance of the two versions for a sequence of deletions from a complete graph, issuing a query after each deletion. Observe from Figure 7(e) that use of primary supports results in a more than 3-fold reduction in evaluation time.

5   Related Work

The materialized view maintenance problem has been extensively researched (see, e.g. [8,12] for surveys). Most of the works in recursive views maintenance generate rules that are similar in spirit to those of DRed [7] and are subsumed by DRed (as compared in [8]).

The relationship of our work to the DRed algorithm [7] has been explained in sections 2 and 3. We handle programs with stratified negation in the same way as DRed algorithm. It should be noted that the idea of counts has been used in other works such as [6,17] but has not been used to avoid recomputing subgoals in recursive rules. The transformation rules for supporting addition are similar to those of [7,18] but we evaluate the incremental rules top-down and on-demand. We also use specialized data structures to efficiently generate new answers and avoid propagation of generation of old answers.

Our techniques are also closely related to the incremental model checking algorithm (MCI) of [17]. We have adopted MCI's use of counts to efficiently compute truth values of nodes during incremental evaluation. The MCI algorithm constructs a *product graph* where each node is associated with a truth value, and the edges denote the dependencies between the nodes' values. Its product graph corresponds to propositional logic program. MCI algorithm falsifies and rederives same number answers as DRed does with respect to this program. Hence, our improvement over DRed carries over to MCI also.

Straight Delete (StDel) algorithm [11] eliminates the rederivation phase of DRed by keeping the entire proof with every answer. While such an approach may be feasible for constraint databases, it is prohibitively expensive for logic programs. For instance, while the support set size for a context free grammar parser is cubic in the length of the string, the number of distinct proofs may be exponential. Thus a succinct representation such as a support graph is essential. However, since we do not keep all the proofs, we cannot avoid rederivation.

A top-down algorithm for incrementally checking integrity constraints (which can be seen as views) is presented in [16]. This algorithm first computes the set of integrity constraints that are possibly affected by the changes to the facts. It then evaluates the integrity constraints top-down. The method works only for non-recursive predicates. However, the idea of using a bottom-up propagation phase to mark the goals that may need to be evaluated is an interesting aspect that we plan to study in the future.

6   Concluding Remarks

We presented, to the best of our knowledge, the first techniques for incrementally evaluating tabled logic programs. Our implementation shows that incremental evaluation in the presence of addition of facts and rules can be added without any overhead whereas there is a tradeoff between memory overhead and performance in presence of deletion of facts and rules. This work opens up numerous interesting research questions, a few of which are enumerated below.

We handle deletions in a purely bottom-up fashion. It would be interesting to propagate answer deletions lazily, only on demand. Furthermore, the support sets that we use to handle deletion can be very large, and we seek ways to reduce the storage requirement. First of all, we need to design clever data structures to share components of different supports. Secondly, we can let the support sets be incomplete (i.e. not store all the supports), thereby trading space for time (for proof searches on rederivation). Thirdly, certain base facts may be "indelible": i.e., can never be deleted. Answers derived solely based on such facts can be also be simply marked "indelible", and we need not keep any supports for them.

For handling deletion in the presence of non-tabled predicates, we can build supports for a non-tabled answer, say β, on the stack, and include these supports whenever a tabled answer α is generated based on β. This approach mimics the way delay lists are propagated across non-tabled predicates when evaluating the well-founded model of a non-stratified program [2].

Finally, we have not considered *updates* to rules and facts as an independent operation. For instance, consider the problem of incremental parsing. A change in the input string can be considered in terms of a set of deletions and additions. However, such a formulation results in the reparsing of a large segment of the string: deletions "cut" the string into pieces which has a profound effect on the parse tree; additions "join" the pieces back, making large-scale changes to the parse tree again. Designing incremental evaluation techniques by considering update as a basic operation is an interesting and important open problem.

406 D. Saha and C.R. Ramakrishnan

References

1. R. Bol and L. Degerstadt. Tabulated resolution for well-founded semantics. In *ILPS*, 1993.
2. W. Chen, T. Swift, and D. S. Warren. Efficient implementation of general logical queries. *J. Logic Prog.*, 1995.
3. W. Chen and D. S. Warren. Tabled evaluation with delaying for general logic programs. *Journal of the ACM*, 43(1):20–74, 1996.
4. L. Damas and V. S. Costa. The YAP prolog system, 2002. http://www.ncc.up.pt/~vsc/Yap/.
5. S. Dawson, C. R. Ramakrishnan, and D. S. Warren. Practical program analysis using general purpose logic programming systems — a case study. In *PLDI*, 1996.
6. A. Gupta, D. Katiyar, and I. S. Mumick. Counting solutions to the view maintenance problem. In *Workshop on Deductive Databases, JICSLP*, pages 185–194, 1992.
7. A. Gupta, I. S. Mumick, and V. S. Subrahmanian. Maintaining views incrementally. In *Proceedings of ACM SIGMOD*, pages 157–166, 1993.
8. A. Gupta and I.S. Mumick. Maintenance of materialized views: Problems, techniques, and appfications. *IEEE Data Engineering Bulletin*, 18(2):3–18, 1995.
9. G. Gupta H-F. Guo. A simple scheme for implementing tabled logic programming systems based on dynamic reordering of alternatives. In *ICLP*, volume 2237 of *LNCS*, pages 181–196, 2001.
10. Y. Liu and S. Stoller. From Datalog rules to efficient programs with time and space guarantees. In *PPDP*, 2003.
11. J. Lu, G. Moerkotte, J. Schue, and V. S. Subrahmanian. Efficient maintenance of materialized mediated views. In *ACM SIGMOD*, pages 340–351, 1995.
12. E. Mayol and E. Teniente. A survey of current methods for integrity constraint maintenance and view updating. In *ER Workshops*, pages 62–73, 1999.
13. R. Paige and S. Koenig. Finite differencing of computable expressions. *ACM TOPLAS*, 4(3):402–454, 1982.
14. C.R. Ramakrishnan, I.V. Ramakrishnan, S.A. Smolka, Y. Dong, X. Du, A. Roychoudhury, and V.N. Venkatakrishnan. XMC: A logic-programming-based verification toolset. In *CAV*, volume 1855 of *LNCS*, pages 576–580, 2000.
15. I. V. Ramakrishnan, P. Rao, K. Sagonas, T. Swift, and D. S. Warren. Efficient tabling mechanisms for logic programs. In *ICLP*, pages 697–711, 1995.
16. R.R. Seljee and H.C.M. de Swart. Three types of redundancy in integrity checking; an optimal solution. *Journal of Data and Knowledge Enigineering*, 30:135–151, 1999.
17. O. V. Sokolsky and S. A. Smolka. Incremental model checking in the modal mu-calculus. In *CAV*, volume 818 of *LNCS*, pages 351–363, 1994.
18. M. Staudt and M. Jarke. Incremental maintenance of externally materialized views. In *The VLDB Journal*, pages 75–86, 1996.
19. H. Tamaki and T. Sato. OLDT resolution with tabulation. In *ICLP*, pages 84–98, 1986.
20. XSB. The XSB logic programming system. Available from http://xsb.sourceforge.net.
21. G. Yang and M. Kifer. Flora: Implementing an efficient dood system using a tabling logic engine. In *Computational Logic*, volume 1861 of *LNCS*, pages 1078–1093, 2000.
22. N.-F. Zhou, Y.-D. Shen, L.-Y. Yuan, and J.-H. You. Implementation of a linear tabling mechanism. *Journal of Functional and Logic Programming*, 2001(10), 2001.

On Deterministic Computations in the Extended Andorra Model

Ricardo Lopes[1], Vítor Santos Costa[2], and Fernando Silva[1]

[1] DCC-FC and LIACC, Universidade do Porto, Portugal
{rslopes,fds}@ncc.up.pt
[2] COPPE/Sistemas, Universidade Federal do Rio de Janeiro, Brasil
vitor@cos.ufrj.br

Abstract. Logic programming is based on the idea that computation is controlled inference. The Extended Andorra Model provides a very powerful framework that supports both co-routining and parallelism. In this work we show that David H. D. Warren's design for the EAM with Implicit Control does not perform well for deterministic computations and we present several optimisations that allow the BEAM to achieve performance matching or even exceeding related systems. Our optimisations refine the original EAM control rule demonstrate that overheads can be reduced through combined execution rules, and show that a good design and emulator implementation is relevant, even for a complex system such as the BEAM.

Keywords: Logic Programming, Extended Andorra Model, Language Implementation.

1 Introduction

Logic programming [11] is based on the idea that computation is controlled inference. It provides a high-level view of programming where programs are fundamentally seen as a collection of statements that define a model of the intended problem, and queries may be asked against this model. Prolog [3] is the most popular example of a logic programming language. Prolog relies on SLD resolution [7] and uses a straightforward left-to-right selection function and depth-first search rule. This computation rule is simple to understand and efficient to implement but, unfortunately, it is not the ideal rule for every logic program. The limitations of Prolog may lead programmers to convoluted and non-declarative programs. Prolog may also perform badly for automatically generated programs [20].

Ideally, we would like the execution of logic programs to achieve the following goals, presented by David H. D. Warren [24] as, in order of priority:

- *Minimum number of inferences*: this is achieved by trying never to repeat the same execution step (inference) in different locations of the execution tree.
- *Maximum parallelism*: this is achieved by allowing goals to execute as independently as possible, and combining all solutions as late as feasible.

C. Palamidessi (Ed.): ICLP 2003, LNCS 2916, pp. 407–421, 2003.

Towards these goals, Warren, Haridi and others proposed the Extended Andorra Model [23], or *EAM*. The key ideas for this model are:

- Goals can execute (in parallel) as long as they are deterministic or *they do not need to bind external variables*;
- If a goal must bind external variables non-deterministically, the computation of this goal will *split*.

The Extended Andorra Model addresses the main limitations found in the implementations of the Basic Andorra Model (BAM) [22], such as Andorra-I [21, 18]. It provides very elegant support for data-driven execution of logic programs (co-routing) and for parallelism, both between deterministic reductions and between alternative branches for non-deterministic goals.

Work in the EAM progressed in two directions. In the SICS AGENTS system [10,9], it was argued that control should be provided explicitly by the programmer, through annotations such as guards. In Warren's EAM with Implicit Control, the Extended Andorra Model was proposed as a computational model for the execution of logic programs. Annotations can be used to improve search, but are not required. Warren's EAM supports traditional logic programs, seen as a collection of Horn clauses while AKL provides a new programming paradigm where control is embedded in the fabric of the language. Each clause includes a guard and a body. The body can only execute when the guard is entailed by the current environment.

To study whether the EAM with implicit control was practical, we have proposed and implemented the *BEAM* (Basic Design for the EAM), a novel system that refines Warren's original design [13]. For the BEAM to be relevant, we wanted it to perform well. The BEAM will perform best if it substantially reduces the search space. On the other hand, we expected the BEAM to perform worse than Prolog, and even Andorra-I, on non-deterministic programs where we cannot reduce the search space. The reason is that splitting is much more inefficient, even if more general, that the choice-points mechanism used in Prolog and Andorra-I. The main issue for us was therefore how the BEAM would perform for deterministic computations. Performing well for deterministic programs is an important issue, because it makes the BEAM relevant for applications we expect to achieve mostly deterministic computations, with a few non-determinism goals (e.g., constraint-style applications [8]). Of course, Prolog does not need to support co-routing, hence has less overheads and should have better performance. Andorra-I has execution closer to Prolog. AGENTS benefits from user effort in coding the guards, so it might perform much better than the BEAM.

In this work we demonstrate that the Warren's design for the EAM with implicit control would indeed not perform well for deterministic computations, and present several optimisations that allowed the BEAM to have performance matching or even exceeding related systems. Our optimisations refine the original EAM control rule, demonstrate that overheads can be reduced through combined execution rules, and show that a good design and emulator implementation is relevant, even for a complex system such as the BEAM.

The paper is organised as follows. First, we present the BEAM design. Next, we discuss our main optimisations. We then present our performance results, comparing the BEAM with related systems.

2   The BEAM

We briefly present the BEAM. The BEAM model has been implemented for the Herbrand domain [12].

2.1   BEAM Concepts

A BEAM *computation* is a series of rewriting operations, performed on an And-Or Trees. And-Or Trees contain two kinds of nodes:

- *and-boxes* represent a conjunction of positive literals; they consist of a conjunction of goals which define new *local variables*, of constraints (bindings in the Herbrand Domain), and of control information.

$$[\exists X_1, \ldots, X_m : \sigma \& G_1 \& \ldots \& G_n]$$

  And-box corresponding to a clause with subgoals G_1 to G_n. The variables X_1 to X_m represent the variables created in the box and σ represents the constraints on external variables imposed by the and-box.
- *or-boxes* represent alternative clauses for a selected literal; each or-box contains a set of and-boxes.

$$\{C_1 \vee \ldots \vee C_n\}$$

Each C_i represents an alternative clause for the goal.

A *configuration* is a And-Or Tree, describing a state of the computation. A *computation* is a sequence of configurations obtained by successive applications of rewrite rules that define valid state transitions. The *initial configuration* is an and-box containing the initial sequence of atomic goals that represent the query and the empty set of constraints. The constraints over the top-and box on a final configuration are called an answer. An *answer* describes a set of assignments for variables for which the initial configuration holds. We define an And-Or Tree as *compact* when all children of and-boxes are or-boxes and when all children of or-boxes are and-boxes.

A goal is said to be *deterministic* when there is at most one candidate that succeeds for the goal. Otherwise it is said to be *non-deterministic*.

A variable is said to be *external* to an and-box when not defined in that and-box, and *local* otherwise. Moreover, a box is said to be *suspended* if the computation on it cannot progress deterministically and the box is currently waiting for an event that will allow it to resume computation.

2.2   Rewrite Rules

Execution in the EAM proceeds as a sequence of rewrite operations on configurations. The BEAM's rewrite rules are based on the David Warren's rules. They are designed to be correct and complete, and to allow for efficient implementation. The BEAM rewrite rules are:

1. **Reduction**: reduction resolves the goal G against the heads of all clauses defining the procedure for G.

$$G \rightarrow \{[\exists Y_1 : \sigma_1 \ \& \ C_1] \vee \ldots \vee [\exists Y_n : \sigma_n \ \& \ C_n]\}$$

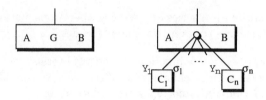

Fig. 1. BEAM reduction rule.

Figure 1 shows this rule. Resolution expands the tree by matching a non-expanded goal G in an and-box, and then replaces G by a new or-box with several alternatives to be explored.

2. **Promotion**: an and-box that is a single alternative to an or-box can promote its variables and its bindings to the parent and-box (see figure 2):

$$[\exists X : \sigma \ \& \ A \ \& \ \{[\exists Y : \theta \ \& \ W]\} \ \& \ B]\} \rightarrow [\exists X, Y : \sigma\theta \ \& \ A \ \& \ \{[W]\} \ \& \ B]$$

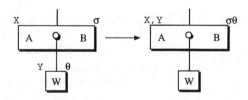

Fig. 2. BEAM promotion rule.

As in the original EAM promotion rule, promotion propagates results from a local computation to the level above. However, promotion in the BEAM does not merge the two and-boxes because the structure of the computation may be required towards pruning: if we discard intermediate and-boxes we may have no detail on the scope of a cut. This contrasts to the original EAM and to AGENTS which require choice-boxes for this purpose.

3. **Propagation**: this rule allows us to propagate constraints from an and-box to all subtrees below. This rule is thus symmetrical to the promotion rule.

$$[\exists X, Z : Z = \sigma(X) \; \& \ldots \& \; \{\ldots \vee [\exists Y : G] \vee \ldots\} \; \& \ldots] \rightarrow$$

$$[\exists X, Z : Z = \sigma(X) \; \& \ldots \& \; \{\ldots \vee [\exists Y : Z = \sigma(X) \; \& \; G] \vee \ldots\} \; \& \ldots]$$

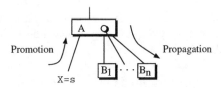

Fig. 3. BEAM propagation rule.

We call the and-box that propagates the constraint the *top and-box*. Figure 3 shows how the propagation and promotion rules work in tandem: promotion promotes a constraint to the top and-box, and propagation makes the constraint available to the underlying and-boxes. The propagation rule is expensive and therefore we do not apply to every box under the top and-box. Instead, we apply it on demand to the and-boxes that consume a binding for the variable. Whenever an and-box is trying to apply a constraint to a variable, all and-boxes that are trying to apply the constraint are signalled to indicate that their constraint must be consistent with the constraint on the top and-box. Local consistency will then be performed.

4. **Splitting** (non-determinate promotion): splitting distributes a conjunction across a disjunction, in a way similar to the forking rule of the original EAM.

$$[\exists X : \sigma \; \& \; A \; \& \; \{C_1 \vee \ldots \vee [\exists Y : \theta \; \& \; C_i] \vee \ldots \vee C_n\} \; \& \; B] \rightarrow$$

$$\{[\exists X : \sigma \; \& \; A \; \& \; \{[\exists Y : \theta \; \& \; C_i]\} \; \& \; B] \vee$$
$$[\exists X : \sigma \; \& \; A \; \& \; \{C_1 \vee \ldots \vee C_{i-1} \vee C_{i+1} \vee \ldots \vee C_n\} \; \& \; B]\}$$

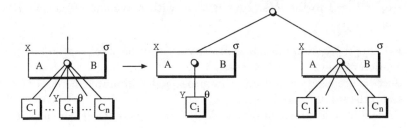

Fig. 4. BEAM splitting rule.

In contrast to Warren's original forking rule, the BEAM does not merge the split and-box (represented as C_i in figure 4) with the parent and-box. The merge will be performed later by an application of a simplification rule to the and-box C_i. The BEAM also does not implement the *global forking* as proposed in Gupta's interpreter [6]. This rule would split the conjunction across all the disjunctions, and is much more expensive to implement in a sequential system.

The previous rules give the main principles for the EAM. An actual implementation must be able to simplify the And-Or Tree in order to propagate success and failure and to recover space by discarding boxes. Our kernel design for the EAM, the BEAM, therefore includes additional simplification rules that generate compact configurations. Extra rules further allow us to optimise the computation process by early pruning of branches, resulting in early detection of failure. Due to space considerations, we give a brief overview next and refer the reader to [12] for the full explanation:

1. *Success Propagation:* an *empty box* $[\exists X :]$ may always be discarded. An and-box is called *empty box* when all the local computations have been completed and the and-box does not contain constraints on external variables. The BEAM supports a more aggressive rule, called *true-in-or simplification* which allows one to simplify a disjunction of the form $\dots \vee [\exists X :] \vee \dots$ to $[\exists X :]$, at the cost of breaking Prolog semantics.
2. *Failure Propagation:* an empty or-box removes all and-boxes above, and the current branch in the nearest ancestor or-box.
3. *And-Compression:* two nested and-boxes may be merged into a single and-box, if the inner and-box has no pruning operators. This rule plus the propagation rule correspond to Warren's original and-compression rule.

2.3   Control in the BEAM

A rewrite operation *matches* an And-Or Tree if the left-hand side matches a subtree in the configuration. If a number of rewrite-rules match, one must decide which one to choose. Arguably, one could choose the same rule as Prolog, and clone Prolog execution. The real power of the EAM is that we have the flexibility to use different strategies. In particular, we will try to use the one which, we believe, will lead to the least computation with maximum efficiency. The key ideas are:

1. Failure propagation rules have priority over all the other rules to allow propagation of failure as fast as possible.
2. Success propagation and and-compression should always be done next, because they simplify the tree.
3. Promotion and propagation should follow, because their combination may force some boxes to fail.
4. Splitting is the most expensive operation, and should be avoided. Therefore:

a) Deterministic reductions, that is, reductions that do not create or-boxes and thus will never lead to splitting, or reductions which do not constrain external variables, should go ahead first;

b) Non-deterministic reductions that constrain external variables should be avoided because they lead to splitting. The exception is if the user explicitly says that non-deterministic reduction will be eventually required [14].

c) Splitting should be used when no deterministic reductions are available.

2.4   BEAM Architecture

The BEAM was built on top of the YAP [4] Prolog system. It reuses most of the YAP *compiler* and its *builtin library*. The BEAM stores data in different memory spaces. The *Code Space* stores the data-base with the predicate/clause information, plus the bytecode to be interpreted by BEAM's *Abstract Machine Emulator* (which we refer shortly as *Emulator*). The *Global Memory* stores the And-Or Tree, and it is further subdivided into the *Heap* and the *Box Memory*. The *Box Memory* stores dynamic data structures including boxes and variables. The *Heap* holds Prolog terms, such as lists and structures. The *Heap* uses term copying to store compound terms and is thus very similar to the WAM's *Heap*. The major difference is that on the BEAM, *Heap* memory can not be recovered after backtracking. A *Garbage Collector* is thus necessary to recover space in this area. More details on memory management and on the garbage collecting algorithm can be found on [15].

The BEAM relies on two main components:

Emulator: runs WAM-like code to perform unification and to setup boxes. Unification code is similar to the WAM. Control instructions follow a compilation scheme similar to the WAM but result in a rather different execution pattern.

And-Or Tree Manager: applies the BEAM rewriting rules to the existing and-boxes and or-boxes until WAM-like execution for the selected goal can start.

The *And-Or Tree Manager* handles most of the complexity in the EAM. It uses a *Code Space* area to determine how many alternatives a goal has and how many goals a clause calls. With this information the *And-Or Tree Manager* constructs the tree and uses the EAM rewriting rules to manipulate it. The Manager requests memory for the boxes from the *Global Memory Areas*. The *Emulator* is called by the *And-Or Tree Manager* in order to execute and unify the arguments of the goals and clauses. As an example consider the clause: p(X,Y):- g(X), f(Y). When running this clause the *And-Or Tree Manager* transforms the p(X,Y) into one and-box, and calls the *Emulator* to create the subgoals and or-boxes for g(X) and f(Y). Control returns to the *And-Or Tree Manager* if the boxes need to suspend.

The details on how BEAM stores the And-Or Tree, the design of the *Emulator* and of the *And-or Tree manager* are described in more detail in [12].

3   Deterministic Execution of And-Boxes

We expect that most execution time in the EAM will be spent performing deterministic reductions, or reductions that do not constrain the external environment. Their implementation is therefore crucial to system performance.

3.1 Determinacy

Warren's EAM proposal states that an and-box should immediately suspend when trying to non-deterministically constrain an external variable whose scope is above the closest or-box. Unfortunately, the original EAM control rule may lead to difficulties. We next discuss two examples, a small data-base, ancestor/2, and a well-known Prolog procedure, partition/4.

```
parent(john, richard).      partition([X|L],Y,[X|L1],L2) :- X =< Y,
parent(john, mary).                 partition(L,Y,L1,L2).
parent(patrick, paul).      partition([X|L],Y,L1,[X|L2]) :- X > Y,
parent(patrick, susan).             partition(L,Y,L1,L2).
                            partition([],_,[],[]).
```

Consider the query ?- parent(X,mary). The query is deterministic, as it only matches the second clause. Unfortunately, a naive implementation of Warren's rule would not recognise the goal as deterministic. Instead, all four clauses would be tried, as parent/2 would try to bind a value to X, and all and-boxes would suspend. The same problem may happen with the query:
?- partition([4,3,5],2,A,B).
Although the calls are deterministic, the EAM would suspend when unifying [X|L1] to A. The suspension would eventually lead to splitting and thus to unnecessarily poor performance.

AGENTS addresses this issue by relying on the guard operators to explicitly control when goals can execute. Arguably, this should allow for the best execution. On the other hand, AGENTS performance may be vulnerable to user errors, and logic programs need to be pre-processed in order to perform well [1]. Andorra-I addresses a similar problem through its compiler. Unfortunately, coding all possible cases of determinacy grows exponentially [17,21]. In the end, Andorra-I manages code size explosion by imposing a limit on the combinations of arguments that it tries, thus losing completeness. This scheme further becomes a source of inefficiency as Andorra-I often has to execute the same unifications twice: initially, when checking for determinacy, and later, after committing to a clause.

To address this problem, we propose a different control rule to define when a reduction should suspend:

> Reduction of an and-box cannot proceed and should therefore *suspend* if and only if (i) the head and immediate built-ins have been completely reduced (the flat guard); and (ii) unification of the head arguments have generated one or more constraints on external variables; and (iii) some other clause may match.

Conditions (i) and (ii) provide a more aggressive determinacy scheme than the one in Warren's EAM. One first advantage is that our scheme is simpler to implement, since the suspension may only occur at a fixed point of the code thus reducing the number of tests one needs to make in order to determine whether the current and-box should or not suspend.

Condition (iii) can be optimised by filtering through an indexing algorithm. One further advantage of our scheme is that such an algorithm needs may be conservative. Indeed, imagine an indexing algorithm that says N clauses may match a deterministic goal. But in this case, evaluation of condition (i) will result in at least $N-1$ clauses failing. Thus, condition after satisfying condition (i) and (ii), condition (iii) cannot hold for the remaining clause, if any. Our indexing algorithm can therefore be designed for being efficient in the common case. In contrast, a badly classified deterministic goal might block a whole deterministic computation in Andorra-I, and a badly chosen guard may block a deterministic computation in AGENTS.

3.2   Deterministic-Reduce-and-Promote

A second important observation is that performance of Prolog programs, and namely of recursive programs, heavily depends on optimisations such as Last Call Optimisation. In the best case, such optimisations allow tail-recursive programs to execute with the same costs that iterative programs would.

Both EAM and AGENTS create an and-box when performing reduction on deterministic predicates. The newly created and-box is promoted immediately afterwards because it is deterministic. The creation of boxes that are immediately promoted is expensive, both in memory usage and in time.

The BEAM address this problem through the *Deterministic-reduce-and-promote* rule. This rule allows for a reduction to expand directly in the home and-box. More precisely, whenever a deterministic goal B is to be reduced to a single alternative with goals $G_1, \ldots, G_n$, the reduction takes place in the parent's and-box. Figure 5 shows an example of this rule.

$$[\exists X : \sigma \& A \& B \& C] \to [\exists X, Y : \sigma\theta \& A \& G_1 \& \ldots \& G_n \& C]$$

As explained before, the BEAM cannot apply the reduce-promote rule if there is a pruning operator, such as cut, in the inner and-box.

4   Results

We next discuss the performance of the BEAM for deterministic programs. Throughout, we have used a group of well-known benchmarks. For each benchmark we present the best execution time from a series of ten runs. We present runtimes in milliseconds. Timings were measured an AMD Thunderbird 900Mhz (200Mhz FSB) with 256Kb *on chip* cache, equipped with 512MB at 100Mhz SDRAM and running Red Hat Linux 7.1. The BEAM was configured with 64Mb of *Heap* plus 32Mb of *Box Memory*.

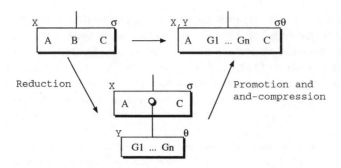

Fig. 5. BEAM deterministic-reduce-and-promote rule.

4.1   The Determinacy Control Rule

We start by showing why determinacy is critical for efficient EAM execution. We use the qsort benchmark, a well known Prolog benchmark. Most of the running time for qsort/2 is spent executing partition/4, which we discussed in the previous section, so this is a good example of how much the control rule may impact execution time.

Table 1. Qsort: EAM vs BEAM.

qsort	BEAM-SoF	BEAM-SoL
Time	58.19	0.49
Number of Splits	2368	0

Table 1 presents the execution time and the number of splits for qsort comparing two different configurations of BEAM:

- **BEAM-SoF**: BEAM suspending on the first constraint. With this configuration BEAM suspends immediately after the generation of the first constraint during the head unification (as David H. D. Warren originally proposed).
- **BEAM-SoL**: BEAM suspending on the last constraint. This version is the default configuration of BEAM. BEAM uses the control rule proposed in 3.1, that is, suspension only occurs if one or more constraint on external variables have been generated and only after the head and immediate built-ins have been completely reduced.

Our results do show that this control rule is critical for performance: the BEAM-SoF is more than two orders of magnitude slower than the BEAM-SoL. As we had discussed, the partition predicate instantiates variables that belong to upper boxes, and thus the EAM suspends the execution. This results in 2368 splits performed by the EAM that affect the performance directly. The number of splits would increase for larger queries, possibly leading to even slower executions.

The results show that our control rule is indeed necessary for efficient execution. We next discuss whether it would be sufficient.

4.2   The BEAM vs. Other Systems

In this section we compare the performance results of the prototype BEAM system with the latest versions of SICStus Prolog, YAP, Andorra-I and AGENTS. We use SICStus Prolog 3.8.6, Yap 4.4.0 and Yap98, Andorra-I v1.14, and SICS AGENTS v1.0. Yap98 is the version of Yap we based our work in. We ran the sequential version of Andorra-I, using the pre-processor to pre-compile the benchmarks. All benchmarks were also rewritten to execute deterministically in AGENTS. Being a prototype, we should observe that the BEAM does not provide the same set of built-ins as the other systems. Namely, the BEAM only supports constraints on the Herbrand domain. Experience with the implementation of other finite domain-constraints systems [2] lead us to believe this will not have a major impact on performance.

Table 2 gives a small description of the benchmarks used in this section. We selected a group of well known deterministic programs commonly used to evaluate Prolog systems.

Table 2. The benchmarks.

Name	Description
cal	last 10000 FoolsDays arithmetic benchmark.
deriv	symbolically differentiates four functions of a single variable.
qsort	quick-sort of a 50-element list using difference lists.
serialise	calculate serial numbers of a list.
reverse	smart reverse of a 1000-element list.
nreverse	naive reverse of a 1000-element list.
kkqueens	smart finder of the solutions for the n-queens problem.
tak	heavily recursive with lots of simple integer arithmetic.

Table 3. Deterministic benchmarks (time in milliseconds).

Benchs.	BEAM	AGENTS	Andorra-I	YAP 98	YAP 4.4	SICStus 3.8.6
cal	0.010	0.020	0.020	0.009	0.005	0.012
deriv	0.060	0.380	0.050	0.019	0.013	0.024
qsort	0.49	1.07	0.46	0.18	0.11	0.38
serialise	0.23	0.69	0.38	0.08	0.06	0.18
reverse_1000	0.30	1.60	0.37	0.13	0.12	0.17
nreverse_1000	130	780	140	50	40	60
kkqueens	240	460	240	127	40	70
tak	110	154	140	60	30	50

Table 3 and Table 4 show how the BEAM performs versus Andorra-I, AGENTS, and several Prolog systems for deterministic applications. Neither the BEAM nor AGENTS ever perform splitting. Andorra-I always executes deterministically.

Table 4. Deterministic benchmarks relative speed comparison to SICStus.

Benchs.	BEAM	AGENTS	Andorra-I	YAP 98	4.4	SICStus 3.8.6
cal	120%	60%	60%	133%	240%	100%
deriv	40%	6%	48%	126%	185%	100%
qsort	78%	36%	83%	211%	345%	100%
serialise	78%	26%	47%	175%	300%	100%
reverse_1000	57%	11%	46%	131%	142%	100%
nreverse_1000	46%	8%	43%	120%	150%	100%
kkqueens	29%	15%	29%	55%	175%	100%
tak	45%	32%	36%	83%	167%	100%
average	62%	24%	49%	136%	213%	100%

The YAP and SICStus Prolog systems are considered some of the fastest Prolog systems on the x86 architectures. The difference between Yap98 (on which the BEAM is based) and Yap4.4 shows that there is scope for improvement even for the rather mature technology used in Prolog systems. We believe the same improvements should also apply to a prototype system such as the BEAM. Yap4.4 is the fastest system, being between 2 and 5 times faster than the BEAM. SICStus Prolog and Yap98 are not as fast, indeed for cal the BEAM gets very close to SICStus Prolog and Yap98. This is quite a good result for the BEAM, considering the extra complexity of the Extended Andorra Model.

Our results also show that, surprisingly, the BEAM tends to perform better than the AGENTS, especially on tail-recursive computations. There were two possible explanations: either the emulator was more efficient, or the BEAM was taking advantage of the special rule for performing tail-recursive computation. We experimented slowing down the interpreter by disabling the deterministic-reduce-and-promote rule (**BEAM-NoRP**), and by disabling the emulator's threaded code (**BEAM-NoTh**).

The results in Table 5 show that the major source of efficiency of the system is in fact the deterministic-reduce-and-promote rule, which improves the performance by a factor of more than 30% in average, and indeed almost doubles performance in some cases. The system is not as dependent on the emulator as Prolog systems are [19,5]. This suggests that further work on execution rules may improve execution times even further.

Performance of the BEAM is very close to the performance of Andorra-I. Andorra-I beats BEAM on two benchmarks: deriv and qsort. Andorra-I also tries to optimise tail recursion, and the difference now depends on determinacy

Table 5. BEAM without reduce-and-promote and no threaded code.

Benchs.	BEAM	BEAM-NoRP	BEAM-NoTh
cal	100%	100%	91%
deriv	100%	60%	90%
qsort	100%	57%	95%
serialise	100%	–	94%
reverse_1000	100%	60%	98%
nreverse_1000	100%	54%	98%
kkqueens	100%	79%	95%
tak	100%	89%	100%
average	100%	71%	95%

detection performed by the Andorra-I pre-processor. Consider the following code from the qsort benchmark:

```
partition([X|L],Y,[X|L1],L2) :- X =< Y, partition(L,Y,L1,L2).
partition([X|L],Y,L1,[X|L2]) :- X  > Y, partition(L,Y,L1,L2).
```

In this case, Andorra-I classifies this code as deterministic, and never has to create a choice point. The BEAM does not perform extensive determinacy analysis. As a result:

– if $X \leq Y$: the BEAM creates an or-box with two alternatives. It performs the head unification for the first alternative and it succeeds executing the test comparing X with Y. Execution then immediately suspends, because head unification generates bindings to variables external to the box. Execution then continues with the second alternative that will fail when comparing X to Y. This failure makes the first alternative the unique alternative in the or-box, and a promotion will occur allowing the suspended computation to resume.
– $X > Y$: the BEAM creates an or-box with two alternatives. The first alternative will fail when comparing X and Y. This failure makes the second alternative unique in its or-box. Promotion thus will occur, allowing the second alternative to run deterministically without suspending.

In general, the BEAM's performance on deterministic programs seems to be somewhat better than AGENTS and very close to Andorra-I. In some code the BEAM still has greater overheads than Andorra-I, suggesting that BEAM performance may be improved further.

5   Conclusions

We have shown that the BEAM, an implementation of the Warren's EAM with Implicit Control, can perform quite well on deterministic logic programs. Indeed, the BEAM performance often exceeds the performance of Andorra-I and

AGENTS, and for some benchmarks compares well with Prolog implementations. Analysis showed that our results were the results of two major optimisations techniques, redefining the control rules to avoid unnecessary suspensions, and implementing new combined rules that optimise common cases of determinacy.

We believe that the BEAM provides an excellent vehicle for research on novel control strategies for logic programs, and can be an excellent complement to traditional Prolog systems. Work on the BEAM thus continues. We are integrating the BEAM with recent releases of the YAP Prolog system, so that it will be available to a larger audience. We are studying how user defined annotations and other control techniques can be used to improve search. Namely, we are studying stability, originally proposed for AGENTS, as a further technique for optimising execution of non-deterministic programs. We are also researching into the integration of tabulation with the EAM model [12], and on the exploitation of parallelism [16].

Acknowledgments. We would like to gratefully acknowledge the contributions we received from Salvador Abreu, Gopal Gupta and Enrico Pontelli. The work presented in this paper has been partially supported by project APRIL (Project POSI/SRI/40749/2001) and funds granted to *LIACC* through the *Programa de Financiamento Plurianual, Fundação para a Ciência e Tecnologia* and *Programa POSI*.

References

1. F. Bueno and M. V. Hermenegildo. An Automatic Translations Scheme from Prolog to the Andorra Kernel Language. In *International Conference on Fifth Generation Computer Systems 1992*, pages 759–769. ICOT, Tokyo, Japan, June 1992.
2. B. Carlson, S. Haridi, and S. Janson. AKL(FD)-A concurrent language for FD programming. In *Logic Programming: Proceedings of the 1994 International Symposium*, pages 521–535. MIT Press, 1994.
3. A. Colmerauer, H. Kanoui, R. Pasero, and P. Roussel. Un système de communication homme–machine en francais. Technical report cri 72–18, Groupe Intelligence Artificielle, Université Aix-Marseille II, October 1973.
4. L. Damas, V. Santos Costa, R. Reis, and R. Azevedo. *YAP User's Guide and Reference Manual*, 1998.
5. B. Demoen and P.-L. Nguyen. So Many WAM Variations, So Little Time. In *LNAI 1861, Proceedings Computational Logic – CL 2000*, pages 1240–1254. Springer-Verlag, July 2000.
6. G. Gupta and D. H. D. Warren. An Interpreter for the Extended Andorra Model. Internal report, University of Bristol, 1991.
7. R. Hill. LUSH-Resolution and its Completeness. Dcl memo 78, Department of Artificial Intelligence, University of Edinburgh, 1974.
8. J. Jaffar and J.-L. Lassez. Constraint logic programming. In *Proceedings Fourtheenth Annual ACM Symposium on Principles of Programming Languages*, pages 111–119. "ACM", 1987.

9. S. Janson. *AKL – A Multiparadigm Programming Language*. PhD thesis, SICS Swedish Institute of Computer Science, Uppsala University, 1994.
10. S. Janson and J. Montelius. Design of a Sequential Prototype Implementation of the Andorra Kernel Language. Sics research report, Swedish Institute of Computer Science, 1992.
11. J. W. Lloyd. *Foundations of Logic Programming*. Springer-Verlag, second edition, 1987.
12. R. Lopes. *An Implementation of the Extended Andorra Model*. PhD thesis, Universidade do Porto, September 2001.
13. R. Lopes, V. S. Costa, and F. Silva. A novel implementation of the extended andorra model. In I. V. Ramakrishnan, editor, *Pratical Aspects of Declarative Languages*, volume 1990 of *Lecture Notes in Computer Science*, pages 199–213. Springer-Verlag, March 2001.
14. R. Lopes and V. Santos Costa. The BEAM: Towards a first EAM Implementation. In *ILPS97 Workshop on Parallelism and Implementation Technology for (Constraint) Logic Programming Languages, Port Jefferson*, October 1997.
15. R. Lopes and V. Santos Costa. Memory Management for the BEAM. In *CL2000 First Workshop on Memory Management in Logic Programs*, Technical Report of Dept. Comp. Science, K.U.Leuven, July 2000.
16. R. Lopes, F. Silva, V. Santos Costa, and S. Abreu. The RAINBOW: Towards a Parallel Beam. In *Workshop on Parallelism and Implementation Technology for (Constraint) Logic Languages*, July 2000.
17. D. Palmer and L. Naish. NUA-Prolog: an Extension to the WAM for Parallel Andorra. In K. Furukawa, editor, *Proceedings of the Eighth International Conference on Logic Programming*. MIT Press, 1991.
18. V. Santos Costa. *Compile-Time Analysis for the Parallel Execution of Logic Programs in Andorra-I*. PhD thesis, University of Bristol, August 1993.
19. V. Santos Costa. Optimising bytecode emulation for prolog. In *LNCS 1702, Proceedings of PPDP'99*, pages 261–267. Springer-Verlag, September 1999.
20. V. Santos Costa, A. Srinivasan, and R. Camacho. A note on two simple transformations for improving the efficiency of an ILP system. In *Proceedings of ILP'2000*, July 2000. Proceedings to appear in Springer-Verlag LNAI series.
21. V. Santos Costa, D. H. D. Warren, and R. Yang. The Andorra-I Preprocessor: Supporting full Prolog on the Basic Andorra model. In *Proceedings of the Eighth International Conference on Logic Programming*, pages 443–456. MIT Press, June 1991.
22. D. H. D. Warren. The Andorra model. Presented at Gigalips Project workshop, University of Manchester, March 1988.
23. D. H. D. Warren. Extended Andorra model. PEPMA Project workshop, University of Bristol, October 1989.
24. D. H. D. Warren. The Extended Andorra Model with Implicit Control. Presented at ICLP'90 Workshop on Parallel Logic Programming, Eilat, Israel, June 1990.

Timed Concurrent Constraint Programming: Decidability Results and Their Application to LTL

Frank D. Valencia*

Dept. of Information Technology, Uppsala University
Box 337 SE-751 05 Uppsala, Sweden
frankv@it.uu.se Fax: +46 18 511 925

Abstract. The ntcc process calculus is a timed *concurrent constraint programming* (ccp) model equipped with a first-order *linear-temporal logic* (LTL) for expressing process specifications. A typical behavioral observation in ccp is the *strongest postcondition (sp)*. The ntcc sp denotes the set of all infinite output sequences that a given process can exhibit. The *verification problem* is then whether the sequences in the sp of a given process satisfy a given ntcc LTL formula.

This paper presents new positive decidability results for timed ccp as well as for LTL. In particular, we shall prove that the following problems are decidable: (1) The *sp equivalence* for the so-called *locally-independent* ntcc fragment; unlike other fragments for which similar results have been published, this fragment can specify *infinite-state systems*. (2) *Verification* for locally-independent processes and negation-free *first-order* formulae of the ntcc LTL. (3) *Implication* for such formulae. (4) *Satisfiability* for a first-order fragment of Manna and Pnueli's LTL. The purpose of the last result is to illustrate the applicability of ccp to well-established formalisms for concurrency.

1 Introduction

Concurrent constraint programming (ccp) [21] is a model of concurrency for systems in which agents interact with one another by telling and asking information in a shared medium, a so-called *store*. Timed ccp [18] extends ccp by allowing agents to be constrained by time requirements. Its distinctive feature is that it combines in one framework the operational and algebraic view based upon process calculi with a declarative view based upon *linear-temporal logic* (LTL). So, processes can be treated as computing agents, algebraic terms and LTL formulae. This allows timed ccp to benefit from the large body of techniques of well established theories used in the study of concurrency and, in particular, reactive computations. In fact, timed ccp has been studied extensively as a model for reactive systems [4,8,14,15,16,17,18,19,20,23].

The ntcc process calculus [15] is a generalization of the timed ccp model tcc [18]. The calculus can represent timed concepts such as unit delays, unbounded finite delays, time-outs, pre-emption, synchrony and asynchrony. Furthermore, ntcc is equipped with an LTL to specify timed properties and with an *inference system* for the verification problem (i.e., for proving whether a given process fulfills a given LTL specification).

---

* This work was supported by the **PROFUNDIS** Project.

C. Palamidessi (Ed.): ICLP 2003, LNCS 2916, pp. 422–437, 2003.

This paper presents new decidability results for infinite-state ntcc processes, the ntcc LTL (here called *constraint* LTL or **CLTL** for short), and for the standard first-order LTL (here called **LTL** for short) described by Manna and Pnueli [10]. The description and relevance of these results are outlined next:

- *On the sp equivalence and verification problem.* The strongest-postcondition (sp) behavior of a given ntcc process P denotes the set of all infinite sequences of outputs that P can exhibit. Thus, P fulfills a given specification (i.e., a **CLTL** formula) F iff each sequence in its sp satisfies F. In Section 3, we show that for a substantial fragment of ntcc and the negation-free first-order fragment of **CLTL**: (1) the sp equivalence is decidable and (2) the verification problem is decidable.
  - A noteworthy aspect of these two results is that the ntcc fragment above admits *infinite-state processes*. All other ntcc fragments for which similar results has been published [14,16] are restricted to finite-state processes.
  - Another noteworthy aspect is that **CLTL** is first-order. Most first-order LTLs in computer science are not recursively axiomatizable let alone decidable [1].
- *On the ntcc LTL.* In Section 3 we prove that: (3) the validity of implication is decidable for the negation-free first-order fragment of **CLTL**.
  - As for Hoare logic, the ntcc inference system [15] mentioned above has the so-called consequence rule which queries an oracle about (**CLTL**) implication. This causes the completeness of the system to be relative to the capability of determining the validity of implication, thus making our third result of relevance to ntcc.
  - As a corollary of this result, we obtain the decidability of *satisfiability* for the negation-free first-order fragment of **CLTL**. This is relevant for specification purposes since, as remarked in [25], a specification is "interesting" only if it is satisfiable.
- *On the standard first-order LTL.* In Section 4 we prove that: (4) the satisfiability problem in **LTL** is decidable for all negation-free first-order formulae without rigid variables. This result is obtained from a reduction to **CLTL** satisfiability.
  - Since first-order **LTL** is not recursively axiomatizable [1], satisfiability is undecidable for the full language of **LTL**. Recent work [9] and also [11], however, have taken up the task of identifying first-order decidable fragments of **LTL**. Our fourth result contributes to this task.
  - The reduction from the standard **LTL** satisfiability to **CLTL** satisfiability also contributes to the understanding of the relationship between (timed) ccp and (temporal) classic logic.

In brief, this paper argues for timed ccp as a convenient framework for reactive systems by providing positive decidability results for behavior, specification and verification (1–3), and by illustrating its applicability to the well-established theory of LTL (4).

2   An Overview of ntcc

In ntcc, time is conceptually divided into *discrete intervals (or time units)*. In a particular timed interval, a process P gets an input (an item of information represented as a *constraint*) c from the environment, it executes with this input as the initial *store*, and when it reaches its resting point, it *outputs* the resulting store d to the environment. The resting point determines a residual process Q, which is then executed in the next time interval. In the rest of this section we shall briefly recall ntcc concepts given in [15].

Definition 1 (Constraint System). *A* constraint system (cs) *is a pair* (Σ, Δ) *where* Σ *is a signature of function and predicate symbols, and* Δ *is a decidable theory over* Σ *(i.e., a decidable set of sentences over* Σ *with a least one model).*

Given a cs (Σ, Δ), let $(\Sigma, \mathcal{V}, \mathcal{S})$ be its underlying first-order language, where $\mathcal{V}$ is a set of variables $x, y, \ldots$, and $\mathcal{S}$ is the set of logic symbols $\neg, \wedge, \vee, \Rightarrow, \exists, \forall, \text{true}$ and false. *Constraints* $c, d, \ldots$ are formulae over this first-order language. We say that c *entails* d in Δ, written $c \models d$, iff $c \Rightarrow d$ is true in all models of Δ. The relation $\models$, which is decidable by the definition of Δ, induces an equivalence $\approx$ given by $c \approx d$ iff $c \models d$ and $d \models c$. Henceforth, $\mathcal{C}$ denotes *the set of constraints under consideration* modulo $\approx$ in the underlying cs. Thus, we simply write $c = d$ iff $c \approx d$.

Definition (Processes, *Proc***).** *Processes* $P, Q, \ldots \in Proc$ *are built from constraints* $c \in \mathcal{C}$ *and variables* $x \in \mathcal{V}$ *in the underlying cs by:*

$$P, Q, \ldots ::= \textbf{tell}(c) \mid \sum_{i \in I} \textbf{when } c_i \textbf{ do } P_i \mid P \parallel Q \mid (\textbf{local } x)\, P$$
$$\mid \quad \textbf{next } P \mid \textbf{unless } c \textbf{ next } P \quad \mid \; \star\, P \quad \mid \, !\, P \quad \mid \quad \textbf{abort}$$

Intuitively, $\textbf{tell}(c)$ adds an item of information c to the store in the current time interval. The *guarded-choice summation* $\sum_{i \in I} \textbf{when } c_i \textbf{ do } P_i$, where I is a finite set of indexes, chooses in the current time interval one of the P_i's whose c_i is entailed by the store. If no choice is possible, the summation is precluded from execution. We write $\textbf{when } c_{i_1} \textbf{ do } P_{i_1} + \ldots + \textbf{when } c_{i_n} \textbf{ do } P_{i_n}$ if $I = \{i_1, \ldots, i_n\}$ and, if no ambiguity arises, omit the "$\textbf{when } c \textbf{ do}$" when $c = \text{true}$. So, $\sum_{i \in I} P_i$ denotes the *blind-choice* $\sum_{i \in I} \textbf{when true do } P_i$. We omit the "$\sum_{i \in I}$" if $|I| = 1$ and use $\textbf{skip}$ for $\sum_{i \in \emptyset} P_i$.

The process $P \parallel Q$ represents the *parallel execution* of P and Q. $\prod_{i \in I} P_i$, where $I = \{i_1, \ldots, i_n\}$, denotes $((P_{i_1} \parallel P_{i_2}) \parallel \ldots P_{i_{n-1}}) \parallel P_{i_n}$. The process $(\textbf{local } x)\, P$ declares an x *local* to P, and thus we say that it *binds* x in P. The *bound variables* $bv(Q)$ (*free variables* $fv(Q)$) are those with a bound (a not bound) occurrence in Q.

The *unit-delay* process $\textbf{next } P$ executes P in the next time interval. The *time-out* $\textbf{unless } c \textbf{ next } P$ is also a unit-delay, but P will be executed only if c cannot eventually be entailed by the store during the current time interval. Note that $\textbf{next } P$ is not the same as $\textbf{unless false next } P$ since an inconsistent store entails false. We use $\textbf{next}^n(P)$ for $\textbf{next}(\textbf{next}(\ldots(\textbf{next } P)\ldots))$, where $\textbf{next}$ is repeated n times.

The operator "$\star$" represents an *arbitrary (or unknown) but finite delay* (as "ϵ" in SCCS [12]) and allows asynchronous behavior across the time intervals. Intuitively, $\star\, P$ means $P + \textbf{next } P + \textbf{next}^2 P + \ldots$, i.e., an unbounded finite delay of P. The *replication* operator "!" is a delayed version of that of the π-calculus [13]: $!\, P$ means $P \parallel \textbf{next } P \parallel \textbf{next}^2 P \parallel \ldots$, i.e., unboundedly many copies of P but one at a time.

For technical and unification purposes we add to the syntax of ntcc in [15] the tcc process $\textbf{abort}$ [18] which causes all interactions with the environment to cease.

SOS Semantics. The structural operational semantics (SOS) of ntcc considers *transitions* between process-store *configurations* of the form $\langle P, c \rangle$ with stores represented as constraints and processes quotiented by $\equiv$ below.

Definition 2 (Structural Congruence). *Let $\equiv$ be the smallest congruence satisfying: (1) $P \parallel \textbf{skip} \equiv P$, (2) $P \parallel Q \equiv Q \parallel P$, and (3) $P \parallel (Q \parallel R) \equiv (P \parallel Q) \parallel R$. Extend $\equiv$ to configurations by decreeing that $\langle P, c \rangle \equiv \langle Q, c \rangle$ iff $P \equiv Q$.*

Following standard lines, we extend the syntax with a construct $\textbf{local}\,(x, d)\,\textbf{in}\,P$, to represent the evolution of a process of the form $\textbf{local}\,x\,\textbf{in}\,Q$, where d is the local information (or store) produced during this evolution. Initially d is "empty", so we regard $\textbf{local}\,x\,\textbf{in}\,P$ as $\textbf{local}\,(x, \textbf{true})\,\textbf{in}\,P$.

The transitions of the SOS are given by the relations $\longrightarrow$ and $\Longrightarrow$ defined in Table 1. The *internal* transition $\langle P, d \rangle \longrightarrow \langle P', d' \rangle$ should be read as "P with store d reduces, in one internal step, to P' with store d' ". The *observable transition* $P \xrightarrow{(c,d)} R$ should be read as "P on input c, reduces in one *time unit* to R and outputs d". The observable transitions are obtained from terminating sequences of internal transitions.

Table 1. Rules for internal reduction $\longrightarrow$ (upper part) and observable reduction $\Longrightarrow$ (lower part). $\gamma \nrightarrow$ in OBS holds iff for no γ', $\gamma \longrightarrow \gamma'$. $\equiv$ and F are given in Definitions 2 and 3.

$$\text{TELL}\ \frac{}{\langle \textbf{tell}(c), d \rangle \longrightarrow \langle \textbf{skip}, d \wedge c \rangle} \qquad \text{SUM}\ \frac{d \models c_j\ j \in I}{\langle \sum_{i \in I} \textbf{when}\ c_i\ \textbf{do}\ P_i, d \rangle \longrightarrow \langle P_j, d \rangle}$$

$$\text{PAR}\ \frac{\langle P, c \rangle \longrightarrow \langle P', d \rangle}{\langle P \parallel Q, c \rangle \longrightarrow \langle P' \parallel Q, d \rangle} \qquad \text{LOC}\ \frac{\langle P, c \wedge \exists_x d \rangle \longrightarrow \langle P', c' \rangle}{\langle (\textbf{local}\,x, c)\,P, d \rangle \longrightarrow \langle (\textbf{local}\,x, c')\,P', d \wedge \exists_x c' \rangle}$$

$$\text{UNL}\ \frac{}{\langle \textbf{unless}\ c\ \textbf{next}\ P, d \rangle \longrightarrow \langle \textbf{skip}, d \rangle}\ \text{if}\ d \models c$$

$$\text{REP}\ \frac{}{\langle !\,P, d \rangle \longrightarrow \langle P \parallel \textbf{next}\,!\,P, d \rangle} \qquad \text{STAR}\ \frac{}{\langle \star\,P, d \rangle \longrightarrow \langle \textbf{next}^{\,n} P, d \rangle}\ \text{if}\ n \geq 0$$

$$\text{STR}\ \frac{\gamma_1 \longrightarrow \gamma_2}{\gamma_1' \longrightarrow \gamma_2'}\ \text{if}\ \gamma_1 \equiv \gamma_1'\ \text{and}\ \gamma_2 \equiv \gamma_2' \qquad \text{ABORT}\ \frac{}{\langle \textbf{abort}, d \rangle \longrightarrow \langle \textbf{abort}, d \rangle}$$

$$\text{OBS}\ \frac{\langle P, c \rangle \longrightarrow^* \langle Q, d \rangle \nrightarrow}{P \xrightarrow{(c,d)} R}\ \text{if}\ R \equiv F(Q)$$

We shall only describe some of the rules of in Table 1 due to space restrictions (see [15] for further details). As clarified below, the seemingly missing cases for "next" and "unless" processes are given by OBS. The rule STAR specifies an arbitrary delay of P. REP says that $!P$ creates a copy of P and then persists in the next time unit. ABORT realizes the intuition of **abort** causing the interactions with the environment to cease by generating infinite sequences of internal transitions. We shall dwell a little upon the description of Rule LOC as it may seem somewhat complex. Let us consider the process

$$Q = (\mathbf{local}\, x, c)\, P$$

in Rule LOC. The global store is d and the local store is c. We distinguish between the *external* (corresponding to Q) and the *internal* point of view (corresponding to P). From the internal point of view, the information about x, possibly appearing in the "global" store d, cannot be observed. Thus, before reducing P we should first hide the information about x that Q may have in d. We can do this by existentially quantifying x in d. Similarly, from the external point of view, the observable information about x that the reduction of internal agent P may produce (i.e., c') cannot be observed. Thus we hide it by existentially quantifying x in c' before adding it to the global store corresponding to the evolution of Q. Additionally, we should make c' the new private store of the evolution of the internal process for its future reductions.

Rule OBS says that an observable transition from P labeled with (c, d) is obtained from a terminating sequence of internal transitions from $\langle P, c \rangle$ to a $\langle Q, d \rangle$. The process R to be executed in the next time interval is equivalent to $F(Q)$ (the "future" of Q). $F(Q)$ is obtained by removing from Q summations that did not trigger activity and any local information which has been stored in Q, and by "unfolding" the sub-terms within "next" and "unless" expressions.

Definition 3 (Future Function). *Let* $F : Proc \rightharpoonup Proc$ *be defined by*

$$F(Q) = \begin{cases} \mathbf{skip} & \text{if } Q = \sum_{i \in I} \mathbf{when}\ c_i\ \mathbf{do}\ Q_i \\ F(Q_1)\ \|\ F(Q_2) & \text{if } Q = Q_1\ \|\ Q_2 \\ (\mathbf{local}\,x)\,F(R) & \text{if } Q = (\mathbf{local}\,x, c)\,R \\ R & \text{if } Q = \mathbf{next}\ R\ \text{or } Q = \mathbf{unless}\ c\ \mathbf{next}\ R \end{cases}$$

Remark 1. F need no to be total since whenever we need to apply F to a Q (OBS in Table 1), every $\mathbf{tell}(c)$, $\mathbf{abort}$, $\star R$ and $!\,R$ in Q will occur within a "next" or "unless" expression.

2.1 Observable Behavior: The Strongest Postcondition

We now recall the notions of observable behavior for $\mathtt{ntcc}$ introduced in [16], in particular that of the *strongest postcondition* (sp), central to this paper.

Notation 1 *Throughout this paper C^ω denotes the set of infinite (or ω) sequences of constraints in the underlying set of constraints C. We use $\alpha, \alpha', \dots$ to range over C^ω.*

Let $\alpha = c_1.c_2.\dots$ and $\alpha' = c_1'.c_2'.\dots$. Suppose that P exhibits the following infinite sequence of observable transitions (or *run*): $P = P_1 \xrightarrow{(c_1, c_1')} P_2 \xrightarrow{(c_2, c_2')} \dots$. Given this run of P, we shall use the notation $P \xrightarrow{(\alpha, \alpha')}{}_\omega$.

IO and Output Behavior. Observe the above run of P. At the time unit i, the environment *inputs* c_i to P_i which then responds with an output c_i'. As observers, we can see that on α, P responds with α'. We refer to the set of all (α, α') such that $P \xrightarrow{(\alpha, \alpha')}{}^\omega$ as the *input-output (io) behavior* of P. Alternatively, if $\alpha = \mathtt{true}^\omega$, we interpret the run as an interaction among the parallel components in P *without the influence of any (external) environment*; as observers what we see is that P produces α on its own. We refer to the set of all α' such that $P \xrightarrow{(\mathtt{true}^\omega, \alpha')}{}^\omega$ as the *output* behavior of P.

Quiescent Sequences and SP. Another observation we can make of a process is its quiescent input sequences. These are sequences on input of which P can run without adding any information; we observe whether $\alpha = \alpha'$ whenever $P \xrightarrow{(\alpha,\alpha')} \omega$.

In [15] it is shown that the set of quiescent sequences of a given P can be alternatively characterized as *the set of infinite sequences that P can possibly output under arbitrary environments*; the strongest postcondition (sp) of P.

Definition (SP and SP-Equivalence). *The* strongest postcondition *of P, $sp(P)$, is given by $sp(P) - \{\alpha \mid P \xrightarrow{(\alpha',\alpha)} \omega$ for some $\alpha'\}$ and its induced observational equivalence $\sim_{sp}$ is given by $P \sim_{sp} Q$ iff $sp(P) = sp(Q)$.*

2.2   LTL Specification and Verification

We now look at the `ntcc` LTL [15]. This particular LTL expresses properties over sequences of constraints and we shall refer to it as **CLTL**. We begin by giving the syntax of LTL formulae and then interpret them with the **CLTL** semantics.

Definition 4 (LTL Syntax). *The formulae $F, G, \ldots \in \mathcal{F}$ are built from constraints $c \in \mathcal{C}$ and variables $x \in \mathcal{V}$ in the underlying cs by:*

$$F, G, \ldots := c \mid \texttt{true} \mid \texttt{false} \mid F \,\dot\wedge\, G \mid F \,\dot\vee\, G \mid \dot\neg F \mid \dot\exists_x F \mid \circ F \mid \square F \mid \Diamond F$$

The constraint c (i.e., a first-order formula in the cs) represents a *state formula*. The dotted symbols represent the usual (temporal) boolean and existential operators. As clarified later, the dotted notation is needed as in **CLTL** these operators do not always coincide with those in the cs. The symbols $\circ$, $\square$, and $\Diamond$ denote the LTL modalities *next*, *always* and *eventually*. We use $F \Rightarrow G$ for $\dot\neg F \,\dot\vee\, G$. Below we give the formulae a **CLTL** semantics. We first introduce some notation and the notion of x-*variant*. Intuitively, d is an x-variant of c iff they are the same except for the information about x.

Notation 2 *Given a sequence $\alpha = c_1.c_2.\ldots$, we use $\exists_x \alpha$ to denote the sequence $\exists_x c_1 \exists_x c_2 \ldots$. We shall use $\alpha(i)$ to denote the $i - th$ element of α.*

Definition 5 (x-variant). *A constraint d is an x-variant of c iff $\exists_x c = \exists_x d$. Similarly α' is an x-variant of α iff $\exists_x \alpha = \exists_x \alpha'$.*

Definition 6 (CLTL Semantics). *We say that α satisfies (or that it is a model of) F in* **CLTL***, written $\alpha \models_{\text{CLTL}} F$, iff $\langle \alpha, 1 \rangle \models_{\text{CLTL}} F$, where:*

$\langle \alpha, i \rangle \models_{\text{CLTL}} \texttt{true}$		$\langle \alpha, i \rangle \not\models_{\text{CLTL}} \texttt{false}$
$\langle \alpha, i \rangle \models_{\text{CLTL}} c$	*iff*	$\alpha(i) \models c$
$\langle \alpha, i \rangle \models_{\text{CLTL}} \dot\neg F$	*iff*	$\langle \alpha, i \rangle \not\models_{\text{CLTL}} F$
$\langle \alpha, i \rangle \models_{\text{CLTL}} F \,\dot\wedge\, G$	*iff*	$\langle \alpha, i \rangle \models_{\text{CLTL}} F$ *and* $\langle \alpha, i \rangle \models_{\text{CLTL}} G$
$\langle \alpha, i \rangle \models_{\text{CLTL}} F \,\dot\vee\, G$	*iff*	$\langle \alpha, i \rangle \models_{\text{CLTL}} F$ *or* $\langle \alpha, i \rangle \models_{\text{CLTL}} G$
$\langle \alpha, i \rangle \models_{\text{CLTL}} \circ F$	*iff*	$\langle \alpha, i+1 \rangle \models_{\text{CLTL}} F$
$\langle \alpha, i \rangle \models_{\text{CLTL}} \square F$	*iff*	*for all* $j \geq i$ $\langle \alpha, j \rangle \models_{\text{CLTL}} F$
$\langle \alpha, i \rangle \models_{\text{CLTL}} \Diamond F$	*iff*	*there is a* $j \geq i$ *such that* $\langle \alpha, j \rangle \models_{\text{CLTL}} F$
$\langle \alpha, i \rangle \models_{\text{CLTL}} \dot\exists_x F$	*iff*	*there is an x-variant α' of α such that* $\langle \alpha', i \rangle \models_{\text{CLTL}} F$.

Define $[\![F]\!]=\{\alpha\,|\,\alpha\models_{\mathrm{CLTL}} F\}$. *F is* **CLTL** *valid iff* $[\![F]\!]=C^{\omega}$, *and* **CLTL** *satisfiable iff* $[\![F]\!]\neq\emptyset$.

Let us discuss a little about the difference between the boolean operators in the cs and the temporal ones to justify our dotted notation. A state formula c is satisfied only by those $e.\alpha'$ such that $e\models c$. So, the state formula `false` has at least one sequence that satisfies it; e.g. `false`$^{\omega}$. On the contrary the temporal formula `false` has no models whatsoever. Similarly, $c\vee d$ is satisfied by those $e.\alpha'$ such that either $e\models c$ or $e\models d$ holds. Thus, in general $[\![c\,\dot{\vee}\,d]\!]\neq[\![c\vee d]\!]$. The same holds true for $\neg c$ and $\dot{\neg}\,c$.

Example 1. Let $e=c\vee d$ with $c=(x=42)$ and $d=(x\neq 42)$. One can verify that $C^{\omega}=[\![c\vee d]\!]\ni e^{\omega}\notin[\![c\,\dot{\vee}\,d]\!]$ and also that $[\![\neg c]\!]\ni$ `false`$^{\omega}\notin[\![\dot{\neg}\,c]\!]$. □

From the above example, one may be tempted to think of **CLTL** as being intuitionistic. Notice, however, that statements like $\dot{\neg}\,F\,\dot{\vee}\,F$ and $\dot{\neg}\,\dot{\neg}\,F\Rightarrow F$ are **CLTL** valid.

Process Verification. Intuitively, $P\models_{\mathrm{CLTL}} F$ iff every sequence that P can possibly output, on inputs from arbitrary environments, satisfies F.

Definition 7 (Verification). P satisfies F, written $P\models_{\mathrm{CLTL}} F$, iff $sp(P)\subseteq[\![F]\!]$.

For instance, $\star\,\mathbf{tell}(c)\models_{\mathrm{CLTL}}\Diamond c$ as in every sequence output by $\star\,\mathbf{tell}(c)$ there must be an e entailing c. Also $P=\mathbf{tell}(c)+\mathbf{tell}(d)\models_{\mathrm{CLTL}} c\vee d$ and $P\models_{\mathrm{CLTL}} c\,\dot{\vee}\,d$ as every e output by P entails either c or d. Notice, however, that $Q=\mathbf{tell}(c\vee d)\models_{\mathrm{CLTL}} c\vee d$ but $Q\not\models_{\mathrm{CLTL}}(c\,\dot{\vee}\,d)$ in general, since Q can output an e which certainly entails $c\vee d$ and still entails neither c nor d - take e,c and d as in Example 1. Therefore, $c\,\dot{\vee}\,d$ distinguishes P from Q. The reader may now see why we wish to distinguish $c\,\dot{\vee}\,d$ from $c\vee d$.

3 Decidability Results for `ntcc`

We first present our decidability result for sp equivalence. We then show, with the help of this first result, our decidability result for the `ntcc` verification problem. Finally, we present the decidability results for validity and satisfiability in **CLTL**.

The theory of Büchi FSA [2] is central to our results. These FSA are ordinary automata with an acceptance condition for infinite (or ω) sequences: an ω sequence is accepted iff the automaton can read it from left to right while visiting a final state infinitely often. The language recognized by a Büchi automaton A is denoted by $L(A)$. Regular ω-languages are those recognized by Büchi FSA.

For a better exposition of our results, it is convenient to look first into previous approaches to the decidability of the `ntcc` observational equivalences. First, we need the following definition.

Definition (Derivatives). *Define* $P\Longrightarrow Q$ *iff* $P\xrightarrow{(c,d)}Q$ *for some* c,d. *A process* Q *is a* derivative *of* P *iff* $P=P_1\Longrightarrow\ldots\Longrightarrow P_n=Q$ *for some* $P_1,\ldots,P_n$.

Restricted Nondeterminism: Finitely Many States. Nielsen et al [16] show the decidability of output equivalence for the *restricted-nondeterministic* fragment of ntcc which only allows ⋆-*free processes* whose *summations are not in the scope of local operators*. First, the authors show that each process in this fragment has a *finite number of derivatives* (up-to output equivalence). Then, they show how to construct for any given restricted-nondeterministic P, a Büchi automaton that recognizes P's output behavior as an $\omega-$ language. Since language equivalence for Büchi FSA is decidable [22] the decidability of output equivalence follows. In his PhD dissertation [24] the author proved the decidability of the sp (and input-output) equivalence for restricted-nondeterministic processes by a reduction to that of output equivalence.

More Liberal Nondeterminism: Infinitely Many States. The above-mentioned FSA have states representing processes and transitions representing observable reductions. The automata are generated by an *algorithm* that uses the ntcc *operational semantics* to generate all possible observable reductions. Hence, the finiteness of the set of derivatives is crucial to guarantee termination. In fact, the algorithm may diverge if we allow arbitrary ⋆ processes, or summations within local operators because, as illustrated below, they can have *infinitely many derivatives* each with different observable behavior.

Example 2. (1) Notice that $\star P$ has *infinitely many derivatives* of the form $\mathbf{next}^{n} P$ and each of them may exhibit different observable behavior. (2) Let $R =!!P$ with $P =$ **when** $x = 1$ **do** $\star$ **tell**$(y = 1)$. Notice that we could have the following sequence $R \Longrightarrow !P \,\|!!P \Longrightarrow !P \,\|!P \,\|!!P \Longrightarrow \dots$. Now, for any $n > 0$, let $D_n = \prod_n !P \,\|!!P$ (i.e., the n-th derivate). One can verify that on input $(x = 1)$. $\mathbf{true}^{\omega}$, D_k can tell c at $k + 1$ different time units but D_{k-1} can only do it at k different units. The same occurs if $P =$ **when** $x = 1$ **do** δ**tell**(c) where δQ denotes an arbitrary *possibly infinite* delay of Q. This delay operator can be recursively defined as $\delta Q \stackrel{\text{def}}{=} Q + \mathbf{next}\, \delta Q$ and such a kind of definitions can be derived in ntcc using replication together with *blind choice summations within local processes* [15]. □

3.1 Decidability of SP Equivalence

We shall show a Büchi FSA characterization of the sp for processes that can exhibit infinitely many, observationally different, derivatives—of the kind illustrated in Example 2. One particular difference with the work previously mentioned is that, to get around the algorithmic problems illustrated above, the characterizations will be guided by the *sp denotational semantics* of ntcc [14] rather than its operational semantics.

The ntcc denotational semantics $[\![\cdot]\!] : Proc \to \mathcal{P}(\mathcal{C}^{\omega})$, given in Table 2 by taking $[\![\cdot]\!] = [\![\cdot]\!]^{\mathcal{C}}$, is meant to capture the sp. From [5], however, we know that there cannot be a $f : Proc \to \mathcal{P}(\mathcal{C}^{\omega})$, compositionally defined, such that $f(P) = sp(P)$ for all P. Nevertheless, Palamidessi et al [17] showed that $[\![P]\!] = sp(P)$ for all P in the so-called *locally-independent* fragment. This fragment forbids non-unary summations (and "unless" processes) whose guards depend on local variables.

Definition 8 (Locally-Independent Processes). P *is* locally-independent *iff for every* **unless** c **next** Q *and* $\sum_{i \in I}$ **when** c_i **do** Q_i $(|I| \geq 2)$ *in* P, *neither* c *nor the* c_i's *contain variables in* $bv(P)$ *(i.e., the bound variables of* P*).*

Theorem 1 (Palamidessi et al [17]). *If P is locally-independent then $\llbracket P \rrbracket = sp(P)$.*

The locally-independent fragment allows $\star$ processes and also blind-choice within local operators which may exhibit infinitely many observationally different derivatives, as illustrated in Example 2. Furthermore, every summation whose guards are either all equivalent or mutually exclusive can be encoded in this fragment [24]. The applicability of this fragment is witnessed by the fact all the ntcc application examples in [15,16,24] can be model as local-independent processes.

SP Büchi FSA. We shall give a Büchi characterization of $sp(P)$ from its denotation $\llbracket P \rrbracket$. We then benefit from the simple set-theoretical and compositional nature of $\llbracket \cdot \rrbracket$ as well as the closure properties of regular ω−languages. A technical problem arises: There can be infinitely many c's such that $c.\alpha \in \llbracket P \rrbracket$ as $\mathcal{C}$ may be infinite, but the alphabets of Büchi FSA are finite. It is therefore convenient to confine $\llbracket P \rrbracket$ to a suitable finite set $S \subseteq_{fin} \mathcal{C}$ including its so-called *relevant constraints*.

Definition (Relevant Constraints). *Given $S \subseteq \mathcal{C}$, let $\overline{S}$ be the closure under conjunction and implication of S. Let $C : Proc \rightarrow \mathcal{P}(\mathcal{C})$ be defined as:*

$$C(\mathbf{skip}) = \{\mathbf{true}\} \qquad\qquad C(\mathbf{abort}) = \{\mathbf{true}\}$$
$$C(\textstyle\sum_{i \in I} \mathbf{when}\ c_i\ \mathbf{do}\ P_i) = \bigcup_{i \in I}\{c_i\} \cup C(P_i) \quad C(\mathbf{tell}(c)) = \{c\}$$
$$C(P \parallel Q) = C(P) \cup C(Q) \qquad\qquad C(\mathbf{next}\ P) = C(P)$$
$$C(!\,P) = C(P) \qquad\qquad C(\star P) = C(P)$$
$$C((\mathbf{local}\ x)\,P) = \{c, \exists_x c, \forall_x c \mid c \in \overline{C(P)}\}$$

Define the relevant constraints *for $P_1, ..., P_n$, written $\mathcal{C}(P_1, \ldots, P_n)$, as the closure under conjunction of $\overline{C(P_1)} \cup \ldots \cup \overline{C(P_n)}$.*

The interested reader is referred to the author's PhD dissertation [24] for the intuition behind the notion of relevant constraints. Now, consider two locally-independent processes P and Q. Clearly, $\mathcal{C}(P, Q)$ is finite. Moreover, it contains the constraints that are indeed relevant for the sp equivalence of P and Q.

Theorem 2 (Relevant SP Denotational Characterization). *Let P and Q be locally-independent. Then $\llbracket P \rrbracket^{\mathcal{C}(P,Q)} = \llbracket Q \rrbracket^{\mathcal{C}(P,Q)}$ iff $P \sim_{sp} Q$.*

Proof. (Outline) Let $S = \mathcal{C}(P, Q)$. Verify by induction on P that $c_1.c_2.\ldots \in \llbracket P \rrbracket$ iff $c_1(S).c_2(S).\ldots \in \llbracket P \rrbracket^S$, where $c_i(S)$ is the strongest $e \in S$ wrt $\models$ such that $c_i \models e$ ($c_i(S)$ is well-defined as S is closed under $\wedge$). By symmetry the same holds for Q. Then conclude that $\llbracket P \rrbracket^S = \llbracket Q \rrbracket^S$ iff $\llbracket P \rrbracket = \llbracket Q \rrbracket$. The result follows from Theorem 1 . $\qquad \square$

Büchi Constructions. Having identified our finite set of relevant constraints for the sp equivalence characterization, we now proceed to construct for each P and $S \subseteq_{fin} \mathcal{C}$, a Büchi automaton A_P^S recognizing $\llbracket P \rrbracket^S$. Each A_P^S will be *compositionally* constructed in the sense that it will be built solely from information about FSA of the form A_Q^S where Q is a subprocess of P. The most interesting case of this construction is replication, as described in the proof of the lemma below.

Table 2. SP Denotation. Above $S \subseteq C$ and $\beta.\alpha'$ is the concatenation of the finite sequence β followed by α'. The sequence $\exists_x \alpha$ results from applying $\exists_x$ to each constraint in α. In DSUM if $I = \emptyset$, the indexed union and intersection are taken to be $\emptyset$ and S^ω, respectively.

DABORT: $[\![\mathbf{abort}]\!]^S = \emptyset$

DTELL: $[\![\mathbf{tell}(c)]\!]^S = \{d.\alpha \in S^\omega \mid d \models c\}$

DSUM: $[\![\sum_{i \in I} \mathbf{when}\ c_i\ \mathbf{do}\ P_i\,]\!]^S = \bigcup_{i \in I} \{d.\alpha \in S^\omega \mid d \models c_i \text{ and } d.\alpha \in [\![P_i]\!]^S\}$

$\cup$

$\bigcap_{i \in I} \{d.\alpha \in S^\omega \mid d \not\models c_i\}$

DPAR: $[\![P \parallel Q]\!]^S = [\![P]\!]^S \cap [\![Q]\!]^S$

DLOC: $[\![(\mathbf{local}\ x)\ P]\!]^S = \{\alpha \in S^\omega \mid \text{there exists } \alpha' \in [\![P]\!]^S \text{ such that } \exists_x \alpha' = \exists_x \alpha\}$

DNEXT: $[\![\mathbf{next}\ P]\!]^S = \{d.\alpha \in S^\omega \mid \alpha \in [\![P]\!]^S\}$

DUNL: $[\![\mathbf{unless}\ c\ \mathbf{next}\ P]\!]^S = \{d.\alpha \in S^\omega \mid d \models c\}$

$\cup$

$\{d.\alpha \mid d \not\models c \text{ and } \alpha \in [\![P]\!]^S\}$

DREP: $[\![!\,P]\!]^S = \{\alpha \in S^\omega \mid \text{for all } \beta, \alpha' \text{ such that } \alpha = \beta.\alpha', \text{ we have } \alpha' \in [\![P]\!]^S\}$

DSTAR: $[\![\star\,P]\!]^S = \{\beta.\alpha \in S^\omega \mid \alpha \in [\![P]\!]^S\}$

Lemma 1. *Given P and $S \subseteq_{fin} C$ one can effectively construct a Büchi automaton A_P^S over the alphabet S such that $L(A_P^S) = [\![P]\!]^S$.*

Proof. We shall give the construction of each A_P^S by case analysis on the structure of P. We only describe some of the cases. The others are similar or simpler.

Replication Automaton. $P = !Q$: We have $\alpha \in [\![!Q]\!]^S$ iff every suffix of α is in $[\![Q]\!]^S$. We then need to construct a $A_{!P}^S$ that accepts an infinite sequence α iff *every suffix* of it is accepted by A_Q^S. At first, such a construction may seem somewhat complex to realize. Nevertheless, notice that the process $!Q$ is *dual* to $\star Q$ in the sense expressed in [17]:

$$[\![!Q]\!] = \nu_X([\![Q]\!] \cap \{d.\alpha \mid \alpha \in X\}) \quad \text{while} \quad [\![\star Q]\!] = \mu_X([\![Q]\!] \cup \{d.\alpha \mid \alpha \in X\})$$

where ν, μ are the greatest and least fixpoint (resp.) in the complete lattice $(\mathcal{P}(C^\omega), \subseteq)$. In fact, $\alpha \in [\![\star Q]\!]^S$ iff *there is a suffix* of α in $[\![Q]\!]^S$. So, given an automaton B define $\star B$ as the automaton that accepts α iff *there is a suffix* of α accepted by B. The construction of $\star B$ is simple and similar to that of $A_{\star Q}^S$ below. Now, given A, one can construct the automaton $\overline{A}$ for the complement of $L(A)$ [22]. Hence, keeping duality in mind, we can take $A_{!Q}^S$ to be $\overline{\star \overline{A_Q^S}}$.

Unbounded but Finite Delay Automaton. $P = \star Q$: The states of $A_{\star Q}^S$ are those of A_Q^S plus an additional state s_0. Its final states are those of A_Q^S. Its initial states are those of A_Q^S plus s_0. The transitions are those of A_Q^S plus transitions labelled with c, for each $c \in S$, from s_0 to itself and from s_0 to each initial state of A_Q^S. The transitions "looping" into the initial state s_0 model the "arbitrary but finite delay" of $\star Q$.

Local Automaton. $P = (\textbf{local}\,x)\,Q$: The states of $A^S_{(\textbf{local}\,x)\,Q}$ are those of A^S_Q. Its initial and final states are those of A_Q. For each $c \in S$, $A^S_{(\textbf{local}\,x)\,Q}$ has a transition from p to q labeled with c iff A^S_Q has a transition from p to q labelled with d for some $d \in S$ such that $\exists_x d = \exists_x e$.

Parallel Automaton. $P = Q \parallel R$: The theory of Büchi FSA gives us a construction for the intersection of ω languages: Given A^S_Q and A^S_R one can construct an automaton that recognizes $L(A^S_Q) \cap L(A^S_R)$ [3]. Take $A^S_{Q\parallel R}$ to be such an automaton.

Skip and Tell Automata. $P = \textbf{skip}$: $A^S_{\textbf{skip}}$ has a single (initial, accepting) state, and for each $c \in S$, there is a transition labeled with c from this single state to itself. $P = \textbf{tell}(c)$: $A^S_{\textbf{tell}(c)}$ has exactly two states: one is its initial state and the other is its accepting one: the unique state of $A^S_{\textbf{skip}}$. The transitions of $A^S_{\textbf{tell}(c)}$ are those of $A^S_{\textbf{skip}}$ plus a transition from the initial state to the state of $A^S_{\textbf{skip}}$ labeled with d for each $d \in S$ such that $d \models c$.

One can verify the correctness of A^S_P using induction on the structure of P. It is easy to see that A^S_P can be effectively constructed, thus concluding the proof.   □

We now state our first decidability result: The decidability of the sp equivalence.

Theorem 3 (Decidability of $\sim_{sp}$). *Given two locally-independent process P and Q, the question of whether $P \sim_{sp} Q$ is decidable.*

Proof. From Theorem 2, Lemma 1 and the decidability of language equivalence for Büchi FSA [22].

3.2 Decidability Results for Verification and CLTL

Here we show the decidability results for the verification problem (i.e., given P and F whether $P \models_{\text{CLTL}} F$, see Definition 7) as well as for **CLTL** (Definition 6).

Recall the **CLTL** models of a given formula F are in C^ω. Thus, for our decidability results we may attempt to give a Büchi characterization of **CLTL** formulae facing therefore the problem pointed out in the previous section: C may be infinite but Büchi FSA only have finite alphabets. One could try to restrict $[\![F]\!]$ to its "relevant" constraints as we did for $[\![P]\!]$. This appears to be possible for negation-free formulae but we do not know yet how to achieve this for the full language.

Nevertheless, for negation-free formulae there is an alternative to obtain the results by appealing to Theorem 3 and the correspondence between processes and LTL formulae. More precisely, we show that one can construct a locally-independent R_F whose sp corresponds to $[\![F]\!]$ if F is a restricted-negation formula in the following sense:

Definition 9 (Restricted-Negation LTL). *F is a* restricted-negation *formula iff whenever $\dot{\neg}\, G$ appears in F then G is a state formula (i.e., $G = c$ for some c).*

Recall that in **CLTL** $\dot{\neg} c$ and the state formula $\neg c$ do not match (Example 1). In fact, we need $\dot{\neg} c$ should we want to express the minimal implication form $c \Rightarrow D = \dot{\neg} c \,\dot{\vee}\, D$.

Lemma 2. *Let F be a restricted-negation formula. One can effectively construct a locally-independent R_F such that $[\![F]\!] = sp(R_F)$.*

Proof. Take $R_F = h(F)$ where h is the map from restricted-negation formulae to locally-independent processes given by

$$
\begin{array}{ll}
h(\mathtt{true}) = \mathbf{skip} & h(\mathtt{false}) = \mathbf{abort} \\
h(c) = \mathbf{tell}(c) & h(\dot{\neg}\, c) = \mathbf{when}\ c\ \mathbf{do\ abort} \\
h(F \wedge G) = h(F)\ \|\ h(G) & h(F \vee G) = h(F) + h(G) \\
h(\dot{\exists}\, xF) = (\mathbf{local}\, x)\, h(F) & h(\bigcirc F) = \mathbf{next}\, h(G) \\
h(\Box F) =\ !\, h(F) & h(\Diamond F) = \star h(F)
\end{array}
$$

Obviously, $h(F)$ can be effectively constructed. One can verify that $[\![F]\!] = [\![h(F)]\!]$ by induction on the structure of F. From Theorem 1 we obtain $[\![F]\!] = sp(h(F))$.   □

Notice that the map h above reveals the close connection between ntcc and LTL. We can now state the decidability of the verification problem for ntcc.

Theorem 4 (Decidability of Verification). *Let F be a restricted-negation formula. Let P be locally-independent. The question of whether $P \models_{\mathrm{CLTL}} F$ is decidable.*

Proof. From Theorem 3 by using the following reduction to sp equivalence:

$$
\begin{array}{llll}
P \models_{\mathrm{CLTL}} F & \text{iff } sp(P) \subseteq [\![F]\!] & \text{(Definition 7)} \\
& \text{iff } sp(P) \subseteq [\![R_F]\!] & \text{(Lemma 2)} \\
& \text{iff } [\![P]\!] \subseteq [\![R_F]\!] & \text{(Theorem 1)} \\
& \text{iff } [\![P]\!] = [\![R_F]\!] \cap [\![P]\!] \\
& \text{iff } [\![P]\!] = [\![R_F\ \|\ P]\!] & \text{(Definition of } [\![\cdot]\!]) \\
& \text{iff } P \sim_{sp} R_F\ \|\ P & \text{(Theorem 2)} & \square
\end{array}
$$

We can reduce the validity of implication to the verification problem. Therefore,

Theorem 5 (Decidability for Validity of Implication). *Let F and G be restricted-negation formulae. The question of whether $F \Rightarrow G$ is **CLTL** valid is decidable.*

Proof. $F \Rightarrow G$ iff $[\![F]\!] = sp(R_F) \subseteq [\![G]\!]$ by Definition 6 and Lemma 2. Then $F \Rightarrow G$ iff $R_F \models_{\mathrm{CLTL}} G$ by Definition 7. The result follows from Theorem 4.   □

As an immediate consequence of the above theorem we obtain the following:

Corollary 1 (Decidability of CLTL Satisfiability and Validity). *Let F be an arbitrary restricted-negation formula. The questions of whether F is **CLTL** valid and whether F is **CLTL** satisfiable are both decidable.*

Proof. F is **CLTL** valid iff $\mathtt{true} \Rightarrow F$ is **CLTL** valid, and F is **CLTL** satisfiable iff $F \Rightarrow \mathtt{false}$ is not **CLTL** valid. The result follows from Theorem 5.   □

4   An Application to Manna and Pnueli's LTL

We now apply the previous results on our ntcc LTL (**CLTL**) to standard first-order LTL, henceforth called **LTL**, as presented by Manna and Pnueli in [10]. Namely, we obtain a new positive decidability result on the satisfiability of a first-order fragment of **LTL** by a reduction to that of **CLTL**. The relevance of our result is that **LTL** is not recursively axiomatizable [1] and, therefore, the satisfiability problem is undecidable for the full language of **LTL**. We confine ourselves to having $\bigcirc$, $\square$, and $\Diamond$ as modalities. This is sufficient for making a recursive axiomatization impossible [11].

We shall recall briefly some LTL notions given in [10]. We presuppose an underlying first-order language $\mathcal{L}$ (including equality) with its (nonlogical) symbols interpreted over some concrete domains such as the natural numbers.

A *state* s is an interpretation that assigns to each variable x in $\mathcal{L}$ a value $s[x]$ over the appropriate domain. The interpretation is extended to $\mathcal{L}$ expressions in the usual way. For example, if f is a function symbol of arity 1, $s[f(x)] = f(s[x])$. We write $s \models c$ iff c is true wrt s in the given interpretation of the $\mathcal{L}$ symbols. For instance, if $+$ is interpreted as addition over the natural numbers and $s[x] = 42$ then $s \models \exists_y(x = y + y)$. We say that c is *state valid* iff $s \models c$ for every state s.

A *model* is an infinite sequence of states. We shall use σ to range over models. The variables of $\mathcal{L}$ are partitioned into *rigid* and *flexible* variables. Each model σ must satisfy the *rigidity* condition: If x is rigid and s, s' are two states in σ then $s[x] = s'[x]$.

The syntax of **LTL** is to that of **CLTL** given in Definition 4. In this case, however, x is a variable in $\mathcal{L}$ and c represents a first-order formula over $\mathcal{L}$.

The semantics of **LTL** is similar that of **CLTL** (Definition 6) except that now the formulae are satisfied by sequences of states. We then need to extend the notion of x-variant (Definition 5) to states: s is x-*variant* of s' iff $s[y] = s'[y]$ for every variable y in $\mathcal{L}$ different from x.

Definition (LTL Semantics). *A model σ satisfies F in* **LTL**, *notation $\sigma \models_{LTL} F$, iff $\langle \sigma, 1 \rangle \models_{LTL} F$ where $\langle \sigma, i \rangle \models_{LTL} F$ is obtained from Definition 6 by replacing α and $\models_{CLTL}$ with σ and $\models_{LTL}$, respectively. We say that F is* **LTL** *satisfiable iff $\sigma \models_{LTL} F$ for some σ, and that F is* **LTL** *valid iff $\sigma \models_{LTL} F$ for all σ.*

In order to prove our decidability result, *we assume that state validity (the set of valid state formulae) is decidable.* From [9] we know that even under this assumption the **LTL** defined above is undecidable. In contrast, under the assumption, **LTL** satisfiability is decidable for the fragment in which temporal operators are not allowed within the scope of quantifiers as it can be reduced to that of propositional LTL [1].

Example 3. Let us now illustrate the interaction between quantifiers, modalities, flexible and rigid variables in **LTL**. The formula $\square \dot{\exists}_u(x = u \wedge \bigcirc x = u+1)$, where x is flexible and u is rigid, specifies sequences in which x increases by 1 from each state to the next. This example also illustrates that existential quantification over rigid variables provides for the specification of counter computations, so we may expect their absence to be important in our decidability result. In fact, we shall state the **LTL** decidability for the *restricted-negation* fragment (Definition 9) with flexible variables only. $\square$

Removing Existential Quantifiers. One might be tempted to think that, without universal quantification and without rigid variables, one could remove the existential quantifiers rather easily: Pull them into outermost position with the appropriate α-conversions to get a prenex form, then remove them since $\dot{\exists}_x F$ is **LTL** satisfiable iff F is **LTL** satisfiable. But this procedure does not quite work; it does not preserve satisfiability:

Example 4. Let $F = (x = 42 \wedge \bigcirc x \neq 42)$, $G = \dot{\exists}_x \Box F$ and $H = \Box \dot{\exists}_x F$ where x is flexible. One can verify that unlike H, $\Box F$ and thus G are not **LTL** satisfiable. Getting rid of existential quantifiers is not as obvious as it may seem.   □

Relating **CLTL** *and* **LTL** *Satisfiability.* Let us give some intuition on how to obtain a *reduction* from **LTL** satisfiability to **CLTL** satisfiability. In what follows we confine ourselves to restricted-negation formulae without rigid variables. One can verify that $\neg c$ and $\dot{\neg} c$ have the same **LTL** models. So, in the reduction we can assume wlg that F has no $\dot{\neg}$ symbols. Notice that $F = (x = 42 \dot{\vee} x \neq 42)$ is **LTL** valid but not **CLTL** valid (Example 1). However, F is satisfiable in both logics. In general, if F is **LTL** satisfiable then F is **CLTL** satisfiable. The other direction does not necessarily hold. $\Diamond \texttt{false}$ is not **LTL** satisfiable but it is **CLTL** satisfiable—recall from Section 2.2 that in **CLTL** $\texttt{false}$ is not the same as $\texttt{false}$. For example, $\texttt{false}^\omega \models_{\text{CLTL}} \Diamond \texttt{false}$. However, we can get around this mismatch by using $\Box \dot{\neg} \texttt{false}$ to exclude **CLTL** models containing $\texttt{false}$ as shown in the lemma below.

Recall that (Σ, Δ) (Definition 1) denotes the underlying cs and $\mathcal{L}$ denotes the underlying first-order language of state formulae. Also recall that both Δ and the set of valid state formulae are required to be decidable.

Lemma 3. *Assume that the cs* (Σ, Δ) *has* $\mathcal{L}$ *as first-order language and* Δ *is the set of valid state formulae. Then*

$$F \text{ is } \textbf{LTL} \text{ satisfiable} \quad \text{iff} \quad F \wedge \Box \dot{\neg} \texttt{false} \text{ is } \textbf{CLTL} \text{ satisfiable,}$$

if F is a restricted-negation formula with no occurrences of $\dot{\neg}$ and with no rigid variables.

Proof. (Outline) "If" direction: Verify that if $\alpha = c_1.c_2. \ldots \models_{\text{CLTL}} F \wedge \Box \dot{\neg} \texttt{false}$ then for any $\sigma = s_1.s_2. \ldots$ where $s_i \models c_i$ $(i \geq 1)$, we have $\sigma \models_{\text{LTL}} F$. Conclude the result by using the observation that if $\alpha \models_{\text{CLTL}} F \wedge \Box \dot{\neg} \texttt{false}$ then α contains no $\texttt{false}$. "Only if" direction: Verify that if $\sigma = s_1.s_2 \ldots \models_{\text{LTL}} F$ then there is an $\alpha = c_1.c_2 \ldots$ with $s_i \models c_i$ $(i \geq 1)$ such that $\alpha \models_{\text{CLTL}} F \wedge \Box \dot{\neg} \texttt{false}$. Each c_i can be taken to be the strongest constraint (under $\models$) satisfied by s_i in the closure under conjunction of the constraints in F.   □

We can now state the decidability result we claimed for first-order LTL.

Theorem 6 (Decidability of LTL Satisfaction). *Let F be a restricted-negation formula without rigid variables. The question of whether F is* **LTL** *satisfiable is decidable.*

Proof. From Lemma 3 and Corollary 1, and the fact that one can freely replace $\dot{\neg}$ by $\neg$ in F and the resulting formula will have the same **LTL** models than the original F.   □

5   Concluding Remarks

We presented positive decidability results for the sp behavioral equivalence, the ntcc verification problem, and the ntcc specification first-order temporal logic **CLTL**. These results apply to *infinite-state* processes. A somewhat interesting aspect is that for proving the results it turned out to be convenient to work with the ntcc *denotational semantics* rather than with its operational counterpart. Also the use of Büchi automata-theoretic techniques in these results highlights the automata-like flavor of ntcc.

Furthermore, by using a reduction to **CLTL** satisfiability, we identified a first-order fragment of the standard LTL [10] for which satisfiability is decidable. The result contributes to the understanding of the relation between (timed) ccp and (temporal) classic logic and also illustrates the applicability of timed ccp to other theories of concurrency.
Related Work. Nielsen et al [14] proved the decidability of the sp equivalence and other behavioral equivalences for several deterministic timed ccp languages. In another work Nielsen et al [16] showed that output equivalence is decidable for a restricted nondeterministic ntcc fragment. The results in [14,16] are obtained by showing that the processes in these languages are indeed *finite-state*. Nielsen et al [14] also show that the sp equivalence is *undecidable* if recursion is present in the language.

Saraswat et al [21] showed how to compile parameterless recursion tcc processes (basically finite-state deterministic ntcc processes) into FSA in a compositional way. Such FSA provide a simple and useful execution model for tcc but not a direct way of verifying sp (or input-output) equivalence. In fact, unlike our FSA constructions, the standard language equivalence between these FSA does not necessarily imply sp equivalence (or input-output) of the processes they represent.

Another interesting approach to timed ccp verification is that by Falaschi et al [8]. The authors show how to construct structures (models) of tcc processes which then, by restricting the domains of variables to be finite, can be used for model-checking. Notice that in our results we make no assumptions about the domains of variables being finite.

The notion of constraint in other declarative formalisms such as Constraint Logic Programming (CLP) and Constraint Programming (CP) has also been used for the verification of infinite-state systems. Delzanno and Podelski [6] showed how to translate infinite-state systems into CLP programs to verify safety and liveness properties. Esparza and Melzer [7] used CP in a semi-decision algorithm to verify 1-safe Petri Nets.

Merz [11] and Hodkinson et al [9] identified interesting decidable first-order fragments of LTL. These fragments are all monadic and without equality. A difference with our work is that these fragments do not restrict the use of negation or rigid variables, and our fragment is not restricted to be monadic or equality-free.
Future Work. The author believes that we can dispense with the restriction on the occurrences of negation in our results. If the claim is true, then the inference system for ntcc [17] would be complete for locally-independent processes (and not just relative complete). This is because we would be able to determine the validity of arbitrary ntcc LTL implication as required by the consequence rule. It will be, therefore, interesting to be able to prove this claim.

In our Büchi FSA constructions we were not concerned with state space issues (e.g., see the "double complementation" construction for the replication automaton in Section 3.1). For verification purposes, it is important to look into these issues.

Acknowledgments. Many thanks to Catuscia Palamidessi, Mogens Nielsen, Joachim Parrow, Jiri Srba, Igor Walukiewicz, Martin Abadi, Ian Hodkinson, Stephan Merz, Richard Mayr, Gerardo Schneider and Martin Leucker for helpful comments.

References

1. M. Abadi. The power of temporal proofs. *Theoretical Computer Science*, 65:35–84, 1989.
2. J. R. Buchi. On a decision method in restricted second order arithmetic. In *Proc. Int. Conf. on Logic, Methodology, and Philosophy of Science*, pages 1–11, 1962.
3. Y. Choueka. Theories of automata on ω-tapes: A simplified approach. *Computer and System Sciences*, 10:19–35, 1974.
4. F. de Boer, M. Gabbrielli, and M. C. Meo. A timed concurrent constraint language. *Information and Computation*, 161:45–83, 2000.
5. F. de Boer, M. Gabbrielli, E. Marchiori, and C. Palamidessi. Proving concurrent constraint programs correct. *ACM Transactions on Programming Languages and Systems*, 19(5), 1997.
6. G. Delzanno and A. Podelski. Model checking in CLP. *TACAS'99*. LNCS 1579, 1999.
7. J. Esparza and S. Melzer. Model checking LTL using constraint programming. In *Proc. of ICATPN'97*. LNCS 1248, 1997.
8. M. Falaschi, A. Policriti, and A. Villanueva. Modelling timed concurrent systems in a temporal concurrent constraint language - I. ENTCS 48, 2001.
9. I. Hodkinson, F. Wolter, and M. Zakharyasche. Decidable fragments of first-order temporal logic. *Ann. Pure. Appl. Logic*, 106:85–134, 2000.
10. Z. Manna and A. Pnueli. *The Temporal Logic of Reactive and Concurrent Systems, Specification*. Springer, 1991.
11. S. Merz. Decidability and incompleteness results for first-order temporal logics of linear time. *Journal of Applied Non-Classical Logic*, 2(2), 1992.
12. R. Milner. A finite delay operator in synchronous ccs. TR CSR-116-82, Univ. of Edinburgh.
13. R. Milner. *Communicating and Mobile Systems: the π-calculus*. 1999.
14. M. Nielsen, C. Palamidessi, and F. Valencia. On the expressive power of concurrent constraint programming languages. In *PPDP 2002*, pages 156–167. ACM Press, October 2002.
15. M. Nielsen, C. Palamidessi, and F. Valencia. Temporal concurrent constraint programming: Denotation, logic and applications. *Nordic Journal of Computing*, 9(2):145–188, 2002.
16. M. Nielsen and F. Valencia. *Temporal Concurrent Constraint Programming: Applications and Behavior*. LNCS 2300:298–324, 2002.
17. C. Palamidessi and F. Valencia. A temporal concurrent constraint programming calculus. In *Proc. of CP'01*. LNCS 2239, 2001.
18. V. Saraswat, R. Jagadeesan, and V. Gupta. Foundations of timed concurrent constraint programming. In *Proc. of LICS'94*, pages 71–80, 1994.
19. V. Saraswat, R. Jagadeesan, and V. Gupta. Programming in timed concurrent constraint languages. In *Constraint Programming: Proc. 1993*, pages 361–410. Springer-Verlag, 1994.
20. V. Saraswat, R. Jagadeesan, and V. Gupta. Timed default concurrent constraint programming. *Journal of Symbolic Computation*, 22:475–520, 1996.
21. V. Saraswat, M. Rinard, and P. Panangaden. The semantic foundations of concurrent constraint programming. In *POPL '91*, pages 333–352, 1991.
22. A. Sistla, M. Vardi, and P. Wolper. The complementation problem for buchi automata with applications to temporal logic. *Theoretical Computer Science*, 49:217–237, 1987.
23. S. Tini. On the expressiveness of timed concurrent constraint programming. ENTCS 27, 1999.
24. F. Valencia. *Temporal Concurrent Constraint Programming*. PhD thesis, BRICS Univ. of Aarhus, 2003. Available online via http://www.brics.dk/~fvalenci/publications.html.
25. M. Vardi. An automata-theoretic approach to linear temporal logic. LNCS 1043, 1996.

Is There an Optimal Generic Semantics for First-Order Equations?

Jan-Georg Smaus

Institut für Informatik, Universität Freiburg, Georges-Köhler-Allee 52,
79110 Freiburg im Breisgau, Germany, smaus@informatik.uni-freiburg.de

Abstract. Apt [1] has proposed a denotational semantics for first-order logic with equality, which is an instance of the *computation as deduction* paradigm: given a language $\mathcal{L}$ together with an interpretation $\mathcal{I}$ and a formula ϕ in $\mathcal{L}$, the semantics consists of a (possibly empty) set of substitutions θ such that $\phi\theta$ is true in $\mathcal{I}$, or it may contain *error* to indicate that there might be further such substitutions, but that they could not be computed. The definition of the semantics is generic in that it assumes no knowledge about $\mathcal{I}$ except that a ground term can effectively be evaluated. We propose here an improvement of this semantics, using an algorithm based on syntactic unification. Although one can argue for the optimality of this semantics informally, it is not optimal in any formal sense, since there seems to be no satisfactory formalisation of what it means to have "no knowledge about $\mathcal{I}$ except that a ground term can effectively be evaluated". It is always possible to "improve" a semantics in a formal sense, but such semantics become more and more contrived.

1 Background

The *computation as deduction* paradigm states that a computation is a *constructive* proof of a logic formula, meaning that the result of the computation is a substitution that makes the formula true. More specifically, one may distinguish between a formula called *query* and a formula called *program*, and compute instantiations of the query that are true in (certain or all) models of the program.

The *formulas as programs* approach [1,2] is an instance of this paradigm and the theoretical foundation of the programming language Alma-0 [3]. Alma-0 combines aspects of logic, constraint and imperative programming. *Formulas as programs* relates logical constructs to imperative programming language constructs, e.g., conjunction to sequential composition. The motivation for the approach has been discussed in the above works.

In particular, Apt [1] has given a *denotational* semantics for first-order formulas over arbitrary interpretations. At the heart of this semantics is the problem of solving equations $s = t$ written in an arbitrary first-order language over an arbitrary algebra $\mathcal{J}^1$. That is, we seek an instantiation of the variables in s and t

---

[1] Recall that an algebra assigns a meaning to terms. An interpretation extends an algebra by assigning a meaning to formulas.

C. Palamidessi (Ed.): ICLP 2003, LNCS 2916, pp. 438–450, 2003.

such that the equation becomes true in $\mathcal{J}$. In full generality, the problem cannot be addressed properly. For example, $x^2 - 1 = 0$ has one solution $\{x/1\}$ if we take $\mathcal{J}$ to be the set of arithmetic expressions interpreted over the natural numbers, but two solutions $\{x/1\}$ and $\{x/-1\}$ if we assume the integers.

The question Apt addressed is: how far can one go in defining a semantics, i.e., a set of solutions for an equation $s = t$, *for an arbitrary algebra*? This means that the definition must not refer to any particular algebra (or language) or use any knowledge about it other than how to evaluate a ground term.

A note on terminology: in contrast to Apt, one could define *the* semantics of an equation as the set of all solutions, with no concern for whether it can be computed or not. But we follow Apt's terminology by which a semantics could be any function assigning a possibly incomplete set of solutions to an equation. The viewpoint is that logic is used as a programming language.

Apt's semantics computes a set of *correct* solutions, where a special *error* element indicates that the set may be incomplete. When presenting his work, Apt expressed the suspicion that his semantics could be proven optimal in a well-defined sense.

The original aim of this work was to provide this proof. However, during our attempts to formalise what "for an arbitrary algebra" means, we gradually discovered more and more "improvements" of the allegedly optimal semantics. We now devise a procedure, based on the standard syntactic unification algorithm, for finding solutions for an equation. We give some evidence that this semantics is the best for an arbitrary algebra, in that the procedure tries all conceivable manipulations based on syntactic criteria and evaluation of ground terms. However, this is not a formal statement. It seems that one can "improve" a semantics ad infinitum, at the cost of making it more and more contrived.

For example, try finding a solution to $x + 1 = 2$ without using any knowledge of the algebra of arithmetic except how to evaluate a ground term.

1. Clearly, subtracting 1 from both sides to resolve the equation by x would not be within the capabilities of a semantics defined for arbitrary algebras.
2. How about a semantics that enumerates all ground terms of the language $(162, 0, -17, \ldots)$ and tries to substitute them for the variables in an equation until a solution is found? It is doubtful if this is acceptable since the enumeration cannot be described without explicitly referring to the language.
3. How about a semantics that considers as solution candidates all substitutions defined by the replacement of each variable x occurring in the equation by a ground subterm r also occurring in the equation? Formally, the semantics would be the set of such substitutions that are indeed solutions. This is an unambiguous description independent of any particular language, and for $x + 1 = 2$, it even works. In fact, such a semantics would be "better" than the one we propose, but it would be unacceptably contrived.

Hence a formal notion of an "optimal" semantics seems out of sight.

2   Apt's Semantics [1]

We consider a first-order language $\mathcal{L}$ of terms and an algebra $\mathcal{J}$. We denote by D the domain of $\mathcal{J}$, and for each function symbol f, we denote by $f_{\mathcal{J}}$ its interpretation in $\mathcal{J}$. We now define "hybrid" objects mixing syntax and semantics.

Definition 2.1. A **generalised term (g-term)** is an object obtained from a term in $\mathcal{L}$ by replacing zero or more of its variables with elements of D. A **generalised substitution (g-substitution)** is a finite mapping from variables to g-terms, denoted $\{x_1/h_1, \ldots, x_n/h_n\}$. The empty g-substitution is denoted $\emptyset$. The application of a g-substitution θ to a g-term t is defined as usual and denoted $t\theta$.

Given a g-term t, its $\mathcal{J}$-**evaluation** $[\![t]\!]_{\mathcal{J}}$ is obtained by replacing as many times as possible each sub-object of the form $f(d_1, \ldots, d_n)$, where $n \geq 0$ and each $d_i \in D$, with the domain element $f_{\mathcal{J}}(d_1, \ldots, d_n)$. A $\mathcal{J}$-**term** is the $\mathcal{J}$-evaluation of some g-term.

A $\mathcal{J}$-**substitution** is a g-substitution $\{x_1/h_1, \ldots, x_n/h_n\}$ where each h_i is a $\mathcal{J}$-term. The **composition** of two $\mathcal{J}$-substitutions θ and η, denoted $\theta\eta$, is the $\mathcal{J}$-substitution γ such that $x\gamma = [\![(x\theta)\eta]\!]_{\mathcal{J}}$ for all variables x. Note that $\theta\eta$ is uniquely defined since for each variable x, $x\theta$ and in turn $(x\theta)\eta$ are uniquely defined g-terms and so $[\![(x\theta)\eta]\!]_{\mathcal{J}}$ is a uniquely defined $\mathcal{J}$-term. We say that θ is **more general than** γ if $\gamma = \theta\eta$ for some η. We denote by $Subs$ the set of $\mathcal{J}$-substitutions.

Note that for a ground term t, the $\mathcal{J}$-evaluation $[\![t]\!]_{\mathcal{J}}$ coincides with the interpretation $\mathcal{J}(t)$.

The notation $\theta\eta$ always refers to the composition of $\mathcal{J}$-substitutions as defined above, never to the usual composition of substitutions. Note also that the application of a $\mathcal{J}$-substitution to a $\mathcal{J}$-term does not necessarily yield a $\mathcal{J}$-term.

The language of arithmetic expressions, with the usual precedences and interpretation $\mathcal{J}$ of all symbols, will be our running example. We denote the domain elements corresponding to the constants $0, 1, \ldots$ by $\mathbf{0}, \mathbf{1}, \ldots$. Then, $[\![x+1]\!]_{\mathcal{J}} = x + \mathbf{1}$. Moreover, $\theta = \{x/y+\mathbf{1}\}$ and $\eta = \{y/\mathbf{1}\}$ are $\mathcal{J}$-substitutions, and $\theta\eta = \{x/\mathbf{2}, y/\mathbf{1}\}$. Moreover, $(x+1)\theta\eta = \mathbf{2}+\mathbf{1}$, but note that $\mathbf{2}+\mathbf{1}$ is not a $\mathcal{J}$-term, while $[\![\mathbf{2}+\mathbf{1}]\!]_{\mathcal{J}} = \mathbf{3}$.

Apt remarks that the above construction could be rendered completely syntactical by introducing a constant for each domain element, but that this is not done to keep the notation simple. However, one could argue that replacing variables in a term by domain elements implies that one regards those domain elements as syntactic objects, so why not call them constants? In any case, the construction is convenient to capture (partial) evaluation of expressions.

The following proposition will be needed in the proof of Lemma 2.4.

Proposition 2.2. For all g-terms t and g-substitutions η, we have $[\![[\![t]\!]_{\mathcal{J}}\eta]\!]_{\mathcal{J}} = [\![t\eta]\!]_{\mathcal{J}}$.

Proof. The proof is by structural induction on t. If t is a variable, we have $[\![t]\!]_{\mathcal{J}} = t$ and so the statement holds.

Now suppose $t = f(t_1, \ldots, t_n)$. If t is ground, we have $[\![[\![t]\!]_{\mathcal{J}}\eta]\!]_{\mathcal{J}} = [\![[\![t]\!]_{\mathcal{J}}]\!]_{\mathcal{J}} = [\![t]\!]_{\mathcal{J}} = [\![t\eta]\!]_{\mathcal{J}}$. If t is non-ground, we have (using the appropriate definitions)

$$[\![[\![f(t_1, \ldots, t_n)]\!]_{\mathcal{J}}\eta]\!]_{\mathcal{J}} = [\![f([\![t_1]\!]_{\mathcal{J}}, \ldots, [\![t_n]\!]_{\mathcal{J}})\eta]\!]_{\mathcal{J}} = [\![f([\![t_1]\!]_{\mathcal{J}}\eta, \ldots, [\![t_n]\!]_{\mathcal{J}}\eta)]\!]_{\mathcal{J}} =$$

$$f([\![[\![t_1]\!]_{\mathcal{J}}\eta]\!]_{\mathcal{J}}, \ldots, [\![[\![t_n]\!]_{\mathcal{J}}\eta]\!]_{\mathcal{J}}) \overset{\text{ind. hyp.}}{=} f([\![t_1\eta]\!]_{\mathcal{J}}, \ldots, [\![t_n\eta]\!]_{\mathcal{J}}) =$$
$$[\![f(t_1\eta, \ldots, t_n\eta)]\!]_{\mathcal{J}} = [\![f(t_1, \ldots, t_n)\eta]\!]_{\mathcal{J}}.$$

$\square$

Given an equation, we are interested in substitutions that make the equation true in $\mathcal{J}$. For generality, the following definition is for a *set* of equations.

Definition 2.3. Let Eq be a finite set of equations and $\Theta \subseteq Subs \cup \{error\}$. A $\mathcal{J}$-substitution η is a **solution for** Eq if $[\![s\eta]\!]_{\mathcal{J}} = [\![t\eta]\!]_{\mathcal{J}}$ for all $s = t \in Eq$. We say Θ is **correct for** Eq if each $\gamma \in \Theta \setminus \{error\}$ is a solution for Eq. We say Θ is **complete for** Eq if for each η that is a solution for Eq, there exists $\gamma \in \Theta$ that is more general than η. We say Θ is **quasi-complete** if either Θ is complete or $error \in \Theta$.

By abuse of notation, we also use the above notions for a single equation $s = t$.

Correctness is an obvious requirement for a semantics. Completeness cannot be achieved in general, but at least solutions should be quasi-complete: *error* should indicate the fact that some solutions might have been lost.

The following lemma will be useful in showing completeness of the semantics.

Lemma 2.4. Let Eq be a set of equations. If $s = t \in Eq$ such that s is a variable, then for any solution η for Eq, we have that $\{s/[\![t]\!]_{\mathcal{J}}\}$ is more general than η.

Proof. Suppose η is a solution for Eq. We show that $\{s/[\![t]\!]_{\mathcal{J}}\}\eta = \eta$. For a variable x other than s, clearly $(x\{s/[\![t]\!]_{\mathcal{J}}\})\eta = x\eta$ and so $[\![(x\{s/[\![t]\!]_{\mathcal{J}}\})\eta]\!]_{\mathcal{J}} = [\![x\eta]\!]_{\mathcal{J}}$; for the variable s, using Prop. 2.2, we have $[\![(s\{s/[\![t]\!]_{\mathcal{J}}\})\eta]\!]_{\mathcal{J}} = [\![[\![t]\!]_{\mathcal{J}}\eta]\!]_{\mathcal{J}} = [\![t\eta]\!]_{\mathcal{J}} = [\![s\eta]\!]_{\mathcal{J}}$. Therefore $\{s/[\![t]\!]_{\mathcal{J}}\}\eta = \eta$. $\square$

Note that s may properly occur in t, and it is not claimed that $\{s/[\![t]\!]_{\mathcal{J}}\}$ is always a solution for $s = t$. For example, $\{x/x \cdot 1\}$ is not a solution for $x = x \cdot 1$, but $\{x/x \cdot 1\}$ is more general than any solution for $x = x \cdot 1$, say, $\{x/5\}$.

We now recall Apt's definition of the semantics $[\![.]\!]$ of an equation between two g-terms [1]. It maps an equation to a subset of $Subs \cup \{error\}$.

Definition 2.5.

$$[\![s = t]\!] := \begin{cases} \{\{s/[\![t]\!]_{\mathcal{J}}\}\} & \text{if } s \text{ is a variable not occurring in } t, & (i) \\ \{\{t/[\![s]\!]_{\mathcal{J}}\}\} & \text{if } t \text{ is a variable not occurring in } s, \\ & \text{and } s \text{ is not a variable}, & (ii) \\ \{\emptyset\} & \text{if } [\![s]\!]_{\mathcal{J}} = [\![t]\!]_{\mathcal{J}}, & (iii) \\ \emptyset & \text{if } s \text{ and } t \text{ are ground and } [\![s]\!]_{\mathcal{J}} \neq [\![t]\!]_{\mathcal{J}}, & (iv) \\ \{error\} & \text{otherwise.} & (v) \end{cases}$$

Apt's original definition is parametrised by a $\mathcal{J}$-substitution θ, with the intuitive meaning that s and t should be evaluated in context θ. We modified the definition in such a way that θ is effectively the empty substitution, and so we can omit it.

The following lemma states correctness and quasi-completeness of Def. 2.5. Essentially, it is a corollary of the Soundness Theorem 1 in [1], but we prefer to give our own formulation and proof here, for three reasons: (1) Apt does not explicitly introduce the concept of a correct and quasi-complete set; (2) our definition of $[\![.]\!]$ is not identical to Apt's; (3) Apt's result is more general, but a proof that our lemma is a corollary would be more complicated than our proof.

Lemma 2.6. $[\![s = t]\!]$ is correct and quasi-complete for $s = t$.

Proof. Consider the cases of Def. 2.5. Correctness is trivial for all five cases.

Completeness for case i follows from Lemma 2.4, and for case ii by symmetry. In case iii, $\{\emptyset\}$ is complete since $\emptyset$ is more general than any substitution. In case iv, since s and t are ground, there exists no substitution η such that $[\![s\eta]\!]_{\mathcal{J}} = [\![t\eta]\!]_{\mathcal{J}}$, and therefore $\emptyset$ is complete. In case v, quasi-completeness is trivial. $\square$

3   Our Improvement of Apt's Semantics

When is one subset of $Subs \cup \{error\}$ *better* than another? The more solutions the better, and not containing *error* is better than containing *error*.

Definition 3.1. Given $\Theta, \Theta' \subseteq Subs \cup \{error\}$, we say Θ' is **better than** Θ, written $\Theta' \geq \Theta$, if

- for each $\gamma \in \Theta \setminus \{error\}$, there exists a $\gamma' \in \Theta'$ that is more general; and
- $error \in \Theta'$ implies $error \in \Theta$.

We have $\{\gamma\} > \{\gamma, error\} > \{error\}$. Note that we understand *better* as *containing more information*, but computing better solutions may also be more expensive.

We propose a semantics based on syntactic unification [12]. For example, given $s = f(x, x, x, x)$ and $t = f(1 + 2, 2 + 1, 1 + y, z + 1)$, the semantics of $s = t$ contains the solution $\{x/3, y/2, z/2\}$. It uses an algorithm defined as rewrite rules on sets of equations with the special elements *fail* and *error*. The current equation set has to be matched against the pattern $\{s = t\} \uplus Eq$, meaning that $s = t$ is selected from it ($\uplus$ denotes disjoint union).

Given a g-substitution $\{s/t\}$, we denote by $Eq!\{s/t\}$ any equation set obtained from Eq by replacing *exactly one* occurrence of s with t. Note that this implies that case 4 below is not applicable if Eq contains no occurrence of s.

Definition 3.2. The relation $\longrightarrow$ is defined by the following rules.

$\{s = t\} \uplus Eq \longrightarrow$

$$
\begin{cases}
\{s_1 = t_1, \ldots, s_n = t_n\} \cup Eq & \text{if } s = f(s_1, \ldots, s_n),\ t = f(t_1, \ldots, t_n), \\
& \quad [\![s]\!]_{\mathcal{J}} \neq [\![t]\!]_{\mathcal{J}},\ \text{and } s,\ t \text{ are not both ground, (1)} \\
fail & \text{if } s \text{ and } t \text{ are ground and } [\![s]\!]_{\mathcal{J}} \neq [\![t]\!]_{\mathcal{J}}, \qquad (2) \\
Eq & \text{if } [\![s]\!]_{\mathcal{J}} = [\![t]\!]_{\mathcal{J}}, \qquad (3) \\
\{s = t\} \uplus Eq!\{s/t\} & \text{if } s \text{ is a variable and } s \neq t, \qquad (4) \\
\{t = s\} \uplus Eq & \text{if } t \text{ is a variable and } s \text{ is not,} \qquad (5) \\
error & \text{if } [\![s]\!]_{\mathcal{J}} \neq [\![t]\!]_{\mathcal{J}},\ \text{and } s,\ t \text{ are both non-} \\
& \quad \text{variable and not both ground, or } s \text{ is a} \\
& \quad \text{variable properly occurring in } t. \qquad (6)
\end{cases}
$$

An equation set Eq is in **solved form** if it has the form $\{x_1 = t_1, \ldots, x_n = t_n\}$ where the x_i are all different variables not occurring in any t_j.[2]

Unlike for the usual unification algorithm, non-determinism matters, so different choices may lead to different solutions. Case 1 is a subcase of 6. The rationale is that decomposition may lead to solutions, but alternative solutions may be lost. In case 4, the choice of the occurrence of s is non-deterministic. Also, since case 4 contains no *occurs check*, it overlaps with case 6. Note that if required simultaneous replacement of *all* occurrences of s in case 4, or if we imposed the occurs check, we would lose solutions. This is demonstrated in Ex. 3.6.

We will also see that due to the absence of the occurs check, there may be infinite $\longrightarrow$ sequences. We suspect that this termination problem is inherent, i.e., it is undecidable in general if an equation set reaches a solved form. One could have considered to impose the occurs check to achieve termination. The resulting semantics would still be an improvement over Apt's (see Ex. 3.6).

For a solved equation set $Eq = \{x_1 = t_1, \ldots, x_n = t_n\}$, we denote by $[\![Eq]\!]_{\mathcal{J}}$ the $\mathcal{J}$-substitution $\{x_1/[\![t_1]\!]_{\mathcal{J}}, \ldots, x_n/[\![t_n]\!]_{\mathcal{J}}\}$. We define a semantics $[\![s = t]\!]$.

Definition 3.3.

$$
[\![s = t]\!] := \{[\![Eq]\!]_{\mathcal{J}} \mid \{s = t\} \longrightarrow^* Eq,\ Eq \text{ is a solved equation set}\} \cup
$$
$$
\{error \mid \{s = t\} \longrightarrow^* error\}.
$$

In Sec. 4, we will see that it is crucial for our informal claim of optimality that the semantics is only defined for a *single* equation, not a set of equations.

One can argue how "natural" our semantics is. As the examples will show, in some cases it seems a mere coincidence if solutions are found or not. Nevertheless, our algorithm is plausible. This will be discussed further in the conclusion.

We compare $[\![.]\!]$ and $[\![.]\!]$.

Proposition 3.4. Consider the cases of Def. 2.5.

$$
\begin{aligned}
\text{In cases } i\text{-}iv, &\quad [\![s = t]\!] = [\![s = t]\!]; \\
\text{in case } v, &\quad [\![s = t]\!] \subseteq [\![s = t]\!].
\end{aligned}
$$

---

[2] This means that no $\longrightarrow$-step is possible from Eq.

Proof. In case i, $\{s = t\}$ is in solved form and so $[\![s = t]\!] = \{\{s/[\![t]\!]_{\mathcal{J}}\}\}$. In case ii, $\{s = t\} \longrightarrow \{t = s\}$ is the only rewrite sequence for $\{s = t\}$ and so $[\![s = t]\!] = \{\{t/[\![s]\!]_{\mathcal{J}}\}\}$. In case iii, the only rewrite sequence is $\{s = t\} \longrightarrow \emptyset$, and so $[\![s = t]\!] = \{\emptyset\}$. In case iv, the only rewrite sequence is $\{s = t\} \longrightarrow \textit{fail}$, and so $[\![s = t]\!] = \emptyset$. In case v, $\{s = t\} \longrightarrow^* \textit{error}$ and so $\{\textit{error}\} \subseteq [\![s = t]\!]$. $\square$

The proposition has the following theorem as consequence.

Theorem 3.5. For any terms s and t, $[\![s = t]\!]$ is better than $[s = t]$.

The following examples illustrate the algorithm and show that $[\![.]\!]$ is sometimes strictly better than $[.]$.

Example 3.6. We underline the selected equation and indicate for each step the applied case of Def. 3.2. The constant f should be thought of as (uninterpreted) tuple constructor. Note that the decomposition steps following the third line both add $1 = 1$, so we wrote a redundant second occurrence for clarity.

$$\{\underline{f(x,x,x,x) = f(1+2, 2+1, 1+y, z+1)}\} \xrightarrow{\ 1\ }^{2}$$
$$\{x = 1+2,\ x = 2+1,\ \underline{x = 1+y},\ x = z+1\} \xrightarrow{\ 4\ }^{2}$$
$$\{\underline{1+y = 1+2},\ z+1 = 2+1,\ x = 1+y,\ x = z+1\} \xrightarrow{\ 1\ }^{2}$$
$$\{\underline{1 = 1},\ y = 2,\ z = 2,\ (1 = 1,)\ x = 1+y,\ x = z+1\} \xrightarrow{\ 3\ }$$
$$\{y = 2,\ \underline{z = 2},\ x = 1+y,\ x = z+1\} \xrightarrow{\ 4\ }^{2}$$
$$\{y = 2,\ z = 2,\ x = 1+2,\ \underline{x = 2+1}\} \xrightarrow{\ 4\ }$$
$$\{y = 2,\ z = 2,\ \underline{2+1 = 1+2},\ x = 2+1\} \xrightarrow{\ 3\ }$$
$$\{y = 2,\ z = 2,\ x = 2+1\}.$$

In the next example, non-determinism leads to two different solutions:

$$\{\underline{f(x+y, x+y) = f(1+3, 2+2)}\} \xrightarrow{\ 1\ }$$

$$\{\underline{x+y = 1+3},\ x+y = 2+2\} \xrightarrow{\ 1\ } \qquad\qquad \{x+y = 1+3,\ \underline{x+y = 2+2}\} \xrightarrow{\ 1\ }$$
$$\{\underline{x = 1},\ y = 3,\ x+y = 2+2\} \xrightarrow{\ 4\ }^{2} \qquad \{x+y = 1+3,\ \underline{x = 2},\ y = 2\} \xrightarrow{\ 4\ }^{2}$$
$$\{x = 1,\ y = 3,\ \underline{1+3 = 2+2}\} \xrightarrow{\ 3\ } \qquad\ \{\underline{2+2 = 1+3},\ x = 2,\ y = 2\} \xrightarrow{\ 3\ }$$
$$\{x = 1,\ y = 3\}. \qquad\qquad\qquad\qquad\qquad \{x = 2,\ y = 2\}.$$

In the next example, we reach a solved form starting from an equation set that would fail in usual unification due to the occurs check.

$$\{\underline{f(x, 1 \cdot x) = f(x \cdot 1, x)}\} \xrightarrow{\ 1\ } \{\underline{x = x \cdot 1},\ 1 \cdot x = x\} \xrightarrow{\ 4\ }$$
$$\{x = x \cdot 1,\ \underline{1 \cdot x = x \cdot 1}\} \xrightarrow{\ 1\ } \{x = x \cdot 1,\ 1 = x,\ \underline{x = 1}\} \xrightarrow{\ 4\ }^{3}$$
$$\{\underline{1 = 1 \cdot 1},\ \underline{1 = 1},\ x = 1\} \xrightarrow{\ 3\ }^{2} \{x = 1\}.$$

Starting from the same equation, we can also get an infinite $\longrightarrow$ sequence due to case 4:

$$\{f(x, 1 \cdot x) = f(x \cdot 1, x)\} \xrightarrow{1} \{\underline{x = x \cdot 1},\ 1 \cdot x = x\} \xrightarrow{4}$$
$$\{\underline{x = x \cdot 1},\ 1 \cdot (x \cdot 1) = x\} \xrightarrow{4} \{\underline{x = x \cdot 1},\ 1 \cdot (x \cdot 1 \cdot 1) = x\} \longrightarrow \dots$$

In all examples, there is also a sequence leading to *error*. This adequately reflects that our algorithm misses some existing solutions.

Apt states that the aim of a semantics of an equation is to exhibit a *most general solution* if one exists, but that this problem cannot be dealt with in full generality [1], e.g. see the equation $x^2 = 1$. Even within the setting of not knowing anything about the algebra except how to evaluate ground terms, it may be possible to compute two different solutions to an equation. This is seen in the second example above, and it is in contrast to Apt's original semantics.

We will now show the correctness of the algorithm.

Proposition 3.7. Let Eq_0 be a set of equations. If $Eq_0 \longrightarrow Eq'$ and η is a solution for Eq', then η is a solution for Eq_0. If $Eq_0 \longrightarrow fail$ then Eq_0 has no solution.

Proof. If Eq_0 is empty, the statement is vacuously true. We adopt the notation of Def. 3.2: $Eq_0 = \{s = t\} \uplus Eq$. We go through the cases of Def. 3.2.

In case 1, a solution η has to fulfil $[\![s_i\eta]\!]_{\mathcal{J}} = [\![t_i\eta]\!]_{\mathcal{J}}$ for all $i \in \{1, \dots, n\}$. But then $[\![s\eta]\!]_{\mathcal{J}} = [\![f([\![s_1\eta]\!]_{\mathcal{J}}, \dots, [\![s_n\eta]\!]_{\mathcal{J}})]\!]_{\mathcal{J}} = [\![f([\![t_1\eta]\!]_{\mathcal{J}}, \dots, [\![t_n\eta]\!]_{\mathcal{J}})]\!]_{\mathcal{J}} = [\![t\eta]\!]_{\mathcal{J}}$ and so η is also a solution for $\{s = t\} \uplus Eq$.

In case 3, trivially $\{s = t\} \uplus Eq$ and Eq have the same solutions.

For case 4, let η be a solution for $\{s = t\}$, so $[\![s\eta]\!]_{\mathcal{J}} = [\![t\eta]\!]_{\mathcal{J}}$. Let r be any g-term and r' any g-term obtained from r by replacing 0 or more occurrences of s with t. It is straightforward that $[\![r\eta]\!]_{\mathcal{J}} = [\![r'\eta]\!]_{\mathcal{J}}$. But this implies that η is a solution for Eq iff η is a solution for $Eq!\{s/t\}$. Hence $\{s = t\} \uplus Eq$ and $\{s = t\} \uplus Eq!\{s/t\}$ have the same solutions.

In case 5, trivially $\{s = t\} \uplus Eq$ and $\{t = s\} \uplus Eq$ have the same solutions.

The second statement follows immediately from Def. 2.3. $\qquad\square$

Although a step by case 4 does not change the set of solutions, the choices of case 4 are critical for subsequent steps and hence for finding a solution (see Ex. 3.6).

Lemma 3.8. $[\![s = t]\!]$ is correct and quasi-complete for $\{s = t\}$.

Proof. Correctness follows from Prop. 3.7. Quasi-completeness follows from Prop. 3.4 and Lemma 2.6. $\qquad\square$

4 How Good Is Our Semantics?

Apt remarks that his semantics is sometimes weaker than that of logic programming, since an *error* may be returned where logic programming would compute a unifier and hence a solution. Our semantics mitigates this problem.

Proposition 4.1. Let Eq be a set of equations. If Eq has a most general unifier γ, then $Eq \longrightarrow^* Eq'$ where $[\![Eq']\!]_{\mathcal{J}} = \gamma$. Consequently, if $s = t$ has an mgu γ, then $\gamma \in [\![s = t]\!]$.

Proof. It is easy to see that for any rewrite sequence of the standard unification algorithm [12] ending in a solved form, there exists a rewrite sequence of our algorithm ending in the same solved form. □

Note however that the usual unification algorithm may reach *fail* where our algorithm reaches *error* or a solution.

A good semantics should avoid the *error* case. Now our algorithm specifies that whenever a step by case 1 is possible, a step going to *error* is also possible. The following lemma states that this must be so to ensure quasi-completeness: it is impossible in general to know if a step by case 1 has lost a solution.

Lemma 4.2. Let Eq be a set of equations and $s = f(s_1,\ldots,s_n)$, $t = f(t_1,\ldots,t_n)$.

There exists an algebra such that $\{s = t\} \uplus Eq$ and $\{s_1 = t_1,\ldots,s_n = t_n\} \cup Eq$ have the same solutions.

If moreover $s \neq t$, then there exists an algebra $\mathcal{J}$ and $\mathcal{J}$-substitution η such that η is a solution for $s = t$ but not for $\{s_1 = t_1,\ldots,s_n = t_n\}$.

Proof. For the first part, simply take $\mathcal{J}$ being the Herbrand algebra.

On the other hand, we show that there exists a $\mathcal{J}$ and a $\mathcal{J}$-substitution η such that η is a solution for $\{s = t\}$ but not for $\{s_1 = t_1,\ldots,s_n = t_n\}$. Without loss of generality assume that s is not a subterm of any t_i (otherwise reverse the roles of s and t). Let D_V be the set containing a unique "constant" c_x, not in $\mathcal{L}$, for each variable x in $s = t$. Let D be the set of ground terms of $\mathcal{L} \cup D_V$. Let η be the $\mathcal{J}$-substitution $\{x/c_x \mid c_x \in D_V\}$. We construct $\mathcal{J}$ so that it is essentially a Herbrand algebra (but note that $\mathcal{J}$ is still defined for the language $\mathcal{L}$), except in one point. Namely, for any function symbol h in $\mathcal{L}$:

$$\mathcal{J}(h(r_1,\ldots,r_m)) := \begin{cases} f(t_1,\ldots,t_n)\eta & \text{if } h(r_1,\ldots,r_m) = f(s_1,\ldots,s_n)\eta, \\ h(\mathcal{J}(r_1),\ldots,\mathcal{J}(r_m)) & \text{otherwise.} \end{cases}$$

By construction, $s_i \neq t_i$ implies $[\![s_i\eta]\!]_{\mathcal{J}} \neq [\![t_i\eta]\!]_{\mathcal{J}}$ for all $i \in \{1,\ldots,n\}$, but $[\![s\eta]\!]_{\mathcal{J}} = [\![t\eta]\!]_{\mathcal{J}}$. Since $s \neq t$, there is at least one i such that $s_i \neq t_i$, and so η is a solution for $s = t$ but not for $\{s_1 = t_1,\ldots,s_n = t_n\}$. □

The fact that we speak of "constructing" $\mathcal{J}$ may be misleading. In fact, one should read the second part of the lemma as follows: if all we know is that s and t are not both ground and that $[\![s]\!]_{\mathcal{J}} \neq [\![t]\!]_{\mathcal{J}}$, so cases 2 and 3 can be excluded, then it is impossible to be sure that $\mathcal{J}$ is not the contrived algebra of our proof.

The construction does not generalise to a statement about $\{s = t\} \uplus Eq$ and $\{s_1 = t_1,\ldots,s_n = t_n\} \cup Eq$. If "by chance" $\{s_1 = t_1,\ldots,s_n = t_n\} \subseteq Eq$, then $\{s = t\} \uplus Eq$ and $\{s_1 = t_1,\ldots,s_n = t_n\} \cup Eq$ have the same solutions. In fact, the second part of the lemma does not hold for a set of more than one equation. For example, if $Eq = \{x^2 = 1^2, \; x = 1\}$, clearly $\{x/\mathbf{1}\}$ is the most general solution, and so it is "sub-optimal" to allow for $Eq \longrightarrow error$. However, starting from a set $\{s = t\}$, the only way to arrive at a set of more than one element is by a first rewriting step by case 1. And then, there is also a rewriting step to $error$ by case 6. So we have $error \in [\![s = t]\!]$ anyway.

The following lemma shows that also in the cases that lead to failure in usual unification, it is justified that our algorithm has a rewrite step going to $error$.

Lemma 4.3. Let Eq be a set of equations. If $Eq = \{s = t\}$ such that either

- $s = f(\ldots)$ and $t = g(\ldots)$ are not both ground, where $f \neq g$, or
- s is a variable properly occurring in t,

then there exists an algebra $\mathcal{J}$ such that Eq has no solution. On the other hand, there exists an algebra $\mathcal{J}$ and $\mathcal{J}$-substitution η such that η is a solution for Eq.

Proof. For the first part, simply take $\mathcal{J}$ being the Herbrand algebra.

On the other hand, if $\mathcal{J}$ is the algebra that maps all ground terms to the same domain element, then any η making Eq ground is a solution. □

Summarising, all the rewriting steps guarantee correctness of computed solutions by Prop. 3.7. Moreover, Lemmas 4.2 and 4.3 show that the initial set $\{s = t\}$ can be rewritten to $error$ only in cases where it is impossible to be sure that other rewriting steps would not lose a solution.

Does this mean that our semantics is optimal? Yes, if one is prepared to accept that the semantics is based on rewriting sets of equations, and that the algorithm of Def. 3.2 tries all conceivable manipulations based on syntactic criteria and $\mathcal{J}$-evaluation of ground terms in an exhaustive way.

But in a formal sense, it is always possible to "improve" a semantics. An example is stated in item 3 in the introduction. Since 1 happens to occur in $x + 1 = 2$, eureka!, we would compute the solution $\{x/\mathbf{1}\}$. But we still cannot solve $x + 1 = 3$. Well then, maybe the semantics should be improved by considering replacements using any terms that can be formed from the symbols in the equation. $1 + 1$ is such a term, and indeed, $\{x/\mathbf{2}\}$ is a solution . . .

5 Conclusion, Related Work, and Outlook

Original aims of this work. The motivating question of Apt's [1] work is: within the computation as deduction paradigm, how can one effectively define computations that take place on arbitrary interpretations, rather than the Herbrand interpretation? We focused here on the problem of solving first-order equations.

Our aim was to prove that Apt's semantics of first-order logic with equality is optimal in the sense that it is the best one can do for an arbitrary algebra. Such a result would hinge on the formalisation of "for an arbitrary algebra".

This paper should have concluded Apt's work with a formal result stating to what extent one can define computations that take place on arbitrary interpretations. It would then be clear that computations that go further can only be described on a more abstract, non-constructive level, or the description can apply only to a specific interpretation. It was hoped that this would be a contribution to our understanding of what can be implemented in first-order logic.

Achievements. We have missed our aim of proving that Apt's semantics is optimal. While working out the formalisation of "for an arbitrary algebra", we discovered improvements of his allegedly optimal semantics. We have argued for an improved semantics, but we cannot claim that this semantics is optimal in a formal sense, since there are always strictly better, but contrived, semantics.

Apt remarks that his semantics is sometimes weaker than that of logic programming. Our improvement mitigates this problem (see Prop. 4.1).

Being modelled on syntactic unification, our algorithm is plausible, in contrast to the algorithm suggested in item 3 in the introduction. Nevertheless, looking at Ex. 3.6, it seems somewhat coincidental under which circumstances our algorithm achieves a proper improvement compared to Apt's semantics. One cannot imagine that our algorithm could be the core of an efficient solver for arithmetic equations, which is something one might have hoped for. Under efficiency aspects, our algorithm is probably already taking the principle of domain-independence too far.

Extensions to arbitrary formulas. We have given a semantics for equations. This semantics may be extended to a semantics for arbitrary formulas as this has been done for $[\![.]\!]$ in [1], but our informal optimality claim does not necessarily hold for this extension. The main reason is that conjunction is interpreted as *sequential* composition, rather than *parallel* composition. For example, $[\![x = 1 \wedge x^2 = 1]\!] = \{\{x/1\}\}$ but $[\![x^2 = 1 \wedge x = 1]\!] = \{error\}$.

Apt and Vermeulen [5] have recently proposed a more general framework of semantics, regarding first-order logic as a constraint programming language. In this framework, equations (and other atoms) are handled by a procedure *infer*. As an example, the authors instantiate the framework so that it exactly models the semantics $[\![.]\!]$. It would be straightforward to do the same for the semantics $[\![.]\!]$ developed here.

It would also be possible to instantiate the framework so that the constraint solving power on a particular equation is exactly that of $[\![.]\!]$, but in addition, equations can be treated as *passive* constraints. For example, in the formula above, the processing of $x^2 = 1$ would be postponed until after the equation $x = 1$ has been processed. This would have the advantage that *error* is avoided in more cases, but the general limitations of how much one can compute over an arbitrary algebra still apply.

Other approaches. One difference between the *formulas as programs* approach [1,2] and (constraint) logic programming ((C)LP) [9,10] is that the latter is based on a smaller subset of first-order logic. However, it has previously been admitted [2] that this difference is not so essential due to other approaches to extending the formula set covered by LP [7,11,14]. It is also said that the approach of [14] could be applied to *constraint* LP provided that negation [6,10] is added. However, Apt and Vermeulen [5] argue that the formulas as programs approach provides a more direct answer to the question of how first-order formulas can be given a semantics than [14].

Generally, Apt's semantics [1] is weaker than that of CLP for any given specialised domain and solver; e.g., his semantics returns *error* for the equation $x - 1 = 0$ where an arithmetic constraint solver may return the solution $\{x/1\}$. On the other hand, Apt's semantics is more general than Prolog in its treatment of arithmetic, since, e.g., $1 = x \land y = x + 1$ will compute the result $\{x/1, y/2\}$.

Apt and Bezem [2] say that logic programming is a restriction of the formulas as programs approach in that terms are interpreted over the Herbrand domain, but that on the other hand, this allows one to solve effectively (without resorting to *error*) all equality atoms. Although the treatment of equations in [1] generalises that of [2], and we generalise it further here, this argument still applies in principle. Our semantics contains all unifiers but also *error* to indicate possible missing solutions.

Apt [1] remarks that previous approaches did not provide a satisfactory answer to the question of computing over an arbitrary algebra. For CLP, the reason is that the computation depends on external procedures that have to be implemented separately for each interpretation. We would alleviate this criticism. First, one could argue that the evaluation of ground terms in the algebra (which we presuppose) is also a kind of external procedure. More importantly, while it is interesting to study the question to which extent computations over an arbitrary algebra can be defined constructively, at some point one will have to study *specific* algebras and devise *specific* solving procedures for them.

In the context of constraint programming, it has already been observed in [13] that some equations (constraints) such as $U = 3$ are independent of any particular structure and can be solved without invoking a constraint solver.

Apt [1] also remarks that the programming language Gödel [8] provides a special interpretation for certain built-in types, e.g. arithmetic types, but user-defined types are always given the Herbrand interpretation. He criticises that equality is treated differently depending on the type without a proper account for this in the theoretical model. However, Gödel interprets equality as the identity relation on the domain. The seemingly different treatment of equality is simply a consequence of the fact that some types are given a special interpretation.

Outlook. Be it Apt's original semantics or our improvement — ultimately, one cannot be satisfied with the "programming language" presented here, and so we will now outline a more general computation formalism, on an abstract level.

We consider a first-order language together with an algebra $\mathcal{J}$. Among the predicate symbols, we distinguish *user-defined* predicates, also called *procedures*, and *built-in* predicates, the latter including the symbol $=$.

There is an interpretation $\mathcal{I}$, extending the algebra $\mathcal{J}$ and defined for all built-in predicates, such that $=_{\mathcal{I}}$ is the identity on the domain. For an atom $p(t_1, \ldots, t_n)$ where p is built-in, the semantics $[\![p(t_1, \ldots, t_n)]\!]$ should contain $\mathcal{J}$-substitutions γ such that $p_{\mathcal{I}}([\![t_1\gamma]\!]_{\mathcal{J}}, \ldots, [\![t_n\gamma]\!]_{\mathcal{J}})$ is true. For example, if `member` is a built-in list membership predicate, $[\![\texttt{member}(x, [3])]\!]$ should contain the $\mathcal{J}$-substitution $\{x/3\}$.

Still considering built-in predicates, one could envisage that whenever a set of $\mathcal{J}$-substitutions cannot effectively be computed for an atom, then the treatment of this atom should be postponed. In this view, built-in predicates are *constraint* predicates and the corresponding atoms are put in a *constraint store* [5].

Concerning procedures, the semantics should be parametrised by a set of definitions (given by the user) of the form $p(x_1, \ldots, x_n) \leftrightarrow \psi$ where ψ is a formula that may contain p. The semantics of an atom $p(t_1, \ldots, t_n)$ is then obtained by replacing the atom with the formula $\psi\{x_1/t_1, \ldots, x_n/t_n\}$.

This setting can be related to imperative programming, and be shown to be a generalisation of (C)LP. Developing this setting has partly been done [1,2,3,4, 5], and partly it is the topic for future work.

References

1. K. R. Apt. A denotational semantics for first-order logic. In J. Lloyd et al., editors, *Proceedings of the First International Conference on Computational Logic*, volume 1861 of *LNAI*, pages 53–69. Springer-Verlag, 2000.
2. K. R. Apt and M. Bezem. Formulas as programs. In K. R. Apt, V. Marek, M. Truszczynski, and D. S. Warren, editors, *The Logic Programming Paradigm: A 25 Years Perspective*, pages 75–107. Springer-Verlag, 1999.
3. K. R. Apt, J. Brunekreef, A. Schaerf, and V. Partington. Alma-0: An imperative language that supports declarative programming. *ACM Transactions on Programming Languages and Systems*, 20(5):1014–1066, 1998.
4. K. R. Apt and J.-G. Smaus. Rule-based versus procedure-based view of logic programming. *Joint Bulletin of the Novosibirsk Computing Center and Institute of Informatics Systems; Series: Computer Science*, 16:75–97, 2001.
5. K. R. Apt and C. F. M. Vermeulen. First-order logic as a constraint programming language. In M. Baaz and A. Voronkov, editors, *Proceedings of the 9th International Conference on Logic for Programming, Artificial Intelligence and Reasoning*, volume 2514 of *LNCS*, pages 19–35. Springer-Verlag, 2002.
6. F. S. de Boer, A. Di Pierro, and C. Palamidessi. An algebraic perspective of constraint logic programming. *Journal of Logic and Computation*, 7(1):1–38, 1997.
7. K. L. Clark. Negation as failure. In H. Gallaire and J. Minker, editors, *Advances in Data Base Theory*, pages 293–322. Plenum Press, 1978.
8. P. M. Hill and J. W. Lloyd. *The Gödel Programming Language*. MIT Press, 1994.
9. J. Jaffar and M. J. Maher. Constraint logic programming: A survey. *Journal of Logic Programming*, 19/20:503–581, 1994.
10. J. Jaffar, M. J. Maher, K. Marriott, and P. J. Stuckey. The semantics of constraint logic programs. *Journal of Logic Programming*, 37(1-3):1–46, 1998.
11. K. Kunen. Negation in logic programming. *Journal of Logic Programming*, 4(4):289–308, 1987.
12. J.-L. Lassez, M. J. Maher, and K. Marriott. Unification revisited. In J. Minker, editor, *Proceedings of Foundations of Deductive Databases and Logic Programming*, pages 587–625. Morgan Kaufmann, 1988.
13. P. Lim and P. J. Stuckey. A constraint logic programming shell. In P. Deransart and J. Małuszynski, editors, *Proceedings of the 2nd International Workshop on Programming Language Implementation and Logic Programming*, volume 456 of *LNCS*, pages 75–88. Springer-Verlag, 1990.
14. J. W. Lloyd and R. W. Topor. Making Prolog more expressive. *Journal of Logic Programming*, 1(3):225–240, 1984.

Loop Formulas for Disjunctive Logic Programs

Joohyung Lee and Vladimir Lifschitz

Department of Computer Sciences
University of Texas, Austin, USA
{appsmurf,vl}@cs.utexas.edu

Abstract. We extend Clark's definition of a completed program and the definition of a loop formula due to Lin and Zhao to disjunctive logic programs. Our main result, generalizing the Lin/Zhao theorem, shows that answer sets for a disjunctive program can be characterized as the models of its completion that satisfy the loop formulas. The concept of a tight program and Fages' theorem are extended to disjunctive programs as well.

1 Introduction

Among the theories proposed to explain the semantics of "negation as failure" in logic programming, influential are the completion semantics [Clark, 1978] and the stable model or the answer set semantics [Gelfond and Lifschitz, 1988]. It is well known that an answer set for a logic program is also a model of its completion, while the converse, generally, does not hold.[1]

When are the two semantics equivalent to each other? François Fages [1994] showed that a certain syntactic condition, which is now called "tightness", is sufficient for establishing the equivalence between them. Esra Erdem and Vladimir Lifschitz [2003] generalized Fages' theorem and extended it to programs with nested expressions (in the sense of [Lifschitz et al., 1999]) in the bodies of rules.

In view of Fages' theorem, answer sets for a tight program can be computed by a satisfiability solver (SAT solver) [Babovich et al., 2000]. CMODELS[2], a system based on this idea, uses SAT solvers to compute answer sets for finite nondisjunctive logic programs that are tight or that can be turned into tight programs by simple equivalent transformations. In several benchmark examples, it found answer sets faster than SMODELS[3], a general-purpose answer set solver.

On the other hand, Fangzhen Lin and Yuting Zhao [2002] were interested in the relationship between completion and answer sets from a different point of view. They showed that a rather simple extension of a program's completion gives a set of formulas that describes the program's answer sets correctly in all cases—even when the program is not tight. We just need to extend the completion by

---

[1] In this paper, we study propositional (grounded) logic programs only, and refer to the propositional case of Clark's completion.

[2] http://www.cs.utexas.edu/users/tag/cmodels/.

[3] http://www.tcs.hut.fi/Software/smodels/.

C. Palamidessi (Ed.): ICLP 2003, LNCS 2916, pp. 451–465, 2003.
© Springer-Verlag Berlin Heidelberg 2003

adding what they call "loop formulas." According to their main theorem, models of the extended completion are identical to the program's answer sets. Their system ASSAT[4] is similar to CMODELS in the sense that it uses SAT solvers for computing answer sets, but it is not limited to tight programs.

However, the concepts of completion and a loop formula have been defined so far for nondisjunctive programs only. In some cases disjunctive rules can be equivalently turned into nondisjunctive rules (see, for instance, [Erdem and Lifschitz, 1999]). But a complexity result tells us that there is no efficient translation from arbitrary disjunctive programs to nondisjunctive programs: the problem of the existence of an answer set for a disjunctive program is Σ_2^P-hard [Eiter and Gottlob, 1993, Corollary 3.8], while the same problem for a nondisjunctive program is in class NP.

In this note, we extend Clark's completion and the definition of a loop formula due to Lin and Zhao to disjunctive logic programs and, more generally, to arbitrary programs with nested expressions. Our main theorem generalizes the Lin/Zhao theorem mentioned above and shows that answer sets for a disjunctive program can be characterized as the models of its completion that satisfy the loop formulas. We extend the concept of a tight program to disjunctive programs as well. For a tight program, adding the loop formulas does not affect the models of completion. This fact leads to extending Fages' theorem to disjunctive programs.

A puzzling feature of Lin and Zhao's extension of completion with loop formulas is that even though their procedure is essentially a reduction of one NP-complete problem to another NP-complete problem, it is not a polynomial time reduction. The number of loop formulas can grow exponentially in the worst case. Our result explains this phenomenon: since a small modification of the definition of a loop formula is applicable to a Σ_2^P-hard problem, the possibility of exponentially many loop formulas is natural.

Another reason why our extension of the Lin/Zhao theorem may be interesting is that it provides an alternative method of computing answer sets for programs more general than those that are currently handled by ASSAT. Yuliya Babovich and Marco Maratea are using this idea to adapt the ASSAT algorithm to programs with cardinality constraints (personal communication). It would be interesting to extend their implementation to disjunctive programs and compare its performance with that of DLV[5], an existing answer set solver that can deal with disjunctive programs.

We begin with a review of the definition of answer sets in the next section, and extend Clark's completion to disjunctive programs in Section 3. The concepts of a loop formula and the main result of [Lin and Zhao, 2002] are extended to disjunctive programs in Section 4, and the definition of tightness is extended to disjunctive programs in Section 5. Related work is discussed in Section 6, and some of the proofs are presented in Section 7.

---

[4] http://assat.cs.ust.hk/.

[5] http://www.dbai.tuwien.ac.at/proj/dlv/.

2   Review of the Answer Set Semantics

This section is a review of the answer set semantics for finite programs with nested expressions, but without classical negation.[6]

We first define the syntax of formulas, rules and logic programs. *Formulas* are formed from propositional atoms and 0-place connectives $\top$ and $\bot$ using negation (*not*), conjunction (,) and disjunction (;). If $m = 0$ then $F_1, \ldots, F_m$ is understood as $\top$ and $F_1; \ldots; F_m$ is understood as $\bot$.

A *rule* is an expression of the form

$$Head \leftarrow Body$$

where *Head* and *Body* are formulas. A rule of the form *Head* $\leftarrow \top$ can be abbreviated as *Head*.

A *(logic) program* is a finite set of rules.

The *satisfaction relation* $X \models F$ between a set X of atoms and a formula F is defined recursively, as follows:

- for an atom a, $X \models a$ if $a \in X$
- $X \models \top$
- $X \not\models \bot$
- $X \models (F, G)$ if $X \models F$ and $X \models G$
- $X \models (F; G)$ if $X \models F$ or $X \models G$
- $X \models not\ F$ if $X \not\models F$.

This definition is equivalent to the usual definition of satisfaction in propositional logic if we agree (as we do in this note) to identify '*not*' with '$\neg$', ',' with '$\wedge$', and ';' with '$\vee$'.

We say that a set X of atoms *satisfies* a rule *Head* $\leftarrow$ *Body* if $X \models Head$ whenever $X \models Body$, and say that X *satisfies* a program Π (symbolically, $X \models \Pi$) if X satisfies every rule of Π.

The *reduct* F^X of a formula F with respect to a set X of atoms is defined recursively, as follows:

- if F is an atom or a 0-place connective, then $F^X = F$
- $(F, G)^X = F^X, G^X$
- $(F; G)^X = F^X; G^X$
- $(not\ F)^X = \begin{cases} \bot, & \text{if } X \models F, \\ \top, & \text{otherwise.} \end{cases}$

The *reduct* Π^X of a program Π with respect to X is the set of rules

$$F^X \leftarrow G^X$$

for all rules $F \leftarrow G$ in Π.

---

[6] The syntax of a program defined in [Lifschitz *et al.*, 1999] is more general than the syntax defined here in that a program can be infinite and can contain classical negation ($\neg$). Classical negation can be easily eliminated by introducing auxiliary atoms as explained in [Lifschitz *et al.*, 2001, Section 5].

Finally, a set X of atoms is an *answer set* for a program Π if X is minimal among the sets of atoms that satisfy the reduct Π^X [Lifschitz *et al.*, 1999].[7]

A program Π_1 is *strongly equivalent* to a program Π_2 if, for every program Π, $\Pi_1 \cup \Pi$ has the same answer sets as $\Pi_2 \cup \Pi$ [Lifschitz *et al.*, 2001]. Section 4 of [Lifschitz *et al.*, 1999] contains a number of examples of strongly equivalent programs. (The equivalence relation defined in that paper is even stronger than strong equivalence.)

We understand the term *clause* to mean a disjunction of distinct atoms $a_1; \ldots; a_n$ $(n \geq 0)$, and we identify a clause with the corresponding set of its atoms.

Using Propositions 3–6 of [Lifschitz *et al.*, 1999], it is easy to prove the following fact.

Fact 1 *Any rule is strongly equivalent to a finite set of rules of the form*

$$A \leftarrow Body \tag{1}$$

where A is a clause and Body is a formula.

The form of rules can be made even more special:

Fact 2 *Any rule is strongly equivalent to a finite set of rules of the form*

$$A \leftarrow B, F \tag{2}$$

where A is a clause, B is a conjunction of atoms and F is a formula in which every occurrence of each atom is in the scope of negation as failure.

We can further specialize the form of F and require that it be a formula of the form
$$not\ a_1, \ldots, not\ a_m, not\ not\ a_{m+1}, \ldots, not\ not\ a_n$$
$(0 \leq m \leq n)$, where a_i $(1 \leq i \leq n)$ are atoms.

3 Completion

Let Π be a logic program whose rules have the form (1). The *completion* of Π, $Comp(\Pi)$, is defined to be the set of propositional formulas that consists of the implication

$$Body \supset A \tag{3}$$

for every rule (1) in Π, and the implication

$$a \supset \bigvee_{\substack{A \leftarrow Body\ \in\ \Pi \\ a \in A}} \left(Body \wedge \bigwedge_{p \in A \setminus \{a\}} \neg p \right) \tag{4}$$

---

[7] In this definition, minimality is understood as minimality relative to set inclusion. In other words, we say that X is an answer set for Π if X satisfies Π^X but no proper subset of X satisfies Π^X.

for each atom a. When the head of every rule of Π is a single atom, $Comp(\Pi)$ is equivalent to the propositional case of completion defined in [Lloyd and Topor, 1984].

For instance, let Π_1 be the program:

$$p \ ; \ q.$$

The answer sets for Π_1 are $\{p\}$ and $\{q\}$. $Comp(\Pi_1)$ is

$$p \vee q$$
$$p \supset \neg q$$
$$q \supset \neg p$$

and its models are $\{p\}$ and $\{q\}$ also.[8]

Π_2 is the following program that adds two rules to Π_1:

$$p \ ; \ q$$
$$p \leftarrow q$$
$$q \leftarrow p.$$

The only answer set for Π_2 is $\{p, q\}$. $Comp(\Pi_2)$ is

$$p \vee q$$
$$q \supset p$$
$$p \supset q$$
$$p \supset \neg q \vee q$$
$$q \supset \neg p \vee p,$$

and its only model is $\{p, q\}$ also.

The following proposition generalizes the property of completion familiar from [Marek and Subrahmanian, 1989] to disjunctive programs:

Proposition 1 *For any program Π whose rules have the form (1) and any set X of atoms, if X is an answer set for Π then X is a model of $Comp(\Pi)$.*

It is well known that the converse of Proposition 1 does not hold; the one-rule program $p \leftarrow p$ is a standard counterexample. The following program Π_3 is another example of this kind, which contains a disjunctive rule:

$$p \ ; \ r \leftarrow q$$
$$q \leftarrow p$$
$$p \leftarrow not \ r$$
$$r \leftarrow r.$$

---

[8] We identify an interpretation with the set of atoms that are true in it.

The only answer set for $\varPi_3$ is $\{p, q\}$. $Comp(\varPi_3)$ is

$$
\begin{aligned}
q &\supset p \lor r \\
p &\supset q \\
\neg r &\supset p \\
r &\supset r \\
p &\supset (q \land \neg r) \lor \neg r \\
q &\supset p \\
r &\supset (q \land \neg p) \lor r
\end{aligned}
\tag{5}
$$

and its models are $\{p, q\}$ and $\{r\}$.

In the next section, the method of strengthening the completion defined in [Lin and Zhao, 2002] is extended to any program whose rules have the form (2).

4   Loop Formulas

For any formula F, by $pa(F)$ we denote the set of its "positive atoms": the set of all atoms a such that at least one occurrence of a in F is not in the scope of negation as failure.

Let $\varPi$ be a program. The *positive dependency graph* of $\varPi$ is the directed graph G such that

- the vertices of G are the atoms occurring in $\varPi$, and
- for every rule *Head* ← *Body* in $\varPi$, G has an edge from each atom in $pa(Head)$ to each atom in $pa(Body)$.

For instance, if all rules of $\varPi$ have the form (2), then the edges of G go from atoms in A to atoms in B.

A nonempty set L of atoms is called a *loop* of $\varPi$ if, for every pair a_1, a_2 of atoms in L, there exists a path of nonzero length from a_1 to a_2 in the positive dependency graph of $\varPi$ such that all vertices in this path belong to L. For example, for the programs in Section 3, $\varPi_1$ has no loops; $\varPi_2$ has one loop: $\{p, q\}$; $\varPi_3$ has two loops: $\{p, q\}$ and $\{r\}$.

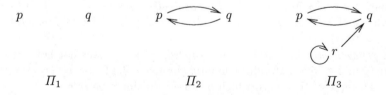

$$\varPi_1 \qquad\qquad\qquad \varPi_2 \qquad\qquad\qquad \varPi_3$$

Fig. 1. Positive dependency graphs

The definition of a loop is essentially equivalent to the corresponding definition from [Lin and Zhao, 2002] in the case when the program is nondisjunctive.[9]

The rest of this section assumes that every rule of $\varPi$ has the form (2).

---

[9] A program is *nondisjunctive* if the head of every rule in it is either an atom or $\bot$.

For any loop L of Π, by $R(L)$ we denote the set of formulas

$$B \wedge F \wedge \bigwedge_{p \in A \setminus L} \neg p$$

for all rules (2) in Π such that $A \cap L \neq \emptyset$ and $B \cap L = \emptyset$.[10] By $CLF(L)$ we denote the *conjunctive loop formula* for L:

$$CLF(L) = \bigwedge L \supset \bigvee R(L).\text{[11]} \tag{6}$$

By $CLF(\Pi)$ we denote the set of all conjunctive loop formulas for Π:

$$CLF(\Pi) = \{CLF(L) \; : \; L \text{ is a loop of } \Pi\}.$$

For instance, $CLF(\Pi_1)$ is $\emptyset$ because Π_1 has no loops. For the only loop $L = \{p, q\}$ of Π_2, $R(L)$ is $\{\top\}$, so that $LF(\Pi_2) = \{p \wedge q \supset \top\}$, which is tautological. For the two loops $L_1 = \{p, q\}$ and $L_2 = \{r\}$ of Π_3, $R(L_1)$ is $\{\neg r\}$ and $R(L_2)$ is $\{q \wedge \neg p\}$, so that $CLF(\Pi_3) = \{p \wedge q \supset \neg r, \; r \supset q \wedge \neg p\}$.

An alternative (stronger) definition of a loop formula replaces $\bigwedge$ in the antecedent of (11) with $\bigvee$. Let's call this formula $DLF(L)$ (*disjunctive loop formula*):

$$DLF(L) = \bigvee L \supset \bigvee R(L). \tag{7}$$

This second definition is a direct generalization of the Lin/Zhao definition of a loop formula to disjunctive programs. $DLF(\Pi)$ is the set of all disjunctive loop formulas for Π.

Syntactically, the loop formulas (11), (7) are somewhat similar to completion formulas (4). One difference is that their antecedent may contain several atoms, rather than a single atom. Accordingly, each multiple conjunction in the consequent of a loop formula extends over the atoms in $A \setminus L$, instead of the atoms in $A \setminus \{a\}$. Second, the multiple disjunction in the consequent of a loop formula is limited to the rules satisfying the condition $B \cap L = \emptyset$; this condition has no counterpart in the definition of completion.

Intuitively, each disjunct in the consequent of a completion formula (4) characterizes a source of support for the atom a, whereas each disjunct in the consequents of loop formulas (11), (7) characterizes a source of support for the loop L where the support comes from outside of L. For instance, if a model X of loop formula (11) contains the loop L, then the program contains a rule (2) such that

- L contains an atom from the head of the rule ($A \cap L \neq \emptyset$), but no positive atoms from the body ($B \cap L = \emptyset$),
- X satisfies the body of the rule ($X \models B \wedge F$) but not the atoms in the head that do not belong to L ($X \models \neg p$ for all $p \in A \setminus L$).

---

[10] Here we identify the conjunction B with the set of its atoms.

[11] The expression $\bigwedge L$ in the antecedent stands for the conjunction of all elements of L. The expression in the consequent has a similar meaning.

We are now ready to state our main theorem.

Theorem 1 *For any program Π whose rules have the form (2) and any set X of atoms, the following conditions are equivalent:*

(a) X is an answer set for Π,
(b) X is a model of $Comp(\Pi) \cup CLF(\Pi)$,
(c) X is a model of $Comp(\Pi) \cup DLF(\Pi)$.

The theorem tells us that answer sets for any logic program Π can be found by computing the models of the corresponding propositional theory $Comp(\Pi) \cup CLF(\Pi)$ (or $Comp(\Pi) \cup DLF(\Pi)$). For example, the answer sets for each of the programs Π_1, Π_2 can be found by computing the models of its completion. The only answer set for Π_3 is the first of the two models $\{p, q\}$ and $\{r\}$ of its completion (5) because that model satisfies the loop formulas $p \wedge q \supset \neg r$, $r \supset q \wedge \neg p$; the second model of the completion does not have this property.

From the fact that (b) and (c) are equivalent to each other we can infer that the antecedent of a loop formula can be allowed to be more general. For any loop L, let F_L be a formula formed from atoms in L using conjunctions and disjunctions. For instance, F_L can be any single atom that belongs to L or a conjunction or disjunction of several atoms from L. It is clear that F_L entails $\bigvee L$ and is entailed by $\bigwedge L$. We conclude:

Corollary 1 *For any program Π whose rules have the form (2) and any set X of atoms, the condition that X is a model of*

$$Comp(\Pi) \cup \left\{ F_L \supset \bigvee R(L) \; : \; L \text{ is a loop of } \Pi \right\}$$

is equivalent to each of conditions (a)–(c) from Theorem 1.

5   Tight Programs

About a program we say that it is *absolutely tight* if it has no loops. For instance, program Π_1 from Section 3 is absolutely tight, and programs Π_2, Π_3 are not. In the case when the program is nondisjunctive, this definition has the same meaning as the definition from [Erdem and Lifschitz, 2003, Section 5]. On the other hand, the latter is more general in the sense that it is applicable to infinite programs and programs with classical negation.

It is clear from Theorem 1 that for any absolutely tight program Π whose rules have the form (2), X is an answer set for Π iff X satisfies $Comp(\Pi)$. This corollary can be extended to programs of a more general form:

Proposition 2 *For any absolutely tight program Π whose rules have the form (1) and any set X of atoms, X is an answer set for Π iff X satisfies $Comp(\Pi)$.*

This proposition is a generalization of Corollary 6 from [Erdem and Lifschitz, 2003] to disjunctive programs. It shows that the method of computing answer sets based on completion [Babovich *et al.*, 2000] can be extended to tight programs whose rules have the form (1). In view of the following proposition, the restriction on the form of rules of the program is not essential.

Proposition 3 *Any absolutely tight program is strongly equivalent to an absolutely tight program whose rules have the form (1).*

Besides absolute tightness, Erdem and Lifschitz [2003] define also tightness relative to a set. That definition can be extended to disjunctive programs as follows.

Let Π be a program, and let X be a set of atoms. By Π_X we denote the set of rules of Π whose bodies are satisfied by X. We say that Π is *tight* on a set X of atoms if the subgraph of the positive dependency graph of Π_X induced by X has no loops.

This definition is equivalent to the corresponding definition from [Erdem and Lifschitz, 2003] in the case when the program is nondisjunctive. The following two propositions are similar to Propositions 2, 3.

Proposition 4 *For any program Π whose rules have the form (1) and any set X of atoms such that Π is tight on X, X is an answer set for Π iff X satisfies $Comp(\Pi)$.*

Proposition 5 *For any set X of atoms, any program tight on X is strongly equivalent to a program tight on X whose rules have the form (1).*

Proposition 4 is a generalization of Corollary 2 from [Erdem and Lifschitz, 2003] to disjunctive programs.

6 Related Work

Baral and Gelfond [1994] and Inoue and Sakama [1998] extended the definition of a supported set to the case of disjunctive programs. In application to programs whose rules have the form (1), their definition can be stated as follows: a set X of atoms is *supported by Π* if, for each atom $a \in X$, there exists a rule (1) in Π such that $X \cap A = \{a\}$ and $X \models Body$. It is easy to check that X satisfies $Comp(\Pi)$ iff X satisfies Π and is supported by Π. In view of this fact, Proposition 1 is similar to Proposition 4.1 from [Baral and Gelfond, 1994] and to Theorem 5.3 from [Inoue and Sakama, 1998], which assert that every answer set is supported.

Rachel Ben-Eliyahu and Rina Dechter [1996] showed that a certain class of disjunctive programs (called head-cycle-free), that includes all nondisjunctive programs, can be translated into propositional theories. Their translation may introduce extra atoms, while ours does not, just as the original Lin/Zhao translation.

7 Selected Proofs

The following facts are stated in [Erdem and Lifschitz, 2003] as Lemma 1 and Lemma 3(i).

Fact 3 *Given a formula F without negation as failure and two sets X, Y of atoms such that $Y \subseteq X$, if $Y \models F$ then $X \models F$.*

Fact 4 *For any formula F and any set X of atoms, $X \models F$ iff $X \models F^X$.*

7.1 Proof of Proposition 1

Lemma 1 *If X is a minimal set of atoms that satisfies a set Γ of clauses, then for each $a \in X$ there exists a clause A in Γ such that $X \cap A = \{a\}$.*

Proof If this is not the case, then there exists an atom $a \in X$ such that every clause in Γ that contains a also includes another atom that is in X. It follows that $X \setminus \{a\}$ also satisfies Γ, which contradicts with the minimality of X. ∎

Lemma 2 *Let Π be a program whose rules have the form (1), let X be a set of atoms, and let Γ be the set of the heads of the rules in Π whose bodies are satisfied by X. If X is an answer set for Π, then X is a minimal set of atoms that satisfies Γ.*

Proof Let X be an answer set for Π. First we will prove that X satisfies Γ. Take any clause A in Γ and consider a corresponding rule $A \leftarrow Body$ in Π such that $X \models Body$. By Fact 4, $X \models Body^X$. Since X is an answer set for Π, X satisfies $A \leftarrow Body^X$. Consequently, $X \models A$. It follows that X satisfies Γ.

Next we will prove that X is minimal among the sets of atoms that satisfies Γ. Let Y be any subset of X that satisfies Γ. We will show that Y satisfies Π^X. Take any rule $A \leftarrow Body$ from Π, and assume that Y satisfies the body of the corresponding rule

$$A \leftarrow Body^X \tag{8}$$

from Π^X. By Fact 3, $X \models Body^X$. By Fact 4, it follows that $X \models Body$, so that $A \in \Gamma$. Since Y satisfies Γ, we conclude that Y satisfies the head A of (8).

Since Y is a subset of an answer set for Π^X and Y satisfies Π^X, $Y = X$. ∎

Proposition 1 *For any program Π whose rules have the form (1) and any set X of atoms, if X is an answer set for Π, then X is a model of $Comp(\Pi)$.*

Proof Let X be an answer set for Π. Take any rule $A \leftarrow Body$ in Π, and assume that X satisfies the antecedent $Body$ of the corresponding formula (3). Then A belongs to set Γ from the statement of Lemma 2. According to the lemma, it follows that X satisfies the consequent A of (3).

Now assume that X satisfies an atom a; we need to show that X satisfies the consequent of the corresponding formula (4). According to Lemma 2, X is a minimal set of atoms satisfying Γ. By Lemma 1, it follows that there exists a clause A in Γ such that $X \cap A = \{a\}$. By the definition of Γ, there is a rule $A \leftarrow Body$ in Π such that $X \models Body$. Then X satisfies the disjunctive term in the consequent of (4)

$$Body \wedge \bigwedge_{p \in A \setminus \{a\}} \neg p$$

that corresponds to this rule. ∎

7.2   Proof of Theorem 1

Theorem 1 *For any program Π whose rules have the form (2) and any set X of atoms, the following conditions are equivalent:*

(a) X is an answer set for Π,
(b) X is a model of $Comp(\Pi) \cup CLF(\Pi)$,
(c) X is a model of $Comp(\Pi) \cup DLF(\Pi)$.

Proof From (c) to (b): use the fact that $DLF(\Pi) \models CLF(\Pi)$.

From (a) to (c): Let X be an answer set for Π. Then X is a model of $Comp(\Pi)$ by Proposition 1. It remains to show that X satisfies every formula in $DLF(\Pi)$. Assume that X satisfies the antecedent $\bigvee L$ of a disjunctive loop formula (7); we want to show that X satisfies the consequent of this formula. Since X is an answer set for Π^X, its proper subset $X \setminus L$ does not satisfy Π^X. Consequently, there is a rule (2) in Π such that $X \setminus L$ satisfies the body of the corresponding rule

$$A \leftarrow B, F^X \tag{9}$$

of Π^X, but does not satisfy its head. From Fact 3, X satisfies the body of (9) also. Consequently, X satisfies the head of (9), that is, $X \cap A \neq \emptyset$. But $X \setminus L$ does not satisfy the head of (9), that is

$$(X \setminus L) \cap A = \emptyset. \tag{10}$$

From these two facts we can conclude that $A \cap L \neq \emptyset$. On the other hand, from the fact that $X \setminus L$ satisfies the body of (9), we can conclude that all atoms in B belong to $X \setminus L$, so that $B \cap L = \emptyset$. Consequently, the formula

$$B \wedge F \wedge \bigwedge_{p \in A \setminus L} \neg p$$

belongs to $R(L)$, and is one of the disjunctive terms in the consequent of (7). We will now check that X satisfies this formula. From the fact that X satisfies the body of (9) and Fact 4, we see that X satisfies both B and F. Formula (10) can be rewritten as $X \cap (A \setminus L) = \emptyset$. Consequently, X doesn't contain atoms from $A \setminus L$, so that it satisfies $\bigwedge_{p \in A \setminus L} \neg p$.

From (b) to (a): Let X be a model of $Comp(\Pi) \cup CLF(\Pi)$. First, we will prove that $X \models \Pi^X$. Take any rule

$$A \leftarrow Body^X \tag{11}$$

in Π^X such that $X \models Body^X$. Then $X \models Body$ by Fact 4. Since X is a model of $Comp(\Pi)$, X satisfies every implication (3). Consequently, $X \models A$, so that X satisfies (11). It follows that X satisfies Π^X.

Next, we will prove that X is minimal among the sets of atoms that satisfy Π^X. Suppose that this is not the case, and consider a proper subset Y of X that satisfies Π^X. We will show that there exists an infinite sequence $p_1, p_2, \ldots$ of elements of $X \setminus Y$ with the following two properties for every $k > 0$:

(i) the positive dependency graph of Π contains a path of nonzero length from p_k to p_{k+1} such that all atoms in the path belong to $\{p_1, \ldots, p_{k+1}\}$;
(ii) if L is a loop of Π such that

$$p_k \in L \subseteq \{p_1, \ldots, p_k\} \tag{12}$$

then $p_{k+1} \notin L$.

The sequence $p_1, p_2, \ldots$ with these properties is defined recursively, as follows. Recall that Y is a proper subset of X; take p_1 to be any element of $X \setminus Y$. To select p_{k+1} given the sequence $p_1, \ldots, p_k$ such that $p_1, \ldots, p_k \in X \setminus Y$, consider two cases.

Case 1: Π has a loop satisfying condition (12). Take the union L_{max} of all such loops L. It is clear that L_{max} is a loop, and

$$p_k \in L_{max} \subseteq \{p_1, \ldots, p_k\}. \tag{13}$$

Since $p_1, \ldots, p_k \in X \setminus Y$, X satisfies $\bigwedge L_{max}$. On the other hand, by the choice of X, X satisfies all conjunctive loop formulas of Π, including $CLF(L_{max})$. Consequently, X satisfies one of the disjunctive terms

$$B \wedge F \wedge \bigwedge_{p \in A \setminus L_{max}} \neg p \tag{14}$$

of $R(L_{max})$. For the corresponding rule (2) of Π,

$$A \cap L_{max} \neq \emptyset \tag{15}$$

and

$$B \cap L_{max} = pa(B, F) \cap L_{max} = \emptyset. \tag{16}$$

Since X satisfies (14),

$$X \models B, F \tag{17}$$

and

$$Y \cap (A \setminus L_{max}) \subseteq X \cap (A \setminus L_{max}) = \emptyset. \tag{18}$$

From (13),

$$Y \cap L_{max} \subseteq Y \cap \{p_1, \ldots, p_k\} \subseteq Y \cap (X \setminus Y) = \emptyset,$$

so that $Y \cap L_{max} = \emptyset$. In combination with (18), this formula shows that

$$Y \cap A \subseteq Y \cap ((A \setminus L_{max}) \cup L_{max}) = (Y \cap (A \setminus L_{max})) \cup (Y \cap L_{max}) = \emptyset,$$

so that $Y \cap A = \emptyset$, which means that $Y \not\models A$. But by the choice of Y, Y satisfies every rule in Π^X, including $A \leftarrow B, F^X$. Consequently,

$$Y \not\models B, F^X. \tag{19}$$

Since all occurrences of atoms in F are in the scope of negation as failure, F^X doesn't contain atoms. It follows that F^X is either satisfied by every set of atoms or is not satisfied by any of them. From (17) and Fact 4 we see that F^X is satisfied by X. Consequently, F^X is satisfied by Y also. By (19), we can conclude that $Y \not\models B$, that is to say, one of the atoms in B doesn't belong to Y. Take this atom to be p_{k+1}. By (17), every atom in B belongs to X, so that p_{k+1} is indeed an element of $X \setminus Y$.

Case 2: Π does not have a loop satisfying condition (12). Consider the implication (4) in $Comp(\Pi)$ whose antecedent is p_k. We know that $p_k \in X \setminus Y \subseteq X$ and X satisfies $Comp(\Pi)$. It follows that X satisfies one of the disjunctive terms

$$B \wedge F \wedge \bigwedge_{p \in A \setminus \{p_k\}} \neg p \tag{20}$$

of this implication, so that (17) holds and

$$X \cap (A \setminus \{p_k\}) = \emptyset. \tag{21}$$

Since $Y \subseteq X$, $Y \cap (A \setminus \{p_k\}) = \emptyset$ also; since $p_k \in X \setminus Y$, $Y \cap \{p_k\} = \emptyset$. Consequently, $Y \cap A = \emptyset$, which means that $Y \not\models A$. By the same reasoning as in Case 1, we can conclude that one of the atoms in B belongs to $X \setminus Y$. Take this atom to be p_{k+1}.

Let us check that the sequence $p_1, p_2, \ldots$ satisfies (i). Assume that p_{k+1} was chosen according to Case 1. By (15), there is an atom p that belongs both to the head A of (2) and to L_{max}. Since $p_{k+1} \in pa(B, F)$, the positive dependency graph of Π contains an edge from p to p_{k+1}. Since both p_k and p belong to the loop L_{max}, this graph contains a path from p_k to p such that all atoms in the path belong to $\{p_1, \ldots, p_k\}$. Consequently, the graph contains a path of nonzero length from p_k to p_{k+1} such that all atoms in the path belong to $\{p_1, \ldots, p_{k+1}\}$.

Assume now that p_{k+1} was chosen according to Case 2. Since X satisfies (20) and the formula (3) corresponding to the rule $A \leftarrow B, F$, X satisfies A, that is, $X \cap A \neq \emptyset$. In view of (21), it follows that $p_k \in A$. But p_{k+1} was chosen as one of conjunctive terms of B. Consequently, there is an edge from p_k to p_{k+1} in the positive dependency graph of Π.

Next we will prove that the sequence satisfies (ii). If a loop L of Π satisfies condition (12), then p_{k+1} was chosen according to Case 1. Since $p_{k+1} \in B$, from (16) we conclude that $p_{k+1} \notin L_{max}$. Since $L \subseteq L_{max}$, it follows that $p_{k+1} \notin L$.

Notice that an atom may belong to X only if it occurs in the head of one of the rules of Π. Indeed, for any other atom a, the consequent of (4) is the empty disjunction $\bot$, so that X satisfies $a \supset \bot$. Since Π has finitely many rules, it follows that X is finite. Since $p_1, p_2, \ldots \in X \setminus Y$, this sequence must contain repetitions. Assume that $p_j = p_{k+1}$ for $j \leq k$. From property (i) we see that the positive dependency graph of Π contains a path from p_j to p_k whose vertices belong to $\{p_1, \ldots, p_{k+1}\}$. This property implies also that there is such a path of nonzero length from p_k to p_{k+1}. Since $p_j = p_{k+1}$, it follows that this graph contains a loop L such that

$$p_k, p_{k+1} \in L \subseteq \{p_1, \ldots, p_{k+1}\} = \{p_1, \ldots, p_k\},$$

which contradicts property (ii). ∎

7.3 Proof of Proposition 2

In logic programming, any formula can be converted to "disjunctive normal forms" in the following sense. A *simple conjunction* is a formula of the form

$$p_1, \ldots, p_k, not\ p_{k+1}, \ldots, not\ p_m, not\ not\ p_{m+1}, \ldots, not\ not\ p_n$$

where $0 \leq k \leq m \leq n$ and all p_i are atoms.

The following fact is essentially Proposition 5(i) from [Lifschitz et al., 1999].

Fact 5 *Any formula can be equivalently rewritten as a formula of the form $F_1; \ldots; F_n$ ($n \geq 0$) where each F_i is a simple conjunction.*

Proposition 2   *For any absolutely tight program Π whose rules have the form (1) and any set X of atoms, X is an answer set for Π iff X satisfies $Comp(\Pi)$.*

Proof If the rules of Π have the form (2), then the set of loop formulas of Π is empty, and the assertion to be proved follows from Theorem 1. On the other hand, any program whose rules have the form (1) can be rewritten as a strongly equivalent program whose rules have the form (2) by the following procedure: convert each body to a disjunctive normal form (Fact 5) and transform the rule into a set of rules whose bodies are simple conjunctions [Lifschitz et al., 1999, Proposition 6(ii)]. This can be done without changing the positive dependency graph, so that the resulting program will be absolutely tight. ∎

Acknowledgments. We are grateful to Fangzhen Lin and Yuting Zhao for providing us with access to the journal version of [Lin and Zhao, 2002], to Yuliya Babovich, Selim Erdoğan, Paolo Ferraris, Michael Gelfond and Hudson Turner for useful discussions related to the subject of this paper, and to the anonymous referees for their comments. This work was partially supported by the Texas Higher Education Coordinating Board under Grant 003658-0322-2001.

References

[Babovich *et al.*, 2000] Yuliya Babovich, Esra Erdem, and Vladimir Lifschitz. Fages' theorem and answer set programming.[12] In *Proc. Eighth Int'l Workshop on Non-Monotonic Reasoning*, 2000.

[Baral and Gelfond, 1994] Chitta Baral and Michael Gelfond. Logic programming and knowledge representation. *Journal of Logic Programming*, 19,20:73–148, 1994.

[Ben-Eliyahu and Dechter, 1996] Rachel Ben-Eliyahu and Rina Dechter. Propositional semantics for disjunctive logic programs. *Annals of Mathematics and Artificial Intelligence*, 12:53–87, 1996.

[Clark, 1978] Keith Clark. Negation as failure. In Herve Gallaire and Jack Minker, editors, *Logic and Data Bases*, pages 293–322. Plenum Press, New York, 1978.

[Eiter and Gottlob, 1993] Thomas Eiter and Georg Gottlob. Complexity results for disjunctive logic programming and application to nonmonotonic logics. In Dale Miller, editor, *Proc. ILPS-93*, pages 266–278, 1993.

[Erdem and Lifschitz, 1999] Esra Erdem and Vladimir Lifschitz. Transformations of logic programs related to causality and planning. In *Logic Programming and Non-monotonic Reasoning: Proc. Fifth Int'l Conf. (Lecture Notes in Artificial Intelligence 1730)*, pages 107–116, 1999.

[Erdem and Lifschitz, 2003] Esra Erdem and Vladimir Lifschitz. Tight logic programs. *Theory and Practice of Logic Programming*, 3:499–518, 2003.

[Fages, 1994] François Fages. Consistency of Clark's completion and existence of stable models. *Journal of Methods of Logic in Computer Science*, 1:51–60, 1994.

[Gelfond and Lifschitz, 1988] Michael Gelfond and Vladimir Lifschitz. The stable model semantics for logic programming. In Robert Kowalski and Kenneth Bowen, editors, *Logic Programming: Proc. Fifth Int'l Conf. and Symp.*, pages 1070–1080, 1988.

[Inoue and Sakama, 1998] Katsumi Inoue and Chiaki Sakama. Negation as failure in the head. *Journal of Logic Programming*, 35:39–78, 1998.

[Lifschitz *et al.*, 1999] Vladimir Lifschitz, Lappoon R. Tang, and Hudson Turner. Nested expressions in logic programs. *Annals of Mathematics and Artificial Intelligence*, 25:369–389, 1999.

[Lifschitz *et al.*, 2001] Vladimir Lifschitz, David Pearce, and Agustin Valverde. Strongly equivalent logic programs. *ACM Transactions on Computational Logic*, 2:526–541, 2001.

[Lin and Zhao, 2002] Fangzhen Lin and Yuting Zhao. ASSAT: Computing answer sets of a logic program by SAT solvers. In *Proc. AAAI-02*, 2002.

[Lloyd and Topor, 1984] John Lloyd and Rodney Topor. Making Prolog more expressive. *Journal of Logic Programming*, 3:225–240, 1984.

[Marek and Subrahmanian, 1989] Victor Marek and V.S. Subrahmanian. The relationship between logic program semantics and non-monotonic reasoning. In Giorgio Levi and Maurizio Martelli, editors, *Logic Programming: Proc. Sixth Int'l Conf.*, pages 600–617, 1989.

---

[12] http://arxiv.org/abs/cs.ai/0003042 .

Default Knowledge in Logic Programs with Uncertainty

Yann Loyer[1] and Umberto Straccia[2]

[1] Laboratoire PRiSM, Université de Versailles Saint Quentin
45 Avenue des Etats-Unis, 78035 Versailles FRANCE
[2] I.S.T.I. - C.N.R., Via G. Moruzzi,1 I-56124 Pisa (PI) ITALY

Abstract. Many frameworks have been proposed to manage uncertain information in logic programming. Essentially, they differ in the underlying notion of uncertainty and how these uncertainty values, associated to rules and facts, are managed. The goal of this paper is to allow the reasoning with *non-uniform default assumptions*, i.e. with any arbitrary assignment of default values to the atoms. Informally, rather than to rely on the same default certainty value for all atoms, we allow arbitrary assignments to complete information. To this end, we define both epistemologically and computationally the semantics according to any given assumption. For reasons of generality, we present our work in the framework presented in [17] as a unifying umbrella for many of the proposed approaches to the management of uncertainty in logic programming. Our extension is conservative in the following sense: (i) if we restrict our attention to the usual uniform Open World Assumption, then the semantics reduces to the Kripke-Kleene semantics, and (ii) if we restrict our attention to the uniform Closed World Assumption, then our semantics reduces to the well-founded semantics.

1 Introduction

The management of uncertainty is an important issue whenever the real world information to be represented is of imperfect nature and the classical crisp *true, false* approximation is not adequate (which is likely the rule rather than an exception). Numerous frameworks for logic programming with uncertainty have been proposed. Essentially, they differ in the underlying notion of uncertainty (e.g. probability theory [8,16,23, 24,25], fuzzy set theory [3,27,29], multi-valued logic [7,12,13,14,17,28], possibilistic logic [4,32,33]) and how uncertainty values, associated to rules and facts, are managed.

Recently, Lakshmanan and Shiri [17] have proposed a general framework, called *Parametric Deductive Databases with Uncertainty* (PDDU), that captures and generalizes many of the precedent approaches, permitting various forms of uncertainty to be manipulated in different ways. Informally, in [17], a rule is of the form $A \xleftarrow{\alpha} B_1, ..., B_n$. Computationally, given an assignment I of certainties, taken from a certainty lattice $\mathcal{L}$, to the B_is, the certainty of A is computed by taking the "conjunction" of the certainties $I(B_i)$ and then somehow "propagating" it to the rule head, taking into account the certainty α of the implication. The term 'parametric' in the PDDU framework derives from the fact it is possible to select, individually for each rule, the aggregation operators, i.e. how conjunction, disjunction and rule propagation are interpreted and, thus, admitting a certain amount of flexibility. Our motivation to consider the PDDU framework comes from its generality. We will just recall that Lakshmanan and Shiri [17] essentially

C. Palamidessi (Ed.): ICLP 2003, LNCS 2916, pp. 466–480, 2003.

motivate their parametric approach by the need (i) to permit various forms of uncertainty to be manipulated in different ways, and (ii) to allow for the fact that certain manipulations amount to treating different derivations of an atom as a set (see, e.g. [4, 15,29]) while others amount to treating it as a multiset (e.g.[16]).

The main topic of this study is to extend the PDDU framework, and thus the approaches captured by that framework, with *non-uniform default assumptions*. Informally, rather than to rely on the same default value for all atoms, we allow arbitrary assignments of default certainty values. An assumption defines default knowledge to be used to complete the available knowledge provided by the facts and rules of a program. As shown in [21], the usual semantics of logic programs can be obtained through a unique computation method, but using different *uniform* assumptions, i.e. assumptions that assign the same default truth-value to all the atoms. Well-known are (i) the *Closed World Assumption* (CWA), which asserts that any atom whose truth-value cannot be inferred from the facts and rules is supposed to be false, and (ii) the *Open World Assumption* (OWA), which asserts that every such atom is supposed to be unknown or undefined. In the first case, fall the approaches, which end up with a *stable model* [9,10], or *well-founded* [31] semantics, like [5,19,23,24], while in the latter case fall the others, including [17] as well. Exceptions are a previous attempt [19] and those works related to Extended and Disjunctive Logic Programs [10], where some non-uniformity is allowed (see, e.g. [32, 33]). In those works, some atoms are allowed to be interpreted according to the OWA, while others are allowed to be interpreted according to the CWA and, thus, roughly the choice of the default is restricted to the value *unknown* and/or *false*. The general case, where *any* assignment may be considered as the default knowledge, is approached in [22], but relying on a weak evaluation of formulas (based on the possible values of unknown atoms), and thus leads to a weaker semantics than the one presented here (that relies on classical formulas evaluation). To the best of our knowledge there is no other work addressing the general case. To illustrate the idea of non-uniform assumptions, consider the following example. Examples motivating the need for combining OWA and CWA can be found in [10,22,32,33] and in [8].

Example 1. A judge is collecting information from two sources, the public prosecutor and the counsel for the defence, in order to decide whether to charge a person named Ted, accused of murder[1]. The judge first collects a set of facts $F = \{\neg\texttt{has\_witness(Ted)},$ $\texttt{friends(John, Ted)}\}$. Then he combines them with his own set of rules R (described below) in order to make a decision.

$$
\begin{aligned}
\texttt{suspect(X)} \quad &\leftarrow \texttt{motive(X)} \\
\texttt{suspect(X)} \quad &\leftarrow \texttt{has\_witness(X)} \\
\texttt{cleared(X)} \quad &\leftarrow \texttt{alibi(X,Y)} \wedge \neg\texttt{friends(X,Y)} \\
\texttt{cleared(X)} \quad &\leftarrow \texttt{innocent(X)} \wedge \neg\texttt{suspect(X)} \\
\texttt{friends(X,Y)} &\leftarrow \texttt{friends(Y,X)} \\
\texttt{friends(X,Y)} &\leftarrow \texttt{friends(X,Z)} \wedge \texttt{friends(Z,Y)} \\
\texttt{charge(X)} \quad &\leftarrow \texttt{suspect(X)} \\
\texttt{charge(X)} \quad &\leftarrow \neg\texttt{cleared(X)}
\end{aligned}
$$

The question is: What should the value of charge(Ted) be? According to that set of rules, Ted should be charged if he has been proved effectively suspect or not cleared. Using F and R (and intuition), it appears that uniform default assumption are not appropriate

---

[1] For ease, we omit any association of uncertainty numbers to the rules and facts.

in such a case. If the judge relies on the CWA, then he will decide that Ted is not cleared and must be charged despite the absence of proof. Relying on the OWA, the atoms suspect(Ted), cleared(Ted) and charged(Ted) will be unknown, and the judge cannot take a decision (approaches based on OWA are often too weak). Assuming that by default the atoms motive(Ted), has_witness(Ted) and suspect(Ted) are false, that the atom innocent(Ted) is true and that the others are unknown seems to be an appropriate assumption here. Relying on this assumption, the judge will infer that Ted is cleared, not suspect and should not be charged. If the set of certainty values is the unit interval $[0, 1]$, then assuming that by default the value of motive(Ted), has_witness(Ted) and suspect(Ted) is 0.1, that the value of innocent(Ted) is 0.9 and that the others are unknown would be a way to use uncertainty values to distinguish the notion of proved innocence from the notion of presumption of innocence.

Motivation for allowing the use of any assignment of truth values as an assumption, apart from proposing a general framework for reasoning with incomplete information, comes mainly from the area of information integration. Information is now usually scattered in many different sources, and then has to be integrated before to be used. But an information source that received knowledge from other sources may want to privilege its own knowledge. To this end, the source should have the possibility to use the "external" information just to complete its own "internal" knowledge, but without 'removing' it. It follows that the source should have the possibility of considering the external knowledge provided by other sources as an assumption over its own universe. Let us consider the following example to illustrate that situation.

Example 2. Consider an insurance company that has information about its customers (data grouped into a set F of facts, and a set R of rules, i.e. a logic program). That information is used to determine, or to re-evaluate, the risk coefficient in $[0, 1]$ of each customer in order to fix the price of the insurance contracts. In presence of incomplete information, the insurance company may use knowledge provided by other sources such as the risk coefficient of a new customer provided by its precedent insurance company. Such knowledge should be seen as "assumed" or "possible" knowledge for completing the knowledge given by the program, but without overwriting it.

We will rely on the central notion of *support*, which is roughly speaking the maximal knowledge provided by an assumption that can be "safely" added to a program. That notion will be used to define new families of models, called *supported models* which are models that can not be completed anymore by the assumption. As a side effect, our approach extends PDDU, and thus the underlying formalisms, by allowing negation, and generalizes to those frameworks the usual semantics of logic programs with negation. Indeed, our extension of the PDDU framework to non-uniform default assumptions is conservative, i.e. if we restrict our attention to the uniform OWA, then our semantics reduces to the Kripke-Kleene semantics [6]. On the other hand, if we restrict our attention to the uniform CWA, then our semantics captures the well-founded semantics [31].

In the following section, we introduce the syntax of PDDU with negation, called normal parametric programs. Section 3 contains the definitions of interpretation and model of a program. Section 4 presents both epistemic and fixpoint characterizations of the intended semantics of normal parametric programs with respect to any given default assumption. Section 5 presents some concluding remarks.

2 Preliminaries

We start with some basic definitions related to PDDU [17]. Consider an arbitrary first order language that contains infinitely many variable symbols, finitely many constants, and predicate symbols, but no function symbols. The predicate symbol $\pi(A)$ of an atom A given by $A = p(X_1, \ldots, X_n)$ is defined by $\pi(A) = p$. Let $\mathcal{L} = \langle \mathcal{T}, \preceq, \otimes, \oplus \rangle$ be a *certainty lattice* (a complete lattice) and $\mathcal{B}(\mathcal{T})$ the set of finite multisets over $\mathcal{T}$. A multiset is indicated with $\{ \cdot \}$. With $\perp$ and $\top$ we denote the least and greatest element in $\mathcal{T}$, respectively. Essentially, as we will see in the next section, an atom will be mapped into a certainty value in $\mathcal{T}$. Typical certainty lattices are: given a set of real values $\mathcal{T}$, define $\mathcal{L}_\mathcal{T} = \langle \mathcal{T}, \preceq, \otimes, \oplus \rangle$, $\alpha \preceq \beta$ iff $\alpha \leq \beta$, $\alpha \otimes \beta = \min(\alpha, \beta)$, $\alpha \oplus \beta = \max(\alpha, \beta)$, $\perp = \inf(\mathcal{T})$ and $\top = \sup(\mathcal{T})$, respectively. Then $\mathcal{L}_{\{0,1\}}$ corresponds to the classical truth-space, while $\mathcal{L}_{[0,1]}$, which relies on the unit interval, is quite frequently used as certainty lattice. While the language does not contain function symbols, it contains symbols for families of propagation ($\mathcal{F}_p$), conjunction ($\mathcal{F}_c$) and disjunction functions ($\mathcal{F}_d$), called *combination functions*. The intention is that a conjunction function (e.g. $\otimes$) determines the certainty of a conjunction in the body of a rule, the propagation function (e.g. $\otimes$) determines how to "propagate" the certainty resulting from the evaluation of the body of a rule to the head, by taking into account the certainty associated to the rule, while the disjunction function (e.g. $\oplus$) dictates how to combine the certainties in case an atom appears in the heads of several rules. Combination functions have to satisfy some restrictions to reflect their use. Formally, a *propagation function* is a mapping from $\mathcal{T} \times \mathcal{T}$ to $\mathcal{T}$ and a *conjunction* or *disjunction* function is a mapping from $\mathcal{B}(\mathcal{T})$ to $\mathcal{T}$. Each combination function is monotonic and continuous w.r.t. (with respect to) each one of its arguments. Conjunction and disjunction functions are commutative and associative. Additionally, each kind of function must verify some of the following properties (for simplicity, we formulate the properties treating any function as a binary function on $\mathcal{T}$):

(i) bounded-above: $f(\alpha_1, \alpha_2) \preceq \alpha_i$, for $i = 1, 2, \forall \alpha_1, \alpha_2 \in \mathcal{T}$;
(ii) bounded-below: $\alpha_i \preceq f(\alpha_1, \alpha_2)$, for $i = 1, 2, \forall \alpha_1, \alpha_2 \in \mathcal{T}$;
(iii) $f(\{\alpha\}) = \alpha, \forall \alpha \in \mathcal{T}$;
(iv) $f(\emptyset) = \perp$;
(v) $f(\emptyset) = \top$; and
(vi) $f(\alpha, \top) = \alpha, \forall \alpha \in \mathcal{T}$.

The following should be satisfied:

- a conjunction function in $\mathcal{F}_c$ should satisfy properties (i), (iii), (v) and (vi);
- a propagation function in $\mathcal{F}_p$ should satisfy properties (i) and (vi); while
- a disjunction function in $\mathcal{F}_d$ should satisfy properties (ii), (iii) and (iv).

Note that, condition (iii) accounts for the evaluation a one-element conjunction or disjunction; condition (v) deals with a conjunction of an empty body, i.e. a fact, and, thus, the body is evaluated to $\top$, while condition (iv) specifies that a disjunction of an empty set of literals is evaluated to $\perp$ (for instance, in case an atom is head of no rule). We also assume that there is a function from $\mathcal{T}$ to $\mathcal{T}$, called *negation function*, denoted $\neg$, that is anti-monotone w.r.t. $\preceq$ and satisfies $\neg\neg\alpha = \alpha, \forall \alpha \in \mathcal{T}$. E.g., in $\mathcal{L}_{[0,1]}$, $\neg\alpha = 1 - \alpha$ is quite typical. Finally, a literal is an atomic formula or its negation.

In the following definition of normal parametric program, we extend [17] by allowing literals to appear in the body of a rule. But, as we will clarify later on, in this special case, the role of a literal $\neg A$ depends on the default assumption made on the atom A. If it is the OWA, i.e. by default A's value is unknown, then $\neg A$ behaves classically, if it is the CWA, i.e. by default A's value is false, then $\neg A$ behaves like *not A* (negation as failure). Note that A's default value may well be any other value, e.g. 0.7 in $\mathcal{L}_{[0,1]}$.

Definition 1 (Normal parametric program). *A normal parametric program P (np-program) is a 5-tuple $\langle \mathcal{L}, \mathcal{R}, \mathcal{C}, \mathcal{P}, \mathcal{D} \rangle$, whose components are defined as follows:*

1. *$\mathcal{L} = \langle \mathcal{T}, \preceq, \otimes, \oplus \rangle$ is a complete lattice, where $\mathcal{T}$ is a set of certainties partially ordered by $\preceq$, $\otimes$ is the meet operator and $\oplus$ the join operator;*
2. *$\mathcal{R}$ is a finite set of normal parametric rules (np-rules), each of which is a statement of the form: $r : A \xleftarrow{\alpha_r} L_1, ..., L_n$ where A is an atom, $L_1, ..., L_n$ are literals or values in $\mathcal{T}$ and $\alpha_r \in \mathcal{T} \setminus \{\perp\}$ is the certainty of the rule;*
3. *$\mathcal{C}$ maps each np-rule into a conjunction function in $\mathcal{F}_c$;*
4. *$\mathcal{P}$ maps each np-rule into a propagation function in $\mathcal{F}_p$;*
5. *$\mathcal{D}$ maps each predicate symbol in P into a disjunction function in $\mathcal{F}_d$.*

For ease of presentation, we write $r : A \xleftarrow{\alpha_r} L_1, ..., L_n; \langle f_d, f_p, f_c \rangle$ to represent an np-rule in which $f_d \in \mathcal{F}_d$ is the disjunction function associated with $\pi(A)$ and, $f_c \in \mathcal{F}_c$ and $f_p \in \mathcal{F}_p$ are the conjunction and propagation functions associated with r, respectively. Note that under the above representation, rules involving the same predicate symbol in the head, should have the same disjunction function associated. The *Herbrand base* $\mathcal{B}_P$ of an np-program P is the set of all instantiated program atoms and, P^* is the *Herbrand instantiation of P*, i.e. the set of all ground instantiations of the rules in P (P^* is finite). Note that any Datalog program with negation can be seen as an np-program.

We recall from [17] the following examples, which both might help informally the reader to get confidence with the formalism and show how PDDU may capture different approaches to the management of uncertainty in logic programming. Consider the following generic program with the four rules r_i, $(r_1: A \xleftarrow{\alpha_1} B)$, $(r_2: A \xleftarrow{\alpha_2} C)$, $(r_3: B \xleftarrow{\alpha_3})$, $(r_4: C \xleftarrow{\alpha_4})$ where A, B, C are ground atoms, where α_i is the certainty of the rule r_i.

Example 3 (Classical case). Consider $\mathcal{L}_{\{0,1\}}$ and $\alpha_i = 1$, for $1 \leq i \leq 4$. Suppose the propagation and conjunction functions associated with r_i are both min, and the disjunction function associated with each atom is max. Then, P is a program in the standard logic programming framework.

Example 4 ([4]). Consider $\mathcal{L}_{[0,1]}$. Suppose $\alpha_1 = 0.8, \alpha_2 = \alpha_3 = 0.7$, and $\alpha_4 = 0.8$ are possibility/necessity degrees associated with the implications. Suppose the conjunction, propagation, and disjunction functions are the same as in the above example. Then P is a program in the framework proposed by Dubois et al. [4], which is founded on Zadeh's possibility theory [35]. In a fixpoint evaluation of P, the possibility/necessity degrees derived for A, B, C are $0.7, 0.7, 0.8$, respectively.

Example 5 ([29]). Consider $\mathcal{L}_{[0,1]}$ and suppose α_i as defined in Example 4. Suppose the conjunction and disjunction functions are as before, but the propagation function is multiplication ($\cdot$). Then P is a program in van Emden's framework [29], which is mathematically founded on the theory of fuzzy sets proposed by Zadeh [34]. In a fixpoint evaluation of P, the values derived for A, B, C are $0.56, 0.7, 0.8$, respectively.

Example 6 (MYCIN [2]). Consider $\mathcal{L}_{[0,1]}$, and suppose α_i's are probabilities defined as in the previous example. Suppose $(\cdot)$ is the propagation and conjunction function associated with every rule in P, and $f_d(\alpha, \beta) = \alpha + \beta - \alpha \cdot \beta$ is the disjunction function associated with every atom in P (algebraic sum). Viewing an atom as an event, f_d returns the probability of the occurrence, of any one of two independent events, in the probabilistic sense. Note that f_d is the disjunction function used in MYCIN [2]. Let us consider a fixpoint evaluation of P. In the first step, we derive B and C with probabilities 0.7 and 0.8, respectively. In step 2, applying r_1 and r_2, we obtain two derivations of A, the probability of each of which is 0.56. The probability of A is then defined as $f_d(0.56, 0.56) = 0.8064$. Note that, in this example, collecting derivations as a multiset is crucial; if the derivations were collected as a set, the certainty obtained for A would be 0.56, which is incorrect.

Finally, let us extend the introductory Example 1 to an np-program formulation.

Example 7. Consider the certainty lattice is $\mathcal{L}_{[0;1]}$. Consider $f_d(\alpha, \beta) = \alpha + \beta - \alpha \cdot \beta$, $f_c(\alpha, \beta) = \alpha \cdot \beta$, $f_p = f_c$ and $\neg\alpha = 1 - \alpha$. Let P be the set of rules in Example 1, rewritten as np-program by including uncertainty values, and extended as follows.

$$
\begin{aligned}
\texttt{suspect(X)} &\overset{0.6}{\leftarrow} \texttt{motive(X)} \;\langle f_d, \otimes, \otimes\rangle \\
\texttt{suspect(X)} &\overset{0.8}{\leftarrow} \texttt{has\_witness(X)} \;\langle f_d, \otimes, \otimes\rangle \\
\texttt{cleared(X)} &\overset{1}{\leftarrow} \texttt{alibi(X, Y)} \wedge \neg\texttt{friends(X, Y)} \;\langle f_d, f_p, \otimes\rangle \\
\texttt{cleared(X)} &\overset{1}{\leftarrow} \texttt{innocent(X)} \wedge \neg\texttt{suspect(X)} \;\langle f_d, f_p, \otimes\rangle \\
\texttt{friends(X, Y)} &\overset{1}{\leftarrow} \texttt{friends(Y, X)} \;\langle \oplus, f_p, \otimes\rangle \\
\texttt{friends(X, Y)} &\overset{0.7}{\leftarrow} \texttt{friends(X, Z)} \wedge \texttt{friends(Z, Y)} \;\langle \oplus, f_p, f_c\rangle \\
\texttt{charge(X)} &\overset{1}{\leftarrow} \texttt{suspect(X)} \;\langle \oplus, f_p, \otimes\rangle \\
\texttt{charge(X)} &\overset{1}{\leftarrow} \neg\texttt{cleared(X)} \;\langle \oplus, f_p, \otimes\rangle \\
\texttt{motive(Ted)} &\overset{1}{\leftarrow} 1 \;\langle \oplus, f_p, \otimes\rangle \\
\texttt{alibi(Ted, John)} &\overset{1}{\leftarrow} 1 \;\langle \oplus, f_p, \otimes\rangle \\
\texttt{friends(Ted, John)} &\overset{1}{\leftarrow} 0.8 \;\langle \oplus, f_p, \otimes\rangle
\end{aligned}
$$

Note that e.g. for predicate $\texttt{suspect}$, the disjunction function is f_d to take into account that if there are different ways for inferring that someone is suspect, then we would like to increase (summing up) our suspicion and not just to choose the maximal value.

3 Interpretations of Programs

An *interpretation* I of an np-program P is a function that assigns to all atoms of the Herbrand base of P a value in $\mathcal{T}$. The semantics of a program P is usually an interpretation chosen in the set of models of P. In Datalog programs, as well as in PDDU, that chosen model is generally the least model of P w.r.t. $\preceq$.[2] Due to the non-monotone negation operator on lattices, some logic programs do not have a unique minimal model anymore, as shown in the following example.

---

[2] $\preceq$ is extended to the set of interpretations as follows: $I \preceq J$ iff $I(A) \preceq J(A)$ for all atoms A.

Example 8. Consider the certainty lattice $\mathcal{L}_{[0,1]}$ and the program $P = \{(A \leftarrow \neg B),$ $(B \leftarrow \neg A), (A \leftarrow 0.2), (B \leftarrow 0.3)\}$. Informally, an interpretation I is a model of the program if it satisfies every rule, while I satisfies a rule $X \leftarrow Y$ if $I(X) \succeq I(Y)$. So, this program has an infinite number of models I_x^y, where $0.2 \preceq x \preceq 1$, $0.3 \preceq y \preceq 1$, $y \geq 1 - x$, $I_x^y(A) = x$ and $I_x^y(B) = y$. (those in the A area below). There are also an infinite number of minimal models (those on the thin diagonal line). The minimal models I_x^y are such that $y = 1 - x$.

Concerning the previous example we may note that the certainty of A in any minimal models of P belongs to the interval $[0.2, 0.7]$, while for B the interval is $[0.3, 0.8]$. An obvious question is: what should be the answer to a query A to the program proposed in Example 8? There are at least two answers:

1. the certainty of A is *undefined*, as there is no unique minimal model. This is a conservative approach, which in case of ambiguity prefers to leave A unspecified;
2. the certainty of A is in $[0.2, 0.7]$, which means that even if there is no unique value for A, in all minimal models the certainty of A is in $[0.2, 0.7]$. In this approach we still try to provide some information. Of course, some care should be used. Indeed from $I(A) \in [0.2, 0.7]$ and $I(B) \in [0.3, 0.8]$ we should not conclude that $I(A) = 0.2$ and $I(B) = 0.3$ is a model of the program.

Applying a usual approach, like the well-founded semantics [31] or the Kripke-Kleene semantics [6], would lead us to choose the conservative solution 1. This was also the approach taken in [19]. Such a semantics seems to be too weak, in the sense that it loses some knowledge (e.g. the value of A should be at least 0.2). In this paper we rely on the more informative solution 2.

There is a well-known solution to it that consists in relying on the induced *interval bilattice* (these bilattices are obtained in a standard way as product of a lattice by itself –see, for instance [5,11]). Indeed, we propose to rely on $\mathcal{T} \times \mathcal{T}$. Any element of $\mathcal{T} \times \mathcal{T}$ is denoted by $[a; b]$ and interpreted as an interval on $\mathcal{T}$, i.e. $[a; b]$ *is interpreted as the set of elements* $x \in \mathcal{T}$ *such that* $a \preceq x \preceq b$. For instance, turning back to Example 8 above, in the intended model of P, the certainty of A is "approximated" with $[0.2; 0.7]$, i.e. the certainty of A lies in between 0.2 and 0.7 (similarly for B). Formally, given a complete lattice $\mathcal{L} = \langle \mathcal{T}, \preceq, \otimes, \oplus \rangle$, we construct a *bilattice* over $\mathcal{T} \times \mathcal{T}$. We recall that a bilattice is a triple $\langle \mathcal{B}, \preceq_t, \preceq_k \rangle$, where $\mathcal{B}$ is a nonempty set and $\preceq_t, \preceq_k$ are both partial orderings giving to $\mathcal{B}$ the structure of a lattice with a top and a bottom [11]. In our setting, we consider $\mathcal{B} = \mathcal{T} \times \mathcal{T}$ with the two following orderings:

– the *truth ordering* $\preceq_t$, where $[a; b] \preceq_t [a'; b']$ iff $a \preceq a'$ and $b \preceq b'$;
– the *knowledge ordering* $\preceq_k$, where $[a; b] \preceq_k [a'; b']$ iff $a \preceq a'$ and $b' \preceq b$.

The intuition of those orders is that truth increases if the interval contains greater values (e.g. $[0.1; 0.4] \preceq_t [0.2; 0.5]$), whereas the knowledge increases when the interval (i.e. in our case the approximation of a certainty value) becomes more precise (e.g. $[0.1; 0.4] \preceq_k$

$[0.2; 0.3]$, i.e. we have more knowledge)[3]. The least and greatest elements of $\mathcal{T} \times \mathcal{T}$ are respectively (i) $f = [\bot; \bot]$ (false) and $t = [\top; \top]$ (true), w.r.t. $\preceq_t$; and (ii) $\bot = [\bot; \top]$ (unknown – the less precise interval, i.e. the atom's certainty value is unknown) and $\top = [\top; \bot]$ (inconsistent – the empty interval) w.r.t. $\preceq_k$. The meet, join and negation on $\mathcal{T} \times \mathcal{T}$ w.r.t. both orderings are defined by extending the meet, join and negation from $\mathcal{T}$ to $\mathcal{T} \times \mathcal{T}$ in the natural way: let $[a; b], [a'; b'] \in \mathcal{T} \times \mathcal{T}$, then

- $[a; b] \otimes^t [a'; b'] = [a \otimes a', b \otimes b']$ and $[a; b] \oplus^t [a'; b'] = [a \oplus a', b \oplus b']$;
- $[a; b] \otimes^k [a'; b'] = [a \otimes a', b \oplus b']$ and $[a; b] \oplus^k [a'; b'] = [a \oplus a', b \otimes b']$;
- $\neg[a; b] = [\neg b; \neg a]$.

$\otimes^t$ and $\oplus^t$ ($\otimes^k$ and $\oplus^k$) denote the meet and join operations on $\mathcal{T} \times \mathcal{T}$ w.r.t. the truth (knowledge) ordering, respectively. For instance, in $\mathcal{L}_{[0,1]}$,

$$[0.1; 0.4] \oplus^t [0.2; 0.5] = [0.2; 0.5] \ ,$$
$$[0.1; 0.4] \otimes^t [0.2; 0.5] = [0.1; 0.4] \ ,$$
$$[0.1; 0.4] \oplus^k [0.2; 0.5] = [0.2; 0.4] \ ,$$
$$[0.1; 0.4] \otimes^k [0.2; 0.5] = [0.1; 0.5] \ ,$$
$$\neg[0.1; 0.4] = [0.6; 0.9] \ .$$

Finally, we extend in a similar way the combination functions from $\mathcal{T}$ to $\mathcal{T} \times \mathcal{T}$. Let f_c (resp. f_p and f_d) be a conjunction (resp. propagation and disjunction) function over $\mathcal{T}$ and $[a; b], [a'; b'] \in \mathcal{T} \times \mathcal{T}$, then

- $f_c([a; b], [a'; b']) = [f_c(a, a'), f_c(b, b')]$;
- $f_p([a; b], [a'; b']) = [f_p(a, a'), f_p(b, b')]$;
- $f_d([a; b], [a'; b']) = [f_d(a, a'), f_d(b, b')]$.

It is easy to verify that the combination functions above preserve the original properties of combination functions and that the negation function is monotone w.r.t. $\preceq_k$.

Theorem 1. *Consider $\mathcal{T} \times \mathcal{T}$ with the orderings $\preceq_t$ and $\preceq_k$. Then*

1. *$\otimes^t, \oplus^t, \otimes^k, \oplus^k$ and the extensions of combination functions are continuous (and, thus, monotonic) w.r.t. $\preceq_t$ and $\preceq_k$;*
2. *any extended negation function is monotonic w.r.t. $\preceq_k$;*
3. *if the negation function satisfies the de Morgan laws, i.e. $\forall a, b \in \mathcal{T}.\neg(a \oplus b) = \neg a \otimes \neg b$ then the extended negation function is continuous w.r.t. $\preceq_k$.*

We extend interpretations based on $\mathcal{T}$ to $\mathcal{T} \times \mathcal{T}$ as follows.

Definition 2 (Approximate interpretation). *Let P be an np-program. An approximate interpretation of P is a total function I from the Herbrand base $\mathcal{B}_P$ to the set $\mathcal{T} \times \mathcal{T}$. The set of all the approximate interpretations of P is denoted $\mathcal{C}_P$.*

---

[3] An alternative to the interval bilattice is used in [5,11], where a pair $[a; b]$ is interpreted as degree of doubt and degree of belief, or, similarly, as degree of falsity and degree of truth, respectively. Of course definitions of orders and extensions of functions would then be different, but the whole theory presented in the paper would still hold.

Intuitively, assigning the logical value $[a; b]$ to an atom A means that the exact certainty value of A lies in between a and b w.r.t. $\preceq$. $I(A) = [a; b]$ can also be understood as the specification of a *lower bound and upper bound constraint* on the admissible certainty values of A. Our goal will be to determine for each atom of the Herbrand base of P the most precise interval that can be inferred.

The two orderings on $\mathcal{T} \times \mathcal{T}$ can be extended to the set of approximate interpretations $\mathcal{C}_P$ in a usual way: let I_1 and I_2 be in $\mathcal{C}_P$, $I_1 \preceq_t I_2$ iff $I_1(A) \preceq_t I_2(A)$, for all ground atoms A; and $I_1 \preceq_k I_2$ iff $I_1(A) \preceq_k I_2(A)$, for all ground atoms A. Under these two orderings $\mathcal{C}_P$ becomes a complete bilattice. The meet and join operations over $\mathcal{T} \times \mathcal{T}$ for both orderings are extended to $\mathcal{C}_P$ in the usual way (e.g. for any atom A, $(I \oplus^k J)(A) = I(A) \oplus^k J(A)$). Negation is extended similarly, for any atom A, $\neg I(A) = I(\neg A)$, and approximate interpretations are extended to $\mathcal{T}$, for any $\alpha \in \mathcal{T}$, $I(\alpha) = [\alpha; \alpha]$. With $\mathtt{I_f}$ and $\mathtt{I_t}$ we will denote the bottom and top approximate interpretation under $\preceq_t$ (they map any atom into $\mathtt{f}$ and $\mathtt{t}$, respectively). With $\mathtt{I_\perp}$ and $\mathtt{I_\top}$ we will denote the bottom and top approximate interpretation under $\preceq_k$ (they map any atom into $\perp$ and $\top$, respectively).

Definition 3 (Model of a logic program). *Let P be an np-program and let I be an approximate interpretation of P.*

1. *I satisfies a ground np-rule r: $A \xleftarrow{\alpha_r} L_1, ..., L_n; \langle f_d, f_p, f_c \rangle$ in P, denoted $\models_I r$, iff $I(A) \succeq_t f_p([\alpha_r; \alpha_r], f_c(\{I(L_1), \ldots, I(L_n)\}))$;*
2. *I is a model of P, or I satisfies P, denoted $\models_I P$, iff for all atoms $A \in \mathcal{B}_P$, $I(A) \succeq_t f_d(X)$ where f_d is the disjunction function associated with $\pi(A)$ and*

$$X = \{f_p([\alpha_r; \alpha_r], f_c(\{I(L_1), \ldots, I(L_n)\})): A \xleftarrow{\alpha_r} L_1, ..., L_n; \langle f_d, f_p, f_c \rangle \in P^*\}.$$

4   Assumption-Based Semantics

In this section we define the semantics of an np-program w.r.t. a given assumption.

Definition 4 (assumption). *An assumption H is an approximate interpretation.*

Informally, we propose to complete our knowledge using an approximate interpretation over the Herbrand base. The term assumption is used in order to stress the fact that it represents "default" knowledge and not the usual "sure" knowledge.

At first, we give the definition of the immediate consequence operator over approximate interpretations, which does not take into account assumptions.

Definition 5. *Let P and I be an np-program and an approximate interpretation, respectively. The immediate consequence operator T_P is defined as follows: for every atom A, $T_P(I)(A) = f_d(X)$, where f_d is the disjunction function associated with $\pi(A)$ and*

$$X = \{f_p([\alpha_r; \alpha_r], f_c(\{I(L_1), \ldots, I(L_n)\})): A \xleftarrow{\alpha_r} L_1, ..., L_n; \langle f_d, f_p, f_c \rangle \in P^*\}.$$

Note that by property (iv) of combination functions satisfied by all disjunction functions, it follows that if an atom A does not appear as the head of a rule, then $T_P(I)(A) = \mathtt{f}$. It can be shown that

Theorem 2. *For any np-program P, T_P is monotonic and, if the de Morgan laws hold, continuous w.r.t. $\preceq_k$.*

It is worth noting that the least fixpoint of T_P with respect to $\preceq_k$ (which exists as T_P is monotonic w.r.t. $\preceq_k$) corresponds to an extension of the classical Kripke-Kleene semantics [6] of Datalog programs with negation to np-programs. Indeed, if we restrict our attention to Datalog with negation, then we have to deal with four values $[0; 0], [1; 1], [0; 1]$ and $[1; 0]$ that correspond to the truth values *false, true, unknown* and *inconsistent*, respectively. In such a setting, our bilattice coincides with Belnap's bilattice $\mathcal{FOUR}$ [1] and for any Datalog program with negation P, the least fixpoint of T_P w.r.t. $\preceq_k$ is a model of P that coincides with the Kripke-Kleene semantics of P.

Example 9. Consider $P = \{(A \leftarrow B, C), (C \leftarrow C, D), (B \leftarrow 0.7), (D \leftarrow 0.9)\}^4$, and $\mathcal{L}_{[0,1]}$ as certainty lattice. The maximal knowledge I that can be inferred from that program (without any extra knowledge such as assumptions) is that the (minimal) values of B and D are exactly 0.7 and 0.9 respectively, while the values of A and C are at most 0.7 and 0.9 respectively, i.e. $I(A) = [0; 0.7], I(B) = [0.7; 0.7], I(C) = [0; 0.9]$ and $I(D) = [0.9; 0.9]$. Using an assumption H asserting that the value of C is by default at least 0.6, i.e. $H(C) = [0.6; 1]$, then we should come up with a more precise characterisation of A and C by stating that A is in $[0.6, 0.7]$ and C is in $[0.6, 0.9]$.

The formalisation of the above concept relies on the notion of safe approximation and support. Intuitively, the notion of *support* provided by a hypothesis H to an np-program P and an interpretation I, denoted $s_P^H(I)$, can be explained as follows. We regard I as what we already know about an intended model of P. On the basis of both the current knowledge I and the information expressed by the rules of P, we want to complete our available knowledge I, by using the hypothesis H. We regard the hypothesis as an additional source of information to be used to complete I. The support of I, $s_P^H(I)$, indeed determines in a principled way the amount of information provided by the hypothesis H that can be joined to I. The concept of support has been extensively discussed in [20] in relation to an alternative, epistemic based, characterization of the well-founded semantics over bilattices. But, in [20], the 'hypothesis' is *fixed* to the approximate interpretation $H = \mathbf{I_f}$. That is, by default the certainty of any atom is $\mathbf{f}$. We base our work on [20], rather than try to extend the well-know Gelfond-Lifschitz transformation [9,10], for two main reasons. First the Gelfond-Lifschitz transformation provides only a computational definition of the semantics whereas our approach provides also an epistemic definition, and thus lights the role of the assumption. Second, the limits of the Gelfond-Lifschitz transformation for reasoning with general assumptions have been shown in [18], where that transformation has been extended for reasoning with any given assumption over Belnap's bilattice $\mathcal{FOUR}$ [1]. It is shown that properties of extremal fixpoints of monotone operators over lattices (and bilattices), on the one hand, allow the use of any such assumption instead of the CWA, but, on the other hand, restrict the set of default values to the set of extremal values only and thus do not allow the use of any assumption over a lattice *different* from $\mathcal{FOUR}$.

Formally, at first, we extend T_P to take an assumption into account as well.

Definition 6. *The* immediate consequence operator T_P^H *is defined as* T_P, *except that rather than mapping into* $\mathbf{f}$ *all atoms that do not appear as the head of any rule in P, T_P^H maps every such atom A into its default value $H(A)$.*

---

[4] For ease of presentation, we omit combination functions.

Definition 7 (safe approximation). *Let P, I and H be an np-program, an approximate interpretation and an assumption, respectively. An approximate interpretation J is safe w.r.t. P, H and I iff both $J \preceq_k H$ and $J \preceq_k T_P^H(I \oplus^k J)$ hold.*

In the above definition, the first condition dictates that a safe interpretation J must not be more informative than a given assumption H. If $J = H$, then every ground atom assumes its default value. But, given I and P, not necessarily the value of every atom may be given by its default (e.g., for some atoms we may infer something else) and, thus, we have to consider some weaker assumption $J \preceq_k H$. The second item dictates that a safe interpretation must be *cumulative*, i.e. that the accumulated amount of information provided by the assumption should be preserved and lead to more precise approximations of an intended model of P.

Example 10. Consider Example 9 and the following table of approximate interpretations I, J_1, J_2, J and assumption H.

	A	B	C	D
I	$[0; 0.7]$	$[0.7; 0.7]$	$[0; 0.9]$	$[0.9; 0.9]$
H	$[0.4; 0.5]$	$[0; 1]$	$[0.6; 1]$	$[0; 0]$
J_1	$[0.3; 0.7]$	$[0; 1]$	$[0.6; 1]$	$[0; 0.9]$
J_2	$[0.4; 0.8]$	$[0; 1]$	$[0.6; 1]$	$[0; 0.9]$
J	$[0.4; 0.7]$	$[0; 1]$	$[0.6; 1]$	$[0; 0.9]$

Then both J_1 and J_2 are safe w.r.t. P, H and I. It is easy to see that the maximal safe approximate interpretation w.r.t. the knowledge order is $J = J_1 \oplus^k J_2$.

Given an assumption H assigning a default value to any atom of the Herbrand base, we can not expect it to be safe, and thus we have to relax the assumption and consider a safe interpretation w.r.t. H, i.e. weaker than H. Among all possible safe approximate interpretations w.r.t. H, we will privilege the maximal one under $\preceq_k$ as our goal is to use it to complete the knowledge provided by P and I.

Definition 8 (support). *Let P be an np-program, let I be an approximate interpretation and consider an assumption H. The support, denoted $s_P^H(I)$, provided by H to P and I is the maximal safe interpretation w.r.t. P, H and I under $\preceq_k$.*

It can be shown that if J_1 and J_2 are two safe interpretations w.r.t. P, H and I, then $J_1 \oplus^k J_2$ is safe w.r.t. P, H and I. It follows that the support is a well-defined concept and that we have $s_P^H(I) = \bigoplus^k \{J: J$ is safe w.r.t. P, H and $I\}$.

The following theorem provides an algorithm for computing the support.

Theorem 3. *Let P be an np-program. $s_P^H(I)$ can be computed as the iterated fixpoint of $F_{P,I}^H$ beginning the computation with H, where $F_{P,I}^H(J) = H \otimes^k T_P^H(I \oplus^k J)$.*

From Theorems 1 and 2, it can be shown that $F_{P,I}^H$ is monotone and, if the de Morgan laws hold, continuous w.r.t. $\preceq_k$. It follows that the iteration of the function $F_{P,I}^H$ starting from H decreases w.r.t. $\preceq_k$ and reaches a fixed point.

Example 11 (Example 10 cont.). Below, the computation of the support is shown.

	A	B	C	D
I	$[0; 0.7]$	$[0.7; 0.7]$	$[0; 0.9]$	$[0.9; 0.9]$
$J_0 = H$	$[0.4; 0.5]$	$[0; 1]$	$[0.6; 1]$	$[0; 0]$
$J_1 = J_2 = s_P^H(I)$	$[0.4; 0.7]$	$[0; 1]$	$[0.6; 1]$	$[0; 0.9]$

Intuitively, the support of an assumption represents the maximal knowledge that can be considered "compatible" with the program and that can be used "safely" to *complete* the knowledge inferred from the program. Given an assumption H, this intuition leads to the definition of a family of models, those models that already integrate their own support provided by H, i.e. the models of P "supported" by H.

Definition 9 (*H-supported models*). *Let P be an np-program and let H be an assumption. A model I of P is supported by H if $s_P^H(I) \preceq_k I$. The semantics of P supported by H is the least model under $\preceq_k$ of P supported by H, denoted A_P^H.*

Example 12 (Example 11 cont.). Below, the semantics, A_P^H, of P supported by H is shown. Note that $s_P^H(A_P^H) \preceq_k H$ and $s_P^H(A_P^H) \preceq_k A_P^H$, i.e. A_P^H contains all the default information that can be used to complete the knowledge provided by the program.

	A	B	C	D
H	$[0.4; 0.5]$	$[0; 1]$	$[0.6; 1]$	$[0; 0]$
$s_P^H(A_P^H)$	$[0.4; 0.7]$	$[0; 1]$	$[0.6; 1]$	$[0; 0.9]$
A_P^H	$[0.6; 0.7]$	$[0.7; 0.7]$	$[0.6; 0.9]$	$[0.9; 0.9]$

Note that there are two special cases of assumptions that are closely related to the interpretation of negation : given an atom A, then if $H(A) = \mathbf{f}$ then $\neg A$ is interpreted as negation-as-failure *not* A, whereas if $H(A) = \perp$ then we revert to the classical interpretation of negation. These two particular cases may be seen as strictly related to Extended and Disjunctive Logic Programs [10], in which you may consider to add a rule of the form $\neg A \leftarrow not\ A$ or not, respectively.

Supported models have also a fixed point characterization. Given an approximate interpretation I, an assumption H and an np-program P, there are two ways of inferring information from an np-program P: (i) using T_P^H; and (ii) using s_P^H. We propose to combine them in order to infer as much knowledge as possible: that is (i) first we compute $s_P^H(I)$, i.e. the most precise approximation of the assumption H that can be used safely; (ii) we add that approximate interpretation to I (that represents the available knowledge) and obtain $I \oplus^k s_P^H(I)$; and finally (iii) we activate the rules of the program by applying the immediate consequence operator, i.e. we compute $T_P^H(I \oplus^k s_P^H(I))$.

Definition 10. *Let P, H and I be an np-program, an assumption and an approximate interpretation, respectively. The assumption-based immediate consequence operator, denoted Γ_P^H, is defined as $\Gamma_P^H(I) = T_P^H(I \oplus^k s_P^H(I))$.*

From the monotonicity (continuity) of T_P^H and s_P^H over the complete lattice $\mathcal{C}_P$, w.r.t. $\preceq_k$, by the well-known Knaster-Tarski theorem, it follows that

Theorem 4. *Let P be an np-program and let H be an assumption. Then Γ_P^H is monotone and, if the de Morgan laws hold, continuous w.r.t. the knowledge order $\preceq_k$. Therefore, Γ_P^H has a least fixpoint w.r.t. the knowledge order $\preceq_k$.*

Γ_P^H provides a fixed point characterization of supported models and, thus, A_P^H can be computed as the iterated fixpoint of Γ_P^H starting with $I_\perp$.

Theorem 5. *Let P be an np-program and let H be an assumption. An interpretation I is a model of P supported by H iff I is a fixpoint of Γ_P^H.*

Example 13 (Example 11 cont.). Below, the computation of the semantics A_P^H is shown.

	A	B	C	D
H	$[0.4; 0.5]$	$[0; 1]$	$[0.6; 1]$	$[0; 0]$
$I_0 = I_\perp$	$[0; 1]$	$[0; 1]$	$[0; 1]$	$[0; 1]$
$s_P^H(I_0)$	$[0; 1]$	$[0; 1]$	$[0; 1]$	$[0; 0.9]$
I_1	$[0; 1]$	$[0.7; 0.7]$	$[0; 0.9]$	$[0.9; 0.9]$
$s_P^H(I_1)$	$[0.4; 0.7]$	$[0; 1]$	$[0.6; 1]$	$[0; 0.9]$
I_2	$[0.6; 0.7]$	$[0.7; 0.7]$	$[0.6, 0.9]$	$[0.9; 0.9]$
$s_P^H(I_2)$	$[0.4; 0.7]$	$[0; 1]$	$[0.6; 1]$	$[0; 0.9]$
$I_3 = I_2 = A_P^H$	$[0.6; 0.7]$	$[0.7; 0.7]$	$[0.6; 0.9]$	$[0.9; 0.9]$

Example 14. Consider the program P given in Example 7. Let H be the assumption that assigns to the atoms `motive(Ted)`, `has_witness(Ted)` and `suspect(Ted)` the value $[0; 0]$, to the atom `innocent(Ted)` the value $[1; 1]$, and to the other atoms the value $[0; 1]$. Then it can be shown that the semantics of P for the three different assumptions, $H_1 = I_\perp$ (i.e. everything unknown), $H_2 = I_f$ (i.e. everything false) and H are:

	suspect(Ted)	cleared(Ted)	charge(Ted)
$A_P^{H_1}$	$[0.6; 0.92]$	$[0.2; 0.52]$	$[0.6; 0.92]$
$A_P^{H_2}$	$[0.6; 0.6]$	$[0.2; 0.2]$	$[0.8; 0.8]$
A_P^H	$[0.6; 0.6]$	$[0.52; 0.52]$	$[0.6; 0.6]$

Note that using the assumption that everything is unknown by default gives obviously a less precise semantics than using any other assumption. As anticipated in Example 1, the OWA, i.e. H_1, does not provide precise information, and the CWA, i.e. H_2, decreases the degree of innocence in presence of incomplete information and leads to charge a person despite the absence of evidence for or against the guiltyness of that person, while the assumption H respects the principle of presumption of innocence and leads to expected results.

A first attempt to give a semantics to PDDU with negation under non-uniform assumptions is described in [19]. It is based on an extension of the alternating fixpoint semantics of van Gelder [30], i.e. on a separated management of positive and negative literals. The approach proposed here is based on a more intuitive management of negation where no distinction is made between positive and negative literals. Moreover, our approach is more general: in fact (i) in [19], some knowledge is lost whenever the value of an atom oscillates between two different uncertainty values, while in our approach, an approximation (interval) of the uncertainty value is assigned. For instance, with respect to Example 8 under the assumption $I_\perp$, [19] assigns $\perp = [0, 1]$ to both A and B, while our approach assigns $[0.2, 0.7]$ to A and $[0.3, 0.8]$ to B; and (ii) our approach does not impose any restriction on the kind of interpretations that can be used as assumptions (any value, even an interval, can be considered as a default value).

If we restrict our attention to PDDU and consider the assumption $H = I_f$, then our approach captures the semantics proposed in [17] for PDDU.

Theorem 6. *Let P be a program as defined in [17]. If $H = I_f$, then the semantics A_P^H assigns exact values to all atoms and coincides with the semantics presented in [17].*

The following theorem states that our approach extends the usual semantics of normal logic programs to the PDDU framework.

Theorem 7. *Let P be a Datalog program with negation. Then we have:*

1. *the semantics of P w.r.t. $H = \mathbf{I_f}$, A_P^H, is the well-founded semantics of P;*
2. *if the assumption H is such that, for all atoms A, if A is not the head of any rule in P^*, then $H(A) = \mathbf{f}$ else $H(A) = \perp$, then the semantics A_P^H of P coincides with the Kripke-Kleene semantics of P.*
3. *a stable model of P [9] is a model of P supported by $H = \mathbf{I_f}$.*

5   Conclusions

PDDU [17] has been proposed as a unifying umbrella for many existing approaches towards the manipulation of uncertainty in deductive databases. We introduced non-uniform assumptions into this context, which allows to assign any default value to the atoms. The well known OWA, CWA and the combination of both are, thus, special cases. A main topic for further research is to generalize the introduced concept within a more fundamental work in which we deal with bilattices, disjunctive programs, assumptions and stable models [9,10,26] in place of our current setting.

References

1. N. D. Belnap. How a computer should think. In Gilbert Ryle, editor, *Contemporary aspects of philosophy*, pages 30–56. Oriel Press, Stocksfield, GB, 1977.
2. B.G. Buchanan and E.H. Shortli. A model of inexact reasoning in medicine. *Mathematical Bioscience*, 23:351–379, 1975.
3. T. H. Cao. Annotated fuzzy logic programs. *Fuzzy Sets and Systems*, 113(2):277–298, 2000.
4. D. Dubois, J. Lang, and H. Prade. Towards possibilistic logic programming. In *Proc. of ICLP-91*, pages 581–595. MIT Press, 1991.
5. M. Fitting. The family of stable models. *J. of Logic Programming*, 17:197–225, 1993.
6. M. Fitting. A Kripke-Kleene-semantics for general logic programs. *J. of Logic Programming*, 2:295–312, 1985.
7. M. Fitting. Bilattices and the semantics of logic programming. *J. of Logic Programming*, 11:91–116, 1991.
8. N. Fuhr. Probabilistic Datalog: Implementing logical information retrieval for advanced applications. *J. of the American Society for Information Science*, 51(2):95–110, 2000.
9. M. Gelfond and V. Lifschitz. The stable model semantics for logic programming. In *Proc. of ICLP-88*, pages 1070–1080, 1988. MIT Press.
10. M. Gelfond and V. Lifschitz. Classical negation in logic programs and disjunctive databases. *New Generation Computing*, 9(3/4):365–386, 1991.
11. M. L. Ginsberg. Multi-valued logics: a uniform approach to reasoning in artificial intelligence. *Computational Intelligence*, 4:265–316, 1988.
12. M. Kifer and Ai Li. On the semantics of rule-based expert systems with uncertainty. In *Proc. of ICDT-88*, LNCS 326, pages 102–117, 1988.
13. M. Kifer and V. S. Subrahmanian. Theory of generalized annotated logic programming and its applications. *J. of Logic Programming*, 12:335–367, 1992.

14. L. Lakshmanan. An epistemic foundation for logic programming with uncertainty. In LNCS 880, pages 89–100, 1994.
15. L. Lakshmanan and F. Sadri. Uncertain deductive databases: a hybrid approach. *Information Systems*, 22(8):483–508, 1997.
16. L. Lakshmanan and N. Shiri. Probabilistic deductive databases. In *Int'l Logic Programming Symposium*, pages 254–268, 1994.
17. L. Lakshmanan and N. Shiri. A parametric approach to deductive databases with uncertainty. *IEEE Transactions on Knowledge and Data Engineering*, 13(4):554–570, 2001.
18. Y. Loyer and N. Spyratos and D. Stamate. Integration of Information in Four-valued Logics under Non-Uniform Assumptions. In *Proc. of the 30th IEEE Int. Symp. on Multi-Valued Logics*, IEEE Press, pages 185–191, 2000.
19. Y. Loyer and U. Straccia. Uncertainty and partial non-uniform assumptions in parametric deductive databases. In *Proc. of JELIA-02*, LNCS 2424, pages 271–282,
20. Y. Loyer and U. Straccia. The well-founded semantics of logic programs over bilattices: an alternative characterisation. TR ISTI-2003-TR-05, ISTI-CNR, Pisa, Italy, 2003. Submitted.
21. Y. Loyer, N. Spyratos and D. Stamate. Parametrized Semantics of Logic Programs - a unifying approach. *Theoretical Computer Science*, to appear.
22. Y. Loyer, N. Spyratos and D. Stamate. Hypotheses-Based Semantics of Logic Programs in Multi-Valued Logics. *ACM Transactions on Computational Logic*, to appear.
23. T. Lukasiewicz. Fixpoint characterizations for many-valued disjunctive logic programs with probabilistic semantics. In *Proc. of LPNMR-01*, LNCS 2173, pages 336–350, 2001.
24. R. Ng and V. S. Subrahmanian. Stable model semantics for probabilistic deductive databases. In *Proc. of ISMIS-91*, LNCS 542, pages 163–171, 1991.
25. R. Ng and V. S. Subrahmanian. Probabilistic logic programming. *Information and Computation*, 101(2):150–201, 1993.
26. T. C. Przymusinski. Extended stable semantics for normal and disjunctive programs. In *Proc. of ICLP-90*, pages 459–477. MIT Press, 1990.
27. Ehud Y. Shapiro. Logic programs with uncertainties: A tool for implementing rule-based systems. In *Proc. of IJCAI-83*, pages 529–532, 1983.
28. V.S. Subramanian. On the semantics of quantitative logic programs. In *Proc. of 4th IEEE Symp. on Logic Programming*, pages 173–182. Computer Society Press, 1987.
29. M.H. van Emden. Quantitative deduction and its fixpoint theory. *J. of Logic Programming*, 4(1):37–53, 1986.
30. A. van Gelder. The alternating fixpoint of logic programs with negation. In *Proc. of ACM PODS-89*, pages 1–10, 1989.
31. A. van Gelder, K. A. Ross, and J. S. Schlimpf. The well-founded semantics for general logic programs. *J. of the ACM*, 38(3):620–650, January 1991.
32. G. Wagner. A logical reconstruction of fuzzy inference in databases and logic programs. In *Proc. of IFSA-97*, Prague, 1997.
33. G. Wagner. Negation in fuzzy and possibilistic logic programs. In *Logic programming and Soft Computing*, Research Studies Press, 1998.
34. L. A. Zadeh. Fuzzy sets. *Information and Control*, 8(3):338–353, 1965.
35. L. A. Zadeh. Fuzzy sets as a basis for a theory of possibility. *Fuzzy Sets and Systems*, 1(1):3–28, 1965.

A Generic Persistence Model for (C)LP Systems

J. Correas[1], J.M. Gómez[1], M. Carro[1], D. Cabeza[1], and M. Hermenegildo[1,2]

[1] School of Computer Science, Technical University of Madrid (UPM)
[2] Depts. of Comp. Science and El. and Comp. Eng., U. of New Mexico (UNM)

Mutable state is traditionally implemented in Prolog and other (C)LP systems by performing dynamic modifications to predicate definitions at runtime, i.e. to *dynamic predicates* of the *internal database*. Dynamic facts are often used to store information accessible per module or globally and which can be preserved through backtracking. These database updates, despite the obvious drawback of their non-declarative nature, have practical applications and they are given a practical semantics by the so-called logical view of (internal) database updates.

On the other hand, the lifetime of the data in the Prolog internal database is that of the Prolog process, i.e., the Prolog database lacks *persistence*. In this context persistence means that program state modifications will survive across program executions, and may even be accessible to other programs—atomically and concurrently. Traditionally, this has been taken care of explicitly by the programmer by, e.g., periodically reading and writing state to an external device (a file or an external database through a suitable interface) and providing locking for concurrency. This approach offers a workable but very tedious solution, where significant modifications to programs are needed and where, unless substantial effort is invested, only limited functionality is achieved.

The fundamental idea that we propose is to make persistence be *a character-istic of certain dynamic predicates*, which encapsulate the persistent state, and to automate implementation by coding persistence once and for all in a reusable (system) library providing the class of *persistent predicates*. The main effect of *declaring a predicate persistent* (a process for which we propose a suitable syntax, compatible with the Ciao system's assertion language) is that *any changes made to such predicates persist from one execution to the next one, and are transactional, and, optionally, externally visible*. The model allows associating an external, persistent storage medium (a file, a database table, etc.) to each such predicate, which will "reside" in that medium. Notably, persistent predicates appear to a program as ordinary (dynamic) predicates: calls to them do not need to be coded or marked specially, and the builtins to update them are (suitably modified versions of) the same used with the internal database (e.g., asserta/1, assertz/1, retract/1, etc.). Thus, only minor modifications to the program code (often independent of its internal logic) are needed to achieve persistence. Also, when using persistent predicates the external storage is at all times *in sync* with the internal database. This provides security against, e.g., system crashes or abnormal termination. Also, transaction atomicity allows *concurrent access* to be handled with only limited effort. Thus, files and/or external databases can be used to communicate and share data among programs, which each view as part of their internal databases. Quite interestingly, since persistent predicates are viewed as regular dynamic Prolog predicates, analyzers (and

C. Palamidessi (Ed.): ICLP 2003, LNCS 2916, pp. 481–482, 2003.
© Springer-Verlag Berlin Heidelberg 2003

related tools) can deal with them with no additional effort. In turn, information deduced by analysis tools (such as, e.g., types and modes) can be used to *optimize* accesses to external storage (the full paper provides performance data for such optimizations in the context of a relational, SQL database).

Finally, perhaps the most interesting advantage of the notion of persistent predicates is that it *abstracts away* the storage mechanism. This allows developing applications which can store data alternatively on, e.g., files or databases with only a few simple changes to a declaration stating the location and modality used for persistent storage. It also minimizes impact on the host language, as the semantics of the access to the database is *compatible* with that of Prolog. We also argue that the conceptual model of persistence developed provides one of the most natural ways of interfacing logic programs with databases.

A number of current Prolog systems offer features which are related to the capabilities offered by our approach: Quintus Prolog has *ProDBI* (also available for SICStus under the generic name *Prodata*), which allows queries (but not updates) on tables in a similar way to Prolog predicates. SICStus Prolog has also special interfaces to database systems. XSB and SWI include *PrologSQL*, which can compile on demand a conjunction of literals to SQL using the compiler by Draxler, also used in our approach, but which do not provide transparent persistence. However, we argue that none of these approaches achieve the same level of flexibility, conceptual simplicity, and seamless integration with Prolog achieved by our proposal.

Implementations of our proposed model have been used in several non-trivial applications, such as the WebDB *deductive database engine*, a generic database system with a highly customizable *html interface*. WebDB allows creating and maintaining Prolog databases stored in a variety of mediums by means of persistent predicates and using a WWW interface. They have also been used in real-world applications such as the Amos tool, aimed at facilitating the reuse of Open Source code through the use of an ontology-based search engine working on a large database of code information.

Full details are available in the full paper, where also experimental data and examples can be found [CGC+03].

Acknowledgments. This work has been partially supported by the EU IST Project IST-2001-34717, Amos and by MCYT project TIC 2002-0055, CUBICO. Thanks are due to I. Caballero, J. F. Morales, S. Genaim, and C. Taboch for their collaboration and feedback.

References

[CGC+03]   J. Correas, J. M. Gomez, M. Carro, D. Cabeza, and M. Hermenegildo. A Generic Model for Persistence in CLP Systems. Technical Report CLIP3/2003.0, Technical University of Madrid, School of Computer Science, UPM, August 2003. http://clip.dia.fi.upm.es/papers/persdb-tr.pdf.

Definitions in Answer Set Programming

(Extended Abstract)

Selim T. Erdoğan and Vladimir Lifschitz

Department of Computer Sciences
University of Texas, Austin, USA
{selim, vl}@cs.utexas.edu

The work described here is motivated by our interest in the methodology of answer set programming (ASP). The idea of ASP is to solve a problem by writing a logic program the answer sets of which correspond to solutions.

An ASP program usually contains a group of rules written to generate answer sets corresponding to an easily described superset of the set of solutions of the problem we want to solve (we call these rules the "generate" part of the program). Then some constraints are added to eliminate the "bad" potential solutions. Before adding the constraints, it is often convenient (and sometimes necessary) to define some auxiliary atoms in terms of the atoms which occur in the generate part. These new atoms are then used in the constraints.

To prove that the answer sets of a program designed according to this plan correspond to the solutions of the problem we want to solve, we need to describe, among other things, how adding the definitions of the auxiliary atoms affects the answer sets of the generate part of the program. In some cases this can be done using the splitting set theorem [Lifschitz and Turner, 1994], which allows us, under certain conditions, to split a logic program into two parts and then determine how the answer sets of the first part are affected by adding the second part. In application to proving the correctness of an ASP program, the first part would consist of the generate rules and the second part would be the definitions.

When we write a program in the input language of the SMODELS[1] system, the generate part often includes rules of the form

$$\{p_1, \ldots, p_n\} \tag{1}$$

where $p_1, \ldots, p_n$ are atoms. Unfortunately, the splitting set theorem in [Lifschitz and Turner, 1994] is limited to programs with rules of a simple form, with only disjunctions of literals allowed in the head, and conjunctions of literals, possibly prefixed with *not*, in the body. Thus it is not applicable to a program containing a rule with braces, such as (1).

We resolve this difficulty by extending the splitting set theorem to programs with nested expressions [Lifschitz *et al.*, 1999]. Such programs allow negation as failure (*not*), conjunction (,) and disjunction (;) to be nested arbitrarily, in both heads and bodies of rules. According to [Ferraris and Lifschitz, 2003], expressions of the form (1), as well as cardinality and weight constraints, can be viewed as nested expressions. In particular, (1) is equivalent to

---

[1] http://www.tcs.hut.fi/Software/smodels.

C. Palamidessi (Ed.): ICLP 2003, LNCS 2916, pp. 483–484, 2003.

$$(p_1; not \ p_1), \ldots, (p_n; not \ p_n). \tag{2}$$

(The old theorem from [Lifschitz and Turner, 1994] does not apply to programs with rules of the form (2), which contain negation as failure in the head.)

To state the new splitting set theorem we need some terminology and notation. A *regular* occurrence of a literal is defined in [Lifschitz *et al.*, 1999]. We will use $head(r)$ to denote the set of all the literals that occur regularly in the head of a rule r, and $lit(r)$ to denote the set of all such literals in the whole rule.

A *splitting set* for a program Π is any set U of literals such that, for every rule $r \in \Pi$, if $head(r) \cap U \neq \emptyset$ then $lit(r) \subseteq U$. The set of rules $r \in \Pi$ such that $lit(r) \subseteq U$ is denoted by $b_U(\Pi)$.

The function e_U defined below represents the process of "partial evaluation" of a formula. Consider two sets of literals U, X and a formula F. For each regular occurrence of a literal L in F such that $L \in U$, if $L \in X$ replace L with $\top$, otherwise replace L with $\bot$. The new formula obtained will be denoted by $e_U(F, X)$. For a program Π, we will denote by $e_U(\Pi, X)$ the program obtained by replacing each rule $F \leftarrow G$ of Π by $e_U(F, X) \leftarrow e_U(G, X)$.

Splitting Set Theorem. *Let U be a splitting set for a program Π. A consistent set of literals is an answer set for Π iff it can be written as $X \cup Y$ where X is an answer set for $b_U(\Pi)$ and Y is an answer set for $e_U(\Pi \setminus b_U(\Pi), X)$.*

Using the splitting set theorem, it can be proved that, under some conditions, adding definitions extends the answer sets of a program conservatively:

Proposition. *Let Π_1 be a program and Q be a set of atoms that do not occur in Π_1. Let Π_2 be a program that consists of rules of the form $q \leftarrow F$, where $q \in Q$, and F does not contain any element of Q in the scope of negation as failure. Then $Z \mapsto Z \setminus Q$ is a 1-1 correspondence between the answer sets for $\Pi_1 \cup \Pi_2$ and the answer sets for Π_1.*

See http://www.cs.utexas.edu/users/vl/papers/defs.ps for the proofs.

We are grateful to Paolo Ferraris for his comments and suggestions. This work was partially supported by the Texas Higher Education Coordinating Board under Grant 003658-0322-2001.

References

[Ferraris and Lifschitz, 2003] Paolo Ferraris and Vladimir Lifschitz. Weight constraints as nested expressions.[2] *Theory and Practice of Logic Programming*, 2003. To appear.

[Lifschitz and Turner, 1994] Vladimir Lifschitz and Hudson Turner. Splitting a logic program. In Pascal Van Hentenryck, editor, *Proc. Eleventh Int'l Conf. on Logic Programming*, pages 23–37, 1994.

[Lifschitz *et al.*, 1999] Vladimir Lifschitz, Lappoon R. Tang, and Hudson Turner. Nested expressions in logic programs. *Annals of Mathematics and Artificial Intelligence*, 25:369–389, 1999.

---

[2] http://www.cs.utexas.edu/users/vl/papers/weight.ps.

A New Mode Declaration for Tabled Predicates[*]

Hai-Feng Guo[1] and Gopal Gupta[2]

[1] Department of Computer Science, University of Nebraska at Omaha, USA
haifengguo@mail.unomaha.edu
[2] Department of Computer Science, University of Texas at Dallas, USA
gupta@utdallas.edu

A tabled logic programming (TLP) system can be thought of as an engine for efficiently computing fixed points. In a TLP system, a global data structure *table* is introduced to memorize the answers of any subgoals to tabled predicates, whose purpose is to never do the same computation twice. Consider the tabled predicate reach/2 defined as follows for the reachability relation. Given a query reach(a,X), a TLP system returns answers X=b, X=c and X=a, albeit the predicate is defined left-recursively.

```
:- table reach/2.                          :- table reach/3.
                                           reach(X, Y, E) :-
reach(X, Y) :- reach(X, Z), arc(Z, Y).       reach(X, Z, E1), arc(Z, Y, E2),
reach(X, Y) :- arc(X, Y).                     append(E1, E2, E).
                                           reach(X, Y, E) :- arc(X, Y, E).
arc(a, b).    arc(a, c).    arc(b, a).     arc(a, b, [(a,b)]).    arc(a, c, [(a,c)]).
                                           arc(b, a, [(b,c)]).
```

Now the question is that since multiple nodes are reachable from a, can the system return the corresponding paths as well to justify the query results? Traditionally, logic programming makes it convenient to build a representation of evidence by adding an extra argument whose instantiation becomes the evidence. Unfortunately, putting evidences as extra tabled predicate arguments results in recording evidences as part of the answers to tabled calls, which might dramatically increase the size of global table space because there could be many explanations for a single answer in the original program. For the reachability instance, we can introduce a new transformed tabled predicate reach/3 shown as above, where the third argument E is used to generate the path from X to Y. Obviously, there are infinite number of paths from a to any node due to the cycle between a and b. Similar problems are raised on generating parsing trees. Therefore, from a complexity standpoint, tabling predicates has certain drawbacks.

In this paper, we introduce a special mode declaration for tabled predicates to overcome these drawbacks. This mode declaration emphasizes only the indexed arguments in a tabled predicate for variant checking. The new mode declaration for tabled predicates can be described in a form of ":- table_mode $p(a_1, ..., a_n)$.", where p is a predicate name, $n \geq 0$, and each a_i has one of the following forms:

+ denotes that this argument should be used for variant checking;
− denotes that this argument should not be used for variant checking.

---

[*] Research partially supported by Nebraska EPSCoR award.

C. Palamidessi (Ed.): ICLP 2003, LNCS 2916, pp. 485–486, 2003.
© Springer-Verlag Berlin Heidelberg 2003

Consider the reachability example again. Suppose we declare the mode as ":- table_mode $reach(+, +, -)$". It means that only the first two arguments of the predicate reach/3 are used for variant checking. We use DRA (dynamic re-ordering of alternatives) resolution to illustrate how the table_mode declaration affects the query results.

As shown in Figure 1, the computation of reach(a,Y,E) is divided into three stages: normal, looping and complete. The purpose of the normal stage is to find all the looping alternatives (the clause (1) leading to a variant sub-goal reach(a,Z,E1)) and record all the answers generated from the non-looping alternatives (the clause (2)) into the table. The new_answer indicates that the new answer generated from that successful path should be added into the table. Then, in the looping stage only the looping alternative (clause (1)) is per-formed repeatedly to consume new tabled answers until a fixed point is reached, that is, no more answers for reach(a,Y,E) can be found. Since only the first two arguments of reach/3 are used for variant checking, the last two answers "Y=b, E=[(a,b),(b,a),(a,b)]" and "Y=c, E=[(a,b),(b,a),(a,c)]", shown on the rightmost two sub-branches, are variant answers to "Y=b, E=[(a,b)]" and "Y=c, E=[(a,c)]" respectively. Therefore, no new answers are added into the table at those points. Afterwards, the complete stage is reached. As a result, each reachable node from a has a simple path.

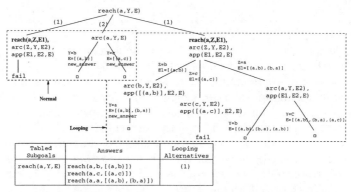

Fig. 1. DRA Resolution with Table Mode Declaration

The directive table_mode makes it easy and efficient to extract evidences for tabled predicates as their arguments. Those generated evidences can be shown concisely without involving any self-dependency among tabled subgoals. For the reachability instance, each returned path is simple in that all nodes on the path are distinct (except the first and the last, which could be the same).

Essentially, if we regard tabled predicates as functions, then a function is con-sidered to be uniquely defined by its input arguments. The mode declaration for tabled predicates exactly decides which arguments are the input ones for func-tions. Therefore, in the previous example, the first two arguments of reach/3 will be the input arguments, and variant checking should be done w.r.t. only those arguments in tabled resolution. From this viewpoint, the new mode declaration also makes tabled resolution more efficient and flexible.

Adding the Temporal Relations in Semantic Web Ontologies

Kwanho Jung[1], Hyunjang Kong[1], Junho Choi[1], Yoojin Moon[2], and Pankoo Kim[1,*]

[1] Dept. of Computer Science and Engineering
Chosun University, Gwangju 501-759, Korea
{khjung,kisofire,spica}@mina.chosun.ac.kr
pkkim@chosun.ac.kr
[2]Hankuk Univ. of Foreign Studies, yjmoon@hufs.ac.kr

Abstract. In studying the semantic web, the main area is to build web ontologies and create the relationships between concepts. Until now, the capabilities of markup languages for expressing the relationships have improved a great deal but it is insufficient for representing the temporal relationships. In this paper, we define the new axioms for representing the temporal relationships.

1 Introduction

As the web advances, the businesses are made throughout the web and most of the businesses have their business rules. It is very important to manage the temporal rules in the many business rules. Until now, the representation of the temporal relations is not good enough to use the existing markup languages' capabilities. Therefore, in this paper, we suggest the method to express the temporal relations. Our idea is based on the Temporal Description Logic. In our study, we select the basic temporal relations that is 'before' and 'after' from the Allen's 13 interval relations. And then, we add the new axioms to represent the temporal relations in semantic web ontologies.

2 Defining the New Axioms for Representing the Temporal Relationships Based on the Description Logic

In this paper, the temporal relationships are defined based on the Temporal Description Logic, which are used to construct the web ontologies. However, it is too difficult to define all the temporal relationships. Therefore, this paper basically defines the two Temporal Description Logics that are 'Before' and 'After'.

This study suggests that the *ALC(D)* Description Logic is more suitable for describing the temporal relationships. In Allen's interval, the relationships are internally defined using a set of real numbers, *R* together with the predicates $<, \leq, >, \geq, =, \neq$. The interval concept can be defined as an ordered pair of real numbers by referring to the concrete predicate, $\leq$, applied to the features, **LEFT-HAS-TIME** and **RIGHT-HAS-TIME**.

---

* Corresponding author

C. Palamidessi (Ed.): ICLP 2003, LNCS 2916, pp. 487–488, 2003.

Interval ≡ ∃ (LEFT-HAS-TIME, RIGHT-HAS-TIME). ≤

Allen's relationships are binary relationships between two intervals and are represented by the **Pair** concept, which uses the features, **FIRST** and **SECOND**.

Pair ≡ ∃FIRST.Interval ⊓ ∃SECOND.Interval

Now Allen's relationships regarding 'Before' and 'After' can be easily defined.

Table 1. Definition of 'Before' and 'After' in the Temporal Description Logic

Before ≡ Pair ⊓ (FIRST∘RIGHT-HAS-TIME, SECOND∘LEFT-HAS-TIME). <
After ≡ Pair ⊓ (FIRST∘RIGHT-HAS-TIME, SECOND∘LEFT-HAS-TIME). >

Based on the above Allen's relationships regarding 'Before' and 'After', new axioms used to represent the temporal relationships are defined.

Table 2. Definition of the new axioms

beforeClassOf ≡ Pair ⊓ (FIRST∘Class, SECOND∘Class). <
afterClassOf ≡ Pair ⊓ (FIRST∘Class, SECOND∘Class). >

The new axioms, 'beforeClassOf' and 'afterClassOf', make it possible to represent the temporal relationships when each class has a temporal relationship.

3 Conclusions and Future Studies

In our research, we define the new axioms based on temporal description logic for representing the temporal relations. Our research, however, is not perfect and needs more detail studies for expressing the temporal relations. We will study to define more complex temporal relations and make many temporal axioms and then we will represent the E-Business rules and the ontology by markup language in the future.

References

1. Peter F. Patel-Schneider, Patrick Hayes, Ian Horrocks, "OWL Web Ontology Language Semantics and Abstract Syntax, W3C Working Draft 31 March 2003",
2. http://www. w3.org/TR/2003/WD-owl-semantics-20030331.
3. Alessandro Artale and Enrico Franconi, "A survey of temporal extensions of description logic", Annals of Mathematics and Artificial Intelligence, 2000.
4. Alessandro Artale and Enrico Franconi. Temporal Description Logics. Chapter in Handbook of Time and Temporal Reasoning in Arti cial Intelligence, edited by Dov Gabbay, Michael Fisher and Lluis Vila, MIT Press. Alessandro Artale Dept. of. Pages 2–22.

Polynomial-Time Learnability from Entailment

M.R.K. Krishna Rao

Information and Computer Science department
King Fahd University of Petroleum and Minerals,
Dhahran 31261, Saudi Arabia. krishna@ccse.kfupm.edu.sa

1 Introduction

The framework of *learning from entailment* introduced by Angluin (1988) and Frazier and Pitt (1993) allows the following types of queries. Through an *entailment equivalence query* $EQUIV(H)$, the learner asks the teacher whether his theory (a set of first-order formulas) H is logically equivalent to the target theory H^* or not. The teacher answers 'yes' to this query if H and H^* are equivalent, i.e., $H \models H^*$ and $H^* \models H$. Otherwise, the teacher produces a formula C such that $H^* \models C$ but $H \not\models C$ or $H^* \not\models C$ but $H \models C$. The request-for-hint query $REQ(C)$ returns (1) an answer 'not-entailed' if $H^* \not\models C$, or (2) an answer 'subsumed' if C is subsumed by a formula in H^*, or (3) a formula (hint) B in the proof of $H^* \models C$ if C is not subsumed by any formula in H^* but $H^* \models C$.

Recently, Arimura, Sakamoto and Arikawa [1,2] have studied learnability of term rewriting systems in this framework and claimed that class of terminating k-variable linear tree translation systems $LTT(k)$ is polynomial time learnable from entailment. This claim is very strong compared to the known results about polynomial time learnability of logic programs. There are many translations from logic programs to term rewriting systems and vice versa. If the above claim were correct, these translations provide better results about polynomial time learnability of logic programs. In this paper, we refute the above claim.[1]

2 Counterexample to Polynomial-Time Learnability

The following learning algorithm is presented in [1].

Algorithm EntLearn;
begin $R := \phi$;
    while $EQUIV(R)$ returns a counterexample $s \Rightarrow^* t$ **do**
        begin
            while $REQ(s \Rightarrow^* t)$ returns a hint u **do**
                if $s \Rightarrow_R^* u$ **then** $s := u$ **else** $t := u$;
            /* The above **while** loop terminates when $s \Rightarrow_{\mathcal{R}_*}^* t$ is of length 1. */
            if C is a largest context such that $s = C[u]$, $t = C[v]$

---

[1] The author gratefully acknowledges the generous support provided by the King Fahd University of Petroleum and Mineral in conducting this research.

and $u \not\Rightarrow_R v$ but $REQ(u \Rightarrow v) =$ "subsumed" **then**
  if $\exists D \in R$ such that $REQ(lgg(u \rightarrow v, D)) =$ "subsumed"
    then $R := (R - \{D\}) \cup \{lgg(u \rightarrow v, D)\}$ **else** $R := R \cup \{u \rightarrow v\}$
end; $Return(R)$;
end;

The number of iterations of the **while** loop requesting for hints is bounded the length of the derivation $s \Rightarrow_{\mathcal{R}_*}^* t$ (the counterexample returned by the equivalence query) – a rule $l \rightarrow r$ in R can only be generalized at most $size(l \rightarrow r)$ times. Therefore to obtain polynomial-time complexity of $EntLearn$, it requires that

1. length of the derivation $s \Rightarrow_{\mathcal{R}}^* t$ should be bounded by a polynomial in the sizes of terms s and t for any counterexample returned by the equivalence queries and
2. the decision problem $s \Rightarrow_{\mathcal{R}}^* u$ (in the **while** loop requesting for hints) should have polynomial-time complexity.

Definition 1 (from [1,2])

A term $t \in \mathcal{T}(\Sigma, \mathcal{X})$ is *linear* if no variable occurs more than once in t. A rewrite rule $l \rightarrow r$ is a *k-variable linear tree translation rule* if $|Var(r)| = |Var(l)| \leq k$ and both l and r are linear terms. A rewrite system is a *k-variable linear tree translation* $LTT(k)$ *system* if all rules in it are k-variable linear tree translation rules.

The following example shows that (a) $LTT(k)$ systems have exponentially long derivations and (b) the decision problem $s \Rightarrow_{\mathcal{R}}^* u$ cannot be decided in polynomial time.

Example 1 Consider the following term rewriting system in $LTT(k)$, where $k = 1$.

$$d(0) \rightarrow 0$$
$$d(s(x)) \rightarrow s(s(d(x)))$$
$$m3(s(s(s(y)))) \rightarrow m3(y)$$

Here, m3 stands for "mod 3" and $m3(s^n(0))$ reduces to $s^m(0)$ where $m = n$ mod 3 in $n/3$ steps.

It is easy to see that $m3(d^n(s(0))$ reduces to $s^m(0)$ where $m = 2^n$ mod 3 in approximately $(2^n + n - 1) * 4/3$ steps, i.e., $2^n + n - 1$ steps to reduce $m3(d^n(s(0))$ to $m3(s^{2^n}(0))$ and $(2^n)/3$ steps to reduce $m3(s^{2^n}(0))$ to $s^m(0)$. The derivation $m3(d^n(s(0))) \Rightarrow_{\mathcal{R}}^* s^m(0)$ is of exponential length.

The decision problem $m3(d^n(s(0))) \Rightarrow_{\mathcal{R}}^* s(0)$ of size $n + 5$ can only be decided in $(2^n + n - 1) * 4/3$ steps. Therefore, this decision problem is **exponential-time decidable, but not polynomial time decidable**. Note that $m3(d^n(s(0))) \Rightarrow_{\mathcal{R}}^*$ $s(0)$ is sometimes TRUE and sometimes FALSE depending on the value of n. It is TRUE for $n = 2$ and FALSE for $n = 3$.   □

References

1. H. Arimura, H. Sakamoto, and S. Arikawa (2000), *Learning Term Rewriting Systems from Entailment*, the 10th International Conference on Inductive Logic Programming (ILP'2000) Work-in-Progress. Also available at
   http://www.i.kyushu-u.ac.jp/ arim/papers/arimura-ILP2000-WIP.ps.gz.
2. H. Sakamoto, H. Arimura, S. Arikawa (2000), *Identification of Tree Translation Rules from Examples*, Proc. the 5th International Colloquium on Grammatical Inference (ICGI'2000), Lecture Notes in Artificial intelligence **1891**, pp. 241–255, Springer-Verlag.

Integration of Semantic Networks for Corpus-Based Word Sense Disambiguation*

Yoo-Jin Moon[1], Kyongho Min[2], Youngho Hwang[3], and Pankoo Kim[4]

[1] Hankuk University of Foreign Studies
270 Imun-dong Tongdaemun-Gu
Seoul, Korea
yjmoon@hufs.ac.kr
[2] Auckland Univ. of Technology, New Zealand
Kyongho.min@aut.ac.nz
[3] Kunsan University, Cheonbuk 573-701, Korea
[4] Chosun University, Kwangju 506-741, Korea
pkkim@chosun.ac.kr

Abstract. This paper presents an intelligent method for corpus-based word sense disambiguation (WSD), which utilizes the integrated noun and verb semantic networks through the selectional restriction relations in sentences. Experiments show that the presented intelligent method performs the verb translation better than the concept-based method and the statistics-based method. Integration of noun semantic networks into verb semantic networks will play an important role in both computational linguistic applications and psycholinguistic models of language processing.

1 Introduction

Extraction of word senses has been one of the most popular research themes in the application fields of knowledge discovery, NLP and information retrieval etc.[1]. In order to solve the problem, semantic networks for verbs and nouns contribute as knowledge bases for simulation of human psycholinguistic models in this paper. Also, they can play an important role in both computational linguistic applications and psycholinguistic models of language processing. There have been researches for supervised WSD and unsupervised WSD[2].

2 Integration of Semantic Networks for WSD

Integrated database of noun semantic networks into verb semantic networks is called Database for Integration of Semantic Networks (DISNet). The presented corpus-based method for WSD simulates the way how human beings resolve WSD utilizing

* This work was supported by Hankuk University of Foreign Studies Research Fund of 2003.

C. Palamidessi (Ed.): ICLP 2003, LNCS 2916, pp. 492–493, 2003.

DISNet. Humans generally consider the prdicate-argument structure of verbs to disambiguate an ambiguous verb in a sentence.

1) There is a parsed input sentence which contains an ambiguous verb(AV).
2) The algorithm refers to DISNet.
   2-1) It tries to match the predicate argument structure of AV in input to that of AV in DISNet.
   2-2) If it succeeds, then return the translated word of AV from DISNet.
   2-3) Otherwise, it tries to match the predicate argument structure of AV in input to the hyponymous predicate-argument structure of AV in DISNet.
   2-4) If it succeeds, then return the translated word of AV from DISNet.
3) It refers to noun semantic networks to calculate word similarities in sequence between the logical constraint of AV and that of the collocation list. It selects the translated word of AV with the maximum value of the word similarity beyond the critical value.
4) It refers to statistical information to calculate co-occurrence similarities in sequence between the logical constraint of AV and that of the collocation list. It selects the translated word of AV with the maximum value of the co-occurrence similarity beyond the critical value.
5) If the result of 3) and that of 4) are the same, return the selected word.
   If the result of the stage 3) is not null, return the selected word of the stage 3).
   If the result of the stage 4) is not null, return the selected word of the stage 4).
6) Return the default value of the translated word of AV.

The presented method for WSD spans calculation of word similarities only to the exact upper node of the human psycholinguistic model. Therefore, experiments show that the presented intelligent method performs the verb translation better than the concept-based method and the statistics-based method.

3 Conclusions

This paper utilized the integrated noun and verb networks for extraction of word-senses, through the selectional restriction relations in sentences. Future works are to update and extend DISNet to all of the verbs and to apply them to NLP.

References

1. Mihalcea, R. F., Modovan, D. I.: A Highly Accurate Bootstrapping Algorithm for Word Sense Disambiguation. International Journal on Artificial Intelligence Tools, vol.10:1. (2001) 5–21
2. Agirre, E., Atserias, J., Padr, L., Rigau, G.: Combining Supervised and Unsupervised Lexical Knowledge Methods for Word Sense Disambiguation. Computers and the Humanities, Special Double Issue on SensEval. eds.34:1, 2. (2000)

Development and Application of Logical Actors Mathematical Apparatus for Logic Programming of Web Agents[*]

Alexei A. Morozov

Institute of Radio Engineering and Electronics RAS
Mokhovaya 11, Moscow 125009, Russia
AlexeiMorozov@netscape.net, morozov@mail.cplire.ru

One of the most interesting and promising approaches to programming Internet agents is logic programming of agents. This approach has good prospects, because the ideology and principles of logic programming are very convenient for searching, recognition, and analysis of unstructured, poorly structured, and hypertext information. Many ideas and methods of logic programming of Internet agents based on various modifications of Prolog and non-classical logic (linear, modal, etc.) were developed during the recent decade. Nevertheless, there has been no mathematical apparatus providing sound and complete operation of logic programs in the dynamic Internet environment (i.e., under conditions of permanent update and revision of information). To solve this problem, we have created a mathematical apparatus based on the principle of repeated proving of sub-goals (so-called logical actors).

Our mathematical apparatus for logic programming of Internet agents includes:

1. A model of intelligent agents that operate in a dynamical environment;
2. A classical declarative (model-theoretic) semantics of agents;
3. Control strategies for executing logic programs (Internet agents) that are sound and (under some conditions) complete with respect to the model-theoretic semantics of these agents.

Within the framework of our model of intelligent agents, an Internet agent (a group of Internet agents) is a logic program controlled by a special strategy. The control strategy is a modification of standard control strategy of Prolog, enhanced by so-called repeated proving of sub-goals.

The idea of repeated proving consists in dividing the program into separate sub-goals (called logical actors) [2,3] that have the following properties:

1. Common variables are the single channel of data exchange between the actors.
2. Proving of separate actors can be fulfilled independently in arbitrary order.
3. One can defeat the results of proving of any actor while keeping all other sub-goals of the program.

[*] This work was supported by the Russian Foundation for Basic Research, project no. 03-01-00256.

C. Palamidessi (Ed.): ICLP 2003, LNCS 2916, pp. 494–495, 2003.

After cancelling the results of proving an actor, its proving can be repeated. Thus, one can implement a modification of reasoning; the logical inference can be partially modified. This makes it possible to eliminate the contradictions between the results of the logical reasoning and new information received from the outside.

The most complicated and interesting problem to be solved for implementing the idea of logical actors and repeated proving is the development of control strategies supporting repeated proving that are sound and (if possible) complete. We have developed several control strategies supporting repeated proving.

One of the first control strategies was created for the execution of sequential logic programs with logical actors [2]. However, further experiments on visual logic programming have shown that it is expedient to develop concurrent control strategies as well.

To the present day, we have expanded our computing model by introducing concurrent processes and asynchronous messages. Our computing model is based on two kinds of messages in contrast to the standard OOP model. There are so-called flow and direct messages in our computing model [3]. The composition of messages of these two kinds helps us to describe the complex behaviour of agents without means of synchronisation of concurrent processes.

The main advantage of our computing model is that it provides a classical declarative (model-theoretic) semantics of concurrent logic programs. The logic programs are sound and (under some special conditions) complete with respect to their model-theoretic semantics. The completeness of logic programs means that the programming language guarantees that a program will found all solutions of a problem.

We have created an object-oriented logic language Actor Prolog on the basis of our mathematical apparatus (the definition of the language, including all new means, is available at our Web Site [1]). We have also introduced some special means that support programming of Internet agents in recent versions of the language. There are predefined classes implementing the HTTP and FTP protocols, some means for visual programming based on translation of Structured Analysis and Design Technique (SADT) diagrams into Actor Prolog [3], and syntactical features supporting component-oriented programming. Now, we have a working version of Actor Prolog. It supports the development of agents that automate of retrieval and analysing information on the Internet.

I am grateful to Prof. Yuri V. Obukhov, who is a co-author of the project.

References

1. Actor Prolog Web Site. http://www.cplire.ru/Lab144.
2. A.A. Morozov. Actor Prolog: an object-oriented language with the classical declarative semantics. In K. Sagonas and P. Tarau, editors, *Proc. of the IDL'99 Int. Workshop*, pages 39–53, Paris, France, September 1999.
3. A.A. Morozov and Yu.V. Obukhov. An approach to logic programming of intelligent agents for searching and recognizing information on the Internet. *Pattern Recognition and Image Analysis*, 11(3):570–582, 2001.

A Real Implementation for Constructive Negation

Susana Muñoz and Juan José Moreno-Navarro

LSIIS, Facultad de Informática
Universidad Politécnica de Madrid
Campus de Montegancedo s/n Boadilla del Monte
28660 Madrid, Spain **
{susana,jjmoreno}@fi.upm.es

Keywords: Constructive Negation, Negation in Logic Programming, Constraint
Logic Programming, Implementations of Logic Programming.

Logic Programming has been advocated as a language for system specification, especially for logical behaviours, rules and knowledge. However, modeling problems involving negation, which is quite natural in many cases, is somewhat restricted if Prolog is used as the specification/implementation language. These constraints are not related to theory viewpoint, where users can find many different models with their respective semantics; they concern practical implementation issues. The negation capabilities supported by current Prolog systems are rather limited, and a correct and complete implementation there is not available. Of all the proposals, constructive negation [1,2] is probably the most promising because it has been proven to be sound and complete [4], and its semantics is fully compatible with Prolog's.

Intuitively, the constructive negation of a goal, $cneg(G)$, is the negation of the frontier $Frontier(G) \equiv C_1 \vee ... \vee C_N$ (formal definition in [4]) of the goal G. After running some preliminary experiments with the constructive negation technique following Chan's description, we realized that the algorithm needed some additional explanations and modifications.

Our goal is to give an algorithmic description of constructive negation, i.e. explicitly stating the details and discussing the pragmatic ideas needed to provide a real implementation. Early results for a concrete implementation extending the Ciao Prolog compiler are also presented.

Constructive negation was, in fact, announced in early versions of the Eclipse Prolog compiler, but was removed from the latest releases. The reasons seem to be related to some technical problems with the use of coroutining (risk of floundering) and the management of constrained solutions. It is our belief that these problems cannot be easily and efficiently overcome. Therefore, we decided to design an implementation from scratch. One of our additional requirements is that we want to use a standard Prolog implementation (to be able to reuse thousands of existing Prolog lines and maintain their efficiency), so we will avoid implementation-level manipulations.

We provide an additional step of **simplification** during the generation of frontier terms. We should take into account terms with universally quantified variables (that

---

** This work was partly supported by the Spanish MCYT project TIC2000-1632.

C. Palamidessi (Ed.): ICLP 2003, LNCS 2916, pp. 496–497, 2003.
© Springer-Verlag Berlin Heidelberg 2003

were not taken into account in [1,2]) because without simplifying them it is impossible to obtain results. We also provide a variant in the **negation of terms with free variables** that entails universal quantifications. There is a detail that was not considered in former approaches and that is necessary to get a sound implementation: the existence of universally quantified variables by the iterative application of the method.

An instrumental step for managing negation is to be able to handle disequalities between terms with a "constructive" behaviour. Moreover, when an equation $\exists \overline{Y}. X = t(\overline{Y})$ is negated, the free variables in the equation must be universally quantified, unless affected by a more external quantification, i.e. $\forall \overline{Y}. X \neq t(\overline{Y})$ is the correct negation. As we explained in [3], the inclusion of disequalities and constrained answers has a very low cost.

Our constructive negation algorithm and the implementation techniques admit some additional optimizations that can improve the runtime behaviour of the system.
- **Compact representation of the information**. The advantage is twofold. On the one hand constraints contain more information and failing branches can be detected earlier (i.e. the search space could be smaller). On the other hand, if we ask for all solutions instead of using backtracking, we are cutting the search tree by offering all the solutions in a single answer.
- **Pruning subgoals**. The frontiers generation search tree can be cut with a double action over the ground subgoals: removing the subgoals whose failure we are able to detect early on, and simplifying the subgoals that can be reduced to true.
- **Constraint simplification**. During the whole process for negating a goal,the frontier variables are constrained. In cases where the constraints are satisfiable, they can be eliminated and where the constraints can be reduced to fail, the evaluation can be stopped with result *true*.

Having given a detailed specification of algorithm in a detailed way we proceed to provide a real, complete and consistent implementation. The results that we have reported are very encouraging, because we have proved that it is possible to extend Prolog with a constructive negation module relatively inexpensively and we have provided experimental results. Nevertheless, we are working to improve the efficiency of the implementation. This include a more accurate selection of the frontier based on the demanded form. Other future work is to incorporate our algorithm at the WAM machine level. We are testing the implementation and trying to improve the code, and our intention is to include it in the next version of Ciao Prolog [1].

References

1. D. Chan. Constructive negation based on the complete database. In *ICLP'88*, pages 111–125. The MIT Press, 1988.
2. D. Chan. An extension of constructive negation and its application in coroutining. In *Proc. NACLP'89*, pages 477–493. The MIT Press, 1989.
3. S. Muñoz and J. J. Moreno-Navarro. How to incorporate negation in a prolog compiler. In E. Pontelli and V. Santos Costa, editors, *PADL'2000*, volume 1753 of *LNCS*, pages 124–140, Boston, MA (USA), 2000. Springer-Verlag.
4. P. Stuckey. Negation and constraint logic programming. In *Information and Computation*, volume 118(1), pages 12–33, 1995.

---

[1] http://www.clip.dia.fi.upm.es/Software

Simulating Security Systems Based on Logigrams

Kaninda Musumbu

LaBRI (UMR 5800 du CNRS),
Université Bordeaux I, France
351, cours de la Libération, F-33.405 TALENCE Cedex,
musumbu@labri.fr

Abstract. We describe a model for managing time-oriented security system and methods to perform simulation on this systems like forward and backward-chaining. Ad hoc solutions may be obtained but often fail to address various issues. Or method in pratice, provides a new trend for design and verify a security system, to ensure themselves of maintain integrite walls of compartments and to ensure of the correct operation of those, while verifiant that the good configuration of the syteme allows resiter well to predefined temperatures.

1 Introduction

The objective of our paper is to discuss a number of important issues for the design of timed security systems and to contribute to give a backward semantics. We use the concept of *logigram* to describe a model of several security systems. A logigram is a set of rules that define the behavior of such systems, where the time is very important. In these system, events are not raised or canceled, they are *scheduled*. To give a formal description of logigrams, at any time, the current event of system can be described by a simple structure called *script*. Scripts have many properties that seem to make them a useful support for working on problems like backward-chaining. We insist of its wide applicability and theoretical soundness and we also provide a short discussion about the nontrivial problem of backward-chaining.

Let us consider a security system. Let us suppose a malfunction occurs in any device. Then, the system turns on an emergency device $\mathcal{E}$, and schedules a test after a *delay*. Assuming that an event E_functionning or E_malfunctionning has been set by the emergency system when it is turned on. The test occurs after delay has expired. If the emergency system is not functionning, there is an alert. Note that our logic is monotonic. *i.e* there is no negation. An event can be set at a given time, and can be rescheduled, but never canceled, which makes the problem simpler. We have to compute a simulator capable of doing Forward-Chaining, backward-chaining, traces on logigrams. The simulator, as mentioned above, must offer many interaction with the user. In fact, the user must be able to control every part of simulation, at every stage. For instance,

C. Palamidessi (Ed.): ICLP 2003, LNCS 2916, pp. 498–499, 2003.

setting an event like E_functioning should lead the simulator to ask the user a choice: E is functioning or not. all this interaction stuff must be correctly integrated in the core of processes like forward and backward chaining. By examining small examples, we can see that computing the backward-chaining is a nontrivial problem. We must make hypothesis, and apply rules backwards. With no further control, complexity of this "method" is exponential, and there is no way to easily reduce it, without being confronted to choice problem. In the future, we think to investigate genetic algorithms.

2   Forward-Chaining (FC)

Let us sketch the approach from a general point of view. The operational semantics of any system consists of (or can be rephrased as)

1. a set of events Σ (events are noted σ);
2. an immediate transition relation between events denoted $\longmapsto$ where $\sigma \longmapsto \sigma'$ means that σ' is a possible successor event of σ;
3. a delay associate with transition which presents a temporal constraint. unary predicate on events, denoted final(σ),
4. a unary predicate on events, denoted final(σ), meaning that execution terminates in event σ.

In the case of our simplified language, we can give a mathematical meaning as the least fixpoint of transformation τ [1] such that: $(\tau f)(S) = \mathrm{FS}(S) \cup f(\mathrm{DR}(S))$.

It is straightforward to show from the operational semantics that this definition correctly maps each set of events into the set of final events reachable from them.

3   Backward-Chaining (BC)

Assuming that we can easily compute FC, it is also easy to verify if a given script s is such that $\tau f(s) = s'$ (where s' is the goal script).

The great problem of the BC is that there is a great number of potential solutions. We have to determine which ones are really useful. This could be done by clearly identifying properties of such scripts. A certain amount of improvements can be done , but we see that the rule-backward-following method has defaults. In order to improve accuracy and complexity, it is better to look for a good characterization of scripts, which seem to be actual reasonable structure to work with.

References

1. R. Alur and A.L. Dill A theory of timed automata. *Theoretical Computer Science*, 126(2):183–235, 1994.

---

[1] FS and DR stand for "Final Events" and "Directly reachable", respectively.

Online Justification for Tabled Logic Programs

Giridhar Pemmasani[1], Hai-Feng Guo[2], Yifei Dong[1], C.R. Ramakrishnan[1], and
I.V. Ramakrishnan[1]

[1] Department of Computer Science, SUNY, Stony Brook, NY, 11794, U.S.A.
{giri,ydong,cram,ram}@cs.sunysb.edu
[2] Department of Computer Science, University of Nebraska at Omaha
Omaha, NE, 68182, USA
haifengguo@mail.unomaha.edu

Justification is the process of computing an evidence for the truth or falsity of
an answer to a query in a logic program. There are two well known approaches
for computing the evidence: Post-processing based techniques that use tabling
engine [3,1] and trace-based techniques such as 4-port debuggers.

The naturalness of using a tabled engine system for justification is that the
evidence supporting the result can be readily constructed from the answer tables
created during query evaluation. The justification for logic programs is computed
by meta-interpreting the clauses of the program and post-processing these answer
tables. There are two drawbacks with this approach. The meta-interpreter keeps
a history of goals visited as it searches for an explanation and rejects any goal
that will lead to a cyclic explanation. In the worst case, this cycle checking can
take quadratic time in the size of evidence. Moreover, meta interpretation is
considerably slower than the original query evaluation.

Trace-based techniques require fine-grained control from the user to display
the execution trace. This is very error-prone and cumbersome to use (e.g., the
debugger may have to be restarted many times).

In this work we use *online justification* to address these drawbacks. The idea
is to transform the given program in such a way that the query evaluation in the
transformed program automatically builds the evidence which can be explored
later. For each literal in the program, we create two transformed literals: one to
generate the evidence for its truth, and the other for its falsity.

There are two cases to consider while transforming a literal for true justification. For non-tabled literals, the transformation adds an extra argument in
the predicate definitions. The idea is to capture the evidence in the argument
as the query is evaluated. However, the extra argument causes serious problems
when used to hold evidences for tabled literals. Tabled evaluation may take only
polynomial time to evaluate goals even though the number of proofs may be
exponential. To avoid this problem we do not introduce the extra argument in
tabled predicates. We only find the *first* evidence of a tabled predicate and store
it in a database.

Justification of false literals is more difficult than that of true literals in logic
programming systems. The main reason is that the evaluation of false literal fails
without providing any information regarding the failure. Therefore the idea of
using an extra argument will not work in this case. Instead, for justification of

C. Palamidessi (Ed.): ICLP 2003, LNCS 2916, pp. 500–501, 2003.

a false literal, we generate the *dual* definition for each predicate defined in the program. The dual predicates are generated in two steps. In the first step, for each literal L, we compute a dual literal $\overline{L}$ which is equivalent to $\neg L$. In the second step, we apply the above transformation rule for the true literals to $\overline{L}$. This ensures that the cycle detection in the presence of negated literals is again handled by the tabling engine itself. A new program is obtained based on those dual predicates and the original program. Justifying a false literal in the original program amounts to justifying its dual is true in the transformed program.

Online justification possesses the following advantages compared to trace-based debuggers and post-processing based justifiers. Efficiency is improved, since the transformed program is evaluated using tabling engine, thus avoiding cycle checking, and evidence is generated during query evaluation, thus avoiding meta-interpretation. Moreover, as the evidence generation is separated from evidence exploration, once the query evaluation is finished, the user can explore the evidence as and when necessary, thus giving greater flexibility in utilizing the evidence.

A similar source-to-source transformation technique is used in [4] to transform logic programs in the context of deductive databases. This technique uses semi-naive approach to compute the evidence in bottom-up evaluation for non-tabled programs. where cycles in the evidence are detected explicitly. Consequently, it suffers from problem of quadratic time overhead for generating evidences.

We have implemented online justifier and integrated it into the XSB logic programming system. We have used the online justifier, in particular, to build evidences in a complex XSB application, the XMC model checking environment [2]. Preliminary performance evaluation indicates that the online justifier for the XMC adds overhead of less than 8% in the case of true literal justification and at most 50% in the case of false literal justification, compared to 4 to 10 *times* overhead for post-processing based justifier.

References

1. H.-F. Guo, C. R. Ramakrishnan, and I. V. Ramakrishnan. Speculative beats conservative justification. In *International Conference on Logic Programming (ICLP)*, volume 2237 of *Lecture Notes in Computer Science*, pages 150–165, Paphos, Cyprus, November 2001. Springer.
2. C. Ramakrishnan, I. Ramakrishnan, S. A. Smolka, Y. Dong, X. Du, A. Roychoudhury, and V. Venkatakrishnan. XMC: A logic-programming-based verification toolset. In *Proceedings of the 12th International Conference on Computer-Aided Verification (CAV '00)*, pages 576–580. Springer-Verlag, 2000.
3. A. Roychoudhury, C. R. Ramakrishnan, and I. V. Ramakrishnan. Justifying proofs using memo tables. In *Second International ACM SIGPLAN Conference on Principles and Practice of Declarative Programming (PPDP)*, pages 178–189, Montreal, Canada, September 2000. ACM Press.
4. G. Specht. Generating explanation trees even for negations in deductive database systems. In M. Ducassé, B. L. Charlier, Y.-J. Lin, and U. Yalcinalp, editors, *Proceedings of ILPS'93 Workshop on Logic Programming Environments*, 1993.

Inducing Musical Rules with ILP

Rafael Ramirez

Technology Department
Pompeu Fabra University
Ocata 1, 08003 Barcelona, Spain
rramirez@iua.upf.es

1   Introduction

Previous research in learning sets of rules in a musical context has included a broad spectrum of music domains. Widmer [8] has focused on the task of discovering general rules of expressive classical piano performance from real performance data via inductive machine learning. The performance data used for the study are MIDI recordings of 13 piano sonatas by W.A. Mozart performed by a skilled pianist. In addition to these data, the music score was also coded. When trained on the data the inductive rule learning algorithm discovered a small set of 17 quite simple classification rules [8] that predict a large number of the note-level choices of the pianist.

Morales has reported research on learning counterpoint rules [5] using inductive logic programming (ILP). The goal of the reported system is to obtain standard counterpoint rules from examples of counterpoint music pieces and basic musical knowledge from traditional music. The system was provided with musical knowledge which includes the classification of intervals into consonances and dissonances, the description of whether two notes of different voices form a perfect or imperfect consonance or a dissonance, and whether two notes from the same voice form a valid or invalid interval. The rules learned by the system, resulting in a Prolog program, were tested for analysis of simple counterpoint pieces.

Igarashi et al. describe the analysis of respiration during musical performance by inductive logic programming [4]. Using a respiration sensor, respiration during cello performance was measured and rules were extracted from the data together with musical knowledge such as harmonic progression and bowing direction. The data was obtained from four skill cello players by asking each of them to perform the same representative cello piece. As background knowledge fifteen kinds of predicates concerned with musical structure and playing styles were defined.

Other inductive logic programming approaches to rule learning and musical analysis of music include [3] and [2]. In [3], Dovey analyzes piano performances of Rachmaniloff pieces using inductive logic programming and extracts rules underlying them. In [2], Van Baelen extended Dovey's work and attempted to discover regularities that could be used to generate MIDI information derived from the musical analysis of the piece.

2   Learning Harmonization Rules in Popular Music

We describe a simple inductive approach for learning rules from popular music harmonizations. As opposed to most of the existing work on harmonization in computer music

C. Palamidessi (Ed.): ICLP 2003, LNCS 2916, pp. 502–504, 2003.

which views harmonization as deriving/analyzing a four voice score for a particular voice, our view is on the sequence of chords that harmonize a melody. In this context, the process of harmonization is difficult to formalize and the way a given melody is harmonized normally varies from person to person according to her taste and background. Thus, the approach presented here makes no attempts at providing a definite set of rules but to learn generic rules from a set of examples.

The data used in our experimental investigations were collected from popular music scores with chord annotations. We used 42 scores mainly of western pop-songs. The data included information about position of a particular bar in the score (initial, middle or last), notes in the bar, harmonization of the bar, harmonizations of preceding bars (chords assigned to previous four bars) and some music theory background knowledge. We used the inductive logic programming system Aleph [7] to induce Horn clauses. We applied Aleph's default greedy set cover algorithm that constructs hypothesis one clause at a time. In the search for any single clause, Aleph selects the first uncovered positive example as the seed example, saturates it, and performs an admissible search over the space of clauses that subsume this saturation, subject to a user-specified clause length bound. In a companion paper we have reported on the application of the C4.5 decision tree learning algorithm [6] and the Apriori rule learning algorithm [1] to induce classification rules and association rules, respectively.

We chose to provide the learning algorithm with harmonic knowledge at the bar level, as opposed to at the note level, in order to capture common chord patterns in popular music. This information would have been lost if we only analyzed the harmonization of melodies at a note level. We also structured our data by musical phrases. We manually segmented the pieces into phrases and provided harmonization knowledge for each segment. This, we believe, is closer to the process of harmonizing a melody by a musician. All the data provided to the learning algorithms was coded by hand which explains the relatively small number of musical scores considered. However, despite of the reduced number of training data some of the rules generated by the learning algorithm turned out to be of musical interest and correspond to intuitive musical knowledge. In order to illustrate the types of rules found let us consider an example:

RULE: harmonize(X,Y) ← notes(Y,Z), member(X,Z).

"A chord harmonizes a note if the note belong to the set of notes in the chord"

The induced rules turned out to be extremely simple and very general, e.g. the above rule predicts 62% of all the cases. Other interesting rules were discovered which we expect to be the basis of a system for automatically harmonize popular music melodies. These rules and their implementation in a Prolog-based system will be reported in a companion paper.

Future work: This paper presents work in progress so there is future work in different directions. The manual segmentation and coding of training data is obviously not scalable so a (semi) automatic method to do this is necessary. We also plan to experiment with different information encoded in the training data. Extending the information in the training data and combining this extended data with background musical knowledge will very likely generate a more complete set of rules. Another issue to be considered is how to implement the rules most efficiently.

References

1. Agrawal, R.T. (1993). Mining association rules between sets of items in large databases. International Conference on Management of Data, ACM, 207,216.
2. Van Baelen, E. and De Raedt, L. (1996). Analysis and Prediction of Piano Performances Using Inductive Logic Programming. International Conference in Inductive Logic Programming, 55–71.
3. Dovey, M.J. (1995). Analysis of Rachmaninoff's Piano Performances Using Inductive Logic Programming. European Conference on Machine Learning, Springer-Verlag.
4. Igarashi, S., Ozaki, T. and Furukawa, K. (2002). Respiration Reflecting Musical Expression: Analysis of Respiration during Musical Performance by Inductive Logic Programming. Proceedings of Second International Conference on Music and Artificial Intelligence, Speinger-Verlag.
5. Morales, E. (1997). PAL: A Pattern-Based First-Order Inductive System. Machine Learning, 26.
6. Quinlan, J.R. (1993) C4.5: Programs for Machine Learning, San Francisco, Morgan Kaufmann.
7. Srinivasan, A. (2001). The Aleph Manual.
8. Widmer, G. (2002). Machine Discoveries: A Few Simple, Robust Local Expression Principles. Journal of New Music Research 31(1), 37–50.

A Distinct-Head Folding Rule

David A. Rosenblueth

Instituto de Investigaciones en Matemáticas Aplicadas y en Sistemas
Universidad Nacional Autónoma de México
Apdo. 20-726, 01000 México D. F.
México

1 Introduction

Tamaki and Sato were perhaps among the first to study folding in logic programs. These authors considered the folding of a single clause (E) using a single-clause definition (D) to give a folded clause (F):

$$\frac{B \leftarrow Q \quad \text{(D)} \qquad A \leftarrow Q\theta, R \quad \text{(E)}}{A \leftarrow B\theta, R \quad \text{(F)}} \ \text{fold}$$

plus some syntactic conditions, later refined by Gardner and Shepherdson. Here and throughout, A and B denote atoms, and Q and R denote tuples of literals.

Subsequently, Pettorossi, Proietti, and Renault [1] exploited an extended folding of multiple-clause predicates and derived the search part of the Knuth–Morris–Pratt string-matching algorithm from a naive, nondeterministic specification. Their folding, when limited to two clauses, can be viewed as the following extension of single-clause folding:

$$\frac{B_1 \leftarrow Q_1 \ (\text{D}_1) \quad A \leftarrow Q_1\theta_1, R \ (\text{E}_1) \quad B_2 \leftarrow Q_2 \ (\text{D}_2) \quad A \leftarrow Q_2\theta_2, R \ (\text{E}_2)}{A \leftarrow B, R \ (\text{F})}$$

where $B = B_1\theta_1 = B_2\theta_2$, requiring both clauses to be folded (E$_1$) and (E$_2$), to have the same head A and the same part of the body R which is not an instance of the bodies of the definition (D$_1$) and (D$_2$). This kind of folding was sufficient for the purposes of [1], where the authors start from a left-associative list concatenation as specification. However, if we associate to the right, which is arguably an equally naive specification, we may arrive at a situation in which we would like to fold, but the above multiple-clause folding is not applicable. This example shows the need for a more elaborate folding rule, perhaps closer to an inverse of unfolding.

2 A More General Kind of Folding

Note first that an *unfolding* with respect to an atom that unifies with two clause heads can be viewed as composed of two independent resolution steps (i.e. single-clause unfoldings). This suggests a two-clause *folding* rule composed of two independent single-clause foldings. In addition, the fact that unfolding uses instantiation suggests a folding rule using generalization. We thus first (incorrectly)

C. Palamidessi (Ed.): ICLP 2003, LNCS 2916, pp. 505–506, 2003.
© Springer-Verlag Berlin Heidelberg 2003

extend single-clause folding as two independent single-clause foldings, followed by the *most specific generalization* (msg) of the two folded clauses:

$$\frac{B_1 \leftarrow Q_1 \qquad A_1 \leftarrow Q_1\theta_1, R_1}{A_1 \leftarrow B_1\theta_1, R_1} \text{ fold} \qquad \frac{B_2 \leftarrow Q_2 \qquad A_2 \leftarrow Q_2\theta_2, R_2}{A_2 \leftarrow B_2\theta_2, R_2} \text{ fold}$$
$$\frac{}{A \leftarrow B, R} \text{ msg}$$

In the following example, we illustrate the fact that the variables appearing only in the heads of the definition (D_1), (D_2) may cause an overgeneralization when computing the msg of the folded clauses. Let us first unfold (F'), below, w.r.t. $b(0, Z)$ unifying with the head of two clauses (D_1), (D_2), giving (E_1), (E_2):

$$\frac{b(X, X) \leftarrow q_1 \ (D_1) \qquad a \leftarrow b(0, Z), r(Z) \ (F') \qquad b(0, 1) \leftarrow q_2 \ (D_2)}{a \leftarrow q_1, r(0) \ (E_1) \qquad a \leftarrow q_2, r(1) \ (E_2)} \text{ unf.}$$

Let us now fold (E_1), (E_2) giving (F_1), (F_2), and then compute their msg:

$$\frac{b(X, X) \leftarrow q_1 \qquad a \leftarrow q_1, r(0)}{a \leftarrow b(X, X), r(0) \ (F_1)} \text{ fold} \qquad \frac{b(0, 1) \leftarrow q_2 \qquad a \leftarrow q_2, r(1)}{a \leftarrow b(0, 1), r(1) \ (F_2)} \text{ fold}$$
$$\frac{}{a \leftarrow b(U, V), r(W) \ (F)} \text{ msg}$$

Since unfolding is a correct rule, w.r.t. the least Herbrand model semantics, say, the inferred clause (F) is clearly incorrect. The reason is that the substitution received by head-only variables of the definition (i.e. X in (D_1)) when unfolding is lost upon folding. This suggests instantiating head-only variables like X before computing the msg. (In this case, X in (F_1) should be instantiated to 0.)

We distinguish two kinds of head-only variable instantiation: (a) *coverage*, taking a function symbol or variable from the substitutions ϕ_i, where (A_i, R_i) = msg$((A_1, R_1), (A_2, R_2))\phi_i$ $(i = 1, 2)$, and (b) *matching*, taking the function symbol from the corresponding position in the clause of the other folding.

Algorithm *msg'*: Instantiation of head-only variables and computation of the msg.

Input. Clauses $A_i \leftarrow B_i\theta_i, R_i$, $i = 1, 2$, resulting from two single-clause foldings.
Output. Folded clause $A \leftarrow B, R$, if it exists.

1. Compute $(A, R) = $ msg$((A_1, R_1), (A_2, R_2))$ and ϕ_i, s.t. $(A, R)\phi_i = (A_i, R_i)$.
2. Compute $B = $ msg$(B_1\theta_1\sigma_1, B_2\theta_2\sigma_2)$ where σ_i instantiates head-only variables of (D_i) with coverage, if possible, or with matching otherwise.

We are currently studying this folding in the context of [2].

References

1. A. Pettorossi, M. Proietti, and S. Renault. Enhancing partial deduction via unfold/ fold rules. In *Proc. 6th Int. Workshop on Logic Program Synthesis and Transformation*, pages 146–168, Stockholm, Sweden, 1996. Springer-Verlag. LNCS 1207.
2. A. Roychoudhury, K. Narayan Kumar, C. R. Ramakrishnan, and I.V. Ramakrishnan. Beyond Tamaki-Sato style unfold/fold transformations for normal logic programs. *Intl. Journal of Foundations of Computer Science*, 13(3):387–403, 2002.

Termination Analysis of Logic Programs
Extended Abstract

Alexander Serebrenik

Department of Computer Science, K.U. Leuven
Celestijnenlaan 200A, B-3001, Heverlee, Belgium
Alexander.Serebrenik@cs.kuleuven.ac.be

Termination is well-known to be one of the most intriguing aspects of program verification. Since logic programs are Turing-complete, it follows by the undecidability of the halting problem that there exists no algorithm which, given an arbitrary logic program, decides whether the program terminates. However, one can propose both conditions that are equivalent to termination and their approximations that imply termination and can be verified automatically. This paper briefly discusses these kinds of conditions that were studied in [2].

Our achievements are twofold. First, a framework has been developed for integration of general orderings within the well-known context of acceptability with respect to a set. The methodology, earlier reported in [1], allowed us to bridge a gap between two major approaches to termination analysis: the transformational approach and the direct approach. A transformational approach first transforms the logic program into a term-rewrite system and then uses general orderings to prove termination of the latter. Direct approaches do not include such a transformation, but prove the termination on the basis of the logic program itself, and are usually based on *level mappings*—functions which map atoms to corresponding natural number. We have shown that from the theoretical perspective termination can be proved via general orderings if and only if, it can be proved via level mappings. In practice, however, for many interesting examples a general ordering required for a termination proof is easier to find than a level mapping. We provide a methodology to construct such an ordering.

The framework developed plays a key role in the study of the termination behaviour of meta-interpreters [4]. Our main contribution is in providing a technique linking termination behaviour of an interpreted program with a termination behaviour of the meta-program. We have shown that for a wide variety of meta-interpreters, a relatively simple relation can be defined between the ordering that can be used to prove termination of an interpreted program and the ordering that can be used to prove termination of the meta-interpreter extended by this interpreted program and a corresponding set of queries. The relationship allows a termination proof obtained for an interpreted program to be reused for showing termination of the meta-program and vice versa. If level mappings were used, no such reuse could have been possible.

Secondly, we turned our attention to programs with numerical computations. We started by considering integer computations [3], the crucial obstacle there being the lack of well-foundedness of integers. The proposed approach is based on transforming a program in a way that allows the integration and the extension of the techniques which were originally developed for analysis of numerical computations in the framework of

C. Palamidessi (Ed.): ICLP 2003, LNCS 2916, pp. 507–508, 2003.

query-mapping pairs with the well-known framework of acceptability, mentioned above. Moreover, we observed that the same approach can be used to determine values of integer arguments of the query such that the query terminates. This ability makes to the best of our knowledge this work is unique. Our technique has been implemented in the HASTA-LA-VISTA system, that turns out to be powerful enough to analyse correctly a broad spectrum of programs, while the time spent on the analysis never exceeds 0.30 seconds. Furthermore, our technique can be used to strengthen many approaches to termination of symbolic computations.

Then this work was extended to computations which depend on floating point numbers [5]. Imprecision and rounding errors are intrinsic to computations involving floating point numbers. As the floating-point numbers have been a subject of an intensive standardisation process, we base our work on the existing standards that provide us with some means to estimate the rounding errors occurring during the computation. We established that with this background knowledge, the termination of floating point computations can be analysed automatically. To the best of our knowledge, the results presented constitute the first work on termination in the context of floating point computations. It should also be stressed that although the results are stated in logic programming language, they are not bound to logic programming, because the matters considered do not depend on the logical aspects of the language.

References

1. D. De Schreye and A. Serebrenik. Acceptability with general orderings. In A. C. Kakas and F. Sadri, editors, *Computational Logic. Logic Programming and Beyond. Essays in Honour of Robert A. Kowalski, Part I*, volume 2407 of *LNCS*, pages 187–210. Springer Verlag, July 2002.
2. A. Serebrenik. *Termination analysis of logic programs*. PhD thesis, Department of Computer Science, K.U.Leuven, Leuven, Belgium, July 2003. xiv++228+x.
3. A. Serebrenik and D. De Schreye. Inference of termination conditions for numerical loops in Prolog. In R. Nieuwenhuis and A. Voronkov, editors, *Logic for Programming, Artificial Intelligence, and Reasoning, 8th International Conferencerence, Proceedings*, volume 2250 of *Lecture Notes in Computer Science*, pages 654–668. Springer Verlag, 2001.
4. A. Serebrenik and D. De Schreye. On termination of meta-programs. In R. Nieuwenhuis and A. Voronkov, editors, *Logic for Programming, Artificial Intelligence, and Reasoning, 8th International Conferencerence, Proceedings*, volume 2250 of *Lecture Notes in Computer Science*, pages 517–530. Springer Verlag, 2001.
5. A. Serebrenik and D. De Schreye. On termination of logic programs with floating point computations. In M. V. Hermenegildo and G. Puebla, editors, *9th International Static Analysis Symposium*, volume 2477 of *Lecture Notes in Computer Science*, pages 151–164. Springer Verlag, 2002.

Refactoring Logic Programs

Extended Abstract

Alexander Serebrenik and Bart Demoen

Department of Computer Science, K.U. Leuven
Celestijnenlaan 200A, B-3001, Heverlee, Belgium
{Alexander.Serebrenik,Bart.Demoen}@cs.kuleuven.ac.be

Program changes take up a substantial part of the entire programming effort. Often a preliminary step of improving the design without altering the external behaviour can be recommended. This is the idea behind *refactoring*, a source-to-source program transformation that recently came to prominence in the OO-community [1]. Unlike the existing results on automated program transformation, refactoring does not aim at transforming the program entirely automatically. The decision on whether the transformation should be applied and how it should be done is left to the program developer. However, providing automated support for refactoring is useful and an important challenge.

Logic programming languages and refactoring have already been put together at different levels [4,5]. None of these papers, however, consider applying refactoring techniques to logic programs. To the best of our knowledge the current work is the first one to consider this problem.

Most of the refactorings developed for object-oriented languages are applicable to logic languages, if we understand *methods* as *predicates* and *classes* as *modules*. One of the most interesting techniques, "predicate extraction", corresponding to "method extraction" of [1], is based on discovering a common functionality, encapsulating it in a new predicate and replacing it with a call to the new predicate (folding). Some refactoring techniques, originally designed for OO languages become even more prominent for logic languages: simplifying conditionals seems to be one of the most important refactoring techniques applicable to CLP. Furthermore, since logic programs make heavy use of recursion, clarifying and simplifying recursive programs becomes essential. In this context we suggest *mutual recursion elimination* and *replacing recursion with logical loops* [3]. Finally, refactoring techniques can be designed in particular for logic programming. These techniques can be based on techniques (*higher-order programming*) or constructs (*cut*) specific for this programming paradigm.

Identifying potential refactoring can be a difficult task on its own. One can resolve this may by trying and predicting further refactorings based on the transformations already applied. Eventually useful sequences of refactoring steps can be learned analogously to automated macro construction.

The ideas of refactoring have been applied to a Prolog-CLP(FD) program designed by one of our students. Given a soprano melody the program computes the scores for alto, tenor and bass. The aim of the refactoring was to *simplify* the program to allow a continuation project to be based on it. As the first

C. Palamidessi (Ed.): ICLP 2003, LNCS 2916, pp. 509–510, 2003.
© Springer-Verlag Berlin Heidelberg 2003

step in the refactoring process, constraints were simplified and a number of unfolding steps were performed. Next, common functionality has been identified and implemented as a separate predicate. These transformations allowed us to improve significantly the structure of the program, making it better suited for further intended extensions. The overall size has been reduced by more than 20%.

Based on this preliminary study we believe that the ideas of refactoring are applicable and important for logic programming. Refactoring promises to bridge the existing gap between prototypes and real-world applications by step-by-step refactoring and extending a prototype with new functionality. We believe that the experience of the logic programming community on program transformation is a good basis for a significant contribution to further development of the refactoring techniques.

Further work on refactoring can proceed in different directions. We plan to start with composing a comprehensive catalogue of the refactoring techniques. Next, a theoretical study of confluence of these techniques should be conducted. Finally, a tool supporting refactoring should be built, similarly to the Refactoring Browser for SmallTalk [2].

References

1. M. Fowler, K. Beck, J. Brant, W. Opdyke, and D. Roberts. *Refactoring: improving the design of existing code.* Object Technology Series. Addison-Wesley, 1999.
2. D. Roberts, J. Brant, and R. Johnson. A refactoring tool for Smalltalk. *Theory and Practice of ObjectSystems (TAPOS)*, 3(4):253–263, 1997.
3. J. Schimpf. Logical loops. In P. J. Stuckey, editor, *Logic Programming, 18th International Conference, ICLP 2002, Copenhagen, Denmark, July 29 – August 1, 2002, Proceedings*, volume 2401 of *LNCS*, pages 224–238. Springer Verlag, 2002.
4. P. Tarau. Fluents: A refactoring of Prolog for uniform reflection an interoperation with external objects. In J. Lloyd, V. Dahl, U. Furbach, M. Kerber, K.-K. Lau, C. Palamidessi, L. Moniz Pereira, Y. Sagiv, and P. J. Stuckey, editors, *Computational Logic – CL 2000, First International Conference, London, UK, July 2000, Proceedings*, volume 1861 of *LNAI*, pages 1225–1239. Springer Verlag, 2000.
5. T. Tourwé and T. Mens. Identifying refactoring opportunities using logic meta programming. In *7th European Conference on Software Maintenance and Reengineering, Proceedings*, pages 91–100. IEEE Computer Society, 2003.

Termination of Logic Programs for Various Dynamic Selection Rules

Jan-Georg Smaus

Institut für Informatik, Universität Freiburg, Georges-Köhler-Allee 52, 79110
Freiburg im Breisgau, Germany, smaus@informatik.uni-freiburg.de

The standard selection rule in logic programming always selects the leftmost
atom in each query. But for some applications this rule is not adequate, and
dynamic scheduling, i.e. a mechanism to determine the selected atom at runtime, is needed. The complex (non-)termination behaviour related to dynamic
scheduling has first been observed by Naish [3].

We believe that *modes* (input and output) are the key to understanding dynamic scheduling and ensuring termination. We have proposed *input-consuming
derivations* (where in each resolution step, the input arguments of the selected
atom do not become instantiated) as a reasonable minimum assumption about
the selection rule, which abstracts from programming language constructs [4]. We
have argued that the majority of real programs terminates for input-consuming
derivations, and given a sufficient and necessary criterion for termination [1].

Here, we consider various *additional* assumptions on the permissible derivations. In one dimension, we consider derivations parametrised by any property
$\mathcal{P}$ that the selected atoms must have, e.g. being ground in the input positions.
In another dimension, we consider local vs. non-local derivations (a derivation is
local if in each resolution step, the most recently introduced atoms are resolved
first). The dimensions can be freely combined, yielding a uniform framework for
proving termination for various dynamic selection rules. This work builds on
[1]. In particular, we make use of a special notion of *model*, which captures the
substitutions that may be computed by input-consuming derivations.

This work was motivated by our impression that it is sometimes necessary to
make stronger assumptions about the selection rule than just assuming input-
consuming derivations, but often, authors have made assumptions that are *too*
strong [2,3]: (1) they cannot easily be implemented using existing constructs; (2)
they impede or prevent coroutining, which is one of the main reasons for using
dynamic scheduling; (3) they are not formally necessary — they are required by
the methods that are used to *show* termination, not for termination itself.

We now give the five most important insights that this work provides:

1. There is a class of recursive clauses, using a natural pattern of programming, that narrowly misses the property of termination for input-consuming
   derivations. Put simply, theses clauses have the form $p(X) \leftarrow q(X, Y), p(Y)$,
   where the mode is $p(I)$, $q(I, O)$. Due to the variable in the head, an atom
   using p may always be selected, and hence we have non-termination. Sometimes, just requiring the argument of p to be at least non-variable is enough
   to ensure termination. This can be captured in our approach by setting $\mathcal{P}$ to

C. Palamidessi (Ed.): ICLP 2003, LNCS 2916, pp. 511–512, 2003.
© Springer-Verlag Berlin Heidelberg 2003

$\{p(t) \mid t$ is non-variable$\}$. The well-known PERMUTE program (in a particular version) can be used to illustrate this.

2. Some programs require for termination that selected atoms must be bounded wrt. a level mapping $|.|$. This is related to *speculative output bindings*, and the PERMUTE program (in another version than the one in the previous point) is the standard example [3]. This can be captured in our approach by setting $\mathcal{P}$ to the set of bounded atoms.

3. A method for showing termination of programs with delay declarations has been proposed in [2], assuming local selection rules. This assumption is usually *too* strong in the above sense. No implementation of local selection rules is mentioned. Local selection rules do not permit any coroutining. But most importantly, while "the class of local selection rules [...] supports simple tools for proving termination" [2], in practice, it does not seem to make programs terminate that would not terminate otherwise. In fact, we can show termination for PERMUTE without requiring local selection rules.

4. In spite of point 3, there are programs that crucially rely on the assumption of local selection rules for termination. We are only aware of artificial examples, but our treatment of local selection rules helps us to understand the role this assumption plays in proving termination.

5. For some programs it is useful to consider "hybrid" selection rules, where differently strong assumptions are made for different predicates. This can be captured by setting $\mathcal{P}$ accordingly. An example is the NQUEENS program in an implementation using the test-and-generate paradigm:

```
nqueens(N,Sol) ←
    sequence(N,Seq), permute(Sol,Seq), safe(Sol).
```

To ensure termination, permute(Sol, Seq) should only be selected once Seq is *ground*. To achieve efficiency, safe(Sol) should be selected as soon as Sol is *non-variable*.

Four of these points correspond to our initial impression. Point 4 was initially an open question for us. Details can be found in [5].

References

1. A. Bossi, S. Etalle, S. Rossi, and J.-G. Smaus. Semantics and termination of simply moded logic programs with dynamic scheduling. *Transactions on Computational Logic*, 2003. To appear. Available from
http://www.dsi.unive.it/%7Esrossi/papers.html.

2. E. Marchiori and F. Teusink. On termination of logic programs with delay declarations. *Journal of Logic Programming*, 39(1-3):95–124, 1999.

3. L. Naish. Coroutining and the construction of terminating logic programs. Technical Report 92/5, Department of Computer Science, University of Melbourne, 1992.

4. J.-G. Smaus. Proving termination of input-consuming logic programs. In D. De Schreye, editor, *Proc. of the International Conference on Logic Programming*, pages 335–349. MIT Press, 1999.

5. J.-G. Smaus. Termination of logic programs for various dynamic selection rules. Technical Report 191, Insitut für Informatik, Universität Freiburg, 2003.

Adding Preferences to Answer Set Planning

Tran Cao Son and Enrico Pontelli

Knowledge Representation, Logic, and Advanced Programming Laboratory
Department of Computer Science
New Mexico State University
Las Cruces, NM 88003, USA
{tson,epontell}@cs.nmsu.edu

Planning—in its classical sense—is the problem of finding a sequence of actions that achieves a predefined goal. As such, much of the research in AI planning has been focused on methodologies and issues related to the development of efficient planners. To date, several efficient planning systems have been developed (e.g., see [3] for a summary of planners that competed in the International Conference on Artificial Intelligent Planning and Scheduling). These developments can be attributed to the discovery of good domain-independent heuristics, the use of domain-specific knowledge, and the development of efficient data structures used in the implementation of the planning algorithms. Logic programming has played a significant role in this line of research, providing a declarative framework for the encoding of different forms of knowledge and its effective use during the planning process [5].

However, relatively limited effort has been placed on addressing several important aspects in real-world planning domains, such as *plan quality* and *preferences about plans*. In many real world situations, the space of feasible plans to achieve the goal is dense, but many of such plans, even if executable, may present undesirable behavior. In these situations, it may not be difficult to find a solution; rather, the challenge is to produce a solution that is considered satisfactory w.r.t. the needs and preferences of the user. Thus, feasible plans may have a measure of quality and only a subset may be considered acceptable. These issues can be illustrated with the following example:

Example 1. It is 7 am and Bob, *a Ph.D. student, is at home. He needs to be at school at 8am to take his qualification exam. His car is broken and he cannot drive to school. He can take a bus, a train, or a taxi to go to school, which will take him 55, 45, or 15 minutes respectively. Taking the bus or the train will require* Bob *to walk to the nearby station, which may take 20 minutes. However, a taxi can arrive in only 5 minutes. When in need of a taxi,* Bob *can call either the* MakeIt50 *or the* PayByMeter *taxi company.* MakeIt50 *will charge a flat rate of $50 for any trip, while* PayByMeter *has a fee schedule of $20 for the trip to school. If he takes the bus or the train, then* Bob *will spend only $2. Furthermore,* Bob, *being a student, prefers to pay less whenever possible.*

It is easy to see that there are only two feasible *plans for* Bob *to arrive at the school on time for his exam: calling one of the two taxi companies. However, a* PayByMeter *taxi would be preferable, as* Bob *wants to save money. In this case, both plans are feasible but* Bob's *preference is the deciding factor to select which plan he will follow.*

The example demonstrates that users' preferences play a deciding role in the choice of a plan. Thus, we need to be able to evaluate plan components at a finer granularity than

C. Palamidessi (Ed.): ICLP 2003, LNCS 2916, pp. 513–514, 2003.
© Springer-Verlag Berlin Heidelberg 2003

simply as consistent or violated. In [4], it is argued that users' preferences are likely to be more important in selecting a plan for execution, when a planning problem has too many solutions. It is worth noticing that, with a few exceptions, like the system SIPE-2 with metatheoretic biases [4], most planning systems *do not* allow users to specify their preferences and to use them in finding the plans. As such, the responsibility in selecting the most appropriate plan for their purpose rests solely on the users. It is also important to observe that *preferences* are different from *goals* in a planning problem; they might or might not be satisfied by a plan. The distinction is similar to the separation between *hard* and *soft* constraints [1]. For instance, if *Bob*'s goal is to spend at most $2 to go to school, then he does not have any feasible plans to arrive at school on time.

In this paper, we will investigate the problem of integrating users' preferences into a logic programming-based planner. We develop a language, called $\mathcal{PP}$ [6], for the specification of user preferences. We divide the preferences that a user might have into different categories:

- *Preference about a state:* the user prefers to be in a state s that satisfies a property ϕ rather than a state s' that does not satisfy it, even though both satisfy his/her goal;
- *Preference about an action:* the user prefers to perform the action a, whenever it is feasible and it allows the goal to be achieved;
- *Preference about a trajectory:* the user prefers a trajectory that satisfies a certain property ψ over those that do not satisfy this property;
- *Multi-dimensional Preferences:* the user has a *set* of preferences about the trajectory, with an ordering among them. A trajectory satisfying a higher priority preference is preferred over those that satisfy lower priority preferences.

It is important to observe the difference between ϕ and ψ in the above definitions. ϕ is a *state* property, whereas ψ is a formula over the whole *trajectory* (from the initial state to the state that satisfies the given goal).

We also provide a logic programming implementation of the language, based on answer set programming [2]. As demonstrated in this work, normal logic programs with answer set semantics provide a natural and elegant framework to effectively handle planning with preferences

References

1. S. Bistarelli et al. Labeling and Partial Local Consistency for Soft Constraint Programming. In *Practical Aspects of Declarative Languages*, Springer Verlag, 2000.
2. V. Lifschitz. Answer set planning. In *International Conference on Logic Programming*, pages 23–37, 1999.
3. D. Long, M. Fox, D.E. Smith, D. McDermott, F. Bacchus, and H. Geffner. International Planning Competition.
4. K.L. Myers and T.J. Lee. Generating Qualitatively Different Plans through Metatheoretic Biases. In *AAAI*, 1999.
5. T.C. Son, C. Baral, and S. McIlraith. Domain dependent knowledge in planning - an answer set planning approach. In *LPNMR*, Springer, pages 226–239, 2001.
6. T.C. Son and E. Pontelli. Planning with Preferences using Logic Programming. Technical Report CS-2003-007, New Mexico State University, 2003. http://www.cs.nmsu.edu/TechReports.

Controlling Semi-automatic Systems with FLUX

Michael Thielscher

Dresden University of Technology
mit@inf.tu-dresden.de

The programming of agents that are capable of reasoning about their actions is a major application of logic programming in Artificial Intelligence. FLUX is a recent, constraint logic programming-based method for designing reasoning agents that can sense, act, and plan under incomplete information [3]. An agent program in this language consists of a background theory, which endows the agent with the necessary knowledge of its actions, along with a high-level acting and planning strategy. The reasoning facilities are provided by a constraint solver, which is formally based on the action theory of the fluent calculus and its solution to the frame problem under incomplete states.

We have extended FLUX by a method that allows agents to reason, plan and act in semi-automatic environments, in which actions can initiate whole chains of indirect or delayed effects. Our approach addresses complex issues such as simultaneous, additive changes of state variables under incomplete information. As a case study, we have developed a control program for a complex dynamic environment of a steam boiler. A model of a real system, the domain involves uncertainty in form of varying output of the water pumps, which requires the agent to reason and plan under incomplete information. Moreover, simple actions in this system, such as turning off a pump, may trigger a whole chain of indirect effects: Another pump may automatically change to high capacity, which in turn may cause a valve to open, etc. Furthermore, every one of these changes has a specific effect on the water level in the boiler, which in turn affects the quantity of steam that is produced.

As an innovative and versatile way of modelling additive fluents and delayed effects, we introduce the notion of a **momentum fluent**. Such a fluent describes a property of the momentum in a physical system rather than a static property. An action may cause several momentum fluents to become true, each of which represents a specific contribution to the same fluent (such as the water level in the steam boiler). Additive fluents can thus be modelled. In a similar fashion, an action which has a delayed effect can be specified as bringing about a momentum fluent that eventually causes the actual delayed effect. Having triggered this effect, the momentum fluent itself may either automatically terminate, or continue to hold in case of recurring effects. On the other hand, the agent may have at its disposal the intervening action of terminating the momentum fluent before it produces the delayed effect.

The ramifications of an action in a semi-automatic environment are the consequence of causal connections among the components. In general, the occurrence of an indirect effect depends on the both the current state and the effects that have already been caused. To specify the causal relations among the

C. Palamidessi (Ed.): ICLP 2003, LNCS 2916, pp. 515–516, 2003.
© Springer-Verlag Berlin Heidelberg 2003

components of a dynamic system, we have extended FLUX by the predicate causes(Z1,P1,N1,Z2,P2,N2). Its intuitive meaning is that if positive and negative effects P1 and N1, respectively, have just occurred in state Z1, then this causes an automatic update to state Z2 with positive and negative effects P2 and N2, respectively.

On the basis of the individual causal relationships of a domain, the indirect consequences of an action are inferred as "causal chains." To this end, the causal relationships together are viewed as a graph in which each node represents a state and each edge represents the transformation from one state into another as a consequence of a single indirect effect. Sinks in this graph are nodes which have no outgoing edges, thus representing a stable state that admits no (further) indirect effect. To infer all indirect effects of an action one therefore has to find a sink, starting in the node which represents the status of the environment after the direct effect of the respective action. To this end, we have defined the new FLUX predicate ramify(Z1,P,N,Z2) for updating a (possibly incomplete) state Z1 by positive and negative effects P and N, respectively, and then automatically leading to a sink Z2 through a chain of causally triggered transitions.

The formal underpinnings of our method are given by a solution to the ramification problem in the action theory of fluent calculus [2]. Using the notion of causal propagation, this extensive solution accounts for mutually dependent components (such as connected controls of pumps) and multiple changes of state variables (such as needed for additive changes). In comparison with previous approaches of modelling semi-automatic environments using solutions to the ramification problem [4,1], our method addresses complex issues such as simultaneous, additive changes of state variables and delayed effects. Moreover, our solution has been embedded in programming language for agents that reason about their actions and sensor information and that can plan under incomplete information.

The full paper as well as the FLUX program for steam boiler control are available for download at our web site

fluxagent.org

References

1. S. McIlraith. An axiomatic solution to the ramification problem (sometimes). *Artificial Intelligence*, 116(1–2):87–121, 2000.
2. M. Thielscher. Ramification and causality. *Artificial Intelligence*, 89(1–2):317–364, 1997.
3. M. Thielscher. FLUX: A Logic Programming Method for Reasoning Agents. *Theory and Practise of Logic Programming*, 2004.
4. R. Watson. An application of action theory to the space shuttle. In *Proc. of PADL*, vol. 1551 of *LNCS*, 290–304, 1998.

The Language Model LMNtal

Kazunori Ueda and Norio Kato

Dept. of Computer Science, Waseda University, Tokyo, Japan
{ueda,n-kato}@ueda.info.waseda.ac.jp

LMNtal is a simple language model based on the rewriting of hierarchical graphs that use logical variables to represent links. The two major goals of the model are (i) to unify various computational models featuring multisets and (ii) to serve as the basis of a truly general-purpose language covering various platforms ranging from wide-area to embedded computation. Another contribution of the model is it greatly facilitates programming with dynamic data structures. The "four elements" of LMNtal are *logical links, multisets, nested nodes, and transformation.*

LMNtal is an outcome of the attempt to unify two extensions of concurrent logic programming, namely concurrent constraint programming and Constraint Handling Rules, where our focus has been multiset rewriting (rather than constraint handling). At the same time, LMNtal can be regarded as a nested multiset rewriting language augmented with *logical* links, and many computational models including Petri Nets, Gamma, the π-calculus, etc., can be encoded into LMNtal. Although developed independently and from different backgrounds and focuses, LMNtal and Bigraphical Reactive Systems exhibit some commonality.

Yet another view of LMNtal is a constructor-free linear concurrent logic language in which data structures are encoded as process structures. Constructor-freeness means that LMNtal links are *zero-assignment* variables, where the purpose of a variable is to connect two points using a private identity. Multisets are supported by the *membrane* construct that allows both nesting and mobility. Logical links can represent (among other things) communication channels, but the key differences from π-calculus channels are that (i) a message sent through a link changes the identity of the link and (ii) links are always private.

Syntax and Semantics. The syntax of LMNtal is given in Fig. 1, where two syntactic categories, *links* (denoted by X) and *names* (denoted by p), are presupposed. The name = is reserved for atomic processes for connecting two arguments.

A process P must observe the following *link condition*: Each link in P (excluding those links occurring in rules) can occur *at most twice*.

Intuitively, **0** is an inert process; $p(X_1, \ldots, X_m)$ $(m \geq 0)$ is an *atom* with m links; P, P is parallel composition called a *molecule*; $\{P\}$, a *cell*, is a process grouped by the membrane { }; and $T :- T$ is a rewrite rule for processes. Rewrite rules must observe several syntactic conditions (details omitted) on possible occurrences of symbols, which are to guarantee that reduction preserves the link condition. A *rule context*, @p, is to match a (possibly empty) multiset of rules within a cell, while a *process context*, $\$p[X_1, \ldots, X_m | A]$ $(m \geq 0)$, is to match processes other than rules within a cell. The arguments of a process context specify what links may or must occur free. The final form, $p(*X_1, \ldots, *X_n)$ $(n > 0)$, represents an *aggregate* of processes.

C. Palamidessi (Ed.): ICLP 2003, LNCS 2916, pp. 517–518, 2003.
© Springer-Verlag Berlin Heidelberg 2003

$$\begin{array}{lll} \text{(Process)} & P ::= \mathbf{0} \quad | \quad p(X_1,\ldots,X_m) \quad | \quad P,P \quad | \quad \{P\} \quad | \quad T\text{:-}T \\ \text{(Process template)} & T ::= \mathbf{0} \quad | \quad p(X_1,\ldots,X_m) \quad | \quad T,T \quad | \quad \{T\} \quad | \quad T\text{:-}T \\ & \qquad | \quad @p \quad | \quad \$p[X_1,\ldots,X_m\,|\,A] \quad | \quad p(*X_1,\ldots,*X_n) \\ & A ::= [] \quad | \quad *X \end{array}$$

Fig. 1. Syntax of LMNtal

(E1) $\mathbf{0},P \equiv P$ (E2) $P,Q \equiv Q,P$ (E3) $P,(Q,R) \equiv (P,Q),R$

(E4) $P \equiv P[Y/X]$ if X is a local link of P

(E5) $P \equiv P' \Rightarrow P,Q \equiv P',Q$ (E6) $P \equiv P' \Rightarrow \{P\} \equiv \{P'\}$

(E7) $X = X \equiv \mathbf{0}$ (E8) $X = Y \equiv Y = X$

(E9) $X = Y,\; P \equiv P[Y/X]$ if P is an atom and X is a free link of P

(R1) $\dfrac{P \longrightarrow P'}{P,Q \longrightarrow P',Q}$ (R2) $\dfrac{P \longrightarrow P'}{\{P\} \longrightarrow \{P'\}}$ (R3) $\dfrac{Q \equiv P \quad P \longrightarrow P' \quad P' \equiv Q'}{Q \longrightarrow Q'}$

(R4) $\{X = Y,P\} \longrightarrow X = Y, \{P\}$ if X and Y are different and do not occur in P

(R5) $X = Y, \{P\} \longrightarrow \{X = Y,P\}$ if X occurs in P and outside any rule

(R6) $T\theta,(T\text{:-}U) \longrightarrow U\theta,(T\text{:-}U)$ if $T\theta$ does not contain = outside any rule

Fig. 2. Structural Congruence and Reduction Relation

The operational semantics of LMNtal (Fig. 2) consists of two parts, namely structural congruence (E1)–(E9) and the reduction relation (R1)–(R6). (E4) represents α-conversion and (E9) is an absorption/emission rule of =.

Computation proceeds by rewriting processes using rules collocated in the same 'place' of the nested membrane structure. (R1)–(R3) are structural rules, and (R4)–(R5) are the mobility rules of =. The central rule of LMNtal is (R6). The substitution θ in (R6) (details omitted) is used to 'instantiate' rule contexts, process contexts and aggregates.

Examples. Two lists, represented by c (cons) nodes and n (nil) nodes, can be concatenated using the following two rules:

```
append(X0,Y,Z0), c(A,X,X0) :- c(A,Z,Z0), append(X,Y,Z)
append(X0,Y,Z0), n(X0) :- Y=Z0
```

N-to-1 stream merging can be programmed as follows:

```
{i(X0),o(Y0),$p[|*Z]}, c(A,X,X0) :- c(A,Y,Y0), {i(X),o(Y),$p[|*Z]}
```

Here, the membrane of the left-hand side records n (≥ 1) input streams with the name i and one output stream with the name o. The process context $p[|*Z] is to match the rest of the input streams and pass them to the right-hand side.

Conclusion. There is a lot of ongoing and future work. The most important language issue is to equip LMNtal with useful type systems. Experimental implementation of LMNtal is underway. Scheduling of active cells (cells with rules), rule compilation and distributed implementation are some of the challenging topics in our implementation project.

Author Index

Lecture Notes in Computer Science

For information about Vols. 1–2821
please contact your bookseller or Springer-Verlag

Vol. 2859: B. Apolloni, M. Marinaro, R. Tagliaferri (Eds.), Neural Nets. Proceedings, 2003. X, 376 pages. 2003.

Vol. 2860: D. Geist, E. Tronci (Eds.), Correct Hardware Design and Verification Methods. Proceedings, 2003. XII, 426 pages. 2003.

Vol. 2861: C. Bliek, C. Jermann, A. Neumaier (Eds.), Global Optimization and Constraint Satisfaction. Proceedings, 2002. XII, 239 pages. 2003.

Vol. 2862: D. Feitelson, L. Rudolph, U. Schwiegelshohn (Eds.), Job Scheduling Strategies for Parallel Processing. Proceedings, 2003. VII, 269 pages. 2003.

Vol. 2863: P. Stevens, J. Whittle, G. Booch (Eds.), «UML» 2003 – The Unified Modeling Language. Proceedings, 2003. XIV, 415 pages. 2003.

Vol. 2864: A.K. Dey, A. Schmidt, J.F. McCarthy (Eds.), UbiComp 2003: Ubiquitous Computing. Proceedings, 2003. XVII, 368 pages. 2003.

Vol. 2865: S. Pierre, M. Barbeau, E. Kranakis (Eds.), Ad-Hoc, Mobile, and Wireless Networks. Proceedings, 2003. X, 293 pages. 2003.

Vol. 2867: M. Brunner, A. Keller (Eds.), Self-Managing Distributed Systems. Proceedings, 2003. XIII, 274 pages. 2003.

Vol. 2868: P. Perner, R. Brause, H.-G. Holzhütter (Eds.), Medical Data Analysis. Proceedings, 2003. VIII, 127 pages. 2003.

Vol. 2869: A. Yazici, C. Şener (Eds.), Computer and Information Sciences – ISCIS 2003. Proceedings, 2003. XIX, 1110 pages. 2003.

Vol. 2870: D. Fensel, K. Sycara, J. Mylopoulos (Eds.), The Semantic Web - ISWC 2003. Proceedings, 2003. XV, 931 pages. 2003.

Vol. 2871: N. Zhong, Z.W. Raś, S. Tsumoto, E. Suzuki (Eds.), Foundations of Intelligent Systems. Proceedings, 2003. XV, 697 pages. 2003. (Subseries LNAI)

Vol. 2873: J. Lawry, J. Shanahan, A. Ralescu (Eds.), Modelling with Words. XIII, 229 pages. 2003. (Subseries LNAI)

Vol. 2874: C. Priami (Ed.), Global Computing. Proceedings, 2003. XIX, 255 pages. 2003.

Vol. 2875: E. Aarts, R. Collier, E. van Loenen, B. de Ruyter (Eds.), Ambient Intelligence. Proceedings, 2003. XI, 432 pages. 2003.

Vol. 2876: M. Schroeder, G. Wagner (Eds.), Rules and Rule Markup Languages for the Semantic Web. Proceedings, 2003. VII, 173 pages. 2003.

Vol. 2877: T. Böhme, G. Heyer, H. Unger (Eds.), Innovative Internet Community Systems. Proceedings, 2003. VIII, 263 pages. 2003.

Vol. 2878: R.E. Ellis, T.M. Peters (Eds.), Medical Image Computing and Computer-Assisted Intervention - MICCAI 2003. Part I. Proceedings, 2003. XXXIII, 819 pages. 2003.

Vol. 2879: R.E. Ellis, T.M. Peters (Eds.), Medical Image Computing and Computer-Assisted Intervention - MICCAI 2003. Part II. Proceedings, 2003. XXXIV, 1003 pages. 2003.

Vol. 2880: H.L. Bodlaender (Ed.), Graph-Theoretic Concepts in Computer Science. Proceedings, 2003. XI, 386 pages. 2003.

Vol. 2881: E. Horlait, T. Magedanz, R.H. Glitho (Eds.), Mobile Agents for Telecommunication Applications. Proceedings, 2003. IX, 297 pages. 2003.

Vol. 2883: J. Schaeffer, M. Müller, Y. Björnsson (Eds.), Computers and Games. Proceedings, 2002. XI, 431 pages. 2003.

Vol. 2884: E. Najm, U. Nestmann, P. Stevens (Eds.), Formal Methods for Open Object-Based Distributed Systems. Proceedings, 2003. X, 293 pages. 2003.

Vol. 2885: J.S. Dong, J. Woodcock (Eds.), Formal Methods and Software Engineering. Proceedings, 2003. XI, 683 pages. 2003.

Vol. 2886: I. Nyström, G. Sanniti di Baja, S. Svensson (Eds.), Discrete Geometry for Computer Imagery. Proceedings, 2003. XII, 556 pages. 2003.

Vol. 2887: T. Johansson (Ed.), Fast Software Encryption. Proceedings, 2003. IX, 397 pages. 2003.

Vol. 2888: R. Meersman, Zahir Tari, D.C. Schmidt et al. (Eds.), On The Move to Meaningful Internet Systems 2003: CoopIS, DOA, and ODBASE. Proceedings, 2003. XXI, 1546 pages. 2003.

Vol. 2889: Robert Meersman, Zahir Tari et al. (Eds.), On The Move to Meaningful Internet Systems 2003: OTM 2003 Workshops. Proceedings, 2003. XXI, 1096 pages. 2003.

Vol. 2891: J. Lee, M. Barley (Eds.), Intelligent Agents and Multi-Agent Systems. Proceedings, 2003. X, 215 pages. 2003. (Subseries LNAI)

Vol. 2893: J.-B. Stefani, I. Demeure, D. Hagimont (Eds.), Distributed Applications and Interoperable Systems. Proceedings, 2003. XIII, 311 pages. 2003.

Vol. 2894: C.S. Laih (Ed.), Advances in Cryptology - ASIACRYPT 2003. Proceedings, 2003. XIII, 543 pages. 2003.

Vol. 2895: A. Ohori (Ed.), Programming Languages and Systems. Proceedings, 2003. XIII, 427 pages. 2003.

Vol. 2897: O. Balet, G. Subsol, P. Torguet (Eds.), Virtual Storytelling. Proceedings, 2003. XI, 240 pages. 2003.

Vol. 2898: K.G. Paterson (Ed.), Cryptography and Coding. Proceedings, 2003. IX, 385 pages. 2003.

Vol. 2899: G. Ventre, R. Canonico (Eds.), Interactive Multimedia on Next Generation Networks. Proceedings, 2003. XIV, 420 pages. 2003.

Vol. 2901: F. Bry, N. Henze, J. Maluszyński (Eds.), Principles and Practice of Semantic Web Reasoning. Proceedings, 2003. X, 209 pages. 2003.

Vol. 2902: F. Moura Pires, S. Abreu (Eds.), Progress in Artificial Intelligence. Proceedings, 2003. XV, 504 pages. 2003. (Subseries LNAI).

Vol. 2903: T.D. Gedeon, L.C.C. Fung (Eds.), AI 2003: Advances in Artificial Intelligence. Proceedings, 2003. XVI, 1075 pages. 2003. (Subseries LNAI).

Vol. 2904: T. Johansson, S. Maitra (Eds.), Progress in Cryptology – INDOCRYPT 2003. Proceedings, 2003. XI, 431 pages. 2003.

Vol. 2905: A. Sanfeliu, J. Ruiz-Shulcloper (Eds.), Progress in Pattern Recognition, Speech and Image Analysis. Proceedings, 2003. XVII, 693 pages. 2003.

Vol. 2916: C. Palamidessi (Ed.), Logic Programming. Proceedings, 2003. XII, 520 pages. 2003.